THE ROUGH GUIDE TO

Costa Rica

This seventh edition updated by

Keith Drew, Steven Horak and Shafik Meghji

ROUGH
GUIDES

roughguides.com

Contents

Introduction to
Costa Rica

Hemmed in between the Pacific and Atlantic oceans near the narrowest point of the Central American isthmus, the diminutive republic of Costa Rica is often pictured as an oasis of political stability in the midst of a turbulent region. This democratic and prosperous nation is also one of the most biodiverse areas on the planet, an ecological treasure-trove whose wide range of habitats – ranging from rainforests and beaches to volcanoes and mangrove swamps – support a fascinating variety of wildlife, much of it now protected by an enlightened conservation system widely regarded as a model of its kind.

Though this idyllic image might not do justice to the full complexities of contemporary Costa Rican society, it's true that the country's long democratic tradition and complete absence of military forces (the army was abolished in 1948) stand in sharp contrast to the brutal internal conflicts that have ravaged its neighbours. This reputation for peacefulness has been an important factor in the spectacular growth of Costa Rica's tourist industry – over two million people visit the country annually, mainly from North America. Most of all, though, it is Costa Rica's outstanding natural beauty, and the wildlife that accompanies it, that has made it one of the world's prime **ecotourism** destinations, with visitors flocking here to hike trails through ancient rainforest, peer into active volcanoes or explore the Americas' last vestiges of high-altitude cloudforest, home to jaguars, spider monkeys and resplendent quetzals.

Admittedly, tourism has made Costa Rica less of an "authentic" experience than some travellers would like: some towns seemingly exist purely to provide visitors with a place to sleep and a tour to take, while previously remote spots are being bought up by foreign entrepreneurs. And as more hotels open, malls go up and potholed tracks tarmacked over, there's no doubt that Costa Rica is experiencing a significant social change, while the darker side of outside involvement in the country – sex tourism,

ABOVE PLAYA CARRILLO **OPPOSITE** VOLCÁN IRAZÚ

conflicts between foreign property-owners and poorer locals and, in particular, drug trafficking – are all on the increase.

Costa Rica's **economy** is the most diversified in Central America, and has become even more so since the country finally entered into the then-controversial Central American Free Trade Agreement (CAFTA) in 2009, enhancing its economic ties with the US in the process. Computer processors and medical supplies now sit alongside coffee and bananas as key exports, although the country's revenue from tourism still outstrips everything else. It is thanks to this money, in particular, that Costa Ricans – or Ticos, as they are generally known – now enjoy the highest rate of literacy, health care, education and life expectancy in the isthmus. That said, Costa Rica is certainly not the middle-class country that it's often portrayed to be – a significant percentage of people still live below the poverty line – and while it is modernizing fast, its character continues to be rooted in **distinct local cultures**, from the Afro-Caribbean province of Limón, with its Creole cuisine, games and patois, to the traditional *ladino* values embodied by the

BIODIVERSITY UNDER PROTECTION

Despite its small size, Costa Rica possesses over five percent of the world's total **biodiversity**, around 165 times the amount of life forms it might otherwise be expected to support. This is in part due to its position as a transition zone between temperate North and tropical South America, and also thanks to its complex system of interlocking **microclimates**, created by differences in topography and altitude. This biological abundance is now safeguarded by one of the world's most enlightened and dedicated conservation programmes – about 25 percent of Costa Rica's land is protected, most of it through the country's extensive network of national parks and wildlife refuges.

Costa Rica's **national parks** range from the tropical jungle lowlands of Corcovado on the Osa Peninsula to the grassy volcanic uplands of Rincón de la Vieja in Guanacaste, an impressive and varied range of terrain that has enhanced the country's popularity with ecotourists. Outside the park system, however, land is assailed by **deforestation** – ironically, there are now no more significant patches of forest left anywhere in the country outside of protected areas.

N

Peñas Blancas
Lago de Nicaragua
Islas Solentiname

REFUGIO NACIONAL DE VIDA SILVESTRE JUNQUILLAL
La Cruz
Los Chiles
Cuajiniquil
PARQUE NACIONAL GUANACASTE
Upala
REFUGIO NACIONAL DE VIDA SILVESTRE CAÑO NEGRO
PARQUE NACIONAL SANTA ROSA
PARQUE NACIONAL RINCÓN DE LA VIEJA
ALAJUELA

INTERAMERICANA

Liberia
PARQUE NACIONAL VOLCÁN TENORIO
Playa del Coco
PARQUE NACIONAL VOLCÁN ARENAL
La Fortuna
RESERVA BIOLÓGICA LOMAS DE BARBUDAL
Laguna de Arenal
1
Tilarán
PARQUE NACIONAL MARINO LAS BAULAS
PARQUE NACIONAL PALO VERDE
Cañas
RESERVA BIOLÓGICA BOSQUE NUBOSO MONTEVERDE
BOSQUE ETORNO DE LOS NIÑOS
GUANACASTE
Monteverde

Tamarindo
Santa Cruz
P. N. BARRA HONDA
REFUGIO NACIONAL DE VIDA SILVESTRE CIPANCÍ
MONTEVERDE
San Ramo
PARQUE NACIONAL DIRIÁ
Nicoya
Isla Chira
Puntarenas
1
Nosara
Carmona
Caldera
Orotina
REFUGIO NACIONAL DE VIDA SILVESTRE OSTIONAL
Nicoya Peninsula
PUNTARENAS
Golfo de Nicoya
Naranjo
PARQU NACION CARAR
Sámara
Carrillo
Paquera
REFUGIO NACIONAL DE VIDA SILVESTRE CAMARONAL
REFUGIO NACIONAL DE VIDA SILVESTRE CURÚ
Tárcoles
Jacó

Santa Teresa
Montezuma
Mal País
RESERVA NATURAL ABSOLUTA CABO BLANCO

PACIFIC OCEAN

Isla del Coco
Bahía Chatham
Bahía Wafer
PARQUE NACIONAL ISLA DEL COCO
Bahía Yglesias
0   3
kilometres
Isla del Coco is 535 kilometres southwest of Costa Rica

Isla del Coco (see inset)

FACT FILE

• The Republic of Costa Rica lies on the Central American isthmus between the Atlantic and Pacific oceans, consisting of a mountainous backbone – known as the **Continental Divide**, which rises to 3819m at the summit of Cerro Chirripó, its highest point – flanked by low-lying coastal strips. The country's **area** of 51,100 square kilometres (which includes the 24 square kilometres of Isla del Coco, 535km southwest of the mainland) makes it slightly larger than the Netherlands, slightly smaller than West Virginia.

• Costa Rica's **population** is largely of Spanish extraction, though there's a substantial community of English-speaking Costa Ricans of African origin around the Caribbean coast, along with 64,000 indigenous peoples. Costa Rica is a young country: out of its population of 4.7 million, around a quarter are aged under 15; men currently enjoy a life expectancy of 77, women 82.

• The country's main **exports** are **coffee** and **bananas**, though in recent years income from these products has been overtaken by that from **tourism**. Despite widespread poverty (around twenty percent of the population), the free and compulsory primary education system means that the country boasts a **literacy** rate of 96 percent, the best in Central America.

• Costa Rica's **wildlife** is mindboggling: the country is home to around 250 species of mammal (including ten percent of the world's bat population), over 400 varieties of reptile and amphibian, nearly 900 species of bird and a staggering 250,000 types of insect, including a quarter of the world's known butterflies.

sabanero, or cowboys, of Guanacaste. Above all, the country still has the highest rural population density in Latin America, and society continues to revolve around the twin axes of countryside and family: wherever you go, you're sure to be left with mental snapshots of rural life, whether it be horsemen trotting by on dirt roads, coffee-plantation day-labourers setting off to work in the mists of the highlands or avocado-pickers cycling home at sunset.

Where to go

Although almost everyone passes through it, hardly anyone falls in love with **San José**, Costa Rica's underrated capital. Often dismissed as an ugly urban sprawl, "Chepe" enjoys a dramatic setting amid jagged mountain peaks and is home to the country's finest museums, as well as some excellent cafés and restaurants, a lively university district and a burgeoning arts scene. The surrounding **Valle Central**, Costa Rica's agricultural heartland and coffee-growing region, supports the vast majority of the country's population and features several of its most impressive volcanoes, including steaming Volcán Poás and Volcán Irazú, its deep-green crater lake set in a strange lunar landscape high above the regional capital of Cartago.

While nowhere in the country is further than nine hours' drive from San José, the far north and the far south are less visited than other regions. The broad alluvial plains of the **Zona Norte** are dominated by the now-dormant cone of Volcán Arenal, which looms large over the friendly tourist hangout of La Fortuna, while the dense rainforest of the Sarapiquí region harbours monkeys, poison-dart frogs and countless species of bird, including the endangered great green macaw. Up by the border with Nicaragua, the seasonal wetlands of the Refugio Nacional de Vida Silvestre Caño Negro provide a haven for water birds, along with gangs of basking caimans.

Author picks

Our authors have tramped around towns and trekked through jungles, rafted down rivers and paddled up canals, and generally consumed more coffee than is probably good for them. Here are a few of their favourite things…

Basílica de Nuestro Señora de Los Ángeles In a country not necessarily known for its architectural heritage, Cartago's showpiece church (p.146) is a stunner, with a gilded interior to match.

Time with the OTS Spend a few days with the Organization of Tropical Studies at their biological stations in La Selva (p.234) or Palo Verde (p.249) and you'll see why their guides are rated some of the best in the country.

Little-known beaches Escape the crowds at the gorgeous beaches of Playa Junquillal in Guanacaste (p.271) and Playas Esterillos on the central Pacific coast (p.349).

Sodas Basic, cheap and unfailingly friendly, Costa Rica's ubiquitous *sodas* are a great place to tuck into a plate of *gallo pinto* or a traditional *cassado*. Try *La Casona Típica* in San José (p.110), *Soda Luz* in Orosí (p.151) or *D'Angel* in Manuel Antonio (p.356).

Off-the-beaten-track reserves The most famous national parks can get crowded in peak season, so try Parque Nacional Juan Castro Blanco (p.134), take a multi-day hike in the Bosque Eterno de los Niños (p.312) or visit Parque Nacional Los Quetzales, home of the iconic, resplendent quetzal (p.368).

Kayaking around Curú There are few more enjoyable ways of watching wildlife than paddling a kayak through the limpid waters of the southern Nicoya Peninsula (p.331), camping on beaches and spotting monkeys, sloths and sea birds along the way.

Our author recommendations don't end here. We've flagged up our favourite places – a perfectly sited hotel, an atmospheric restaurant, a tour operator that goes the extra mile – throughout the Guide, highlighted with the ★ symbol.

FROM TOP SEA-KAYAKING, REFUGIO DE VIDA SILVESTRE CURÚ; EATING AT A *SODA*; BIRDWATCHING, PARQUE NACIONAL PALO VERDE

In the northwest, cowboy culture dominates the cattle-ranching province of **Guanacaste**, with exuberant ragtag rodeos and large cattle haciendas occupying the hot, baked landscape that surrounds the attractive regional capital of Liberia. The province's beaches are some of the best – and, in parts, most developed – in the country, with Sámara and Nosara, on the Nicoya Peninsula, providing picture-postcard scenery and superb sunsets without the crowds.

Further down the **Pacific coast**, the quieter, surf-oriented sands of Montezuma and Santa Teresa/Mal País, on the southern Nicoya Peninsula, draw travellers looking to kick back for a few days (or weeks), while popular Parque Nacional Manuel Antonio, Costa Rica's smallest national park, also enjoys a sublime ocean setting and has equally tempting beaches. Further inland, nestled in the cool highlands of the Tilarán Cordillera, Monteverde has become the country's number-one tourist attraction, pulling in the visitors who flock here to walk through some of the most famous cloudforest in the Americas.

Limón Province, on the Caribbean coast, is markedly different to the rest of the country. It's home to the descendants of the Afro-Caribbeans who came to Costa Rica at the end of the nineteenth century to work on the San José–Limón railroad – their language (Creole English), religion (Protestantism) and West Indian traditions remain relatively intact to this day. The reason most visitors venture here, however, is for Parque Nacional Tortuguero, and the three species of marine turtle that lay their eggs on its beaches each year.

Travellers looking to venture off the beaten track will be happiest in the rugged **Zona Sur**, home to Cerro Chirripó, the highest point in the country, and, further south on the outstretched feeler of the Osa Peninsula, Parque Nacional Corcovado, which protects the last significant area of tropical wet forest on the Pacific coast of the isthmus. Corcovado is probably the best destination in the country for walkers – and also one of the few places where you have a fighting chance of seeing some of the more exotic wildlife for which Costa Rica is famed.

When to go

Although Costa Rica lies between eight and eleven degrees north of the equator, temperatures (see box, p.82), governed by the vastly varying altitudes, are by no means universally high, and can plummet to below freezing at higher altitudes. Local microclimates predominate and make weather unpredictable, though to an extent you can depend upon the **two-season rule**. In the dry season (roughly mid-Nov to April), most areas are just that: dry all day, with occasional northern winds blowing in during January or February and cooling things off; otherwise, you can depend on sunshine and warm temperatures. In the wet season (roughly May to mid-Nov), you'll have sunny mornings and afternoon rains. The rains are heaviest in September and October and, although they can be fierce, will impede you from travelling only in the more remote areas of the country – the Nicoya Peninsula and Zona Sur especially – where dirt roads become impassable to all but the sturdiest 4WDs.

Costa Rica is generally booked solid during the peak season, the North American winter months, when bargains are few and far between. The crowds peter out after Easter, but return again to an extent in July and August. Travellers who prefer to play it by ear are much better off coming during the low or rainy season (euphemistically called the "green season"), when many hotels offer discounts. The months of November, April (after Easter) and May are the **best times to visit**, when the rains have either just started or just died off, and the country is refreshed, green and relatively untouristy.

> ## RUMBLE IN THE JUNGLE
>
> Costa Rica is set in one of the most **geologically active** areas on earth. Ringed by the convergence of five major tectonic plates, it sits on the western edge of the Caribbean plate, at the point where it slides beneath the Cocos plate; this subduction (where one plate sinks into the earth's mantle) formed a chain of volcanoes that stretches 1500km from Guatemala to northern Panama. Costa Rica itself is home to some 112 **volcanoes**, though only five (including the major visitor attractions of Volcán Poás and Volcán Irazú) are considered active – Volcán Arenal, for so long the most active volcano in the country, has been in a resting phase since July 2010.
>
> The ongoing friction between the Caribbean and Cocos plates causes around 1500 **earthquakes** in Costa Rica each year, although only a small proportion of these are actually felt and even fewer still are strong enough to cause significant damage – the worst incident in recent times was the earthquake that struck near Cinchona, 50km north of San José, in January 2009, when forty people were killed.

OPPOSITE RAINFOREST NEAR VOLCÁN ARENAL

23

things not to miss

It's not possible to see everything that Costa Rica has to offer in one trip – and we don't suggest you try. What follows is a selective and subjective taste of the country's highlights: stunning national parks, brooding volcanoes, gorgeous beaches and exhilarating outdoor activities. All highlights have a page reference to take you straight into the Guide, where you can find out more. Coloured numbers refer to chapters in the Guide section.

1

1 TREKKING IN PARQUE NACIONAL CORCOVADO
Page 392
Straddling the Osa Peninsula in the far south of the country, this biologically rich, coastal rainforest is one of Costa Rica's finest destinations for walking and wildlife-spotting.

2 TEATRO NACIONAL, SAN JOSÉ
Page 93
Central America's grandest theatre, extravagantly done out in gold and marble and built in imitation of the Paris Opéra.

3 TURTLE-WATCHING
Pages 175, 267, 280 & 301
View some of the thousands of turtles – leatherbacks, hawksbill, olive ridleys and greens – that come ashore to lay their eggs each year, and, if you're lucky, watch their hatchlings' perilous journeys back to sea.

3

4 VOLCÁN ARENAL
Page 217

The lava may have stopped spewing, but Arenal is still a magnificent sight, and the surrounding area is one giant adventure playground – soak in volcanic hot springs, zipwire through the forest canopy or sign up for any number of other outdoor activities.

5 PARQUE NACIONAL SANTA ROSA
Page 265

This magnificent park protects a rare stretch of dry tropical rainforest – and the wildlife that calls it home.

6 MUSEO DE ORO PRECOLOMBINO
Page 92

One of the country's best museums, with a dazzling display that features over fifteen hundred pre-Columbian gold pieces.

7 COMMUNITY TOURISM
Pages 224, 325 & 197

Learn how the Maleku use medicinal plants, shop for crafts at a women's co-operative in the Gulf of Nicoya or take a walking tour with the Bribrí – just some of the ways of gaining a better insight into Costa Rica's remaining indigenous communities.

10

11

---

16 WHITEWATER RAFTING

Whitewater rafting is one of Costa Rica's most exciting outdoor activities, whether you're floating down the Peñas Blancas or riding Class V rapids on the Pacuaré.

17 EL DÍA DE LA RAZA, PUERTO LIMÓN

Young bloods and grandparents alike take to the streets during Costa Rica's raciest carnival.

18 RESERVA BIOLÓGICA BOSQUE NUBOSO MONTEVERDE

Experience the bird's-eye view – and a touch of vertigo – from a suspended bridge in the lush Monteverde cloudforest.

19 VOLCÁN POÁS

Poás is one of the world's more easily accessible active volcanoes, with a history of eruptions that goes back eleven million years.

16

17

18

19

20 SURFING
Page 70

Boasting nearly 1300km of palm-fringed coastline, and a variety of beach breaks, reef breaks, long lefts and river mouths, Costa Rica has a wave for just about every surfer out there.

21 COFFEE
Page 59

Sample an aromatic cup of Costa Rica's most famous export, and the foundation of the country's prosperity.

22 PARQUE NACIONAL RINCÓN DE LA VIEJA
Page 256

Clouds of sulphurous smoke and steaming mudpots dot the desiccated slopes of Volcán Rincón de la Vieja, one of the country's more thermally active areas.

23 EXPLORING THE TORTUGUERO CANAL
Page 178

Take a slow boat north from Puerto Limón along the Tortuguero Canal, past luxuriant vegetation and colourful wooden houses on stilts.

20

21

Itineraries

The following itineraries will give you a taste of everything that's addictive about Costa Rica. From the wildlife-rich wetlands of the north to the remote rainforests of the south, from surf-lashed Pacific beaches to nesting turtles on the Atlantic coast, there is something for everyone, whether you're stringing together a hit-list of the country's must-see sights or looking to get back to Mother Nature for a week or two.

CLASSIC COSTA RICA

All the big hitters, from volcanoes to beaches via wildlife-rich national parks, can be ticked off on a simple, fairly central two-week circuit.

❶ **San José** The oft-overlooked capital has Costa Rica's best museums and its widest range of restaurants, and is worth at least a night at the beginning or end of your trip. **See p.84**

❷ **Poás or Irazú** Two active volcanoes lie a short hop from San José: choose Volcán Poás for its boiling acid pools, Volcán Irazú for its milky-green crater lake and views of both oceans. **See p.136 & p.148**

❸ **Parque Nacional Tortuguero** Even if you're not here for the turtle-nesting seasons, you'll see plenty of other jungle wildlife as you paddle around the network of forest-fringed canals. **See p.175**

❹ **The Arenal region** Volcán Arenal itself may be quiet, but the bustling town of La Fortuna is still an essential stop for walks in the national park and all manner of other outdoor activities. **See p.209**

❺ **Monteverde** Arguably the most famous reserve in Costa Rica, where you can hike through the cloudforest in search of resplendent quetzals. **See p.317**

❻ **Parque Nacional Manuel Antonio** Further south along the coast, Manuel Antonio is Costa Rica's smallest national park (but also its most popular). Finish your trip spotting sloths and squirrel monkeys. **See p.357**

WILDLIFE-WATCHING

Diverse and abundant, Costa Rica's wildlife is the country's single biggest attraction. Allow a minimum of three weeks for the below, longer if you want to go deeper into Corcovado.

❶ **Parque Nacional Tortuguero** Green, hawksbill and giant leatherback turtles, plus howler monkeys, sloths and caimans – not a bad way to start any trip. **See p.175**

❷ **Reserva Rara Avis** Remote jungle lodge in the heart of the Sarapiquí region, with an impressive birdlist and a bounty of unusual reptiles and amphibians. **See p.235**

❸ **Refugío Nacional de Vida Silvestre Mixto Maquenque** This important wedge of protected rainforest on the border with Nicaragua represents the country's last refuge of the stunning, great green macaw. **See p.240**

❹ **Refugío Nacional de Vida Silvestre Caño Negro** Wily caimans basking on the riverbanks during the dry season; migratory birds swell the resident populations during the wet. **See p.228**

ABOVE HUMMINGBIRDS

❺ Refugio Nacional de Vida Silvestre Ostional At certain times of the year, thousands of olive ridley turtles storm the beaches at Ostional in one of nature's most spectacular sights. **See p.301**

❻ Parque Nacional Carara The hot northern lowlands meet the humid southern Pacific at Carara, meaning even greater varieties of wildlife, from armadillos and agoutis to both types of toucan. **See p.341**

❼ Parque Nacional Corcovado The one place in the country where you have a realistic chance of seeing a tapir, an ocelot or even the famously elusive jaguar. **See p.392**

OUTDOOR ACTIVITIES

Costa Rica is one giant natural playground. You could spend months just surfing the waves at Santa Teresa and Mal País, but three weeks should be enough to cover the below.

❶ Raft the Río Pacuaré Start by tackling one of the wildest rivers in Central America and some-time host of the World Whitewater Rafting Championships. **See p.155**

❷ Arenal Hike the old lava-flow trails of Parque Nacional Volcán Arenal and take a dip in volcano-fed hot springs: the pricey Balneario Tabacón is the most popular, the smaller Ecotermales Fortuna the most relaxed. **See p.209**

❸ Monteverde Birdwatching tours and guided night walks, of course, but also hanging bridges and zip lines – the canopy-tour craze that has swept the country (and the world) started in Monteverde. **See p.308**

❹ Santa Teresa and Mal País Popular surfer hangouts on the southern tip of the Nicoya Peninsula, offering a variety of beginner-friendly and much more challenging beach and reef breaks. **See p.336**

❺ Isla del Coco It's a long way to go and expensive to get there, but Isla del Coco, 535km off mainland Costa Rica (and some 36hr in a boat from Puntarenas), is simply the best scuba-diving destination in the country. **See p.326**

❻ Parque Nacional Chirripó Climb up through cloudforest and alpine paramo, and past crestones and glacial lakes as you tackle Cerro Chirripó, Costa Rica's highest point. **See p.370**

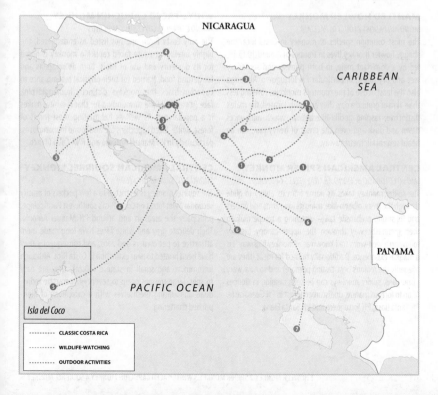

Wildlife

Thanks to Costa Rica's celebrated position as a land bridge between the temperate Nearctic zone to the north and the Neotropics to the south, the country's varied animal life features tropical forms like the jaguar, temperate-zone animals such as deer and some unusual, seemingly hybrid combinations like the coati. Many of the country's more exotic mammals (*mamíferos*) are either nocturnal, endangered or have been made shy through years of hunting and human encroachment, and you are far more likely to come into contact with some of the smaller and more abundant species. Amphibians and reptiles (*anfibios y reptiles*) are much more evident, though, and birdlife is particularly numerous, with 850 species of bird (*ave*), more than the US and Canada combined.

This field guide helps you identify some of the more common and distinctive animals that you might spot in Costa Rica, together with their Spanish names. The abbreviations used below are PN: Parque Nacional; RNA: Reserva Natural Absoluta; EB: Estación Biológica; RBBN: Reserva Biológica Bosque Nuboso; RB: Reserva Biológica; and RNdVS: Refugio Nacional de Vida Silvestre.

MONKEYS

Costa Rica is home to four species of monkey. As their diets consist of slightly different foods, it is not unusual to see mixed-species groups foraging together, with spider monkeys on the lookout mainly for fruit, howler monkeys favouring leaves, and white capuchin and squirrel monkeys feeding mostly on insects. Although comparatively prevalent, Costa Rican monkeys are threatened by habitat loss, which limits their movement and exposes them to disease.

MANTLED HOWLER MONKEY (*MONO CONGO* or *MONO AULLADOR*) *ALOUATTA PALLIATA*

The most common species of monkey in Costa Rica, the shaggy howler monkey lives in troupes of around 10 to 15, led by a dominant male, in both primary and secondary wet and dry forest, in particular PN Tortuguero. Although also the least active of the country's monkeys, covering less than 1km of ground a day, they are easily located: the male's distinctive, rasping gorilla-like bellow, which announces dawn and dusk and even the onset of heavy rain, can be heard several kilometres away.

WHITE-FACED CAPUCHIN MONKEY (*MONO CARABLANCO*) *CEBUS CAPUCINUS*

The only Costa Rican ape not listed as endangered, the highly intelligent white-faced capuchin monkey is noted for its dexterity and use of tools, both as weapons and for getting food. Named for their physical resemblance to Capuchin friars, the monkeys' distinctly humanoid pink face (it's actually the surrounding fur that is white) makes it a popular pet. As well as habituating most forms of forest, white-faced capuchins are also found in mangroves, particularly in PN Manuel Antonio and RNA Cabo Blanco.

CENTRAL AMERICAN SPIDER MONKEY (*MONO COLORADO* or *MONO ARAÑA*) *ATELES GEOFFROYI*

The spider monkey takes its name from its ability to glide through the trees, gibbon-like, using its long arms and fingers and its strong prehensile tail – watching a troupe making their gymnastic way through the upper canopy (usually following a well-worn trail known as a "monkey highway") is a magical experience. Traditionally hunted for meat (they are allegedly the region's best-tasting primate) and so now wary of humans, spider monkeys can be seen ranging in troupes of up to forty in mature, undisturbed forest in PN Guanacaste, PN Santa Rosa, PN Tortuguero and PN Santa Elena.

CENTRAL AMERICAN SQUIRREL MONKEY (*MONO TITÍ*) *SAIMIRI OERSTEDII*

The squirrel monkey is restricted to a few pockets of mostly secondary wet forest on Costa Rica's southwest Pacific slope, principally the areas in and around PN Manuel Antonio. Their delicate grey and white faces have long made them attractive to pet owners and zoos, and consequently they have been hunted to near extinction in Costa Rica. Although uncommon, and small in stature (30cm), they are easy to spot, large troupes of up to seventy hyperactive individuals announcing themselves with a cacophony of high-pitched chattering.

SLOTHS

True to their name, Costa Rica's two species of sloth (*perezoso*, which means "lazy" in Spanish) are inherently adverse to movement, with an extremely slow metabolism that allows them to sleep for up to twenty hours a day. Their sharp, taloned claws are best suited to the arboreal world, and yet once a week, risking life and limb, they descend to the forest floor to defecate – exactly why they do this remains a zoological mystery.

HOFFMANN'S TWO-TOED SLOTH
(PEREZOSO DE DOS DEDOS) CHOLOEPUS HOFFMANNI

Mostly nocturnal, the two-toed sloth is common in both primary and secondary wet forest, and more mobile than its three-toed cousin, but is still difficult to spot – the greasy green algae that often covers their brown hair camouflages them from their main predators, eagles, and means that, from a distance, they can easily be mistaken for a hornet's nest. They prefer disturbed growth, particularly in PN Tortuguero, RBBN Monteverde and EB La Selva – look for them hanging out in the mid- and upper branches of cecropia and guarumo trees.

BROWN-THROATED THREE-TOED SLOTH
(PEREZOSO DE TRES DEDOS) BRADYPUS VARIEGATUS

Diurnal and nocturnal, the three-toed sloth is the one you're more likely to see on the move, but even then they can spend more than eighty percent of the time asleep. They also prefer disturbed growth, and can often be seen curled around the V-shaped intersections between branches in PN Manuel Antonio, PN Corcovado, PN Cahuita and PN Tortuguero. Apart from the difference in digits on their hands (both species have three toes on their feet), they have greyer, wirier hair than two-toed sloths, with a brown stripe on their back, black eye masks and a stubby tail (two-toed sloths are tail-less).

CATS

Costa Rica has half of the New World's dozen wild cat species, which in descending size order are the jaguar, puma (*puma*), jaguarundi (*león breñero*), ocelot, margay (*caucel*) and oncilla (*tigrillo*); the very rare black panther is in fact a melanistic (dark) form of jaguar. Nocturnal and shy at the best of times, they are incredibly difficult to spot – indeed, all six are listed as endangered – and require areas of (rapidly disappearing) pristine wilderness to thrive.

JAGUAR *(TIGRE) FELIS ONCA*

The largest of Costa Rica's cats, the semi-sacred jaguar was once common throughout Central America, especially in the lowland forests and mangroves of coastal areas, but is now an endangered species, hunted by man – incredibly, right up until the 1980s – for its valuable pelt and because of its reputation as a predator of calves and pigs. A solitary nocturnal hunter, the jaguar stalks its prey – whatever's most abundant, from turtles to tapirs – often killing it by biting straight through the skull. You may spot tracks (four rounded toe prints, about 10cm wide) in the morning mud, though deep-forest hiking in PN Corcovado offers the only real (and very rare) chance of seeing one in the wild.

OCELOT *(MANIGORDO) FELIS PARDADIS*

The sleek and elegant-looking ocelot, with its beautiful roseate patterning, is similar in appearance to the jaguar, though considerably smaller, and is another animal you are very unlikely to see – it is threatened due to habitat loss and a slow reproductive cycle. Mostly nocturnal, ocelots spend up to twelve hours roaming through primary and secondary forest (occasional sightings include PN Tortuguero and RB Tirimbina) and across open country for a variety of prey, particularly rodents. Its tracks are fairly easy to distinguish, with the forepaw print wider than the hind paw – hence its Spanish name ("Fat Hand").

RACCOON FAMILY

There are seven members of the raccoon (or Procyonidae) family in Costa Rica, an omnivorous group of New World species that have long tails to aid their arboreal antics and are united by their strong night vision and hearing and their excellent sense of smell. The most unusual-looking species is the brilliantly named kinkajou, though the one you're most likely to see is the ubiquitous coati.

KINKAJOU *(MARTILLA) POTOS FLAVUS*

Ranging in colour from russet orange to grey brown, the kinkajou uses its long, narrow tongue to eat fruit, nectar and insects, and is most often seen hanging from branches by its prehensile tail. Common in primary and secondary forests, including RBBN Monteverde and EB La Selva, it is one of the most frequently seen of Costa Rica's nocturnal mammals; look out for the orange reflection of its eyes in torchlight. The kinkajou is slightly bigger than the similar-looking olingo, which is absent from the Pacific slope, and uses its tail like a fifth limb as it moves about the forest canopy (olingos favour jumping).

WHITE-NOSED COATI *(PIZOTE) NASUA NARICA*

With its long muzzle and ringed tail, held aloft to aid its balance, the coati (often mistakenly called coatimundi) looks like a confused combination of a raccoon, domestic cat and an anteater. The coati is very common, and its habituation to humans and comparative abundance makes it easy to spot: coatis are regularly seen in roadside bands of a dozen or more, on the scrounge for food, or scavenging in national-park car parks. Groups are made up of females and their young only, save for mating season, when a solitary male joins them temporarily – he is banished soon after, as he will harm the pups.

RODENTS

There are 47 species of rodent in Costa Rica, ranging from pocket gophers and spiny rats to the Mexican hairy porcupine. The majority are common across the country, with most of them contributing to their surrounding environment by dispersing seeds and providing an important link on the food chain for larger carnivores; the important exceptions are the black rat, brown rat and house mouse, introduced species that are responsible for contaminating food, spreading disease and often adversely affecting native ecosystems.

CENTRAL AMERICAN AGOUTI *(GAUTUSA) DASYPROCTA PUNCTATA*

Often seen on trails or foraging along the forest floor, the rabbit-like agouti is common in both primary and secondary forest, and – thanks to their comparative abundance and diurnal activities – is the Costa Rican rodent you are most likely to come across, particularly if you're spending much time in PN Manuel Antonio or PN Carara. Agoutis spend most of their time alone (though monogamous pairs will share territory), and will follow troupes of white-faced capuchin and spider monkeys, feeding on fallen tidbits. They make their dens in hollow trees or log piles.

PACA *(TEPEZCUINTLE) AGOUTI PACA*

Roughly fifty percent larger than the agouti, the solitary paca is nocturnal and uncommon, and so less readily seen. They make their dens near forest rivers; their burrows contain one or more secret exits (known as *uzús*), through which a paca will burst if cornered, often jumping into the water to escape danger. Pacas are easily distinguishable thanks to their rows of white spots, but can sometimes be mistaken for baby tapirs (see p.32), though the latter has a longer snout, a more defined streak patterning and white-tipped ears.

1

2

3

4

BATS

With 109 species in Costa Rica, bats make up over half of the country's mammal species; most of them are spotted whizzing about at dusk, though you can also see them hanging out by day, sleeping on the underside of branches, where they look like rows of small grey triangles. For the best bat-viewing opportunities, head to PN Barra Honda caves on the Nicoya Peninsula, where they roost in huge numbers.

GREATER FISHING BAT (MURCIÉLAGO PESCADOR) NOCTILIO LEPORINUS

Costa Rica is home to both species of fishing bat (also known as bulldog bats, due to their stout heads, folded faces and large canines), although it is easy enough to tell the two apart – as the name suggests, the greater fishing bat is much larger than the lesser variety (about 12cm in length, compared to 6cm), its clawlike feet are proportionately much bigger, and it is only found below elevations of around 200m. You may see one skimming the water in PN Tortuguero, casting its aural net in front of it in search of food: being blind, it fishes by sonar.

WHITE TENT BAT (MURCIÉLAGO BLANCO) ECTOPHYLLA ALBA

One of only two whitish bats in Costa Rica (the other is the larger northern ghost bat), the furry, ball-like white tent bat roosts in small groups underneath the leaves of heliconia plants, rattlesnake plants and banana plants. Look for folded-down midsections in horizontal leaves that are close to the ground; the bats create their protective "tents" by gnawing through the leaf veins. White tent bats only inhabit forests on the Atlantic slope, and, although generally uncommon, are relatively abundant in EB La Selva.

OTHER MAMMALS

NORTHERN TAMANDUA (COLLARED ANTEATER) (OSA HORMIGUERO) TAMANDUA MEXICANA

Of the two species of anteater that inhabit Costa Rica (the giant anteater, a third, was once found on both the Caribbean and Pacific slopes but is now thought to be extinct), you're more likely to see the northern tamandua or collared anteater, which is more prevalent than the silky anteater, though largely nocturnal. It hunts ants, occasionally bees, and termites, digging into nests using its sharp claws and vacuuming them up with its proboscis-like sticky tongue. Good places to spy one include PN Rincón de la Vieja and Reserva Rara Avis – look for large gashes in termite mounds (smaller scuffs are usually the work of other animals) – and its distinctive interlocking paw tracks.

COLLARED PECCARY (SAÍNO) TAYASSU TAJACU

Of the two barely distinguishable species of peccary, a kind of wild boar, that forage through the rainforest undergrowth in Costa Rica, the collared peccary is the much more frequently seen, particularly in PN Corcovado, PN Santa Rosa and PN Braulio Carrillo. While they may clack their teeth when aggravated, collared peccaries are much less aggressive than the more elusive white-lipped variety (chancho de monte), which are essentially restricted to PN Corcovado. Longer haired than their cousins, they can travel in battalions of several hundred and are dangerous when threatened; the best route of escape is to climb a tree.

BAIRD'S TAPIR (DANTA) TAPIRUS BAIRDII

One of the largest, most extraordinary looking mammals in the Neotropics, the Baird's tapir resembles an overgrown pig with a sawn-off elephant's trunk stuck on its face. Their antediluvian look comes from their prehensile snout, small ears and delicate cloven feet; adults have a stout reddish-brown body, young have additional white streaks. Weighing as much as 300kg (and vegetarian), they are extremely shy in the wild, largely nocturnal, and stick to densely forested or rugged land. Consequently, they are very rarely seen by casual rainforest walkers, though you may spot one in the inner reaches of PN Corcovado, and there have been occasional sightings at Rara Avis – look in muddy areas around water.

WEST INDIAN MANATEE (MANATÍ or VACA MARINA) TRICHECHUS MANATUS

Among Costa Rica's marine mammals, the sea cow or manatee is arguably the most beguiling, an amiable herbivore that is elephantine in size and well intentioned, not to mention endangered. Manatees all over the Caribbean are declining in number, due to the disappearance and pollution of the fresh- and saltwater riverways in which they live. Your only reasonable chance of seeing one is in the Tortuguero canals in Limón Province, where they sometimes break the surface (main sightings are early morning), though there are a few in the more recently protected lagoons of the RNdVS Mixto Maquenque, near the border with Nicaragua – at first, you might mistake it for a tarpon, but the manatee's overlapping snout and long whiskers are quite distinctive.

TURTLES

Five species of marine turtle visit Costa Rica's shores: greens, hawksbills, leatherbacks and olive ridleys, while the strange blunt-nosed loggerhead, which seems not to nest in Costa Rica, can sometimes be seen in Caribbean coastal waters. Nesting takes place mostly at night, when hundreds of turtles come ashore at a certain time of year, visiting the same beach each time (the same beach, in fact, on which they themselves hatched) and laying hundreds of thousands of eggs. They are found in shallow and (in the case of the leatherback and olive ridley) deep ocean, and shallow bays, estuaries and lagoons.

LEATHERBACK TURTLE (TORTUGA BAULA)
DERMOCHELYS CORIACEA

The leatherback turtle (see box, p.281) is the largest of Costa Rica's sea turtles, growing to a length of around 2m and weighing around 300kg. Leatherbacks have a soft, dark-grey ridged carapace – not a shell like other sea turtles, but actually a network of bones overlaid with a very tough leathery skin (hence the name). Although they nest in most numbers at PN Marino Las Baulas on the western Nicoya Peninsula (Oct–Feb), leatherbacks also come ashore elsewhere, including PN Tortuguero and RNdVS Gandoca-Manzanillo (March–May). Their numbers have dwindled considerably due to loss of beachfront habitat and manmade hazards such as rubbish dumping (they can choke on plastic bags, which they mistake for jellyfish), and they are now listed as endangered.

GREEN TURTLE (TORTUGA VERDE) CHELONIA MYDAS

The green turtle, long prized for the delicacy of its flesh, has become nearly synonymous with its favoured nesting grounds in PN Tortuguero (Pacific greens, as opposed to Atlantic greens, nest at PN Santa Rosa and PN Manuel Antonio), with some turtles travelling 2000km to reach their breeding beaches (they nest July–Oct). Green turtles have a heart-shaped shell and are similar in appearance to the hawksbill, which have closer mosaic patterns on their flippers. Green turtles were classified as endangered as long ago as the 1950s, but are making a bit of a comeback thanks in part to the protection offered by areas like Tortuguero.

HAWKSBILL TURTLE (TORTUGA CAREY)
ERETMOCHELYS IMBRICATA

The hawksbill turtle, so-named for its distinctive hooked "beak", is found all over the tropics, often preferring rocky shores and coral reefs. It used to be hunted extensively on the Caribbean coast for its meat and shell, but this is now banned; poaching does still occur, however, despite their being listed as endangered, and you should avoid buying any tortoiseshell that you see for sale. Hawksbills have heart-shaped shells, like green turtles, but with mottled tortoise-shell patterns. Unlike greens and olive ridleys, hawksbills prefer to nest alone, coming ashore on beaches in PN Tortuguero, PN Santa Rosa and PN Marino Ballena (July–Oct).

OLIVE RIDLEY TURTLE (TORTUGA LORA)
LEPIDOCHELYS OLIVACEA

Growing to around 70cm, the olive ridley is the smallest of Costa Rica's sea turtles. Like greens and hawksbills, they also have a heart-shaped shell, although their distinctive colouring tells them apart. They nest (July–Nov) on just a few beaches along the Pacific coast, principally Playa Nancite in PN Santa Rosa and RNdVS Ostional, coming ashore in their thousands (an event known as an *arribada*; see box below), unusually, often during the day. Despite these seemingly huge *arribadas*, olive ridleys are also unfortunately listed as endangered.

ARRIBA THE ARRIBADA!

Olive ridley turtles are one of only two species of marine turtle that nest in vast numbers (Kemp's ridleys being the other), a mass gathering of up to eight thousand turtles known as an **arribada** (Spanish for "arrival"). *Arribadas* can last over twelve hours, with a steady stream of females crawling slowly out of the water to a free patch of sand beyond the high tide line where they will begin to lay their eggs. Each individual will lay around one hundred eggs over the course of a few days; according to estimates, more than **eleven million eggs** may be deposited during a single *arribada*. It is the sheer number of eggs that is the evolutionary reason behind the unusual behaviour of the olive ridleys: with so many eggs and hatchlings for predators to prey on, the likelihood of a hatchling making it out to sea increases dramatically. Despite the mass layings, however, the odds are still stacked overwhelmingly against the young turtles – only one out of every three hundred hatchlings from the protected beaches of the Refugio Nacional de Vida Silvestre Ostional, for example, will reach adulthood.

1 LEATHERBACK TURTLE 2 GREEN TURTLE 3 HAWKSBILL TURTLE 4 OLIVE RIDLEY TURTLE >

CROCODILIANS AND LIZARDS

AMERICAN CROCODILE (*COCODRILO*)
CROCODYLUS ACUTUS

Travelling along Costa Rica's waterways, you may well see crocodiles hanging out on the riverbanks, basking in the sun, or lounging in the muddy shallows – you have a decent chance of spotting one in PN Tortuguero, RNdVS Mixto Maquenque and RNdVS Gandoca-Manzanillo, and are virtually guaranteed to see them under the so-called Crocodile Bridge near Tárcoles on the Pacific coast (see p.342). Crocodiles live in both freshwater and brackish water, mostly in lowland rivers, lagoons and estuaries but also occasionally in the sea, near the mouth of rivers. They are aggressive and dangerous, and have been known to kill humans in Costa Rica. Crocodiles have a longer, more pointed snout than caimans, with two projecting teeth, one on either side of the lower jaw, which caimans lack.

SPECTACLED CAIMAN (*CAIMÁN* or *GUAJIPAL*)
CAIMAN CROCODILUS

Smaller and lighter in colour (tan or brown) than "flatter"-looking crocodiles, and with a shorter snout, caimans inhabit lowland rivers, swamps and wetlands, particularly PN Tortuguero, PN Palo Verde and RNdVS Caño Negro, where they will sometimes perch on submerged tree branches, scuttling away at your approach; in the dry season, large numbers gather in diminishing pools of water with only their eyes and snout visible. Caimans feed on various aquatic wildlife and carrion, and will even eat other young caimans. Although common locally, caimans (like crocodiles) are under constant threat from hunters, who sell their skin to make shoes and handbags.

GREEN IGUANA (*IGUANA VERDE* or *GALLINA DE PALO*)
IGUANA IGUANA

Pot-bellied iguanas are the most ubiquitous of Costa Rica's lizards, as common here as chickens are in Europe or the US (indeed, their Spanish name means "tree chicken", though this is a reference more to the taste of their meat). Masters of camouflage, they like basking on high branches over water, or on riverbank rocks. Their colours vary from lime green to orangey brown (a yellow or orange head indicates a breeding male). Green iguanas are distinguished from their spiny-tailed cousins by the comb-like yellow crest along their spine; a large, circular scale below their ear; and a hanging throat sac (dewlap), which is used to regulate body temperature and for courtship and territorial displays. Despite their size (they can grow up to 2m), they are very shy, and when you do spot them, it's likely that they'll be scurrying away in an ungainly fashion.

SPINY-TAILED IGUANA (BLACK IGUANA)
(*IGUANA NEGRA*) *CTENOSAURAS IMILIS*

More terrestrial than the green iguana, the tetchier spiny-tailed or black iguana can often be seen on or by the side of roads, or at the back of Pacific-coast beaches, basking on logs on the forest floor. Apart from the difference in colour, they can be told apart from the green iguana by the bands of spiny scales that encircle their tail and the black stripes that extend to their dorsal crest. They are the world's fastest lizard, escaping predators by hitting speeds of up to 35kph.

EMERALD BASILISK LIZARD (*BASILISCA VERDE*)
BASILISCUS PLUMIFRONS

One of the more incredible reptilian sights in and around the rivers and wetlands of Costa Rica is the tiny form of a basilisk lizard skittering across the water: its partially webbed hind feet, and the speed at which it can move them, enable the basilisk to "walk" on water (for up to 4.5m), earning it the nickname "Jesus Christ" lizard. When not in flight, basilisks are regularly seen in damp leaf litter and on low-hanging branches. Emerald basilisk lizards – which are easy to spot in PN Palo Verde and RNdVS Caño Negro – are more colourful than brown (Pacific slope) and striped (Caribbean slope) basilisks. It's also easy enough to differentiate between the sexes: males have three crests along their back, females have two.

SNAKES

Of the 162 species of snake (*serpientes* or *culebras*) that call Costa Rica home, only 22 are venomous. These are usually well camouflaged, but some, such as the highly venomous coral snake (*coralillo*), advertise their danger with a flamboyance of colour: although retiring, they are easily spotted (and avoided) thanks to their bright rings of carmine red, yellow and black (though note that the many-banded coral snake has only red and black rings). Snakes are largely nocturnal, and for the most part far more wary of you than you are of them, so the chances of actually spotting one – let alone getting bitten (see p.61) – are very slim.

FER-DE-LANCE (*TERCIOPELO*) *BOTHROPS ASPER*

The fer-de-lance pit viper has adapted quite well to cleared areas and grassy uplands, although you are far more likely to see them in places that have heavy rainfall (such as the Limón coast) and near streams or rivers at night (they are absent from Guanacaste's dry forest and the Nicoya Peninsula). Though it can reach more than 2m in length, the *terciopelo* ("velvet") is very difficult to spot – its brown body, marked with cream chevrons and dark triangles resembling "X"s (sometimes an hourglass), resembles a big pile of leaves. Along with the bushmaster, the fer-de-lance is one of the few snakes that may attack without provocation, and is extremely dangerous (its venom can kill within 2hr).

CENTRAL AMERICAN BUSHMASTER
(*MATABUEY*) *LACHESIS STENOPHRYS*

The largest venomous snake in the Americas (reaching 3m), the bushmaster is extremely aggressive and packs a highly potent bite (its Spanish name translates as "bull killer").

Fortunately, it is rarely spotted, as it is restricted to remote primary wet forests on the Caribbean slope (the black-headed bushmaster is endemic to the Osa Peninsula), prefers dense and mountainous territory and is nocturnal. Bushmasters are recognized by their thick, triangular head, with a broad, dark stripe running behind the eye, and the dark triangles that run down from the ridge along their back.

EYELASH VIPER (*BOCARACÁ*) *BOTHRIECHIS SCHLEGELII*

The very pretty eyelash viper is usually tan or bright green or decked out in a lichen-like pattern of browns, greys and mottled green, but is sometimes brilliant yellow when inhabiting golden palm-fruit groves. Largely arboreal and generally well camouflaged, it takes its name from the raised scales around its eyes – other notable features are its large triangular head, which is clearly distinguishable from its neck, and vertical pupils. Eyelash vipers are quite venomous to humans and should be given a wide berth if seen hanging from a branch or negotiating a path through the groves.

FROGS

There are many, many frogs (*ranas*) in Costa Rica, the most famous of which are the brilliantly coloured miniature poison-dart frogs. With markings as varied as wallpaper, they are relatively easy to see, but you should never touch one – these frogs secrete some of the most powerful natural toxins known to man through their skin, directly targeting the heart muscle, paralysing it and causing immediate death. You will most likely see Costa Rica's frogs around dusk or at night; some of them make a regular and dignified procession down paths and trails, sitting motionless for long periods before hopping off again.

RED-EYED TREE FROG (*RANA CALZONUDA*)
AGALYCHNIS CALLIDRYAS

The nocturnal red-eyed tree frog is physically striking: relatively large, it is an alarming bright green, with orange hands and feet and dark blue thighs; its eyes are pure red, to scare off potential predators. Very common and abundant in wet forest, swamps and small pools, red-eyed tree frogs are particularly active during the wet season, and on humid nights you can often hear breeding males calling (a short "chuck" or "chuck-chuck") for the larger female.

FLEISCHMANN'S GLASS FROG (*RANA DE CRISTAL*) *HYALINO BATRACHIUM FLEISCHMANNI*

The extraordinary Fleischmann's glass frog is a living biological lesson – their inexplicably transparent belly affords you the dubious pleasure of observing its viscera and digestive processes through its skin. Glass frogs are fairly common and widespread in moist and wet forest,

where they are usually found on leaves overhanging fast-flowing water, so you have a good chance of spotting one; they are most active on rainy nights, when the male calls (a whistle-like "wheet") from the underside of a leaf.

STRAWBERRY POISON-DART FROG
(*RANA VENENOSA ROJA Y AZUL*) *OOPHAGA PUMILIO*

If you're spending any time on the Caribbean side of the country, you are almost guaranteed to see the diminutive but extravagantly coloured strawberry poison-dart frog, also known as the "Blue Jeans" thanks to its dark-blue hind legs. They are very common and abundant in wet forest, particularly the Sarapiquí – look in the leaf litter round the base of trees for them feeding on ants (if their colouring doesn't give them away, their loud "buzz-buzz-buzz" croak will). If you're lucky, you may even spot a female carrying her tadpoles, piggy-back style, one at a time, to take refuge in small water pools that form in treetop plants.

1 FER-DE-LANCE 2 BUSHMASTER 3 EYELASH VIPER 4 RED-EYED TREE FROG 5 FLEISCHMANN'S GLASS FROG
6 STRAWBERRY POISON-DART FROG >

BIRDS

Birds, both migratory and indigenous, are abundant in Costa Rica – indeed, with nearly 900 different species, the country is home to more varieties than in all of North America – and most visitors take a bird-watching trip (see p.73) of one sort or another while they're here. Costa Rica's national bird is the rather dour-looking clay-coloured robin (*el yigüirro*), a somewhat surprising choice given that the competition includes some of the most colourful species in the Americas. Many birds are best observed while feeding – quetzals, for instance, are most often sighted when they are foraging from their favoured aguacatillo tree, and you might catch a glimpse of a hummingbird hovering over a flower as it sups on its nectar.

MAGNIFICENT FRIGATEBIRD (*RABIHORCADO MAGNO*) *FREGATA MAGNIFICENS*

The magnificent frigatebird is a very common sight along the Pacific coast (less so on the Caribbean side of the country), where they are often spotted just offshore or in mangrove keys, or circling over fishing boats at harbours and docks – they are easily recognized by their sleek forked tail and large wingspan (up to 2m). Due to its absorbent plumage, the frigatebird rarely dives underwater, instead feeding by snatching food from the sea or other birds. The male is the more "magnificent" of the two, inflating its enormous scarlet pouch (gular sac) to attract females.

BOAT-BILLED HERON (*PICO CUCHARA*) *COCHLEARIUS COCHLEARIUS*

The chunky, funny-looking boat-billed heron is fairly common in Costa Rica's wetlands, mangroves and coastal lowlands. Its large eyes and sensitive bill enable the heron to hunt at night, but it is easier to see during the day, resting in trees near the water's edge. Its call is a throaty croak, which will help locate it amid the branches, but there's little chance of a confusing sighting, thanks to the eponymous beak, which it snaps when disturbed.

ROSEATE SPOONBILL (*ESPATULA ROSADA*) *PLATALEA AJAJA*

As the only pink bird in Costa Rica, there is no mistaking the roseate spoonbill. Common in coastal waters and open wetland in the Pacific lowlands, particularly around the Río Tempisque and in the Gulf of Nicoya, it is restricted to RNdVS Caño Negro on the Caribbean side of the country – birds are usually seen feeding in groups in both shallow fresh- and saltwater, trawling for food with their flattened, spatula-shaped bill. The spoonbill's unique pink plumage is attained through its diet of crustaceans.

NORTHERN JACANA (*JACANA CENTROAMERICANA*) *JACANA SPINOSA*

Anyone spending much time in the wetlands of PN Palo Verde and RNdVS Caño Negro and the waterways of PN Tortuguero will come to know the northern jacana rather well – it is common in wetlands, ponds and rivers across the country but is particularly prevalent in these three protected areas. A rather ungainly looking bird, the northern jacana's giant spindly feet and elongated toes enable it to walk on floating vegetation in search of insects and seeds. It is easily agitated, displaying its recognizable lemon-yellow underwings when taking flight. Northern jacanas are usually seen in pairs, though the female mates with several males, who care for separate clutches of eggs.

LAUGHING FALCON (*GUACO*) *HERPETOTHERES CACHINNANS*

Of Costa Rica's raptors, the laughing falcon, found all over the country, probably has the most distinct call, which sounds exactly like its Spanish name – the "laughing" bit comes from a much lower-pitched variation, which resembles muted human laughter. The falcon preys on reptiles, including venomous snakes, biting off the head before bringing the body back to its eyrie, where it drapes it over a branch, sings a duet with its mate and proceeds to dine.

RED-CAPPED MANAKIN (*SALTARIN CABECIRROJO*) *PIPRA MENTALIS*

The diminutive star of many a wildlife documentary, the red-capped manakin is famous for its flamboyant leks, where males gather to woo females with elaborate courtship displays that range from short swoops to a variety of nifty tree-branch moves. Aside from the eponymous "helmet", males are also easily identified by their bright yellow thighs; like most manakins, the female is a dull green colour. They are common in primary rainforest on the Caribbean and central and southern Pacific slopes, and are regularly filmed at EB La Selva.

MONTEZUMA OROPENDOLA (*OROPÉNDOLA DE MOCTEZUMA*) *PSAROCOLIUS MONTEZUMA*

You are unlikely to visit Costa Rica without seeing a Montezuma oropendola. These large, russet-coloured birds are very common in gardens, wet forests and forest fringes of the Caribbean lowlands (less so higher up, and rarer on the northwest Pacific slope) and are easily distinguished thanks to their outsized beaks, pretty facial markings and golden tails. Courting males are even more noticeable, tipping off their perch and flicking their wings while uttering a long, warbling call that ends with a loud gurgle. Oropendolas live in noisy colonies of skillfully woven hanging nests (*oropéndola* means "gold pendulum"), which dangle from tall trees like Christmas decorations.

1 MAGNIFICENT FRIGATEBIRD 2 BOAT-BILLED HERON 3 ROSEATE SPOONBILL 4 NORTHERN JACANA 5 LAUGHING FALCON
6 RED-CAPPED MANAKIN 7 MONTEZUMA OROPENDOLA >

SCARLET MACAW (*LAPA ROJA*) *ARA MACAO*

The endangered scarlet macaw, with its liberal splashes of red, yellow and blue, was once common on the Pacific coast of southern Mexico and Central America. The birds, which are easily distinguished from the rest of Costa Rica's predominantly green parrot species, live in lowland forested areas, but these days your best chance of spotting them is in the dense cover of PN Corcovado and the Osa Peninsula, although their numbers are on the increase in PN Carara and the RNdVS Curú, and to a lesser extent PN Palo Verde and RB Lomas Barbudal. They are usually spotted in or near their tree-trunk nesting holes, wrestling seeds, fruit and nuts from the upper branches, or while flying high in pairs (they are monogamous) and calling to one another with their distinctive raucous squawk.

VIOLET SABREWING (*ALA DE SABLE VOLÁCEO*) *CAMPYLOPTERUS HEMILEUCURS*

Of the fifty-plus species of hummingbird (*colibrí*) in Costa Rica, the violet sabrewing is the largest, and one of the most beautiful, its deep, iridescent purple plumage shimmering like sequins. Its wings are big enough for you to hear them beating, but despite its size, the sabrewing is timid and easily scared off feeding sites by smaller birds. Sabrewings prefer the forest understorey but are often seen hovering around heliconia and banana plants and are a regular at nectar-feeders – RBBN Monteverde is a good place to spot them.

RESPLENDENT QUETZAL (*QUETZAL*) *PHAROMACHRUS MOCINNO*

With a range historically extending from southern Mexico to northern Panama, the dazzling resplendent quetzal was highly prized by the Aztecs and the Maya. In the language of the Aztecs, quetzali means, roughly, "beautiful", and along with jade, the jewel-coloured feathers were used as currency in Maya cities. Top of most visitors' birdwatching wish-list, the quetzal is unfortunately endangered due to the destruction of its favoured cloudforest habitat, and the male in particular – who possesses the distinctive streamer-like feather train of up to 1.5m long – is still pursued by poachers. These days the remaining cloudforests, particularly RBBN Monteverde, PN Los Quetzales and the area around San Gerardo de Dota in the Zona Sur, are among the best places to see them (March–May is most favourable).

BLUE-CROWNED MOTMOT (*BARRANQUERO*) *MOMOTUS MOMOTA*

The blue-crowned motmot is readily seen in gardens and forest fringes of the Valle Central, and also in the Pacific lowlands. As its name suggests, this particular member of the motmot family sports a turquoise-blue cap, though it is more noticeable for its distinctive pendulous tail, which ends in twin racket-shaped tips. The blue-crowned motmot nests in burrows in earthbanks and is able to sit motionless for a long time, perched on a branch in the lower canopy, before darting out for prey such as insects and small lizards.

CHESTNUT-MANDIBLED TOUCAN (*DIOS TEDÉ*) *RAMPHASTOS SWAINSONII*

Costa Rica is home to six members of the toucan family, which include toucanets and aracaris, the largest of which is the chestnut-mandibled toucan. Named for the two-tone brown colour in their bill, which differentiates them from the flamboyantly adorned keel-billed toucan (*tucán pico iris*), chestnut-mandibled toucans are fairly common in coastal lowlands, wet forests and clearings across the country, although they're generally easier to see on the Pacific slope (you are most likely to see keel-billed toucans, however, in the Caribbean lowlands, particularly the Sarapiquí area); both varieties are often spotted at dawn and in the afternoon as early as 4 or 4.30pm – although dusk is best – sitting in the open upper branches of secondary forest. The chestnut-mandibled toucan's Spanish name is derived from its onomatopoeic call; the keel-billed toucan's is more of a monotonous croak.

THREE-WATTLED BELLBIRD (*CAMPENERO TRICARUNCULADO*) *PROCNIASTRICA RUNCULATUS*

Spend a few days in the cloudforests of PN Santa Elena and RBBN Monteverde and you're likely to hear the distinctly unbell-like metallic "eenk" of the three-wattled bellbird, a strange-looking bird whose appearance is defined by the black, wormlike strands that dangle from its beak; audible from almost a kilometre away, its call is considered one of the loudest bird songs on earth. Despite a variety of ongoing conservation efforts, the bellbird is becoming increasingly less common in wet and humid forests; between March and June, you may also spot them in the Tilarán and Talamanca *cordilleras*, to which they migrate during the breeding season.

BARE-NECKED UMBRELLABIRD (*PÁJARO-SOMBRILLA CUELLINUDO*) *CEPHALOPTERUS GLABRICOLLIS*

Endemic to Costa Rica and western Panama, the bare-necked umbrellabird is a difficult species to spot – confined to a strip along the Caribbean slope from Volcán Miravalles south, it is uncommon, and generally silent. But there's no mistaking this bizarre-looking bird if you are lucky enough to see one: it has a cropped, overhanging crest, which makes it look like it's sporting a bad basin-style hairpiece, whilst during the breeding season (March–June), the male is even more distinctive, inflating his impressive scarlet throat sac during courting displays. Usually found in wet-forest lowlands, but migrates to higher altitudes to breed.

1 SCARLET MACAW 2 VIOLET SABREWING 3 RESPLENDENT QUETZAL 4 BLUE-CROWNED MOTMOT 5 CHESTNUT-MANDIBLED TOUCAN
6 THREE-WATTLED BELLBIRD 7 BARE-NECKED UMBRELLABIRD >

HOTEL BED AND BREAKFAST SIGN

Basics

Getting there

Costa Rica has two international airports. Juan Santamaría (SJO), just outside San José, receives the majority of flights, while Daniel Oduber (LIR), near the northern city of Liberia, handles some flights from the US and Canada. Although there are a few direct flights from Europe, the vast majority of routes pass through the US, meaning that passengers have to comply with US entry requirements, even if merely transiting the country.

Airfares always depend on the **season**, with the highest being around July, August and December to mid-January; you'll get the best prices during the wet summer (May–Nov). Note, too, that although prices are steepest during the Christmas period (mid-Dec until the first week in Jan) when flying from the US, in Europe this can be the cheapest time to travel. Also, flying at weekends is usually more expensive; price ranges quoted below assume midweek travel.

From the UK and Ireland

There are no direct flights **from the UK** to Costa Rica, and you will have to fly via either Madrid (with Iberia), the US (with British Airways, American Airlines, Delta, United and US Airways) or Canada (with Air Canada). United tends to have the lowest fares (from as little as £480 in high season) and offers a good service, AA and BA the shortest flights (around 14hr 15min, including changing planes in the US); Iberia's daily flight avoids the US but is normally much more expensive.

There are no direct flights **from Ireland** to Costa Rica. Delta and United both fly from Dublin via New York daily (from 15hr 30min with Delta), and offer comparable fares starting at around €750.

From the US and Canada

Daily direct flights depart **for San José** from numerous cities in **the US**, including Miami (2hr 45min), Orlando (3hr 5min), Dallas (3hr 55min), Houston (3hr 40min), Denver (5hr 15min), New York (5hr 30min) and Los Angeles (6hr). American Airlines usually offers the cheapest fares **from Miami** and **Dallas** (starting at $450 in high season), while United's flights **from Houston** start at around $615; American Airlines and United both fly from many US cities to Dallas, Miami or

Houston to connect with flights to Costa Rica. Frontier Airlines flies from **Denver** from $500, while jetBlue and Spirit Airlines run services from **Florida** (both from Orlando and Fort Lauderdale), with fares around $375 for a flight from Orlando but as low as $190 on one of Spirit's early morning departures from Fort Lauderdale. The best fares **from New York** are on Avianca (via San Salvador), which cost $450; Spirit Airlines has the cheapest flights at $350, though these involve a long wait in Fort Lauderdale in either direction. **From LA**, the best deals are with Avianca (again via San Salvador); flights start at $595. jetBlue also flies from New York **to Liberia** (5hr 15min), from around $385.

There are no nonstop flights to San José **from Canada**. The cheapest fare (and quickest route) **from Toronto** is with American Airlines via Miami (Can$665), which can take as little as 7hr 30min, including the stopover in Florida. American Airlines is also the best bet from **Montréal**, with flights (7hr 35min) also requiring a plane change, in Miami (Can$690); Delta provide the best route and fares from **Vancouver**, with a change of planes in Los Angeles (Can$830; 6hr 15min).

From Australia, New Zealand and South Africa

There are no direct flights from Australia, New Zealand or South Africa to Costa Rica – the quickest and easiest option is to fly via the US. Note that it's best to book several weeks ahead.

From Australia, the cheapest fares **to San José** from Sydney are via Los Angeles with Delta (from Aus$2015 in high season); American Airlines' fares to San José via LA are slightly higher (Aus$2215). Fares from all eastern Australian cities are generally the same; fares from Perth and Darwin are more (only Aus$125, with Delta, though that requires flying via Melbourne as well).

From New Zealand, the best through-tickets **to San José** are with Delta, departing from either

---

A BETTER KIND OF TRAVEL

At Rough Guides we are passionately committed to travel. We believe it helps us understand the world we live in and the people we share it with – and of course tourism is vital to many developing economies. But the scale of modern tourism has also damaged some places irreparably, and climate change is accelerated by most forms of transport, especially flying. All Rough Guides' flights are carbon-offset, and every year we donate money to a variety of environmental charities.

Auckland or Christchurch and travelling via Sydney/Brisbane and Los Angeles (from NZ$2485 in high season).

From **South Africa**, the least convoluted route to San José is with Delta from Johannesburg via Atlanta (ZAR14,400); flights from Cape Town to Jo'burg with a South African domestic carrier such as Mango cost from ZAR1850.

Overland to Costa Rica

Costa Rica's main international bus company, Tica Bus (☎ 2221 0006, ✆ ticabus.com), runs a good **overland bus** service between Mexico (Tapachula), Guatemala, El Salvador, Honduras, Nicaragua and Costa Rica, continuing on south to Panama. It's a very popular route, and you'll need to reserve your tickets up to a month in advance in the high season (up to three months in Dec).

Tica Bus leaves **Tapachula** daily (except Good Friday) for San José at 7am, arriving in **Guatemala City** at noon and departing at 2pm (there's also a 6am service from Guatemala City); from here, it's a two-and-a-half-day trip, entailing nights (at your own expense) in San Salvador (El Salvador) and Managua (Nicaragua); a one-way fare is $93 ($83 from Guatemala City). From **Tegucigalpa** in Honduras, the bus leaves for San José ($46) daily at 9.30am, travelling via Managua (where you'll need to make an overnight stop, again at your own expense). From **Managua**, buses depart daily for San José at 6am, 7am & noon ($23); alternatively, TransNica (☎ 2223 4242, ✆ transnica.com) runs daily buses to San José from Managua at 5am, 7am, 10am & 1pm (from $28.75), while Central Line (☎ 2221 9115, ✆ transportescentralline.com) runs services via Granada at 4.30am and 10.30am

($28.75). From **Panama City**, Tica Bus leaves daily for San José at 11am and 11.55pm (from $40); alternatives include Expreso Panamá (☎ 507 314 6837, ✆ expresopanama.com), whose daily service departs at 11pm. Transportes Bocatareños (☎ 2227 9523) and Panaline (☎ 2256 8721) each run a daily bus from Changuinola (Bocas del Toro) to San José, while Tracopa (☎ 2221 4214, ✆ tracopacr.com) run a couple of services from David to the capital, leaving at 8.30am and noon.

The main northern **border crossing** with Nicaragua is at Peñas Blancas (see p.274) on the Interamericana. Further east, another crossing at Los Chiles (see p.237) involves a boat trip (and usually an overnight stop to catch it in the morning) to/from San Carlos on the shores of Lago Nicaragua, although (diplomatic tensions with Nicaragua notwithstanding) a bridge is allegedly in the pipeline. The main route south to and from Panama is again along the Interamericana, at Paso Canoas (see p.407). On the Caribbean coast, Sixaola is a smaller crossing, across one of the most decrepit bridges in the world, while in the southern highlands a little-used route links San Vito with the border town of Río Sereno.

Airlines, agents and operators

Airlines

Air Transat ✆ airtransat.ca
American Airlines ✆ aa.com
Avianca ✆ avianca.com
British Airways ✆ britishairways.com
Delta ✆ delta.com
Frontier Airlines ✆ flyfrontier.com
Iberia ✆ iberia.com
jetBlue ✆ jetblue.com
Spirit Airlines ✆ spirit.com
United Airlines ✆ united.com

TRAVEL AGENTS

eBookers UK ☎ 0203 320 3320, ✆ ebookers.com. Low fares on an extensive range of scheduled flights.
Flightcentre UK ☎ 0870 499 0040, US ☎ 1 877 992 4732, Canada ☎ 1 877 967 5302, Australia ☎ 13 31 33, New Zealand ☎ 0800 243544, South Africa ☎ 0877 405000; ✆ flightcentre.com. Rock-bottom fares worldwide.
Harvey World Travel New Zealand ☎ 0800 758787, ✆ harveyworld.co.nz; South Africa ☎ 0860 626364, ✆ harveyworld.co.za. Excellent deals on flights and holidays.
Journey Latin America UK ☎ 0203 603 8765, ✆ journeylatin america.co.uk. Latin American specialists, adept at arranging unusual itineraries at competitive fares. They also offer tours (see opposite).

North South Travel UK ☎ 01245 608 291, ⓦ northsouthtravel .co.uk. Friendly, competitive travel agency, offering discounted fares worldwide. Profits are used to support projects in the developing world, especially the promotion of sustainable tourism.

STA Travel UK ☎ 0333 321 0099, US ☎ 1800 781 4040, Australia ☎ 13 47 82, New Zealand ☎ 0800 474 400, South Africa ☎ 0861 781781; ⓦ statravel.co.uk. Worldwide specialists in independent travel; also student IDs, travel insurance, car rental, rail passes, and more. Good discounts for students and under-26s.

Tico Travel US ☎ 1 800 493 8426, ⓦ ticotravel.com. Costa Rican travel specialists who also offer discount airfares.

Trailfinders UK ☎ 0207 368 1200, Ireland ☎ 021 464 8800; ⓦ trailfinders.com. One of the best-informed and most efficient agents for independent travellers.

Travel CUTS Canada ☎ 1 800 667 2887, ⓦ travelcuts.com. Canadian youth and student travel firm.

USIT Ireland ☎ 01 602 1906, ⓦ usit.ie. Ireland's main student and youth travel specialists.

TOUR OPERATORS

In addition to the below, there are some excellent tour operators in Costa Rica itself (see p.54).

Adventure Associates Australia ☎ 02 8916 3000, ⓦ adventureassociates.com. A couple of escorted small-group tours from San José, including a week-long trip focusing on Parque Nacional Corcovado (Aus$2450).

Adventures Abroad UK ☎ 01142 473400, US & Canada ☎ 1 800 665 3998, Australia ☎ 2 9680 2828; ⓦ adventures-abroad.com. Adventure specialists, with one- to three-week trips throughout Costa Rica and other Central American countries (from £1680).

Backroads US ☎ 1 800 462 2848, ⓦ backroads.com. Cycling and multi-sport tours (from $2500) designed for the young at heart, with the emphasis on going at your own pace. Accommodation ranges from "casual inns" to luxury hotels. Also family-friendly options and singles trips.

Contours Australia ☎ 1 300 135391, ⓦ contourstravel.com.au. Specialists in Latin America, with a decent range of trips across Costa Rica – their two-week Discover Costa Rica tour takes in Parque Nacional Tortuguero, Puerto Viejo de Talamanca, Volcán Arenal and Monteverde (Aus$1430).

★ **Costa Rican Adventures US** ☎ 1 800 5517887, ⓦ costaricanadventures.com. Small-group and private trips, with a company dedicated to creating a healthier and more sustainable Costa Rica through eco-centred travel.

★ **Costa Rica Undiscovered** ⓦ costaricaundiscovered.com. Fully independent tour operator specializing in Costa Rican sustainable tourism, and following the code of ethics outlined by Sustainable Travel International and the Rainforest Alliance. Offers everything from day-tours in Parque Nacional Tortuguero ($99) to week-long yoga breaks ($1460).

Exodus UK ☎ 0845 287 7562, ⓦ exodus.co.uk. Experienced adventure-tour operators offering a range of Central American itineraries, with a popular sixteen-day Discover Costa Rica tour including visits to Parque Nacional Tortuguero, Reserva Santa Elena and Parque Nacional Piedras Blancas (£2399).

GAP Adventures UK ☎ 0844 272 0000, Ireland ☎ 01 697 1360, US & Canada ☎ 1 888 800 4100, Australia ☎ 1300 796618, NZ ☎ 0800 333307, South Africa ☎ 11 463 1170; ⓦ gapadventures .com. Over two dozen public-transport and self-drive trips, including kayaking adventures and continental odysseys (from £649).

GeoEx US ☎ 1 888 570 7108, ⓦ geoex.com. Luxury adventure travel and cultural tours, including rainforest and river trips, plus customized itineraries (from $5645).

Global Exchange US ☎ 415 255 7296, ⓦ globalexchange.org. Human rights organization offering "Reality Tours" to meet local activists and participate in educational workshops. They run three trips a year to Costa Rica (one to the Caribbean coast, two to the Pacific) concentrating on ecotourism and sustainability ($1650).

Journey Latin America UK ☎ 0203 432 3949, ⓦ journey latinamerica.co.uk. Specialist in flights, packages and adventurous, tailor-made trips to Latin America, including sixteen varied tours of Costa Rica, from week-long language courses in Monteverde (£317) to a five-week "Isthmus Crossing" that also takes in Belize, El Salvador, Guatemala, Nicaragua and Panama (£5420).

Journeys International US ☎ 1 800 255 8735, ⓦ journeys .travel. Prestigious, award-winning operator focusing on ecotourism and small-group trips, a couple specializing in photography and writing (from $2250).

Nature Expeditions International US ☎ 1 800 869 0639, ⓦ naturexp.com. Small-group expeditions led by specialists in anthropology, biology and natural history; Costa Rican trips offer optional lectures on the environment, ecotourism and local cultures (from $2850).

Peregrine UK ☎ 0808 274 5438, ⓦ peregrineadventures.com. Experienced small-group adventure specialists offering a number of good-value tours, from seven to 25 days (from £765).

Rainbow Tours UK ☎ 020 7666 1260, ⓦ rainbowtours.co.uk. Highly respected and experienced tour operator with a strong focus on wildlife-watching; their dozen itineraries include family-friendly options (from £2395).

Road Scholar US ☎ 1 800 454 5768, ⓦ roadscholar.org. Extensive selection of educational and activity programmes, including photography trips, birdwatching tours and "study cruises". Participants must be over 55, though companions may be younger (from $1500 for an eight-day wildlife-watching trip).

Sunvil Holidays UK ☎ 0208 568 4499, ⓦ sunvil.co.uk. Flexible fly-drive itineraries and tailor-made tours, specializing in luxury and wildlife-watching trips, with accommodation in a number of areas including Caño Negro, Santa Teresa and the Osa Peninsula (from £2755 for a two-week trip, though late deals are often available).

Wildlife Worldwide UK ☎ 0845 130 6982, ⓦ wildlifeworldwide .com. Tailor-made trips for wildlife and wilderness enthusiasts, visiting more off-the-beaten-track places such as Parque Nacional Braulio Carrillo and Refugio Nacional de Vida Silvestre Gandoca-Manzanillo (from £2345).

Getting around

Costa Rica's public bus system is excellent, cheap and relatively frequent, even in remote areas. Taxis regularly do long- as well as short-distance trips and are a fairly inexpensive alternative to the bus, at least if you're travelling in a group. Car rental is more common here than in the rest of Central America, but is quite expensive, especially if you're hiring a 4WD, and driving can be quite a hair-raising experience, with precipitous drops in the highlands and potholed roads just about everywhere else.

Domestic airlines are reasonably economical and can be quite a time-saver, especially since Costa Rica's difficult terrain makes driving distances longer than they appear on the map. A number of tour operators in San José organize individual itineraries and packages with transport included, well worth checking out before making any decisions about heading out on your own.

By bus

Travelling by bus is by far the cheapest way to get around Costa Rica – the most expensive journey in the country (from San José to Paso Canoas on the Panamanian border) costs just $15. San José is the hub for virtually all bus services in the country (see p.104); indeed, it's often impossible to travel from one place to another without backtracking to the capital. Tickets for some of the popular routes ought to be booked in advance, though you may be lucky enough to get on without a reservation. Tickets on most mid- to long-distance and popular routes are issued with a date and a seat number; make sure the date is correct, as you cannot normally change your ticket or get a refund. Neither can you buy return bus tickets on Costa Rican buses, which can be quite inconvenient if you're heading to very popular destinations like Monteverde or Manuel Antonio at busy times – you'll need to buy your return ticket as soon as you arrive to assure yourself a seat.

Bus schedules change with impressive frequency, so be sure to check in advance; you can download a comprehensive timetable from the ICT website (Ⓦ visitcostarica.com) or for updated information on schedules, check Ⓦ thebusschedule.com/EN/cr.

The majority of the country's buses are in good shape, although most lack air conditioning and there's very little room for luggage, or long legs. Most comfortable are the Tica Buses – modern air-conditioned vehicles with good seats, adequate baggage space and very courteous drivers – that run from San José to Panama City and Managua, and on to Tegucigalpa, San Salvador, Guatemala City, and Tapachula in Mexico (see p.46). Most buses in Costa Rica have buzzers or bells to signal to the driver that you want to get off, though you may still find a few people using the old system of whistling, or shouting "*¡Parada!*" ("Stop!") – despite signs requesting

---

FINDING YOUR WAY AROUND COSTA RICAN TOWNS

As in most Central American countries, Costa Rica's major urban areas are laid out on a **grid system**, with the main plaza in the middle of town. Calles run north–south, avenidas east–west. Generally, calles east of the plaza are odd-numbered, while those to the west are even-numbered; avenidas are even-numbered south of the park and odd-numbered to the north. However, there are a number of peculiarities that are essential to get to grips with if you want to find your way around with ease. The following rules apply to all cities except Limón…

Exact street numbers tend not to exist, and you'll typically see **addresses** written as follows: *Bar Esmeralda*, Av 2, C 5/7, which means that *Bar Esmeralda* is on Avenida 2, between Calle 5 and Calle 7. *Bar Lotto*, C 5, Av 2, on the other hand, is on the corner of Calle 5 and Avenida 2. Apartado (Aptdo) means "postbox", and bis means, technically, "encore": if you see "Av 6 bis" in an address, for example, it refers to another Avenida 6, right next to the original one.

Many **directions**, in both written and verbal form, are given in terms of metres rather than blocks (in general, one block is equivalent to 100m). Thus "de la Escuela Presidente Vargas, 125 metros al sur, cincuenta metros al oeste", translates as "from the Presidente Vargas School, 125 metres south [one block and a quarter] and 50 metres west [half a block]". More confusingly, verbal directions are commonly given in relation to landmarks that everyone – except the visitor – knows and recognizes. Even more frustratingly, some of these landmarks may not even exist any longer. This is something to get the hang of fast: taxi drivers will often look completely bewildered if given street directions, but as soon you come up with a landmark (the town church, the *parque central*, a *Pops Heladería*), the proverbial light bulb goes on.

otherwise. The atmosphere on board is generally friendly, and while there are no **toilets** on the buses, drivers make (admittedly infrequent) stops on longer runs. Often, there'll be a lunch or dinner stop at a roadside restaurant or service station; failing that, there is always a bevy of hardy food and drinks sellers who leap onto the bus proffering their wares.

The **local buses** that make short hops between towns and nearby villages and attractions, such as the services that run from Heredia to Santa Barbara, are less comfortable and more crowded, though they can be convenient to use, and the journeys are short. Finding the bus stop you need, however, can be difficult, as they tend to move about town with alarming frequency – you'll probably need to ask around to find the current departure point.

In recent years, travellers have begun to make much more use of the network of air-conditioned **shuttle buses** that connect most of Costa Rica's main tourist destinations. While these cost more than five times as much as the public buses, they are significantly faster, more comfortable and will pick up and drop off at hotels. The main operator is **Interbus** (☏ 4100 0888, ⊛ www.interbusonline .com), with comprehensive routes across the country; their fares range from $37 to $57. The similar but slightly more expensive **Gray Line** (☏ 2220 2126, ⊛ graylinecostarica.com) runs direct services between many tourist spots, with fares from $49 to $92 one way; they also offer a variety of passes that offer unlimited use of their routes, starting from $180 for a week.

By car

Although there's little traffic outside San José and the Valle Central, the common perception of **driving** in Costa Rica is of endless dodging around cows and potholes, while big trucks nudge your rear bumper in an effort to get you to go faster around the next blind bend. The reality is somewhat different. While many minor roads are indeed badly potholed and unsurfaced, driving is relatively easy, and with your own vehicle you can see the country at your own pace without having to adhere to bus or plane schedules – road signage, however, is poor, particularly in the Valle Central, so a good map (see p.80) is essential.

You only need a **valid driver's licence** issued in your home country to drive a car in Costa Rica (for up to three months). The general **speed limit** on highways is 80kph, reducing to 40kph elsewhere and 25kph in built-up areas; the speed limit is marked on the road surface or on signs. Fines (*multas*) for

---

> ### SOME USEFUL ROAD-SIGN MEANINGS
> **No Hay Paso** No Entry
> **Ceda El Paso** Give Way
> **Una Via** One Way
> **Despacio** Slow
> **Peligroso** Danger
> **Carretera En Mal Estado** Road In Bad Condition
> **Hombres Trabajando En La Via** Men Working In The Road
> **Salida De Camiones** Truck Exit

---

motoring offences are steep: talking on a mobile phone or driving without a seatbelt can incur fines of $185, running a red light could cost you $370, while if you're caught speeding (speed traps are fairly common), you may have to pay a fine up to $550 (the same amount, oddly, that you can be fined if caught making a "U" turn). If a motorist – especially a trucker – in the oncoming direction flashes his headlights at you, you can be almost certain that traffic cops with speed-trapping radar are up ahead. Although traffic cops routinely accept bribes to tear up tickets, it's a very serious offence and should not be attempted under any circumstances.

Petrol is comparatively expensive (though still cheap by European standards) at about $1.40 per litre or $5.30 per gallon (fuel prices are regulated by the government, so you'll pay the same at all petrol stations). Most cars take regular; all petrol stations (*bomboneras* or *gasolineras*) are serviced.

If you're unlucky enough to have an **accident** in Costa Rica, don't attempt to move the car until the traffic police (☏ 2222 9330 or ☏ 2222 9245) arrive: call the National Insurance Institute (☏ 2287 6000, ⊛ ins-cr.com), who will send an inspector to check the vehicles involved to assess who caused the accident – vital if you're using a rental car.

Car rental

There's no two ways about it: **car rental** in Costa Rica is expensive. Expect to pay from about $395 per week for a regular vehicle, and up to $570 for an intermediate 4WD (both including full insurance); extras such as additional driver, child seats, mobile phone and cool box will push the price up further – though note that the excellent Vamos Rent A Car (see p.52) include these as standard. Rental days are calculated on a 24-hour basis: thus, if you pick up your car on a Tuesday at 3pm for a week, you have to return it before that time the following Tuesday.

DISTANCE CHART (IN KM)

	Alajuela	Cahuita	Cartago	Dominical	Golfito	Guápiles	Heredia	Jacó	Liberia	Limón
Alajuela	-	192	40	179	331	64	12	100	200	148
Cahuita	192	-	195	334	486	128	175	287	392	44
Cartago	40	195	-	139	291	70	35	131	240	151
Dominical	179	334	139	-	152	219	174	118	309	290
Golfito	331	486	291	152	-	371	326	270	461	442
Guápiles	64	128	70	219	371	-	47	159	264	84
Heredia	12	175	35	174	326	47	-	112	205	131
Jacó	100	287	131	118	270	159	112	-	191	243
Liberia	200	392	240	309	461	264	205	191	-	348
Limón	148	44	151	290	442	84	131	243	348	-
Nicoya	185	377	225	295	442	249	197	161	83	333
Paso Canoas	337	492	291	162	54	379	332	284	471	448
Peñas Blancas	277	469	317	377	524	341	289	259	77	425
Puerto Jiménez	354	509	314	175	127	394	349	293	454	465
Puerto Viejo de Sarapiquí	79	168	119	241	393	57	67	179	272	124
Puerto Viejo de Talamanca	209	17	212	351	503	145	192	304	409	61
Puntarenas	98	290	138	187	339	162	103	75	132	246
Quepos	175	377	182	43	195	239	187	75	263	333
San Carlos	56	225	96	235	387	97	68	144	185	181
San Isidro de El General	153	308	111	28	180	180	146	251	351	264
San José	17	175	23	162	309	47	12	117	217	131
Tamarindo	257	449	297	357	524	321	269	239	69	405
Tilarán	174	366	214	274	421	236	186	156	70	322
Turrialba	85	150	45	187	336	70	80	176	285	106

Nicoya	Paso Canoas	Peñas Blancas	Puerto Jiménez	Puerto Viejo de Sarapiquí	Puerto Viejo de Talamanca	Puntarenas	Quepos	San Carlos	San Isidro de El General	San José	Tamarindo	Tilarán	Turrialba
185	337	277	354	79	209	98	175	56	153	17	257	174	85
377	492	469	509	168	17	290	377	225	308	175	449	366	150
225	291	317	314	119	212	138	182	96	111	23	297	214	45
295	162	377	175	241	351	187	43	235	28	162	357	274	187
442	54	524	127	393	503	339	195	387	180	309	524	421	336
249	379	341	394	57	145	162	239	97	180	47	321	236	70
197	332	289	349	67	192	103	187	68	146	12	269	186	80
161	284	259	293	179	304	75	75	144	251	117	239	156	176
83	471	77	454	272	409	132	263	185	351	217	69	70	285
333	448	425	465	124	61	246	333	181	264	131	405	322	106
-	452	160	465	264	394	118	242	210	336	202	72	95	272
452	-	534	159	399	509	355	209	393	186	320	534	431	342
160	534	-	547	383	486	210	334	223	428	304	146	173	355
465	159	547	-	416	526	362	218	410	203	332	527	444	359
264	399	383	416	-	185	170	254	57	201	67	336	253	164
394	509	486	526	185	-	307	394	242	325	192	466	383	167
118	355	210	362	170	307	-	150	108	249	115	190	107	183
242	209	334	218	254	394	150	-	119	326	192	314	231	227
210	393	223	410	57	242	108	119	-	209	73	272	115	141
336	186	428	203	201	325	249	326	209	-	134	408	325	156
202	320	304	332	67	192	115	192	73	134	-	274	191	68
72	534	146	527	336	466	190	314	272	408	274	-	139	335
95	431	173	444	253	383	107	231	115	325	191	139	-	252
272	342	355	359	164	167	183	227	141	156	68	335	252	-

The **minimum age** for rental is usually 21, though sometimes as low as 18, and you'll need a credit card, either Visa or MasterCard, which has sufficient credit for the entire cost of the rental. Most **car-rental companies** are located in San José and at or around the international airports near Alajuela and Liberia (note that airport rentals incur an additional twelve percent charge), though you can also rent cars in various towns around the country. Local agencies invariably provide a much better deal than the major overseas operators (Vamos and Adobe are particularly recommended), and while prices vary considerably from agency to agency, renting outside San José is usually a bit more expensive. During peak season (especially Christmas, but any time from December to March), it's wise to reserve a car before you arrive. Picking up your car in another part of Costa Rica and dropping it off at the airport when you leave normally entails a charge of $30 or more, though it may be waived if you're taking the vehicle for more than a few days.

Buying basic **insurance** is mandatory, even if you have your own. "Basics" insurance in Costa Rica tends to only cover damage by you to other people's vehicles, not your own, and given the rudimentary state of some of the roads and the aggressive driving of some of the people on them, it is worth paying extra for full insurance, although this will add to your car-rental costs considerably (full insurance starts at around $27 per day).

If you're planning to visit the Nicoya Peninsula, Santa Elena and Monteverde or remote parts of the Zona Sur, it's definitely worth paying the extra money for a **4WD**; indeed, in some areas of the country during the rainy season (May–Nov), it's a necessity. While a 4WD doesn't grant you immunity to the laws of physics, it does provide greater traction in the wet and higher clearance for rough roads and river crossings. Furthermore, in smaller vehicles, punctures are a depressingly regular experience, and although getting them repaired is a matter of a couple of minutes' hammering at the rim at the local garage, you've got better things to be doing on your holiday.

RENTAL COMPANIES AROUND SAN JOSÉ

Adobe 10 Plaza Aventura ☎ 2542 4848, ⓦ adobecar.com
Alamo Paseo Colón ☎ 2242 7733, ⓦ alamocostarica.com
Budget Paseo Colón, C 30 ☎ 2255 4240, ⓦ budget.co.cr
Hertz Paseo Colón, C 38 ☎ 2221 1818, ⓦ hertz.com
National Paseo Colón ☎ 2242 7878, ⓦ natcar.com
Payless Juan Santamaría International Airport ☎ 2432 4747, ⓦ paylesscr.com
Vamos Rent A Car C 4, Plaza Aeropuerto ☎ 2432 5258, ⓦ vamos4x4.com

CAR SAFETY IN COSTA RICA

Although the majority of the country's roads are fairly light on traffic, the **road accident** rate is phenomenal – while most Ticos blame bad road conditions, the real cause is more often poor driving. Sections of washed out, unmarked or unlit road add to the hazards, as do big trans-isthmus trucks. Another hazard is **car crime** (break-ins are an unfortunately regular occurrence) and **scams**, such as thieves puncturing your tyres and then robbing you after stopping to "help". Most people have a memorable, and uneventful, time driving around Costa Rica, but it will help if you consider the following:

- Drive defensively.
- Keep your doors locked and windows shut, especially in San José.
- Keep valuables in the boot or out of sight, and your car locked at all times.
- Avoid driving at night, when wild animals are more active.
- If someone suspicious approaches your vehicle at a red light or stop sign, sound your horn.
- Do not pull over for flashing headlights – note that an emergency or police vehicle has red or blue flashing headlights.
- If you get lost, find a public place, like a service station, to consult your map or ask for directions.
- If someone tells you something is wrong with your vehicle, do not stop immediately. Drive to the nearest service station or other well-lit public area.
- Do not park at remote trailheads – leave your car at the nearest manned ranger station.
- Be aware of steep roadside gullies used to channel rainwater runoff when turning or reversing.
- Do not pick up hitchhikers.
- In case of emergency, call ☎ 911.

CAR RENTAL ESSENTIALS

You have to exercise caution when **renting a car** in Costa Rica. While the agencies listed above are all recommended for their service, it is not uncommon for rental companies to claim for "damage" they insist you inflicted on the vehicle, and you may wish to rent a car through a Costa Rican ICT-accredited **travel agent** (see p.54), which could work out cheaper than renting on your own and will help guard against false claims of damage and other accusations.

Make sure to **check the car** carefully before you sign off the damage sheet. Scan the bodywork for dents and scuffs, and check the oil, brake fluid and fuel gauge (to make sure it's full) and that there is a spare tyre with good air pressure and a jack. Look up the Spanish for "scratches" (*rayas*) and other relevant terminology first, so you can at least scrutinize the rental company's assessment. Keep a copy of this document on you.

Take the full **insurance**, not just the basic CDW (Collision Damage Waiver); because of the country's high accident rate, you need to be covered for damage to the vehicle, yourself and any third party, and public property.

By motorcycle

For riders with a decent amount of experience, a **motorcycle** is one of the best ways to discover the diversity of Costa Rica. You will need a valid motorcycle licence or endorsement in order to rent a bike: smaller motorcycles for day-trips (125–155cc) can be rented in some beach towns (ie Jacó and Tamarindo), with daily rates around $50.

Those who want to tour the country can rent larger motorcycles (250cc and above) or book **guided tours** out of San José. Once outside the metropolitan area, an endless number of curvy back-roads and scenic gravel trails await – while the notorious road conditions of Costa Rica can be tiring in a car, they are usually great fun on a dual-sport motorcycle (Enduro motorcycle) with its large suspension.

RENTAL COMPANIES IN SAN JOSÉ

Costa Rica Motorcycle Tours ☎ 2225 6000, ⓦ costaricamotor cycletours.com. Rental (from $140/day) and tours on new BMWs (650–1200cc).

Wild Rider Motorcycles Paseo Colón, C 30/32 ☎ 2258 4604 or ☎ 8844 6568, ⓦ wild-rider.com. Very helpful German-run motorcycle rental (from $65/day for 3 days) and tours, using Honda and Suzuki bikes from 250cc to 650cc.

By bicycle

Costa Rica's terrain makes for easy **cycling** compared with neighbouring countries, and as there's a good range of places to stay and eat, you don't need to carry the extra weight of a tent, sleeping bag and stove. Always bring warm clothes and a cycling jacket, however, wherever you are. As for **equipment**, rear panniers and a small handlebar bag (for maps and camera) should be enough.

Bring a puncture repair kit, even if your tyres are supposedly unbustable. You'll need a bike with a triple front gear – this gives you 15 to 21 gears, and you will really need the low ones, especially if cycling in the highlands. Make sure, too, that you carry and drink lots of water – five to eight litres a day in the coastal lowlands.

There is very little **traffic** outside the Valle Central, and despite their tactics with other cars (and pedestrians), Costa Rican drivers are some of the most courteous in Central America to cyclists. That said, however, bus and truck drivers do tend to forget about you as soon as they pass, sometimes forcing you off the road. **Roads** are generally good for cyclists, who can dodge the potholes and wandering cattle more easily than drivers. Bear in mind that if you cycle up to Monteverde, one of the most popular routes in the country, you're in for a slow trip: besides being steep, there's not much traction on the loose gravel roads. Although road signs will tell you that cycling on the Interamericana (Panamerican Highway, or Hwy-1) is not permitted, you will quickly see that people do so anyway.

San José's best **cycle shop** is Ciclo Los Ases, 100m east of the Gimnasio Nacional, Av 10 (☎2255 0535, ⓔinfo@ciclosasescr.com). They have all the parts you might need, can fix your bike and may even be able to give you a bicycle carton for the plane.

By plane

Costa Rica's two **domestic carriers**, Sansa and NatureAir, offer reasonably economical flights between San José and many beach destinations and provincial towns, and can be particularly handy for accessing the more remote corners of the country – the flight from San José to Puerto

Jiménez on the Osa Peninsula, for example, takes just fifty minutes compared to four and a half hours on the bus. Both carriers fly small twin-propeller aircraft (so bad weather can have an impact on schedules) and service more or less the same destinations.

Of the two, **NatureAir** (☎ 2299 6000, ⓦ natureair .com), which flies from Tobías Bolaños Airport in Pavas, 7km west of San José, is generally more reliable and has more frequent services on some runs. **Sansa** (☎ 2290 4100, ⓦ flysansa.com) flies from Juan Sàntamaría airport, 17km northwest of San José, and is cheaper but less dependable. Rates start at around $60 for the shortest hops, though NatureAir will often reduce its cheapest fares to $30 on flights that aren't fully booked. On both airlines, make your reservations as far as possible in advance (at least two weeks in high season), and even then be advised that a booking means almost nothing until the seat is actually paid for. Reconfirm your flight in advance of the day of departure and again on the day of travel, if possible, as their **schedules** (see p.104) can change at short notice. Note that the airports at Arenal ($7), Tambor ($2.50) and Quepos ($3) charge **departure/arrival taxes**.

If you're planning to cover a lot of ground in a limited amount of time, the **Nature Air Pass** ($309/529 for one/two weeks) gives you unrestricted use of all thirteen of their services.

If you're travelling in a large group, **air-charter taxis** can prove a reasonably cheap way to get to the country's more remote areas. NatureAir and Alfa Romeo Air (☎ 8632 8150, ⓦ alfaromeoair.com) both run charters, on five- to eighteen-seater planes; Alfa Romeo's flight from San José to Tortuguero, for example, costs $550.

Tour operators

There are scores of **tour operators** in Costa Rica, some very good, some not so – bear in mind that although you may save a few dollars by going with the cheapest agency, you could end up on a badly organized tour with poor accommodation and under-qualified guides. Go with a reputable tour operator – such as those listed below, which are all licensed (and regulated) by the ICT, and in the relevant sections of each chapter – and not with one of the freelance "guides" who may approach you at the bus station or on the street. The following is not a comprehensive list, but all those that we've listed are experienced and recommended, offering a good range of services and tours.

TOUR OPERATORS IN SAN JOSÉ

★**ACTUAR** 250m north of Parque La Amistad, Pavas ☎ 2290 7514, ⓦ actuarcostarica.com. The Costa Rican Association of Community-based Rural Tourism, whose highly rewarding trips give a real insight into co-operatives, locally owned coffee farms and indigenous reserves, among other grassroot organizations. Day-trips from $20.

Camino Travel ☎ 1, Av 0/1 ☎ 2234 2530, ⓦ caminotravel.com. Young, enthusiastic staff with high standards (and a mainly European clientele) offering upmarket and independent travel, including individual tours with quality accommodation. They can also help with transport information and car rental. From $25 for a day-tour of Santa Cruz and the pottery village of Guaitil.

Cooprena Simbiosis Tours 200m west and 75m south of CNFL, Sabana Sur ☎ 2290 8646, ⓦ turismoruralcr.com. Tour company offering community-based rural tourism and volunteer programmes alongside various day-trips; some of their excellent hiking trips are held in conjunction with local co-operatives, and involve staying in community lodges.

★**Costa Rica Expeditions** C Central, Av 3 ☎ 2257 0766, ⓦ costaricaexpeditions.com. The longest-established and most experienced of the major tour operators, with superior accommodation in Tortuguero, Monteverde and Corcovado, a superlative staff of guides and tremendous resources. You can drop into the busy downtown office and talk to a consultant about individual tours.

Ecole Travel C 7, Av 0/1 ☎ 2234 1669, ⓦ ecoletravel.com. Small agency, popular with backpackers, offering well-priced tours to Tortuguero (2/3 days; from $219) and the Osa Peninsula (3/4 days; from $375). They work with ACTUAR on their community-based tourism trips and boast a maximum Certificate of Sustainable Tourism rating (see p.431).

Expediciones Tropicales Av 11/13, C 3 bis ☎ 2257 4171, ⓦ costaricainfo.com. Well-regarded agency with knowledgeable guides who run popular combination day-tours of Volcán Poás and nearby sights (from $73), as well as a host of other trips from San José at competitive prices. They can also organize short-term minivan or bus rental (including driver).

Horizontes Nature Tours C 28, Av 1/3 ☎ 2222 2022, ⓦ horizontes.com. Highly regarded agency concentrating on rainforest walking and hiking, volcanoes and birdwatching, all with an emphasis on natural and cultural history; their eight-day tour of Carara and Palo Verde national parks costs $1600.

Serendipity Adventures Apdo 90 7150, Turrialba ☎ 2556 5852, ⓦ serendipityadventures.com. This superior travel agency offers individual custom-made tours for self-formed groups with a sense of adventure, mostly to undiscovered parts of Costa Rica. They're experts in canyoning and rappelling, and are the only operators in Costa Rica to offer hot-air balloon trips ($345).

Specops ☎ 504 289 5988, ⓦ specops.com. Adventure education group, comprising US Special Forces veterans and expert Costa Rican guides, which specializes in white-knuckle thrills, jungle-survival courses and extreme photography.

Accommodation

Most towns in Costa Rica have a wide range of places to stay, and even the smallest settlements usually have simple lodgings. Prices are higher than you'd pay in other Central American countries, but they're by no means exorbitant, and certainly not when compared with the US or Western Europe. Budget accommodation runs the gamut from the extremely basic, where $20 will get you little more than a room and a bed, to reasonably well-equipped accommodation with a clean, comfortable en-suite room, a fan and possibly even a TV for around $35 a night. In the middle and upper price ranges, facilities and services are generally of a very good standard throughout the country. When considering the cost, remember that not all hotels list the hotel tax (13 percent) in the published price.

The larger places to stay in Costa Rica are usually called **hotels**. Posadas, **hostals**, **hospedajes** and **pensiones** are smaller, though *posadas* can sometimes be quite swanky, especially in rural areas. **Casas** tend to be private guesthouses or

ACCOMMODATION PRICES

All the prices quoted for accommodation in this book are for the least expensive double room or dorm bed in high season, and include the thirteen percent national tax that is automatically added onto hotel bills. Unless otherwise stated, breakfast is included in the price.

B&Bs, while **albergues** are the equivalent of lodges. **Cabinas** are common in Costa Rica, particularly in coastal areas: they're usually either a string of motel-style rooms in an annexe away from the main building or, more often, separate self-contained units. Usually – although not always – they tend towards the basic, and are most often frequented by budget travellers. More upmarket versions may be called "villas" or "chalets". Anything called a **motel** – as in most of Latin America – is unlikely to be used for sleeping.

Few hotels at the lower end of the price range have double beds, and it's more common to find two or three single beds. **Single travellers** will generally be charged the single rate even if they're occupying a double room, though this is sometimes not the case in popular beach towns and at peak seasons.

STAYING WITH A COSTA RICAN FAMILY

There's no better way to experience life off the tourist trail and to practise your Spanish than by **staying with a Tico family**. Usually enjoyable, sometimes transformative, this can be a fantastic experience, and at the very least is sure to provide genuine contact with Costa Ricans.

Most **homestay programmes** are organized by the country's various **language schools** and cater mainly to students. However, some schools may be willing to put you in contact with a family even if you are not a student at the school in question. The **Ilisa Language School** (☎ 2280 0700, ☒ ilisa.com), one of San José's largest, is particularly helpful in this regard. Stays can last from one week to several months, and many travellers use the family home as a base while touring the country. You'll have your own key, but in most cases it would be frowned upon if you brought someone home for the night. The one rule that always applies is that guests and hosts communicate in Spanish. Packages, including accommodation, meals, laundry and internet access start from $1370 a month for four hours of group classes a day.

For a **non-study-based option**, try **Bells' Home Hospitality** (☎ 2225 4752, ☒ homestay -thebells.com), run by long-time resident Vernon Bell and his wife Marcela, who arrange for individuals, couples and families to stay in private rooms in a family home, with private or shared bathroom; singles cost $35, doubles $60, reduced rates for stays of two weeks or longer (breakfast is included in the price). Another recommended organization is the **Monteverde Institute** (☎ 2645 5053, ☒ monteverde-institute.org), which offers accommodation in a range of rural family homes near the Santa Elena and Monteverde reserves for $22 per night including meals and laundry.

Other points of contact for homestays as well as longer-term **apartment rentals and houseshares** include adverts in the *Tico Times* (although homestays and flats listed here tend to be expensive), the (Spanish) classifieds in *La Nación* and the notice boards of hostels and guesthouses.

TOP 5 ECOLODGES

As the original ecotourist destination (see p.426), Costa Rica has some of the best **ecolodges** in the Americas, and there can be few more gratifying ways to spend your holiday than by lushing it up in a luxury lodge in the middle of the rainforest, safe in the knowledge that you're having no negative impact on your surroundings and that your money is going to a good cause.

Finca Rosa Blanca Coffee Plantation & Inn Gorgeous, idiosyncratically designed rooms and suites on an organic coffee plantation in the Valle Central. Solar heating and recycling (including a vermiculture compost) are just some of their sustainable practices. See p.142.

Lapa Ríos Upmarket lodge built using renewable resources on the diversity-rich Osa Peninsula. Protects its own thousand-acre conservancy, invests heavily in the local community and regional wildlife projects and is completely locally staffed. See p.392.

Rancho Margot Self-sufficient organic farm and holistic retreat with a range of accommodation to suit all budgets – join in with milking the cows or help in the herb garden. See p.220.

Rara Avis Rainforest Lodge & Reserve Remote rainforest lodge that doubles as a research station, set in thick primary forest that's home to a variety of unique flora and thrilling fauna. See p.235.

El Silencio Lodge & Spa Inviting hillside cabins overlooking swathes of cloudforest (much of it the lodge's private reserve). Carbon-offsetting initiatives and waste-management programmes, plus most of the staff, including the management, is local; profits go towards primary school projects. See p.134.

Bear in mind that in Costa Rican hotels, the term "**hot water**" can be misleading. Showers are often equipped with squat plastic nozzles (water heaters), inside which is an electric element that heats the water to a warm, rather than hot, temperature. Some of the nozzles have a button that actually turns on the element. Under no circumstances should you touch this button or get anywhere near the nozzle when wet – these contraptions may not be quite as bad as their tongue-in-cheek name of "suicide showers" suggests, but there's still a distinct possibility you could get a nasty shock. The trick to getting fairly hot water is not to turn on the pressure too high. Keep a little coming through to heat the water more efficiently.

Reservations

Costa Rica's hotels tend to be chock-full in high season (Nov–April), especially at Christmas, New Year and Easter, so **reserve well ahead**, particularly for youth hostels and good-value hotels in popular spots; the easiest and surest way is with a credit card by email. Once on the ground, phone or email again to reconfirm your reservation. Some establishments will ask you to reserve and pay in advance – the more popular hotels and lodges require you to do this as far as thirty days ahead, often by money transfer.

If you prefer to be a little more spontaneous, travelling in the low season, from roughly after Easter to mid-November, can be easier, when you can safely wait until you arrive in the country to make reservations. During these months, it's even possible to show up at hotels on spec – there will probably be space, and possibly even a low-season discount of as much as thirty to fifty percent.

Pensiones and hotels

When travelling, most Costa Ricans and nationals of other Central American countries stick to the lower end of the market and patronize traditional **pensiones** (a fast-dying breed in Costa Rica, especially in San José) or established Costa Rican-owned hotels. If you do likewise, you may well get a better price than at the tourist or foreign-owned hotels, although this is not a hard-and-fast rule. Though standards are generally high, you should expect to get what you pay for: usually clean but dim, spartan rooms with cold-water showers. If you've got the option of looking at several places, it's perfectly acceptable to ask to see the room first.

The majority of accommodation catering to foreigners is in the **middle range**, and as such is reasonably priced – although still more expensive than similar accommodation in other Central American countries. Hotels at the lower end of this price category will often offer very good value, giving you private bathroom with hot water, perhaps towels, and maybe even air conditioning (which, it has to be said, is not really necessary in most places; a ceiling fan generally does fine). At the upper end of this price range, a few extras, like TV, may be thrown in.

Resorts, lodges and B&Bs

Costa Rica's many "resorts" range from swanky hotels in popular places like Manuel Antonio to lush **rainforest ecolodges** in areas of outstanding natural beauty – the sort of hideaways that have their own jacuzzis, swimming pools, spas, gourmet restaurants and private stretches of jungle. These rank among the finest – and most expensive – places to stay in the country (see box opposite), though prices can fall dramatically out of season, when you might be able to get yourself a night of luxury for as little as $150.

A new breed of **B&Bs** (often owned by expats) has sprung up in recent years, similar to their North American or UK counterparts, offering rooms in homes or converted homes with a "family atmosphere", insightful local advice and a full breakfast. As well as those listed in the Guide, you can search online for Costa Rican B&Bs at ⓦbedandbreakfast .com/costa-rica.html.

Camping

Though **camping** is fairly widespread in Costa Rica, gone are the days when you could pitch your tent on just about any beach or field. With the influx of visitors, local residents (especially in small beachside communities) have grown tired of campers leaving rubbish on the beach – you'll have a far better relationship with them if you ask politely whether it's OK to camp first.

In beach towns, you'll usually find at least one well-equipped **private campsite**, with good facilities including toilets, drinking water and cooking grills; staff may also offer to guard your clothes and tent while you're at the beach. You may also find hotels, usually at the lower end of the price scale, where you can pitch your tent on the grounds and use the showers and washrooms for a fee. Though not all **national parks** have campsites, the ones that do usually offer high standards and at least basic facilities, with toilets, water and cooking grills – all for around $5 per person per day. In some national parks, you can bunk down at the **ranger station** if you call well in advance (see p.65).

There are three general **rules of camping** in Costa Rica: never leave your tent (or anything of value inside it) unattended, or it may not be there when you get back; never leave your tent open

A CAMPING CHECKLIST

- Tent
- Backpack (with waterproof cover)
- Lightweight (summer) sleeping bag, except for climbing Chirripó, where you may need a three-season bag
- Sleeping-bag liner (optional)
- Rain gear
- Mosquito net
- Maps
- Torch
- Knife
- Camping stove (bought once in Costa Rica)
- Matches, in a waterproof box
- Firelighter
- Compass
- Insect repellent
- Water bottles
- Toilet paper
- Hat
- Hiking boots
- Sunglasses
- Sunblock
- Plastic bags (for wet clothes/rubbish)

except to get in and out, unless you fancy sharing your sleeping quarters with snakes, frogs, insects or curious coati; and always take your rubbish with you when you leave.

Youth hostels

Costa Rica has over two hundred **hostels** and **backpackers**, offering dorm beds for as little as $5 a night; most have a range of double (from around $20), triple and family rooms, and many offer additional services including free wi-fi, laundry and luggage storage. Bed linen, towels and soap are generally included in the price. There are only three **official youth hostels** affiliated with Hostelling International – *Jardines Arenal* in La Fortuna, *Vista Serena Hostel* in Manuel Antonio (see p.353) and *Hostel Casa Yoses* in San José – which cost from $11 per night. As with all accommodation in Costa Rica, bookings should ideally be made several months in advance if you're visiting in high season.

YOUTH HOSTEL ASSOCIATIONS

UK AND IRELAND

Youth Hostel Association (YHA) UK ☎ 0800 019 1700, ⓦyha .org.uk

Scottish Youth Hostel Association UK ☎ 0845 293 7373, ⓦ syha.org.uk

Irish Youth Hostel Association Ireland ☎ 01 830 4555,
Ⓦ anoige.ie
Hostelling International Northern Ireland Northern Ireland
☎ 028 9032 4733, Ⓦ hini.org.uk

US AND CANADA

Hostelling International–American Youth Hostels US
☎ 240 650 2100, Ⓦ hiusa.org
Hostelling International Canada Canada ☎ 1800 663 5777,
Ⓦ hihostels.ca

AUSTRALIA, NEW ZEALAND AND SOUTH AFRICA

Australian Youth Hostels Association Australia Ⓦ yha.com.au
Youth Hostelling Association New Zealand New Zealand
☎ 0800 278 299, International ☎ 0643 379 9970, Ⓦ yha.co.nz
Hostelling International South Africa South Africa
Ⓦ hisouthafrica.com

Food and drink

**Costa Rican food – called comida típica
("native" or "local" food) by Ticos – is best
described as unpretentious. Simple it
may be, but tasty nonetheless, especially
when it comes to the interesting regional
variations found along the Caribbean
coast, with its Creole-influenced cooking,
and in Guanacaste, where there are
vestiges of the ancient indigenous
peoples' use of maize. For more on the
cuisine of these areas, see the relevant
chapters in the Guide.**

Típico dishes you'll find all over Costa Rica include
rice and some kind of meat or fish, often served as
part of a special plate with coleslaw salad and
plantain, in which case it's called a **casado** (literally,
"married person"). The ubiquitous **gallo pinto**
("painted rooster"), often described as the national
dish of Costa Rica, is a filling breakfast combination
of red and white beans with rice, sometimes served
with *huevos revueltos* (scrambled eggs). The heavy
concentration on starch and protein reveals the
rural origins of Costa Rican food: *gallo pinto* is food
for people who are going out to work it off.

Of the dishes found on menus all over the country,
particularly recommended are *chicarrones* (fried pork
rind), **ceviche** (raw fish "marinated" in lime juice with
coriander and peppers), **pargo** (red snapper),
corvina (sea bass) and any of the ice creams and
desserts, though these can be too sickly for many
tastes. The fresh **fruit** is especially good, either eaten
by itself or drunk in *refrescos* (see opposite). Papayas,

pineapple and bananas are all cheap and plentiful,
along with some less familiar fruits like *mamones
chinos* (a kind of lychee), *anona* (custard fruit),
pejibaye (peach palm fruit) and *marañón*, whose seed
is the cashew nut. Look out, too, for fresh strawberries around Volcán Poás and sweet, fleshy *guanábana*
(soursop) along the Caribbean coast.

Eating out

Eating out in Costa Rica will cost more than you
might think, and has become even more expensive
over the past few years. Main dishes start at around
$10 in San José, and can be double that in some of
the more popular coastal towns, and then there are
those sneaky **extra charges**: the service charge (10
percent) and the sales tax (13 percent), which bring
the meal to a total of 23 percent more than the
menu price. Add this all up, and dinner for two can
easily come to $25 for a single course and a couple
of beers. **Tipping** (see p.82) is not necessary,
however. Costa Rica's best restaurants are on the
outskirts of San José, and in popular tourist destinations such as Tamarindo, Manuel Antonio and
around La Fortuna, where demand has created
some excellent gourmet options.

The cheapest places to dine in Costa Rica – and
where most workers eat lunch, their main meal –
are the ubiquitous **sodas**, halfway between the
North American diner and the British greasy spoon.
Sodas offer filling set *platos del día* (daily specials) for
about $5, as well as *casados* and other hearty *típico*
classics; most do not add sales tax. You usually have
to go to the cash register to get your bill. *Sodas* also
often have takeaway windows where you can pick
up snacks such as *churros*, delicious little fingers of
fried dough and sugar. Many *sodas* are vegetarian,
and in general **vegetarians** do quite well in Costa
Rica – most menus will have a vegetable option, and
asking for dishes to be served without meat is
perfectly acceptable.

Because Costa Ricans start the day early, they
are less likely to hang about late in restaurants in
the evening, and establishments are usually empty
or **closed** by 10pm. Nonsmoking sections are
uncommon, to say the least, except in the most
expensive establishments, but in general Ticos don't
smoke much in restaurants.

Drinking

Costa Rica is famous for its **coffee**, and it's usual to
end a meal with a small cup, traditionally served in
a pitcher with heated milk on the side. Most of the

best blends are exported, so premium coffee is generally only served in high-end restaurants and sold in shops.

Always popular are **refrescos**, cool drinks made with fresh fruit, ice and either milk (*leche*) or water (*agua*), all whipped up in a blender; you can buy them at stalls or in cartons, though the latter tend to be sugary. **Batidos** (smoothies) are a thicker, tastier variation. You'll find **herb teas** throughout the country; those served in the Caribbean province of Limón are especially good. In Guanacaste, you can sample the distinctive **corn-based drinks** *horchata* and *pinolillo*, made with milk and sugar, and with a grainy consistency.

Costa Rica has several local brands of **lager**, a godsend in the steamy tropics. Most popular is Imperial, with its characteristic eagle logo, but Bavaria Gold is the best of the bunch, with a cleaner taste and more complex flavour; they also produce a decent dark beer, while Pilsen and the lemon-flavoured Rock Ice are also worth a try. Of the local low-alcohol beers, Bavaria Light is the best tasting.

Wine, once a rare commodity, has become far more common in mid- and top-range restaurants, where you'll often find good Chilean and Argentinian varieties on offer, as well as (for a premium) Spanish brands. **Spirits** tend to be associated with serious drinking, usually by men in bars, and are rarely consumed by local women in public; the indigenous sugarcane-based drink, **guaro**, of which Cacique is the most popular brand, is a bit rough but good with lime sodas or in a cocktail. For an after-dinner tipple, try Café Rica, a creamy **liqueur** made with local coffee.

Bars

Costa Rica has a variety of **places to drink**, from shady macho domains to pretty beachside bars, with some particularly cosmopolitan nightspots in San José. The capital is also the place to find the country's last remaining **boca bars**, atmospheric places that serve *bocas* (tasty little tapas-like snacks) with drinks (see box, p.114); though historically these were free, nowadays even in the most traditional places you'll probably have to pay for them. In even the smallest town with any foreign population – either expat or tourist – you'll notice a sharp split between the places frequented by locals and those that cater to foreigners. Gringo grottoes abound, especially in beach towns, and tend to have a wide bar stock, at least compared to the limited *guaro*-and-beer menu of the local joints. In many places, especially port cities like Limón, Puntarenas and Golfito, there is the usual contingent of rough-and-ready bars where testosterone-fuelled men go to drink gallons and fight; it's usually pretty obvious which ones they are – they advertise their seediness with a giant Imperial placard parked right in front of the door so you can't see what's going on inside.

Most bars typically **open** in the morning, any time between 8.30 and 11am, and **close** at around 11pm or midnight. Sunday night is usually dead: many bars don't open at all and others close early, around 10pm. Though Friday and Saturday nights are the busiest, the **best nights** to go out are often weeknights (particularly Thursdays), when you can enjoy live music, happy hours and other

COFFEE

There are two types of coffee available in Costa Rica: **export quality** (*grano d'oro*, literally the "golden bean"), typically packaged by either Café Britt or Café Rey and served in good hotels and restaurants; and the **lower-grade blend**, usually sold for the home market. Costa Rica's export-grade coffee is known the world over for its mellowness and smoothness. The stuff produced for the domestic market, however, is another matter entirely; some of it is even pre-sweetened, so if you ask for it with sugar (*con azúcar*), you'll get a saccharine shock.

All coffee in Costa Rica is Arabica; it's illegal to grow anything else. Among the best brews you'll find are **La Carpintera**, a smooth, rich, hard bean grown on Cerro de la Carpintera in the Valle Central, and **Zurqui**, the oldest cultivated bean in the country, grown for over 150 years on the flanks of Volcán Barva. Strong, but with a silky, gentle taste, **Café el Gran Vito**, grown by Italian immigrants near San Vito in the extreme south of the country, is an unusual grade of export bean, harder to find than those grown in the Valle Central.

Several small coffee producers run **tours** of their plantations, allowing you to see the coffee-cultivating process up close and to try their home-grown roasts on site. The Valle Central, home to five of the country's eight regional varieties, offers the greatest range (see box, p.125), though there are also a couple of tours worth trying near Monteverde (see box, p.311).

specials. **Karaoke** is incredibly popular, and if you spend much time in bars, you'll soon pick out the well-loved Tico classics. The **drinking age** in Costa Rica is 18, and many bars will only admit those with ID (*cédula*); a photocopy of your passport page is acceptable.

Health

Health-wise, travelling in Costa Rica is generally very safe. Food tends to be hygienically prepared, so bugs and upsets are normally limited to the usual "traveller's tummy". Water supplies in most places are clean and bacteria-free, and outbreaks of serious infectious diseases such as cholera are rare.

In general, as in the rest of Latin America, it tends to be local people, often poor or without proper sanitation or access to healthcare, who contract infectious diseases. Although Costa Rica's **healthcare** is of a high standard, the facilities at its major public hospitals vary widely, and while some, such as the Hospital Nacional de Niños in San José (see p.74), are very good, you are advised to use private hospitals and clinics where possible – and get extensive health insurance before you travel (see p.79). The capital's two excellent **private hospitals**, CIMA San José and Clínica Biblica (see p.117), are equipped to handle medical, surgical and maternity cases, and have 24-hour emergency rooms; the latter also has a good paediatric unit.

Inoculations

No compulsory **inoculations** are required before you enter Costa Rica unless you're travelling from a country that has yellow fever, such as Colombia, in which case you must be able to produce a current inoculation certificate. You may, however, want to make sure that your polio, tetanus, typhoid, diphtheria and hepatitis A jabs are up to date, though none of the diseases is a major risk. Rabies, a potentially fatal illness, should be taken very seriously if you're going to be spending a significant amount of time in the countryside. There is a vaccine comprising a course of three injections that has to be started at least a month before departure – though it's expensive and serves only to shorten the course of treatment you need. If you're not vaccinated, stay away from dogs, monkeys and any other potentially biting or scratching animals. If you do get scratched or bitten, wash the wound at once, with alcohol or iodine if possible, and seek medical help immediately.

The sun

Costa Rica is just eight to eleven degrees north of the Equator, which means a blazing-hot sun directly overhead. To guard against **sunburn** take at least factor-15 sunscreen (start on factor-30) and a good hat, and wear both even on slightly overcast days, especially in coastal areas. Even in places at higher altitudes where it doesn't feel excessively hot, such as San José and the surrounding Valle Central, you should protect

---

A TRAVELLER'S FIRST-AID KIT

Among the items you might want to carry with you, especially if you're planning to go hiking, are:

- Antiseptic cream
- Plasters/Band-Aids
- Imodium for emergency diarrhoea treatment
- Paracetamol/Aspirin
- Rehydration sachets
- Calamine lotion
- Hypodermic needles and sterilized skin wipes
- Iodine soap for washing cuts (guards against humidity-encouraged infections)
- Insect repellent
- Sulphur powder (fights the sand fleas/chiggers that are ubiquitous in some of Costa Rica's beach areas)

Note that most of Costa Rica's major towns have well-stocked **pharmacies** (*farmacias* or *boticas*) where trained pharmacists are licensed to dispense a wide range of drugs (essentially anything other than antibiotics or psychotropic drugs, for which you'll need a prescription).

yourself. **Dehydration** is another possible problem, so keep your fluid level up, and take rehydration salts (Gastrolyte is readily available) if necessary. **Diarrhoea** can be brought on by too much sun and heat sickness, and it's a good idea to bring an over-the-counter remedy such as Imodium from home – it should only be taken for short periods, however, and only when really necessary (such as travelling for long periods on a bus) as extensive use leads to constipation and only serves to keep whatever is making you ill inside you.

Drinking water

The only areas of Costa Rica where it's best not to drink the tap water (or ice cubes, or drinks made with tap water) are the port cities of **Limón** and **Puntarenas**. Bottled water is available in these towns; drink from these and stick with known brands, even if they are more expensive. Though you'll be safe drinking tap water elsewhere in the country, it is possible to pick up **giardia**, a bacterium that causes stomach upset and diarrhoea, by drinking out of streams and rivers – campers should stock up on water supplies from the national parks waterspouts, where it's been treated for drinking.

The time-honoured method of **boiling** will effectively sterilize water, although it will not remove unpleasant tastes. A minimum boiling time of five minutes (longer at higher altitudes) is sufficient to kill microorganisms. Boiling water is not always convenient, however, as it is time-consuming and requires supplies of fuel or a travel kettle and power source – **chemical sterilization** can be carried out using either chlorine or iodine tablets or (better) a tincture of iodine liquid; add five drops to one litre of water and leave to stand for thirty minutes. **Pregnant women** or people with **thyroid problems** should consult their doctor before using iodine sterilizing tablets or iodine-based purifiers. Inexpensive iodine-removal filters are recommended if treated water is being used continuously for more than a month or if it is being given to babies.

Malaria and dengue fever

Although some sources of information – including perhaps your GP – will tell you that you don't need to worry about **malaria** in Costa Rica, there is a small risk if you're travelling to the **southern Caribbean coast**, especially Puerto Limón and south towards Cahuita and Puerto Viejo de Talamanca. Less than one hundred cases of malaria are reported annually, and the World Health Organization is optimistically predicting Costa Rica could eradicate the disease by 2018, but if you want to make absolutely sure of not contracting the illness, and intend to travel extensively anywhere along the southern Caribbean, you should take a course of prophylactics (usually chloroquine rather than mefloquine), available from your doctor or clinic.

Dengue fever is perhaps more of a concern, and in 2013 there were a record 50,000 cases reported in the country, more than double the amount of the previous year; the Nicoya Peninsula was the worst area affected. Most cases occur during the rainy season when the mosquito population is at its height, and usually in urban or semi-urban areas; note that, unlike malaria, the dengue-carrying mosquito often bites during the day. The symptoms are similar to malaria, but with extreme aches and pains in the bones and joints, along with fever and dizziness. On rare occasions, the illness may develop potentially fatal complications, although this usually only affects people who have caught the disease more than once. The only cure for dengue fever is rest and painkillers, and, as with malaria, the best course of action is **prevention**: to avoid getting bitten by mosquitoes (*zancudos*), cover up with long sleeves and long trousers, use insect repellents (containing DEET) on exposed skin and, where necessary, sleep under a mosquito net.

Snakes

Snakes abound in Costa Rica, but the risk of being bitten is incredibly small – there has been no instance of a tourist receiving a fatal bite in recent years. Most of the victims of Costa Rica's more venomous snakes such as the fer-de-lance and the dreaded bushmaster (see p.38) are field labourers who do not have time or the resources to get to a hospital (there are around five such deaths each year). Just in case, however, travellers hiking off the beaten track may want to take specific **antivenins** plus sterile hypodermic needles; if you're worried, you can buy antivenin at the Instituto Clodomiro Picado, the University of Costa Rica's snake farm in Coronado, outside San José (☎2511 7888, 🌐icp.ucr.ac.cr), where herpetologists (people who study snakes) are glad to talk to visitors about precautions.

If you have no antivenin and are unlucky enough to get bitten, do not try to catch or kill the specimen for identification, as you only risk getting bitten again. Clean the wound with soap and water (do not try to suck out the venom), immobilize the bitten limb (do not apply a tourniquet) and get to the nearest hospital as soon as possible.

In general, **prevention** is better than cure. As a rule of thumb, you should approach rainforest cover and grassy uplands – the kind of terrain you find in Guanacaste and the Nicoya Peninsula – with caution. Always watch where you put your feet and, if you need to hold something to keep your balance, make sure the "vine" you're grabbing isn't, in fact, a surprised snake. Be particularly wary at dawn or dusk – before 5.30am or after 6pm – though note that many snakes start moving as early as 4.30pm, particularly in dense cloudforest cover. In addition, be careful in "sunspots", places in thick rainforest where the sun penetrates through to the ground or onto a tree; snakes like to hang out here, absorbing the warmth. Above all, though, don't be too alarmed: thousands of tourists troop through Costa Rica's rainforests and grasslands each year without encountering a single snake.

Spiders

Most spiders in Costa Rica are harmless, but one species that's definitely worth avoiding is the Brazilian wandering spider or **banana spider**, a large, aggressive arachnid that hides under logs, dried banana leaves and other dark places during the daytime, coming out at night to stalk the forest floor in search of prey. It is recognized as the most venomous spider in the world, carrying a cocktail of toxins that can cause priapism, convulsions and paralysis; bites are rare in Costa Rica (banana plantation workers, rather than tourists, are most at risk), but if you are bitten, you should seek medical attention immediately.

Pujarras, chiggers, ants and bees

Costa Rica is home to a quarter of a million different species of **insect** (*bicho*), and while most are perfectly harmless there are a few that can give you a nasty bite or sting. In hot, slightly swampy lowland areas, such as coastal Osa and southern Nicoya peninsulas, you may come across **purrujas**, similar to blackflies or midges. They can inflict itchy bites, as can the **chiggers** (*colorados*) that inhabit scrub and secondary-growth areas, attaching themselves to the skin, leech-like, in order to feed.

Of the country's numerous species of ant, the ones to watch out for are the enormous **bullet ants**, which resemble moving blackberries. Prevalent in low-lying forests, they hold the distinction of causing the world's most painful insect sting – their colloquial name of *veinticuatro* ("24") refers to the fact that if you get bitten by one it will hurt for 24 hours.

Among Costa Rica's many bee species (*abejas*) are aggressive **Africanized bees**, which migrated from Africa to Brazil and then north to Costa Rica, where they have colonized certain localities. Although you have to disturb their nests before they'll bother you, people sensitive or allergic to bee-stings should avoid Parque Nacional Palo Verde.

Sharks

Sharks (*tiburón*) are generally found on beaches where turtles nest, especially along the northern Caribbean coast, on Playa Ostional in the Nicoya Peninsula (although not as far south as Playa Nosara) and in the waters surrounding Parque Nacional Corcovado. **Bull sharks**, an aggressive species and one of the few sharks that can live in both fresh water and sea water, have been known to enter the rivers here (see p.393), as well as the Río San Juan on their way between Lago Nicaragua and the sea.

HIV and AIDS

HIV and **AIDS** (in Spanish, SIDA) are present in the country (an estimated 9800 adults in Costa Rica are living with HIV), but aren't prevalent. That said, the same common-sense rules apply here as all over the world: sex without a condom, especially in some of the popular beach towns, is a serious health risk. **Condoms** sold in Costa Rica are not of the quality you'll find at home; it's best to bring them with you. Though hospitals and clinics use sterilized equipment, you may want to bring sealed hypodermic syringes anyway.

MEDICAL RESOURCES

Canadian Society for International Health Canada ☎ 613 241 5785, ⓦ csih.org. Extensive list of travel health centres.

CDC US ☎ 1800 232 6348, ⓦ cdc.gov/travel. Official US government travel health site.

Hospital for Tropical Diseases Travel Clinic UK ⓦ thehtd.org. Pre- and post-trip advice and help with the prevention, diagnosis and treatment of tropical diseases and travel-related infections.

International Society for Travel Medicine US ☎ 1404 373 8282, ⓦ istm.org. Has a full list of clinics specializing in international travel health. Publishes outbreak warnings, suggested inoculations, precautions and other background information for travellers.

MASTA (Medical Advisory Service for Travellers Abroad) UK Ⓦ masta-travel-health.com for the nearest clinic.
NHS UK Ⓦ fitfortravel.nhs.uk. Information and advice on recommended inoculations, malaria risk and the general health situation in listed countries.
The Travel Doctor Ⓦ traveldoctor.com.au. Lists travel clinics in Australia, New Zealand and South Africa.
Tropical Medical Bureau Ireland ☏ 1850 487 674, Ⓦ tmb.ie.

The media

Though the Costa Rican media generally pumps out relatively anodyne and conservative coverage of local and regional issues (shadowing the antics of the president and the political elite with dogged tenacity), it's possible to find good investigative journalism, particularly in the daily La Nación. There are also a number of interesting local radio stations, though TV coverage leaves a lot to be desired.

Newspapers

In San José, all **domestic newspapers** are sold on the street by vendors. Elsewhere, you can find them in newsagents and *pulperías* (general stores). All are tabloid format, with colourful, eye-catching layouts and presentation.

Though the Costa Rican press is free, it does indulge in a certain follow-the-leader journalism. Said leader is the daily **La Nación** (Ⓦ nacion.com), voice of the (right-of-centre) establishment and owned by the country's biggest media consortium; other highbrow dailies and television channels more or less parrot its line. Historically, *La Nación* has featured some good investigative reporting, as in the Banco Anglo corruption scandal and in highlighting Costa Rica's continuing drug-trafficking problems. It also comes with a useful daily pull-out arts section, **Viva**, with listings of what's on in San José, and the classifieds are handy for almost anything, including long-term accommodation.

Also quite serious is **La República** (Ⓦ larepublica .net), even if they do have a tendency to slap a football photo on the front page no matter what's happening in the world. Alternative voices include **El Heraldo** (Ⓦ elheraldo.net), a small but high-quality daily, and **La Prensa Libre** (Ⓦ prensalibre .cr), the very good left-leaning evening paper. **Al Día** (Ⓦ aldia.cr) is a popular daily sports paper (read national and international football, plus occasional surf pieces).

The weekly **Semanario Universidad** (Ⓦ semanario .ucr.ac.cr), the voice of the University of Costa Rica, certainly goes out on more of a limb than the big dailies, with particularly good coverage of the arts and the current political scene; you can find it on or around campus in San José's university district of San Pedro, and also in libraries.

The well-regarded English-language paper **Tico Times** (Ⓦ ticotimes.net) ended its print edition in 2012 and is now an online-only publication, though it is still a good source of information for travellers. As for the **foreign press**, you can pick up recent copies of *The New York Times*, *International Herald Tribune*, *USA Today*, *Miami Herald*, *Newsweek*, *Time* and sometimes the *Financial Times* in the souvenir shop beside the *Gran Hotel Costa Rica* in downtown San José and at La Casa de Revistas in San José. Of the capital's bookstores, Librerías Lehmann and Librería Internacional keep good stocks of mainstream and non-mainstream foreign magazines (see p.116); the Mark Twain Library at the Centro Cultural Costarricense Norteamericano (see p.117) also receives English-language publications.

Radio

There are lots of **commercial radio stations** in Costa Rica, all pumping out techno and house, along with a bit of salsa, annoying commercials and the odd bout of government-sponsored pseudo propaganda promoting the general wonder that is Costa Rica. Some of the more interesting **local radio stations** have only a limited airtime, such as Radio Costa Rica (930AM), while others, such as Radio Alajuela (1120AM), stop broadcasting early on Sundays. A fascinating programme is *El Club del Taxista Costarricense* – the "Costa Rican Taxi Driver's Club" – broadcast by Radio Actual FM (107.1FM) on Mondays to Fridays from 6 to 7pm. This social and political talk show, which started broadcasting in 1973, was initially directed only at taxi drivers, but its populist appeal has led to it being adopted by the general population. Radio Dos (99.5FM) has a weekday English-language morning show, *Good Morning Costa Rica*, which runs from 6 to 9am.

Television

Most Costa Rican households have a **television**, beaming out a range of wonderfully awful Mexican or Venezuelan *telenovelas* (soap operas) and some not-so-bad domestic news programmes. On the downside, Costa Rica is also the graveyard for 1970s American TV, the place where *The Dukes of Hazzard* and other such delights, dubbed into Spanish, come back to haunt you.

Canal 7, owned by Teletica, is the main national station, particularly strong in local and regional news. Other than its news show, **Telenoticias**, Costa Rica has few home-grown products, and Canal 7's programming comprises a mix of bought-in shows from Spanish-speaking countries plus a few from the US. Repretel's **Canal 6** is the main competitor, very similar in content, while **Canal 19** mostly shows US programmes and movies dubbed into Spanish. The **Mexican cable channels** are good for news, and even have reports from Europe. Many places also subscribe to CNN and other cable channels, such as HBO, Fox and ESPN, which show wall-to-wall reruns of hit comedy shows and films.

Holidays and festivals

Though you shouldn't expect the kind of colour and verve that you'll find in fiestas in Mexico or Guatemala, Costa Rica has its fair share of lively holidays and festivals, or feriados, when all banks, post offices, museums and government offices close. In particular, don't try to travel anywhere during Semana Santa, Holy (Easter) Week: the whole country shuts down from Holy Thursday until after Easter Monday, and buses don't run. Likewise, the week from Christmas to New Year is invariably a time of traffic nightmares, overcrowded beach towns and suspended transport services.

Provincial holidays, such as Independence Day in Guanacaste (July 25) and the Limón Carnival (the week preceding Oct 12) affect local services only, but nonetheless the shutdown is drastic, with municipal shutdowns similar to those experienced at festival time.

January 1 New Year's Day. Celebrated with a big dance in San José's Parque Central.

January Fiesta de Palmares. Two weeks of dancing, music and horse parades in the small town of Palmares.

February Puntarenas Carnival. Ten days of parades, music and fireworks around the middle of the month.

February/March Monteverde Music Fest. National and international musicians gather in the cloudforest town for a month of song and dance.

March Festival Imperial. Alajuela's annual rock festival is the biggest of its kind in Costa Rica, attracting over thirty thousand revellers.

March El Día de los Boyeros. The Escazú barrio of San José celebrates the historical importance of oxcart drivers on the second Sunday in March with colourful parades of painted oxcarts and driving competitions, plus plenty of traditional food and dancing.

March 19 El Día de San José (St Joseph's Day). The patron saint of San José Province is celebrated with fairs, parades and church services.

Ash Wednesday Countrywide processions; in Guanacaste, they're marked by horse, cow and bull parades, with bullfights (in which the bull is not harmed) in Liberia.

Holy Week (Semana Santa) Dates vary annually, but businesses will often close for the entire week preceding Easter weekend.

April International Arts Festival. Every two years (even numbers), San José plays host to ten days of theatre shows, concerts, dance performances and art exhibitions.

April 11 El Día de Juan Santamaría. Public holiday (and longer festivities) to commemorate the national hero who fought at the Battle of Rivas against the American adventurer William Walker in 1856.

May 1 El Día del Trabajo (Labour Day). The president delivers his annual "state of the nation" address while everyone else heads to the beach.

May 29 Corpus Christi Day. Countrywide national holiday, typically focused around a traditional feast.

June 29 St Peter's and St Paul's Day. Street festivities in towns named after these saints (Pedro and Pablo).

July Virgen del Mar (Virgin of the Sea). Elaborately decorated boats fill the Gulf of Nicoya on the Saturday nearest to the 16th, celebrating the patron saint of Puntarenas.

July 25 El Día de Guanacaste (Guanacaste Province only). Celebrations mark the annexation of Guanacaste from Nicaragua in 1824.

August 2 El Día de La Negrita (Virgin of Los Angeles Day). Worshippers make a pilgrimage to the basilica in Cartago to venerate the miraculous Black Virgin of Los Ángeles (La Negrita), the patron saint of Costa Rica.

August 15 Assumption Day and Mother's Day. Family get-togethers and occasional street parades and community events mark what is traditionally a big deal in Costa Rica.

September 15 Independence Day. Big patriotic parades celebrating Costa Rica's independence from Spain in 1821. The highlight is a student relay race across the entire Central American isthmus, carrying a "freedom torch" from Guatemala to Cartago (the original capital of Costa Rica).

October 12 El Día de la Raza (Columbus Day; Limón Province only). Celebrations to mark Christopher Columbus' landing at Isla Uvita are centred on the Limón Carnival, which takes place in the week prior to October 12.

November 2 El Día de los Muertos (All Souls' Day). Families visit cemeteries to pay their respects to their ancestors.

Christmas Week The week before Christmas is celebrated in San José with fireworks, bullfights and funfairs.

December 25 Christmas Day. Family-oriented celebrations with trips to the beach.

December 27 San José Carnival. Huge parade with colourful floats and plenty of music.

National parks and reserves

Costa Rica protects just over a quarter of its total territory under the aegis of a carefully structured system of national parks, wildlife refuges and biological reserves – in all, there are nearly two hundred designated protected areas. Gradually established over the last 45 years or so (see p.426), the role of these parks in conserving the country's rich fauna and flora is generally lauded.

In total, the parks and reserves harbour approximately five percent of the world's total **wildlife species** and **life zones**, among them rainforests, cloudforests, paramo (high-altitude moorlands), swamps, lagoons, marshes and mangroves, and the last remaining patches of tropical dry forest in the isthmus. Also protected are areas of historical significance, including a very few pre-Columbian settlements, a number of active volcanoes and places considered to be of immense scenic beauty – valleys, waterfalls, dry lowlands and beaches. Costa Rica has also taken measures to safeguard beaches where marine turtles lay their eggs.

Definitions

A **national park** (*parque nacional*) is typically a large chunk of relatively untouched wilderness – usually more than 2500 acres – dedicated to preserving features of outstanding ecological, environmental or scenic interest. These are generally the most established of the protected areas, typically offering walking, hiking or snorkelling opportunities. Though habitation, construction of hotels and hunting of animals is prohibited in all national parks (indeed, since 2012, trophy hunting has been prohibited in Costa Rica full stop), "**buffer zones**" are increasingly being designated around them, where people are permitted to engage in a limited amount of agriculture. In most cases, park boundaries are surveyed but not demarcated – rangers and locals know what land is within the park and what is not – so don't expect fences or signs to tell you where you are.

Although it also protects valuable ecosystems and conserves areas for scientific research, a **biological reserve** (*reserva biológica*) generally has less of scenic or recreational interest than a national park, though fishing is usually still prohibited. A **national wildlife refuge** (*refugio nacional de vida silvestre* or *refugio nacional de fauna silvestre*) is designated to protect the habitat of wildlife species. It will not be at all obviously demarcated, with few, if any, services, rangers or trails, and, the Refugio Nacional de Vida Silvestre Caño Negro notwithstanding, is generally little visited by tourists. An "**absolute**" **reserve** (*reserva absoluta*) is purely dedicated to scientific research, with no public entry permitted – the one exception being the Reserva Natural Absoluta Cabo Blanco, on the tip of the southern Nicoya Peninsula, which was Costa Rica's first piece of nationally protected land and grants visitors similar access to a national wildlife refuge or national park.

There are also a number of **privately owned reserves**, chief among them community-initiated projects such as the now famous reserves at Monteverde and nearby Santa Elena. While the money you pay to enter these does not go directly to the government, they are almost always not-for-profit places; the vast majority are conscientiously managed and have links with national and international conservation organizations.

Visiting the parks

Despite their role in attracting tourists to the country, national parks – and the national park system in general – are underfunded, and facilities at some of the more remote and less visited parks (such as Juan Castro Blanco el Agua, Volcán Turrialba and La Cangreja) can be surprisingly threadbare or even nonexistent. Most parks, however, have an entrance **puesto**, or ranger station, often little more than a small hut where you pay your fee (usually around $10) and pick up a general map. Typically, the main ranger stations – from where the internal administration of the park is carried out, and where the rangers (or *guardaparques*) sleep, eat and hang out – are some way from the entrance *puesto*; it's a good idea to pay these a visit, as you can talk to the *guardaparques* (if your Spanish is good) about local terrain, conditions and recent wildlife spottings, enquire about drinking water and use the bathroom. In some parks, such as Corcovado, you can sleep in or camp near the main stations, which usually provide basic but adequate accommodation, be it on a campsite or a bunk, in a friendly atmosphere.

In general, the **guardaparques** are extremely knowledgeable and informative and are happy to tell you about their encounters with fearsome bushmasters or placid tapirs. Independent travellers and hikers might want to ask about the possibility

NATIONAL PARKS AT A GLANCE

National Park	Location	Topography	Wildlife	Activities
La Amistad*	border with Panama	rainforest	mammals, birds	hiking
Ballena**	190km SE of San José	marine coral	mammals, marine life	diving, snorkelling
Barbilla	100km E of San José	rainforest	birds, mammals	hiking
Barra Honda	330km W of San José	subterranean caves	bats, reptiles, birds	caving
Las Baulas**	300km NW of San José	beach, marine	turtles	turtle-watching
Braulio Carrillo	20km N of San José	cloudforest, rainforest	birds, reptiles, mammals	hiking, birdwatching
Cahuita	195km SE of San José	marine, beaches	marine life, reptiles, mammals	swimming, walking snorkelling
La Cangreja	85km SW of San José	rainforest	birds, mammals	hiking
Carara	90km S of San José	rainforest, tropical dry forest	birds, mammals, reptiles	birdwatching, hiking
Chirripó	150km SE of San José	mountain peaks, paramo	mammals, birds (incl. quetzal)	hiking, climbing
Corcovado	380km SE of San José	rainforest	mammals, amphibians, reptiles	hiking
Diriá	285km W of San José	tropical dry forest	mammals, birds	hiking
Guanacaste	250km NW of San José	rainforest, tropical dry forest	butterflies, moths, birds, mammals	hiking
Guayabo***	85km E of San José	rainforest	mammals, birds	archeology, history, walking
Isla del Coco	535km offshore	volcanic, rainforest	marine life	diving
Juan Castro Blanco el Agua	65km NW of San José	rainforest	birds, mammals	hiking
Manuel Antonio	130km S of San José	rainforest, mangroves, beaches	mammals, marine life, reptiles	hiking, swimming
Palo Verde	240km NW of San José	seasonal wetlands, savanna	birds, mammals	birdwatching, hiking
Piedras Blancas	320km SE of San José	rainforest, beach	birds, mammals, marine life	hiking, swimming
Los Quetzales	75km S of San José	cloudforest	mammals, birds (incl. quetzal)	birdwatching, hiking
Rincón de la Vieja	255km NW of San José	rainforest, savanna	birds	hiking, volcano-watching
Santa Rosa	260km NW of San José	tropical dry forest	mammals, turtles	hiking, history, turtle-watching
Tapantí-Macizo Cerro de la Muerte	40km SE of San José	primary montane forests	mammals, birds	hiking
Tortuguero	255km NE of San José	rainforest, beach	turtles, mammals, birds	turtle-watching
Volcán Arenal	135km NW of San José	volcanic	birds, mammals	volcano-watching, hiking
Volcán Irazú	55km E of San José	volcanic	birds	volcano-watching
Volcán Poás	55km N of San José	volcanic, dwarf cloudforest	mammals, birds	volcano-watching
Volcán Tenorio	160km NW of San José	volcanic	birds	volcano-watching, hiking
Volcán Turrialba	65km E of San José	volcanic	birds	volcano-watching, hiking

* Parque Nacional Internacional   ** Parque Nacional Marino   *** Monumento Nacional

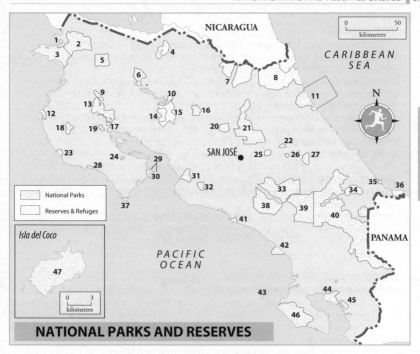

NATIONAL PARKS AND RESERVES

NATIONAL PARKS AND PRINCIPAL BIOLOGICAL RESERVES, WILDLIFE REFUGES AND PRIVATE RESERVES

1 Refugio Nacional de Vida Silvestre Junquillal
2 Parque Nacional Guanacaste
3 Parque Nacional Santa Rosa
4 Refugio Nacional de Vida Silvestre Caño Negro
5 Parque Nacional Rincón de la Vieja
6 Parque Nacional Volcán Tenorio
7 Refugio Nacional de Vida Silvestre Mixto Maquenque
8 Refugio Nacional de Vida Silvestre Barra del Colorado
9 Reserva Biológica Lomas de Barbudal
10 Parque Nacional Volcán Arenal
11 Parque Nacional Tortuguero
12 Parque Nacional Marino Las Baulas
13 Parque Nacional Palo Verde
14 Reserva Biológica Bosque Nuboso Monteverde & Reserva Santa Elena
15 Bosque Etorno de los Niños
16 Parque Nacional Juan Castro Blanco
17 Refugio Nacional de Vida Silvestre Cipancí
18 Parque Nacional Diriá
19 Parque Nacional Barra Honda
20 Parque Nacional Volcán Poás
21 Parque Nacional Braulio Carrillo
22 Parque Nacional Volcán Turrialba
23 Refugio Nacional de Vida Silvestre Ostional
24 Refugio Nacional de Vida Silvestre Reserva Karen Mogensen

25 Parque Nacional Volcán Irazú
26 Monumento Nacional Guayabo
27 Parque Nacional Barbilla
28 Refugio Nacional de Vida Silvestre Camaronal
29 Reserva Biológica de Guayabo y Negritos
30 Refugio Nacional de Vida Silvestre Curú
31 Parque Nacional Carara
32 Parque Nacional La Cangreja
33 Parque Nacional Tapantí-Macizo Cerro de la Muerte
34 Reserva Biológica Hitoy-Cerere
35 Parque Nacional Cahuita
36 Refugio Nacional de Vida Silvestre Gandoca-Manzanillo
37 Reserva Natural Absoluta Cabo Blanco
38 Parque Nacional Los Quetzales
39 Parque Nacional Chirripó
40 Parque Internacional La Amistad (Costa Rica & Panama)
41 Parque Nacional Manuel Antonio
42 Parque Nacional Marino Ballena
43 Reserva Biológica Isla del Caño
44 Parque Nacional Piedras Blancas
45 Refugio Nacional de Vida Silvestre Golfito
46 Parque Nacional Corcovado
47 Parque Nacional Isla del Coco

of joining them on patrol during the day (you'll probably have to speak some Spanish), while the more adventurous can volunteer to help out at remote ranger stations (see p.76); you have to be pretty brave to do this, as you are expected to do everything that a ranger does, which includes patrolling the park (often at night) against poachers.

Outside the most visited parks – Volcán Poás, Volcán Irazú, Santa Rosa and Manuel Antonio –

opening hours are erratic. Most places are open daily, from around 8am to 3.30 or 4pm, though there are exceptions, while other parks may open a little earlier in the morning. In all cases, especially the volcanoes, you should aim to arrive as early in the morning as possible to make the most of the day and, in particular, the weather (especially in the wet season); early morning is also the best time to spot the wildlife that the parks protect. You'll usually

TOP 5 HIKES

Costa Rica's national parks and wildlife refuges are home to some truly spectacular **trails**, enabling you to hike deep into verdant rainforest, past bubbling mud pools or along surf-lashed beaches. Below are a few of our favourites.

Cerro Chirripó A long, cold and sometimes wet slog up and across alpine-esque moorland rewards you (on a clear day) with superb views from Costa Rica's highest point. See p.371.

Estación Biológica Pocosol Arguably the most adventurous trek in the country, the two-day hike from Monteverde to this research station on the eastern edge of the Bosque Eterno de los Niños traverses unmarked trails and is accompanied by armed rangers. See p.312.

Sendero Laguna Meándrica Perhaps the finest birding trail of any national park (and that's saying something), this 4.3km round-trip in the western half of Parque Nacional Carara leads through transitionary terrain to a croc-filled lake that's home to myriad birdlife. See p.342.

Sendero Las Pailas Terrific 6km circuit, taking in the best of Parque Nacional Rincón de la Vieja: sulphur pools, geothermal "stoves" and thermal mud pots, all within the shadow of a smoking volcano. See p.357.

Sendero Los Patos–Sirena Tough 20km trek through the dense rainforest cover of Parque Nacional Corcovado, offering experienced hikers the chance to spot some of Costa Rica's more elusive large mammals, including tapir and collared peccary. See p.395.

find a *guardaparque* somewhere, even if he or she is not at the ranger station – if you hang around for a while and call "¡Upe!" (what people say when entering houses and farms in the countryside), someone will usually appear.

Costa Rica's protected areas are overseen by the Sistema Nacional de Areas de Conservación (National System of Conservation Areas), or **SINAC** (☎2522 6500, ⓦwww.sinac.go.cr), which operates within MINAE and can provide information on individual parks, transport and camping facilities. The only central office where you can make reservations and buy **permits**, where required, is the **Fundación de Parques Nacionales** (Av 15, C 25, Barrio Escalante, San José ☎2257 2239, ⓔfpncr@ ice.co.cr), who will contact those parks for which you sometimes need reservations, chiefly Santa Rosa, Corcovado and Chirripó (see the individual accounts in the Guide for more details); other parks can be visited on spec.

Outdoor activities

Costa Rica is famous for year-round adventure tourism and its variety of adrenaline-fuelled outdoor activities, with numerous operators running well-organized packages and guided outings (see p.54). For further information on sporting activities, pick up the bi-monthly Costa Rica Outdoors magazine or visit ⓦcostaricaoutdoors.com – they specialize in fishing, but cover other sports, too.

Hiking

Almost everyone who comes to Costa Rica does some sort of **hiking** or **walking**, whether it be multi-day hikes through remote rainforest, scaling Cerro Chirripó or ambling along beaches and well-maintained national park trails.

Make sure you **bring** sturdy shoes or hiking boots, and lightweight rain gear. It helps to have binoculars, too, even if you don't consider yourself an avid birder or animal-spotter. In certain areas, like Parque Nacional Corcovado – where you'll be doing more walking than you've probably ever done before, unless you're in the Marines – most people also bring a tent. In the high paramo of Chirripó, you'll need to bring at least a sleeping bag.

There are a number of things you have to be careful of when hiking in Costa Rica. The chief danger is **dehydration**: always carry lots of water with you, preferably bottled, or a canteen, and bring a hat and sunscreen to protect yourself against sunstroke (and use both, even if it's cloudy).

Each year many hikers **get lost**, although they're nearly almost always found before it's too late. If you're venturing into a remote and unfamiliar area, bring a map and compass and make sure you know how to use both. To lessen anxiety if you do get lost, make sure you have matches, a torch and, if you are at a fairly high altitude, warm clothing. It gets cold at night above 1500m, and it would be ironic (and put quite a dampener on your holiday) to end up with hypothermia in the tropics.

Whitewater rafting

After hiking, **whitewater rafting** is probably the single most popular activity in Costa Rica. Some of the best rapids and rivers to be found south of the Colorado are here, and there's a growing mini-industry of rafting outfitters, most of them in San José, Turrialba and La Virgen.

Whitewater rafting entails getting in a rubber dinghy with about eight other people (including a guide) and paddling, at first very leisurely, down a river, before negotiating exhilarating rapids of varying difficulty. Overall it's very safe, and the ample life jackets and helmets help. **Wildlife** you are likely to see from the boat includes caimans, lizards, parrots, toucans, herons and kingfishers. Most trips last a day, though some companies run overnight or multi-day excursions; **costs** range between $65 and $130 for a day, including transport, equipment and lunch. Dress to get wet, with a bathing suit, shorts and surfer sandals or gym shoes.

Rafters classify their rivers from Class I (easiest) to Class V (pretty hard – don't venture onto one of these unless you know what you're doing). The **most difficult** rivers in Costa Rica are the Class III–IV+ Pacuare and Reventazón, both reached from Turrialba (see box, p.155); the Río Naranjo, near Quepos (see p.349); and the Class V Upper Balsa, accessed from La Fortuna (see p.209). The **moderately easy** Río Sarapiquí (see box, p.239) is a Class II river with some Class III rapids and a fearsome Class IV upper section; the Río Savegre, near Quepos (see p.349) runs Class II–III rapids. The **gentlest** of all is the Río Corobicí (see box, p.248), a lazy ride along Class I flat water.

OUTFITTERS

Aguas Bravas ☎ 2292 2072, ⓦ costaricaraftingvacation.com. One of the largest rafting specialists in the country, operating on the Balsa, the Sarapiquí, the Pacuare and the Chirripó, close to San José.

Aventuras Naturales ☎ 2225 3939, ⓦ adventurecostarica.com. Focuses on running the Sarapiquí and the Pacuare rivers – its two- to seven-day trips on the latter include an overnight stay at their sumptuous *Pacuare Jungle Lodge*.

Exploradores Outdoors ☎ 2222 6262, ⓦ exploradoresoutdoors .com. A focussed selection of one- and two-day trips on the Pacuare and the Reventazón (El Carmen section).

Ríos Tropicales ☎ 2233 6455, ⓦ riostropicales.com. One of the larger outfitters, with challenging one- to four-day trips on the Pacuare, plus day-rides on half a dozen other rivers, including the Reventazón, the Tenorio and the Cucaracho in Guanacaste – a good choice for experienced rafters.

RIPTIDES

Riptides are always found on beaches with relatively heavy surf, and can also form near river estuaries; some are permanent, while others "migrate" up and down a beach. If caught in a riptide – and you'll know when you're in one as they can move at an alarming rate of up to 10kph – you should follow the advice below:

Don't panic While riptides may drag you out to sea a bit, they won't take you far beyond the breakers, where they lose their energy and dissipate. They also won't drag you under (that's an undertow), and there are far fewer of those on Costa Rica's beaches. Relax as much as possible – panicking will exhaust you fast and cause you to take in water.

Don't swim against the current This is a pointless exercise. Instead, float, call for help and wait until the current dies down. Then swim back towards the beach at a 45-degree angle, not straight in; by swimming at an angle, you'll avoid getting caught in the current again.

BEACHES WITH RIPTIDES

Some of the most popular and frequented **beaches** in Costa Rica are, ironically, also the worst for riptides. Take extra care when swimming at the following destinations:

Playa Avellana (Guanacaste)
Playa Bonita (Limón)
Playa Cahuita (the first 400m of beach; Limón)
Playa Doña Ana (Central Pacific)
Playa Espadilla (Manuel Antonio, Central Pacific)
Playa Jacó (Central Pacific)
Playa Junquillal (Guanacaste)
Playa Tamarindo (Guanacaste)
Punta Uva (Limón)

Kayaking

More than twenty rivers in Costa Rica offer good **kayaking** opportunities, especially the Sarapiquí, Reventazón, Pacuare and Corobicí, while several tour operators run paddling trips among the wildlife-rich mangroves of islas Damas and Bahía Drake. The small town of La Virgin in the Zona Norte is a good base for customized kayaking tours, with a number of specialist operators or lodges renting boats, equipment and guides (see box, p.239). The "Week of Rivers" trip run by Costa Rica Rios (US & Canada ☎1 888 434 0776, UK ☎0800 612 8718; ⓦcostaricarios.com) takes in four of the country's best kayaking rivers and includes three days on the Pacuare ($1650).

Sea kayaking has become increasingly popular in recent years. This is an activity for experienced kayakers only, and should never be attempted without a guide – the number of rivers, rapids and streams pouring from the mountains into the oceans on both coasts can make currents treacherous, and kayaking dangerous without proper supervision. One of the best operators is Seascape Kayak Tours (☎8314 8605, ⓦseascapekayaktours.com), who run recommended trips around the Refugio Nacional de Vida Silvestre Curú on the southern Nicoya Peninsula (see p.330).

Canopy tours, hanging bridges and aerial trams

The **canopy tour** craze that started in Monteverde in the early 1990s has taken the country by storm, and now pretty much any tourist town worth its salt has a zip line or two. The standard tour consists of whizzing from lofty platform to platform via traverse cables, and while you're moving too fast to see much wildlife, it's definitely a thrill. In recent years, Tarzan swings and Superman cables (which you ride horizontally, arms stretched out like the eponymous superhero) have upped the ante, and several places now let you zip-line at night. Monteverde (see box, p.314) and the area around Volcán Arenal (see box, p.211) have some of the best canopy tours in Costa Rica.

More sedate, and more worthwhile for wildlife-watching, are the **hanging bridges** complexes, where you can experience spectacular views – if not a touch of vertigo – as you walk across the wobbly structures over serious heights. Several bridges take you right alongside the canopy of tall trees; most places offer tours with a naturalist guide, which can be a great way of gaining a better insight into life in the treetops. Again, Monteverde and Volcán Arenal are recommended places to take a "sky walk".

For an even more relaxing meander through the canopy, you could try riding on an **aerial tram**, a gondola-like cable car that slowly circuits the upper reaches of the rainforest. Several places that operate canopy tours and hanging bridges also have aerial trams, though the most famous is the Rainforest Aerial Tram (now known as the Rainforest Adventures Costa Rica Atlantic), just outside Parque Nacional Braulio Carrillo (see p.145); there's also a Pacific branch, just north of Jacó (see p.344).

Swimming

Costa Rica has many lovely **beaches**, most of them on the Pacific coast. You do have to be careful swimming at many of them, however, as around 250 **drownings** occur each year – about five a week. Most are the result of **riptides**, strong, swift-moving currents that go from the beach out to sea in a kind of funnel (see box, p.69). It's also important to be aware of fairly heavy **swells**. These waves might not look that big from the beach but can have a mighty pull when you get near their break point. Many people are hurt coming out of the sea, backs to the waves, which then clobber them from behind – it's best to come out of the sea sideways, so that there is minimum body resistance to the water.

In addition to the above **precautions**, never swim alone, don't swim at beaches where turtles nest (this means, more often than not, sharks), never swim near river estuaries (pollution and riptides) and always ask locals about the general character of the beach before you swim.

Surfing

Surfing is one of Costa Rica's biggest draws and is very good on both coasts, although there are certain beaches that are suitable during only parts of the year. You can surf all year round on the **Pacific**: running north to south the most popular beaches are Naranjo, Tamarindo, Boca de Barranca, Jacó, Hermosa, Quepos, Dominical and, in the extreme south near the Panama border, Pavones. On the **Caribbean** coast, the best beaches are at Puerto Viejo de Talamanca and Punta Uva, further down the coast.

If you're interested in **learning to surf**, there are several surf camps and schools in Tamarindo (see box, p.284), Santa Teresa/Mal País (see box, p.338) and Jacó (see box, p.345). You can check **tide**

times online at Ⓦ crsurf.com. Costa Rica is small enough that if things are quiet on one coast, it's fairly easy to pack up your kit and hit the other (buses will take your board for an additional $2 or so, more on shuttle buses). Serious surfers spending some time in the country will find *The Surfer's Guide to Costa Rica and SW Nicaragua* by Mike Parise an invaluable guide.

The Pacific

The **north Pacific coast and Nicoya Peninsula** are the country's prime surfing areas, with a wide variety of reef and beach breaks, and lefts and rights of varying power and velocity. **Playa Potrero Grande** (also known as Ollie's Point and made famous in the surf flick *Endless Summer II*) is only accessible by boat from Playas del Coco and

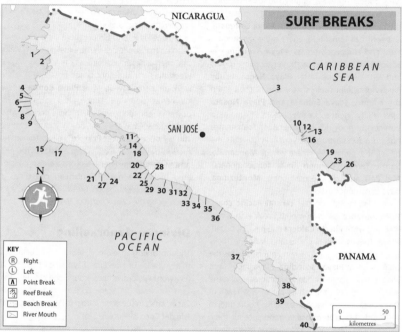

MAJOR SURF BREAKS

1 Petrero Grande (Ollie's Point) Ⓡ Ⓐ
2 Playa Naranjo (Witch's Rock) Ⓡ Ⓛ ☐
3 North Caribbean Coast Ⓡ Ⓛ ☐
4 Playa Grande Ⓡ Ⓛ
5 Playa Tamarindo Ⓡ Ⓛ Ⓐ ◇
6 Playa Langosta Ⓡ Ⓛ Ⓐ
7 Playa Avallena Ⓡ Ⓛ ☐
8 Playa Negra Ⓡ Ⓐ
9 Playa Junquillal Ⓡ Ⓛ Ⓐ
10 Portete Ⓡ ▨
11 Boca Barranca Ⓛ ◇
12 Isla Uvita Ⓛ ▨
13 Playa Bonita Ⓛ Ⓐ ▨
14 Puerto Caldera Ⓛ Ⓐ
15 Playa Nosara Ⓡ Ⓛ ☐
16 Westfalia Ⓡ Ⓛ
17 Playa Sámara Ⓡ Ⓛ ☐
18 Playa Tivives/Valor Ⓡ Ⓛ ☐ ▨
19 Playa Negra Ⓡ Ⓛ ☐
20 Playa Escondida Ⓛ Ⓐ

21 Santa Teresa, Playa Carmen & Mal País Ⓡ Ⓛ ☐ ▨
22 Playa Jaco Ⓡ Ⓛ ☐
23 Puerto Viejo de Talamanca (La Salsa Brava) Ⓡ Ⓛ ▨
24 Montezuma Ⓡ Ⓛ Ⓐ ☐
25 Roca Loca Ⓡ ▨
26 Manzanillo Ⓡ Ⓛ ☐
27 Cabuya Ⓛ Ⓐ ▨
28 Playa Hermosa Ⓡ Ⓛ ☐
29 Playa Esterillos Oeste Ⓡ Ⓛ ☐
30 Playa Esterillos Este Ⓡ Ⓛ ☐
31 Playa Bejuco Ⓡ Ⓛ ☐
32 Boca Damas Ⓡ Ⓛ ☐
33 Quepos Ⓛ ◇
34 Playa Espadilla Ⓡ Ⓛ ☐
35 Playa El Rey Ⓡ Ⓛ ☐
36 Playa Dominical Ⓡ Ⓛ ☐
37 Bahía Drake Ⓡ Ⓛ ▨
38 Matapalo Ⓡ
39 Pavones Ⓛ Ⓐ
40 Punta Burica Ⓡ Ⓛ ▨

offers a very fast, right point break. Within Parque Nacional Santa Rosa, **Playa Naranjo** (or Witch's Rock) gives one of the best breaks in the country and has the added attraction of good camping facilities, though you'll need your own 4WD to reach them.

Moving down to the long western back of the Nicoya Peninsula, **Playa Tamarindo** has three (very popular) sites for surfing, though they don't offer a really demanding or wild ride and parts of the beach are plagued by rocks. **Playa Langosta**, just south of Tamarindo, offers more demanding right and left beach breaks. **Playa Avellana** has a good beach break, with very hollow rights and lefts, while the faster **Playa Negra** nearby has a right point break that is one of the best in the country. **Playa Sámara and Playa Nosara** offer fairly gentle beach breaks (Sámara is particularly good for beginners), though things hot up a bit as you work your way towards the tip of the peninsula, where *playas* **Manzanillo**, **Santa Teresa**, **Carmen** (best for beginners), **Mal País** and, on the east coast, **Montezuma**, have consistent breaks.

Near Puntarenas on the **central Pacific coast**, **Boca Barranca** is a river-mouth break with a very long left, while **Puerto Caldera** also has a good left. **Playa Tivives** (beach break) and **Valor** (a rocky point break) have good lefts and rights, as does the point break at **Playa Escondida**. **Playa Jacó** is not always dependable for good beach breaks, and the surf is not too big, though it's within easy reach of **Roca Loca**, a rocky point break to the north, and, to the south, **Playa Hermosa**, a good spot for more experienced surfers, with a very strong beach break. The adjacent *playas* **Esterillos Oeste**, **Esterillos Este**, **Bejuco** and **Bocas Damas** offer similarly good beach breaks.

On the **south Pacific coast**, the river mouth at **Quepos** has a small left point break, while **Playa Espadilla** at Manuel Antonio is good when the wind is up, with beach breaks and left and right waves. Southwards from here, **Playa El Rey** offers left and right beach breaks, but you're best off continuing to **Dominical** and some really great surfing, with strong lefts and rights and beautiful surroundings. Down at the very south of the country, **Bahía Drake** gets going on a big swell. A much more reliable wave hits the shore at **Playa Pavones**, allegedly the longest left point in the world, very fast and with a good formation; it's offset by the nearby right point break at **Matapalo**. Only hardcore surfers tend to tackle the remote reef break at **Punta Burica**.

The Caribbean

The best surfing beaches on the **Caribbean coast** lie in the south, from Cahuita to Manzanillo villages. **Playa Negra** at Cahuita has an excellent beach break, with the added bonus of year-round waves. **Puerto Viejo de Talamanca** is home to **La Salsa Brava**, one of the few legitimate "big waves" in Costa Rica, a very thick, tubular wave formed by deep water rocketing towards a shallow reef. Further south, **Manzanillo** has a very fast beach break in lovely surroundings.

Up towards Puerto Limón, there are a couple of beaches that, while not in the class of Puerto Viejo, can offer experienced surfers a few good waves. **Westfalia**'s left and right beach breaks only really work on a small swell, while **Playa Bonita**, a few kilometres north of Limón, is known for its powerful and dangerous left; only people who really know what they are doing should try this. The right point break at **Portete** is easier to handle, though the left-breaking waves at **Isla Uvita**, just off the coast from Puerto Limón, are also considered tricky. The **north Caribbean coast** has a number of decent beach breaks, which you can reach along the canals north of Moín.

Diving and snorkelling

Though **diving** is less of a big deal in Costa Rica than in Belize or Honduras' Bay Islands, there are a few worthwhile dive sites around the country; the best, however, lie some 535km off Costa Rica's Pacific coast in the waters around **Parque Nacional Isla del Coco** (see box, p.326).

You can also theoretically **snorkel** all along the Pacific coast – Playa Flamingo in northern Guanacaste has clear waters though not a lot to see, while Playa Panama and Bahía Ballena also have good snorkelling. For people who want to see an abundance of underwater life, the small **reef** near Manzanillo on the Caribbean coast is the best; the nearby reef at Cahuita has suffered in recent years from erosion and is now dying.

OUTFITTERS

Aquamor Talamanca Adventures ☎ 2759 9012, ⓦ greencoast .com/aquamor2.htm. Excellent dive operation situated within the Refugio Nacional de Vida Silvestre Gandoca-Manzanillo. Employs local captains and works in alliance with the Talamanca Dolphin Foundation.
Bill Beard's Costa Rica ☎ 1 877 853 0538, ⓦ billbeards.com. Experienced operator running trips in the northern Guanacaste region, including around Isla Murciélago in Parque Nacional Santa Rosa, as well as trips to Isla del Caño off the Osa Peninsula. PADI certification courses available.

Costa Rica Adventure Divers ☎ 2231 5806, ⓦ costaricadiving .com. Boat dives, dive courses and snorkelling around Bahía Drake and the pristine reef of nearby Isla del Caño.

Ocotal Beach Resort and Marina ☎ 2670 0321, ⓦ ocotaldiving .com. PADI certification courses and day- and night-dive trips to Catalina and Murciélago islands; five- to eight-day packages also available.

Rich Coast Diving ☎ 2670 0176, ⓦ richcoastdiving.com. Snorkelling and scuba-diving trips in northern Guanacaste, plus PADI certification courses.

Fishing and sportfishing

Costa Rica is one of the biggest sportfishing grounds in the Neotropics. Both coasts are blessed with the kind of big fish serious anglers love, marlin (*aguja*), sailfish (*pez vela*), tarpon (*sábalo*) and snook (*robalo*) among them. Sportfishing is just that: sport, with the vast majority of fish returned to the sea alive. Its most obvious characteristic, though, is its tremendous **expense** – day-trips start at around $400, while multi-day packages can cost upwards of $3500. **Quepos** (p.349) and **Golfito** (p.398) have long been good places to do some fishing, while **Barra del Colorado** (p.182) in the northeast and **Playa Flamingo** (p.278) in Guanacaste have turned into monothematic costly sportfishing destinations. Although good fishing is possible all year round, the catch is seasonal (Pacific marlin, for example, can only be caught between Nov & April); January and February are the most popular months.

Casual anglers can find cheaper and more low-key fishing opportunities in the country's many trout-rich **freshwater rivers**, or in **Laguna de Arenal** and the **Refugio Nacional de Vida Silvestre Caño Negro**, where fishing for rainbow bass (*guapote*) is especially good.

Birdwatching

One oft-repeated statistic you'll hear about Costa Rica is that the country boasts more than 885 species of bird (including migratory ones), a higher number than all of North America. Consequently, the **birding** is hugely impressive, and it's likely that you'll spot hummingbirds, toucans, kingfishers and a variety of trogons (the best time to see migratory birds is the dry season). The iconic resplendent quetzal, found in the higher elevations of Monteverde and the Cordillera de Talamanca, is elusive, but can still be spotted – the tiny hamlet of San Gerardo de Dota (see p.367), close to Cerro de la Muerte, and the nearby Parque Nacional Los Quetzales are by far the best places to see them.

A good **guide** is worth its weight in gold and will be able to pick out all sorts of species that you might otherwise miss; the wildlife guide at the start of this book (see p.26) will help you identify some of the more common and unusual birds, but anyone with more than a casual interest will probably also want to carry a more comprehensive birdwatching **field guide** with them (see p.434).

Most **lodges** include some sort of birdwatching trip among their excursions, and several cater specifically for birders, including *Rancho Naturalista* (see p.156) and *Bosque de Paz* (see p.134), organizing day-trips and multi-day tours of various nearby habitats.

SPECIALIST OPERATORS

Costa Rica Gateway ☎ 2433 8278, ⓦ costaricagateway.com. Long-established operator running a dozen one- and two-week tours using birder-friendly lodges; can also help put together tailor-made trips including transport, accommodation and local guides.

Costa Rican Bird Route ☎ 1 608 3448, ⓦ costaricanbirdroute .com. Network of eighteen private reserves and lodges in the Zona Norte, including *Selva Verde Lodge*, *Laguna del Lagarto* and the Estación Biológica La Selva, which harbours over five hundred of the country's bird species. Their four-day Great Green Macaw tour is the only multi-day trip in the country that focuses on observing, photographing and learning about this endangered species. See box, p.238.

★ **Organization of Tropical Studies** ☎ 2524 0607, ⓦ ots.ac.cr. Custom-made itineraries taking in the three research stations operated by the OTS (Las Cruces, La Selva and Palo Verde), and their varying habitats and species, with some of the best naturalist guides in the country. Also offers day-long birdwatching workshops at La Selva and Las Cruces – an excellent introduction to birdwatching in the tropics.

Mountain biking

Only certain places in Costa Rica lend themselves well to **mountain biking**. In general, the best areas for extensive biking are Parque Nacional Corcovado, the road from Montezuma to the Reserva Natural Absoluta Cabo Blanco on the southern Nicoya Peninsula and Parque Nacional Santa Rosa. The La Fortuna and Volcán Arenal area is also increasingly popular: you can bike to see the volcano (although not up it) and around the pretty Laguna de Arenal. Some tour operators, such as Desafío (ⓦ desafiocostarica.com), also offer mountain biking as part of the transfer from La Fortuna to Monteverde.

There are plenty of bike **rental shops** throughout the country, and you may also be able to rent one from local tour agencies; bike rental costs around $5 an hour or between $10 and $20 for the day.

TOUR OPERATORS

Bike Arenal ☎ 2479 7150, Ⓦ bikearenal.com. Exciting week-long rides through the Zona Norte and along the Pacific coast, with a paved-road option for the less adventurous. Their scenic one-day tour around Laguna de Arenal is the closest you can get to Volcán Arenal on two wheels.

Coast to Coast Adventures ☎ 2280 8054, Ⓦ ctocadventures .com. Multi-activity operator with mountain-bike sections in the Valle Orosí and across the southern Nicoya Peninsula.

Serendipity Adventures ☎ 2556 5852, Ⓦ serendipity adventures.com. Adventure specialists offering all-inclusive customized biking tours along the Caribbean coast, around the Valle Central and in the Zona Norte.

Horseriding

Almost everywhere you go in Costa Rica, with the exception of waterlogged northern Limón Province, you should be able to hook up with a **horseriding tour**. Guanacaste is probably the best area in the country for riding, with a cluster of excellent haciendas (working cattle ranches) that also cater to tourists, offering bed and breakfast and horse hire.

Riding **on the beach** on the Nicoya Peninsula, especially in Montezuma in the south and Sámara on the west coast, is also very popular; however, there has been a history of mistreatment of horses in these places (if you see any extreme cases of mistreatment, complain to the local tourist information centre or local residents), so don't expect the animals here to be in great shape.

TOUR OPERATORS

★ **Horsetrek Monteverde** ☎ 1 866 811 0522 or ☎ 8359 3485, Ⓦ horsetrekmonteverde.com. Trips on well-cared-for horses around Monteverde and horseriding as part of a multi-day transfer between the cloudforest and La Fortuna; their eight-day Trails of the Campesinos takes in Monteverde, Guanacaste and Arenal. They can also arrange bespoke horse tours across the country.

Mr Big J ☎ 2755 0328, ✉ hbigjoe@cahuita.cr. Friendly tour company in Cahuita that organizes rides to waterfalls and along the lovely black-sand beach of Playa Negra.

Travelling with children

Costa Rica is arguably the most child-friendly destination in Central America: historically peaceful, easy to get around and with a good healthcare system, it boasts a bounty of exotic wildlife and enough outdoor activities to keep even the most adrenaline-fuelled teenager quiet for a week or two.

Like most other Latin countries, children are a fundamental part of society in Costa Rica, and you'll be made to feel more than welcome in **hotels and restaurants** and on guided tours and trips. Very few hotels do not accept children (we've noted in the Guide those that don't), and you'll find that the comparatively early opening hours in restaurants actually favour the routines of younger families.

Costa Rica is also a very **safe** destination to travel around, with a long history of political stability and far less crime than in neighbouring countries. You don't need specific inoculations to visit (and malaria is only present in the southern Caribbean) and most tourist places have a high standard of food hygiene, so **health** problems (see p.60) are rarely an issue – though Costa Rica's position near the equator means that you should take the necessary precautions with the sun. In the unlikely scenario that you do require medical help, note that the (private) healthcare system in Costa Rica is excellent, with a couple of top-notch clinics in San José (see p.117), while the capital's Hospital Nacional de Niños at C 14, Av Central (☎ 2222 0122) has the best paediatric specialists in Central America.

Activities

Costa Rica's incredible **wildlife** will undoubtedly provide your children with the most abiding memories of their trip, and you'd struggle to spend a couple of weeks in the country and not see a blue morpho butterfly, a colourful keel-billed toucan or a sloth or howler monkey working their way through the rainforest canopy – the latter two are particularly prevalent in Tortuguero and Manuel Antonio national parks. Most parks have well-maintained **trails**, many of which are short circuits; travellers with very young children will find pushchair-friendly paths at Poás (see p.136) and Carara (see p.341) national parks and the Reserva Santa Elena (see p.320), while the main-crater viewpoint at Parque Nacional Volcán Irazú (see p.148) is also reachable with a buggy.

Butterfly farms are a big hit for younger children. It can sometimes seem that every small rural village has its own finca de la mariposa, but one of the best – and most interesting for the adults – is the Butterfly Conservatory at El Castillo, near La Fortuna (see p.219), the biggest in the country. Similarly, **frog gardens**, or ranariums, should also appeal thanks to the variety of croaking, whirring, garishly coloured species that are easily spotted hopping about; most major tourist centres, such as Monteverde, have a frog garden, while several private wildlife reserves run evening frog walks.

Costa Rica's two long coastlines are backed by some beautiful beaches, though **swimming** should be supervised at all times – the same waves that make the country so popular with surfers can be dangerous for children, while some of the best beaches are plagued by riptides (see p.69). Older children can rent **bodyboards and surfboards** in major surfing resorts such as Tamarindo and Santa Teresa/Mal País.

Taking a dip in an outdoor **hot spring** is a novel experience likely to be enjoyed by young children and teenagers alike. Most complexes have a variety of pools (of varying temperatures), many "fed" by waterfalls that you can perch under, and some have water slides as well; the springs around Volcán Arenal (see p.209) make great spots for a thermally heated soak.

The variety of outdoor activities available to teenagers is seemingly endless, and few will be able to resist hurtling through the treetops attached to cables on a **zip line** (see p.70); **hanging bridges** (see p.70) offer a more relaxing alternative to exploring the upper canopy. You can go **bungee-jumping** in the Valle Central (see p.130) and at Jacó on the Pacific coast (see box, p.345), and **caving** in Parque Nacional Barra Honda (see p.292) and Venado, near La Fortuna (see p.224). Older teenagers can try their hand at **whitewater rafting** (see p.69) by tackling the raging rapids of the Pacuare and Reventazón rivers among others, though there are also "safari floats" on much calmer waters that will appeal to all the family.

Studying and volunteering

Costa Rica is a great place to broaden your mind, and an increasing number of visitors kick off their travels through the country with an immersive language course, or break up their vacation with a few days of volunteering, which can range from helping maintain trails in a cloud-forest reserve to measuring turtles on the Pacific coast. There are also a great number of opportunities for travellers with more time and a scientific interest in the country's flora and fauna to enrol in a variety of research projects.

Study programmes and learning Spanish

There are over 125 language schools in Costa Rica, with San José and the Valle Central offering a wealth of **Spanish courses**. Though you can arrange a place through organizations based in your home country (see below), the best way to choose (at least in the low season, from May to November) is to visit a few, perhaps sit in on a class or two, and judge the school according to your own needs; in the high season, many classes will have been booked in advance. Note that courses in Costa Rica generally cost more than in Mexico or Guatemala.

Some of the **language schools** listed here are Tico-run; some are branches of international (usually North American) education networks. Instructors are almost invariably Costa Ricans who speak some English. School notice boards are an excellent source of information and contact for travel opportunities, apartment shares and social activities. Most schools have a number of Costa Rican families on their books with whom they regularly place students for **homestays**. If you want **private tuition**, any of the places listed below can recommend a tutor – rates run from $21 to $30 per hour.

LANGUAGE SCHOOLS

Academia Latinoamericana de Español ☎ 2224 9917, ⓦ alespanish.com. Friendly school running small-group courses (20hr weekly; $175), with morning or afternoon schedules; homestay programmes (which includes breakfast, dinner and laundry) cost a further $160 per week; all materials included.

Conversa ☎ 2203 2071, ⓦ conversa.com. Well-established institute whose classes have a maximum of four students (5hr 30min daily for a super-intensive course) with thorough teaching that puts the emphasis on grammar; stay either with a Tico family or at the centre's five-acre former dairy farm, 10km outside San José. Not cheap at $795–895 per week, though the price also includes Latin dance and cooking classes and community activities.

Costa Rican Language Academy (CRLA) ☎ 2280 1685, ⓦ spanishandmore.com. Small, friendly and Costa Rican-owned school, with a conversational approach to learning, based on current affairs, and with a variety of options (3–6hr/day, 4–5 days/week). One-week (4hr/day) programme, including Latin dance and cooking classes, costs just $448 including homestay accommodation.

Costa Rica Spanish Institute (COSI) ☎ 2234 1001, ⓦ cosi.co.cr. Small classes in San José, as well as a "Beach and Rainforest Programme" in Parque Nacional Manuel Antonio ($50–75 extra/week). Homestays are arranged (or you can stay in an apartment or hotel), as are tours and cultural activities. One-week (4hr per day) programme costs $515 including homestay accommodation.

Instituto Para Estudiantes Extranjeros ☎ 2030 7855, ⓦ ipee.com. Small school that prides itself on a cosy atmosphere, total-immersion methodology and small groups (max six people), with year-round courses, from one week to six months or more. Facilities include free internet, and they can also arrange field trips and excursions and homestays. One-week (4hr/day) programme costs $440 including homestay accommodation.

Montaña Linda Spanish School ☎ 2533 3640, ⓦ montana linda.com. Popular school in the gorgeous Valle Orosí run by a friendly and knowledgeable team. Tuition is either one-to-one (nine months of the year) or in tiny classes up to a maximum of three people (3hr/day), with the choice of grammar or conversation. Accommodation is provided in a nearby hostel, homestay or guesthouse (starting from $195 for one week in the hostel), and a wide range of tours and sightseeing activities are available.

Universal de Idiomas ☎ 2257 0441, ⓦ universal-edu.com. Well-established school with programmes offering three to six hours of tuition daily. Tours can also be arranged. One-week (4hr/day) programme costs $435 including homestay accommodation.

Volunteer work and research projects

There's a considerable choice of **volunteer work** and **research projects** in Costa Rica – some include food and lodging, and many can be organized from overseas. You'll be required to spend at least a week working on a project (such as monitoring sea turtles, helping conserve endangered parrots or working with rural communities), sometimes up to three months, though the extra insight you'll gain – and, of course, the enormous sense of achievement – are ample rewards.

A good resource **in the US** for volunteer work programmes is *Transitions Abroad* (☎1 802 442 4827, ⓦtransitionsabroad.com), a bimonthly magazine and website focusing on living and working overseas. Prospective **British** volunteers should contact the Costa Rican Embassy in London (see p.78). In **Australia**, details of current student exchanges and study programmes are available either from the Costa Rican consul (see p.78), or from the American Field Service (AFS) in Sydney (☎02 9215 0077, ⓦafs.org.au); in **New Zealand** and **South Africa**, you should contact the AFS, in Wellington (☎04 494 6020, ⓦafsnzl .org.nz) and Johannesburg (☎011 447 2673, ⓦafs .org.za), respectively.

VOLUNTEER PROGRAMMES

In addition to the programmes recommended below, many private reserves take volunteers direct, including the Reserva Biológica Bosque Nuboso Monteverde and the Reserva Santa Elena (see box, p.317).

ASVO ☎ 2258 4430, ⓦ asvocr.org. Nonprofit association enabling volunteers to work in national parks and wildlife refuges, local schools or communities, from monitoring turtle nests in the Refugio Nacional de Vida Silvestre Gandoca-Manzanillo to helping in a cheese factory in Zapotal.

Earthwatch US ☎ 1 800 776 0188, UK ☎ 01865 318838, Australia ☎ 03 9016 7590; ⓦ earthwatch.org. Studying leatherback turtles in Guanacaste, researching whales and dolphins in the Golfo Dulce; monitoring the effect of climate change on Costa Rica's caterpillars; or tracking mammals in Parque Nacional Peñas Blancas.

Friends of the Osa ☎ 2735 5756, ⓦ osaconservation.org. Hands-on help at a sea-turtle project on the southern tip of the Osa Peninsula, measuring turtles, monitoring nesting sites and hatchlings, and patrolling the beach at night. Minimum one week.

Monteverde Institute ☎ 2645 5053, ⓦ mvinstitute.org. Regular volunteer opportunities on a variety of wildlife and community initiatives in and around Monteverde.

Proyecto Campanario ☎ 2289 8694, ⓦ campanario.org. Research station and ecotourist project on the Osa Peninsula, which sometimes offers free or discounted lodging and meals in exchange for a minimum of three months' work on and around the reserve.

Reserva Rara Avis ☎ 2764 1111, ⓦ rara-avis.com. This off-the-beaten-track rainforest lodge and research station in the Zona Norte (see p.235) regularly requires volunteers to help with guiding, research or conservation projects. Minimum three months.

Sea Turtle Conservancy ☎ 1 352 373 6441, ⓦ conserveturtles .org. Volunteer research work on leatherback and green turtles or Neotropical birds at Parque Nacional Tortuguero.

Travel essentials

Costs

Costa Rica is the most **expensive** country in Central America. Just about everything – from ice-cream cones and groceries to hotel rooms and car rental – costs more than you might expect. Some prices, especially for high-end accommodation, are comparable with those in the US, which never fails to astonish American travellers and those coming from the cheaper neighbouring countries. That said, you can, with a little foresight, travel fairly cheaply throughout the country.

The high cost of living is due in part to the **taxes**, which are levied in hotels (13 percent) and restaurants (23 percent) and also, more recently, to the International Monetary Fund, whose restructuring policies of balancing the country's payments deficit have raised prices. Even on a rock-bottom **budget**, you're looking at spending $40 a day for lodging, three meals and the odd bus ticket. Staying in mid-range accommodation, eating in nice restaurants and taking part in the odd activity will usually cost you over $100 a day, while the sky's the limit at the upper end, where one night in a swanky hotel can set you back over $400 in some places. And that's not including any tipping you might do (see p.82).

The good news is that **bus travel**, geared towards locals, is always cheap – often less than $1 for local buses, and around $7.50 for long-distance buses (3hr or more).

Crime and safety

Costa Rica is one of the safest countries in Latin America, and crime tends to be opportunistic rather than violent. **Pickpockets** and **luggage theft** are the greatest problems, particularly in San José and other larger cities (be extra vigilant in bus terminals and markets). If you do have anything stolen, report it immediately at the nearest police station (*estación de policía*, or *guardia rural* in the countryside).

Car-related crime, especially involving rental vehicles, is on the rise, so make sure you park securely, particularly at night (see box, p.52). A common scam is for people to pre-puncture rental-car tyres, follow the vehicle and then pull over to "offer assistance"; beware of seemingly good Samaritans on the roadside.

Drug-trafficking is a growing problem in Costa Rica (see p.421), and dealers in tourist hangouts such as Jacó and Tamarindo occasionally approach travellers. Drug possession carries stiff penalties in Costa Rica.

Electricity

The **electrical current** in Costa Rica is 110 volts – the same as Canada and the US – although plugs are two-pronged, without the round grounding prong.

Emergencies

The national **emergency number** is ☎911.

Entry requirements

Citizens of the UK, Ireland, the US, Canada, Australia, New Zealand, South Africa and most Western European countries can obtain a ninety-day entry stamp for Costa Rica without needing a **visa**. Whatever your nationality, you must in theory show your passport (with more than six months remaining), a valid onward (or return) air or bus ticket, a visa for your next country (if applicable) and proof of "sufficient funds" (around $500), though if you arrive by air the last is rarely asked for. Most other nationalities need a visa (a thirty-day visa costs $32); always check first with a Costa Rican consulate concerning current regulations. The websites of the ICT (ⓦvisitcostarica.com) and Costa Rica's US embassy (ⓦcostarica-embassy.org) give up-to-date requirements.

Your **entrance stamp** is very important: no matter where you arrive, make sure you get it. You have to carry your passport (or a photocopy) with you at all times in Costa Rica; if you are asked for it and cannot produce it, you may well be detained and fined.

The easiest way to **extend your entry permit** is to leave Costa Rica for 72 hours – to Panama or Nicaragua, say – and then re-enter, fulfilling the same requirements as on your original trip. You should then be given another ninety-day (or thirty-day) stamp, although it is at the discretion of the immigration officer. If you prefer not to leave the country, you can apply for a permit or visa

---

INTO NICARAGUA AND PANAMA

To cross the border from Costa Rica **into Panama** (at Paso Canoas, Sixaola or Río Sereno), most nationalities need a tourist card ($5), valid for thirty days; nationals of the UK, Ireland, the US, Canada, Australia and New Zealand do not need a visa. You may also need a return ticket back to Costa Rica (or an onward ticket out of Panama to another country), but bear in mind that immigration requirements frequently change, seemingly at whim, so always check with the Panamanian consulate before setting off. Panama has no paper currency of its own, and US dollars – called balboas – are used; it does have its own coins, however, which are equivalent to US coins and in wide circulation. Also beware that you cannot take any **fruit or vegetables** across the border (they will be confiscated if you try). Note that Panama is one hour ahead of Costa Rica.

Few nationalities require a visa to cross **into Nicaragua** (at Peñas Blancas or Los Chiles), but if needed, this must be done at the Nicaraguan consulate in San José (see p.117); everyone, however, has to pay the $10 entry fee (it costs $2 going the other way). Note that if you needed a visa to enter Costa Rica, make sure you've got a double-entry stamp or you won't be allowed back into Costa Rica.

The local currency is the *córdoba*, which you can exchange colones or dollars for in Peñas Blancas and Los Chiles before arriving in Sapoa or San Carlos de Nicaragua, respectively.

extension at the *migración* near San José (see p.117), a time-consuming and often costly business. You'll need to bring all relevant documents – passport and four photographs, personal letter, onward air or bus ticket – as well as proof of sufficient funds ($100 for every month's stay); note that requirements change, so check in advance. If you do not have a ticket out of Costa Rica, you may have to buy one in order to get your extension. Bus tickets are more easily refunded than air tickets; some airlines refuse to cash in onward tickets unless you can produce or buy another one out of the country. If you **overstay your limit**, you'll need to go to the Departamento de Migración in San José with your passport and onward ticket and will be charged an overstayers' fee of $100 per month.

COSTA RICAN EMBASSIES AND CONSULATES ABROAD

Australia Consulate-General, Suite 301 B, Level 3, 50 Margaret St, Sydney, NSW 2000 ☎ 02 9262 3883

Canada 350 Spark St, Suite 701 (Office Tower), Ottawa, Ontario, K1R 7S8 ☎ 613 562 2855, ⓦ costaricaembassy.com

Ireland No representation; contact the UK embassy.

New Zealand No representation; contact the Australian Consulate-General.

South Africa 14 Talton Road, Forest Town, Johannesburg ☎ 11 486 4716, ⓔ bish@mega.co.za

UK Flat 1, 14 Lancaster Gate, London W2 3LH ☎ 0207 706 8844, ⓦ costaricanembassy.co.uk

US 2112 S St NW, Washington, DC 20008 ☎ 202 499 2991, ⓦ costarica-embassy.org

Gay and lesbian Costa Rica

Costa Rica has a good reputation among gay and lesbian travellers and continues to be generally hassle-free for gay and lesbian visitors. The country has a large gay community by Central American standards, and to a smaller extent a sizeable lesbian one, too; it's pretty much confined to San José (which holds a **Gay Pride Festival** every June), though there is also a burgeoning scene in Manuel Antonio.

Outside of these two places, macho attitudes still exist, and gay and lesbian travellers should be discreet – there have been some incidents of police harassing gays in bars. That said, there's no need to assume, as some do, that everyone is a raving hetero-Catholic poised to discriminate against homosexuals. Part of this general **tolerance** is due to the subtle tradition in Costa Rican life and politics summed up in the Spanish expression "*quedarbien*", which translates roughly as "don't rock the boat" or "leave well alone". People don't ask you about your

sexual orientation or make assumptions, but they don't necessarily expect you to talk about it unprompted, either.

Where once it was difficult to find an entrée into gay life (especially for women) without knowing local gays and lesbians, there are now several **points of contact** in Costa Rica for gay and lesbian travellers. On the web, try Costa Rica Gay Map (ⓦ costaricagaymap.com), which provides information about gay-friendly accommodation and nightlife, or Costa Rica Gay Vacation (ⓦ costaricagayvacation.com), a travel agent that specializes in gay and lesbian holidays to Costa Rica. For a more informal introduction to the scene in the country itself, head to *Déjà Vu*, a mainly gay disco in San José (ⓦ dejavucity.com).

Information

The best source of information about Costa Rica is the **Instituto Costarricense de Turismo (ICT)** in La Urucain San José (☎ 22915764, ⓦ visitcostarica .com). Pre-trip advice generally amounts to pretty but not particularly informative glossy pamphlets and brochures, and you're better off going in person to their office on the Plaza de la Cultura in central San José (see p.107), where the friendly, bilingual staff will do their best to answer your queries; they can also give you a free city map and a useful bus timetable – which is also available online (see p.48). Outside the capital, there are seven regional ICT tourist offices offering limited information and advice, as well as small booths at the four main entry points to the country: the Juan Santamaría and Daniel Oduber airports and at Peñas Blancas on the Nicaraguan border and Paso Canoas on the Panamanian border; otherwise, you'll have to rely on locally run initiatives, often set up by a small business association or the chamber of commerce, or hotels and tourist agencies.

A number of Costa Rican **tour operators**, based in San José (see p.54), can offer information and guidance when planning a trip around the country, though bear in mind that they may not be as objective as they could be.

USEFUL WEBSITES

In addition to the below, many of Costa Rica's newspapers, such as La Nación, have online editions, which are good resources for current affairs, cultural events and the like (see p.63).

ⓦ **anywherecostarica.com** Useful online guide, with practical advice, destination guides, thematic maps and transport information.

ⓦ **canatur.org** Website of the Costa Rican National Tourism Chamber.

ⓦ **costarica-nationalparks.com** Detailed guide to the country's national parks and wildlife reserves.

Ⓦ **visitcostarica.com** Comprehensive website of the tourist board, including a very handy countrywide bus schedule.

GOVERNMENT WEBSITES

Australian Department of Foreign Affairs Ⓦ dfat.gov.au
British Foreign & Commonwealth Office Ⓦ fco.gov.uk
Canadian Department of Foreign Affairs Ⓦ international.gc.ca
Irish Department of Foreign Affairs Ⓦ dfa.ie
New Zealand Ministry of Foreign Affairs Ⓦ mfat.govt.nz
South African Department of Foreign Affairs Ⓦ dfa.gov.za
US State Department Ⓦ state.gov

Insurance

It's always a good idea to take out **insurance** before travelling. A typical policy usually provides cover for the loss of baggage, tickets and – up to a certain limit – cash or cheques, as well as cancellation or curtailment of your journey. It's particularly important to have one that includes **health cover**, too, since while private medical treatment in Costa Rica is likely to be cheaper than in your home country, it can still be expensive.

You can buy a policy from a specialist travel insurance company, or consider the deal we offer (see box below). When choosing a policy, always check whether **medical benefits** will be paid as treatment proceeds or only after you return home, and if there is a **24-hour medical emergency number**. When securing baggage cover, make sure that the per-article limit – typically under £500 and sometimes as little as £100 – will cover your most valuable possession. Most policies exclude so-called **dangerous sports** unless an extra premium is paid: in Costa Rica, this can mean scuba diving, whitewater rafting, surfing and windsurfing.

If you need **to make a claim**, you should keep receipts for medicines and medical treatment, and in the event you have anything stolen, you must obtain an official statement from the police: tell them "*He sidorobado*" ("I've been robbed") and they'll provide you with the necessary paperwork.

Internet

Most hostels and hotels provide free internet access to their guests, and many places offer wi-fi. The majority of Costa Rican towns have at least one **internet café** (around $1/hr in major towns, more in remote areas where they rely on slower satellite link-up), though these are becoming increasingly rarer with the proliferation of free wi-fi hotspots.

Laundry

There are very few **launderettes** in Costa Rica, and they're practically all in San José (see p.117); in the main tourist towns, though, you'll usually be able to find someone running a small **laundry service**, charging by the kilo (around $1.50). Most hotels can do your laundry, although charges are generally outrageously high.

Mail

Even the smallest Costa Rican town has a **post office** (*correo*), with generally uniform opening hours (see p.81), but the most reliable place to mail overseas is from San José's Correo Central (see p.117). Airmail letters to the US and Canada take around a week to arrive; letters to Europe take ten days or so; letters to Australasia and South Africa take three or four weeks.

Most post offices have a **poste restante** (*lista de correos*) – an efficient and safe way to receive letter mail, especially at the main office in San José. They will hold letters for up to four weeks for a small fee (though in smaller post offices you may not be charged at all). Bring a photocopy of your passport when picking up mail, and make sure that correspondents address letters to you under your name exactly as it appears on your passport.

ROUGH GUIDES TRAVEL INSURANCE

Rough Guides has teamed up with WorldNomads.com to offer great travel insurance deals. Policies are available to residents of over 150 countries, with cover for a wide range of adventure sports, 24hr emergency assistance, high levels of medical and evacuation cover and a stream of travel safety information. Roughguides.com users can take advantage of their policies online 24/7, from anywhere in the world – even if you're already travelling. And since plans often change when you're on the road, you can extend your policy and even claim online. Roughguides.com users who buy travel insurance with WorldNomads.com can also leave a positive footprint and donate to a community development project. For more information, go to Ⓦ roughguides.com/travel-insurance.

One thing you can't fail to notice is the paucity of **mailboxes** in Costa Rica. In the capital, unless your hotel has regular mail pick-up, the only resort is to hike down to the Correo Central. In outlying or isolated areas of the country, you will have to rely on hotels or local businesses' private mailboxes. In most cases, especially in Limón Province, where mail is very slow, it's probably quicker to wait until you return to San José and mail correspondence from there.

Although letters are handled fairly efficiently, **packages** are another thing altogether – the parcel service, both coming and going, gets snarled in paperwork and labyrinthine customs regulations, besides being very expensive and very slow. If you must send parcels, take them unsealed to the post office for inspection.

Maps

The **maps** dished out by Costa Rican embassies and the ICT are basic and somewhat out of date, so arm yourself with some general maps before you go. The best **road maps**, clearly showing all the major routes and national parks, are the *Costa Rica Road Map* (1:650,000; Berndtson & Berndtson; ⓦberndtson.com) and the annually updated *Costa Rica Waterproof Travel Map* (1:470,000; Toucan Maps; ⓦmapcr.com), which also has a very useful, highly detailed section of the Valle Central and San José, plus area maps of Monteverde, Volcán Arenal, Tamarindo and Manuel Antonio, among others.

In Costa Rica, it's a good idea to go to one of San José's big downtown bookstores, such as Librería Internacional (see p.116) and look through their stock of **maps,** which are contoured and show major topographical features such as river crossings and high-tide marks; you can buy them in individual sections. You can also go to the government maps bureau, the **Instituto Geográfico Nacional**, C 9, Av 20/22, San José, which sells more lavishly detailed colour maps of specific areas of the country; while out of date, the smaller-scale series (available in 133 sheets) is useful for serious hiking trips.

Considering it's such a popular hiking destination, there are surprisingly few good maps of Costa Rica's **national parks**. Those given out at ranger stations are very general; your best bet is to get hold of the Fundación Neotrópica (ⓦneotropica.org) 1:500,000 map (available from the major San José bookshops), which shows national parks and protected areas; alternatively, while the maps in the book *National Parks of Costa Rica* (also usually available in San José) suffer from being rather cramped, not too detailed

and of little practical use for walking the trails, they do at least show contours and give a general idea of the terrain, the animals you might see and the annual rainfall.

Money

The official currency of Costa Rica is the **colón** (plural colones), named after Colón (Columbus) himself; you'll often hear them colloquially referred to as "pesos". There are two types of **coins** in circulation: the old silver ones, which come in denominations of 5, 10 and 20, and newer gold coins, which come in denominations of 5, 10, 25, 50, 100 and 500. The silver and gold coins are completely interchangeable, with the exception of public payphones, which don't accept gold coins. **Notes** are available in 1000, 2000, 5000, 10,000 (sometimes called the "rojo"), 20,000 and 50,000 colones. The colón floats freely against the US dollar, which in practice has meant that it devalues by some ten percent per year; at the time of writing, the **exchange rate** was around 510 colones to the dollar, 850 colones to the pound and 705 colones to the euro. Obtaining colones outside Costa Rica is virtually impossible: wait until you arrive and get some at the airport or border posts. While the **US dollar** has long been the second currency of Costa Rica and is accepted almost everywhere (we quote dollar prices throughout the Guide), the vast majority of Costa Ricans get paid in colones, and buy and sell in colones, so it's still a good idea to get the hang of the currency.

Outside San José and Juan Santamaría International Airport, there are effectively no official **bureaux de change**. In general, legitimate money-changing entails going to a bank, a hotel (usually upper-end) or, in outlying areas of the country, to whoever will do it – a tour agency, the friend of the owner of your hotel who has a Chinese restaurant... That said, it's unlikely that you'll need to change US dollars into colones, but if you do, or if you are changing other currencies such as sterling or euros, you'll find that the efficient private banks (such as Banco Popular and the Banco de San José) are much faster but charge scandalous commissions; the state banks such as Banco Nacional don't charge such high commissions but are slow and bureaucratic. All in all, it's far easier to withdraw cash from **ATMs** (*cajeros automático*) as and when you need it; international Visa and MasterCard debit cards are accepted at any ATM, and some dispense dollars as well as colones.

When heading for the more remote areas, try to carry sufficient colones with you, especially in small denominations – banking facilities can be scarcer here, and you may have trouble changing a 5000 note in the middle of the Nicoya Peninsula, for example. Going around with stacks of mouldy-smelling colones may not seem safe, but you should be all right if you keep them in a money belt, and it will save hours of time waiting in line. Some banks may not accept bent, smudged or torn dollars. It's also worth noting that, due to an influx of counterfeit **$100 notes** a few years ago, some shops, and even banks, are unwilling to accept them; if you bring any into the country, make sure that they are in mint condition.

Opening hours

Banks are generally open Monday to Friday 8.30 or 9am to 3 or 4pm, with some of the bigger banks in the bigger towns also open 9am to noon on Saturday. **Post offices** are open Monday to Friday 8am to 4.30 or 5.30pm (sometimes with an hour's break between noon and 1pm), and Saturdays 8am to noon; government offices, Monday to Friday 8am to 5pm; and **shops** Monday to Saturday 9am to 6 or 7pm. In rural areas, shops generally close for lunch. Practically the only places open on Sundays are shopping malls and **supermarkets**, which are generally open daily from 7 or 8am to 8pm, though sometimes they don't close until 9 or 10pm.

Phones

The **country code** for all of Costa Rica is ☎**506**. There are no area codes, and all phone numbers have eight digits: in 2008, a "2" was added to the beginning of landline numbers, and an "8" to mobile numbers, though not all signs, brochures and business cards have been updated. Calls **within Costa Rica** are inexpensive and **calling long-distance** can work out very reasonably if you ring directly through a public telephone network, and avoid calling from your hotel or other private business.

With the proliferation of free wi-fi, free internet phone calls via Skype are by far the best way to make **international calls**. Alternatively, you can purchase a phonecard (*tarjeta telefónica*), available from most grocery stores, street kiosks and pharmacies; you'll need card number 199 (card number 197 is for domestic calls only), which comes in varying denominations. You can also **call collect** to virtually any foreign country from any phone or payphone in Costa Rica; dial ☎09 (or ☎116 to get an English-speaking operator, a more expensive option), then

---

> ### USEFUL PHONE NUMBERS
> **International information** ☎124
> **International operator** (for collect calls) ☎116
>
> #### CALLING HOME FROM ABROAD
> Note that the initial zero is omitted from the area code when dialling the UK, Ireland, Australia and New Zealand from abroad.
> **Australia** international access code + 61
> **Ireland** international access code + 353
> **New Zealand** international access code + 64
> **South Africa** international access code + 27
> **UK** international access code + 44
> **US and Canada** international access code + 1

---

tell them the country code, area code and number; note that this method costs twice as much as dialling direct.

Another way of making calls is by purchasing a prepaid SIM card for your **mobile phone** at the booths in the arrivals area at Juan Santamaría and Daniel Obuder airports or from telecommunications offices around the country; cards start at 2000 colones and can (for a fee) be topped up online; a thirty-day data package costs around $18. Your phone will need to work on the 1800mhz range (any quad band and most tri-band phones; there's an approved list on the ICE website ⓦgrupoice.com) and must be unlocked (check with your provider).

Photography

Film is extremely expensive in Costa Rica, so if you've got a conventional camera bring lots from home. Although the incredibly bright equatorial light means that 100ASA will do for most situations, remember that rainforest cover can be very dark, and if you want to take photographs at dusk you'll need 400ASA or even higher. San José is the main place in the country where you can process film.

Prostitution

Prostitution is legal in Costa Rica, and is particularly prevalent in San José and Jacó. While there is streetwalking (largely confined to the streets of the capital, especially those in the red-light district immediately west and south of the Parque Central), many prostitutes work out of bars. Bars in San José's "Gringo Gulch" (more or less on C 7, Av 0/5) tend to cater to and attract more foreign customers than the bars in the red-light district, which are frequented by Ticos. Streetwalkers around C 12 look like women but are not – *travestís* are transsexual or transvestite prostitutes. In recent years, Costa Rica has gained a reputation as a destination for sex tourism (see p.431), and more specifically for child-sex tourism. The government is trying to combat this with a public information campaign and strict prison sentences for anyone caught having sex with a minor.

Shopping

Compared with many Latin American countries, Costa Rica does not have a particularly impressive crafts or artisan tradition. There are some interesting souvenirs, such as carved wooden salad bowls, plates and trays, however, and wherever you go, you'll see hand-painted wooden **replica ox-carts**, originating from Sarchí in the Valle Central (see p.131) – perennial favourites, especially when made into miniature drinks trolleys.

Reproductions of the **pre-Columbian pendants and earrings** displayed in San José's Museo Nacional, the Museo de Oro and the Museo del Jade are sold both on the street and in shops. Much of it isn't real gold, however, but gold-plated, which chips and peels: check before you buy.

Costa Rican **coffee** (see box, p.58) is one of the best gifts to take home. Make sure you buy export brands Café Britt or Café Rey – or better yet, home-grown roasts straight from the coffee plantations themselves (see boxes, p.125 & p.311) – and not the lower-grade sweetened coffee sold locally. It's often cheaper to buy bags in the supermarket rather than in souvenir shops, and cheaper still to buy beans at San José's Mercado Central. If you want your coffee beans roasted to your own taste, go to the *Café Gourmet* in San José for excellent beans and grinds.

Indigenous crafts are available at places such as the Reserva Indígena Maleku (see p.224) and the Reserva Indígena KéköLdi (see box, p.197), but in the general absence of a real home-grown crafts or textile tradition, generic **Indonesian** dresses and clothing – batiked and colourful printed cloth – are widely sold in the beach communities of Montezuma, Cahuita, Tamarindo and Quepos. In some cases, this craze for all things Indo extends to slippers, silver and bamboo jewellery – and prices are reasonable.

If you have qualms about buying goods made from **tropical hardwoods**, ask the salesperson what kind of wood the object is made from, and avoid mahogany, laurel, purple heart and almond (which is illegal anyway). Other goods to steer clear of are coral, anything made from tortoise shells, and furs such as ocelot or jaguar.

Time

Costa Rica is in North America's **Central Standard time zone** (the same as Winnipeg, New Orleans and Mexico City) and six hours behind **GMT**; daylight saving time is not observed.

Tipping

Unless **service** has been exceptional, you do not need to leave a tip in restaurants, where a ten percent service charge is automatically levied. **Taxi drivers** are not usually tipped, either. When it

AVERAGE TEMPERATURE AND RAINFALL

	Jan	Feb	Mar	Apr	May	Jun	Jul	Aug	Sep	Oct	Nov	Dec
SAN JOSÉ												
min/max (°C)	15/23	15/24	16/25	16/26	17/26	17/26	17/25	17/25	16/24	16/25	16/24	15/23
min/max (°F)	59/73	59/75	60/77	60/78	62/78	62/78	62/77	62/77	60/76	60/77	60/75	59/73
rainfall (mm)	10	5	13	43	226	287	216	249	330	330	142	41
TORTUGUERO												
min/max (°C)	20/31	20/31	21/31	22/31	22/31	22/31	22/31	22/30	22/31	22/31	21/29	21/31
min/max (°F)	68/88	68/88	69/87	71/87	71/87	71/87	71/88	71/86	71/87	71/87	69/85	69/88
rainfall (mm)	318	211	203	277	279	298	427	312	145	208	391	445
MANUEL ANTONIO												
min/max (°C)	21/31	21/31	22/32	22/32	22/32	22/31	21/31	21/30	22/30	22/30	22/30	21/30
min/max (°F)	69/87	69/87	71/89	71/89	71/89	71/87	69/87	69/86	71/86	71/86	71/86	69/86
rainfall (mm)	71	36	64	168	391	432	457	478	528	645	389	170

comes to **nature guides**, however, the rules become blurred. Many people – especially North Americans, who are more accustomed to tipping – routinely tip guides up to $10 per day. If you are utterly delighted with a guide, it seems fair to offer a tip, although be warned that some guides may be made uncomfortable by your offer – as far as many of them are concerned, it's their job.

Toilets

The only place you'll find so-called public conveniences – they're really reserved for customers – is in fast-food outlets in San José, petrol stations and roadside restaurants. When travelling in the outlying areas of the country, you may want to take a roll of **toilet paper** with you. Note that except in the poshest hotels – which have their own sewage system/septic tank – you should not put toilet paper down the toilet. Sewage systems are not built to deal with paper, and you'll only cause a blockage. There's always a receptacle provided for toilet paper.

Travellers with disabilities

While public transport isn't **wheelchair-accessible**, an increasing number of hotels are – we've noted where this is the case in our accommodation reviews. Travellers with disabilities will also find short but **accessible trails** at Poás (see p.136) and Carara (see p.341) national parks, and the Reserva Santa Elena (see p.320), while the main-crater viewpoint at Parque Nacional Volcán Irazú (see p.148) is also accessible to wheelchair users. A good starting point is to contact Serendipity Adventures (see p.54), who can organize dedicated adventure trips for travellers with disabilities that include whitewater rafting and rappelling.

Women travellers

Educated urban women play an active role in Costa Rica's public life and the workforce – indeed, in 2010, the country voted in its **first female president** (see p.421) – while women in more traditional positions are generally accorded the respect due to their role as mothers and heads of families.

Despite this, however, women may be subjected to a certain amount of machismo.

In general, people are friendly and helpful to solo **women travellers**, who get the *pobrecita* (poor little thing) vote, because they're *solita* (all alone), without family or man. Nonetheless, Costa Rican men may throw out unsolicited comments at women in the street: "*mi amor*", "*guapa*", "*machita*" ("blondie") and so on. If they don't feel like articulating a whole word, they may stare or hiss – there's a saying used by local women: "Costa Rica is full of snakes, and they're all men".

Blonde, fair-skinned women are in for quite a bit of this, whereas if you look remotely Latin you'll get less attention. This is not to say you'll be exempt from these so-called compliments, and even in groups, women are targets. Walk with a man, however, and the whole street theatre disappears as if by magic. The accepted wisdom is to pass right by and pretend nothing's happening. If you're staying in Costa Rica for any time, though, you may want to learn a few responses in Spanish; this won't gain you any respect – men will look at you and make *loca* (crazy) whirligig finger gestures at their temples – but it may make you feel better.

None of this is necessarily an expression of sexual interest: it has more to do with a man displaying his masculinity to his buddies than any desire to get to know you. **Sexual assault figures** in Costa Rica are low, you don't get groped and you rarely hear *piropos* outside of towns. But for some women, the machismo attitude can be endlessly tiring, and may even mar their stay in the country.

In recent years, there has been a spate of incidents allegedly involving Rohypnol, the so-called **date-rape drug** (legal and available over the counter in Costa Rica), whereby women have been invited for a drink by a man, or sent a drink from a man in a bar, which turns out to be spiked with the drug (often by the bartender, who's in on the game). In the worst cases, the women have woken up hours later having no recollection of the missing time, and believe they were raped. This is not to encourage paranoia, but the obvious thing to do is not accept opened drinks from men and be careful about accepting invitations to go to bars with unknown men. If you do, order a beer and ask to open the bottle yourself.

San José

TEATRO NACIONAL

1

San José

Sprawling smack in the middle of the fertile Valle Central, San José, the only city of any size and administrative importance in Costa Rica, has a spectacular setting, ringed by the jagged silhouettes of soaring mountains – some of them volcanoes – on all sides. On a sunny morning, the sight of the blue-black peaks piercing the sky is undeniably beautiful. At night, from high up on one of these mountains, the valley floor twinkles like a million Chinese lanterns.

That's where the compliments largely end, however. Costa Ricans can be notoriously hard on the place, calling it, with a mixture of familiarity and contempt, "**Chepe**"– the diminutive of the name José – and writing it off as a maelstrom of stress junkies, rampant crime and other urban horrors. Travellers, meanwhile, tend to view it as an unavoidable stopover jarringly at odds with expectations and impressions of the rest of the country.

Going by first impressions it's easy to see why this is the case. San José certainly doesn't exude immediate appeal, with its nondescript buildings and aggressive street life full of umbrella-wielding pedestrians, narrow streets, noisy food stalls and homicidal drivers. Scratch the surface, though, and you'll find a civilized city, with museums and galleries and plenty of places to walk, meet people, enjoy a meal, and go dancing. It's also relatively manageable, with less of the chaos and crowds that plague most other Latin American cities. San José is a surprisingly green and open city: small, carefully landscaped parks and paved-over plazas punctuate the centre of town. All the attractions lie near each other, and you can cover everything of interest in a couple of days.

San José has a sprinkling of excellent **museums** – some especially memorable for their bizarre locations – a couple of elegant buildings and landscaped parks. Cafés and art galleries line the streets, and as you wander amid the colonial-era wooden houses in the leafy barrios of **Amón** and **Otoya**, you could just as well be in an old European town. Further afield, the comfortable districts of **Escazú** and hip **San Pedro** (home to the Universidad de Costa Rica), merit a visit in their own right.

Of the city's museums, the major draws are the exemplary **Museo de Oro Precolombino**, featuring over two thousand pieces of pre-Columbian gold, and the **Museo del Jade**, the Americas' largest collection of the precious stone. Less visited, the **Museo Nacional** offers a brutally honest depiction of the country's colonization and some interesting archeological finds. The **Museo de Arte y Diseño Contemporáneo** displays some of the most striking contemporary works in the Americas.

Brief history

San José was established in 1737 at the insistence of the Catholic Church in order to give a focal point to the scattered populace living in the area. For the next forty years, **Villa Nueva de la Boca del Monte**, as it was cumbersomely called, remained a muddy village of a few squalid adobe houses, until coffee was first planted in the Valle Central in 1808 (see p.124), triggering the settlement's expansion.

Orientation in San José p.89	Bus companies in San José p.106
Safety in San José p.90	Useful bus routes p.107
Costa Rican gold p.94	Salsa like a Josefino p.113
Luggage on long-distance buses p.105	Boca bars p.114

MERCADO CENTRAL

Highlights

❶ Mercado Central Enormous, labyrinthine food market where crimson sides of beef and crispy *chicharrones* (deep-fried pork skins) share the aisles with teetering mounds of papaya and sacks of pungent coffee beans. **See p.91**

❷ Museo de Oro Precolombino Striking underground collection featuring intricate gold pieces by Diquis masters. **See p.92**

❸ Teatro Nacional Tour San José's most elegant building – and with luck catch a rehearsal. **See p.93**

❹ Parque la Sabana Enjoy a serene respite from the city's congestion, where you can meander amid towering eucalyptus and visit the acclaimed Museo de Arte Costarricense. **See p.102**

❺ Grano de Oro San José's finest gourmet restaurant has a lovely, leafy patio and is the only place in town for piña colada cheesecake. **See p.112**

❻ Bar Jazz Café A consistently stellar slate of live acts and top-notch acoustics makes San Pedro an essential stop for jazz aficionados. **See p.113**

HIGHLIGHTS ARE MARKED ON THE MAPS ON P.88 & PP.92–93

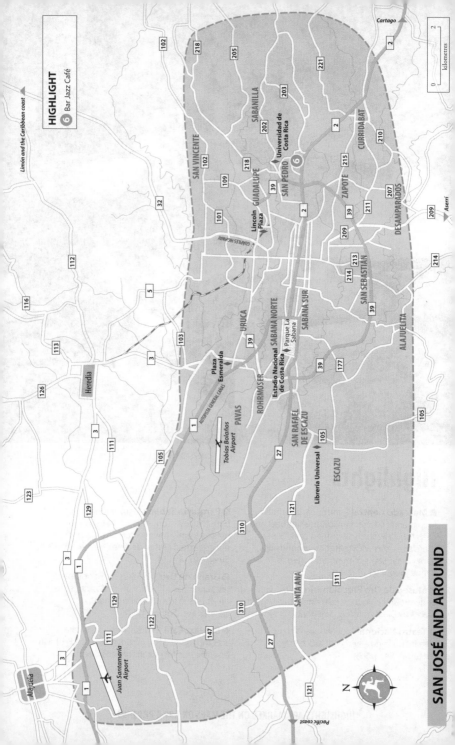

SAN JOSÉ AND AROUND

HIGHLIGHT
6 Bar Jazz Café

1

ORIENTATION IN SAN JOSÉ

The centre is subdivided into little neighbourhoods (*barrios*) that flow seamlessly in and out of one another. Barrios **Amón** and **Otoya**, in the north, are the prettiest, lined with the genteel mansions of former coffee barons. To the east and southeast are **La California** and **Los Yoses**, home to most of the embassies and the Centro Cultural Costarricense Norteamericano. The esteemed Universidad de Costa Rica rises amid the lively student bars and cafés of the **San Pedro** barrio, further east of the city centre.

San José, along with most Costa Rican towns of any size, is planned on a grid system. It's intersected east–west by **Avenida Central** (called Paseo Colón west of La Coca-Cola bus station) and north–south by **Calle Central**. From Avenida Central, parallel avenidas run to the north (odd numbers) and to the south (even numbers). From Calle Central, even-numbered calles run to the west and odd numbers to the east. Avenidas 8 and 9, therefore, are actually quite far apart. Similarly, calles 23 and 24 are at opposite ends of the city. When you see **bis** (literally "encore" – again) in an address it denotes a separate street, usually a dead end (*calle sin salida*), next to the avenida or calle to which it refers. Av 8 bis, for example, is between Av 8 and 10. "**0**" in addresses is shorthand for "Central": thus Av 0, C 11 is the same as Av Central, C 11.

Most times, locals – and especially taxi drivers – won't have a clue what you're talking about if you try to use street numbers to find an address. When possible, give directions in relation to local **landmarks**, buildings, businesses, parks or institutions. In addition, people use **metres** to signify distance: in local parlance 100 metres equals one city block. There are precious few street signs, so it's helpful to count streets as you go along so as not to miss your turn. Note that most roads are one-way, usually (but not always) the opposite direction to the previous road.

The single most crucial event in determining the city's future importance, however, was Costa Rica's **declaration of independence** from the Spanish Crown in 1821. Following the declaration, Mexico's self-proclaimed "emperor", General Agustín de Iturbide, ordered Costa Rica's immediate annexation, a demand which caused a rift between the citizens of Heredia and Cartago, who supported the move, and those of Alajuela and San José, who saw it for what it was: a panicky imperialist attempt to stifle Latin America's burgeoning independence movements. A short **civil war** broke out, won in 1823 by the *independentistas*, who moved the capital from Cartago to San José in the same year.

Into the nineteenth century

Despite its status, San José remained a one-horse town until well into the nineteenth century. The framed sepia photographs in the venerable *Balcón de Europa* restaurant show wide dirt roads traversed by horse-drawn carts, with simple adobe buildings and a few spindly telegraph wires. Like the fictional town of Macondo in García Márquez's *One Hundred Years of Solitude*, this provincial backwater attracted piano-teaching European flotsam – usually young men looking to make their careers in the hinterland – who would wash up in the drawing rooms of the country's nascent bourgeoisie. Accounts written by early foreign tourists to San José give the impression of a tiny, stultifying backwater society: "The president of the republic has to sit with his followers on a wooden bench", they wrote, aghast, after attending a church service. In the city's houses they found dark-skinned young women, bound tight in white crinoline dresses, patiently conjugating French verbs, reflecting the degree to which Costa Rica's earliest cultural affiliations and aspirations lay with France. Even the mansions of former *finqueros* (coffee barons) in San José's Barrio Amón – especially the Alianza Francesa – resemble mansions in New Orleans or Port-au-Prince, with their delicate French ironwork, Moorish-influenced lattices, long, cool corridors of deep-blooded wood and brightly painted exteriors.

By the 1850s, fuelled largely by the tobacco boom, the city's prosperity had become demonstrable, with a profusion of leafy parks, a few paved avenues and some fine examples of European-style architecture. Grand urban houses were built to

1

SAFETY IN SAN JOSÉ

Be particularly wary, even during the day, in the streets around La Coca-Cola bus terminal and Parque Central. A few places have a bad reputation day and night, including Barrio México in the northwest of the city and the red-light districts of C 12, Av 8/10, and Av 4/6, C 4/12, just southwest of the centre. The **dangers** are mainly mugging, purse-snatching or jewellery-snatching rather than serious assault, and many people walk around without encountering any problems at all. However, taxis are cheap enough that it's not worth taking the risk in those areas.

CROSSING STREETS

You have to be careful when crossing the street in San José, as drivers are very aggressive, and pedestrian fatalities are distressingly common (you'll see lots of stories about "*atropellados*" in the national newspaper). There are a few ground rules, however, that can help minimize your chances of ending up in hospital.
- If possible, always try to cross the street at an official crossing point alongside other pedestrians. Note that there are only a handful of pedestrian lights in the entire city.
- Don't expect anyone to stop for you under any circumstances. You have to get out of their way – not vice versa.
- Run if it looks like the light is changing.
- Take particular care negotiating the city's very wide roadside storm-drains.

accommodate the burgeoning middle class of coffee middlemen and industrialists; these Europhile aspirations culminated in 1894 with the construction of the splendid **Teatro Nacional** – for which every molecule of material, as well as the finest craftsmen, were transported from Europe.

The twentieth century and beyond

During the twentieth century, San José came to dominate nearly all aspects of Costa Rican life. As well as being the seat of government, since the 1970s it has become the Central American headquarters for many foreign nongovernmental organizations, which has considerably raised its international profile. Multinationals, industry and agribusiness have based their national and regional offices here, creating what at times seems to be a largely middle-class city, populated by an army of neatly suited, briefcase-toting office and embassy workers.

Central San José

Compact **central San José** contains the lion's share of the city's major attractions, all of which are a short walk from each other on or just off Avenida Central. Despite holding the bustling **Mercado Central**, the regal **Teatro Nacional** and San José's more renowned **museums**, the area has a low-key charm that is punctuated only by the shouts of street hawkers selling their wares.

Parque Central

Av 2, C 0/2

At the heart of the city centre, **Parque Central** is a landscaped square punctuated by tall royal palms and centred on a weird Gaudí-esque bandstand. Green parrots roost nightly in the palms; come twilight, their noisy chatter drowns out the constant rumble of traffic. Less frantic than many of the city's squares, it's a nice place to snack on the lychee-like *mamones chinos* or papayas sold by the nearby fruit vendors. The barely contained hubbub of Calle 2 and its assorted electronics and shoe shops overtakes the park's northwestern corner.

Catedral Metropolitana and Teatro Melico Salazar

Catedral Metropolitana Mon–Sat 6am–noon & 3–6pm, Sun 6am–9pm • Free **Teatro Melico Salazar** Free guided visits can be arranged by appointment • ☎ 2221 5172

At the eastern edge of the Parque Central looms the huge, columnar **Catedral Metropolitana**, nicely restored and well worth a peek inside for its colourful frescoes and gilded columns. On the square's northeastern corner, the Neoclassical **Teatro Melico Salazar** (see p.115) is one of Costa Rica's premier theatres, second only to the Teatro Nacional a few blocks further east.

Avenida Central and Paseo Colón

Two blocks north of Parque Central, the pedestrianized **Avenida Central** bisects the city from east to west. Despite the constant ebb and flow of people pressing onwards, it's a pleasant and surprisingly welcoming stretch of street and makes for a good introduction to the city. Department stores dot the Avenida, including Universal, with a particularly good book department (see p.116), the cavernous book–stationery shop Librería Lehmann (see p.116) and, further down, a clutch of *sodas* and fast-food outlets. The atmosphere changes markedly to the west at C 20, as Avenida Central turns into **Paseo Colón**, a wide boulevard of upmarket shops, restaurants and car dealerships.

Mercado Central

Av 0/1, C 6/8 • Mon–Sat 8am–5pm • Free

Just beyond the western end of Avenida Central's pedestrianized section on the corner of Calle 6, is the squat **Mercado Central**. Though it's more orderly than the usual chickens-and-*campesinos* Latin American city markets, it's still quite an experience. Entering the labyrinthine market, you're assaulted by colourful arrangements of strange fruits and vegetables, dangling sides of beef and elaborate, silvery rows of fish. At certain times of the day (lunch and late afternoon, for example) the Mercado Central can resemble the Eighth Circle of Hell – choking with unfamiliar smells and an almighty crush of people – while at other times you'll be able to enjoy a relaxed wander through wide uncrowded alleys of rural commerce. It's certainly the best place in town to get a cheap bite to eat, and the view from a counter stool is fascinating, as traders and their customers jostle for regional produce from *chayotes* (a pear-shaped vegetable) and *mamones* (a lychee-type fruit) to *piñas* (pineapples) and *cas* (a sweet-sour pale fruit.) With a little Spanish, and a pinch of confidence, shopping for fruit and vegetables here can be miles cheaper than in the supermarket.

The streets surrounding the market, which can look quite seedy even during the day (in sharp contrast to the roads just one or two blocks east), are also full of noisy traders and determined shoppers. All this activity encourages **pickpockets**, and in this environment tourists stick out like sore thumbs. Carry only what you need and be on your guard.

Plaza de la Cultura

Av Central, C 3/5

Just east of the Parque Central, the **Plaza de la Cultura** is one of the few places in San José where you can sit at a pleasant outdoor café – the *Café Parisienne* (see p.110), under the arches of the *Gran Hotel Costa Rica* on the plaza's western edge – and watch the world go by to the accompaniment of buskers. The Neoclassical Teatro Nacional rises elegantly over the plaza's southern side while the (rather poorly signposted) joint-entrance to the city's underground **tourist office** (see p.107) and Museo de Oro Precolombino can be found on the plaza's eastern edge.

SAN JOSÉ

BUS STOPS

Alajuela, Volcán Poás & International Airport	L	
Cahuita, Puerto Viejo de Talamanca & Sixaola	A	
Cartago	N	
Los Chiles & Zarcero	C	
Golfito	F	
Guápiles	A	
Jacó & Quepos	K	
Liberia & Playa del Coco	E	
Limón	A	
Nicoya, Sámara & Tamarindo	I	
Peñas Blancas & La Cruz	J	
Puerto Jiménez	B	
Puerto Viejo de Sarapiquí	A	
Puntarenas	M	
Santa Cruz, Playa Hermosa & North Guanacaste Beaches	G	
Sarchí	H	
Tilarán & Monteverde	D	

Museo de Oro Precolombino

Plaza de la Cultura • Daily 9.15am–5pm • $11 • ☎ 2243 4202, ⊕ museosdelbancocentral.org

The Plaza de la Cultura cleverly conceals one of San José's treasures, the Banco Central-owned **Museo de Oro Precolombino**, or Pre-Columbian Gold Museum. The bunker-like underground museum is unprepossessing but the gold on display is truly impressive – all the more extraordinary if you take into account the relative paucity of pre-Columbian artefacts in Costa Rica (compared with Mexico, say, or Guatemala). Most of the exquisitely delicate goldwork is by the **Diquís**, ancient inhabitants of southwestern Costa Rica.

The gold pieces are hung on transparent wires, giving the impression of floating in space, mysteriously suspended in their perspex cases. Most of the gold pieces are small and unbelievably detailed, with a preponderance of disturbing, evil-looking animals. Information panels (in English and Spanish) suggest that one of the chief functions of these portents of evil – frogs, snakes and insects – was to protect the bearer against illness. The Diquís believed that sickness was transmitted to people through spirits in animal form. The *ave de rapiña*, or bird of prey, seems to have had a particular religious relevance for the Diquís: hawks, owls and eagles, differing only fractionally in shape and size, are depicted everywhere. Watch out, too, for angry-looking arachnids, ready to bite or sting; jaguars and alligators carrying the pathetic dangling legs of human victims in their jaws; grinning bats with wings spread; turtles, crabs, frogs, iguanas and armadillos; and a few spiny lobsters. Museum displays highlight the historical and

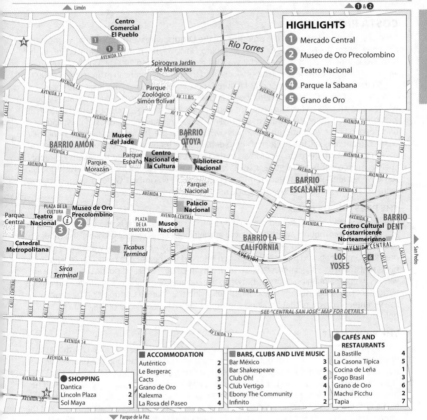

▲ Limón

HIGHLIGHTS
1. Mercado Central
2. Museo de Oro Precolombino
3. Teatro Nacional
4. Parque la Sabana
5. Grano de Oro

ACCOMMODATION
Auténtico	2
Le Bergerac	6
Cacts	3
Grano de Oro	5
Kalexma	1
La Rosa del Paseo	4

SHOPPING
Dantica	1
Lincoln Plaza	2
Sol Maya	3

BARS, CLUBS AND LIVE MUSIC
Bar México	3
Bar Shakespeare	5
Club Oh!	6
Club Vertigo	4
Ebony The Community	1
Infinito	2

CAFÉS AND RESTAURANTS
La Bastille	4
La Casona Típica	5
Cocina de Leña	1
Fogo Brasil	3
Grano de Oro	6
Machu Picchu	2
Tapia	7

SEE "CENTRAL SAN JOSÉ" MAP FOR DETAILS

▼ Parque de la Paz

geographical context of Costa Rican gold. Maps pinpoint gold-production centres and there are models of gold-making settlements.

The **temporary exhibits** tend to branch outside the prevailing gold theme, with attractive displays featuring other artefacts from the pre-Columbian period — often they're just as compelling as the permanent collection, if not more so.

Sharing the building is the marginally interesting **Museo de Numismática** (free with admission to Museo de Oro Precolombino), with a collection of Costa Rican coins. Look out for the old five-colón note, decorated with a delicate, brightly coloured panorama of Costa Rican society.

Teatro Nacional

C 5, Av 2 • May–Nov Mon–Sat 9am–4pm, Dec–April daily 9am–4pm • Guided tours offered • $7 • ⓦ teatronacional.go.cr

Reputedly modelled on the Paris Opéra, San José's heavily colonnaded, grey-brown **Teatro Nacional** is tucked in behind the Plaza de la Cultura and oozes an unmistakable Old World air in the heart of the tropics. Indeed, the theatre's marbled stairways, gilt cherubs and red velvet carpets would look more at home in Europe than in Central America.

Teatro Nacional's story is an intriguing one, illuminating the industrious, no-nonsense attitude of the city's coffee elite, who demonstrated the national pride and yearning for cultural achievement that came to characterize Costa Rican society in the twentieth century. In 1890, the world-famous prima donna Adelina Patti was making a

1

COSTA RICAN GOLD

Little, if anything, is known of the prehistory of the **Diquis**, who were responsible for most of the goldwork at the Museo de Oro Precolombino. However, the history of gold working in the New World is fairly well documented. It was first recorded (around 2000 BC) in Peru, from where it spread northwards, reaching Mexico and the Central American isthmus by 700–900 AD. All the ancient American peoples favoured more or less the same methods and styles, using a gold-copper alloy (called *tumbaga*) and designs featuring extremely intricate shapes, with carefully rendered facial expressions and a preference for ingenious but rather diabolical-looking zoomorphic representations – growling peccaries, threatening birds of prey, and a two-headed figure, each mouth playing its own flute. The precise function of these intricately crafted creations is still the subject of some debate since many of the objects show no sign of having been worn (there are no grooves in the pendant links to indicate they were worn on chains). Archeologists believe they may have been intended for ceremonial burial and, indeed, some were even "killed" or ritually mutilated before being entombed. Others may have been worn as charms protecting the bearer against illness and evil spirits.

THE PRESTIGE OF GOLD

The Diquis would have obtained the gold by panning in rivers, and it is speculated that in Osa, at least, the rivers routinely washed up gold at their feet. Diquis *caciques* (chiefs) and other social elites used their gold in the same way it is used today – to advertise wealth and social prestige. Ornaments and insignias were often reserved for the use of a particular *cacique* and his family, and these special pieces were traded as truce offerings and political gifts between various rulers, maintaining contacts between the *caciques* of distant regions. Indeed, it was the removal of native distinctions of social rank following the Spanish Conquest of the country in the seventeenth century that heralded the almost immediate collapse of the Costa Rican gold-making industry.

THE RICH COAST

Although the Diquis were the undisputed masters of design, archeological digs in the Reventazón Valley suggest that gold working could also be found among the peoples of the Atlantic watershed zone. When Columbus first came ashore in 1502, he saw the local (Talamancan) peoples wearing gold mirror-pendants and headbands and rashly assumed he had struck it rich – hence the country's name. An early document of a subsequent expedition to the Caribbean coastal region of Costa Rica, now housed in archives in Cartago, contains the impressions of native wealth recorded by one gold-crazed Spaniard in Diego de Sojo's 1587 expedition: "The rivers abound with gold… and the Indians extract gold with calabashes in very large grains… from these same hills Captain Muñoz… took from the tombs of the dead… such a great quantity of gold as to swell two large chests of the kind in which shoes and nails for the cavalry are brought over from Castile."

tour through the Americas, but could not stop in Costa Rica as there was no appropriate theatre. Mortified, and determined to raise funds for the construction of a national theatre, the wealthy coffee farmers responded by levying a tax on every bag of coffee exported. Within a couple of years the coffers were full to bursting; European craftsmen and architects were employed, and by 1897 the building was ready for its inauguration, a stylish affair with singers from the Paris Opéra performing *Faust*.

The interior

The theatre itself is lavishly done in red plush, gold and marble, with richly detailed frescoes and statues personifying "Dance", "Music" and "Fame". The upstairs "salons" are decorated in mint and jade-green, trimmed with gold, and lined with heavy portraits of *finqueros*. In the main lobby, look for the mural depicting the coffee harvest (once featured on the five-colón note), a gentle reminder of the agricultural source of wealth that made this urban luxury possible. All in all, the building remains in remarkably good condition, despite the dual onslaught of the climate and a succession of earthquakes. The latest, in 1991, closed the place for two years. Above all it is the details that leave a lasting impression: plump cherubim, elegantly numbered boxes fanning out in a wheel-spoke circle, heavy hardwood doors and intricate glasswork in the washrooms.

Even if you're not coming to see a performance (see p.115) you can wander around the post-Baroque splendor – and just off the foyer is an elegant café (see p.110), which serves good coffee, juices and European-style cakes.

Parque España and around

C 11, Av 3/7 • Daily 24hr

Lined with tall trees, the verdant **Parque España** is surrounded by several excellent museums. On the western corner, facing Avenida 5, stands the **Edificio Metálica** (Metal Building, also known as the "Escuela Metálica"), so-called because its exterior is made entirely out of metal plates shipped from France over a hundred years ago. Though the prospect sounds dour, the effect – especially the bright multicoloured courtyard as seen from the **Museo del Jade**, high above – is very pretty, if slightly military. Just west of Parque España lies **Parque Morazón**, more a concrete-paved square than a park proper. It's centred on the landmark grey-domed bandstand floridly known as the Templo de Música.

Museo del Jade

Av 7, C 9/11 • Mon–Fri 8.30am–3.30pm, Sat 10am–2pm • $8 • ☎ 2287 6034

On the north side of the Parque España rises one of the few office towers in San José: the INS, or Institute of Social Security building. The eleventh floor of this uninspiring edifice contains one of the city's finest museums, the **Marco Fidel Tristan Museo del Jade** (Jade Museum), home to the world's largest collection of American jade.

As in China and the East, jade was much prized in ancient Costa Rica as a stone with religious or mystical significance, and for Neolithic civilizations it was an object of great power. It was and still is considered valuable because of its mineralogical rarity. Only slightly less hard than quartz, it's well known for its durability, and is a good material for weapons and cutting tools like axes and blades. As no quarries of the stone have been found in Costa Rica, the big mystery is how the pre-Columbian societies here got hold of so much of it. The reigning theories are that it came from Guatemala, where the Motagua Valley is home to one of the world's six known jade quarries, or that it was traded or sold down the isthmus by the Olmecs of Mexico. This would also explain the Maya insignia on some of the pieces – symbols that had no meaning for Costa Rica's pre-Columbian inhabitants.

The museum displays are ingenious, subtly back-lit to show off the multicoloured and multi-textured pieces to full effect. Jade exhibits an extraordinary range of nuanced colour, from a milky-white green and soft grey to a deep green; the latter was associated with agricultural fertility and particularly prized by the inhabitants of the Americas around 600 BC. No two pieces in the collection are alike in hue and opacity, though, as in the Museo de Oro, you'll see a lot of **axe-gods**: anthropomorphic bird-cum-human forms shaped like an axe and worn as a pendant, as well as a variety of ornate necklaces and fertility symbols.

Incidentally, the **view** from the museum windows is one of the best in the city, taking in the sweep of San José from the centre to the south, and then west to the mountains.

CENAC

C 15, Av 3/7 • Free • ☎ 2255 3188

Sprawling across the entire eastern border of the Parque España, the former National Liquor Factory, dating from 1887, today houses the **Centro Nacional de la Cultura** (**CENAC**), an arts complex that includes the Museo de Arte y Diseño Contemporáneo, two theatres, a dance studio (wander around during the day for glimpses of dancers

1

and musicians rehearsing) and an amphitheatre. Many Josefinos still refer to the buildings as the old *Liquoría*; indeed you can still see a massive old distilling machine in the grounds, complete with the nameplate of its Birmingham manufacturers.

Museo de Arte y Diseño Contemporáneo

C 15, Av 3 • Mon–Sat 9.30am–5pm • $3 • ☎ 2257 7202, ⓦ madc.cr

The main attraction here is the cutting-edge **Museo de Arte y Diseño Contemporáneo**, or Museum of Contemporary Art and Design. Opened in 1994 under the direction of dynamic artist Virginia Pérez-Ratton, it's a highly modern space, with a cosmopolitan, multimedia approach – there's an area specially designed for outdoor installations by up-and-coming Central American artists.

Parque Nacional and around

Av 1/3, C 15/19

San José's **Parque Nacional**, one of the city's finest open spaces, marks the heart of downtown San José. Overlooked by rows of mop-headed palms and thick deciduous trees, it's popular with courting couples and older men discussing the state of the nation. After gaining notoriety as a hangout for muggers and prostitutes, it was equipped with tall lamps to add extra light – a tactic that has apparently succeeded in drawing the courting couples back to its nocturnal benches. Even so, it's still probably not a good idea to wander around here after dark.

You can hear government debates Costa Rican-style at the **Palacio Nacional**, home to Costa Rica's Legislative Assembly, just south of the park at the corner of Calle 15 and Avenida Central. The fun starts at 4pm, but check first if the Legislature is in session.

Biblioteca Nacional

Library Av 3 bis, C 15/17 • Mon–Fri 8am–6pm • Free **Gallery** Mon–Sat 10am–1pm & 2–5pm • Free

The modernist **Biblioteca Nacional** is Costa Rica's largest and most useful library, at least for readers of Spanish. Anyone can rifle through the newspaper collection to the right of the entrance on the ground floor. At the library's southwest corner, the **Galería Nacional de Arte Contemporáneo** features small and often quirky displays of work by local artists.

Plaza de la Democracía

C 13/17, Av 0/2

A block southwest of the Parque Nacional sits the concrete **Plaza de la Democracía**, yet another of the city's soulless squares which is just one aesthetic notch up from a paved car park. Constructed in 1989 to mark President Oscar Arias's key involvement in the Central American Peace Plan, this expanse of terraced concrete slopes up towards a fountain. At its western end is a row of **artisans' stalls** selling hammocks, thick Ecuadorian sweaters, leather bracelets and jewellery. You can also buy Guatemalan textiles and decorative *molas* (patchwork textiles in vibrant colours) made by the Kuna people of Panama, though at steeper prices than elsewhere in Central America. Other stalls sell T-shirts and wooden crafts and trinkets. The traders are friendly and won't pressure you; a bit of gentle bargaining is a must.

Museo Nacional

C 17, Av 0/2 • Tues–Sat 8.30am–4.30pm, Sun 9am–4.30pm • $8 • ☎ 2257 1433, ⓦ museocostarica.go.cr

The north end of Plaza de la Democracía is crowned by the impressive **Museo Nacional**, occupying the renovated former Bellavista Barracks. Bullet holes from the 1948 insurrection (see p.416) can still be seen on the north side of the building's thick

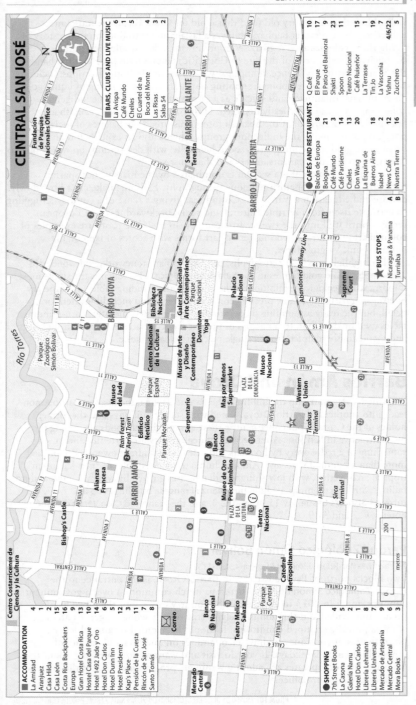

CENTRAL SAN JOSÉ

■ ACCOMMODATION

La Amistad	4
Aranjuez	1
Casa Hilda	2
Casa León	15
Costa Rica Backpackers	16
Europa	9
Gran Hotel Costa Rica	13
Hostel Casa del Parque	10
Hotel 1492 Jade y Oro	14
Hotel Don Carlos	6
Hotel Dunn Inn	5
Hotel Presidente	12
Kap's Place	3
Pensión de la Cuesta	11
Rincón de San José	7
Santo Tomás	8

● SHOPPING

7th Street Books	4
La Casona	5
Galería Namu	2
Hotel Don Carlos	1
Librería Lehmann	8
Librería Universal	7
Mercado de Artesanía	9
Mercado Central	6
Mora Books	3

■ BARS, CLUBS AND LIVE MUSIC

La Avispa	6
Café Mundo	1
Chelles	5
El Cuartel de la Boca del Monte	4
Las Risas	3
Salsa 54	2

● CAFÉS AND RESTAURANTS

Balcón de Europa	8	Q Café	10
Bologna	21	El Parque	17
Café Mundo	3	El Patio del Balmoral	9
Café Parisienne	14	Shakti	23
Chelles	13	Spoon	11
Don Wang	20	Teatro Nacional	15
La Esquina de Buenos Aires	18	Café Ruiseñor	1
Isabel	2	La Terrasse	19
News Café	12	Tin Jo	7
Nuestra Tierra	16	La Vasconia	22
		Vishnu	4/6/22
		Zucchero	5

★ BUS STOPS

Nicaragua & Panama	A
Turrialba	B

Centro Costarricense de Ciencia y la Cultura

Fundación de Parques Nacionales Office

1

walls. More than a century old (and that *is* old for Costa Rica), the museum's collection, though rather haphazard, gives a fascinating introduction to the story of Costa Rica's **colonization**. A grisly series of drawings, deeply affecting in their simplicity, tells the story of the fate of Costa Rica's **indigenous** people at the hands of the Spanish settlers. Violence, it appears, was meted out in both directions, including beheadings, hangings, clubbings, shooting of priests and the pouring of liquid gold down throats. Infanticide and suicide as a means of resistance in the indigenous community are also mercilessly depicted. Displays explain (in both English and Spanish) how the arrival of the Spanish forever disturbed the balance of social and political power among the indigenous groups. There's also an explanation on the function of gold in the indigenous social hierarchy, with descriptions on which objects were used to identify warriors, chiefs and shamans.

The museum's **colonial-era** section is dominated by the massive but spartan furniture and cheesy Spanish religious iconography. Exhibits make clear how slowly culture and education advanced in Costa Rica, giving a sense of a country struggling to extricate itself from terrible cultural and social backwardness – in European terms – until well into the twenty-first century. In the same room are examples of **colonial art**, which replaced indigenous art forms with scores of lamentable gilt-and-pink Virgin Marys.

Other highlights include petroglyphs, pre-Columbian stonework, and wonderful anthropomorphic gold figures in the **Sala Arqueológica**. This remains the single most important archeological exhibition in the country; the grinding tables and funerary offerings, in particular, show precise geometric patterns and incredible attention to detail, but the really astounding pieces are the "flying panel" **metates**, corn-grinding tables used by the Chorotega peoples of present-day Guanacaste, each with three legs and meticulously sculpted from a single piece of volcanic stone.

Barrios Amón and Otoya

Weaving its way north up the hill from the Parque España, the historic **Barrio Amón** leads into another old barrio, **Otoya**. Lined with stately buildings and the former homes of the Costa Rican coffee gentry, these two neighbourhoods are among the most attractive in San José. After decades of neglect they are currently undergoing something of a rediscovery by hoteliers and café and restaurant owners. Established more than a hundred years ago, Amón is home to fine examples of "neo-Victorian" tropical architecture, with low-slung wooden houses girthed by wide verandas and iron railings. Striking examples include the **Alianza Francesa** building, C 5 and Av 7, the turreted **Bishop's Castle**, Av 11 bis and C 3, and the grand old **Casa Verde de Amón** hotel at C 7 and Av 9.

Parque Zoológico Simón Bolívar

Av 11 and C 7/9 • Mon–Fri 8am–3.30pm, Sat & Sun 9am–4.30pm • $3.50

Two blocks north of Parque España, in Barrio Otoya, is the entrance to the **Parque Zoológico Simón Bolívar**. There was much commotion over a government announcement in 2013 to close all of the country's zoos, but the move has predictably stalled and this zoo is likely to stay open a while longer. At any rate, with its pitifully cramped conditions, it should be avoided by animal lovers. Nevertheless, it continues to draw Tico families on Sundays and gaggles of schoolchildren on weekdays. If you do visit and want to do something about the facilities, the zoo operates an "adopt-an-animal" programme – ask at the entrance kiosk or the museum office.

1 El Pueblo and around

Off Av 17, about 200m north of the zoo across the Río Torres · Daily 9am–5pm · ☎ 2221 9434

The cluster of shops, restaurants, bars and discos that make up the **Centro Comercial El Pueblo** is generally known simply as "El Pueblo". For a tourist complex, El Pueblo is well designed and a sensible initiative that gives both tourists and Josefinos – who love it – an attractive, atmospheric place to shop, eat, drink and dance. El Pueblo's whitewashed adobe buildings evoke a type of colonial architecture that has found it hard to survive in Costa Rica, due to the successive tremors of earthquakes. Walking here means running a gauntlet of pedestrian-unfriendly traffic – most people take a taxi, which costs around $3 from the Plaza de la Cultura.

Spirogyra Jardín de Mariposas

Opposite El Pueblo off Av 17 · Daily 8am–4pm · $7 · ☎ 2222 9237, ⓦ butterflygardencr.com

The compact **Spirogyra Jardín de Mariposas** has a wide variety of butterflies fluttering about, with daily guided tours pointing out particularly unusual and pretty ones. For being smack in the middle of San José, it exudes a tranquility far removed from the rest of the city, and the sight of brilliant blue morphos and dense foliage is a good primer for what you'll see once you explore further afield.

Centro Costarricense de la Ciencia y la Cultura

C 4, Av 15 · Tues–Fri 8am–4.30pm, Sat & Sun 9.30am–5pm · $2 · ⓦ museocr.org **Museo de los Niños** Same hours · $3 · ☎ 2258 4929 **Galería Nacional** Same hours · Free

Near El Pueblo, at the end of Calle 4, is the **Centro Costarricense de la Ciencia y la Cultura**. Located in a former prison, this multi-use complex houses a library and small theatre space, as well as the **Galería Nacional de Ciencia y Cultura** (National Gallery of Science and Culture). Making good use of original prison cells restored to their nineteenth-century condition, it showcases contemporary national art, with an emphasis on photography and sculpture. Most of the CCCC, however, is devoted to the mildly interesting **Museo de los Niños** (or Children's Museum), where Costa Rican kids learn about their country's history, culture and science through interactive displays.

Los Yoses and La California

The neighbourhoods of **Los Yoses** and **La California**, facing one another from opposite sides of Avenida Central as it runs east from the Museo Nacional to San Pedro, are oases of calm just blocks from the city centre. Mainly residential, Los Yoses is home to foreign embassies and a few stylish hotels. The commercial La California runs into Barrio Escalante and Barrio Dent, two of San José's nicest residential districts. Walking through Barrio Escalante is the way to head east, and much more pleasant than bus-choked Avenida Central.

Centro Cultural Costarricense Norteamericano

100m north of the Am-Pm supermarket on the corner of Av 0 and C 37, Barrio Dent · Mon–Fri 7am–7pm, Sat 9am–noon · Free · ☎ 2207 7500, ⓦ centrocultural.cr

Homesick North American tourists should head to the **Centro Cultural Costarricense Norteamericano**. The Mark Twain library has English-language publications – including the *Miami Herald*, *The New York Times* and *USA Today* – as well as all the main Costa Rican dailies. There's also an art gallery, the Teatro Eugene O'Neill (see p.115), with jazz festivals and English-language theatre performances, a pleasant café and CNN beamed out on the communal TV.

San Pedro

First impressions of **San Pedro** can be off-putting. Avenida Central (known here also as Paseo de los Estudiantes) appears to be little more than a strip of petrol stations, broken-up pavements and shopping malls. Walk just a block off the Paseo, however, and you'll find a lively university student quarter, plus a few elegant old residential houses. The area has traditionally been home to some of the city's best restaurants and nightlife, but an increasing proliferation of dark bars filled with shouting college students means that it's often not the most relaxing spot to be on a Friday or Saturday night, at least during term time.

Universidad de Costa Rica

C 0, C de Amarguras • ☎ 2511 0000, ⓦ ucr.ac.cr

The leafy campus of the **Universidad de Costa Rica** is one of the finest in Central America, and certainly the most prestigious educational institution in the country. Founded in 1940, the university has in the past been accused of being too rigidly academic and elitist, but the overall campus atmosphere is busy, egalitarian and stimulating.

The best places to hang out on **campus** and meet both young Josefinos and students from other countries are the frenzied and cheap cafeteria in the building immediately to the right of the library (there's also an excellent **bookshop** across from the back entrance of the cafeteria), the Comedor Universitario, or **dining hall**, and the Facultad de Bellas Artes, which has a wonderful open-air **theatre** used for frequent concerts. Notice boards around campus, particularly in front of the Vida Estudiantíl office (Student Life office, Building A, fourth floor), keep you up to date with what's going on; try also to get hold of a copy of *Semana Universitaria*, the campus newspaper, which is sold in most restaurants and bookshops in the area and lists upcoming events. The three or four blocks surrounding the university are lined with lively bars and restaurants, though in most of them you'll feel more comfortable if you're under 30. For Spanish-speakers this is a great place to meet people, watch movies and browse around the several well-stocked bookshops.

Museo de Insectos

Mon–Fri 1–4.45pm • $2 • ⓦ miucr.ucr.ac.cr

Oddly located in the basement of the Facultad de Artes Musicales (School of Music), the

1

excellent **Museo de Insectos** hosts as extensive an insect collection as you're ever likely to see. Pride of place is given to butterflies, which come in a bewildering variety of shapes, sizes and colours. If you're worried you might miss out on spying a harlequin beetle out in the wild – or perhaps you'd rather see one securely mounted on a wall – this is *the* place to go.

Parque la Sabana

Av 0, C 42/68 • Open 24hr • Free

At the very western end of Paseo Colón (see p.91), a solid expanse of green today known as **Parque la Sabana** was San José's airport until the 1940s, and is now home to the country's most prominent museum devoted to national art, as well as the Estadio Nacional de Costa Rica (see p.116).

Concerted efforts to maintain its cleanliness and an ongoing project to introduce hundreds of trees native to Costa Rica provide the verdant Parque la Sabana with a sense of vitality. Its status as San Jose's finest green space was confirmed in May 2010, when the park was chosen as the site of the inauguration of Laura Chinchilla, the country's first female president.

Most people come to the park to enjoy an afternoon stroll amid leafy trees shading a central lake and colourful modern sculptures scattered around. On Sunday afternoons, hordes of local families feed the resident geese and eat ice cream. It's also one of the best places in San José to **jog**. The cement track is usually full of serious runners in training, but if it gets too crowded you can also run quite safely throughout the park.

Just outside the southern boundary of the park is the futuristic air-traffic-control-tower shape of the **Contraloría de la República**: this is the government's administrative headquarters.

Museo de Arte Costarricense

Av 0, C 42 • Tues–Sun 9am–4pm • Free • ☎ 2256 1281, ⊕ musarco.go.cr

The renovated bright white Neocolonial edifice of the old air terminal at the eastern end of Parque la Sabana has been converted into the attractive **Museo de Arte Costarricense**, with a fine collection of mainly twentieth-century Costa Rican paintings displayed in a handsome setting. Highlights of the permanent collection include numerous sculptures and paintings by the celebrated **Juan Manuel Sánchez**, the outstanding landscapes of **Teodorico Quirós**, with their Cézanne-inspired palettes of russets and burnt siennas, along with Enrique Echandi, Margarita Berthau, abstract painter Lola Fernández and a scattershot selection of foreign artists including Diego Rivera and Alexander Calder. The remarkable **Salon Dorado** upstairs features four full walls of bas-relief wooden carvings overlaid with sumptuous gold, portraying somewhat idealized scenes of Costa Rica's history since the Spanish arrived. On the western wall are imagined scenes from the lives of the indigenous peoples, followed on the north wall by Columbus's arrival, to which the indigenous peoples improbably respond by falling to their knees and praying solemnly. Other golden representations include the Costa Rican agrarian gods of horses, oxen and chickens, and an image of this very building when it was San José's airport, little biplanes buzzing around it like mosquitoes.

Museo de Ciencias Naturales La Salle

Av 12, C 68 • Mon–Sat 7.30am–4pm, Sun 9am–5pm • $2 • ☎ 2232 1306, ⊕ lasalle.ed.cr/museo.php

On the southwest corner of Sabana Park, across the road in the Ministry of Agriculture and Livestock complex, is the quirky natural-science museum **Museo de Ciencias Naturales La Salle**. Walk in, and after about 400m you'll see the painted wall proclaiming the museum; the entrance is at the back. It's an offbeat collection, with displays ranging from pickled fish and snakes coiled in formaldehyde to some rather forlorn taxidermy exhibits – age and humidity have taken their toll. Highlights include the model of the huge **baula**, or leatherback turtle, the biggest reptile on earth, and the **dusky grouper** fish, a serious contender for first prize in the Ugliest Animal in the World contest. Tonnes of crumbly fossils and an enormous selection of pinned butterflies (twelve cases alone of titanium-bright Blue Morphos) finish off the collection. Live tortoises, virtually motionless, doze in the courtyard garden.

Escazú

The pleasant suburb of **Escazú**, 9km west of the centre, has a decidedly more exclusive feel to it than much of the rest of San José. It has its fair share of strip malls and dreary international fast-food chains to be sure, but stroll through its trendy pockets and cobblestone streets and it becomes clear why so many expats favour living and going out here. Spreading up along its namesake mountain from a valley floor, Escazú consists of three separate neighbourhoods, each with a tidy central square as its focal point. At the base, modern **San Rafael** is the commercial hub, where most of the upscale shops and galleries are located. Just over a mile up the mountain, **San Miguel** (also known as Escazú Centro) is the site of the original town and still has a laidback and rural character that reflects its ranching origins. Fronting its central square, the gleaming white **Iglesia Escazú** (irregular hours) dates back to the late eighteenth century, though its rebuilt modern front is at odds with the rest of the square's more understated buildings. The square also is the site of Escazú's excellent **farmers' market** (Sat 7am–noon), which draws Josefinos from across the city for the impressive selection of fresh produce and artisanal foods. About half a mile further up the mountain is **San Antonio**, the most residential of the three neighbourhoods and marked by a number of expansive estates and grand mansions.

ARRIVAL AND DEPARTURE   SAN JOSÉ

Arrival in San José, whether by **plane** or **bus**, is straightforward; even if you don't speak Spanish, getting into town is a well-oiled procedure and there's less opportunistic theft than at most other Central and South American arrival points. Though Liberia is gaining tracking as an arrival point for international flights, José is undisputedly the transport hub of Costa Rica. Most bus services, flights and car rental agencies are located here. Chances are, wherever you plan to go – and however you plan to get there – you'll have to first go through San José.

BY PLANE
Most international flights arrive at Juan Santamaría International Airport (☎ 2443 2622), 17km northwest of San José and 3km southeast of Alajuela. The ICT office here (Mon–Fri 9am–5pm; ☎ 2443 1535) can supply maps and give advice on accommodation. There's also a post office

(Mon–Fri 8am–5pm), an ATM machine (handily situated next to the departure tax desk), and a bank, downstairs on the departure level (Mon–Fri 6.30am–6pm, Sat & Sun 7am–1pm); local currency isn't necessary for taxis, but you'll need colones for the bus.

1

AIRPORT TAXIS

The best way to get into central San José from the airport is by taxi, which takes about twenty to thirty minutes in light traffic and costs around $35. Official airport taxis are orange and line up outside the terminal. You'll have no problems getting a cab, as the drivers will stampede for your business while you're practically still in customs. Take a deep breath and make sure to agree on the fare before you get in the cab. Some taxi drivers take travellers who haven't made accommodation bookings to hotels where they get commission – these are often more expensive than you were bargaining for, so be firm about where you want to go. Taxi drivers accept dollars as well as colones, although they tend not to accept notes larger than $20; they now accept credit cards as well.

AIRPORT BUSES

The Alajuela–San José bus (every 10min between 4am & 11pm; every 30min at other times) stops right outside the airport's undercover car park. Though it's much cheaper than a taxi, there are no proper luggage racks inside and the buses are nearly always full – you can just about get away with it if you're carrying only a light backpack or small bag. Drivers will indicate which buses are on their way to San José (a thirty-minute journey) and which to Alajuela. The fare to San José is 500 colones (about $1) – payable in local currency; pay the driver. The bus drops passengers in town at Av 2, C 12/14 near the Hospital de San Juan de Dios, where there are plenty of taxis.

AIRLINE OFFICES

Alitalia, C 38, Av 3 (☎ 2295 6870); American, Paseo Colón, C 26/28 (☎ 2257 1266); Continental, C 19, Av 2 (☎ 2296 4911); Copa, C 1, Av 5 (☎ 2212 6640); Delta, at the airport (☎ 2257 8946); Iberia, C 40, Paseo Colón (☎ 2257 8266); Lacsa, C 1, Av 5 (☎ 2212 9383); LanChile, Sabana Oeste (☎ 2290 5222); Lufthansa, C 5, Av 7/9 (☎ 2243 1818); Mexicana, C 1, Av 2/4 (☎ 2295 6969); SAM, Av 5, C 1/3 (☎ 2233-3066); Sansa, Av 5, C 1/3 (☎ 2221 5774); TACA, C 1, Av 1/3 (☎ 2296 9353); United Airlines, Sabana Sur (☎ 2220 4844); Varig, Av 5, C 1/3 (☎ 2290 5222).

DEPARTURE TAX

The departure tax is $26; it is best to pay in cash as credit card transactions are treated as a cash advance.

DOMESTIC FLIGHTS

Domestic flights from San José are run by Sansa, the state airline, and NatureAir, a commercial company. Sansa (☎ 2257 9444, ⊛ flysansa.com), flies from Juan Santamaría International Airport, 17km northwest of the city. They change their schedules frequently, so it's best to phone ahead or double-confirm when booking. NatureAir (☎ 2220 3054 or ☎ 2296 1102, ⊛ natureair.com), more

reliable in terms of schedules, flies from Tobías Bolaños airport in Pavas, 7km west of the city. Although the information below gives as accurate a rundown of the routes as possible, flight durations are subject to change at the last minute. Both NatureAir and Sansa fly small propeller planes that are often grounded by inclement weather. Keep in mind that, in the event of a cancellation, both airlines offer credit rather than money back. Some of the routings, particularly those to the Nicoya Peninsula, tend to be roundabout, often with one or two stops. Sansa check-in is at their San José office one hour before departure; they run a free bus to get you to the airport, and in some cases offer free transfers to your hotel at the other end. Fares for both airlines generally range from $55 one-way to $110–130 return for most destinations.

Destinations via Sansa Bahía Drake (1 daily; 50min); Golfito (3 daily; 1hr); Nosara (1 daily; 1hr); Palmar Sur (2 daily; 50min); Puerto Jiménez (4 daily; 50min); Quepos (8 daily; 30min); Sámara (1 daily; 1hr); Tamarindo (3 daily; 1hr); Tambor (2 daily; 20min); Tortuguero (1 daily Mon, Wed & Fri; 45min).

Destinations via NatureAir Bahía Drake (4 daily; 45min); Golfito (2 daily; 55min); Liberia (4 daily; 1hr 10min); Nosara (2 daily; 45min); Palmar Sur (1 daily; 1hr); Puerto Jiménez (5 daily; 50min); Quepos (4 daily; 25min); Tamarindo (4 daily; 55min); Tambor (3 daily; 25min); Tortuguero (1 daily; 30min).

BY BUS

From San José there are few places in Costa Rica that can't be reached by bus; get a complete timetable at the ICT office (see p.107) when you arrive or check some routes online at ⊛ thebusschedule.com. As schedules are prone to change, exact departure times are not given here, though some details are given under individual destinations elsewhere in the book. Another possibility is Interbus (see p.49), which offers shuttle service from San José hotels to various destinations further afield. The rates are, of course, far higher than riding a similar route with one of the companies listed below, but their prices are more reasonable than you might expect.

BUS TERMINALS

The closest thing San José has to a main domestic bus station is La Coca-Cola, five blocks west of the Mercado Central at Av 1/3, C 16/18 (the main entrance is on C 16). Named after an old bottling plant, La Coca-Cola not only applies to the station proper – which is quite small and the arrival point for only a few buses, principally those from Jacó, Quepos and Dominical – but also the surrounding area, where many more buses pull in. Like many bus stations, La Coca-Cola is an irredeemable hellhole – noisy, hemmed in by small, confusing streets crammed with busy market traders, and invariably prowled by pickpockets.

LUGGAGE ON LONG-DISTANCE BUSES

Thefts from the luggage compartments of long-distance bus services are not uncommon, especially on the Monteverde and Manuel Antonio routes. The accepted wisdom is, if possible, to **take your luggage onto the bus** with you. Even then, make sure all compartments are locked and that you have nothing valuable inside easily unzipped pockets. If you have to put your bags in the luggage hold, make sure only the driver or his helper handles them, and get a seat from where you can keep an eye on the luggage compartment during stops.

Lugging your bags and searching for your bus stop around here makes it very hard not to look like a confused gringo, thus increasing the chances that you'll become the target of opportunistic theft: best to arrive and leave in a taxi. Buses for the Caribbean coast depart from Gran Terminal del Caribe, C 0 at Av 15/17. Be especially careful of your belongings around the Tilarán terminal, C 12, Av 7/9, which is also used by buses to Monteverde: people waiting here for the 6.30am bus to Monteverde seem to be particularly at risk of attempted theft.

DOMESTIC BUS ROUTES

The buses listed below are express services from San José. Regional bus information is covered in the relevant accounts in the Guide. The initials below correspond to the bus companies (see box, p.106) that serve the route. PN = Parque Nacional; RNdVS = Refugio Nacional de Vida Silvestre; MN = Monumento National.

Destinations Alajuela and the airport (TU; Av 2, C 12/14; every 5min; 35min); Cahuita (ME; C 0, Av 11/13; 4 daily; 4hr); Cartago SA; C 5, Av 18/20 (every 5min; 45min); La Fortuna (for Volcán Arenal; ATSC; C 16, Av 1/3; 12 daily; 4hr 30min); Golfito (TRC; C 14, Av 3/5; 2 daily; 8hr); Guápiles (for PN Braulio Carrillo; EG; C 0, Av 11/13; every 45min; 35min); Heredia (TU/MRA; C 1, Av 7/9 & Av 2, C 12/14; every 5min; 25min); Liberia (PU; C 14, Av 1; 17 daily; 4hr); Limón (TC; C 0, Av 11/13; 25 daily; 2hr 30min); Los Chiles (for RNdVS Caño Negro; ATS; C 12, Av 7/9; 2 daily; 5hr); Monteverde (TIL; C 12, Av 7/9; 2 daily; 3hr 30min); Nicoya (EA; C 16, Av 3/5; 8 daily; 6hr); Nosara (EA; C 14, Av 3/5; 1 daily; 6hr); Palmar (TRA; C 14, Av 5; 7 daily; 5hr); Playa Brasilito (TRA; C 20, Av 3/5; 2 daily; 6hr); Playa Coco (PU; C 24, Av 5/7; 3 daily; 5hr); Playa Flamingo (TRA; C 20,

Av 3/5; 2 daily; 6hr); Playa Hermosa (TRA; C 20, Av 1/3; 2 daily; 6hr); Playa Jacó (TJ; C 16, Av 1/3; 5 daily; 2hr 30min); Playa Junquillal (TRA; C 20, Av 3/51; daily; 5hr); Playa Panamá (TRA; C 20, Av 1/3; 2 daily; 6hr); Playa Potrero (TRA; C 20, Av 3; 2 daily; 6hr); Puerto Jiménez (for PN Corcovado; TB; C 14, Av 9/11; 1 daily; 8hr); Puerto Viejo de Sarapiqui (ME; C 0, Av 15; 10 daily; 2hr); Puerto Viejo de Talamanca (ME; C 0, Av 13; 4 daily; 4hr 30min); Puntarenas (EU; C 16, Av 10/12; 15 daily; 2hr); Quepos (for PN Manuel Antonio; MO; C 16, Av 3/5; 4 daily; 3hr 30min); Sámara (EU; C 14, Av 3/5; 1 daily; 6hr); Ciudad Quesada (ATS; C 12, Av 7/9; 15 daily; 3hr); San Isidro de El General (for PN Chirripó; MU; C 0, Av 22/24; 14 daily; 3hr); Santa Cruz (TRA; Av 3, C 18/20; 9 daily; 5hr); Sarchí (Tuan; Av 3, C 16/18; 30 daily; 1hr 30min); Tamarindo (EA; C 14, Av 5; 2 daily; 6hr); Turrialba (for MN Guayabo; TRS; C 13, Av 6/8;17 daily; 1hr 40min); Volcán Irazú (BM; Av 2, C 1/3; 1 Sat & Sun; 2hr); Volcán Poás (TU; Av 2, C 12/14; 1 daily; 1hr 30min).

INTERNATIONAL BUS ROUTES

Most international buses from Nicaragua, Honduras, Guatemala and Panama pull into the Tica Bus station, C 3 Av 26 (☎ 2221 8954 or ☎ 2221 0006), several blocks south of the city centre. Advance purchase – at least a week in advance, particularly for Managua and Panama City – is necessary for all routes.

Destinations David (TRC; C 5, Av 18/20; 1 daily; 9hr); Guatemala City (Tica; Av 4, C 9/11; 3 daily; 60hr with overnight in Managua & El Salvador); Managua (Nica; C 0, Av 11; 1 daily; 11hr), (Tica; Av 4, C 9/11; 4 daily; 11hr) & (TRN; C 22, Av 3/5; 4 daily; 11hr); Panama City (PA; C 16, Av 3/5; 1 daily; 16hr) & (Tica; Av 4, C 9/11; 2 daily; 16hr); Changuinola, Panama (TBO; C 14/16, Av 5; 1 daily; 6hr).

GETTING AROUND

Once you've got used to the deep gutters and broken pavements, San José is easily negotiated **on foot**. Several blocks in the city centre around the Plaza de la Cultura have been completely pedestrianized. There is little need to take **buses** within the city centre, though the suburban buses are useful, particularly if you are heading out to Parque la Sabana, a 30min walk west along Paseo Colón. Escazú is a 20min ride to the west, and San Pedro and the Universidad de Costa Rica are a 10min ride to the east. Buses stop running between 10–11pm and taxis become the best way to get around. **Street crime** is an issue, and most Josefinos advise against walking alone after dark, women especially.

BY BUS

Fast, cheap and frequent buses connect the centre of the city with virtually all San José's neighbourhoods and

suburbs, and generally run from 5am until 10–11pm everyday. Most buses to San Pedro, Tres Ríos and other points east leave from the stretch of Avenida Central

1

BUS COMPANIES IN SAN JOSÉ

A bewildering number of **bus companies** use San José as their hub. The following is a rundown of their head-office addresses and/or phone numbers, and the abbreviations that we use in our listings.

ATSC	Autotransportes San José-San Carlos, C 12, Av 7/9 (☎2255 4318)
BL	Autotransportes Blanco-Lobo, C 12, Av 9 (☎2771 4744)
BM	Buses Metropoli (☎2530 1064)
EA	Empresa Alfaro, C 14, Av 3/5 (☎2222 2666)
EG	Empresarios Guápileños (☎2710 7780)
EU	Empresarios Unidos (☎2222 0064)
ME	Transportes MEPE, Av 11, C 0/1 (☎2257 8129)
MO	Transportes Delio Morales, C 16, Av 1/3 (☎2223 5567)
MRA	Microbuses Rapiditos Heredianos, C 1, Av 7/9 (☎2223 8392)
MU	MUSOC, C 16, Av 1/3 (☎2222 2422)
Nica	Nicabus (☎2223 0293)
PA	Panaline (☎2256 8721)
PU	Pulmitan, C 14, Av 1/3 (☎2222 1650)
SA	SACSA, C 5, Av 18 (☎2551 0232)
TB	Transportes Blanco, C 14, Av 9/11 (☎2257 4121)
TBO	Transportes Bocatoreños, C 14/16, Av 5 (☎2227 9523)
TC	Transportes Caribeños (☎2221 2596)
Tica	Ticabus, C 9, Av 4/6 (☎2221 8954)
TIL	Transportes Tilarán, C 14, Av 9/11 (☎2222 3854)
TJ	Transportes Jacó (☎2223 1109)
TRA	TRALAPA, C 20, Av 1/3 (☎2221 7202)
TRC	Tracopa-Alfaro, Av 18, C 2/4 (☎2221 4214)
TRN	Transnica (☎2223 4242)
TRS	Transtusa, Av 6, C 13 (☎2556 4233)
TU	Tuasa, C 12, Av 2 (☎2442 9523)
Tuan	Tuan (☎2441 3781)

between C 9 and C 15. You can pick up buses for Paseo Colón and Parque la Sabana (labelled "Sabana-Cementerio") at the bus shelters on Av 2, C 5/7. In an enlightened move, city authorities are hoping to move the bus stops out of the centre proper in order to cut traffic and pollution (most city buses belch depressingly black streams of diesel fumes from their exhaust pipes).

All buses have their routes clearly marked on their windshields, and usually the fare too. This is payable either to the driver or his helper when you board and is usually 200 colones, though the faster, more comfortable *busetas de lujo* (luxury buses) to the suburbs cost upwards of 300 colones; push the bell to signal a desired stop.

BY TAXI

Taxis are cheap and plentiful, even at odd hours of the night and early morning. Licensed vehicles are red with a yellow triangle on the side, and have "SJP" ("San José Público") licence plates. A ride anywhere within the city costs $2–3, and around double that to get out to the suburbs. The starter fare – about $1 – is shown on the red digital read-out, and you should always make sure that the meter is on before you start (ask the driver to

"toca la maría, por favor"). Some drivers may claim that the meter doesn't work – if this is the case, it's best either to agree on a fare before you start out or to find another taxi whose meter is working. Many drivers are honest – don't immediately assume everyone's trying to cheat you. After midnight, taxis from the El Pueblo centre charge forty percent extra. These are institutionalized higher fares, and you shouldn't attempt to negotiate. Tipping is not expected. There are several taxi companies in the city; two of the more reliable are Coopeirazu ☎2254 0533 and Coopetaxi ☎2235 9966.

BY CAR

There's no need to rent a car specifically for getting around San José – indeed, most Josefinos advise foreigners against driving in the city, at least until they're familiar with the aggressive local style of driving. In addition, most of the city's streets are one-way, though sometimes unmarked as such. Cars left on the street anywhere near the city centre are almost certain to be broken into or stolen. If you do rent a car (see p.49), always use the secure *parqueos* (guarded car parks) that dot the city: most close at 8 or 8.30pm, although there are some 24-hour parks, including one on the corner of Av 0, C 19. Some hotels have on-site parking. If you have to leave your car on the street, most areas have a man whose job is to guard the cars – look for the fellow with the truncheon and expect to pay around 300 colones. If driving in the centre of the city, keep your windows rolled up and your doors locked so no one can reach in.

BY BICYCLE
It's unfortunately not a good idea to cycle in San José. Diesel fumes, potholes and aggressive drivers don't make for pleasant cycling, although riding in the suburbs or Parque la Sabana is easier and much less hazardous to your health.

INFORMATION

Tourist office San José's Instituto Costarricense de Turismo (ICT) office is beneath the eastern edge of the Plaza de la Cultura, C 5, Av 0/2 (Mon–Fri 9am–5pm; ☎ 2299 5800, ⓦ visitcostarica.com). It gives out free maps, hotel brochures and – most crucially – comprehensive booklets detailing the national bus schedule. Staff here also hand out the free monthly *Culture Calendar*, which details concerts and festivals throughout the country.

ACCOMMODATION

San José has plenty of quality **hotel** rooms, with reasonable prices in all categories. If you are coming in high season (Dec–May), and especially over busy periods like Christmas and Easter, be prepared to reserve (and, in some cases, even pay) in advance. Room rates vary dramatically between high and low seasons and you can expect to get substantial discounts at less busy times. Unless otherwise indicated, breakfast is usually not included.

Many of San José's rock-bottom hotels have cold-water showers only. Unless you're particularly hardy, you'll want some form of heated water, as San José can get chilly, especially from December to March. At the budget end of the spectrum, so-called "hot" water is actually often no more than a tepid trickle, produced by one of the eccentric electric contraptions you'll find fitted over showers (see p.56) throughout the country.

Though staying in one of the budget hotels in the **city centre** is convenient, the downside is noise and, in many places, a lack of atmosphere. Not too far from downtown, in quieter areas such as Paseo Colón, Los Yoses and **barrios Amón and Otoya**, are more expensive hotels, many of them in old colonial homes. To the west of the city is **Escazú**, the stomping ground of American expats. The vast majority of B&Bs here are owned by foreign nationals, with higher prices than elsewhere in town. East of the city and closer to the centre is studenty **San Pedro**, with better connections to downtown and a more cosmopolitan atmosphere.

CENTRAL SAN JOSÉ
Le Bergerac C 35, Av 0 ☎ 2234 7850, ⓦ bergerachotel .com; map pp.92–93. For luxury without the price tag, this elegant and relaxing top-end hotel is an excellent choice. The 26 spacious rooms all have cable TV and phone, internet access and some also have their own private gardens. The agreeable restaurant, next to an interior courtyard, serves local and North American fare, and there's a travel service that arranges tours.

Continental breakfast included. $98

Casa León Av 6 bis, C 13/15 ☎ 2221 1651, ⓦ hotel casaleon.com; map p.97. This Swiss-run small guesthouse has dorms and basic private rooms with a spotlessly clean shared bathroom and kitchen. There is laundry service and luggage storage. The house is a little hard to find; look for it next to the train tracks and tell your taxi driver it's in a *calle sin salida*. 3-bed dorm $15, double $20

USEFUL BUS ROUTES
The following is a rundown of the main inner-city routes, all of which stop along Avenida Central or Avenida 2 in the centre of town. If in doubt, ask "*¿dónde está la parada para…?*" ("Where is the stop for…?").

Sabana–Cementerio buses travel west along Paseo Colón to Parque la Sabana, and are ideal for going to any of the shops, theatres and restaurants clustered around Paseo Colón, the Museo de Arte Costarricense or Parque la Sabana.

Sabana–Estadio services run basically the same route, with a tour around Parque la Sabana. Good for the neighbourhoods of Sabana norte and Sabana sur.

Sabanilla–Bethania buses run east through Los Yoses and beyond to the quiet residential suburb of Sabanilla.

San Pedro (also **La U**) or **Tres Ríos** buses will also take you east through Los Yoses and on to the Universidad de Costa Rica and the hip neighbourhood of San Pedro. Other buses serving San Pedro are: Vargas Araya, Santa Marta, Granadilla, Curridabat and Cedros.

1

Costa Rica Backpackers Av 6, C 21/23 ☎ 2221 6191, ⓦ costaricabackpackers.com; map p.97. A great place to meet fellow travellers, this is one of the city's best budget guesthouses with both single- and mixed-sex dorms plus a few private double rooms. Facilities include a fully equipped kitchen, a garden with swimming pool, luggage storage, laundry service, a TV room, wi-fi, free parking and airport shuttle service ($24). Dorm $12, double $36

Europa C 0, Av 3/5 ☎ 2222 1222, ⓦ hoteleuropacr.com; map p.97. Mid-range casino-hotel, San José's oldest, located in the heart of downtown, with a restaurant, bar, indoor pool, lots of bright communal areas and a 24-hour Egyptian-themed gaming room. Outer rooms tend to get street noise but more light while inner rooms are quieter but less airy. There's a helpful tour desk with good contacts throughout the country and breakfast is a small additional cost. $56

Gran Hotel Costa Rica Av 0/2, C 3 ☎ 2221 4000, ⓦ granhotelcostarica.com; map p.97. This elegant hotel has over a hundred spotlessly clean but rather unimaginatively furnished rooms – some are enormous, some are small, but all have TV, phone, wi-fi and 24-hour room service. The central location – overlooking the Plaza de la Cultura, and with a popular terrace café below – can be noisy, especially when the buskers are in full swing. Breakfast is included. $145

★**Hostel Casa del Parque** C 19, Av 1/3 ☎ 2233 3437, ⓦ hostelcasadelparque.com; map p.97. With a serene location adjacent to Parque Nacional, this small, family-run hostel is easily one of the city's better budget choices. The dorm has ten full-size beds and there are six private rooms – all are clean and comfortable. The friendly staff can book tours, the common areas are smarter than you'd expect for this category and there's free wi-fi throughout. Dorm $13, double $35

Hotel 1492 Jade y Oro Av 1, C 31/33 ☎ 2256 5913 or ☎ 2225 3752, ⓦ hotel1492.com; map p.97. On a quiet stretch of Av 1, this comfortable hotel has ten well-appointed rooms, some surrounding an elegant antique- and art-filled atrium and others adjoining a small tropical garden. All have private shower and TV. The friendly staff can arrange tours. $68

Hotel Presidente Av 0, C 7 ☎ 2010 0000, ⓦ hotel-presidente.com; map p.97. Plush, immaculate hotel smack in the middle of downtown. Over 90 rooms, each tastefully designed and well-appointed with cable TV, a/c, safe and wi-fi and some have a jacuzzi. There's a spa on-site, as well as a gym, sports lounge and the excellent *News Café* (see p.110). Double $119, spa suite $150

Pensión de la Cuesta Av 1, C 11/15 ☎ 2256 7946, ⓦ pensiondelacuesta.com; map p.97. Tranquil rooms – though some are a bit gloomy – in a pink and blue colonial-style wooden house, with a plant-filled lounge area, gold masks on walls and decorated bedsteads. All rooms have shared bathrooms, plus there's a communal kitchen, laundry service and luggage storage. Staff can arrange tours and car rental. Good deals for weekly stays. Dorm $11, double $37

BARRIOS AMÓN, OTOYA AND ARANJUEZ

La Amistad Av 11, C 13 ☎ 2258 0021, ⓦ hotelamistad.com; map p.97. Set in a large mansion in historic Barrio Otoya, this American-owned hotel has over 30 rooms all with cable TV, wi-fi, in-room safe, private bathroom and queen-sized beds; there are also six penthouse suites with a/c. Serious breakfast buffet included. Double $78, penthouse suite $134

★**Aranjuez** C 19, Av 11/13 ☎ 2256 1825, ⓦ hotelaranjuez.com; map p.97. In quiet Barrio Aranjuez yet still close to the centre, the rooms of this hotel are in converted houses that have been joined with communal sitting areas. Relax in the pretty garden around the back, where organic waste from the hotel is used as fertilizer. They serve a good buffet breakfast (included in the rate) and can arrange package tours to *Laguna Lodge* in Tortuguero (see p.180). The 36 rooms either have shared or private bathroom; all have wi-fi and cable TV. Be sure to reserve ahead. Private bath $50, shared bath $35

Casa Hilda Av 11, C 3 & 3 bis, house no. 353 ☎ 2221 0037, ⓔ c1hilda@racsa.co.cr; map p.97. Small and affordable hotel in an old-style wooden house on a quiet street near the city centre. The five rooms are basic but comfortable and have private bathroom with hot water and fans. Rooms with outside-facing windows are best; the others are a bit dark. There's also a patio garden and communal sitting areas with cable TV. Good single rates. $33

Hotel Don Carlos C 9, Av 7 / 9 ☎ 2221 6707, ⓦ doncarloshotel.com; map p.97. An elegant landmark hotel, once the home of two presidential families, now filled with replicas of pre-Columbian art and a lovely kitsch breakfast terrace/cocktail lounge with a fountain and a pretty tiled mural of the city hand-painted by Costa Rican artist Mario Aroyabe. All rooms have cable TV and safe (some also have private patios) and there's wi-fi and a small pool, plus an excellent gift shop (see p.115) and travel agency. $96

Hotel Dunn Inn Av 11, C 5 ☎ 2222 3232, ⓦ hotel-dunninn.com; map p.97. Attractive and inviting hotel with 28 sunny rooms of various sizes. All are adorned with custom furnishings and have wi-fi and cable TV. There's a pretty restaurant and bar on-site and the staff are a wealth of local information. $72

Kap's Place C 19, Av 11/13 ☎ 2221 1169, ⓦ kapsplace.com; map p.97. One of the city's best mid-range choices, this family-friendly hotel is run by the unstintingly helpful

Karla Arias who is a endless source of information on all things San José. There are several different types of accommodation available; all have private bathrooms, wi-fi, cable TV and all are colourfully decorated. There's a fully equipped communal kitchen. Tours arranged on request. **$50**

Rincón de San José Av 9, C 13/15 ☎2221 9702, ⓦhotelrincondesanjose.com; map p.97. This well-run Dutch-owned hotel in pretty Barrio Amón has 27 clean rooms over four interconnected properties. All offer cable TV, wooden floors and piping-hot showers, plus the use of a computer and safe. Most rooms have wi-fi access. The excellent *Café Mundo* (see p.111) is just across the street. Breakfast included. **$73**

★**Santo Tomás** Av 7, C 3/5 ☎2255 0448, ⓦhotel santotomas.com; map p.97. In quiet, elegant Barrio Amón, near downtown, this American-owned hotel is one of San José's best boutique options. It occupies an old mansion awash in soft lighting and decorated with burnished wood and Persian rugs. 20 rooms vary widely in size, character and price, though all have cable TV, telephone and wi-fi. There's a small swimming pool, hot tub, an excellent open-air restaurant and a travel service. **$60**

WEST OF THE CENTRE

Auténtico C 40, Av 5 bis ☎2222 5266, ⓦautenticohotel .com; map pp.92–93. Recently overhauled boutique hotel in a quiet area just two blocks east of Parque la Sabana. Smallish rooms are comfortably furnished, and all have TV, radio and telephone; the renovated rooms are a bit larger. Facilities include a tiny pool, jacuzzi, gym and sauna and there's a good bar and restaurant. Good low-season discounts. **$113**

Cacts C 28/30, Av 3 bis ☎2221 6546 or 2928, ⓦhotel cacts.com; map pp.92–93. *Cacts* has 25 rooms, all with ceiling fans and TV; all but four have private bathrooms. There's a tropical garden, swimming pool, jacuzzi and a sunny roof terrace, where you can enjoy the complimentary breakfast buffet of fresh fruits and baked goods. The friendly owners run a travel agency and can book tours and reservations. **$72**

★**Grano de Oro** C 30, Av 2/4 ☎2255 3322 ⓦhotel granodeoro.com; map pp.92–93. Elegant converted mansion in a quiet area west of the centre, a block from Paseo Colón. The 40 well-appointed rooms and suites are furnished in faux-Victorian style, with wrought-iron beds and polished wooden floors. Several of the deluxe rooms have lovely private gardens and all rooms have cable TV, minibar, phone and wi-fi. A rooftop sun terrace equipped with twin hot tubs provides expansive views over the centre. The staff are exceedingly helpful, and an excellent breakfast is served in its gourmet restaurant (see p.112). **$170**

La Rosa del Paseo Paseo Colón, C 28/30 ☎2257 3225, ⓦrosadelpaseo.com; map pp.92–93. Converted, late nineteenth-century house on busy Paseo Colón. Rooms have nice touches – sparkling bathrooms, wooden floors and Victorian fittings – and all come with private bathroom and cable TV. Breakfast included. **$96**

ESCAZÚ

Casa de las Tías San Rafael de Escazú, southeast of the El Cruce Shopping Centre; take the east turn by the Restaurante Cerutti ☎2289 5517, ⓦcasade lastias.com; map p.103. Set on a garden estate, this quiet, friendly B&B has just five rooms, each individually decorated with private bathroom, hot water and wi-fi. **$113**

Costa Verde Inn On an unmarked side street off Av 2 ☎2228 4080, ⓦcostaverdeinn.com; map p.103. Exceedingly friendly and airy B&B with large, nicely appointed rooms, small pool, jacuzzi, garden and open dining area. The helpful staff can arrange numerous tours. **$79**

Posada El Quijote 800m south of the El Cruce Shopping Centre, just east of Chango's restaurant ☎2289 8401, ⓦquijote.cr; map p.103. Renovated, tranquil inn with eight spacious rooms adorned in Spanish colonial style and comfortably furnished with bathroom, hot water and cable TV. Breakfast is served in the lovely garden. **$85**

SAN PEDRO

Hotel Milvia 250m northeast of the Muñoz y Nanne supermarket ☎2225 4543, ⓦnovanet.co.cr/milvia; map p.101. Mid-range hotel in a lovely old Caribbean-style plantation house beautifully decorated with antiques and modern Costa Rican art. Located in a residential area, with a soothing fountain, garden, sun terrace and mountain views, plus TV lounge and games room. Lunch and dinner available on request. **$78**

THE CITY OUTSKIRTS

Kalexma La Uruca, 5km northwest of downtown, ☎2290 2624, ⓦkalexma.com; map pp.92–93. Twelve comfortable rooms with shared or private bathroom are offered at this simple B&B. There's a communal kitchen, two TV lounges, laundry service and internet access. Staff can arrange transport, tours, and Spanish classes. Breakfast included. Private bath **$28**, shared bath **$40**

Real Inter-Continental 2km north of Escazú, near the Multiplaza shopping centre ☎2208 2100, ⓦihg.com; map p.103. If you like big fancy hotels, this is one of the best, with a large pool (and pool bar), sauna, gym, two restaurants, internet access and a free shuttle bus into town. Rooms have piping-hot water, cable TV and phone. Breakfast is included in the price. **$203**

EATING

For a Central American city of its size, San José has a surprising variety of restaurants – Italian, Thai and even macrobiotic – along with simple places, such as **sodas**, that offer dishes beginning and ending with rice (rice-and-shrimp, rice-and-chicken, rice-and-meat). For excellent **típico** cooking – try the upmarket restaurants specializing in grills or barbecues (churrascos). **Fast food outlets** in San José are proliferating so rapidly that at times it can look like a veritable jungle of Pizza Huts, Taco Bells and KFCs, not to mention McDonald's. **Cafés** also abound; some, like Giacomín, have old-world European aspirations; others, such as Spoon, are resolutely Costa Rican. Working Josefinos eat their **main meal** between noon and 2pm, and at this time sodas especially get very busy. Many of the more upmarket restaurants close at 3pm and open again in the evening.

CAFÉS AND BAKERIES

Most cafés serve exclusively export Costa Rican coffee (see box, p.59), which has a mild, soft flavour. As is the case with shops and restaurants, some of the best cafés are in the shopping malls outside San José. Bakeries (pastelería, repostería) on every corner sell cakes, breads and pastries, most of them heavy with white refined flour. Worthwhile bakery chains include Musmanni, Spoon, Schmidt and Giacomín.

★ **Café Parisienne** Gran Hotel Costa Rica, Av 2, C 3/5; map p.97. The closest thing in San José to a European street café, complete with wrought-iron chairs and trussed-up waiters. Laze away the afternoon over coffee and cake while taking in the tunes and antics of buskers and performers on Plaza de la Cultura. It's one of the few cafés that serves continental breakfast. Open 24hr.

Café Ruiseñor 250m west of the San Pedro Mall, Los Yoses ☎ 2225 2562; map p.101. This upmarket café (with a pleasant outdoor terrace) serves sandwiches and pastries. The old-fashioned, European-style atmosphere and service are a treat, but you pay for it – sandwiches are around $7. Mon–Fri 7am–10pm, Sat 10am–7pm.

Giacomín Main branch in Escazú; map p.103. Also in Los Yoses and further afield. Comfortable café for chocolate and cake lovers, with lots of seasonal cakes such as stollen and panettone (slices from $3). Mon–Sat 8.30am–noon, 2–6.30pm.

News Café Av 0, C 7/9 in the Hotel Presidente (see p.108) ☎ 2222 3022; map p.97. Refuel over a cup (or two) of Costa Rica's potent coffee at this midtown café. Find a comfortable perch on the balcony and people-watch to your heart's content. Inside, the walls are adorned with pictures that tell the story of Costa Rica's coffee-growing industry. Daily 6am–11pm.

Q Café Av 0, C 2 ☎ 2221 0707; map p.97. Sleek, upmarket café on Avenida Central that's a great spot to idle away a couple of hours, especially while sipping their signature espresso accented with slivers of chocolate or one of their several other house-blend coffee drinks. They also serve hamburgers and various pastries, though prices are high. Mon–Fri 8am–9pm, Sat & Sun 10am–8pm.

Spoon Av 0, C 5/7; map p.97. Other branches throughout San José. Popular chain packed with Josefinos ordering birthday cakes. The coffee, served with mix-it-yourself hot milk, is somewhat bitter, but the choice of cookies and cakes is endless. They serve full breakfasts and lunches at a good price. Mon–Fri 8am–8pm, Sat 9am–8pm, Sun 10am–6pm.

★ **Teatro Nacional Café Ruiseñor** Av 2, C 3/5 ☎ 2221 3262; map p.97. Coffee ($2), fruit drinks, sandwiches ($5) and fantastic cakes ($3.50) served amid a Neoclassical decor of marble, crystal and dark wood. Settle in at a window table and check out the goings-on in Plaza de la Cultura. Mon–Fri 9am–5pm, Sat 9am–4pm.

Zucchero C 33, Av 5, just north of Los Yoses; map p.97. Excellent coffee and French-style pastries and cakes served up in quiet, residential Barrio Escalante. Mon–Sat 6am–10pm.

SODAS AND SNACKS

Sodas generally open early, close late and are cheap – a plato del día lunch will rarely set you back more than $5. They also have empanadas and sandwiches to take away – combine these with a stop at one of the fruit stalls on any street corner and you've got a quick, cheap lunch. The pieces of papaya and pineapple sold in neatly packaged plastic bags have been washed and peeled by the vendors and should be safe, but if in doubt, wash again. Snacks sold at the Mercado Central are as tasty as anywhere, and there's a good cluster of sodas hidden away in the Galería shopping arcade, Av 2, C 5/7.

Bologna Av 8, C 17 ☎ 2222 4950; map p.97. An Italian version of a traditional Costa Rican soda. Fill up on ciabattas and focaccias washed down with super-strong Italian coffee.

La Casona Típica Av 2, C 10 ☎ 2248 0701; map pp.92–93. An incongruous white, blue and red shack that serves up, as the name implies, comida típica at rock-bottom prices. The rice and beans and various casados are all a great deal at around $5. Daily 7am–10pm.

Chelles Av 0, C 9; map p.97. This spartan bar, with bare fluorescent lighting and a TV blaring away in the corner, is a San José institution and a great place to sit and watch your fellow customers or the street action outside. Aproned waitresses serve up cold, cheap beer, snacks and casados. 24hr.

Isabel C 19, Av 9; map p.97. Permanently filled (or so it seems) with locals shooting the breeze, downing endless cups of coffee and munching on tortillas and casados. A street kiosk just outside sells snacks to those too busy to stop. Mon–Sat 7am–10pm.

El Parque C 2, Av 4/6; map p.97. This soda caters to everyone from businessmen grabbing a cup of coffee on their way to work and retail workers popping out for a quick lunchtime snack to late-night bar hoppers looking to eat themselves sober. Try the *pinto con huevo* (rice, beans and eggs), a bargain at just $2. 24hr.

Tapia Southeast corner of Parque la Sabana ☎ 2222 6734; map pp.92–93. Huge place, open to the street with views (across the busy ring road) of Parque la Sabana. Especially handy for late-night snacks, with sandwiches and burgers ($5) for those weary of *casados*. Mon–Thurs 6am–2am, Fri & Sat 24hr, Sun 6am–midnight.

La Vasconia Av 1, C 3/5 ☎ 2223 4857; map p.97. Get off the tourist trail and dig into cheap breakfasts, ceviche and *empanadas* ($3) alongside Costa Rican workers at this casual *soda*. Adorning the walls are thousands of photos of the national football team (some dating back to 1905) and there's karaoke nightly, for better or worse. Mon–Fri 9am–1.30am, Sat 11am–2am.

Vishnu Three central branches at Av 1, C 1/3; Av 3, C1; Av 8, C 9/11; map p.97. These cheery vegetarian *sodas* are an obligatory pit stop for healthy fare in San José. Enjoy delicious, reasonably priced *platos del día* with brown rice and also generous vegetable dishes and soups. The vegetarian club sandwich with chips will set you back a mere $3.50; fruit plates with yoghurt are around $2. Mon–Fri 8am–7pm, Sat & Sun 9am–6pm.

RESTAURANTS

Many of the city's best restaurants are in the relatively wealthy and cosmopolitan neighbourhoods of San Pedro, along Paseo Colón, and in Escazú. Wherever you choose, eating out in San José can set your budget back considerably. Prices are generally steep, and the 23 percent tax on restaurant food (which includes a 10 percent "service charge") make it even pricier to eat out. In central San José, you'll find plenty of cheaper snack bars and *sodas* (see opposite), where the restaurant tax doesn't apply.

CENTRAL SAN JOSÉ

Balcón de Europa C 9, Av 0/1 ☎ 2221 4841; map p.97. The pasta and other Italian staples (most $12–16) are nothing special at this city landmark, but the atmosphere is great. Sepia photos of San José's early days line the wood-panelled walls, along with treacly snippets of "wisdom". Monster cheeses dominate the dining room, as does the strummer who serenades each table. Tues–Sun 11am–11pm.

★**Café Mundo** Av 9, C 15, Barrio Otoya ☎ 2222 6190; map p.97. One of the finest restaurants in San José, the Italian-influenced cuisine is a delight, served in a beautiful dark-wood dining room or, if the weather is nice, on a leafy terrace. The Caesar ($5) and Niçoise ($10) salads are large but a bit overpriced. If you're on a budget, go for the pizza, or just come for a cappuccino ($2). At night the bar attracts a largely gay clientele. Mon–Thurs 11am–10.30pm, Fri 11am–midnight, Sat 5pm–midnight.

Don Wang C 11, Av 6/8 ☎ 2233 6484; map p.97. If you have a craving for dim sum, this authentic Chinese restaurant, with tables set around a koi pond, should be your first and only stop. Hotpots are a speciality and there are several vegetarian and seafood dishes on offer, all at reasonable prices (most mains are around $10). Mon–Thurs 11am–3.30pm & 5.30–10pm, Fri 11am–3.30pm & 5.30–11pm, Sat 11am–11pm, Sun 11am–11pm.

★**La Esquina de Buenos Aires** C 11, Av 4 ☎ 2223 1909; map p.97. A block and a half from Plaza de la Democracia and adjacent to the Iglesia de La Soledad, this is a gem of a steakhouse and easily the best in San José. Well-executed Argentine *parrillas* feature heavily, including *lomito* (tenderloin) and *ojo de bife* (ribeye). Prices are very reasonable, with most mains around $15, and the decor evoking a bygone Buenos Aires can't be beat. Mon–Fri 11.30am–3pm & 6–10.30pm, Sat 12.30–11pm, Sun noon–10pm.

Nuestra Tierra Av 2, C 15 ☎ 2258 6500; map p.97. Hugely popular in spite of its gimmicky feel, *Nuestra Tierra* offers reliable Tico fare and a dining experience that is anything but dull. Expect dancing singers, a persistent din, hefty portions and a bill that is more than you might expect (mains as high as $26). 24hr.

El Patio del Balmoral Av 0, C 7/9 ☎ 2221 1700; map p.97. Smack in the middle of the pedestrianized portion of Av Central, this pleasant open-air restaurant has a wide range of international salads and entrees, such as fish and chips ($16) and *fettuccine Alfredo* ($14). The portions are enormous; a breakfast here could easily carry you through to dinner. Daily 6am–10pm.

★**Shakti** C 13, Av 8 ☎ 2222 4475; map p.97. The self-proclaimed "home of healthy food" offers filling *platos del día* of *sopa negra* or salad, hearty vegetarian *casado*, a *refresco* and tea or coffee, all for only $4. Tasty breakfast specials include granola, fruit juice and coffee or tea for just $2. It's popular for lunch, so go early or late for a seat. Mon–Sat 8am–7pm.

★**La Terrasse** Av 9, C 15, Barrio Otoya ☎ 2221 5742; map p.97. Just a bit north of *Café Mundo*, this handsome, intimate spot in a historic house features rich French-styled dishes, such as veal stew ($16). Reservations recommended. Mon–Fri noon–10pm, Sat 6–10pm.

Tin Jo C 11, Av 6/8 ☎ 2221 7605; map p.97. Quiet, popular and fairly formal Asian restaurant with a choice of Chinese, Indian, Indonesian, Thai, Burmese or Japanese cuisine. The lemongrass soup, bean-thread noodle salad in lime juice and coconut milk curries ($14) are particularly recommended. Dinner with wine is around $40 for two; skip the alcohol, or go for lunch, and you'll get away with half that. Mon–Thurs 11.30am–2.30pm & 6–10pm, Fri 11.30am–2.30pm & 6–11pm, Sat noon–3.30pm & 6–11pm, Sun noon–9pm.

1

CENTRO COMERCIAL EL PUEBLO

Cocina de Leña Centro Comercial El Pueblo ☎ 2222 1003; map pp.92–93. Some see this as an example of Tico food at its best, superb meals cooked in a wooden oven and served in faux-rustic surroundings. Others see it as a glorified *soda* selling overpriced staples to gullible tourists. The truth lies somewhere in between. The succulent chicken dishes are recommended and it's certainly handy if you're making a night of it in the bars and discos of El Pueblo. Dinner for two costs around $40. Mon–Thurs 11am–11pm, Fri & Sat 11am–midnight, Sun 11am–11pm.

WEST OF THE CENTRE

La Bastille Av 0, C 22 ☎ 2255 4994; map pp.92–93. Swanky restaurant-cum-art gallery with a dining room bedecked in garishly coloured modern art, including some strange Gaudí-esque chairs. Though the decor is strictly "love it or hate it", the French-Italian cuisine is some of the finest in the city – the ravioli is particularly recommended. Around $50 for two with wine. Mon–Fri noon–2pm & 6–10pm.

Fogo Brasil 100m north of the Nissan dealership, La Sabana ☎ 2248 1111; map pp.92–93. A true carnivore's delight, this Brazilian steakhouse is a popular stop-off on the way to or from Juan Santamaría. The skewered red meat is adroitly cooked and doled out until you practically have to plead for mercy. Against all odds, there's a massive salad bar, too. It's pricey, though, and dinner for two could cost upwards of $100. Daily 11.30am–11.30pm.

★**Grano de Oro** C 30, Av 2/4 ☎ 2253 3322; map pp.92–93. Upmarket restaurant with beautiful hacienda-style decor and a changing menu. Breakfast (from 6am) includes fresh fruit, eggs Benedict and banana macadamia pancakes. The salads are excellent – try the spinach, avocado and gorgonzola – while main courses feature Costa Rican takes on international staples, such as filet mignon stuffed with tropical fruits. Amazing desserts, including tiramisu and piña colada cheesecake. Book ahead and bring plenty of funds. Daily 7am–10pm.

★**Machu Picchu** C 32, Av 1 ☎ 2222 7384; map pp.92–93. Velvet llamas hang on the walls at this San José favourite, one of the top South American restaurants in town. The appetizers, including ceviche and Peruvian *bocas*, tend to be more interesting than the main dishes. Around $30 for two with beer or wine; the Pisco sour should not be missed. Mon–Sat 10am–10pm, Sun 11am–6pm.

SAN PEDRO AND LOS YOSES

Antojitos Cancún In the Centro Comercial Cocorí, 50m west of the Fuente de la Hispanidad roundabout,

Los Yoses ☎ 2225 9525; map p.101. Cheap, filling Mexican food, not wholly authentic, but good for late-night snacks and cheap all-you-can-eat buffets ($7). Draught beer and an outside terrace where you can sit and watch the 4WDs whizz round the fountain. Mariachi Fri and Sat from 10pm. Mon–Thurs & Sun 11am–midnight, Fri & Sat 11am–12.30am.

Le Chandelier 100m west and 100m south of the ICE (Instituto Costarricense de Electricidad) building in Los Yoses ☎ 2225 3980; map p.101. Exquisite French food prepared by the restaurant's Swiss owner. Try the lobster in pastry ($18) or the delicious trout with almonds ($15). A homely decor of exposed ceiling beams and a crackling fireplace. Mon–Fri 11.30am–midnight, Sat 6.30pm–midnight.

★**Mantras Veggie Café and Teahouse** 200 metres north of the Centro Cultural Costarricense Norte-americano, Barrio Escalante ☎ 2253 6715; map p.101. While *Mantras* definitely draws its share of vegetarians and vegans, it pulls in just as many meat lovers with its colourful and exceedingly tasty dishes. The menu isn't extensive, but there isn't any filler and the entrees, such as raw courgette pasta ($9), pop with flavour. Be sure to save room for the inventive raw and organic desserts. Mon–Fri 8.30am–5pm, Sat 8.30am–3pm.

Marbella In the Centro Comercial Calle Real, San Pedro ☎ 2225 3733; map p.101. Spanish cuisine, including excellent veal dishes and delicious paella ($15 for two) with real rabbit (unusual in Costa Rica). Mon–Thurs 11am–3pm & 6.30–10.30pm, Fri 11am–3pm & 6.30–11pm, Sat 11am–3pm & 6.30–11.30pm, Sun 11am–5pm.

La Mazorca 200m east and 100m north of San Pedro Church; just east of the entrance to UCR; map p.101. Inexpensive macrobiotic meals served in a simple, homely space. The tasty bread, soups, peanut-butter sandwiches and macrobiotic cakes are a welcome change from greasy *arroz con pollo*. Lunch is $5; takeaway is also available. Daily 9am–8pm.

ESCAZÚ

★**La Cascada** Behind the Centro Comercial Trejos Montalegre ☎ 2228 0906; map p.103. This difficult-to-find restaurant (there's no sign) with ho-hum decor is actually one of the best steakhouses in San José. Hugely popular, it's often full of Tico families, especially on Sunday afternoons. The hunks of beef, such as the house tenderloin ($16), are fantastic, and the filling plates all come with rice and veggies. Mon–Fri 11.30am–3pm & 6–10pm, Sat noon–10pm, Sun noon–9pm.

DRINKING AND NIGHTLIFE

San José pulsates with the country's most diverse nightlife, and is home to scores of bars, clubs and live music venues. Most young Josefinos, students and foreigners in the know stay away from downtown (where prostitution is particularly prevalent) and head instead to Los Yoses or San Pedro. Avenida Central in **Los Yoses** is a well-known "yuppie trail" of bars, packed with middle- and upper-middle-class Ticos imbibing and conversing.

San Pedro nightlife is geared more towards the university population, with a strip of studenty bars to the east of the UCR entrance. Those looking to kick back with locals should head to a *boca* bar (see box, p.114) or seek out places to hear *peñas*: slow, acoustic folk songs from the Andean region that grew out of the revolutionary movements of the 1970s and 1980s.

Many bars don't offer music during the week, but change character drastically come Friday or Saturday, when you can hear jazz, blues, up-and-coming local bands, rock 'n' roll, or South American folk music. For full details of what's on, check the *Cartelera* in the *Tiempo Libre* section of *La Nación*, which lists live music along with all sorts of other activities, from swimming classes to cultural discussions. Or for a more hip magazine, try *San José Volando* (w sanjosevolando.com).

BARS AND LIVE MUSIC

★ Bar Jazz Café In San Pedro, near the Banco Popular ☎ 2253 8933; map p.101. The best bar in San José for live jazz, with an air of intimacy and consistently good bands. The cover charge varies from $6 to $10 (sometimes including a glass of wine) and is well worth it. Doors typically open at 8pm; closed Sun.

Bar México C 16, Av 11/13, Barrio México ☎ 2221 8025; map pp.92–93. Strictly off the tourist trail, northwest of the city centre but well worth hunting out, this traditional bar serves tasty *bocas* (around $3–5) to its largely working-class clientele. Devoid of any pretension, it's a great place to mix with locals. Live Latin music on Wednesday. Mon–Fri 3pm–midnight, Sat 11am–midnight.

Bar Río Boulevard Los Yoses ☎ 2225 8371; map p.101. Wildly popular and long-running Los Yoses sports bar with a large terrace. Inside, several large TVs usually show football matches, and in the back is a large dance area. Live music on Tuesday and the occasional weekend. The starchy fast-food menu, such as quesadillas and nachos for around $8, is a good way to soak up the alcohol. Mon & Tues 3pm–midnight, Wed & Thurs 3pm–1am, Fri & Sat noon–4am, Sun 4pm–midnight.

★ Bar Shakespeare Av 2, C 28 ☎ 2258 6787; map pp.92–93. Friendly bar that draws a mix of locals with everything from ambient electronica to classic rock. Popular for a quick drink before heading to a performance at the adjacent Sala Garbo cinema or Laurence Olivier theatre. Occasionally has acoustic sets and live jazz. Tues–Sat 5pm–2am.

Caccio's Calle de la Amargura, 200m east and 25m north of San Pedro Church ☎ 2224 3261; map p.101. This insanely popular student hangout, where guys wearing baseball caps sing along loudly to outdated songs, is a great spot to meet Ticos. Knock back cheap, cold beer while munching on pizza. Daily 11am–1am.

Chelles Av 0, C 9 ☎ 2221 1369; map p.97. This simple, brightly lit, 24hr bar, with football on TV and cheap beers and *bocas* ($6–11), pulls in an eclectic crowd of weary businessmen and late-night revellers. Daily 24hr.

El Cuartel de la Boca del Monte Av 1, C 21/23 ☎ 2221 0327; map p.97. Lively, long-established bar – with great lunch, dinner and *bocas* ($6–18) – that still packs in Josefinos, particularly on Monday and Wednesday when there's live music (Latin, rock and reggae) by up-and-coming bands. Mon–Fri 11.30am–2pm & 6pm–midnight, Sat 6pm–midnight.

Raíces Av 2, C 45 ☎ 2226 9322; map p.101. Dedicated reggae bar with a booming sound system and hordes of dreadlocked Ticos packing the small dancefloor. Drinks are cheap (beers from $2), and there's occasional live music. Thurs–Sat 7pm–2.30am.

★ Las Risas C 1, Av 0/1 ☎ 2223 2803; map p.97. One of the best downtown bars, on three floors in a building that once served as the National Library. A young crowd packs the small dancefloor at the popular top-floor disco; the ground-level bar is much more laidback. Bring ID – a copy of your passport will suffice – or the bouncers won't let you in. The cover charge of $2 will usually get you two drinks or a shot. Saturday is ladies' night. Mon–Sat 4pm–5am.

CLUBS

Club Vertigo Paseo Colón, C 36/38 ☎ 2257 8424; map pp.92–93. When a big-named international DJ tours Central America, a date at *Club Vertigo* is pretty much a certainty. The lines are almost inevitably long – particularly

---

SALSA LIKE A JOSEFINO

One of the best ways to meet people and prepare yourself for San José nightlife is to take a few **salsa lessons** at one of the city's many *academias de baile*. You don't necessarily need a partner, and you can go with a friend or in a group. The tuition is serious, but the atmosphere is usually relaxed. The best classes in San José are at Bailes Latinos, in the Costa Rican Institute of Language and Latin Dance, Av 0, C 25/27 (☎ 2233 8938); at Malecón, C 17/19, Av 2 (☎ 2222 3214); and at Merecumbé, which has various branches, the most central of which is in San Pedro (☎ 2224 3531).

1

BOCA BARS

In Costa Rica, *bocas* (appetizers) are the tasty little snacks traditionally served free in bars. **Boca bars** are a largely urban tradition, and although you find them in other parts of the country, the really famous ones are all in San José. Because of mounting costs, however, and the erosion of local traditions, few places serve *bocas* gratis any more. Several bars have a *boca* menu, among them *El Cuartel de la Boca del Monte* (see p.113) near Los Yoses, but the authentic *boca* bars are concentrated in suburban working- or lower-middle-class residential neighbourhoods. They have a distinctive welcoming feel – friends and family spending the evening together – and are very busy most nights. Saturday is the hardest night to get a table; get there before 7.30pm. You'll be handed a menu of free *bocas* – one beer gets you one *boca*, so keep drinking and you can keep eating. The catch is that the beer costs about twice as much as elsewhere ($2 as opposed to $1) but even so, the little plates of food are generous enough to make this a bargain way to eat out. Typical *bocas* include deep-fried plantains with black-bean paste, small plates of rice and meat, shish kebabs, tacos or *empanadas*.

One of the most authentic and well-known *boca* bars is the working-class, long-established *Bar México* (see p.113) in Barrio México – it's a pretty rough neighbourhood, so go by taxi. Alternatively, you'll find a varied clientele – but conspicuously few foreigners – at *Los Perales* and *El Sesteo* (both Mon–Sat 7pm–midnight) in the eastern suburb of Curridabat. They're about 100m from each other on the same street but hard to find on your own; taxi drivers will know them.

on Saturday night – and the dress code is somewhat strict for San José, but they're small prices to pay for a vibe that can't be matched elsewhere in town. The action is split between two rooms, and the music you'll hear in each differs nightly, with trance and house usually amping up the joint. Daily 10pm–6am.

Ebony The Community El Pueblo ☎ 2223 2195; map pp.92–93. One of the most popular among El Pueblo's glut of discos. Several large dancefloors play salsa and US and European dance music with the odd 1980s/1990s pop hit thrown in. Wed 8pm–3am, Thurs–Sun 8pm–6am.

Infinito El Pueblo ☎ 2223 2195; map pp.92–93. Three dancefloors boom salsa, US and European dance music, as well as 1970s romantic hits spun by excellent DJs. Attracts an older, smarter crowd. Mon–Sat 6pm–6am.

Salsa 54 C 3, Av 1/3 ☎ 2233 3814; map p.97. Downtown alternative to the El Pueblo discos, this lively joint plays the favoured mix of Latin and American tunes but, as the name implies, also goes heavy on the salsa and merengue. The best place to dance in San José proper, attracting the most talented *saleros*. Thurs–Sat 8pm–4am.

Terra U C de la Amargura, one block east of San Pedro Church ☎ 2283 7728; map p.101. With three open-air levels and a heaving dancefloor, this is one of San José's weekend hotspots. Latin and Jamaican dance hits predominate. Music videos (and occasional football match highlights) play on the big-screen TVs. Mon–Sat 10am–2.30am, Sun 3pm–2.30am.

GAY AND LESBIAN NIGHTLIFE

San José is one of the best places in Central (possibly Latin) America for gay nightlife. The spots we've included are the most established, and it helps if you have a local lesbian or gay contact to help you hunt down small local clubs.

La Avispa C 1, Av 8/10 ☎ 2223 5343; map p.97. Friendly, landmark gay and lesbian disco-bar, "The Wasp" has three dancefloors and several pool tables housed in a distinct black-and-yellow building. The big nights are Sunday and Tuesday, while Thursday is karaoke. There's a varying cover charge at weekends, usually $6 or less. Thurs–Sat 8pm–6am, Sun 5pm–6am.

Café Mundo Av 9, C 15, Barrio Otoya ☎ 2222 6190; map p.97. In the restaurant (see p.111) of the same name, this low-key bar-restaurant attracts a mainly gay clientele. Mon–Thurs 11am–10.30pm, Fri 11am–midnight, Sat 5pm–midnight.

Club Oh! C 2, Av 14/16 ☎ 2221 9341; map pp.92–93. A mixed crowd – gay, lesbian and straight – come for the hot and happening scene and music, mostly house and techno with some salsa and reggae. Two large dancefloors plus a quiet bar and a café. The neighbourhood is a little sketchy, so best to take a taxi. Cover charge varies from $3 to $5, though drinks are cheap. Fri & Sat 9pm–3am.

ENTERTAINMENT

Bearing in mind the decreasing financial support from the national government, the quality of the arts in San José is very high. Josefinos especially like **theatre**, and there's a healthy range of venues for a city this size, staging a variety of inventive productions at affordable prices. If you speak even just a little Spanish it's worth checking to see what's on. For details of all performances, check the *Cartelera* section of the *Tiempo Libre* supplement in *La Nación* on Thursday.

THEATRES

The city's premier venues are the Teatro Nacional and the Teatro Melico Salazar; here you can see performances by the National Symphony Orchestra and National Lyric Opera Company (June–Aug), as well as visiting orchestras and singers, usually from Spain or other Spanish-speaking countries.

Eugene O'Neill 1.5 blocks north of the Automercado, Centro Cultural, Los Yoses ☎ 2207 7564. Works by modern playwrights in innovative independent productions in one of the larger theatres in the country.

Facultad de Bellas Artes Universidad de Costa Rica, San Pedro ☎ 2511 8931, ⊛ bellasartes.ucr.ac .cr. Generally excellent and innovative student productions with new spins on classical and contemporary works.

Laurence Olivier Av 2, C 28, in the Sala Garbo building ☎ 2222 1034. Modern theatre specializing in contemporary productions, plus occasional jazz concerts and film festivals.

Melico Salazar C Central, Av 2 ☎ 2295 6032, ⊛ teatro melico.go.cr. San José's "workhorse" theatre stages occasional performances of traditional Costa Rican song and dance, including classic and modern productions by Costa Rica's Compañía Nacional de Danza (National Dance Company); ticket costs are low.

Teatro Nacional C 5, Av 2 ☎ 2010 1111, ⊛ teatro nacional.go.cr. The city's premier theatre hosts opera, ballet and concerts, as well as drama.

CINEMAS

Going to the movies in San José is a bargain ($4–7 a ticket), and most cinemas show the latest American films, which are almost always subtitled. The few that are dubbed will have the phrase "*hablado en Español*" in the newspaper listings or on the posters. For Spanish-language art movies, head to Sala Garbo.

Alianza Francesa Av 7, C 5, Barrio Amón ☎ 2222 2283. Occasional French-language films, usually dubbed or subtitled in Spanish.

Cine Omni C 3, Av 0/1 ☎ 2221 7903. Downtown cinema showing US blockbusters.

Colón Paseo Colón, C 38/40 ☎ 2221 4517. US mall-style cinema, with mainstream Hollywood films.

Multicines San Pedro In San Pedro Mall ☎ 2280 9585. American-style multiplex with ten screens, full surround sound and popcorn on tap.

Sala Garbo Av 2, C 28 ☎ 2223 1960. Popular arthouse cinema showing independent films from around the world usually in the original language with Spanish subtitles.

Variedades C 5, Av 0/1 ☎ 2222 6104. Old but well-preserved downtown movie house with Rococo-style decor showing good foreign and occasionally Spanish-language films.

SHOPPING AND MARKETS

San José's **souvenir** and **crafts shops** are in general fairly pricey; it's best to buy from the larger shops run by government-regulated crafts co-operatives, from which more of the money filters down to the artisans. You'll see an abundance of pre-Columbian gold jewellery copies, Costa Rican liqueurs (Café Rica is the best known), coffee (the supermarkets have just about any variety you could hope to take home), T-shirts with jungle and animal scenes, weirdly realistic wooden snakes, leather rockers from the village of Sarchí (see p.131), walking sticks, simple leather bracelets, hammocks and a vast array of woodcarvings, from miniature everyday rural scenes to giant, colourfully hand-painted Sarchí ox-carts. Look out too for molas, handmade and appliquéd clothes, mostly shirts, occasionally from the Bahía Drake region of southwestern Costa Rica, but more usually made by the Kuna peoples of Panama. A good place to buy any of these handicrafts is at San José's street craftmarket in the Plaza de la Democracia (see p.96). It's worth bargaining, although the goods are already a little cheaper than in shops.

SOUVENIRS AND CRAFTS

La Casona C 0, Av 0/1; map p.97. Large two-floor marketplace with stalls selling the usual local stuff along with Guatemalan knapsacks and bedspreads. It's great for browsing, and the traders are friendly, but quality at some stalls is dismal. Mon–Sat 9.30am–6.30pm.

★**Dantica** Lincoln Plaza shopping mall, third floor, Moravia ☎ 2519 9036; map pp.92–93. Excellent gallery operated by the owners of the lodge of the same name in San Gerardo de Dota (see p.367) and featuring a range of brightly-coloured masks, jewellery and woodwork. To the northeast of downtown and a bit out of the way, but well worth seeking out. Mon–Sat 10am–9pm, Sun 10am–8pm.

Galería Namu Av 7, C 5/7 ☎ 2256 3412; map p.97. Top-notch fair trade gallery specializing in indigenous artwork, such as Wounaan baskets and Brunka masks. Mon–Sat 9am–6.30pm, Jan–April also Sun 1–5pm.

Hotel Don Carlos C 9, Av 9 ☎ 2221 6707; map p.97. A good selection of pre-Columbian artefacts and jewellery reproductions are on sale in the gift shop of this hotel.

Mercado de Artesanía Av 2 C 15 bis; map p.97. A block from Parque Nacional, this orderly market sells souvenirs and crafts, featuring Sarchí ox-carts, and jewellery. Though you can find it cheaper elsewhere in the country, the quality is usually fairly good. Daily 10am–5pm.

Mercado Central Av 0/1, C 6/8; map p.97. *The* place to buy coffee beans, but make sure they're export quality

1

– ask for Grano d'Oro ("Golden Bean"). It's a veritable warren (see p.91) and there's a lot of tacky tourist offerings, but there are some decent handmade items; it's just a real hunt to find them. Mon–Sat 8am–5pm.

★**Plaza Esmeralda** La Uruca, Pavas, about 5m northwest of city centre ☎2296 9042; map p.103. Craft co-operative run by local artisans where you can watch cigars being rolled, necklaces being set and the ubiquitous Sarchí ox-carts being painted. Mon–Sat 10am–6pm.

Sol Maya Paseo Colón, C 18/20 ☎2221 0864; map pp.92–93. Rather pricey indigenous and Guatemalan arts and crafts in La Sabana; the clothes on sale are a better deal. Mon–Fri 8am–6pm.

Tienda de la Naturaleza Av 0, 1km east of San Pedro, Curridabat ☎2253 7230; map p.101. The shop of the Fundación Neotrópica, this is a good place to buy the posters, T-shirts and other paraphernalia painted by English artist Deirdre Hyde that you see all over the country. Mon–Sat 10am–6pm.

BOOKSHOPS

7th Street Books C 7, Av 0/1 ☎2256 8251; map p.97. New and used books, including English literature, as well as a wide selection of books and maps on Costa Rica in both English and Spanish. Mon–Sat 9am–6pm, Sun 10am–6pm.

★**Librería Internacional** In the San Pedro Mall ☎2234 1096; map p.101. Other locations across the city including Av Central and the Multiplaza shopping centre, Escazú. San José's best bookshop, with a well-stocked Latin American literature section, including Costa

Rican authors, and a good selection of both fiction and nonfiction in English as well as maps and tourist guides. Mon–Sat 9am–7pm.

Librería Lehmann Av 0, C 1/3 ☎2223 1212; map p.97. A good selection of mass-market Spanish-language fiction and nonfiction, as well as maps, children's books and a small (mainly secondhand) collection of English-language books.

Librería Universal Av 0, C/1 ☎2222 2222; map p.97. Strong on Spanish fiction, books about Costa Rica (in Spanish) and country maps. Mon–Fri 8.30am–7pm, Sat 9am–6pm, Sun 9am–5pm.

Mora Books Av 1, C 3/5, in the Omni building ☎2255 4136; map p.97. A pleasant shop with a good selection of secondhand English-language books, CDs, guidebooks, magazines and comics.

SHOPPING MALLS

Lincoln Plaza C 55, Av 61/65, Moravia ☎2519 9043; map pp.92–93. San José's newest and slickest mall, with a massive food court, a huge range of national and international shops on its gleaming three floors and one of the best cinemas in the city. Mon–Sat 10am–9pm, Sun 10am–8pm.

San Pedro Mall Where Avenida Central runs into the fountain-roundabout that separates San José proper from San Pedro ☎2283 7540; map p.101. At the very end of Barrio Dent is the truly ugly but wildly popular San Pedro Mall. A ceramic-coloured multistorey building festooned with plants and simulated waterfalls, inside it's a jumble of US chain stores and fast-food outlets. Daily 9am–8.30pm.

SPORTS AND OUTDOOR ACTIVITIES

FOOTBALL

Estadio Nacional de Costa Rica The western edge of Parque la Sabana ☎2284 8700. Opened in 2011, this 35,000-seat venue hosts games by the Costa Rican national football team as well as national clubs. A somewhat controversial project – it was funded by the Chinese government and built exclusively by Chinese workers – it is nonetheless a far more inviting place to see a match than the iconic Estadio Ricardo Saprissa, which is about a 10min drive north of the centre.

PARKS AND SPORTS COMPLEXES

Multispa Cipreses A block north of the Multiplaza shopping centre, Escazú ☎2215 6495. Also in Curridabat, 700m north of the La Galera petrol station. Set in landscaped grounds, this full-service gym offers an $8/day membership that gives access to weights, machines, pools and aerobics classes. Both Mon–Fri 5am–10pm, Sat 8am–4pm, Sun 9am–3pm.

Parque de la Paz Av 46, C 11/21 ☎8345 4970. In the south of the city, this park is a good spot for running and has a velodrome and a roller hockey rink. 24hr.

Parque la Sabana Av 0, C 42/68 ☎2284 8700. The sports complex behind the Museo de Arte Costarricense on Parque la Sabana has a gym, Olympic-size pool and well-maintained running track. The park itself has tennis courts, and is as good a place as any for jogging, with changing facilities and showers. There are lots of runners about in the morning and the afternoon, though the park is best avoided at dusk and later, when muggings have been reported. 24hr.

ROCK CLIMBING

Rocódromo Av 3, C 36/38 ☎2221 6934. An impressive rock-climbing facility, open to the public, at the back of the Mundo Aventura store, with daily passes only $3. Mon–Fri 1–8.30pm, Sat 9am–3pm.

YOGA

Downtown Yoga C 15, Av 3, above Hostel Pensión de la Cuesta, Barrio Otoya ☎6050 1952. Central, friendly yoga studio with at least two mixed-style classes ($10) in English most days. Weather permitting, they host a Saturday morning class in Parque España.

Krama Yoga Center 1km north of the Multiplaza shopping centre roundabout, Escazú ☎2215 3535. It's not easy to reach without a car, but this studio delivers the most complete yoga experience in San José. Single vinyasa and hot classes, among others, are $19. Closed Sun.

DIRECTORY

Embassies and consulates Argentina, 400m south of *McDonald's* in Curridabat (☎2234 6520 or ☎2234 6270); Belize, 400m east of the Iglesia Santa Teresita, Rohrmoser (☎2253 5598); Bolivia, in Rohrmoser (☎2232 9455); Brazil, Paseo Colón, C 20/22 (☎2223 1544); Canada, C 3, Av 1 (☎2296 4149); Chile, 50m east and 225m west of the Automercado, Los Yoses (☎2224 4243); Colombia, 175m west of *Taco Bell*, in Barrio Dent (☎2283 6861); Ecuador, 100m west and 100m south of the Centro Comercial Plaza Mayor, in Rohrmoser (☎2232 1503); El Salvador, Av 10, C 33/35, Los Yoses (☎2256 4047); Guatemala, 100m north and 50m east of *Pizza Hut*, in Curridabat (☎2283 2557); Honduras, 300m east and 200m north of ITAN, in Los Yoses (☎2234 9502); México, Av 7, C 13/15 (☎2257 0633); Nicaragua, Av 0, C 25/27 (☎2222 2373 or ☎2233 8747); Panama, C 38, Av 5/7 (☎2281 2442); Peru, 100m south and 50m west of the San José Indoor Club, in Curridabat (☎2225 1786); UK, 11th floor, Edificio Centro Colón, Paseo Colón, C 38/40 (☎2258 2025); US, opposite the Centro Comercial in Pavas – take the bus to Pavas from Av 1, C 18 (☎2220 3939); Venezuela, Av 2, C 37/39, Los Yoses (☎2225 5813 or 8810). There is no consular representative for Australia or New Zealand. Few nationalities require a visa (see box, p.77) to cross into Nicaragua or Panama.

Hospitals The city's public (social security) hospital is San Juan de Dios, Paseo Colón, C 14/16 (☎2257 6282). Of the private hospitals, foreigners are most often referred to Clínica Biblica, Av 14, C 0/1 (☎2257 5252; emergency and after-hours number ☎2257 0466). CIMA San José, 500m west of the tollbooths on the Prospero Fernández Freeway (☎2208 1000), is also a good private hospital. San José has many excellent medical specialists, too – your embassy will have a list.

Immigration Costa Rican *inmigración* (Mon–Fri 8am–4pm; ☎2220 0355) is on the airport highway opposite the Hospital México; take an Alajuela bus and get off at the stop underneath the overhead walkway. Get there early, if you want visa extensions or exit visas. Larger travel agencies can take care of the paperwork for you for a fee (roughly $10–25).

Internet access Most of the hotels and guesthouses in San José offer internet access, usually for free. You'll also find plenty of internet cafés in town. Expect to pay around 300 colones/30min. Try Café Digital, Av 0, C 5/7, which also

has a snack bar, a cigar shop and a balcony overlooking Av Central; Neotopia Cyber Café, Av 1, C11, or Internet Café Costa Rica, Av 0, C 0/2.

Laundry Burbujas, 50m west and 25m south of the Mas por Menos supermarket in San Pedro, has coin-operated machines and sells soap; Lava y Seca, 100m north of Mas por Menos, next to Autos San Pedro, in San Pedro, will do your laundry for you, as well as dry-cleaning. Other places include Lava Más, C 45, Av 8/10, next to *Spoon* in Los Yoses; Lavamatic Doña Anna, C 13, Av 16; and Sixaola (one of a chain), Av 2, C 7/9.

Libraries and cultural centres Biblioteca Nacional, C 15, Av 3 (Mon–Sat 9am–5pm), and Centro Cultural Costarricense Norteamericano, 100m north of the Am-Pm supermarket in Barrio Dent (Mon–Fri 7am–7pm, Sat 9am–noon; ☎2207 7500, ⓦ cccncr.com).

Money and exchange State-owned banks in San José include the Banco de Costa Rica, Av 2, C 4/6 (Mon–Fri 9am–3pm; Visa only), and Banco Nacional, Av 0/1, C 2/4 (Mon–Fri 9am–3pm; Visa only). Private banks include Banco Mercantil, Av 3, C 0/2 (Mon–Fri 9am–3pm; Visa only); Banco Metropolitano, C 0, Av 2 (Mon–Fri 8.15am–4pm; Visa only); Banco Popular, C 1, Av 2/4 (Mon–Fri 8.30am–3.30pm, Sat 9am–1pm; Visa & MasterCard), Banco de San José, C 0, Av 3/5 (Visa & MasterCard) and BANEX, C 0, Av 1 (Mon–Fri 8am–5pm; Visa only). There's an American Express office at C Av 0/1 (Mon–Fri 8.30am–5pm; ☎2257 1792, ⓦ american express.com).

Pharmacies Farmacia Fischel, Av 3, C 2, underneath Club Unión (Mon–Sat 7am–7pm, Sun 10am–5pm; ☎2248 1692), is one of the oldest pharmacies in the city and has a good stock of both conventional and herbal remedies. There are other locations throughout the city. Other options include Clínica Biblica, Av 14, C 0/1 (open 24hr; ☎2257 5252), and Farmacia del Este, on Av Central near Mas por Menos in San Pedro (open until 8pm); there are many pharmacies in the blocks surrounding the Hospital Calderon Guardia, 100m northeast of the Biblioteca Nacional, in Barrio Otoya.

Post office The Correo Central, C 2, Av 1/3 (Mon–Fri 7am–5pm, Sat 7am–noon; ☎2258 8762), is two blocks east and one block north of the Mercado Central. They'll hold letters for up to four weeks (you'll need a passport to collect your post).

The Valle Central and the highlands

VOLCÁN POÁS

The Valle Central and the highlands

Costa Rica's Valle Central ("Central Valley") and the surrounding highlands form the cultural and geographical fulcrum of the country. Rising between 3000 and 4000m, this wide-hipped intermountain plateau – which is often referred to as the Meseta Central or "Central Tableland" – has a patchwork-quilt beauty, especially when lit up by the early morning sun, with staggered green coffee terraces set in sharp contrast to the blue-black summits of the nearby mountains. Many of these are volcanoes – the Valle Central is edged by a chain of volcanic peaks, running from Poás in the north to Turrialba in the east – and their volatile nature can sometimes give the region an air of unease.

The sight of **Poás**, **Irazú** and **Turrialba** spewing and snorting, raining a light covering of fertile volcanic ash on the surrounding farmland, is a fairly common one, though seismic activity in recent years has been a lot more significant: in January 2009, an earthquake devastated the area around Poás, and a year later Turrialba erupted for the first time in nearly 150 years, causing nearby villages to be evacuated.

Although occupying a relatively small area, the fertile Valle Central supports roughly two-thirds of Costa Rica's population, the majority of whom live in San José (covered in Chapter 1) or one of the provincial capitals of **Alajuela**, **Heredia** and **Cartago**. The tremendous pressure on land is noticeable even on short forays from San José: urban areas, suburbs and highway communities blend into each other, and in some places, every spare patch of soil sprouts coffee bushes, fruit trees or vegetables.

Away from the big cities, the countryside is blanketed by **coffee plantations** – several of which can be explored on tours (see box, p.125) – though sizeable tracts of land have been protected around the valley's fringes, most noticeably at **Parque Nacional Braulio Carrillo** and **Parque Nacional Tapantí-Macizo Cerro de la Muerte**. In addition to the volcanoes and their surrounding **national parks**, the region boasts whitewater rafting on the **Río Pacuare** near Turrialba; craft shopping at **Sarchí**, a convenient if crowded place to stock up on souvenirs; and ancient ruins at **Guayabo**, Costa Rica's most-visited archeological site.

INFORMATION AND GETTING AROUND   THE VALLE CENTRAL

Accommodation While the provincial capitals each have their own strong identity, there is little in them to entice you to linger – with the exception of Alajuela – and most people use San José as a base for forays into the Valle Central or stay at one of the lodges and inns scattered throughout the countryside.

Getting around Many Ticos commute from the Valle Central and the surrounding highlands to work in San José via an efficient bus and train network. However, some interesting areas – notably Irazú and Tapantí – remain frustratingly out of reach of public transport. In many cases the only recourse is to rent a car, though this

WHITEWATER RAFTING NEAR TURRIALBA

Highlights

❶ **Coffee tours** Learn the finer points of coffee tasting – and the whole coffee-making process – on an insightful plantation tour. **See p.125**

❷ **Villa Blanca Cloudforest Hotel and Nature Reserve** Relax by the fireplace in your luxury casita on the edge of the misty cloudforest alive with butterflies and echoing with birdsong. **See p.135**

❸ **Volcán Poás** Take in smoke-shrouded craters at the otherworldly Volcán Poás, easily accessible from Alajuela. **See p.136**

❹ **Orosí** Soak in riverside hot springs or brush up on your Spanish in this beguiling village, that is home to Costa Rica's oldest working church, and is set amid the cool, coffee-studded hills of the Valle Orosí. **See p.149**

❺ **CATIE** Hands-on tours of the excellent Jardín Botánico are just one of the draws at this unique research station. **See p.154**

❻ **Whitewater rafting** Tackle the churning whitewaters of the Reventazón and Pacuare rivers, near Turrialba. **See p.155**

HIGHLIGHTS ARE MARKED ON THE MAP ON PP.122–123

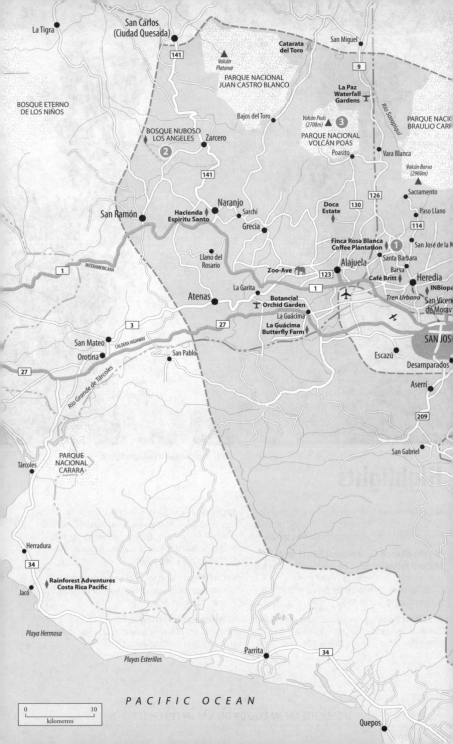

La Tigra

San Carlos
(Ciudad Quesada)

141

San Miguel

Catarata
del Toro

9

Volcán
Platanar

PARQUE NACIONAL
JUAN CASTRO BLANCO

BOSQUE ETERNO
DE LOS NIÑOS

La Paz
Waterfall
Gardens

Bajos del Toro

Volcán Poás
(2708m)   3

PARQUE NACIO
BRAULIO CARF

BOSQUE NUBOSO
LOS ANGELES

Zarcero

2

PARQUE NACIONAL
VOLCÁN POÁS

Poasito

Vara Blanca

Volcán Barva
(2960m)

141

Sacramento

Naranjo

Sarchí

130

Paso Llano

San Ramón

Hacienda
Espíritu Santo

Grecia

Doca
Estate

114

Finca Rosa Blanca
Coffee Plantation

1

San José de la M

Llano del
Rosario

Zoo-Ave

123

Alajuela

Santa Barbara

1

Café Britt

Barva

HEREDIA

INBiopa

INTERAMERICANA

San Ramón

La Garita

La Guácima

Atenas

Botancial
Orchid Garden

La Guácima
Butterfly Farm

Tren Urbano

San Vicen
de Morav

1

3

27

San Mateo

CALDERA HIGHWAY

SAN JOS

Orotina

San Pablo

Escazú

Desamparados

27

Río Grande de Tárcoles

Aserrí

209

San Gabriel

PARQUE
NACIONAL
CARARA

Tárcoles

Herradura

34

Rainforest Adventures
Costa Rica Pacific

Jacó

Playa Hermosa

Parrita

34

Playas Esterillos

PACIFIC OCEAN

0   10
kilometres

Quepos

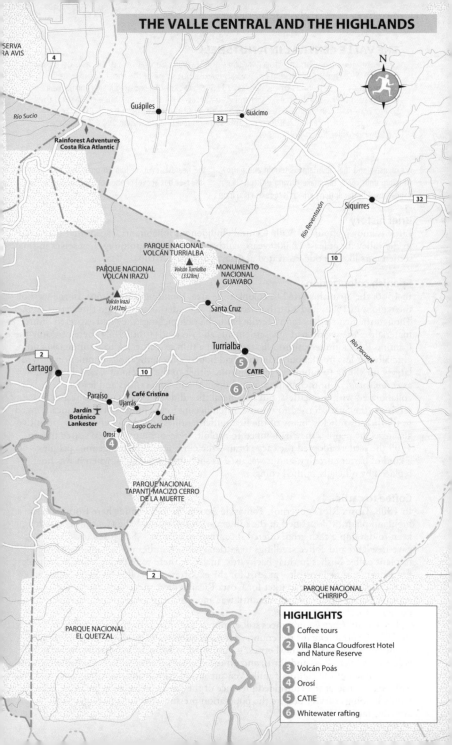

2

THE VALLE CENTRAL IN A NUTSHELL

One easy, albeit fairly whistle-stop way of visiting the Valle Central's major sights is on a **tour** from San José (see p.54). All kinds of packages exist, but some of the most popular are organized by Expediciones Tropicales (☎ 2233 5151, ⓦ expedicionestropicales.com). Their full-day tour of the northern Valle Central visits Volcán Poás, the Doka coffee estate and the La Paz Waterfall Gardens ($105), while their jaunt around the southern highlights takes in Volcán Irazú, the botanical gardens at Lankester and the beautiful Valle Orosí ($87); prices include breakfast, lunch and guide.

is expensive and the mountainous terrain and narrow, winding, unlit roads can make driving difficult, if not dangerous. A better option perhaps is to take a taxi from the nearest town, or join an organized tour from San José (see box above) or one of the provincial capitals.

Brief history

Little is known about the Valle Central's **indigenous** inhabitants, except that they lived in the valley for at least 12,000 years, cultivating corn and grouping themselves in small settlements like the one excavated at **Guayabo**, near Turrialba.

Spanish colonization

In 1560, the Spanish started to **colonize** the area, founding **Garcimuñoz**, in the west of the region, in 1561, and a further settlement at modern-day Cartago three years later. Though the first settlers found fertile land, the rich pickings they had expected didn't materialize: the region had few settlements and no roads (until 1824 there was only the Camino Real, a mule path to Nicaragua, and a thin ox-cart track to Puntarenas) and, crucially, far less **free labour** than they had hoped – the indigenous population proved largely unwilling to submit to Spanish rule, either to the system of slave labour, known as *encomienda*, or to the taxation forced upon them. Some tribes and leaders collaborated with the settlers, but in general they did what they could to resist the servitude the Spanish tried to impose, often fleeing to the jungles of Talamanca. Forced to till their own fields, many of the first settler families ended up living in as "primitive" a state as the peoples they had hoped to exploit. Indeed, money was so scarce that in 1709 the settlers adopted the cacao bean – the currency of the indigenous peoples – as a kind of barter currency, and it was used as such until the 1850s, when it was finally replaced by officially minted coins.

Coffee to cattle

In 1808, Costa Rica's governor, Tomás de Acosta, brought **coffee** here from Jamaica; a highland plant, it flourished in the mineral-rich soil of the Valle Central. Legislators, keen to develop a cash crop, offered incentives to farmers – San José's town council gave free land and coffee seedlings to settlers, while families in Cartago were ordered to plant coffee bushes in their backyards. In 1832, there were enough beans available for export, and real wealth – at least for the exporters and coffee brokers – came in 1844, when the London market for Costa Rican coffee opened up. It was the country's main source of income until war and declining prices devastated the domestic market in the 1930s.

Heredia and Cartago provinces still earn much of their money from coffee, and today the Valle Central remains the country's most economically productive region. **Fruit**, including mangoes and strawberries, is cultivated in Alajuela; **vegetables** thrive in the volcanic soil near Poás and Irazú; and on the slopes of Irazú and Barva, Holstein **cattle** provide much of the country's milk. Venture anywhere outside the urban areas and you will see evidence of the continued presence of the yeoman farmer, as small plots and family holdings survive despite the population pressure that continues to erode available farmland.

Alajuela and around

At first sight, it can be hard to distinguish **ALAJUELA** from San José, but slowly the pleasant realization dawns that you can smell bougainvillea rather than petrol fumes as you walk down the street. The city was founded in 1657 and remains a largely agricultural centre. Its most cherished historical figure is the drummer-boy-cum-martyr **Juan Santamaría**, hero of the 1856 Battle of Rivas (see box, p.269) and subject of his own **museum**, about the only formal attraction in the centre; he also has his own festival, the **Día de Juan Santamaría** (April 11, the anniversary of the great battle), when the townsfolk kick up their heels with bands, parades and fireworks.

Alajuela can be seen in half a day or so, but it makes a convenient base for visiting the surrounding sights (most of the Valle Central's main attractions lie within a 30km radius, and the city is considerably warmer than San José) or a useful place to stay if you've an early-morning flight to catch – the **airport** is just a five-minute bus ride away, compared to forty minutes or more from the capital.

Museo Juan Santamaría

Parque Central • Tues–Sat 10am–6pm • Free • ☎ 2441 4775

Most impressive of the old colonial buildings that fringe the Parque Central is the sturdy whitewashed former jail that now houses the **Museo Juan Santamaría**, entered through a pretty tiled courtyard garden lined with long wooden benches. The curiously monastic atmosphere of the rooms is almost more interesting than the small collection, which runs the gamut from mid-nineteenth-century maps of Costa Rica to crumbly portraits of figures involved in the battle of 1856. Temporary exhibitions showcase local crafts or modern art, while the auditorium hosts cultural lectures (in Spanish) on regional topics.

ANYONE FOR COFFEE?

Some of the world's finest coffee grows on the cultivated slopes of the Valle Central, and a number of the region's fincas and estates run **tours** of their plantations ($15–35; 1–2.5hr), which take you through the process from planting and picking to drying and roasting. The area is home to five of the country's eight regional **coffee varieties**: from west to east, they are the Valle Occidental, the Valle Central, Tres Ríos, Orosí and Turrialba. Differences in altitude, soil composition and production methods mean that the beans harvested from each estate have their own individual characteristics, which a good barista can help you detect. Coffee tasting, or **cupping** (*catación*), is an art in itself, and at the end of most tours you'll learn how to measure a cup's uniformity, its complexity, dry fragrance, wet aroma, brightness (actually its acidity) and body, as well as the finish it leaves on the palate.

The following fincas and estates are open year-round but are best visited during the **picking season** (Oct–Feb), when you can often get involved in harvesting the bright red beans and roasting them yourself:

Café Britt Barva; Valle Central. Slick group tours from the country's largest coffee exporter, including a musical rendition of the history of Costa Rican coffee, plus more-insightful tasting tours for aficionados. See p.139.

Café Christina Paraiso; Orosí. Owner-led tours (by appointment only) of this environmentally-sound family setup on the edge of the beautiful Valle Orosí. See p.152.

Doka Estate San Luis de Sabanilla; Valle Central. Doka, which produces Café Tres Generaciones, boasts the oldest *beneficio* (water mill) in Costa Rica and offers ox-cart rides around its estate. See p.129.

Finca Rosa Blanca Coffee Plantation & Inn Santa Bárbara; Valle Central. Highly personal insight into the workings of a small-scale organic coffee farm – and its sustainable practices – with an experienced and informative barista. See p.140.

Hacienda Espíritu Santo Naranjo; Valle Occidental. Part of a co-operative of producers in the Naranjo area, whose friendly guides lead you on a historical tour through their compact plantation. See p.132.

2

▲ Zoo-Ave (7km), La Garita (14km) & Atenas (23km)

Estadio Alejandro Morera Soto (300m) ▶

La Guácima Butterfly Farm (14km) ▲

Iglesia de Santo Cristo de la Agonía (200m) ▶

San José & Heredia ▶

▲ 1 (3km), 2 (5.5km), 3 (7km), 4 (10km), Doka Estate (10km) & Volcán Poás (38km)

ALAJUELA

AVENIDA 9

AVENIDA 7

AVENIDA 5

Police

Goodlight Books

AVENIDA 3

Banco de San José $

Museo Juan Santamaría

AVENIDA 1

Mercado Central

Banco Nacional $

Tienda Llobet

Parque Central

Catedral

Scotiabank $

Tuasa Teminal

AVENIDA CENTRAL

Estación al Pacífico

Banco de Costa Rica $

Teatro Municipal de Alajuela $

AVENIDA 2

Local Buses

Parque Juan Santamaría

Parque Los Niños

AVENIDA 4

★ **Station Wagon Alajuela Buses**

AVENIDA 6

AVENIDA 8

AVENIDA 8

AVENIDA 10

AVENIDA 10

AVENIDA 16

3

La Radial Transport

Hospital San Rafael

▼ Interamericana & Airport

CALLE 10 · CALLE 8 · CALLE 6 · CALLE 4 · CALLE 2 · CALLE CENTRAL · CALLE 1 · CALLE 3

■ ACCOMMODATION	
Charly's Place Hotel	8
Cortez Azul	6
Hostel Trotamundos	7
Hotel 1915	5
Hotel Mi Tierra	10
Maleku Hostel	11
Pura Vida Retreat & Spa	3
Siempreverde Lodge	4
Villa Pacande	1
Los Volcanes	9
Xandari Resort & Spa	2

● CAFÉS AND RESTAURANTS	
Café Delicias	3
El Chante Vegano	1
Dove Miei Cugini	4
Jalapeños Central	2
Restaurant El Balcón	5
Restaurante Chiwake	6

0 ——— 100
metres

Catedral de Alajuela

Parque Central • No fixed opening hours

Flanking the eastern end of the square, the white-domed **Catedral de Alajuela** possesses no great architectural merit – not helped by the damage it received in an earthquake in 1990 – though it does have pretty floor tiles, round stained-glass windows and a large cupola bizarrely decorated with *trompe l'oeil* balconies.

Iglesia de Santo Cristo de la Agonía

5 blocks east of the Parque Central • No fixed opening hours

The **Iglesia de Santo Cristo de la Agonía** was constructed in 1935, but looks much older, with a Baroque exterior painted in two-tone cream. Head inside for a look at the lovely wooden, gilt-edged altar, with naive Latin American motifs and gilt-painted columns edging the bright tiled floor. Realist murals, apparently painted from life, show various stages in the development of Christianity in Costa Rica, depicting monsignors and indigenous people gathering with middle-class citizens to receive the Word.

ARRIVAL AND INFORMATION

ALAJUELA AND AROUND

BY PLANE

Juan Santamaría International Airport Most international flights arrive at Juan Santamaría International Airport, less than 3km from Alajuela; most hotels and hostels include airport pick-up, or you can take a taxi (around $5–8) or catch a bus (signed, unsurprisingly, "Alajuela") into town.

BY BUS

San José, Heredia and Volcán Poás The Tuasa buses that run to and from San José (every 10min; 20min) and Heredia (every 15min; 45min) use the station on C 8, four blocks west of the Parque Central; Station Wagon Alajuela buses from San José drop you off on Av 4, 50m southwest of Parque Juan Santamaría, a few minutes' walk from the centre. The daily bus to Volcán Poás (departs 9.15am, returns 2.30pm; around 1hr 30min) uses the Tuasa terminal.

Local buses Local services leave from the Estacíon al Pacífico on Av 2, C 8/10, or from one of the surrounding jumble of bus stops.

Destinations Atenas (every 30min; 1hr); Grecia (every 30min; 1hr); La Garita (for Zoo-Ave; every 30min; 15min);

Naranjo (every 30min; 1hr 35min); Sabanilla (for Doka Estate; every 30min; 40min); Sarchí (every 30min; 1hr 15min).

Long-distance buses Buses for destinations further afield depart from La Radial station (officially known as Multicentro La Estacíon), 75m south of the Shell station, on C 4.

Destinations Jacó (3 daily; 2hr 30min); La Fortuna/ Volcán Arenal (3 daily; 3hr 25min); Liberia (frequent; 4hr); Monteverde (7am & 3pm; 4hr–4hr 30min); Puntarenas (every 30min–1hr; 2hr 10min); San Carlos (11 daily; 1hr 55min).

BY CAR

From San José If you're driving from San José, head in the direction of the airport on Hwy-1 (the Interamericana, or Autopista General Cañas); the turn-off to Alajuela is 17km northwest of San José – don't use the underpass or you'll end up at the airport.

INFORMATION

Goodlight Books The best source of information in town – alongside some of the better hotels and hostels – is

---

IN A LIGA THEIR OWN

Football (*fútbol*) is big in Costa Rica, even more so since the country's qualification for the 2014 World Cup, and Alajuela is home to one of the most historic teams in the country: **Liga Deportivo Alajuelense** (☎ 2443 1617, ⓦ lda.cr), who ply their trade at the impressive 18,000-seat Estadio Alejandro Morera Soto, northeast of the centre on C 9, Av 9. One of the original founders of the national league in 1921, LDA have won the Primera División 29 times, most recently in 2013. Their great rivals are Deportivo Saprissa from San José – derbies between the two teams, known as the **Clásico de Costa Rica**, can be fiery affairs, and are certainly worth catching if you can.

Matches are played on Sundays during the winter (late July to late Dec) and summer (mid-Jan to mid-May) championships; **tickets** start around $15 and can be bought at the stadium, or in advance on ☎ 2206 7770 or at ⓦ specialticket.net.

Goodlight Books on Av 3, C 1/3 (daily 9am–6pm; ☎ 2430 4083, ⓦ goodlight.costari.ca), where staff can usually help with public transport questions and the like.

GETTING AROUND

By car Most car rental agencies in and around the airport will bring your car to your hotel in Alajuela; otherwise, try BioTours, contacted through *Hotel 1915* (see below).

ACCOMMODATION

Due to its proximity to the airport, **accommodation** fills up quickly, and it's important to reserve ahead even in the rainy season; the finest options are actually just **outside town**, including the *Xandari Resort & Spa*, one of Costa Rica's loveliest hotels. Most places can organize **tours** of the surrounding attractions.

IN TOWN

Charly's Place Hotel Av 5, C 0/2 ☎ 2441 0115, ⓦ charlysplacehotel.com. This friendly hotel attracts a gringo crowd which often fills up the large, clean dorms and private rooms (some of the latter have attached bathrooms). Hang out in the plant-festooned courtyard or in the decent-sized TV lounge. Dorm ‾$15, double ‾$30

Cortez Azul Av 5, C 2/4 ☎ 2443 6145, ⓔ hotelcorteazul @gmail.com. Comfortable hostel run by a welcoming local artist (whose works hang on the walls), with five rooms (some with private bathrooms), dorm, communal kitchen looking onto a small garden, and laundry facilities. Dorm ‾$13, double ‾$29

Hostel Trotamundos Av 5, C 2/4 ☎ 2430 5832, ⓦ hosteltrotamundos.com. Inexpensive and cheerful, this busy hostel is no palace, but with a communal kitchen and welcoming staff, you won't be complaining. The rooms have shared hot-water bathrooms and there are also dorms. Pack your earplugs though – it can get very noisy. Free airport drop-off on your last night. Dorm ‾$12, double ‾$35

Hotel 1915 C 2, Av 5/7 ☎ 2440 7163, ⓦ 1915hotel .com. Alajuela's oldest hotel is also its finest, with elegantly subtle rooms dotted around a large living area split by an imposing staircase. All the rooms are en suite and come with fridge and cable TV; those with a/c cost an extra $10. The attached Bio Tours agency can also arrange car rental and flights. ‾$65

Hotel Mi Tierra Av 2, C 3/5 ☎ 2441 1974, ⓦ hotel mitierra.net. This perennially popular hotel with a pool is beautifully adorned with paintings by the English-speaking artist owner. The well-kept rooms (triples and quads also available), arranged around an attractive tropical garden, have TVs; ones with private bathrooms cost $5 extra. As well as breakfast, rates include airport transfer and parking. ‾$42

★Maleku Hostel Opposite Hospital San Rafael ☎ 2430 4304, ⓦ malekuhostel.com. This great-value, family-run hostel is the best deal in Alajuela, offering large, spotless rooms (all with shared bathrooms) and comfortable beds. The welcoming proprietor and friendly staff – on hand for travel advice – set the sociable scene. Free airport transfers. Dorm ‾$15, double ‾$38

★Los Volcanes Av 3, C Central/2 ☎ 2441 0525, ⓦ hotel losvolcanes.com. One of Alajuela's oldest buildings, this former Red Cross centre now houses a charming low-cost hotel. Standard rooms (shared bathrooms or en suite) are comfortable enough, but it's worth paying extra to enjoy the a/c and flat-screen TV that comes with the superior ones ($74). The friendly owner runs a travel agency and offers a free shuttle service to/from the airport. ‾$46

OUT OF TOWN

Pura Vida Retreat & Spa 7km north of Alajuela on the road to Carizal ☎ 2483 0033, ⓦ rrresorts.com. Accommodation at this lifestyle retreat for yoga enthusiasts ranges from plush pagodas ($430) with jacuzzis to luxury "tentalows" with shared bathrooms. Most people come here on a package: five-night "Mind, Body & Spirit" retreats start at $1230 for two and include yoga classes, guided tours, a massage at the on-site spa and oodles of nutritious nosh. Rates include three meals a day. ‾$220

Siempreverde Lodge 2km from the school in San Isidro, 8km north of Alajuela on the road to Poás ☎ 2449 5562, ⓦ dokaestate.com/siempreverde_eng .html. Cute, comfortable B&B on the slopes of Volcán Poás, with gardens overlooking the lush Doka Coffee estate (see opposite). A traditional breakfast is accompanied, naturally, by a cup of steaming Café Tres Generaciones. ‾$90

Villa Pacande Opposite Escuela de Hiquis, 3km north of Alajuela on the road to Poás ☎ 2431 0783, ⓦ villa pacande.com. Great budget option if you want to stay in the countryside just outside town. Rooms (triples and quads also available) in this airy villa have comfy beds and smart tiled flooring, and there's a lovely sun-trap garden. The bus into Alajuela passes every 20min, or a taxi costs around $5. ‾$40

★Xandari Resort & Spa 5.5km north of Alajuela, clearly signposted from the main road to Poás ☎ 2443 2020, ⓦ xandari.com. Designed and decorated by its creative owners (he's an architect, she's an artist), this blissfully tranquil luxury hotel sits high above the city, with splendid views over the Valle Central. The 23 spacious villas, each with their own terrace, feel very private, hidden throughout the tropical gardens, and the Star Suite ($622) is aptly named to say the least. Pamper yourself at the spa, splash about in the three swimming pools or wander through the attractive grounds, complete with waterfalls and a verdant coffee plantation. The top-notch restaurant's constantly changing menu features organic vegetables grown in their own greenhouse. One of the villas, an Ultra Plus ($418), can accommodate travellers with disabilities. **$299**

EATING, DRINKING AND ENTERTAINMENT

Alajuela has several decent **restaurants**, and you can dig into particularly tasty ceviche and *casados* at the friendly **Mercado Central** (daily 11am–10pm), around which there are also several inexpensive Chinese joints. **Nightlife**, however, is limited and most bars close around 11pm.

Café Delicias Corner Av 1 & C 1 ☎ 2440 3681, ⌨ cafe delicias.com. Breezy, open-sided café serving good coffee (from $2.25), breakfasts, sandwiches, pastries and cakes. A relaxing spot, despite the colour-clash lime green ceiling and red and yellow walls. Mon–Sat 8am–8pm.

El Chante Vegano Av 5, C 3/5 ☎ 8911 4787, ⌨ facebook .com/ElChanteVegano. If you've overindulged, this vegan (and organic) restaurant is the place to come. The menu features wholesome soups, salads, sandwiches (try the one with portobello mushroom and caramelized red onion), burgers and juices (including a kale and orange combo). Dishes from $5. Tues–Sun 11am–8pm.

Dove Miei Cugini Av 0, C 5 ☎ 2240 6893. Literally "At My Cousin's", this family-run restaurant serves up tasty American-Italian staples ($7–15), including minestrone soup, pastas and, of course, pizza (takeaway available). Wash it down with a beer at the downstairs bar. Daily 5–10pm.

★**Jalapeños Central** C 1, Av 1/3 ☎ 2430 4027. Fajitas, burritos, nachos, quesadillas – this authentic little Tex-Mex has it all. The tasty fare is prepared with love and attitude by a Colombian-American, and there are some great-value lunch and dinner specials ($7–9). Closed Sun.

Restaurant El Balcón Second floor, C 0, Av 0/2 ☎ 2441 4390. Formerly known as La Mansarda, this popular restaurant boasts an extensive menu of international and Tico classics ($8–15), best enjoyed with a glass of wine, and topped off with a cocktail at the bar (till 1am). Daily 10.30am–10pm.

Restaurante Chiwake Av 8, C 3 ☎ 2430 7887. Excellent Peruvian restaurant, authentic down to its Inka Kolas and Pisco sours. Choose from half a dozen or so ceviches, or try one of the delicious chef specials ($10–30), such as *aji de gallina*, shredded chicken in a smooth, spicy sauce, or *jalea de mariscos*, an assortment of lightly breaded seafood. Daily 11am–10pm.

Teatro Municipal de Alajuela Northwest corner of Parque Juan Santamaría ☎ 2436 2300. Fast becoming the city's cultural hub, the 300-seater Teatro Municipal de Alajuela stages regular concerts, dance shows and plays, generally by Costa Rican and Central American performers, in a historic nineteenth-century building.

DIRECTORY

Bookshop Goodlight Books, Av 3, C 1/3 (daily 9am–6pm; ☎ 2430 4083, ⌨ goodlight.costari.ca), carries an extensive selection of used English-language novels, travel guides, maps and phrasebooks; good espresso and pastries are also on offer.
Hospital San Rafael, Av 12 (☎ 2436 1000, ⌨ hospital sanrafael.sa.cr).
Internet access Goodlight Books (see above).

Money and exchange Banco Nacional, opposite the Parque Central; Banco de Costa Rica, C 2, Av 0/2; Scotiabank, Av Central, C1. All have 24hr ATMs and change travellers' cheques.
Police Public ☎ 2440 8889 or ☎ 2440 8890, emergencies ☎ 911.
Post office C 1, Av 5 (Mon–Fri 8am–5.30pm, Sat 8am–noon).

Doka Estate

10km north of Alajuela • Tours daily 9am, 10am, 11am, 1.30pm & 2.30pm, Mon–Fri also 3.30pm; 1hr • $20 • ☎ 2449 5152, ⌨ dokaestate .com • Buses run from Alajuela to the nearby town of Sabanilla, from where a taxi costs around $4 (a taxi direct from Alajuela costs about $22); the estate can also arrange transportation (phone for details)

Set amid rolling coffee fields, the **Doka Estate** is one of the most historic coffee farms in the country. The Vargas family have been growing beans here for over seventy years – their *beneficio* (water mill) is the oldest in Costa Rica – and today produce a variety of roasts for Café Tres Generaciones. Enthusiastic guides cover the entire coffee-making process (the longer Friday-morning tour also includes an ox-cart ride around the plantation), and finish with a free tasting – look out for their Peaberry Estate, a smooth medium roast containing the *caracolillo* bean, a mutation that gives the cup a sweeter flavour. You can also visit their new butterfly farm (included in the price), and grab lunch at the on-site restaurant.

Doka has its own **café** a couple of kilometres beyond the turning off the main road to Poás, where you can sample the estate's various brews in an attractive setting.

Zoo-Ave

7km west of Alajuela • Daily 8.30am–5pm • $20 • ☎ 2433 8989, ⓦ zooavecostarica.org • Frequent La Garita buses from Alajuela pass right by Zoo-Ave (every 30min–1hr; 15min)

Central America's largest aviary, **Zoo-Ave** is just about the best place in the country – besides the wild – to see Costa Rica's fabulous **birds**. The exceptionally well-run rescue and rehabilitation centre has large, clean cages and carefully tended grounds. Many of the birds fly free, fluttering around in a flurry of raucous colours: look out for the kaleidoscopic scarlet macaws and wonderful blue parrots. Other birds include chestnut-mandibled toucans and resplendent quetzals – Zoo-Ave is one of the few places in the world where you can get up close to these mythical creatures – and you'll also see **primates**, from monkeys to marmosets, plus a variety of the country's resident **reptiles**, including crocodiles and iguanas.

La Garita and Atenas

Famed for their wonderful weather, **LA GARITA**, 14km west of Alajuela, and **ATENAS**, a further 9km along Hwy-3, were deemed by *National Geographic* to have the best climate in the world; fruits, ornamental plants and flowers flourish here, as does maize, a fact most evident in the corn restaurants that line the road between the two (see opposite). The area has a few notable attractions, but sees less tourist traffic since the opening of the Caldera Highway in March 2010, which links San José to the Pacific and has superseded Hwy-3 as the quickest route to the coast. At **Llano del Rosario**, just north of La Garita on Hwy-1 (and also accessible on a back road from Atenas), you can try Costa Rica's original **bungee jump**. Rival companies organize leaps from the 70m-high bridge over the Río Colorado and if you require some Dutch courage before taking the leap, there's a large open-air bar.

Botanical Orchid Garden

Off Hwy-3, just beyond La Garita • Tues–Sun 8.30am–5pm, last entry 4.30pm • $12, children $6 • ☎ 2487 8095, ⓦ orchidgardencr.com • Regular buses from Alajuela to Atenas (every 30min; 1hr) can drop you off on Hwy-3, from where it's an 800m walk up to the gardens

A welcome recipient of the area's clement climate, the **Botanical Orchid Garden** is home to some 150 orchid species, half of them native. Walking trails (accessible to wheelchairs and buggies) lead through extensive gardens awash with colour (the blooms are at their peak from Jan–March); keep an eye out for the *Guaria morada*, a delicate purple orchid that is Costa Rica's national flower.

ACCOMMODATION   LA GARITA AND ATENAS

B&B Vista Atenas Sabana Larga, 3km west of Atenas ☎ 2446 4272, ⓦ vistaatenas.com. Up a steep hill in Sabana Larga, this relaxing B&B enjoys lovely views across the Valle Central, particularly from the pool terrace. The welcoming Belgian owner fosters a homely ambience – many of the guests in the *cabinas* and *casitas* ($400–500/week) are long-term, repeat visitors – and is gradually making her property eco-friendly, having installed a solar-powered hot-water system and now adding a freshwater well to the replanted grounds. $65

Orchid Tree Rio Grande, 4km southeast of Atenas ☎ 2477 2314, ⓦ orchidtreecostarica.com. The airy *Orchid Tree* has four tastefully furnished, spacious en suites, with a distinct Balinese influence – for example, the open-sided living areas – and an inviting swimming pool (with a wet bar), set in lush tropical gardens. $80

Vista del Valle Plantation Inn 2km from Llano del Rosario ☎ 2451 1165, ⓦ vistadelvalle.com. The luxury bungalows of the *Vista del Valle Plantation Inn* are poised on the edge of a canyon above the gushing Río Grande.

Accommodation ranges from thatched-roofed suites ($198) with canopy beds and outdoor showers to large villas ($209) with huge stone bathrooms you could get lost in; three cheaper rooms are also available in the main lodge ($113). The property has its own 90m-high waterfall, and there's also horseriding, hiking, pampering services and a swimming pool and jacuzzi to occupy your time. The smart restaurant has an emphasis on organic, locally sourced produce. $113

EATING AND DRINKING

Fiesta del Maíz 3km west of La Garita ☏ 2487 5757. The most popular of the area's corn restaurants, this buzzing fast-food-style *cantina* on the road to Atenas draws swarms of Ticos for its tasty fare (from $5), nearly all of it made from the eponymous grain. Mon, Wed & Thurs 10am–8pm, Fri–Sun 7am–9pm.

ACTIVITIES

Costa Rica Bungee ☏ 2494 5102 or ☏ 8355 7207, ⊛ bungeecostarica.com. Bungee jumps from the Puente Viejo over Río Colorado ($75; free pick-up) are on offer, as well as canyoning adventures down the 60m-high waterfall at Las Cataratas de Los Chorros, a picturesque spot 5km south of Grecia ($75).
Tropical Bungee ☏ 2248 2212, ⊛ bungee.co.cr. Organizes bungee jumps from the same bridge over Río Colorado ($75; free pick-up from San José at 8am & 1pm), as well as rappelling ($75) and rock climbing ($95).

Sarchí and around

Touted as Costa Rica's centre for arts and crafts, **SARCHÍ**, 30km northwest of Alajuela, is famous for producing the brightly painted ox-carts (*carretas*) that have become the country's national symbol. Its setting is pretty enough, between precipitous verdant hills, but don't expect to see picturesque scenes of craftsmen sitting in small historic shops, sculpting marble or carving wood – Sarchí is an overly commercialized, touristy village, and most of the factories are rather soulless showrooms. In a few, however, you

---

THE CARRETA DE SARCHÍ

The **Carreta de Sarchí** or Sarchí ox-cart was first produced by enterprising local families for the immigrant settlers who arrived at the beginning of the twentieth century to run the coffee plantations. The original designs featured simple geometric shapes, though the ox-carts sold today are kaleidoscopically painted, square creations built to be hauled by a single ox or team of two oxen. Moorish in origin, the designs can be traced back to immigrants from the Spanish provinces of Andalucía and Granada. Full-scale carts ($1000-plus) are rarely sold, but many smaller-scale coffee-table-sized replicas are made for tourists ($250–500), while dinky desktop versions can be picked up for around $5.

FÁBRICAS DE CARRETAS

Cooperativa de Artesanas y Mueblerías de Sarchí Sarchí Norte, on the right-hand side of the main road just after the petrol station (look for the large spinning ox-cart wheel out front) ☏ 2454 4050, ⊛ coopears.com. While their prices are generally lower than the rest, they haven't skimped on quality: this is as good a place as any to browse for ox-carts, made by water-wheel-powered machines. They also stock traditional wooden handicrafts and furniture. Mon–Fri 8am–6pm, Sat & Sun 9am–6pm.
Fábrica de Carretas Joaquín Chaverri Sarchí Sur, on the left-hand side of the main road as you enter the village ☏ 2454 4411, ⊛ facebook.com /FabricaDeCarretasJoaquinChaverri. Wander around the painting workshop and see dozens of ox-carts in progress at Sarchí's largest ox-cart factory, which has been in business since 1903. They'll arrange shipping and transport for souvenirs, and accept credit cards. Daily 8am–5pm.
Taller Eloy Alfaro Sarchí Norte, 125m up Calle 1 de Eva, one block east of the football field ☏ 2454 4131, ⊛ fabricadecarretaseloyalfaro.com. Alfaro and his sons have been crafting *carretas* since 1923, and you can watch the younger generation still using age-old methods in their rickety workshop, the last of its kind in Sarchí. Mon–Sat 5.30am–9pm, Sun 6am–9pm.

2

can watch carts and furniture being painted and assembled, and at the very least, the ox-carts and rocking chairs are less expensive here than elsewhere in the country.

Straggling along the road for several kilometres, the village is split by the Río Trojas into **Sarchí Sur**, essentially a collection of roadside workshops (*fábricas*) and furniture stores (*mueblerías*), and **Sarchí Norte**, a residential area further up the hill. Besides the shops and factories, the town's only site of interest is Sarchí Norte's pretty pink-and-white **church**; inside, its tiles are delicate pastel shades of pink and green. The **giant ox-cart** in the little park fronting the church is a record-breaking 14m long and weighs in at two tonnes; it was built in 2006 by Taller Eloy Alfaro, the only workshop in the country still making ox-carts the traditional way (see box, p.131).

Grecia church

12km southwest of Sarchí • Buses run every 30min to Grecia from Alajuela and San José (La Coca-Cola); both take around an hour

The small town of **GRECIA** is noticeable for its remarkable *fin-de-siècle* **church**. After their first church burned down, the prudent residents decided to take no chances and built the second out of pounded sheets of metal, imported from Belgium. The white-trimmed rust-coloured result is surprisingly beautiful, with an altar that's a testament to Latin American Baroque froth, made entirely from intricate marble and rising up into the eaves of the church like a wedding cake.

The World of Snakes

Just east of Grecia on the old Alajuela road • Daily 8am–5pm, last entry 4pm • $11, children $6 • ☎ 2494 3700, ⊛ theworldofsnakes.com • Buses from Alajuela and San José (La Coca-Cola) to Grecia (every 30min; around 1hr) run past the entrance

The World of Snakes is a small collection of fifty species of snake from around the world housed in large glass boxes. The entrance fee includes a highly informative guided tour (in English or Spanish; 1hr), during which you learn all kinds of strange snake information, such as the fact that they are completely deaf, and that they frequently die of stress.

Hacienda Espíritu Santo

5km northwest of Sarchí, just outside the town of Naranjo • Tours 9am, 11am, 1pm & 3pm; 1hr 30min • $25 • ☎ 2450 3838, ⊛ espiritusantocoffeetour.com • Local buses run from Sarchí to Naranjo (every 30min; 20min); Espíritu Santo is a signposted 800m walk west from the Banco Nacional, opposite the Parque Central in the middle of town

The red berries lining the fields at **Hacienda Espíritu Santo**, a co-op coffee plantation, end up in the bags of Café Bandola that you'll see in all the stores around here. Thanks to the local climate, the beans are of the Valle Occidental variety – something that is explored in greater depth on one of the hacienda's tours, which also cover the nursery, mill and roasting room, as well as a walk around the plantation itself. Tours end with that all-important tasting.

ARRIVAL AND DEPARTURE
SARCHÍ AND AROUND

By bus Buses from Alajuela leave for Sarchí every 30min (1hr 15min); buses back can be hailed on the main road from Sarchí Norte to Sarchí Sur. From San José, a daily express service (Mon–Fri 12.15pm, 5.30pm & 5.55pm, Sat noon; 1hr 30min) runs from La Coca-Cola; buses return via Alajuela. Alternatively, you can take the bus to Naranjo from La Coca-Cola (every 30min), and switch there for a local service to Sarchí.

ACCOMMODATION

Hotel Daniel Zamora C 2 ☎ 2454 4596. The best of Sarchí's few hotels is *Hotel Daniel Zamora*, opposite the eastern end of the football field, with simple but clean rooms. If it's full, the owner runs another lodge (with a pool) on the outskirts of town. **$30**

THE CARRETA DE SARCHÍ (P.131) >

DIRECTORY

Money and exchange Banco Nacional, on the main road opposite the football field, changes dollars and travellers' cheques, as does a smaller branch in the Plaza de la Artesanía.

Post office The post office is 50m east of the football field (Mon–Fri 8am–5pm).

Parque Nacional Juan Castro Blanco and around

Just north of the village of Bajos del Toro • Daily 8am–4pm (there's theoretically a $10 entry fee, but there's rarely anyone to collect it)

Harbouring the headwaters for five rivers, the 143-square-kilometre **PARQUE NACIONAL JUAN CASTRO BLANCO** is one of Costa Rica's least-explored national parks, partly due to its isolated location but mostly because of its seemingly permanent status as a national-park-in-waiting – scant marked trails and minimal tourist infrastructure in the surrounding villages has made it something of an off-the-beaten-path destination for **hikers** and **wildlife** enthusiasts. Created in 1992 to protect the Platanar and Porvenir volcanoes from logging, more than half the park consists of lush primary forest. Rare species of bird, such as resplendent quetzal and black guan, can be spotted here, while armadillo, tapir, red brocket deer and white-faced capuchin monkeys also roam the park. If you need a guide, most of the hotels and restaurants in Bajos del Toro – which is not much more than a cluster of corrugated houses – can hook you up with a knowledgeable local.

Catarata del Toro

6km beyond Bajos del Toro • Mon–Sat 8am–5pm • $10, children $6 • ☎ 2761 0681, ⓦ catarata-del-toro.com

Beyond Bajos del Toro the road climbs for another 6km before coming to the **Catarata del Toro**, a private reserve with a hugely impressive waterfall that plunges 100m into the caldera of an extinct volcano. Trails lead through primary forest to the base of the falls (500 steps back up) or around the crater rim; the more adventurous can rappel right alongside the thundering cascade ($60).

ARRIVAL AND TOURS

PARQUE NACIONAL JUAN CASTRO BLANCO

By car If you want to visit independently, you'll need your own car – the smoother road from Sarchí is the easiest approach, the rough roads from San Carlos or Zarcero the more spectacular, providing tremendous views as you zigzag down into Bajos del Toro, 7km from the park entrance.

Tours The best way to visit the park is on a tour with Mapache Tours (☎ 2479 8333, ⓦ mapachetours.com), who run full-day trips from La Fortuna ($80).

ACCOMMODATION

Bajos del Toro Hotel y Villas 300m south of the church ☎ 2761 0284. A compact roadside hotel (although "road" is a bit of an exaggeration), *Bajos del Toro* has spotless en-suite rooms with TVs and balconies that overlook the bubbling Río Gaurion. $50

★**Bosque de Paz** 1.5km west of Bajos del Toro, on the road to Zarcero ☎ 2234 6676, ⓦ bosquedepaz .com. Top birdwatching lodge, set in its own cloudforest reserve that features 22km of walking trails and is home to over 330 species of bird, including quetzal and three-wattled bellbird. Attractively rustic rooms, with wrought-iron beds, look out onto the surrounding forest. $123

★**El Silencio Lodge & Spa** Just south of Bajos del Toro, on the road to Sarchí ☎ 2761 0301, ⓦ elsilenciolodge.com. Nestled at the foot of a thick wall of cloudforest, the ultra-stylish rooms (two wheelchair-accessible) at this tranquil eco-retreat have bamboo-shrouded outdoor jacuzzis and wooden terraces that enjoy glorious jungle views. There are a bevy of treatments available at the therapeutically sited spa, and various guided hikes head off into the lodge's private reserve. Rates include three meals a day at the excellent restaurant. Profits help fund a local social programme. Two-night minimum stay (rates here are per night). $294

San Ramón

At the far western edge of the Valle Central, the colonial town and agricultural centre of **SAN RAMÓN** sits amid verdant rolling hills surrounded by coffee plantations and sugar cane fields. As a crossroads town between San José and La Fortuna, Liberia and the Pacific coast, it receives plenty of tourist traffic, and its leafy Parque Central, home to the imposing Gothic-style **Iglesia de San Ramón** and a couple of museums, makes a decent destination while waiting for onward connections.

Centro Cultural e Histórico José Figueres Ferrer

Opposite the northern side of the church • Tues & Wed 9am–7pm, Thurs–Sat 9am–8pm • Free • ☎ 2447 2178, ⓦ centrojosefigueres.org

Known as the "City of Poets and Presidents", San Ramón has given birth to no fewer than five of Costa Rica's former leaders, most notably the visionary and social reformer **José "Don Pepe" Figueres Ferrer**, who famously abolished the military in 1948. His childhood home has been converted into the **Centro Cultural e Histórico José Figueres Ferrer**, a museum dedicated to his life and politics, which also hosts rolling art and photographic exhibitions.

ARRIVAL AND INFORMATION   SAN RAMÓN

By bus Buses arrive at and depart from C 16, Av 1/3, 150m west of the Mercado Central.

Destinations Alajuela (hourly; 45min), San José (hourly; 1hr) and San Carlos via Zarcero (8 daily; 1hr).

ACCOMMODATION AND EATING

Aromas Café 150m southwest of the Parque Central ☎ 2447 1414. Clean, airy café with a garden courtyard out back; fill up on chicken *empanadas* and the like or indulge in some coconut flan or lemon pie (around $2–4). Sat–Wed 8am–8pm, Thurs 8am–8.15pm, Fri 8.30am–8.15pm.

La Posada Hotel Four blocks north of the church ☎ 2445 7359, ⓦ posadahotel.net. By far the nicest accommodation option in San Ramón, *La Posada Hotel* has rooms with wide-screen TV, super-clean bathrooms and regal decorative flourishes such as ornate wooden bedheads. Breakfast costs extra. **$60**

Reserva Bosque Nuboso Los Ángeles

Around 20km northwest of San Ramón • Daily 8am–4pm • $20, paid at the office, some 500m from the reserve itself • Guides cost around $30–40 and are available from the reserve office • ☎ 2461 0643

The **RESERVA BOSQUE NUBOSO LOS ÁNGELES** is a less crowded alternative to the larger and far more famous cloudforest at Monteverde. Climbing from 700m to nearly 1400m, Los Ángeles' twenty square kilometres contain a number of habitats and microclimates, including dark, impenetrable cloudforest, often shrouded in light misty cloud and resounding with the calls of monkeys.

Both of the easy dirt-track **trails** – Sendero Anastacio Alfaro (2km; 50min) and the longer Sendero Alberto Brenes (4km; 2hr 30min) – give a great introduction to the reserve's flora and fauna, and you'll stand a good chance of spotting coatis and racoons. Additional **activities** include **horseriding** ($20/hr) and a **zip-line canopy tour** ($50).

ARRIVAL   RESERVA BOSQUE NUBOSO LOS ÁNGELES

By car To reach the reserve from San Ramón, take a right fork opposite the hospital towards La Fortuna and follow the road until you reach the hamlet of Los Ángeles Norte, from where

Villa Blanca (see below) and the reserve are well signed (note that the last 9km is down a bumpy potholed track).
By taxi A taxi from San Ramón costs around $20–25.

ACCOMMODATION

★**Villa Blanca Cloudforest Hotel and Nature Reserve** ☎ 2461 0300, ⓦ villablanca-costarica.com. The

traditional en-suite *casitas* at *Villa Blanca* come complete with wood-burning stoves and are set in their own adjoining private reserve, El Silencio de Los Ángeles. The hotel was the first in Costa Rica to host an INBio Research Station, here to investigate the reserve's staggering variety of moths (some 3000 species). You'll spot a fair few of them on the short trail that runs around the forest fringes, while the hotel runs various guided tours deeper into the reserve ($26/2hr). There's also an on-site spa, and a fine-dining restaurant, though its prices cater to a captive audience. **$232**

Zarcero

ZARCERO, 52km northwest of Alajuela on Hwy-141, sits at more than 1700m, almost at the highest point of this stretch of the Cordillera Central in an astounding landscape where precipitous inclines plunge into deep gorges, and contented Holstein cattle munch grass in the valleys. A pleasant mountain town, Zarcero's focal point is its Parque Central, dotted with a motley collection of fabulous, Doctor Seuss-like **topiary sculptures**: an elephant, a helicopter, a dinosaur, along with Gaudí-esque archways of scented hedges, all the work of Costa Rican landscape gardener Evangelisto Blanco.

Zarcero is also known for its organic produce as well as a fresh, white, relatively bland **cheese**, called *palmito* (heart-of-palm, which is what it looks like); you can buy it from any of the shops near the bus stop on the south side of the main square.

ARRIVAL AND DEPARTURE
ZARCERO

By bus Buses leave from C 12, Av 7/9 in San José every 45min and from La Coca-Cola at 9.15am, 12.20pm, 4.20pm and 5.20pm (both 1hr 30min), arriving in Zarcero on the northern side of the main square; they depart from the southwest corner.

Destinations San Carlos (every 30min–1hr; 1hr); San José (every 45min or so); San Ramón (every 2hr; 1hr).

ACCOMMODATION

Hotel Don Beto Northern corner of the Parque Central ☎ 2463 3137, ✇ hoteldonbeto.com. The small, friendly *Hotel Don Beto* has a selection of neat and tidy rooms with TVs and shared bathrooms, as well as a few larger en suites ($45) that can sleep up to three people. **$25**

Parque Nacional Volcán Poás

38km north of Alajuela • Daily 8am–3.30pm • $10, $2 parking • ☎ 2482 2165

PARQUE NACIONAL VOLCÁN POÁS is home to one of the world's most accessible active volcanoes, with a history of eruptions dating back eleven million years. Poás' last gigantic blowout was on January 25, 1910, when it dumped 640,000 tonnes of ash on the surrounding area, and from time to time you may find the volcano off-limits due to sulphurous gas emissions and other seismic activities – it was closed for a while following the **Cinchona Earthquake** in January 2009 (see box, p.138), but has since reopened. It's worth checking conditions with the park before setting off, and regardless you'll still need to get to the volcano before the clouds roll in, which they invariably do at around 10am.

The park

Though measuring just 65-square-kilometres, Poás packs a punch: it's a strange, otherworldly landscape, dotted with smoking fumaroles (steam vents) and tough ferns and trees valiantly surviving regular scaldings with sulphurous gases – the battle-scarred *sombrilla de pobre*, or poor man's umbrella, looks the most woebegone. The volcano itself has blasted out three craters in its lifetime, and due to the more-or-less constant activity, the appearance of the **main crater** changes regularly – it's currently 1500m wide and filled with milky turquoise water from which sulphurous gases waft and bubble (with a pH value of 0.8, this is reputably the most acidic lake on earth).

> ### WATCHING WILDLIFE AT VOLCÁN POÁS
>
> **Birds** ply this temperate forest, from the colourful but shy quetzal to the robin and several species of hummingbird, including the endemic **Poás volcano hummingbird**, distinguished by its iridescent rose-red throat. Although a number of large **mammals** live in the confines of the park, including wildcats such as the margay, you're unlikely to spot them around the crater; one animal you will come across, however, is the small, green-yellow **Poás squirrel**, unique to the region.

Although it's an impressive sight, you only need about fifteen minutes' viewing and picture-snapping; otherwise, you can take one of the short trails that lead off the main route to the crater.

The trails

From the visitor centre, a few very well-maintained, short and unchallenging **trails** lead through a rare type of cloudforest called **dwarf** or **stunted cloudforest**, a combination of pine-needle-like ferns, miniature bonsai-type trees and bromeliad-encrusted ancient arboreal cover, all of which have been kept clipped by the cold weather (temperatures can drop to below freezing), continual cloud cover, and acid rain from the mouth of the volcano.

The **Crater Overlook Trail**, which winds around the main crater along a paved road, is only 750m long and is accessible to wheelchairs and pushchairs. A side trail (830m; 20–30min; last access 2.30pm) heads through the forest to the pretty, emerald **Lago Botos** that fills an extinct crater and is a lovely spot to picnic. Named for the pagoda-like tree commonly seen along its way, the **Escalonia Trail** (1km; 30min) starts at the picnic area (follow the signs), taking you through ground cover less stunted than that at the crater.

ARRIVAL AND INFORMATION   PARQUE NACIONAL VOLCÁN POÁS

By bus A Tuasa bus leaves daily from Av 2, C12/14 in San José at 8.30am, travelling via their terminal in Alajuela (9.15am) and returning from the volcano at 2.30pm.

By car and taxi If you want to reach Poás before the tour buses and, more importantly, dense cloud cover arrive, you'll need to either drive or take a taxi.

Tours Most visitors visit Poás on a pre-arranged tour (see box, p.124) from San José or Alajuela. From San José a tour costs around $50, including return transport and guide.

Visitor centre The park's visitor centre (daily 8.30am–3.15pm) shows film of the volcano – handy if the real thing is covered by cloud – and has a couple of displays explaining the science behind it; there's also a simple snack shop, but you're probably better off packing a picnic or grabbing lunch at one of the nearby restaurants (see p.138).

ACCOMMODATION

No camping is allowed in the park, but if you want to get a really early start to beat the clouds, you'll find plenty of places to stay in the vicinity, including a couple of comfortable **mountain lodges** on working dairy farms (though you'll need a car to get to them) and other, simpler and cheaper *cabinas* lining the road leading up to the volcano and reached on the bus to Poás.

Lagunillas Lodge Signposted 2km south of the park, and down a very steep 1km rutted dirt track, accessible by 4WD only ☎ 8389 5842, ⓦ lagunillaslodge.com. Tico-family-owned, this high-altitude rustic lodge offers rooms and *cabinas* with hot water. The views are simply breathtaking and you can even catch your dinner from the on-site trout pond. For added kicks, take a guided hike or horse trot through the surrounding forest. Double $30, *cabinas* $50

Poás Lodge 6km south of the park on the road from Alajuela ☎ 2482 1091, ⓦ poaslodge.com. Friendly owners run this pleasant little spot on the road up to Poás. Its accommodation options, which include a six-bed dorm and neat and tidy private rooms, seem to hang out over the valley; the restaurant (daily 8am–8pm; mains around $8–11) enjoys the same superb views and makes a great lunchtime stop for cheeseburgers and the like. Free shuttle to the park leaves daily at 8am. Dorm $15, double $45

2

THE CINCHONA EARTHQUAKE

In the early afternoon of January 8, 2009, an **earthquake** measuring 6.2 on the Richter scale struck the area just west of Volcán Poás, leaving at least 34 people dead and making thousands homeless. The worst quake to hit Costa Rica in nearly 150 years, it destroyed the village of **Cinchona** and scythed through nearby **Vara Blanca**; **Poasito** and **Fraijanes** were also damaged, while landslides affected **Parque Nacional Volcán Poás** and buried parts of **La Paz Waterfall Gardens** (see below), stranding some 300 tourists in the process.

The area's return to normality has been slow. Aftershocks continued in the Valle Central throughout the year – more than 2000 **tremors** were registered along the Cinchona fault line in 2009 – and workers were still repairing damage to the region's roads and buildings more than a year on; the vast majority of the work is now complete. The national park and gardens have also reopened and a new community, **Nueva Cinchona** in Cariblanco, 6km from the original, has been built to house 1200 of the survivors who lost their homes in the surrounding area.

Poás Volcano Lodge 6km east of Poasito, which is 10km before the park, on the road from Alajuela; take a right towards Vara Blanca ☎ 2482 2194, ⓦ poasvolcanolodge.com. Set on a working dairy farm, this rustic lodge was severely damaged by the Cinchona Earthquake and was undergoing a stylish-looking renovation at the time of writing. The standard en-suite rooms are nice enough, but it's better to fork out for one with a view of the volcano ($195). Walking trails run through the extensive grounds, and there's a restaurant, bar, library, and basement games room with pool and ping-pong tables. The lodge is 5km from the La Paz Waterfall Gardens and offers discounted tickets to the gardens. **$145**

EATING AND DRINKING

La Casa del Café de la Luis 10km north of Alajuela, on the road to Poás ☎ 2482 1535, ⓦ dokaestate.com. Roadside outlet of the Doka Estate – and thereby serving some mighty smooth Café Tres Generaciones roasts ($2.50–4) – this lovely little café enjoys superb views of the surrounding coffee fields from its breezy balcony. Daily 7am–5pm.

★ **Chubascos** Fraijanes, 12km south of the park on the road from Alajuela ☎ 2482 2280, ⓦ restaurante chubascos.com. This extremely welcoming and relaxed restaurant, overlooking a large garden, draws crowds for its superlative local cuisine – the *gallotes*, huge tortillas heaped with various goodies (from $5–6) take some beating – and top-notch *casados*. The area around the volcano abounds with strawberry fields, and *Chubascos* makes one of the best strawberry *refrescos* in the country. Mon–Fri 10.30am–5pm,

Sat 9.30am–9pm, Sun 9.30am–5.30pm.
Colbert Restaurant About 1km past the Poás Volcano Lodge (see above), in Vara Blanca ☎ 2482 2776, ⓦ colbert.co.cr. It can come as quite a surprise to stumble upon this smart French restaurant, perched on a hill at the eastern end of Vara Blanca, just beyond the petrol station – the menu includes such Gallic delights as French onion soup, rabbit fillet in Dijon mustard, and seafood casserole à La Rochelle, the chef's former haunt. Mains $15–20. Fri–Wed noon–9pm.
Jaulares 15km north of Alajuela, on the road to Poás ☎ 2482 2155, ⓦ jaulares.com. Simple restaurant with *típico* dishes (from $4), using local produce cooked on a wood-burning stove (try the *sopa negra*), and a generous buffet. Live music Saturday. Sun–Thurs 7am–9pm, Fri & Sat 7am–midnight, Sun 7am–8pm.

La Paz Waterfall Gardens

15km east of Poás • Daily 8am–5pm • $38, children $22; jungle cat exhibit $5 extra • ☎ 2482 2720, ⓦ waterfallgardens.com

One of Costa Rica's most popular attractions, the **LA PAZ WATERFALL GARDENS** bore the brunt of the Cinchona Earthquake (see box above), with landslides washing out several of the trails and causing extensive damage to the grounds, closing the gardens for five months. The resulting renovations, however, have returned La Paz to its former glory, and enabled the owners to make a number of improvements and additions.

Self-guided tours meander through a pretty garden planted with native shrubs and flowers, taking in a butterfly observatory; orchid display; frog house; snake garden; hummingbird garden, home to 26 different species; and, the newest attraction, a **jungle cat** exhibit. The 35 felines here were brought to La Paz when the rescue centre housing them closed, and it is now home to five of Costa Rica's six cats (only the oncilla is absent); it's hoped that any future offspring will be released back into the wild.

The waterfalls

Beyond the frog house, an immaculate series of riverside trails links five **waterfalls** on the Río La Paz, starting with Tempio and winding past Magia Blanca – the highest, which crashes deafeningly 40m down into swirling whitewater – before concluding at the top of the eponymous La Paz Waterfall, Costa Rica's most photographed cascade (it can also be seen from the public highway that runs below); viewing platforms at various points along the way place you above and beneath the falls.

ARRIVAL	LA PAZ WATERFALL GARDENS

By bus Buses (10 daily) heading to Puerto Viejo de Sarapiquí (via Heredia) from San José's Terminal del Caribe on Calle Central, Av 15, pass La Paz (around 1hr from San José, 30min from Heredia).

By car If you're driving, take a right at the junction in Poasito towards Vara Blanca and, on reaching the village, take a left at the petrol station and follow the well-marked signs for about 5km.

Tours You can visit the gardens as part of an organized trip – Expediciones Tropicales (see box, p.124) includes La Paz as part of their combination tour.

ACCOMMODATION

Peace Lodge ☎ 2482 2720, ⓦ waterfallgardens.com. Luxurious but expensive option, where the handsome rooms feature handmade canopy beds, stained-glass windows, private bathrooms, hot tubs and balconies overlooking the gardens (and up to Volcán Poás). Staying in the lodge entitles you to entry to the gardens outside the official opening hours, when you can explore its lush expanses away from the otherwise constant crowds. Breakfast not included. **$412**

Heredia and around

Just 11km northeast of San José lies the lively city of **HEREDIA**, boosted by the student population of the Universidad Nacional (UNA), at the eastern end of town. Central Heredia is a little run-down, with the Parque Central flanked by tall palms and the **Basílica de la Inmaculada Concepción**, whose unexciting squat design – "seismic Baroque" – has kept it standing through several earthquakes since 1797. North of the *parque*, the old colonial tower of **El Fortín**, "The Fortress" (closed to the public), features odd gun slats that fan out and widen from the inside to the exterior, giving it a medieval look. Although there's not a great deal to see in town, Heredia is a natural jumping-off point for excursions to **Volcán Barva**, and many tourists also come for the **Café Britt tour**, hosted by the nation's largest coffee exporter, about 3km north of the town centre.

Casa de la Cultura

Av Central, east of El Fortín • Daily 8am–8pm • Free

The **Casa de la Cultura**, a colonial house with a large breezy veranda, was once the home of Alfredo Gonzáles Flores, president of Costa Rica between 1913 and 1917. Today the building displays local art, including sculpture and paintings by Heredia schoolchildren.

Café Britt

Just north of Heredia on the road to Barva • Standard tour daily 11am, plus 3pm Dec–April • $22 • 1hr 30min; Coffee and nature tour Fri–Sun 11am • $68 • 4hr including lunch • ☎ 2777 1600, ⓦ coffeetour.com • The Heredia–Barva bus runs past the turning to Café Britt every 30min, from where it's a 400m walk; otherwise, a pick-up/drop-off from Heredia/San José costs $17

A visit to **Café Britt** gives you an idea of how the modern-day coffee industry operates. The *finca* grows one of the country's best-known brands and is the most important

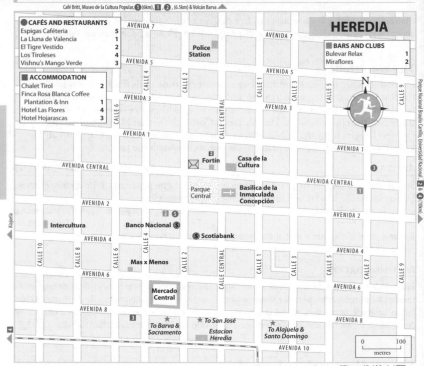

exporter of Costa Rican coffee to the world. Guides take you through the history of coffee growing in Costa Rica, demonstrating how crucial this export crop was to the development of the country, with a rather polished presentation and thorough descriptions of the processes involved in harvesting and selecting the beans. Once you've toured the plantation, roasting factory and drying patios, it's back for a coffee-cupping demo and, of course, the inevitable stop in the gift shop. There's also the extended "Coffee and Nature" tour.

Museo de Cultura Popular

2km beyond the Café Britt turn-off • Groups Mon–Fri 8am–4pm • $7, includes guided tour and one or two cooking workshops, depending on group size; reserve in advance; individuals Sun 10am–5pm • $3 • ☎ 2260 1619, Ⓦ museo.una.ac.cr

The unusual **Museo de Cultura Popular** portrays coffee-plantation life from the late nineteenth and early twentieth centuries. Set in a large house with verandas, and surrounded by coffee fields, it features rooms re-created in the style of that time. The emphasis is firmly on education, a concept that stems to the **restaurant** as well, which serves authentic food of the period, including *torta de arroz* (layered rice casserole), *pan casero* (a type of sweet bread) and *gallos picadillos* (a mixture of meat, vegetables and rice).

Finca Rosa Blanca

On the road between Barva and Santa Bárbara, 6.5km northwest of Heredia • Tours daily 9am & 1pm • $35 • 2hr 30min • Book in advance • ☎ 2269 9392, Ⓦ fincarosablanca.com

For an interesting alternative to large-group **coffee tours** head to **Finca Rosa Blanca Coffee Plantation & Inn**. The plantation at this fantastic hotel (see p.142) is one of the country's few **organic** setups – the beans are fertilized using rich soil from the hotel's vermiculture and compost made from their restaurant refuse, while the fields are planted with various trees and plants that help the crop's growth: *pejibaye* to deter insects, bananas to help retain moisture during the dry season, palms for shade. The resident expert passionately guides visitors through the science behind this, plus there's the chance (in season) to join in the harvesting or roasting, as well as some excellent tasting tips in the cupping sessions that finish off the tours.

INBioparque

Santo Domingo village, 4km southeast of Heredia • Fri 9am–3pm, last admission 2pm, Sat & Sun 9am–4pm, last admission 3pm • $25, children $15; guided tours (included in entry fee) Fri–Sun 9am, 11am & 2pm (reserve in advance) • ☎ 2507 8107, ⊕ inbioparque.com • Local buses (every 30min; 15min) run from Heredia to Santo Domingo

INBioparque is a small educational and recreational centre set up by the not-for-profit Instituto Nacional de Biodiversidad to explain, in simple terms, how biodiversity works and why it's so important. The park comprises a projection room with an audiovisual presentation on Costa Rican flora and fauna, instructive displays, and **guided trails** (30min–2hr) through four small botanical gardens filled with plants and animals from the country's main ecosystems – Valle Central forest, rainforest, tropical dry forest and wetland – as well as a small petting farm. Although mostly aimed at schoolchildren and students, the park is a good place for budding naturalists to learn to identify native species – it's home to 51 species of bird and nearly 600 native plant species. There's a café and restaurant on-site.

ARRIVAL AND INFORMATION

By bus Heredia has no bus terminal, but a variety of well-signed bus stops are scattered around town, with a heavy concentration around the Mercado Central. Buses from San José and Alajuela, arrive in Heredia on Av 8, just east of the market: they leave from here too, as do buses for Santo Domingo (for INBioparque). Local services to Barva (for Café Britt and the Museo de Cultura Popular) and Sacramento (for Volcán Barva) leave from stops along Av 8 and C 1.

HEREDIA AND AROUND

Destinations Alajuela (every 15min; 45min); Barva (for Café Britt and the Museo de Cultura Popular; every 30min; 20min); Sacramento (for Volcán Barva; 3 daily; 1hr 45min); San José (every 5min; 30min); Santo Domingo (for INBioparque; every 10min; 15min).
By train The commuter train, the Tren Urbano (⊕ tren urbano.co.cr), runs from the Estación del Atlántico in San José to Heredia's station, on Av 10, C 0 (Mon–Fri departs every 30min 5.30–8am & 3.30–7.30pm; returns every 30min 6–8.30am & 4–8pm; 20min).

ACCOMMODATION

While decent **accommodation** in downtown Heredia is pretty sparse, it's unlikely, in any case, that you'll need to stay in town; San José is within easy reach, and there are several country hotels nearby, including *Finca Rosa Blanca*, one of the finest in the country.

IN TOWN
Hotel Las Flores Av 12, C 12/14 ☎ 2261 8147, ⊕ hotel -lasflores.com. While it's a bit of a hike or a short taxi ride from the centre, it's more than worth it for *Hotel Las Flores's* simple but bright and immaculate rooms, which come with balconies and spotless hot-water bathrooms. **$30**
Hotel Hojarascas Av 8, C 4/6 ☎ 2261 3649, ⊕ hotel hojarascas.com. The comfortable whitewashed rooms, offset by bright bed linen, are spotless, but it's the incredibly friendly owners who make the difference at this popular spot in the southwest part of town. It's quite a pricey option for Heredia, but you get what you pay for – which includes a delicious buffet of fruits and fresh pastries

plus free airport pick-up/drop-off and luggage storage. Double **$90**, apartment **$160**

OUT OF TOWN
Chalet Tirol 10km north of Heredia, well signposted on the road to Los Ángeles via San Rafael ☎ 2267 6222, ⊕ hotelchaleteltirol.com. Sitting in a lovely pine forest on the edge of the Parque Nacional Braulio Carrillo, this incredibly kitsch hotel with ten alpine chalets was built to accommodate diners at *Los Tiroleses*, its renowned French restaurant (see p.142). The grounds contain a reproduction Tirol (traditional Austrian-style) village church for concerts and events. Guided walking tours also available. **$90**

★**Finca Rosa Blanca Coffee Plantation & Inn** On the road between Barva and Santa Bárbara, 6.5km northwest of Heredia ☎2269 9392, ⓦfinca rosablanca.com. One of Costa Rica's top hotels, this tranquil place is perched above the surrounding coffee fields and has wonderful views across the Valle Central. The thirteen unique suites, four of which can be opened up to form two villas ($610), have been beautifully decorated with hand-painted murals and bamboo-fibre linen; some also have jacuzzis. You can relax in the fairy-tale-esque main lounge or take a dip in the gorgeous tiled pool, set among Higueron trees and seemingly dripping over the hillside. The restaurant is one of the area's best (see below), and a sustainability tour (*Finca Rosa Blanca* has flawless eco-credentials) and a recommended tour of the organic coffee fields (see p.140) are on offer. **$345**

EATING AND DRINKING

With such a large student population, Heredia is crawling with cafés, cake shops, ice-cream joints and vegetarian **restaurants**. The low-key **nightlife** is concentrated around the four blocks immediately to the west of the Universidad Nacional, in the east of Heredia.

IN TOWN

Bulevar Relax Av 0, C 7. One of the "in" places for Heredia's student population, this lively sports bar opens to the street so you can people-watch while downing inexpensive beer-and-*boca* specials (around $5). Daily 11am–1.30am.

Espigas Cafetería Southwest corner of Parque Central ☎2237 3275. You'll find all your hangover needs at this central café: cappuccino, sweet pastries and filling breakfasts (the latter from $6) should get your day off to a good start. Daily 7am–9.30pm.

Miraflores Av 2, C 2/4 ☎2260 2727. Heredians dance salsa and merengue at this lively nightclub – the longest-running disco in the country – which attracts a slightly older, more mellow crowd than some of the other venues in town. Daily 8pm–5.30am, Fri–Sun till 6am.

Vishnu's Mango Verde C 7, Av 0/1 ☎2237 2526. One of a chain of vegetarian eateries, this rustic, plant-filled restaurant has a pretty back garden and serves good vegetarian food (around $5), including sandwiches made to order. Mon–Thurs 8am–6pm, Fri, Sat & Sun 9am–6pm.

OUT OF TOWN

★**La Lluna de Valencia** San Pedro de Barva, 6km northwest of Heredia ☎2269 6665, ⓦlallunade valencia.com. The gregarious owner Vincente works the tables at this top Spanish outpost on the road to Alajuela. Tapas are decent, but the house speciality is, naturally, paella (around $30 for two people), large and lip-smackingly tasty; there are recipes on the website, if you fancy trying to re-create the dishes when you get home. Music (acoustic guitar sets, flamenco) at the weekends. Thurs 7–10pm, Fri & Sat noon–10pm, Sun noon–5pm.

★**El Tigre Vestido** Finca Rosa Blanca Coffee Plantation & Inn, on the road between San Pedro de Barva and Santa Bárbara de Heredia, 6.5km northwest of Heredia ☎2269 9392, ⓦfincarosa blanca.com. The small, smart restaurant at this beautiful hotel specializes in "legacy dining", refined household cooking that celebrates the cuisine of Costa Rica and Central America in general. Eat out on the terrace with beautiful views across the twinkling lights of the Valle Central, where market-fresh food from local organic farmers is served in such dishes as chicken breast in a tangy coffee and tamarind sauce. Mains around $20; reserve a table in advance. Daily 6–10pm.

Los Tiroleses Chalet Tirol, 10km north of Heredia, well signposted on the road to Los Ángeles via San Rafael ☎2267 6222, ⓦhotelchaleteltirol.com. One of Costa Rica's most acclaimed French restaurants (the chef is Cordon Bleu-trained), with an elegant dining area adorned with murals and a large and eclectically stocked wine cellar. Try the excellent bean-heavy *cassoulet*. Mains around $20. Mon noon–7pm, Tues & Wed noon–9pm, Thurs noon–10pm, Fri & Sat noon–11pm, Sun noon–6pm.

DIRECTORY

Language school As befits a university town, Heredia is also home to the excellent Intercultura Spanish language school (☎2260 8480, ⓦinterculturacostarica.com), with rates from $315 a week ($483 including a homestay).

Market The Mercado Central (daily 5am–6pm) is a clean, orderly place, its aisles lined with rows of fruits and veggies, dangling sausages and plump prawns.

Money and exchange The Banco Nacional at C 2, Av 2/4 and Scotiabank at Av 4, C 0/2 both have ATMs, and change currency and travellers' cheques.

Post office The post office (Mon–Fri 8am–5.30pm, Sat 8am–noon) is on the northwest corner of the Parque Central.

Parque Nacional Braulio Carrillo

15km northeast of Heredia • Daily 8am–3.30pm • $8 • ☎ 2268 1039 (Quebrada González section), ☎ 2261 2619 (Volcán Barva section)

PARQUE NACIONAL BRAULIO CARRILLO covers nearly 500 square kilometres of virgin rainforest and dense cloudforest, but draws few visitors on account of its sheer size and lack of facilities – most tourists experience the majestic views of thick foliage only from the window of a bus on their way to the Caribbean coast. Those who do spend any length of time here tend to spend it tackling **Volcán Barva**, which dominates the southwest corner of the park and is accessed from the village of Sacramento.

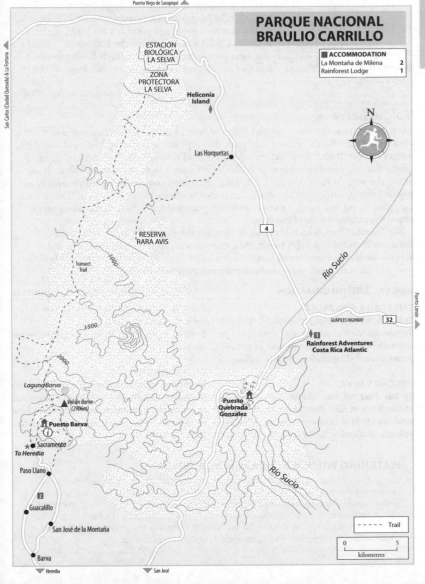

PARQUE NACIONAL
BRAULIO CARRILLO

■ ACCOMMODATION
La Montaña de Milena   **2**
Rainforest Lodge   **1**

The park is named after Costa Rica's third, and rather dictatorial, chief of state, who held office in the mid-1800s. It was established in 1978 to protect the land from the possible effects of the **Guápiles Highway**, then under construction between San José and Limón, a piece of intelligent foresight without which this whole stretch of countryside might have been turned into a solid strip of petrol stations and motels.

Quebrada González

Three short, circular **trails** lead off from the ranger station at **Quebrada González**, on the Guápiles Highway, 2km east of the Río Sucio bridge – though as they are narrow, steep and often ungroomed, they can take longer than you might think to complete. **Las Palmas** (1.6km), just behind the ranger station, is a good bet for birds; directly across the Guápiles Highway, **El Ceibo** (1km) loops down to the Río Sucio, named "Dirty River" due to its discolouration by minerals; while the high-hiking route of **Botarrama** (2.5km) is more likely to provide chance encounters with some of the park's animals.

Volcán Barva

Most people visit the more popular Barva section of the park with just one aim: climbing **Volcán Barva**, a forest-clad peak that tops out at just over 2900m. From the ranger station, **trails** (5km; 4hr round-trip) ascend through dense deciduous cover, giving fleeting panoramic views over the Valle Central and southeast to Volcán Irazú along the way. At the summit, the striking green-blue **Laguna Barva** fills the small, pristine crater, surrounded by dense forest that is often obscured in cloud. Take a compass, water and food, a sweater and rain gear, and leave early in the morning to enjoy the clearest views of the top.

The **Transect Trail**, which leads north through the park from here as far as the Estacíon Biológica La Selva (see p.234), takes around four days to complete and is strictly for highly experienced jungle hikers only; you'd need to be totally self-sufficient, and take all your food, water and camping equipment with you.

ARRIVAL AND INFORMATION

PARQUE NACIONAL BRAULIO CARRILLO

QUEBRADA GONZÁLEZ
By bus Hourly buses from San José's Terminal de Caribe pass the Quebrada González ranger station (about 45min) en route to Limón and Puerto Viejo de Sarapiquí; for the return journey, it's a case of flagging one down on the highway.

back to Heredia leave at 7.30am, 1pm (12.30pm on Sun) and (most conveniently) 5pm.
By car You'll need a 4WD if driving to Volcán Barva, even in the dry season.

INFORMATION
Security Note that, unfortunately, security is a growing problem in the park; if driving, never leave anything in your car, and always use a guide for longer hikes – though these are only available to hire at Quebrada González (around $15–20 for 3–4hr).

VOLCÁN BARVA
By bus Buses run from Heredia (Mon–Sat 6.25am, 11.45am & 3.55pm, Sun 6.30am, 11am & 4pm; 1hr 45min) to the tiny hamlet of Sacramento, from where it's a 3km walk up a steep track to the Barva ranger station; buses

---

WATCHING WILDLIFE IN BRAULIO CARRILLO

Due to its enormous size and varied altitude, Braulio Carrillo has one of the highest levels of biodiversity in Costa Rica, with over 530 species of **bird**, including the rare quetzal (mostly seen at higher elevations), toucans, trogons and eagles, and some 135 species of **mammal**, such as collared peccary, paca, jaguar and ocelot. The park, particularly the Barva area, is one of the few places in the country where the bushmaster, Central America's largest **venomous snake**, makes its home, along with the equally poisonous fer-de-lance.

ACCOMMODATION

La Montaña de Milena 5km south of Volcán Barva ☎ 2266 0015, ⓦ lasardillascostarica.com. The closest lodgings to the park, with eleven log cabins dotted among the trees, each with private bathroom, TV and open fireplace. Rates include use of spa at weekends. Note that there's no restaurant. $85

Rainforest Adventures Costa Rica Atlantic

Just beyond the northeastern boundary of Parque Nacional Braulio Carrillo, 1.5km from the Guápiles Highway • Daily 7am–4pm • Tram $60, children $30, various multi-activity packages available; canopy tour $50, no children under 12; birdwatching and trekking tours from $128, including tram ride; butterfly and frog garden $10 • ☎ 2257 5961, ⓦ rainforesttram.com

The brainchild of American naturalist Donald Perry, the Rainforest Aerial Tram has now been rebranded by some marketing whizz as the **Rainforest Adventures Costa Rica Atlantic**. Funded by private investors, and the product of many years' research, the tram was, when it opened in the mid-1990s, the first of its kind in the world: there's now another one in Costa Rica near Jacó on the Pacific coast (see p.344). In his book, *Life Above the Jungle Floor* (see p.435), Perry tells how he risked life and limb to get the project started. Committed to protecting the rainforest canopy and the jungle floor, he refused to allow the construction firm erecting the tram's high-wire towers to use tractors; they were unable to secure a powerful enough helicopter in Costa Rica, but Nicaragua's Sandinistas came to the rescue, loaning one of their MI-17 combat helicopters (minus the guns) to help erect the poles.

The tram

The tram's premise is beautifully simple: twenty overhead cable cars, each holding five passengers and one guide, run slowly (and largely silently) along the 2.6km aerial track, skirting the tops of the forest and passing between trees, providing eye-level encounters along the way. The ride (45min each way) affords a rare glimpse of birds, animals and plants, including the epiphytes, orchids, insects and mosses that live in the upper reaches of the forest – wear a hat and insect repellent, and bring binoculars, camera and rain gear. For those staying in the lodge (see below), **torchlit night rides** (until 9pm) examine the canopy's nocturnal inhabitants.

Other activities

To view the treetops at a faster pace, you can sign up for the new **canopy tour**, which sends you whizzing through the forest along seven zip lines. More conventionally, you can also explore the park via a network of ground-level trails (included in the price), or on a number of full-day **guided tours**, such as birdwatching and trekking. A **butterfly and frog garden** and a **serpentarium** complete the attractions.

ARRIVAL AND DEPARTURE   RAINFOREST ADVENTURES COSTA RICA ATLANTIC

By bus Hourly buses from San José's Terminal de Caribe to Limón and Puerto Viejo de Sarapiquí can drop you off at the turn-off for the Aerial Tram (about 1hr), from where it's a 1.5km walk; to get back to San José, you'll need to flag down buses on the highway.

Tours It's much easier to take a tour (from around $99), either directly with the tram's San José office on Av 7, C 5/7, or on one of the combination tours offered by several San José-based agencies (see p.54).

ACCOMMODATION

Rainforest Lodge Inside the park ☎ 1 866 759 8736, ⓦ rainforesttram.com. Accommodation at the tram's expensive *Rainforest Lodge* comprises ten luxury bungalows, all with views of the forest. Rates include two tram rides, a morning birdwatching tour, unlimited access to the trails in the company of an expert guide, and three meals a day. $344

Cartago and around

Founded in 1563 by Juan Vásquez de Coronado, **CARTAGO**, meaning "Carthage", was Costa Rica's capital for three hundred years before the centre of power was moved to San José in 1823. Like its ancient namesake, the city has been razed a number of times, although in this case by earthquakes instead of Romans – two, in 1823 and 1910, almost demolished the place. Most of the town's fine nineteenth-century and *fin-de-siècle* buildings were destroyed, and what has grown up in their place – the usual assortment of shops and haphazard modern buildings – is not particularly appealing. Nowadays, Cartago functions mainly as a busy market and shopping centre, with some industry around its periphery. The star attraction is its soaring **cathedral**, or *basílica*.

Las Ruinas

Parque Central

The ruined Iglesia de la Parroquía, known as **Las Ruinas**, dominates the dour, paved Parque Central, and is as popular with a cacophony of roosting great-tailed grackles as it is with the townsfolk. Originally built in 1575, the church was repeatedly destroyed by earthquakes but stubbornly rebuilt every time, until eventually the giant earthquake of 1910 vanquished it for good. Only the elegantly tumbling walls remain, enclosing pretty subtropical gardens; unfortunately, the gardens are locked more often than not, but you can peer through the iron gate at the fluffy blossoms flowering inside. If you inspect the sides and corners of the ruins carefully, you'll see where the earthquake dislodged entire rows of mortar, sending them several centimetres beyond those above and below.

Basílica de Nuestra Señora de Los Ángeles

Av 2, C 16 • No fixed opening hours • Free

Cartago's cathedral, properly named the **Basílica de Nuestra Señora de Los Ángeles**, was built in a decorative Byzantine style after the previous basilica was destroyed in an earthquake in 1926. This huge cement-grey structure with its elaborate wood-panelled

■ ACCOMMODATION		● CAFÉS AND RESTAURANTS	
Casa Aura	1	Cartago Grill	2
San Francisco Lodge	2	Soda Apolo	1

CARTAGO

EL DÍA DE LA NEGRITA

The celebration of the Virgin of Los Ángeles (**El Día de la Negrita**) on August 2 is one of the most important days in the Costa Rican religious calendar, when hundreds of pilgrims make the journey to Cartago to visit the tiny black statue of the Virgin, tucked away in a shallow subterranean antechamber beneath the crypt in the town's *basílica*. It is a tradition in this grand, vaulting church for pilgrims to shuffle down the aisle towards the altar on their knees, rosaries fretting in their hands as they whisper a steady chorus of Hail Marys: indeed, many will have travelled like this from as far away as San José to pay their respects.

2

interior is home to **La Negrita**, the representation of the Virgin of Los Ángeles, patron saint of Costa Rica. On this spot on August 2, 1635, the Virgin reportedly showed herself to a poor peasant girl in the form of a dark doll made of stone. Each time the girl took the doll away to play with it, it mulishly reappeared on the spot where she had found it; this was seen as a sign, and the church was built soon after. In the left-hand antechamber of the cathedral you'll see silver *ex votos* (devotional sculptures) of every imaginable shape and size, including horses, planes, grasshoppers (representing plagues of locusts), hearts with swords driven through them, arms, fingers and hands. This is a Latin American tradition stretching from Mexico to Brazil, whereby the faithful deposit representations of whatever they need cured, or whatever they fear, to the power of the Almighty.

Jardín Botánico Lankester

4km southeast of Cartago • Daily 8.30am–5.30pm, last entry 4.30pm • $7.50 • ☎ 2511 7939, ⓦ jbl.ucr.ac.cr • Take the Paraíso-bound bus (every 10min) from a stop on C 4, Av 1/3 in Cartago; the driver will drop you on the main road, from where it's a (signposted) walk of about 500m

Orchids are the chief attraction at the University of Costa Rica's **Jardín Botánico Lankester**, a research centre southeast of Cartago. The large, attractive gardens (the oldest in the country) are covered with a bewildering array of tropical plant and flower species, including orchids, heliconias and bromeliads – ostentatious elaborate blooms that thrust out from the undergrowth. The most rewarding time to visit is the dry season, particularly in March and April, when the garden explodes with virulent reds, purples and yellows.

ARRIVAL AND DEPARTURE
CARTAGO AND AROUND

By bus LUMACA buses run to and from Av 10, C 5 in San José (every 10min; 45min) and their terminal in Cartago on C 5, Av 6/8, and from stops along Cartago's Av 6. Buses for Turrialba leave from a stop on Av 3, C 8. Local services are frequent and reliable: buses for Paraíso and Orosí use the stops on C 6, Av 1/3; buses for Cachí leave from Av 3, C 4/6. Note that local bus stops do move around town periodically, so check with a local before setting off.

Destinations Cachí (for Ujarrás; roughly hourly; 25min);

Orosí (every 30min–1hr; 45min); Paraíso (for the Jardín Botánico Lankester; every 5min; 15min); Turrialba (Mon–Fri 5.45am, 4pm & 5.45pm, Sat 6.15am, more on Sun; 1hr 20min).

By train The commuter train, the Tren Urbano (ⓦ tren urbano.co.cr), runs between Cartago's railway station, on Av 6, C 3, and San José (Mon–Fri 12/day; 45min).

By taxi Cartago's taxi rank is at Las Ruinas; the journey to Jardín Botánico Lankester costs roughly $6–8.

ACCOMMODATION

Casa Aura C 1, Av 6/8 ☎ 2591 8161, ⓦ casaaura.com. This modest guesthouse, located a short walk from the centre of town, has just four reasonable, though pretty spartan, rooms (though they do have TV and private bathrooms), as well as a garden and a small book swap. **$60**

San Francisco Lodge C 3, Av 6/8, one block north of the Mercado Central ☎ 2551 4804. A cheaper alternative to *Casa Aura*, with perfectly respectable rooms, all with three beds, cable TV, coffee maker, fridge, microwave and private hot-water bathrooms; check-in is insalubriously at the erotic video shop next door (run by the same owners). **$30**

2

EATING AND DRINKING

You'll find a few basic restaurants in Cartago, and a handful of **sodas** where you can fill up for under $5. Your best bet may be to pop into one of the pastry shops and enjoy lunch on a bench in front of the *basílica*.

Cartago Grill In front of the courthouse, Av 1, C 8/10 ☎ 2591 5342. This popular restaurant with cheerful blue and yellow decor has a crowd-pleasing menu, excellent service and pile-on-the-pound portions. Choose between chicken, hamburgers or kebabs (around $5–6), or settle for what they do best – juicy cuts of steak grilled to perfection ($8–16). Daily 11am–9pm,

Sat till 10pm.
Soda Apolo Av 2, C 1. Its bar permanently propped up by locals, this lively street-corner *soda* is a good source of solid, *típico* food (less than $4 for a chicken and drink combo) and (if your Spanish is up to it) gossip. Daily 24hr.

DIRECTORY

Money and exchange Banco de Costa Rica and Banco Nacional have ATMs and will change travellers' cheques.

Post office The post office is 10min from the town centre at Av 2, C 15/17 (Mon–Fri 7.30am–6pm, Sat 7.30am–noon).

Parque Nacional Volcán Irazú

32km north of Cartago • Daily 8am–3.30pm • $10 • ☎ 2200 5025

The blasted lunar landscape of **PARQUE NACIONAL VOLCÁN IRAZÚ** reaches its highest point at 3432m and, on clear days, offers fantastic views all the way to the Caribbean coast. Famous for having had the gall to erupt on the day President John F. Kennedy visited Costa Rica on March 19, 1963, Irazú has been more or less calm ever since. But while its **main crater** is far less active, in terms of bubblings and rumblings, than that of Volcán Poás, its deep depression and the strange algae-green lake that fills it create an undeniably dramatic sight.

The volcano makes for a long and entirely uphill but scenic trip from Cartago, especially in the early morning before the inevitable **clouds** roll in (about 10am). While the main crater draws the crowds, it's worth noting that the shallow bowl to its right, the flat-bottomed and largely unimpressive **Diego de la Haya crater**, is the remnant of Irazú's first and largest eruption: when it blew in 1723, the eruption lasted ten months and showered San José in ash.

There's not much to do around here after viewing the main crater from the *mirador* – no official trails cut through this section of the park, though you can scramble among the grey ash dunes that have built up on **Playa Hermosa**, the buried, older crater that spreads to the left of the walkway and is dotted with what little vegetation can survive in this moon-like environment. Stay behind the barriers at all times, though, as volcanic ash crumbles easily, and you could end up falling into the ominous-looking lake.

ARRIVAL AND DEPARTURE
PARQUE NACIONAL VOLCÁN IRAZÚ

By bus Only one bus runs to the park, leaving from opposite San José's *Gran Hotel Costa Rica* on Av 2, C1/3 at 8am daily (get there early in high season to get a seat; 2hr), stopping to pick up passengers in Cartago (on the corner of Las Ruinas; 45min from San José) at 8.45am;

the bus returns to San José at 12.30pm.
Tours You can also get to Irazú on any number of half-day tours, run by travel agencies in San José (see p.54), which whisk you back and forth in a modern minibus for around $50, not including the entrance fee.

INFORMATION

Facilities At the crater parking area, you'll find toilets, an information board, and a reception centre with a gift shop and snack bar, which serves cakes and hot drinks; there are picnic tables out front, but make sure you keep an eye out for the many white-nosed coatis (members of

the racoon family) who can be a real pain as they scrounge for food.
What to wear It can get both cold and wet at the summit of Volcán Irazú, so bring a sweater and a waterproof jacket.

Valle Orosí

After workaday Cartago, the verdant **VALLE OROSÍ**, occupying a deep bowl just 9km to the southeast, is a veritable Garden of Eden. Passing through **Paraíso**, the road drops down a ski-slope hill to the pretty villages of **Orosí** and, on the other side of Lago Cachí, **Ujarrás**, each with their own lovely church; annoyingly, although they lie less than 8km apart, no bus runs between them, so without your own transport you'll have to backtrack to Paraíso. Southeast of these lies the little-visited **Parque Nacional Tapantí-Macizo Cerro de la Muerte**, a wildlife-rich park that's one of the closest places to the capital for rainforest hiking.

2

Orosí

Nestled in a little topographical bowl between thick-forested hills and coffee plantations, **OROSÍ** is one of the most picturesque villages in Costa Rica. Its bucolic charms have a way of seducing visitors, and many end up staying far longer than they intended – on a clear morning, when the lush hillsides are drenched in sunlight and with Irazú and Turrialba volcanoes hovering on the horizon, Orosí can feel like the most idyllic spot on earth.

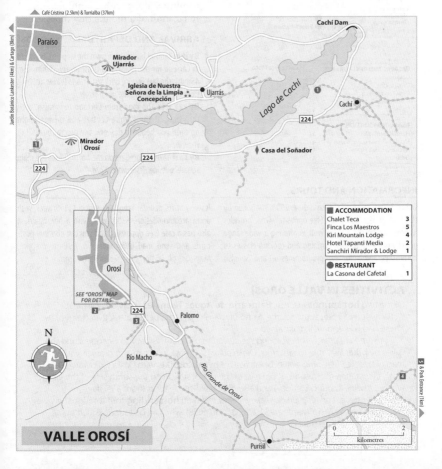

2

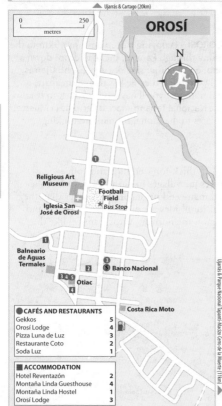

Iglesia San José de Orosí

In the centre of Orosí • Museum Tues–Sat 1–5pm, Sun 9am–5pm • $1

While Orosí's laidback atmosphere is its top attraction, the village does also boast the **Iglesia San José de Orosí** (built in 1735), Costa Rica's oldest church still in use, which sits squat against the rounded hills behind. This simple, low-slung adobe structure, single-towered and roofed with red tiles, has an interior devoid of the hubris and frothy excess of much of Latin American religious decor.

The adjacent **religious art museum** exhibits fascinating *objectos de culto* from the early 1700s such as icons, religious paintings and ecclesiastical furniture, along with a faithful re-creation of a monk's tiny room.

ARRIVAL AND DEPARTURE OROSÍ

By bus Regular buses leave from the stop on C 6, Av 1/3 in Cartago for the journey to Orosí (every 30min–1hr; 45min); the last service back to Cartago leaves at 10pm from the stops along the main street.

By car Take the road from Cartago to Paraíso, then turn right at the Parque Central and drive straight on until you begin to descend the precipitous hill to the village.

By taxi Taxis congregate on the north side of the main square, outside *Restaurante Coto*.

INFORMATION AND TOURS

Otiac 300m south of the church 🕿 2533 3640. Run by the folks at *Montaña Linda* (see opposite), Otiac provides information on the area as well as offering a wide range of activities – from rock climbing and cooking classes to homestays and volunteer programmes – and Spanish

lessons at its popular language school ($199/week with dorm accommodation, $300/week with a homestay). It also has a café (see opposite), and you can also buy postcards and send mail here. Mon–Fri 7.30am–6.30pm, May–Oct till 4.30pm, Sat & Sun 9am–5pm.

ACTIVITIES IN VALLE OROSÍ

Of the two **hot springs** in Orosí, **Balneario de Aguas Termales** (daily except Tues 7.30am–4pm; $3.60), at the southern end of the village, is the better, attractively framed by forest-clad hills and well maintained.

There are various ways of exploring the surrounding countryside: you can ride along the valley by **bike**, available to rent from *Orosí Lodge* ($10/day), who can also provide you with a map of the area featuring points of interest; or by **motorbike**, with Costa Rica Moto (🕿 2533 1442, ⓦcostarica-moto.com), 100m east of the petrol station on the south side of the village, who rent bikes (around $50/day) and also offer tailor-made tours (from $95/day).

For a gentler excursion, you can take an early morning **horseriding** tour through the valley with Francisco "Pancho" Martínez ($10/hr; 🕿 2830 6058), who can be found just left of the Balneario de Aguas Termales.

ACCOMMODATION

IN TOWN

Hotel Reventazón 25m south and 25m east of the Banco Nacional ☎ 2533 3838, ✉ hotelreventazon @gmail.com; map p.150. Small, clean rooms suited to a variety of budgets; all have lovely valley vistas, attached bathrooms and for those who like their creature comforts, one room even comes with funky wall art, a flat-screen TV, stereo, leather couch and desk. $30

Montaña Linda Guesthouse 25m south of Otiac ☎ 2533 3640, ⊛ montanalinda.com; map p.150. These relaxed digs offer large, light-filled rooms with en-suite bathrooms and glorious valley views from the wraparound balcony. The communal kitchen and lounge area – complete with book exchange library, long dining table and inviting couches – is a great space to relax, study or chat with other travellers. Breakfast not included. $30

Montaña Linda Hostel 200m south and 100m east of the football field ☎ 2533 3640, ⊛ montanalinda .com; map p.150. Benefiting from the same chilled-out vibe as its sister accommodation, this is the best budget option in Orosí: in three pretty dorm rooms, private doubles (with shared or attached bathrooms) with valley views, or camping space. All rooms have shared hot-water bathrooms, and there's a communal kitchen. Breakfast not included. Camping $4, dorm $9, double $22

★ **Orosí Lodge** 25m east of Aguas Termales ☎ 2533 3578, ⊛ orosilodge.com; map p.150. Lovely little hotel whose six wood-floored rooms (top three with volcano views, bottom three with an extra bed in each) are equipped with coffee maker, minibar and fan. The split-level chalet around the back makes an excellent base, with a spacious, high-ceilinged lounge and a private balcony looking across Orosí to Irazú and Turrialba, looming on the horizon. Breakfast (which costs extra) can be taken at the on-site café (see below). Double $66, chalet $107

OUT OF TOWN

Chalet Teca 2km outside Orosí, on the road to Tapantí ☎ 2533 3268, ⊛ chaletorosi.com; map p.149. Good-looking wood-and-stone chalet set in compact but attractive grounds on a hill south of the village. There's a well-equipped kitchen and inviting open fireplace, plus fine views from its terrace (complete with jacuzzi). Breakfast costs $8 extra. $110

Hotel Tapantí Media 1km south of the church and 100m up a steep hill ☎ 2533 9090, ✉ tapanti media@gmail.com; map p.149. Fronted by flags flapping in the breeze and offering superb views of the valley, *Tapantí Media* has clean but modest rooms, with TV, phone and private bathrooms. If you can score the top-floor far-corner room with two big bay windows, you've got it made. There's a cosy bar with comfy lounge chairs and fireplace – perfect for those chilly Orosí nights. $60

Sanchirí Mirador & Lodge 6.5km north of Orosí ☎ 2574 5454, ⊛ sanchiri.com; map p.149. The large-windowed rooms at this family-run option make the most of their stupendous position high above the valley, though there are also new comfortable wood cabins in the grounds. The restaurant (with equally jaw-dropping views) serves tasty meals made from locally grown produce, and the hotel's friendly staff can help with local information and tours. $82

EATING AND DRINKING

Gekkos 300m south of the church ☎ 2533 3640; map p.150. Breezy arts café in the Otiac information centre, serving half a dozen breakfast variations (from $3.75), lunch (salads, burgers and the like, from $5) and (local) coffee and cakes. Browse the small library while you wait or make use of the free wi-fi. Daily 6.30am–2pm.

Orosí Lodge 25m east of Aguas Termales ☎ 2533 3578, ⊛ orosilodge.com; map p.150. Top spot for all-day breakfasts, home-made pastries ($2–5) and Orosí coffee (their own brand) while chilling to a backdrop of cool tunes on the 1950s Wurlitzer jukebox or getting competitive on the table football. Good collection of local art and world music CDs for sale. Daily 7am–7pm.

Pizza Luna de Luz Next to the Banco Nacional ☎ 2533 3825; map p.150. Pick up a tasty pizza loaded with fresh toppings ($6–12) at this rustic joint on the main road through the village. There's around a dozen to choose from, including a decent vegetarian. Mon, Tues & Thurs 2–10pm, Fri–Sun 11.30am–10pm.

Restaurante Coto Opposite the football field ☎ 2533 3032; map p.150. You're paying for the central location as much as anything, although the inviting terrace is as good a place as any in town for, albeit pricey, *Típico* food ($8–12). Daily 8am–10pm.

Soda Luz 100m north of the church; map p.150. *Soda Luz* has been going strong for over sixty years, and the proprietors still serve up one of the best *gallo pintos* ($3–5) you'll find anywhere in the country. Daily 7am–4pm, Sat & Sun till 8pm.

COFFEE AT CRISTINA

One of the most interesting activities in the area is visiting **Café Cristina** (☎ 2574 6426, ⓦ www.cafecristina.com), a small-scale organic coffee farm about 9km northeast of Orosí, on the road from Paraíso to Turrialba, which has been toiled by an American family since 1977. The charismatic owners, Linda and Ernie, offer 1hr 30min tours ($15; reservations essential) and take great pride in explaining every stage of the coffee-making process – from growing to milling to roasting. The tour culminates in one of the sweetest cups of coffee you'll taste in Costa Rica.

Ujarrás and around Lago de Cachí

The 30km loop-road from Orosí around **Lago de Cachí** makes for a great half-day trip, ambling through some of the most beautiful scenery in the valley. Heading north out of Orosí you pass a couple of *miradors* before arriving at the agricultural hamlet of Ujarrás, home to a ruined church. Six kilometres beyond Ujarrás, over Cachí Dam and beyond the turn-offs to Cachí itself, you'll come to the charming Casa del Soñador. From here, the road continues along the shore of Lago de Cachí for a few more kilometres before arcing south and running alongside the Río Grande de Orosí until it reaches the hamlet of Paloma; crossing the rickety bridge just beyond here and turning right will lead you back into Orosí.

Iglesia de Nuestra Señora de la Limpia Concepción

If coming by bus, ask to be dropped at the fork for Ujarrás, from where it's a 1km walk

The tiny agricultural hamlet of Ujarrás is home to the evocative ruins of the **Iglesia de Nuestra Señora de la Limpia Concepción**. Built between 1681 and 1693 on the site of a shrine erected by a local fisherman who claimed to have seen the Virgin in a tree trunk, the church was abandoned in 1833 after irreparable damage from flooding; today, the sun-bleached limestone ruins are lovingly cared for, with a full-time gardener who tends the landscaped grounds. The ruined interior, reached through what used to be the door, is now a grassy, roofless enclosure fluttering with parrots; despite its dilapidated state, you can identify the fine lines of a former altar.

Casa del Soñador

Around 2km southwest of Cachí · Daily 8am–6pm · Free · ☎ 2577 1186

The charming **Casa del Soñador** is a wooden and bamboo cottage decorated with local woodcarver Macedonio Quesada's lively depictions of rural people – gossiping women, musicians and farmers – and religious scenes. Señor Quesada passed away in 1995, and his sons now use the house as a workshop, where they create and sell their wood-carvings (about $10), mostly figures etched into coffee-bush roots.

ARRIVAL AND DEPARTURE

UJARRÁS AND AROUND LAGO CACHÍ

By bus Ujarrás and Cachí (for the Casa del Soñador) are accessible by buses from Cartago (every 30min–1hr; 25min to Ujarrás).

By jeep-taxi A tour around the lake in one of Orosí's jeep-taxis costs around $20–25.

By bike If you're fit enough, cycling can be a great way to tour the valley: bikes are available for rent in Orosí (see box, p.150).

EATING AND DRINKING

★ **La Casona del Cafetal** By the lake, around 900m northwest of Cachí ☎ 2577 1414, ⓦ lacasonadelcafe .com; map p.149. Enjoying an idyllic lakeside setting, this is one of the best restaurants in the area. Its menu, strong on fish, includes tilapia *a la plancha* and trout, plus *casados* for shallower pockets (mains $10–30); the all-you-can-eat Sunday buffet is something of an institution round these parts. Daily 11am–6pm.

Parque Nacional Tapantí-Macizo Cerro de la Muerte

12km southeast of Orosí · Daily 8am–3.30pm · $10 · ☎ 2206 5615

Rugged, pristine **PARQUE NACIONAL TAPANTÍ-MACIZO CERRO DE LA MUERTE** is one of Costa Rica's least-visited national parks, covering around 580 square kilometres. Altitude in this watershed area ranges from 1220m to 3490m above sea level and contains three life zones (low mountain and premontane rainforest, and paramo), a range of habitat that provides shelter for a variety of **bird and animal life**, as well as countless species of insect – it's perhaps one of the easiest places in the country to spot the beautiful Blue Morpho butterfly. Flora is equally spectacular, including bromelias, heliconia and numerous ferns and mosses; it has been estimated that each 2.5-acre section contains up to 160 different species of tree. The park is divided into two sectors: **Tapantí**, accessed from Orosí (and described here), and **Macizo Cerro de la Muerte**, approached from the Interamericana.

The trails

Tapantí's three densely wooded **trails** lead off from the main road that cuts through the park and are relatively short. Of the walks that skirt the Río Grande de Orosí, the easiest is the sun-dappled **Sendero La Oropendola** (1.2km), which, true to its name, is a good place to spot Montezuma oropendola – a flock can normally be seen in the trees near where the trail loops back. The slightly harder **Sendero La Pava-Catarata** (1.5km) descends, via a couple of little bridges, to a section of small rapids (Catarata) or a boulder-strewn spot along the river (Pava). On the opposite side of the main road, the steep and difficult **Sendero Natural Arboles Caídos** (2km) is a reliable birdwatching trail.

ARRIVAL

PARQUE NACIONAL TAPANTÍ

By jeep-taxi From Orosí, jeep-taxis from the north side of the village square cost around $20 each way to the park.

By car Follow the main road south of Orosí to the Beneficio Orlich coffee factory, where it bends left across a small bridge; turn right (the park is signposted from here) and continue for 10km along a progressively rugged track (you'll need a 4WD in the rainy season).

INFORMATION

Facilities Despite its low numbers of visitors, the park has good services, with car-parking spaces at the trailheads and toilets and drinking water at regular intervals along the trails themselves.

Climate Tapantí receives one of the highest average annual rainfalls (a whopping 7000mm) in the country. October is the wettest month, but bring rain gear whenever you go, and dress in layers – if the sun is out it can be blindingly hot, whereas at higher elevations, when overcast and rainy, it can feel quite cool.

ACCOMMODATION

Finca Los Maestros 1km from the park entrance ☎ 2533 3312; map p.149. The campsite is run by a friendly and helpful local schoolteacher. Rates are for two people, and meals are available on request. Camping $6

Kiri Mountain Lodge 2.5km from the park ☎ 2533 2272, ☻ kirilodge.net; map p.149. The closest hotel to Tapantí, *Kiri Mountain Lodge* is an isolated, peaceful place with basic but comfortable rooms and a restaurant and bar, and they can also arrange guided walks and trout-fishing excursions for guests. $50

WATCHING WILDLIFE IN TAPANTÍ

Tapantí is chock-full of **mammals**; about 45 species live here, including the elusive tapir, as well as ocelot and margay, although you're more likely to spot paca, coati and, if you're lucky, kinkajou. **Birdlife** is abundant, particularly along the trails that wind up into the hills: look out for black guan, tinamou and chacalaca. The park's high rainfall makes it nirvana for **reptiles** and **amphibians**, too, including eye-lash viper and basilisk lizard.

2

Turrialba and around

The agricultural town of **TURRIALBA**, 45km east of Cartago on the eastern slopes of the Cordillera Central, boasts sweeping views over the rugged eastern Talamancas – and not much else. With the demise of the railroad to the Caribbean and the opening of the Guápiles Highway further north, Turrialba has faded in importance, though there are a number of worthwhile day-trips around town: most visitors come through here en route to the **Monumento Nacional Guayabo** or for a **whitewater rafting** trip on the thrilling *ríos* Pacuare or Reventazón, but there are also the excellent biological gardens at **CATIE** and the smoking cone of **Volcán Turrialba** to explore.

CATIE

4km east of Turrialba • **Jardín Botánico** Mon–Fri 7am–4pm, Sat & Sun 8am–4pm • $10, tours $25, reservations recommended **Bird-banding** Mon, Wed & Fri 5–9.30am • $15, $25; reserve in advance • ☎ 2556 2700 or ☎ 2558 2596, ⓦ catie.ac.cr • Turrialba–Siquirres buses pass by CATIE; Explornatura offers bike tours ($52; ☎ 2556 2070, ⓦ explornatura.com)

Regarded as one of the world's premier tropical research stations, the **Centro Agronómico Tropical de Investigación y Enseñanza**, thankfully otherwise known by its acronym **CATIE**, is unique in Costa Rica. For the last 65 years, the agricultural research

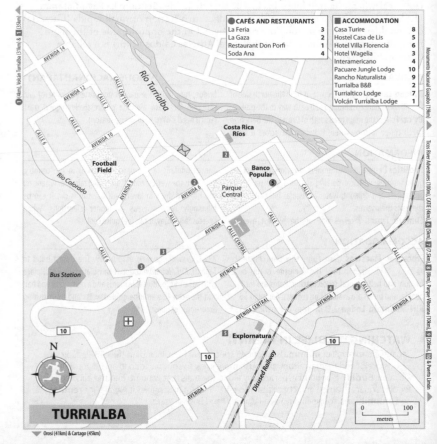

CAFÉS AND RESTAURANTS		ACCOMMODATION	
La Feria	3	Casa Turire	8
La Gaza	2	Hostel Casa de Lis	5
Restaurant Don Porfi	1	Hotel Villa Florencia	6
Soda Ana	4	Hotel Wagelia	3
		Interamericano	4
		Pacuare Jungle Lodge	10
		Rancho Naturalista	9
		Turrialba B&B	2
		Turrialtico Lodge	7
		Volcán Turrialba Lodge	1

TURRIALBA

Orosí (41km) & Cartago (45km)

WHITEWATER: THE PACUARE AND THE REVENTAZÓN

Turrialba is blessed with two of Central America's finest **whitewater rafting** rivers on its doorstep. Indeed, the scenic **Río Pacuare**'s adrenaline-inducing mix of open canyons and narrow passages has made it one of the best on earth – when rapids are called "Double Drop" and "Upper Pinball", you know they've earned their names. Although a controversial hydroelectric-dam project has put paid to some of the most popular sections of the **Río Reventazón**, there is still a lot of world-class water to ride, especially the technical drops that constitute the Pascua section, where you can tackle the "Corkscrew", the "North Sea" and "Frankenstein" (it's a bit of a monster), among others.

Most **day-trips** (around $80, including lunch and transport) on the Pacuare run the 29km stretch of Class-IV rapids on the Lower Pacuare (up to 5hr on the river); trips down the Reventazón tend to hit the Class-III rapids at the Caribbean-side section of Florida (up to 2hr 30min on the river) or, for experienced rafters, the 24km of Class-IV+ rapids at Pascua (up to 3hr 30min on the water). **Multi-day trips** on the Pacuare include overnight accommodation at jungle lodges along the river.

Recommended Turrialba **rafting operators** include Tico's River Adventure (☎2556 1231, ⓦticoriver.com) and Costa Rica Ríos (☎2556 9617, ⓦcostaricarios.com). Several specialists, including Rios Tropicales and Exploradores Outdoors, run trips out of San José (see p.54).

and higher education centre has worked on marrying the needs of Latin America's rural poor with those of the environment – it was here that the technique for producing *palmito* (heart-of-palm) from the *pejibaye* was developed – and at any one time it is involved in over a hundred research and development projects, from tackling climate change to producing disease-resistant tropical crops.

Jardín Botánico

It's this expert knowledge that makes the tours of CATIE's landscaped **Jardín Botánico** so eye-opening. The genial guide will introduce you to some of the 472 species being preserved here, explaining the virtues of the miracle fruit (it makes sour things taste sweet) or divulging some of the 101 benefits of eating noni. The tour is very interactive, so you'll spend much of your time sniffing spices, touching tubers and munching on freshly picked tropical fruit such as mangosteen and pink ornamental bananas.

Wildlife-watching

As well as hosting a number of vital germplasm projects, including one of the most important collections of coffee and cacao plants in the world, CATIE harbours a variety of **wildlife**: armadillos, coatis, sloths and caimans, and, attracted by the myriad tropical plants, 300 species of bird – the central lagoon alone is home to boat-billed heron, northern jacana and purple gallinule, and is the roosting site for a hundred or so great white herons. Keen birders can take part in the **bird-banding** research run by the Programa Monitoreo de Aves, part of an ongoing study into land-use transition – vital when so many Costa Rican farmers are replacing their coffee plantations with sugar cane. Volunteers can help with the catching, weighing and releasing of birds in various habitats across campus.

Parque Viborana

Around 10km east of Turrialba • Daily 8am–4pm; phone for tour times • $10 • ☎ 2538 1510 • Hourly Turrialba–Siquirres buses run past the *parque*

Parque Viborana is a small snake centre run by renowned herpetologist Minor Camacho, who spent years researching snake venom at the University of Costa Rica for medicinal purposes. Minor gives fascinating educational talks, focusing on the deadly fer-de-lance snake, a native (although thankfully not a very common one) of the area.

ARRIVAL   TURRIALBA AND AROUND

By bus Buses from San José (hourly; 2hr), Cartago (every 30min; 1hr 20min) and Monumento Nacional Guayabo (3 daily; 1hr) pull into Turrialba's station, 400m west of the Parque Central.

ACCOMODATION

IN TOWN

Hostel Casa de Lis Av Central, C 2/6 🕿2556 4933, ⓦhostelcasadelis.com. Cheerful Dutch-run "boutique hostel" with smart dorms, as well as private rooms with shared bathrooms (an extra $5 gets you a private bathroom and a TV). There's also a communal kitchen. Rates include tea and coffee, but not breakfast. Dorm $10, double $25

Hotel Wagelia Av 4, C 2/4 🕿2556 1566, ⓦhotel wageliaturrialba.com. *Hotel Wagelia* has tasteful but somewhat overpriced rooms with TV, wi-fi and attached bathrooms set around a tranquil courtyard. Breakfast at the on-site bar-restaurant is included in the room rate. $65

Interamericano Av 1, C 0/1 🕿2556 0142, ⓦhotel interamericano.com. Near the old train station, *Inter-americano* is the town's best budget option – basic but friendly and an excellent place to meet other travellers. There are a variety of rooms on offer, hot water and wi-fi, and they can organize kayaking and various other tours. Breakfast costs extra. $22

★**Turrialba B&B** C 1, Av 6/8 🕿2556 6651, ⓦturrialba bedandbreakfast.com. There's a great vibe at this rafters' crash-pad. Rooms come with queen-size beds and hot-water bathroom, while spacious public areas include a large kitchen, courtyard with bar and jacuzzi, and a roof terrace. Pool and darts are also on offer. $75

OUT OF TOWN

★**Casa Turire** 8km southeast of Turrialba on the road to La Suiza 🕿2531 1111, ⓦhotelcasaturire.com. Elegant, Swiss-owned colonial plantation mansion enfolded by Lago Angostura. The mellow, wood-floored rooms have king-sized bed, cable TV, bathtub and private balcony, while the honeymoon-worthy master suite ($452) runs over two floors and has jacuzzi, couches and breathtaking views. There's a dazzling swimming pool, fine-dining restaurant, bar, games room, and spa. The hotel has its own walking trails, and organizes bird-watching and kayaking, as well as trips to Monumento Nacional Guayabo and Volcán Turrialba. $180

Hotel Villa Florencia 5km east of Turrialba, on the road to Siquirres 🕿2557 3536, ⓦvillaflorencia.com. Set amid coffee fields near CATIE, the large, likeable rooms – wood-floored and featuring two queen-sized beds – open out onto lovely grounds, home to toucans, oropendolas and a variety of other chattering birdlife. Decent restaurant too. $138

Pacuare Jungle Lodge 35km northeast of Turrialba, on the Río Pacuare 🕿2225 3939, ⓦpacuarelodge. com. Archetypal luxury hideaway (palm-thatched river-view suites, vast canopy king-sizes dressed in Egyptian-cotton sheets) with a difference – you paddle yourself there in a raft, negotiating several kilometres of the raging Río Pacuare (see box, p.155) in order to bed down for the night in your own private piece of paradise. The WTO-certified ecolodge part-funds a nearby jaguar research project and has started its own conservation effort by reintroducing howler monkeys into the surrounding area. Rates are for two-night, one-day packages, including rafting in and out. $460

Rancho Naturalista 20km southeast of Turrialba, beyond La Suiza 🕿2554 8100, ⓦcostaricagateway .com. Rustic five-bedroom lodge with four adjacent cabins that is famed among birdwatchers (more than 400 bird species have been spotted in the area). It's not cheap, but the cost includes three gourmet communal meals and guided tours – and the property has its own network of rainforest trails. Rates include all meals. $340

Turrialtico Lodge 7.5km southeast of Turrialba, on the road to Siquirres 🕿2538 1111, ⓦturrialtico.com. Cosy lodge, groaning under the weight of its blossoming bougainvillea. Farmhouse-style rooms are decorated with

---

PARQUE NACIONAL VOLCÁN TURRIALBA

Volcán Turrialba (3328m), around 15km north of Turrialba, erupted for the first time in 145 years on January 5, 2010, blowing a large vent in the crater's upper wall and forcing the evacuation of sixty people from local villages; further activity was recorded in early 2012, and at the time of publication, the park remained closed to the public.

handmade bedspreads and work by local artists; some have balconies overlooking the gorgeous surrounding countryside. They organize tours to Volcán Turrialba and Monumento Nacional Guayabo. **$64**

Volcán Turrialba Lodge 35km northwest of Turrialba ☎ 2273 4335, ⦿ volcanturrialbalodge.com. Simply furnished farmhouse that sits on the very flanks of Volcán Turrialba (see box opposite) – it advertises itself as "the only hotel with a volcano in its garden". The fourteen rooms all have wood-burning stoves and private bath; diversions include birdwatching and horseriding tours to the volcano. There's an on-site restaurant too. **$90**

EATING AND DRINKING

Several *sodas* around the main square in Turrialba offer inexpensive, *Típico* fare. Fresh produce can be bought every Friday and Saturday at the buzzing **farmer's market** held alongside the disused railway tracks (7am–5pm).

La Feria Av 4, just up from Hotel Wagelia ☎ 2556 5550. Decent regional cuisine, including a variety of Caribbean dishes – adventurous diners might give the tongue a try. Mains around $5–8. Wed–Mon 11am–10pm, Tues 11am–2pm.

La Gaza C 0, Av 6/8 ☎ 2556 1073. Long-standing bar and restaurant, located on the northwest corner of the Parque Central, serving inexpensive sandwiches and hamburgers (around $3–4), plus the usual range of chicken, meat and seafood dishes. Daily 10.30am–11pm.

★ **Restaurant Don Porfi** 4km north of Turrialba, on the road to Volcán Turrialba ☎ 2556 9797. *Restaurant Don Porfi* provides the best food in town – expertly prepared international cuisine (from $10) that can be paired with a bottle of fine European or Chilean wine. Daily except Wed 11am–11pm.

Soda Ana Av 1, east of the Interamericana. An intimate, family-run *soda* where the friendly staff serve up impromptu Spanish lessons with the piping-hot *gallo pinto*, *casados* and *arroz cons* (all around $5). Daily 7am–10pm.

DIRECTORY

Money and exchange The Banco Popular on Av 4 has an ATM and changes travellers' cheques.

Post office The post office (Mon–Fri 8am–5.30pm) is just north of the centre, directly above the square.

Monumento Nacional Guayabo

19km northeast of Turrialba and 84km east of San José • Daily 8am–3.30pm • $6; guides cost $10 though English-speakers are not always available • ☎ 2559 1220

The most accessible ancient archeological site in Costa Rica, the **MONUMENTO NACIONAL GUAYABO** was discovered by explorer Anastasio Alfaro at the end of the nineteenth century; the remains of the town of Guayabo, believed to have been

inhabited from about 300 BC to 1400 AD, were only excavated in the late 1960s. Administered by MINAE (which also controls Costa Rica's national park system), Guayabo today suffers from an acute shortage of funds: some of the **montículos** (stone mounds) are in a poor state of repair and only a small part of the site has been excavated. With the withdrawal of the annual US aid grant, the prospects for further exploration look bleak.

2 The site

The **site**, a dairy farm until 1968, is visually disappointing compared to the magnificent Maya and Aztec cities of Mexico or Guatemala – cultures contemporaneous with Guayabo – though it's well to remember that civilizations should not necessarily be judged on their ability to erect vast monuments. Facing the considerable difficulties posed by the density of the rainforest terrain, the Guayabo managed not only to live in harmony with an environment that remains hostile to human habitation, but also constructed a complex system of water management and social organization, and expressed themselves through the "written language" of petroglyphs. Other than this, little is known of them, and there are no clues as to why Guayabo was ultimately abandoned, though hypotheses include an epidemic or war with neighbouring tribes.

The mysteries of Guayabo are amplified by today's site, which lacks anything in the way of information or interpretation; it's a good idea to hire a **guide** to help you decipher what can otherwise look like random piles of stone. Either way, it's best to start at the gloomy **exhibition** space, which has a model showing how the town would have looked, before heading up to the *mirador* for an overview; the trail (1.6km) then weaves its way down among the mounds.

Aqueducts

Most of the heaps of stones and basic structures now exposed were erected between 300 and 700 AD, though the (still working) **aqueducts** at the northwestern end of the site are some 2000 years old. Excavations have shown that the Guayabo were particularly skilled in water conducting – look out for the stone **tanque de captación** near here, where they stored water carried in these subterranean channels from nearby springs.

Mounds and tombs

At the heart of the town is the **central mound**. Of the 43 *montículos* that make up the site, this is the tallest circular base unearthed so far, with two staircases and pottery remains at the very top. Guayabo houses were built to a hierarchial system, and it is likely that this was home to the community chief, a *cacique*, who had both social and religious power. Near the central mound, you can see some of the **tombs** (known as Tumbas de Cajón, or Drawer Tombs) that have been uncovered in various parts of the site. They were constructed in layers of rock (hence their name) brought from surrounding rivers; unfortunately, the tombs discovered so far were plundered by looters long ago. Beyond here, at the eastern end of the site, a paved road, the **Calzada Caragra**, runs for 200m before disappearing into thick jungle; the main entrance to town, this was believed to have once stretched for 20km.

Petroglyphs

The people of Guayabo brought stones to the site from a great distance, probably from the banks of the Río Reventazón, and **petroglyphs** have been found on 53 of these – most are now in the Museo Nacional in San José (see p.96), but you can still see carvings of what appear to be lizard and jaguar gods, and an altogether more intriguingly patterned rock, the so-called **Sky Stone**, believed by some experts to represent a celestial map of the southern skies, and therefore possibly of use as an ancient calendar.

ARRIVAL AND DEPARTURE
GUAYABO

By bus Daily buses make the 1hr journey from Turrialba's main station (Mon–Sat departs 11.15am, 3.10pm & 5.20pm, Sun 9am, 3.30pm & 6.30pm, returns 7am, 12.30pm & 4pm). The inconvenient timetable means you'll probably get too long at the site, so alternatively you can walk back to the main road, a 4km downhill hike, and intercept the bus from Santa Teresita to Turrialba, which passes by at about 1.30pm (double-check the times with the *guardaparques*); if you get stuck, you can always bed down at the monument's small campsite ($5/person).

By car Driving from Turrialba takes about 30min; the last 4km is on a bad gravel road, passable with a regular car, but watch your clearance.

By taxi Taxis charge around $16 from Turrialba (one way).

Tours Most hotels in Turrialba run tours to the site, as do Explornatura (☏ 2556 2070, ⊛ explornatura.com), who offer a guided hike for $65 (including return transport).

Limón Province and the Caribbean coast

TORTUGUERO NATIONAL PARK

Limón Province and the Caribbean coast

The Caribbean coast forms part of the huge, sparsely populated Limón Province, which sweeps south in an arc from Nicaragua to Panama. Hemmed in to the north by dense jungles and swampy waterways, to the west by the mighty Cordillera Central and to the south by the even wider girth of the Cordillera Talamanca, Limón can feel like a lost, remote place.

Those seeking palm-fringed sands and tranquil crystalline waters conjured up by the word "Caribbean" will be disappointed. Limón has very few really good **beaches** to speak of and most are battered, shark-patrolled shores, littered with driftwood. However, you can watch gentle giant sea **turtles** lay their eggs on the wave-raked beaches of **Tortuguero**; snorkel coral reefs at the unspoilt **Cahuita** or Punta Uva; go surfing at **Puerto Viejo de Talamanca**; or go animal- and bird-spotting in the region's many **mangrove swamps**. The interior of Limón Province is crisscrossed by the powerful Río Reventazón and Río Pacuare, two of the best rivers in the Americas for **whitewater rafting**.

Although Limón remains unknown to the majority of visitors – especially those on package tours – it holds much appeal for ecotourists and travellers off the beaten track. The province has the highest proportion of **protected land** in the country, from the **Refugio Nacional de Vida Silvestre Barra del Colorado**, on the Nicaraguan border, to the **Refugio Nacional de Vida Silvestre Gandoca-Manzanillo** near Panama in the extreme south. That said, however, the wildlife reserves and national parks still offer only partial resistance to the considerable ecological threats of full-scale fruit farming, logging, mining and tourism.

The Caribbean coast exudes a greater sense of **cultural diversity** than anywhere else in Costa Rica – a feeling of community and a unique and complex local history. **Puerto Limón**, the only town of any size, is one of several established "black" Central American coastal cities, like Bluefields in Nicaragua and Livingston in Guatemala. A typical Caribbean port, it has a large, mostly Jamaican-descended **Afro-Caribbean** population. In the south, near the Panamanian border, live several communities of indigenous peoples from the **Bribrí** and **Cabécar** groups, none of whom has been well served by the national government.

The area's diverse microclimates mean there is no best **time to visit** the Caribbean coast. In Tortuguero and Barra del Colorado, you'll encounter wet weather year-round, with somewhat drier spells in February, March, September and October. South of Limón, September and October offer the best chance of rain-free days.

PLAYA COCLES

Highlights

❶ **Carnival, Puerto Limón** Revellers in Afro-Caribbean costumes and spangly tops parade through the streets to a cacophony of tambourines, whistles and blasting sound systems. **See p.171**

❷ **Caribbean cuisine** Sample the region's traditional Creole-influenced Caribbean cooking, from coconut-scented rice-and-beans to *rondon*, a vegetable and fish or meat stew cooked with tender plantains and breadfruit. **See p.174**

❸ **Tortuguero Canal** Spot moss-covered sloths, chattering spider monkeys, crocodiles, caimans and local life as you float up the beautiful Tortuguero Canal. **See p.178**

❹ **Snorkelling in Parque Nacional Cahuita** Watch manta rays glide by and iridescent schools of fish shimmer at Costa Rica's largest coral reef. **See p.190**

❺ **ATEC tours** Learn about traditional plant remedies and indigenous history on a tour to the Bribrí and Cabécar villages, led by the grassroots organization ATEC and locals whose families have been in the area since the eighteenth century. **See p.197**

❻ **Playa Cocles, Playa Chiquita and Punta Uva** The idyllic beaches of Cocles, Chiquita and Punta Uva dot one of the most beautiful stretches of Costa Rica's Caribbean coast. **See p.198 & p.199**

HIGHLIGHTS ARE MARKED ON THE MAP ON P.164

Brief history

Although the coast has been populated for at least ten thousand years, little is known of the ancient indigenous **Bribrí** and **Cabécar** peoples who inhabited the area when Columbus arrived just off the coast of present-day Puerto Limón, on his fourth and last voyage to the Americas in 1502. Well into the mid-eighteenth century, the only white people the Limón littoral saw were British **pirates**, rum-runners and seamen from the merchant vessels of the famous Spanish Main, plying the rich waters of the Caribbean, and bringing with them commerce and mayhem. Nefarious buccaneers often found refuge on Costa Rica's eastern seaboard, situated as it was between the two more lucrative provinces of Panama and Nicaragua, from which there was a steady traffic of ships to raid. Their presence, along with the difficult terrain, helped deter full-scale settlement of Limón.

LIMÓN PROVINCE AND THE CARIBBEAN COAST

HIGHLIGHTS

1. Carnival, Puerto Limón
2. Caribbean cuisine
3. Tortuguero Canal
4. Snorkelling in Parque Nacional Cahuita
5. ATEC tours
6. Playa Cocles, Playa Chiquita and Punta Uva

Railways and bananas

The province's development was inextricably linked to two things, themselves related: the **railway and bananas**. In 1871 it was decided that Costa Rica needed a more efficient export route for its coffee crop than the long, meandering river journey from Puerto Viejo de Sarapiquí to Matina (midway between Tortuguero and Puerto Limón) from where the beans were shipped to Europe. From the other main coffee port – Puntarenas on the Pacific coast – boats had to go all the way round South America to get to Europe. **Minor Keith**, an American, was contracted to build a railroad across the Cordillera Central from San José to Puerto Limón; to help pay for the laying of the track, he planted bananas along its lowland stretches. Successive waves of highlanders, Chinese, East Indian (still locally called Hindus) and Italian immigrant labourers were brought in for the gruelling construction work, only to succumb to yellow fever; at least four thousand people died while laying the track for the **Jungle Train**. In the final stages, some ten thousand Jamaicans and Barbadians, thought to be immune to the disease, were contracted, many of them staying on to work on further railroad expansion or in the banana plantations. In 1890, the first Jungle Train huffed its way from San José via Turrialba and Siquirres to Limón, bringing an abrupt end to the Caribbean coast's era of near-total isolation. This also marked the beginning of Costa Rica's **banana boom**. Initially planted as a sideline to help fund the railroad, the fruit prospered in this ideal climate, leading Keith to found the

3

MULTICULTURALISM IN LIMÓN PROVINCE

In his book *Tekkin a Waalk*, journalist and travel writer Peter Ford uses the ingenious term "an anthropological Galápagos" to describe the ethnic and cultural oddities encountered in Limón, where the Caribbean meets Central America. There's no doubt that the province provides a healthy dose of **multiculturalism** lacking in the rest of Costa Rica's relatively homogeneous Latin, Catholic society. In Limón, characterized by intermarriage and racial mixing, it's not unusual to find people who are of combined Miskito, Afro-Caribbean and Nicaraguan ancestry.

ETHNIC DIVERSITY

Though the first black inhabitants of the province were the slaves of the British pirates and mahogany-cutters who had lived in scattered communities along the coast since the mid-1700s, the region's **ethnic diversity** stems largely from the influence of Minor Keith (see above), who brought in large numbers of foreign labourers to work on the construction of the Jungle Train. They were soon joined by turtle fishermen who had settled in Bocas del Toro, Panama, before migrating north to escape the Panamanian war of independence from Colombia in 1903. The settlers brought their respective **religions** with them – unlike in the rest of Costa Rica, most Afro-Caribbeans in Limón Province are Protestant.

Regardless of race or religion, the coastal settlers were resourceful and independent. They not only planted their own **crops**, bringing seeds to grow breadfruit, oranges, mangoes and ackee, all of which flourished alongside native coconuts and cocoa, but also made their own salt, charcoal, musical instruments and shoes, and brewed their own **spirits** – red rum, *guarapo*, cane liquor and ginger beer.

Limón's diversity has never been appreciated by the ruling and economic elite of the country. Until 1949, blacks were effectively forbidden from settling in the Valle Central or the highlands, and while the **indigenous communities** have a degree of autonomy, their traditional territories have long since been eaten up by government-sanctioned mining and banana enterprises. Official discrimination against the province's Afro-Caribbean inhabitants ended in 1949 with a new constitution that granted them full citizenship. Black Limonenses now make up around 30 percent of the province's population.

LANGUAGE

Language can be a problem when travelling around Limón Province. While English is spoken widely along the coast – and there are a fair number of expats, particularly in and around Cahuita and Puerto Viejo – don't expect everyone to know it. Your best bet is to make your first approaches in Spanish, if you can; people can then choose in which language to answer you.

United Fruit Company, whose monopoly of the banana trade throughout Central America made him far wealthier than the railroad ever could.

The 1991 earthquake to today

Traditionally neglected and underfunded by the government, Limón suffered a major blow in the 1991 **earthquake**, which heaved the Caribbean coast about 1.5 metres up in the air. Already badly maintained roads, bridges and banana railroads were destroyed, including the track for the Jungle Train, one of the most scenic train rides in the world. While much has been rebuilt, an air of neglect still hangs over parts of the province, from housing and tourist infrastructure to basic sanitation.

GETTING AROUND   **LIMÓN PROVINCE AND THE CARIBBEAN COAST**

BY CAR

From San José to Puerto Limón, you have a choice of just two roads: the Guápiles Highway (Hwy-32) and the Turrialba Road (Hwy-10). From Puerto Limón south to the Panama border at Sixaola, Hwy-36 is the one decent route (not counting the few small local roads leading to the banana *fincas*). Petrol provision is generally poor; it's best to leave San José (and Puerto Limón, if you're driving towards Panama) with a full tank and fill up at the next station as soon as you reach half a tank.

Canal, dug in the late 1960s in order to bypass the treacherous breakers of the Caribbean. The canal connects the port of Moín, 8km north of Puerto Limón, to the Río Colorado near the Nicaraguan border. La Pavona, not much more than a boat dock about 50km northeast of Guápiles, also provides access to the Tortuguero Canal. A reliable bus network operates in the rest of the province, with the most efficient and modern routes running from San José to Puerto Limón and on to Sixaola.

BY BUS AND BOAT

North of Puerto Limón there is no public land transport at all: instead, private *lanchas* ply the coastal Tortuguero

BY PLANE

There are daily flights from San José to Barra del Colorado and Tortuguero.

The Guápiles Highway

Two land routes head from the capital to Puerto Limón. Though the main route, the **Guápiles Highway** (Hwy-32), remains one of the best-maintained roads in the country, it's still half-jokingly referred to as the "Highway to Heaven" because of its high accident and fatality record. Nevertheless, the vast majority of buses, trucks and cars take this road, which begins in San José at the northern end of Calle 3 and climbs out of the highlands to the northeast. This opening section of the highway is the most impressive, with Barva and Irazú volcanoes looming on either side. In general, however, the road doesn't offer quite the scenery you might expect, because it's hewn from sheer walls of mountain carpeted with thick, intertwining vegetation. While one side is solid rock, the other side, in places, makes a sheer phantasmagoric drop that you can't quite see, with only the enormous, common huge-leaf plant known as "poor man's umbrella" (*sombrilla de pobre*) growing by the roadside to break the monotony.

Guápiles and around

GUÁPILES, about 60km east of San José, is the first town of any size on the Guápiles Highway and functions as a supply point for the Río Frío banana plantations and a way station for the *bananero* workers. Today it's a commotion of shopping malls and stalls – there's even a farmers' market on Saturdays. From here you can continue on Hwy-32 toward Puerto Limón or, if your ultimate destination is Tortuguero, follow the signs left out of town.

Jardín Botánico Las Cusingas

4km down an unmarked road at *Soda Buenos Aires* • Open by appointment • 2hr guided tour $6 • ☎ 2382 5805

Two kilometres east of Guápiles, a dirt road turn-off at *Soda Buenos Aires* leads to the secluded **Jardín Botánico Las Cusingas**, 4km further on. Owned by Costa Ricans, Las Cusingas aims to educate visitors about tropical ecology and conservation. They offer hiking trails, horseriding and a library. Covering fifty acres, the garden features eighty species of stunning orchids, and more than a hundred species of medicinal plants and bromeliads. Over a hundred species of bird have been recorded here.

ARRIVAL AND DEPARTURE

By bus The long-distance bus terminal is on the main road, north of Hwy-32 beyond the Total petrol station.
Destinations Cariari (daily every 30min; 45min);

GUÁPILES AND AROUND

Puerto Limón (10–14 daily; 1hr 30min); Siquirres (20 daily; 40min).

ACCOMMODATION AND EATING

Casa Río Blanco Ecolodge About 7km outside Guápiles, following a well-marked right turn from the highway at the Ponderosa restaurant ☎ 2710 4124, ⓦ casarioblanco.com. A rainforest lodge and bird-lover's paradise with comfortable *cabinas* and lush hiking trails down to the river and its waterfalls. *Cabinas* are perched on a 65ft cliff, with one wall fully screened out to a hammocked veranda overlooking the frothy Río Blanco and its captivating rainforest environs. The owners are passionate about nature and offer birding/hiking tours. Breakfast included. $\overline{\underline{577}}$

Hotel Suerre Across from the Technical College ☎ 2713 3000, ⓦ suerre.com. The few hotels in town cater mainly to plantation workers and have cold water and thin walls. The one exception is the comparatively swish *Hotel Suerre*, a

country club with 55 rooms, a lengthy pool (with waterslides), jacuzzi, gym, tennis/basketball courts and poolside bar (all of which non-guests are welcome to use for around $5). The rooms have a/c and satellite TV. The hotel also features a decent restaurant, two bars and a disco. $\overline{\underline{5124}}$

Jardín Botánico Las Cusingas (see opposite). The botanical gardens rent out a rustic yet well-appointed two-room cabin, which accommodates four people without difficulty. $\overline{\underline{559}}$

Rancho Roberto's At the intersection of Hwy-32 and Hwy-4, 13km west of Guápiles ☎ 2711 0146. This popular roadside restaurant is a welcoming spot to break up the journey from San José to the coast. The menu features heaped plates of *comida típica*, with most mains $5–7. Daily 7am–9pm.

DIRECTORY

Internet It's possible to access the internet at the bus terminal in the small café there ($1/hr).

Money and exchange There's a Banco Nacional three blocks north of the bus terminal.

The Turrialba Road

Slow and narrow, Hwy-10, often called the **Turrialba Road**, runs through Turrialba on the eastern slopes of the Cordillera Central before following the old switchbacking San José–Limón train tracks through a dense and pristine mountainous landscape, gutted by the deep cuts of the Pacuare and Reventazón rivers. It joins the Guápiles Highway near **Siquirres**, about three-quarters of the way to Limón, beyond which the road passes through a final 80km of low flatlands to the coast. Considered dangerous and difficult to drive, the Turrialba Road carries very little traffic, as it takes about four hours as opposed to almost three hours on the Guápiles Highway.

From Siquirres, it's a relatively easy 50km drive east to Puerto Limón along this well-maintained stretch, though beware of truck and bus drivers speeding and overtaking. As you drive, the countryside unfolds with macadamia nut farms set alongside small banana plots, flower nurseries and bare agricultural land dotted with humble roadside dwellings.

Siquirres

As the rusted hulks of freight cars and track-scarred streets show, **SIQUIRRES** – which means "reddish colour" in a Miskito dialect – used to be a major railway hub for the **Jungle Train** that carted people, bananas and cacao to the highlands. Along with Turrialba, this is where black train drivers, engineers and maintenance men would swap positions with their

TOURS AND ACTIVITIES AROUND SIQUIRRES

The Standard Fruit Company of Costa Rica (which exports under the more popular name Dole) runs a tour of its **Bananito banana plantation** ($15; ☎8383 4596, ⓦ bananatourcostarica.com). If bananas are not your fruit of choice, you could always try the **Agri Pineapple Tour** ($20; ☎2765 8189), which offers an inside look at Del Monte's Hacienda Ojo de Agua. Both tours are aimed at bus groups, and while drop-ins are accepted, you should call in advance outside of high season.

About 1km east of the town is the rafting centre for **Exploradores Outdoors** (see box, p.194), which runs white-knuckle trips down the Río Pacuare.

"white" (Spanish, *mestizo*, European or highland) counterparts, who would then take the train into the Valle Central, where blacks were forbidden from travelling until 1949. Though the Jungle Train no longer runs, trains still haul bananas and machinery to and from Siquirres, mainly servicing the innumerable banana towns or *fincas* nearby (easily recognizable on maps from their factory-farm names of Finca 1, 2, a, b and so forth).

These days sleepy Siquirres is increasingly trying to pitch itself as an ecotourism destination; the mighty Río Pacuare is just to the south of town and most regional **whitewater rafting** operators are based here. You won't find much in the way of sights in town itself except for the completely **round church** on the western side of the football field. Built to mirror the shape of a Miskito hut, its authentic indigenous shape shelters a plain, wood-panelled interior.

ARRIVAL AND DEPARTURE   SIQUIRRES

By bus Buses from San José stop at the newer bus terminal, adjacent to the central plaza.
Destinations Guápiles (20 daily; 40min); Puerto Limón (16

daily; 50min); San José (10–12 daily; 1hr 30min); Turrialba (14 daily; 2hr).

ACCOMMODATION AND EATING

Centro Turístico Pacuare On Hwy-32, at the east edge of town ☎2768 8111, ⓦ centroturisticopacuare.com. Squat modern facility with 60 spotless rooms that all have cable TV and wi-fi; some also have a/c ($10 surcharge). There's a large outdoor pool, a decent restaurant that serves *comida típica* as well as burgers ($8) and salads, a café and a lively karaoke bar on-site, too. As you can surmise from the name,

it's possible to book trips down the Pacuare here. $51
Restaurante Hong Kong Next door to the Banco de Costa Rica on the main village road left off Hwy-32 ☎2768 8550. It's not likely you'll need to stop just for a bite to eat in the village, but if you do, make straight for this popular central spot that serves surprisingly tasty – and cheap – Chinese food, with mains around $7. Daily 10am–10pm.

Puerto Limón and around

To the rest of the country, **PUERTO LIMÓN**, more often simply called Limón, is Costa Rica's *bête noire*, a steamy port raddled with slum neighbourhoods, bad sanitation and drug-related crime. The traveller may be kinder to the city than the highland Tico, although Paul Theroux's first impressions in *The Old Patagonian Express* are no encouragement:

The stucco fronts had turned the colour and consistency of stale cake, and crumbs of concrete littered the pavements. In the market and on the parapets of the crumbling buildings there were mangy vultures. Other vultures circled the plaza. Was there a dingier backwater in all the world?

Not much has changed in the thirty-five years or so since Theroux went through town, though the vultures have disappeared. Many buildings, damaged during the 1991 earthquake (the epicentre was just south of Limón), lie skeletal and wrecked, still in the process of falling down. Curiously, however, with its washed-out, peeling oyster-and-lime hues, Limón can be almost pretty, in a sad kind of way, with the pseudo-beauty of all Caribbean "slums of empire", as St Lucian poet Derek Walcott put it.

It's a working port but a neglected one, because most of the big-time banana boats now load at the deeper natural harbour of **Moín**, 6km up the headland toward Tortuguero. Generally, tourists come to Limón for one of three reasons: to get a **boat to Tortuguero** from Moín; to catch a bus south to the **beach towns** of Cahuita and Puerto Viejo to join in the annual **El Día de la Raza** (Columbus Day) carnival during the week preceding October 12; and, increasingly, to explore **Veragua Rainforest**. Less well known, but equally worth a visit, is the **Reserva Selva Bananito**, about thirty minutes to the south and one of the best birdwatching spots on the Caribbean coast. **Playa Bonita**, a few kilometres north of the centre off the road to Moín, is the most appealing spot to base yourself around the city, with a clutch of decent seafront places to stay and eat.

As for **swimming** in town, forget it: one look at the water from the tiny spit of sand next to the *Park Hotel* is discouragement enough. Pollution, sharks, huge banana-carrying ships and sharp, exposed coral make it practically impossible; the nearest possibility is at Playa Bonita, though even that is plagued by dangerous riptides.

Mercado Central

Av 2, C 3/4 • Mon–Sat 6am–8pm

Stroll around Puerto Limón for about fifteen minutes and you've got a decent lay of the land. **Avenida 2**, known locally as the "market street" and for all purposes the main drag, runs along both the north edge of Parque Vargas and the south side of the

3

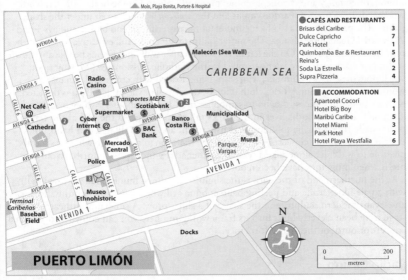

Moín, Playa Bonita, Portete & Hospital

CARIBBEAN SEA

Malecón (Sea Wall)

● CAFÉS AND RESTAURANTS	
Brisas del Caribe	3
Dulce Capricho	7
Park Hotel	1
Quimbamba Bar & Restaurant	5
Reina's	6
Soda La Estrella	2
Supra Pizzeria	4

■ ACCOMMODATION	
Apartotel Cocorí	4
Hotel Big Boy	1
Maribú Caribe	5
Hotel Miami	3
Park Hotel	2
Hotel Playa Westfalia	6

Radio Casino

Net Café @

Cathedral

Cyber Internet @

Supermarket

Transportes MEPE

Scotiabank

BAC Bank

Banco Costa Rica

Municipalidad

Mercado Central

Parque Vargas

Mural

Police

Museo Ethnohistoric

AVENIDA 1

Terminal Caribeños

Baseball Field

Docks

N

0 200 metres

PUERTO LIMÓN

N

Playa Bonita

CARIBBEAN SEA

Moín

240

PORTETE

Tortuguero Canal

Lanchas to Tortuguero

Isla Uvita

Puerto Limón

0 kilometre

PORTETE AND PLAYA BONITA

SEE MAP ABOVE FOR DETAILS

6 , Cahuita, Puerto Viejo, San José & Airport

SAFETY AND ORIENTATION IN LIMÓN

While Limón isn't quite the mugger's paradise as portrayed by the national media, you shouldn't linger on the pavement looking lost nor carry valuables while on the street – most of the better hotels listed have safes. When trying to **find your way around**, bear in mind that even more so than in other Costa Rican towns, nobody refers to **calles** and **avenidas** in Limón. The city does have street numbers, but virtually no signs. To confuse things further, unlike other towns in Costa Rica, calles and avenidas in Limón run sequentially, rather than in separate even- and odd-numbered sequences. Though the city as a whole spreads quite far out, central Limón covers no more than about ten blocks.

Mercado Central. At times, the market seems to contain the entire population of Limón – dowager women mind their stalls while men clutch cigarettes, chattering and gesticulating. The produce looks fresh: chayotes, plantains, cassava, yucca, beans and the odd banana (most of the crop is exported) vie for space with bulb-like cacao fruit, baseball-sized tomatoes and huge carrots. For an inexpensive, quality bite to eat, try the market's numerous *sodas* and snack bars (see p.172).

Parque Vargas and around

C 1, Av 1/2 • Daily 24hr

Limón, often noisy and chaotic, becomes pleasantly languid in the heat of the day, with workers drifting towards **Parque Vargas** and the *malecón* at lunch to sit under the shady palms. The park features a sea-facing **mural** (at the easternmost end of C 1 and avs 1 and 2) by artist Guadalupe Alvarea. The mural swarms with colourful, evocative images of the province's tough history. On the left of the semicircular wall, indigenous people are shown making crafts, which were later destroyed by the Catholic missionaries. Moving right, you'll note the era of Columbus, with ships being loaded with coffee and bananas by women wearing vibrant African cloth. Finally, the arrival of the Jungle Train is depicted with a wonderful Chinese dragon to symbolize the Chinese labourers who worked on it.

A small colony of **sloths** lives in the park's tall royal palms. At the end of the central promenade rises a shrine to sailors and fishermen, and also a dilapidated bandstand, the site of occasional concerts. From here, the **malecón** (a thin ledge where it's hardly possible to walk, let alone take a seaside promenade) winds its way north. Avoid it at night when muggings have been reported.

At the northern end of the park is the slightly run-down **municipalidad** (town hall), with a pale blue facade and peeling belle-époque grillwork. Opposite, on the shore, sits an elegant modern sculpture in the shape of a ship's prow. A small amphitheatre and stage have been cleverly built into its framework, and here you can enjoy the occasional concert or outdoor theatre performance.

Radio Casino

C 4, Av 4

One of the more distinctive buildings in Limón by some margin, the landmark **Radio Casino** is home to an excellent community-service station, broadcast by and for Limonenses, with call-in chat shows, international news and good music, including local and imported reggae. It's generally not possible to go inside, though the exterior has an appealingly faded, fuchsia-coloured grandeur.

ARRIVAL AND DEPARTURE   PUERTO LIMÓN AND AROUND

By plane Limón's tiny Aeropuerto Internacional is along the coast 5km south of the centre off Hwy-36. There is presently no regular NatureAir or Sansa service.

By bus Arriving in Limón after dark can be unnerving – get here in daylight if possible. You should buy your ticket several days in advance during El Día de la Raza (see box below), even though extra buses run at this time. Grupos Caribeños (☎ 2222 0610) buses from San José, Siquirres and Guápiles arrive at Limón's Terminal Caribeños on C 7, Av 1/2. At the same terminal you can catch a bus to Moín ($1), which leaves only when it's full. Arrivals from the south – Cahuita, Puerto Viejo de Talamanca and Panama (via Sixaola) – terminate at the Transportes MEPE (☎ 2257 8129) stop at C 3, Av 4, 100m north of Mercado Central.

Destinations Cahuita (10–14 daily; 1hr); Guápiles (10–14 daily; 1hr 30min); Manzanillo (6 daily; 1hr 45min); Moín (roughly every 30min; 1hr 30min); Puerto Viejo de Talamanca (10–14 daily; 1hr 30min); San José (every 30min; 2hr 30min–3hr); Siquirres (16 daily; 50min); Sixaola (14 daily; 3hr).

By lancha Shallow-bottomed private *lanchas* make the trip up the coastal canal from the docks at Moín to Tortuguero (3hr). It's best to arrive at the docks early (7–9am) although you may find boatmen willing to take you until 2pm. Expect to pay around $50 round-trip for a group of four to six people; if you're travelling alone or in a couple, try to get a group together at the docks.

By taxi Taxis line up on Avenida 2 and around the corner from Terminal Caribeños: they do long-haul trips to Cahuita and Puerto Viejo ($30–40) and beyond. Prices are per car, so if you're in a group, renting a taxi can be far more convenient than taking the bus, and almost as cheap. If you're going to Moín, a taxi (around $5) makes more sense than waiting for the bus (see opposite), which won't leave until it's full.

INFORMATION

Tourist information There's no official tourist office in Limón or the entire province for that matter. Your best bet is to contact ICT in San José (see p.107) in advance of your arrival. Note that during El Día de la Raza carnival, everything shuts for a week, including all banks and the post office (see p.173).

ACCOMMODATION

It's worth shelling out a bit extra for a room in Limón, especially if you're travelling alone. In midweek, hotels fill up quickly with commercial travellers; try to get to Limón as early as possible if you're arriving on a Wednesday or Thursday. **Hotel prices** rise by as much as fifty percent for carnival week, and to a lesser extent during Semana Santa, or Easter week. The **least expensive times** to stay are when rainfall is at its highest, between July and October, and December to February, which (confusingly) are considered high season in the rest of the country. Limón has its share of dives, which tend to get booked when a big ship has docked. None of the places listed below is rock-bottom cheap. If this is what you're after, you'll find it easily enough, but always ask to see the room first and inspect the bathroom in particular.

EL DÍA DE LA RAZA CARNIVAL

Though carnivals in the rest of Latin America are usually associated with the days before Lent, the Limón Carnival celebrates Columbus's arrival in the New World on October 12. The festivity was first introduced to Limón by Arthur King, a local who had been away working in Panama's Canal Zone. He was so impressed with that country's Columbus Day celebrations that he decided to bring the merriment home to Limón. Today, **El Día de la Raza** (Day of the People) basically serves as an excuse to party. Throngs of highland Ticos descend upon Limón – buses fill to bursting, hotels brim and partygoers hit the streets in search of this year's sounds and style. Rap, rave and ragga – in Spanish and English – are hot, and Bob Marley lives, or at least is convincingly resurrected, for carnival week.

Carnival can mean anything you want it to, from noontime displays of Afro-Caribbean dance to calypso music, bull-running, children's theatre, colourful *desfiles* (parades) and massive firework displays. Most spectacular is the **Grand Desfile**, usually held on the Saturday before October 12, when locals in Afro-Caribbean costumes – sequins, spangles and fluorescent colours – parade through the streets to a cacophony of tambourines, whistles and blasting sound systems.

The overall atmosphere – even late at night – remains unthreatening, with teens and grandparents alike enjoying the music. Kiosks dispense steaming Chinese, Caribbean and Tico food, and on-the-spot discos help pump up the volume. **Cultural Street**, which runs from the historic Black Star Line (the shipping company that brought many of the black immigrants here), is an alcohol-free zone, popular with family groups. Kids can play games at small fairgrounds to win candyfloss and stuffed toys. Elsewhere, bars overflow onto the street, and the impromptu partying builds up as the night goes on.

3

LIMÓN PATOIS

Limón patois combines **English phrases**, brought by Jamaican and Barbadian immigrants to the province in the last century, with a Spanish slightly different to that spoken in the highlands. Though used less these days, the traditional greeting of "What happen?" ("Whoppin'?") remains a stock phrase, equivalent to the Spanish "¿Qué pasa?" ("What's going on?"). In Limón, you'll also hear the more laconic "Okay" or "All right" (both hello and goodbye) taking the place of the Spanish "Adiós" ("hello" in Costa Rica rather than goodbye), "Que le vaya bien" and "Que Díos le acompañe".

Yet, English might be spoken at home, and among the older Limón crowd, but Spanish is the language taught at school and used on the street, particularly among the younger generation. Older Limonenses sometimes refer to Spanish speakers as "Spaniamen" (which comes out sounding like "Sponyaman").

IN TOWN

Staying downtown puts you in the thick of things, and many hotels have communal balconies, perfect for relaxing with a cold beer and checking out the lively street activity below. The downside is the noise, especially at night; if you prefer to hear gentle waves lapping, try the *Park Hotel*, which stands alone on a little promontory close to the sea.

Hotel Big Boy Next door to the Transportes MEPE ☎ 8926 4148. While it's undeniably dreary and is overly fond of the colour brown, it is clean and, with its location next door to the MEPE terminal, convenient for onwards bus travel to Cahuita and Puerto Viejo. Rooms have no frills beyond cable TV. $67

Hotel Miami Av 2, C 4/5 ☎ 2758 0490, ✉ hmiami limon@yahoo.com. This friendly, stylish spot near the central market offers large, clean rooms with cable TV, wi-fi and private bathrooms. Most rooms have ceiling fans, though there are a few with a/c ($10 surcharge) and hot water. $55

Park Hotel Av 3, C 1/3 ☎ 2758 4364, ⊕ parkhotellimon .com. Popular with Ticos and travellers alike, this well-appointed hotel has 32 rooms in a range of styles: the more expensive ones come with a sea view, slightly less expensive rooms have a street view, and the cheapest, *plana turista*, have no view at all. There's a good restaurant on-site, and note that it's important to book in advance. $81

AROUND LIMÓN

There's also a group of quieter – and nicer – hotels outside town (about 4km up the spur road to Moín) at Portete and the small, somewhat misnamed Playa Bonita. A taxi here costs less than $1.50, and the bus to and from Moín runs along the road every 20min or so; it's not advisable to walk into town.

Apartotel Cocorí Playa Bonita ☎ 2798 1670. Don't expect any frills from these barebones self-catering apartments, though they are comfortable and have fan or a/c, and a beautiful leafy setting overlooking the ocean. Pluses include friendly staff and a swimming pool. The lively outdoor bar-restaurant, right by the sea, has lovely views. $51

★**Hotel Playa Westfalia** 2km south of Limón airport ☎ 2756 1300, ⊕ hotelplayawestfalia.com. If you're looking for luxury within easy driving distance of Limón, this idyllic beachfront hotel is unquestionably your best choice. The eight well-appointed rooms and suites all have a/c, wi-fi and cable TV, and the hotel has a pool and a pleasant restaurant serving Caribbean cuisine. $102

Maribú Caribe Playa Bonita ☎ 2795 4010, ⊕ maribu -caribe.com. A favourite among banana-company executives, this luxurious seaside complex of round, thatched-roof huts has 1960s decor, a pool and a pleasant but pricey bar-restaurant overlooking the sea. $88

EATING AND DRINKING

Limón has a decent variety of places to eat, with several restaurants focusing on **authentic Caribbean and Creole cuisine**. It's best to heed the warnings and not sit outside at the restaurants in the town centre, particularly around the Mercado Central, where tourists are prime targets for often aggressive beggars. Inside the market, however, it's quite safe and you'll find a host of decent *sodas* serving tasty *casados*. Gringos in general and women especially should avoid most bars, especially those that have a large advertising placard blocking views of the interior, which are often less than salubrious. When you tire of the town, head to relaxing Playa Bonita for lunch or an afternoon beer. In all but the most upmarket places, avoid drinking the tap water; instead use a filter or iodine tablets.

IN TOWN

Brisas del Caribe Hotel Caribe, C 1, Av 2 ☎ 2758 0138. Enjoy the soothing ambience and views of Parque Vargas from this clean bar-restaurant – except when they blast the sound system. The varied menu includes Chinese fare, sandwiches, snacks and a tasty *medio casado* (half *casado*) for around $3. Mon–Fri 7am–11pm, Sat & Sun 10am–11pm.

Dulce Capricho Plaza Nayerith, Av 10, C 6 ☎2710 7255. Cute ice-cream parlour serving all the usual varieties plus several billowing sundaes ($3.50). Easily the most refreshing spot around to beat the heat. Mon–Thurs 10.30am–8.30pm, Fri 10am–5pm, Sat 6pm–8.30pm, Sun 10.30am–8.30pm.

Park Hotel Av 3, C 1, by the malecón. The only restaurant in town where you feel you might actually be in the Caribbean – warm breezes float in through large slatted windows that look out onto vistas of blue seas and clouds as far as the eye can see. Dine on excellent, though pricey, breakfast and standard Costa Rican fare, including *elote* (corn on the cob; $3) and *arroz con pollo* ($8). Daily 7am–10pm.

Soda La Estrella C 5, Av 3/4 ☎2798 4658. The best lunch in town features excellent *soda* staples, delicious *refrescos*, coffee and snacks like *arreglados* (filled puff

pastries; $3), all accompanied by cordial service. Daily 10am–10pm.

Supra Pizzeria Av 3, C 4/5 ☎2758 3371. Located upstairs at the Plaza Caribe, this is a good spot to enjoy pizza (large $10) and pasta with the local set. Open daily till 11pm.

PLAYA BONITA

Quimbamba Bar & Restaurant ☎2795 4805. Dine on excellent – if pricey – fresh fish cooked to order at this hopping split-level beach-bar. Live music at the weekend. Daily 8am–late.

★**Reina's** ☎2795 0879. Stylish beachside restaurant and lounge bar that's equally successful at delivering tasty Caribbean cuisine (particularly the seafood), smooth cocktails and energetic local live acts and DJs. Daily 10am–10pm.

DIRECTORY

Hospital ☎2758 2222. Limón is home to the largest hospital on the coast, which is located on the northern edge of town, along the *malecón*; to get there, follow Av 6.

Internet At the post office; Net Café on Av 4, C 5/6; and Cyber Internet, on Av 3, C 3/4.

Money and exchange The Banco de Costa Rica, on Av 2, C 1, and Scotiabank, on Av 3, C 2, both offer money exchange and have ATMs that accept Visa and Cirrus.

Post office Av 2, C 4 (Mon–Fri 7.30am–5pm, Sat 8am–noon), though the mail service from Limón is dreadful – you're better off posting items from San José.

Veragua Rainforest

Brisas de Veragua • Tues–Sun 8am–3pm • Full tour $65; exhibits only $35 • ☎ 2296 5056, ⓦ veraguarainforest.com

Opened in 2008, **Veragua Rainforest** is a fascinating "research and adventure park" that provides a quick and sleek introduction to some of the region's rich biodiversity. Owned and operated entirely by Costa Ricans, Veragua holds several smartly-designed animal exhibits – including one that mimics a nocturnal habitat for frogs – as well as an aerial tram, a zip line and an elevated trail through the rainforest leading to a waterfall. The highlight, though, is the research facility, where you can talk with the resident biologists and learn more about the ongoing study of the park's stunning collection of butterflies.

ARRIVAL AND DEPARTURE   VERAGUA RAINFOREST

By bus Empresa buses for Siquirres leave Limón's Terminal de Caribeños hourly; get off at the Liverpool town stop, about 12km from Limón – let the bus driver know you're going to Veragua. The road leading to Veragua is signposted about 50m from the bus stop. Call in advance to arrange

pick-up from here, which is possible most days.

By car If you're driving, a 4WD is necessary to negotiate the bone-rattling gravel road that covers the final 3km to the rainforest.

Reserva Selva Bananito

About 8km from the hamlet of Bananito Norte • Daily 7am–6pm • Call for current day-rates and tour options • ☎ 2253 8118 or ☎ 8386 1005, ⓦ selvabananito.com

Twenty kilometres south of Limón, the eight-square-kilometre private **Reserva Selva Bananito** unfolds alongside the Parque Internacional La Amistad (see p.405) and protects an area of mountainous, virgin rainforest. There are several activities on offer, from horseriding and tree-climbing to hiking and birdwatching (toucans, orioles, various raptors and kingfishers have all been spotted in the reserve). Whether or not you're planning to stay at the reserve's lodge, call or email in advance to advise of your estimated arrival time and make tour arrangements.

CREOLE CUISINE IN LIMÓN PROVINCE

Creole cuisine is known throughout the Americas, from Louisiana to Bahía, for its imaginative use of African spices and vegetables, succulent fish and chicken dishes and fantastic sweet desserts. Sample Limón's version at any of the locally run restaurants dotted along the coast. These are often family affairs, usually presided over by respected older Afro-Caribbean women. Sitting down to dinner at a red gingham tablecloth, with a cold bottle of Imperial beer, reggae on the boombox and a plate heaped with coconut-scented rice-and-beans is one of the real pleasures of visiting this part of Costa Rica. Note that many restaurants, in keeping with age-old local tradition, feature Creole dishes at weekends only, serving simpler dishes or the usual highland rice concoctions during the week.

TYPICAL DISHES

Everyone outside Limón will tell you that the local speciality, **rice-and-beans** (in the lilting local accent it sounds like "rizanbin"), is "*comida muy pesada*" (very heavy food). However, this truly wonderful mixture of red or black beans and rice cooked in coconut milk is no more *pesada* – and miles tastier – than traditional highland dishes like *arroz con camarones*, where everything is fried; it's the coconut milk that gives this dish its surprising lift. Another local speciality is **pan bon**, sweet bread glazed and laced with cheese and fruit which is often eaten for dessert, as are ginger biscuits and plantain tarts. *Pan bon* doesn't translate as "good bread", as is commonly thought; "bon" actually derives from "bun", brought by English-speaking settlers. **Rundown** (said "rondon" – to "rundown" is to cook) is a vegetable and meat or fish stew in which the plantains and breadfruit cook for many hours, very slowly, in spiced coconut milk. It may be hard to find, mainly because it takes a long time, at least an afternoon, to prepare. Though some restaurants – *Miss Junie's* (see p.181) in Tortuguero and *Miss Edith's* (see p.190) in Cahuita – have it on their menus as a matter of course, it's usually best to stop by on the morning of the day you wish to dine and request it for that evening.

Right at the other end of the health scale are **herbal teas**, a speciality of the province and available in many restaurants: try wild peppermint, wild basil, soursop, lime, lemon grass or ginger.

THE KEY INGREDIENTS

Favoured **spices** in Limonese Creole cooking include cumin, coriander, peppers, chillies, paprika, cloves and groundspice, while the most common vegetables are those you might find in a street market in West Africa, Brazil or Jamaica. Native to Africa, **ackee** (in Spanish *seso vegetal*) was brought to the New World by British colonists, and has to be prepared by knowledgeable cooks because its sponge-cake-like yellow fruit, enclosed in three-inch pods, is poisonous until the pods open. Served boiled, ackee resembles scrambled eggs and goes well with fish. **Yucca**, also known as manioc, is a long pinkish tuber, similar to the yam, and usually boiled or fried. Local yams can grow as big as 25kg, and are used much like potato in soups and stews. Another native African crop, the huge melon-like **breadfruit** (*fruta de pan*), is more a starch substitute than a fruit, with white flesh that has to be boiled, baked or grated. **Pejiballes** (*pejibaye* in Spanish – English-speaking people in Limón pronounce it "picky-BAY-ah") are small green or orange fruits that look a little like limes. They're boiled in hot water and skinned – and are definitely an acquired taste, being both salty and bitter. You'll find them sold on the street in San José, but they're most popular in Limón. Better known as heart-of-palm, **palmito** is served in restaurants around the world as part of a tropical salad. **Plantains** (*plátanos* in Spanish), the staple of many highland dishes, figure particularly heavily in Creole cuisine, and are deliciously sweet when baked or fried in fritters.

ARRIVAL

RESERVA SELVA BANANITO

By car The reserve is reached via an inland road from the main coastal highway that goes through the banana town of Bananito and then along a very rough track across several rivers (you'll need a 4WD).

By bus If you don't have your own transport, you can call *Selva Bananito Eco Lodge* (see opposite) and arrange to be picked up from the bus stop at Salon Delia in the centre of Bananito Norte. As the bus service to Bananito Norte is irregular, enquire at the lodge for the current timetable.

ACCOMMODATION

★ **Selva Bananito Eco Lodge** ☎ 2253 8118 or ☎ 8386 1005, ⓦ selvabananito.com. The reserve's wonderfully peaceful and remote lodge has eleven attractive, spacious cabins with large verandas overlooking the forest: meals (included in the price) and drinks are served in the main ranch. Owned and run by the environmentally conscious children of a pioneering German farmer, the lodge is built from secondhand wood discarded by loggers, has solar-powered hot water (though no electricity) and donates a percentage of its profits to the Fundación Cuencas de Limón, which helps protect the local area and develop educational programmes. $170

Parque Nacional Tortuguero

Despite its isolation – 254km from San José by road and water – **PARQUE NACIONAL TORTUGUERO** is among the most visited national parks in Costa Rica. Though its biodiversity has few peers in the country, it is most known for its turtles, specifically the **green sea turtle**, one of only eight species of marine turtle. Along with hawksbill turtles, green sea turtles lay their eggs here between July and October in great numbers, making it one of the most important nesting sites in the world for the species.

First established as a protective zone in the 1960s, Tortuguero officially became a national park in 1975. It encompasses 190 square kilometres of protected land, including not only the beach on which the turtles nest, but also the surrounding impenetrable tropical rainforest, coastal mangrove swamps and lagoons, and canals and waterways. Except during the comparatively dry months of February, March, September and October, the park is fairly wet, receiving over 3500mm of rain a year.

As elsewhere in Costa Rica, logging, economic opportunism and fruit plantations have affected the parkland. Sometimes advertised by package tour brochures as a "Jungle Cruise" along "Central America's Amazon", the journey to Tortuguero is indeed Amazonian, taking you past tracts of **deforestation** and lands cleared for cattle – all outside the park's official boundaries but, together with the banana plantations, disturbingly close to its western fringes.

Tortuguero village and around

The peaceful village of **TORTUGUERO**, with a small population of around 700, lies at the northeastern corner of the park, on a thin spit of land between the sea and the canal. The exuberant foliage of wisteria, oleander and bougainvillea imbues the village with a tropical garden feel. Tall palm groves loom over patchy expanses of grass dotted with zinc-roofed wooden houses, often elevated on stilts. This is classic Caribbean style: washed-out, slightly ramshackle and pastel-pretty, with very little to disturb the torpor until after dark.

A dirt path – the "main street" – runs north–south through the village, from which narrow paths lead to the sea and the canal. Smack in the middle of the village stands one of the prettiest churches you'll see anywhere in Costa Rica, tiny and pale yellow, with a small spire and an oval doorway.

Natural History Museum

The northern edge of the village near the beach • Daily 10am–5pm • $2 • ⓦ cccturtle.org

At the north end of the village is the **Natural History Museum** run by the Caribbean Conservation Corporation, with a small but informative exhibition explaining the life cycle of sea turtles. You can watch a rather portentous twenty-minute video explaining the history of turtle conservation in the area and, before you leave, you'll be invited to "adopt a turtle" for $25 for which you'll receive an adoption certificate and information so that you can track the migratory progress of your chosen beast on the internet as it makes its slow, purposeful way across the ocean.

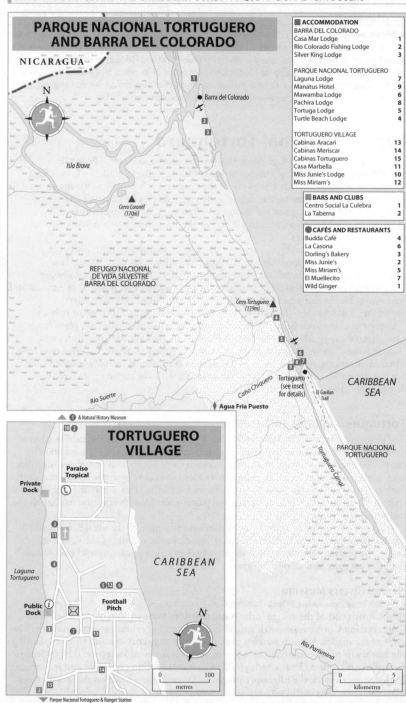

PARQUE NACIONAL TORTUGUERO AND BARRA DEL COLORADO

NICARAGUA

Isla Brava

Cerro Coronel (170m)

REFUGIO NACIONAL DE VIDA SILVESTRE BARRA DEL COLORADO

Cerro Tortuguero (119m)

Río Suerte

Caño Chiquero

Río Parismina

Agua Fría Puesto

Barra del Colorado

Tortuguero (see inset for details)

El Gavilán Trail

CARIBBEAN SEA

PARQUE NACIONAL TORTUGUERO

Tortuguero Canal

■ **ACCOMMODATION**

BARRA DEL COLORADO
Casa Mar Lodge	1
Río Colorado Fishing Lodge	2
Silver King Lodge	3

PARQUE NACIONAL TORTUGUERO
Laguna Lodge	7
Manatus Hotel	9
Mawamba Lodge	6
Pachira Lodge	8
Tortuga Lodge	5
Turtle Beach Lodge	4

TORTUGUERO VILLAGE
Cabinas Aracari	13
Cabinas Meriscar	14
Cabinas Tortuguero	15
Casa Marbella	11
Miss Junie's Lodge	10
Miss Miriam's	12

■ **BARS AND CLUBS**
Centro Social La Culebra	1
La Taberna	2

● **CAFÉS AND RESTAURANTS**
Budda Café	4
La Casona	6
Dorling's Bakery	3
Miss Junie's	2
Miss Miriam's	5
El Muellecito	7
Wild Ginger	1

TORTUGUERO VILLAGE

& Natural History Museum

Paraíso Tropical

Private Dock

Laguna Tortuguero

Public Dock

Football Pitch

CARIBBEAN SEA

Parque Nacional Tortuguero & Ranger Station

0   100
metres

0   5
kilometres

WILDLIFE IN PARQUE NACIONAL TORTUGUERO

Tortuguero is home to a staggering abundance of **wildlife** – fifty kinds of **fish**, numerous **birds**, including the endangered green parrot and the vulture, and about 160 **mammals**, some under the threat of extinction. Due to the waterborne nature of most transport and the impenetrability of the ground cover, it's difficult to spot them, but howler, white-faced capuchin and spider monkeys lurk behind the undergrowth. The park is also home to the fishing bulldog bat, which locates its underwater prey by sonar, and a variety of large rodents, including the window rat, whose internal organs you can see through its transparent skin. Jaguars used to thrive here, but are slowly being driven out by the encroaching banana plantations at the western end of the park. You may also spot the West Indian manatee, or sea cow, or much less likely, bull sharks; as good a reason as any to not try swimming here. It's the **turtles**, however, that draw all the visitors. The sight of the gentle beasts tumbling ashore and shimmying their way up the beach to deposit their heavy load before limping back, spent, into the dark phosphorescent waves can't fail to move.

Cerro Tortuguero

Cerro Tortuguero, an ancient volcanic deposit, looms 119m above the flat coastal plain 6km north of the village. A climb up the gently sloping sides leads you to the "peak", where you can enjoy good views of flat jungle and inland waterways. Accessible only by *lancha*, this is a half-day hike, and you must go with a guide. Of the lodges, only *Laguna Lodge* (see p.180) offers the guided climb as part of its accommodation package.

The park

Main entrance at the south end of the village • Daily 6am–6pm • $10 • ☎ 2710 2929

Most people come to Tortuguero to see the **desove**, or egg-laying of endangered marine turtles. Few are disappointed, as the majority of tours during **laying seasons** (March–May & July–Oct) result in sightings of the surreal procession of the reptiles from the sea to make their egg-nests in the sand. While turtles have been known to lay in the daylight (the hatchlings wait under the cover of sand until nightfall to emerge), it is far more common for them to come ashore in the relative safety of night. Nesting can take place turtle-by-turtle – you can watch a single mother come ashore and scramble up the beach just south of the village or, more strikingly, in groups (*arribadas*) when dozens emerge from the sea at the same time to form a colony, marching up the sands to their chosen spot, safely above the high-tide mark. Each turtle digs a hole in which she lays eighty or more eggs; the collective whirring noise of sand being dug away is extraordinary. Having filled the hole with sand to cover the eggs, the turtles begin their course back to the sea, leaving the eggs to hatch some weeks later; when the hatchlings emerge they instinctively follow the light of the moon on the water, scuttling to safety in the ocean.

Along with the **green** (*verde*) turtle, named for the colour of soup made from its flesh, you might see the **hawksbill** (*carey*), with its distinctive hooked beak, and the ridged **leatherback** (*baula*), the largest turtle in the world, which weighs around 300kg – though some are as heavy as 500kg and reach 2.4m in length. The green turtles and hawksbills nest mainly from July to October (August is the peak month), while the leatherbacks may come ashore from March to May.

El Gavilan trail and beach

The well-maintained **El Gavilan trail** (2 miles round-trip) starts at the ranger station at the park entrance and heads toward the coast where it turns south, paralleling the beach which remains close at hand for the length of the path. It's a mostly shaded walk, and it gives you a good chance of glimpsing lizards and monkeys. As for the long, wild **beach**, you can amble for up to 30km south, spotting crabs and birds along the way, and also looking for turtle tracks, which resemble the two thick parallel lines a truck would leave in its wake.

Swimming is not a good idea, due to heavy waves, turbulent currents and sharks. Remember that you need to pay **park fees** to walk on either the beach or along the trail.

ARRIVAL AND DEPARTURE

BY LANCHA

As the Tortuguero Canal is impassable in most areas to all but the most shallow-bottomed of boats, *lanchas*, which go up the canal from Moín, La Pavona and elsewhere, are effectively the only means of transportation. Expect a 3–4hr trip (sometimes longer), depending upon where you embark – if you're on a package tour, it will probably be Hamburgo de Siquirres on the Río Reventazón; travelling independently, you'll find it logistically easier to leave from La Pavona or Moín. The *lanchas* drop you at Tortuguero dock in the centre of the village, from where you can walk to the village accommodation or take another *lancha* to the more expensive tourist lodges further up the canal.

From Moín If you're travelling independently, you should be able to find a *lancha* at Moín willing to make the 4hr

PARQUE NACIONAL TORTUGUERO

journey ($10) up the canal any time from 6am until as late as 2pm (depending on the tides), although the earlier you travel the better. You can arrange with your boatman your return day and time; get a phone number if possible, so you can call from Tortuguero village if you change return plans.

From Cariari Alternatively, you can do as the locals do and take a 9am or 10.30am bus from San José's Terminal Gran Caribe to Cariari, and then switch to either the noon or 3pm bus to La Pavona (see below), from where *lanchas* depart daily to Tortuguero (a boat is timed to leave shortly after the bus arrives from Cariari). The journey is long, but you'll save money, particularly if you're travelling alone.

From La Pavona The transport hub here is technically at the restaurant/bar *Rancho La Suerte*, but it is known more commonly as La Pavona. *Lanchas* travel from here to

THREATS TO MARINE TURTLES

For hundreds of years the fishermen of the Caribbean coast made their living culling the seemingly plentiful turtle population, selling shell and meat for large sums to middlemen in Puerto Limón. Initially, turtles were hunted for local consumption only, but during the first two decades of the 1900s, the fashion for turtle soup in Europe, especially England, led to large-scale exports.

TURTLE-HUNTING

Turtle-hunting was a particularly brutal practice. Spears were fashioned from long pieces of wood, taken from the apoo palm or the rawa, and fastened with a simple piece of cord to a sharp, barbed metal object. Standing in their canoes, fishermen hurled the spear, like a miniature harpoon, into the water, lodging the spear in the turtle's flesh. Pulling their canoes closer, the fishermen would then reel in the cord attached to the spear, lift the beasts onto the canoes and take them ashore dead or alive. On land, the turtles might be beheaded with a machete or put in the holds of ships, where they could survive a journey of several weeks to Europe if they were given a little water.

CONSERVATION EFFORTS

Today, turtles are protected, their eggs and meat a delicacy. Locals around Tortuguero are officially permitted to take two turtles a week during nesting season for their own consumption – the unlucky green turtles are considered the most delicious. The recent sharp decline in the populations of hawksbill, green and leatherback turtles has been linked, at least in part, to **poaching**. This has prompted the national parks administration to adopt a firm policy discouraging the theft of turtle eggs within the park boundaries and to arm park rangers. Meanwhile, should you find a turtle on its back between July 10 and September 15, do not flip it over, as in most cases it is being tagged by researchers, who work on the northern 8km of the thirty-five-kilometre-long nesting beach.

NATURAL PREDATORS

It is not just the acquisitive hand of humans that endangers the turtles. On land, a cadre of **predators**, among them coati and racoons, regularly ransack the nests in order to eat the unborn reptiles. Once the hatching has started – the darkness giving them a modicum of protection – the turtles really have their work cut out, running a gauntlet of vultures, barracudas, sharks and even other turtles (the giant leatherback has been known to eat other species' offspring) on their way from the beach to the sea. Only about sixty percent – an optimistic estimate – of hatchlings reach adulthood, and the survival of marine turtles worldwide is under question.

Tortuguero (3–5 daily; 1hr 15min to 2hr) and cost around $3–10. The return boat to La Pavona (and then onwards to San José) leaves daily at 6am.

BY CAR

There's a covered parking area at La Pavona (see opposite) if you need to leave a car rental behind during your stay in Tortuguero ($10/day). Take all of your possessions with you and leave no valuables in the car.

BY PLANE

Much less time-consuming, of course, is a flight from San José to the airstrip across the canal from *Tortuga Lodge* (see p.181) 4km north of the village. The trip is a spectacular one, as you rise above the mountains outside the city and are afforded a bird's-eye view of the canals as you approach the park from the south. Sansa (☎ 2290 4100) and NatureAir (☎ 2299 6000) fly regularly from San José. Sansa flights depart at 6am from Juan Santamaría International Airport, while NatureAir flights depart at 6.15am from Tobías Bolaños International Airport in the Pavas district. There are no taxis from the airstrip to the village, though the more upscale lodges will come and pick you up; otherwise you'll have to walk. The purple Paraíso Tropical souvenir shop in the middle of the village doubles as the village's NatureAir agent, and sells tickets to San José.

Destinations San José (2 daily Mon, Tues & Fri; daily Wed, Thurs, Sat & Sun; 30–45min).

INFORMATION

Tourist information A small, somewhat faded display on the turtles' habits, habitat and history surrounds the information kiosk (daily 9am–6pm) in the village centre. This is the official place to buy tickets for turtle tours; park rangers sell the tickets at the kiosk from 5pm to 6pm. Here you can also get contact info for local guides.

TOURS

The most popular way to see Tortuguero is on one of literally hundreds of **tour packages**, many of which are two-night, three-day affairs that use the expensive lodges across the canal from the village. Accommodation, meals and transport (which otherwise can be a bit tricky) are all taken care of. The main difference between tours comes in the standard of accommodation, and most importantly, the quality of your guide. Ask about your guide's accreditations, and don't hesitate to check his level of English. Budget options also tend to involve some form of bus/boat transfer while the more expensive tours fly direct from San José.

TOUR OPERATORS

★ **Costa Rica Expeditions** C Central, Av 3, San José ☎ 2257 0766, ⓦ costaricaexpeditions.com. Exceedingly well-run and attentive outfit offering upscale Tortuguero packages including flights from San José, accommodation at the comfortable *Tortuga Lodge* and three meals a day. Prices start at $548/person for a three-day, two-night package. They also offer trips to Barra del Colorado.

Ecole Travel C 7, Av 0/1, San José ☎ 2234 1669, ⓦ ecole travel.com. One of the longest-established companies offering Tortuguero tours, Ecole has excellent budget tours popular with students and backpackers. Tours ($219 for one night and two days) start from San José; pick-ups can be arranged at your hotel.

Jungle Tom Safaris ☎ 2221 7878, ⓦ jungle tomsafaris.com. Long-running US-owned operator offering some of the more inexpensive tours to Tortuguero. They lead one-, two- and three-day trips from San José from $92.

Riverboat Francesca Tours ☎ 2226 0986, ⓦ tortuguero canals.com. Features two-day, one-night tours of the Tortuguero canals from $200. The price includes bus transportation from San José to Moín (where you embark on the canal tour), meals and lodging.

LOCAL GUIDES

There are numerous local guides in the village who offer tours of the canals and national park. The ones listed below are among the best and most established. Take time to talk with various guides before choosing – it's generally best to not immediately make arrangements with the guides who hover around the *lanchas* when they dock.

Castor Hunter Thomas Enquire at Soda Doña María ☎ 8870 8630. Well-respected local guide whose father was Tortuguero's first to take paying customers out in the surrounding area.

Darryl Loth ☎ 2709 8011, ⓦ casamarbella.tripod.com. Canadian naturalist and local resident Darryl Loth, who runs *Casa Marbella* (see p.180), has a small information centre in the village and can arrange tours, including boat trips and hikes up Cerro Tortuguero (see p.177).

Iguana Verde Tours Operates out of Miss Junie's Lodge ☎ 2231 6803, ⓦ iguanaverdetours.com. Offers a number of tours, including popular canal and national park excursions (from $20), as well as a village tour ($35) that provides an excellent introduction into local and Caribbean culture.

Ross Ballard ☎ 2709 8193, ⓔ srossballard@gmail.com. Canadian botanist Ross Ballard leads informative 3hr tours on the canals and into the national park as well as longer multi-day excursions.

3

3

TURTLE TOURS AND CANAL TOURS

Turtle tours, led by certified guides, leave at 8pm and 10pm every night from the information kiosk in the village. If you're not going with an organized group from one of the lodges, you'll need to buy park entrance tickets from the kiosk. Be sure to get there early because the number of visitors is strictly limited (no more than 200 people are allowed on the beach at any one time); visitors must wear dark clothing, refrain from smoking, and aren't allowed to bring cameras (still or video) or flashlights. Everyone must be off the beach by midnight. There are over a hundred certified guides in Tortuguero; they charge $10 for a turtle tour (roughly half the price of a lodge tour). If you haven't already sorted one out, they conveniently tend to hang around the ticket kiosk at 5pm in search of customers.

Almost as popular as the turtle tours – and with good reason – are Tortuguero's **boat tours** through the *caños*, or lagoons, to spot a jaw-dropping array of wildlife, including caimans, crocodiles and Jesus Christ lizards, as well as birds such as nocturnal herons with bulbous eyes, dignified-looking cranes and kingfishers. You may also glimpse immobile sloths clinging to a tree or perhaps even a troupe of spider monkeys making their leaping, chattering way through the waterfront canopy. Most lodges have **canoes** (some also have hydro-bikes) that you can take out on the canal – a great way to get around if you're handy with a paddle, but stick to the main canal as it's easy to get lost in the complex lagoon system northwest of the village. In the south of the village, 50m north of the ranger station and right by the water, Rubén Aragón Rodrígues rents traditional Miskito-style boats and canoes for about $8 an hour, or $15 with a guide-paddler. The information kiosk has a list of other locals who rent canoes.

ACCOMMODATION

With a little planning you can get to Tortuguero independently and stay in **cabinas** in the village. Basing yourself here allows you to explore the beach at leisure – though you can't swim – and puts you within easy reach of restaurants and bars. If you haven't booked a hotel in advance, be aware that accommodation in the village can fill up quickly during the turtle-nesting seasons (March–May & July–Oct). Staying at Tortuguero's **lodges**, most of which are across the canal from the village, has its drawbacks. Though convenient, and in some cases quite luxurious, life as a lodger can be a rather regimented affair. Guests are shuttled in and out of the lodges with stopwatch precision, there's precious little nightlife and, as all meals are included in most packages, it can be tempting to never leave the grounds. If you want to explore the village and the beach on your own you have to get a *lancha* across the canal (free, but inconvenient). Note, however, that outside the turtle-watching season, most lodges don't operate their boats at night. Owing to Tortuguero's perennial popularity with package tourists, the lodges don't always have space for independent travellers.

TORTUGUERO VILLAGE

Cabinas Aracari South of the information kiosk and football field ☎2709 8006. Run by a local family, these clean, comfortable *cabinas*, all with private bath, cold water and fan, sit amid a beautiful tree-filled garden. $9

Cabinas Meriscar In the southern part of the village where three dirt roads converge ☎2709 8202. Newer cabins come with private bathrooms, while the older, slightly gloomy but clean *cabinas* have shared spick-and-span bathrooms. It's possible to camp in the grounds as well. $8 shared bath; $2 camping

Cabinas Tortuguero South of the village, towards the entry to the national park and across from the supermarket ☎2709 8114, ✉cabinas_tortuguero @yahoo.com. Simple cabins with wi-fi surround a lovely garden at this quiet spot. Tasty meals are offered, including Italian food, as one of the owners is from Bologna. You can also rent canoes. $25 shared bath; $34 private bath

Casa Marbella In front of the Catholic church, next to the information kiosk ☎2709 8011, ⊛casamarbella

.tripod.com. Managed by a committed Canadian environmentalist, an inexhaustible source of info on the regional flora and fauna, this friendly B&B has four large, comfortable en-suite rooms. Breakfast, included, is served on a small terrace overlooking the canal. Tours offered. $45

Miss Junie's Lodge At the north end of the village, just before you reach the Natural History Museum ☎2231 6803, ⊛iguanaverdetours.com/lodge.htm. Tortuguero's most popular cook (see opposite) also offers refurbished, simply decorated, comfortable rooms with hot-water private bath and fans. Excellent breakfast included in the price. $50

Miss Miriam's On the north side of the village football pitch ☎2709 8002. Six simple rooms are available adjacent to the eponymous restaurant; those upstairs have a sea view and are a bit breezier. $17

PARQUE NACIONAL TORTUGUERO

The rates below are all per-night for packages.

Laguna Lodge A little over 1km north of the village ☎2272 4943, ⊛lagunatortuguero.com. This well-equipped lodge has a riverside bar, swimming pool, beach access and a conference centre (which looks like a giant turtle as envisaged by Gaudí). For some, the lodge's regime, with set meal and tour times, may be a bit too constraining. Nevertheless, the rooms are perfectly comfortable and the tour guides extremely knowledgeable. This is one of the few lodges that offers hiking trips through the jungle as well as canal tours. $236

Manatus Hotel 1km south of the village centre ☎ 2709 8197, ⍦ manatuscostarica.com. Glitzy and intimate property with 12 spacious rooms featuring canopy beds, a/c, and flat-screen cable TV. The on-site spa tempts with a variety of treatments and there's a pretty pool and fitness room. Several excursions are offered, including kayaking and fishing, and the service is exemplary throughout. $270

★**Mawamba Lodge** 1km north of the village ☎ 2709 8181, ⍦ grupomawamba.com. This large, ritzy lodge has a daily slide show, environmentally friendly boats and round-the-clock cold beers from room service. The *cabina*-style rooms come with ceiling fans and private bathroom, there's a large pool and jacuzzi, and the village and ocean are just a short walk away. $230

Pachira Lodge Opposite the Natural History Museum at the north end of the village ☎ 2257 2242, ⍦ pachira lodge.com. This luxurious establishment has 88 spacious, attractive rooms in wood cabins, linked by covered walkways, with large en-suite, hot-water bathrooms, along with a pool and imaginative tour options. $229

★**Tortuga Lodge** ☎ 2257 0766, ⍦ tortugalodge.com. Owned by Costa Rica Expeditions, this is the plushest lodge in the area (but among the furthest from the village) with large, attractive en-suite rooms, exemplary service, excellent food, a riverside swimming pool and elegantly landscaped grounds from which several trails depart into the jungle. $279

Turtle Beach Lodge About 2km north of the village ☎ 2248 0707, ⍦ turtlebeachlodge.com. The most removed of the major lodges, this secluded upmarket option has handsome and supremely comfortable rooms and an inviting pool. Being so far away from the village means you're more reliant on the lodge and what it offers, but it's an easy trade-off to make, as the food and tours are top-notch, not to mention the stunning 175-acre grounds. $218

CAMPING

Camping on the beach is not allowed, though you can set up a tent for about $3 per day at the mown enclosure near the ranger station at the southern end of the village, where you enter the park. It's in a sheltered situation, away from the sea breezes, and there's drinking water and toilets. Bring a groundsheet and mosquito net, and make sure your tent is waterproof.

EATING AND DRINKING

Tortuguero village offers homely Caribbean food with a wide selection of fresh fish, as well as more international options. Expect to pay more for a meal here than you would in other parts of Costa Rica, but the standard is comparatively high.

★**Budda Café** In the village centre ☎ 2709 8084. Relaxing spot with seats along the canal, *Budda* offers an assortment of tantalizing crêpes ($5), pizzas and speciality drinks, such as coffee with rum, ice cream and milk. Daily noon–9pm.

La Casona On the north side of the village football pitch. Thatched open-air restaurant that's popular for its palm hearts lasagne ($8) and tasty Caribbean fare such as *casados*. When there's a breeze, this is one of the more idyllic lunch spots in the village. Daily 8.30–11.30am & 1.30–8.30pm.

Centro Social La Culebra Next door to the dock. This social club has a booming nightly disco, though the clientele can be a bit rough. Daily 8pm–late.

Dorling's Bakery Attached to Cabinas Marbella. A very basic interior belies heavenly baked goods, gut-busting breakfasts ($4–5) and coffee strong enough to see you through the morning. The service is friendly, too. Daily 5am–7pm.

Miss Junie's North end of village path, 50m before the Natural History Museum ☎ 2709 8029. Operating out of a dining hall, the town's most revered restaurant offers solid Caribbean food – red beans, jerk chicken, rice, chayote and breadfruit ($11), all on the same plate – dished up by local Miss Junie. Wash it down with an ice-cold beer. The standard, though, isn't quite as high as it once was and meals can be somewhat hit or miss. Daily noon–9pm.

★**Miss Miriam's** On the north side of the village football pitch ☎ 2709 8002. A good spot to watch the village football teams in action, this cheerful, immaculate restaurant serves Caribbean food, including chicken with rice and beans cooked in coconut milk, at very reasonable prices (most dishes around $6). Daily 7.30am–9pm.

El Muellecito In the middle of the village ☎ 2709 8104. One of Tortuguero's best breakfast spots, with tasty pancakes and fruit salad. For lunch and dinner the menu is heavy on Costa Rican regulars like grilled beef with rice and fried plantains. Daily 8am–9pm.

La Taberna Next door to the Bambú supermarket. Tortuguero's best bet for a laidback sundowner, this is the place to come to kick back to a reggae soundtrack and drink $2 beers. Daily 11am–11pm.

★**Wild Ginger** At the north end of the village ☎ 2709 8240. One of Tortuguero's newest restaurants and certainly

3

its most cosmopolitan, ecofriendly *Wild Ginger* exudes an unmistakeable Californian vibe. Its inventive dishes include treats like passionfruit chicken ($10) and wild ginger shrimp ($16); the prices are reasonable across the board.

Presently open only for dinner, but check to see if it's started serving lunch. The cosy on-site bar is open later than most other spots in the village. Restaurant daily 6–9pm; bar 6pm–midnight.

DIRECTORY

Medical services Tortuguero has a weekly medical service; otherwise emergencies and health problems should be referred to the park's administration headquarters, north of the village, near the airstrip.

Money and exchange There are no bank or money-changing facilities – bring all the cash you'll need with you.

Post office Although there's a post office in the middle of the village, mail may take three or four weeks just to make its way to Limón. If villagers are heading to Limón they might offer to carry letters for you and post them from there, which can be useful if you're staying here for any length of time.

Refugio Nacional de Vida Silvestre Barra del Colorado

Created to preserve the area's abundant fauna, the **REFUGIO NACIONAL DE VIDA SILVESTRE BARRA DEL COLORADO** lies at the northern end of Costa Rica's Caribbean coast, 99km northeast of San José near the border with Nicaragua. This ninety-square-kilometre, sparsely populated (by humans, at least) tract of land is crossed by the Río Colorado, which meets the Caribbean sea next to the village of Barra del Colorado. The grand Río San Juan marks the park's northern boundary, which is also the border with Nicaragua. The river continues north of the border all the way to the Lago de Nicaragua and almost all traffic in this area is by water.

Barra del Colorado

The small, quiet village of **Barra del Colorado**, the area's only settlement of any size, is inhabited by a mixed population of Afro-Caribbeans, Miskitos, Costa Ricans and a significant number of Nicaraguans, many of whom spilled over the border during the civil war. The village is divided into two halves: Barra Sur and the larger Barra Norte, which stand opposite each other across the mouth of the Río Colorado. Tropical hardwoods are still under siege from illegal logging around here – you may see giant tree trunks being towed along the river and into the Caribbean, from where they are taken down to Limón. There are no public services in town (no post office, police station, internet café or hospital) except for a couple of public phones outside the souvenir shop next to the airport and near the *Los Almendros* bar.

ACTIVITIES IN BARRA

Very few people come to Barra on a whim. As far as tourism goes, **sportfishing** is its *raison d'être*, and numerous lodges offer packages and transportation from San José. Large schools of tarpon and snook, two big-game fish prized for their fighting spirit, ply these waters, as does the garfish, a primeval throwback that looks something like a cross between a fish and a crocodile. The sportfishing season runs from January to May, and September to October.

Because of the impenetrability of the cover, activities for non-fishing tourists are limited to **wildlife-watching** from a boat in one of the many waterways and lagoons. The usual sloths and monkeys are in residence, and you'll certainly hear the wild hoot of howler monkeys shrieking through the still air. If you are really lucky, and keep your eyes peeled, you might catch sight of a *manatí* (manatee, or sea cow) going by underneath. These large, benevolent seal-like creatures are on the brink of becoming an endangered species. This is **shark** territory so you shouldn't swim here – even though you may see locals taking that risk.

It is extremely **hot** and painfully **humid** around Barra. Wear a hat and sunscreen and, if possible, stay in the shade during the hottest part of the day. It rains throughout the year, though February, March and April are the driest months.

ARRIVAL AND DEPARTURE   BARRA DEL COLORADO

By lancha In terms of the time it takes to get there, Barra is one of the least accessible places in the country. Most people arrive either by *lancha* from Tortuguero (1hr 45min) or Puerto Lindo (45min). For the latter you'll need to catch the 2pm bus from Cariari (2hr), which will drop you at the small dock in Puerto Lindo where a *lancha* will be waiting to pick up passengers for Barra.

Lanchas arrive in Barra Sur, or, if you ask, will take you directly to your accommodation.
By plane The flight (30min) from San José to Barra (landing at Barra Sur) affords stupendous views of volcanoes, unfettered lowland tropical forest and the coast; both Sansa (☎ 2290 4100) and NatureAir (☎ 2290 6000) operate this route.

ACCOMMODATION

Because of Barra's inaccessibility and its emphasis on fishing, hardly anyone comes here for just one night. Most lodges are devoted exclusively to **fishing packages**, although you could, theoretically, call in advance and arrange to stay as an independent, non-fishing guest. The lodges can provide details on their individual packages; generally they comprise meals, accommodation, boat, guide and tackle, and some may offer air transfer to/from San José, boat lunches, drinks and other extras. They do not include fishing licence or tips.

Casa Mar Lodge Across the river from Barra del Colorado ☎ 1 800 543 0282. Luxurious, elegant cabins set in lovely gardens with hiking trails through jungle to the beach. Fishing packages only, seven nights $2950
Río Colorado Fishing Lodge Barra Sur ☎ 2232 4063, ⓦ riocoloradolodge.com. Built on walkways over the river, the oldest lodge in town has lots of character. Comfortable wooden rooms are homely and come with a/c, cable TV and bathrooms. Enjoy good food and pretty Barra Norte views in the dining room, where local musicians

often perform in the evenings. Tours of the rainforest and Tortuguero are also offered and a tame tapir wanders the grounds. Five-night packages $2133; independent rate per night $550
Silver King Lodge ☎ 2794 0139 or ☎ 1 877 335 0755, ⓦ silverkinglodge.net. Efficient, well-equipped fishing lodge, with spacious rooms, a bar, restaurant, swimming pool, jacuzzi and TV with US channels. Closed July & Dec. Three-night packages with fishing $2750; without fishing $1300

THE RÍO SAN JUAN AND THE NICARAGUAN BORDER

Heading to or from Barra via the Sarapiquí area in the Zona Norte entails a trip along the Río Sarapiquí to the mighty **Río San Juan**. Flowing from Lago de Nicaragua to the Caribbean, the San Juan marks most of Costa Rica's border with Nicaragua, and the entire northern edge of the Refugio Nacional de Vida Silvestre Barra del Colorado. It's theoretically in Nicaraguan territory, but Costa Ricans have the right to travel on the river – though this eastern stretch of the San Juan has been the source of a diplomatic dispute between the two countries since late 2010 (see box, p.422). There isn't, however, an official entry point between the two countries so it's technically illegal to cross into either country along this stretch. It is possible to cross into Nicaragua 7km north of Los Chiles (see box, p.227).

One bizarre phenomenon local to this area is the migration of **bull sharks** from the saltwater Caribbean up the Río San Juan to the freshwater Lago de Nicaragua. They are unique in the world in making the transition, apparently without trauma, from being saltwater to freshwater sharks.

You'll notice much evidence of **logging** here, especially at the point where the Sarapiquí flows into the Río San Juan – the lumber industry has long had carte blanche in this area, due to the non-enforcement of existing anti-logging laws. The **Nicaraguan side** of the Río San Juan, part of the country's huge Reserva Indio Maíz, looks altogether wilder than its southern neighbour, with thick primary rainforest creeping right to the edge of the bank. Partly because of logging, and the residual destruction of its banks, the Río San Juan is silting up, and even shallow-bottomed *lanchas* get stuck in this once consistently deep river. It's a far cry from the sixteenth and seventeenth centuries, when pirate ships used to sail all the way along the Río San Juan to Lago de Nicaragua, from where they could wreak havoc on the Spanish Crown's ports and shipping.

Reserva Biológica Hitoy-Cerere

60km south of Limón • Daily 8am–4pm • $10 • ☎ 2795 1446, Ⓦ sinac.go.cr

A three-hour road-trip south of Limón is one of Costa Rica's least visited national reserves, the **RESERVA BIOLÓGICA HITOY-CERERE**. Sandwiched between the Tanyí, Telier and Talamanca indigenous reservations, this very rugged, isolated terrain – ninety-one square kilometres of it – has no campsites, washrooms or any real services to speak of, though there is a ranger station at the entrance.

In the Bribrí language, *hitoy* means "woolly" (the rocks in its rivers are covered with algae, and everything else has grown a soft fuzz of moss); and *cerere* means "clear waters", of which there are many. One of the wettest reserves in all of Costa Rica, it receives a staggering 4m of **rain** per year in some areas, with no dry season at all. Its complicated biological profile reflects the changing altitudes within the park. The top canopy trees loom impressively tall – some as high as 50m – and epiphytes, bromeliads, orchids and lianas grow everywhere beneath the very dense cover. **Wildlife** is predictably abundant, but most of the species are nocturnal and rarely seen, although you might spot three-toed sloths, and perhaps even a brocket deer. You'll probably hear howler monkeys, and may glimpse white-faced monkeys. Pacas and rare frogs abound, many of them shy and little-studied. More visible are the 115 species of **bird**, from large black vultures and hummingbirds to trogons and dazzling blue kingfishers.

Sendero Espavel

Hitoy-Cerere's **Sendero Espavel**, a tough nine-kilometre hike, leads south from the ranger station through lowland and primary rainforest past clear streams, small waterfalls and beautiful vistas of the green Talamanca hills. Only **experienced tropical hikers** should attempt it; bring a compass, rubber boots, rain gear and water. The trail begins at a very muddy hill; after about 1km, in the area of secondary forest, you'll notice the white-and-grey wild cashew trees (*espavel*) after which the trail is named. Follow the sign here; it leads off to the right and cuts through swathes of thick forest before leaving the reserve and entering the Talamanca reservation, which is officially off-limits. At the reserve's boundary, take the trail leading up a steep hill. This ends at the Río Moín, 4.5km from the start. All you can do now is turn back, taking care to negotiate the numerous fallen trees, tumbled rocks and boulders. Many of them were felled by the earthquake in 1991; older casualties are carpeted in primeval plants and mosses. The only possible respite from very dense jungle terrain are the small dried-up river beds that follow the streams and tributaries of the ríos Cerere and Hitoy.

ARRIVAL AND DEPARTURE

RESERVA BIOLÓGICA HITOY-CERERE

By car Having a car is the most convenient way to get to Hitoy-Cerere. From Puerto Limón follow Hwy-36 towards Cahuita. After 33km take the right fork towards Penhurst and follow the signs to the reserve.

By bus and taxi Using public transport, you'll need to take the bus from Limón to Valle de Estrella, and get off at the end of the line at a banana town called (confusingly) both Fortuna and Finca Seis. It's 15km from here to the reserve, most of it through banana plantation. A local 4WD taxi – ask at the plantation office – can take you there, and will return to pick you up at a mutually agreed time for $15–20.

ACCOMMODATION

There is a ranger station at the entrance with a small dormitory where you can bed down for the night ($6/ person). Beyond this, the nearest accommodation is at the *Selva Bananito Eco Lodge* (see p.175) or the Sloth Sanctuary (see p.191).

Cahuita and around

Like other villages on the Talamanca coast, the tiny village of **CAHUITA** has become a byword for relaxed, inexpensive Caribbean holidays, with a laidback atmosphere and great Afro-Caribbean food, not to mention top surfing beaches further south along the coast. The local "dry" season is between March and April, and from September to October, though it's pretty wet all year round. Close to the village, the largely marine **PARQUE NACIONAL CAHUITA** (see p.190) was created to protect one of Costa Rica's few living coral reefs; many people come here to snorkel and take glass-bottom-boat rides.

The sheltered bay was originally filled with *cawi* trees, known in Spanish as *sangrilla* ("bloody") on account of the tree's thick red sap – Cahuita's name comes from the Miskito words *cawi* and *ta*, which means "point". Most of the inhabitants are descended from Afro-Caribbean settlers of the Bocas del Toro area of Panama and from workers brought to help build the Jungle Train. Older residents remember when fishing, small-scale farming and some quadrille-dancing formed the mainstays of local life. These days, Cahuita – along with the rest of the Talamanca coast – has become very popular with backpackers and surfers, its semi-Rasta culture offering an escape from the cultural homogeneity of highland and Pacific Costa Rica. In recent years the community has made huge and largely successful efforts to eradicate the once-notorious drug scene, with extra policemen drafted in to patrol the sandy streets. Still, it's worth being cautious: lock your door and windows, never leave anything on the beach and avoid walking alone in unlit places at night.

Cahuita comprises just two puddle-dotted, gravel-and-sand streets running parallel to the sea, intersected by a few cross-streets. Though it seems like anything nailed down has been turned into some kind of small business, you'll still see a couple of private homes among the haphazard conglomeration of signs advertising *cabinas* and restaurants. The main street runs from the national park's entrance at Kelly Creek to the northern end of the village, marked more or less by the football field. Beyond here it continues two or three kilometres north along **Playa Negra**.

Tree of Life

Northern edge of Playa Negra • Jan to mid-April, Nov & Dec Tues–Sun 9am–3pm; July to late Aug Tues–Sun 11am guided tour; closed mid-April to June & late Aug to Oct • $12, including the tour • ☎ 8610 0490, ⓦ treeoflifecostarica.com

Opened in 2008, Playa Negra's **Tree of Life** has quickly become one of Cahuita's more popular outings. In between towering ginger plants and below a dense canopy, this still-growing wildlife rescue centre is devoted to providing care and comfort to indigenous species from the surrounding region – and sometimes further afield – with the goal of releasing as many as possible back into the wild. The centre lovingly cares for numerous mammals, including capuchin and spider monkeys, kinkajous, peccary and coatis, and also has a walk-in enclosure teeming with brilliantly coloured butterflies. The tours are an excellent source of information not only on regional wildlife, but also on flora from their natural habitats – the centre is set on the grounds of a botanical garden chock-full of endemic plants and trees.

The beaches

You can swim at either of the village's two **beaches**, although neither is fantastic: the first 400m or so of the narrow **Playa Cahuita** (also known as the White Sand Beach or Kelly Creek), just south of the village in the national park, is particularly dangerous because of riptides. At the northern end of the village, **Playa Negra** (or Black Sand Beach) is safe for swimming in most places but also littered with driftwood. The beach south of Punta Cahuita – sometimes called **Playa Vargas** – is better for swimming than those in the village. It's protected from raking breakers by the coral reef and also patrolled by lifeguards. It does, however, take some effort to reach it – you need to follow a trail for half a kilometre or so through thick vegetation and mangrove swamps that back the shore.

Note that nude or topless bathing is definitely unacceptable at either beach, as is wandering through the village in just a bathing suit.

3

PIRATES AND GHOSTS

According to local history, in the 1800s the coastal waters of the Caribbean crawled with pirates. Two **shipwrecks** in the bay on the north side of Punta Cahuita are believed to be pirate wrecks, one Spanish and one French. You can sometimes see the Spanish wreck on glass-bottom-boat tours (see box, p.188) to the reef although it has been (illegally) picked over and the only thing of interest that remains is encrusted manacles – an indication of the dastardly motives of the ship's crew.

In her excellent collection of local folk history and oral testimony, *What Happen*, sociologist Paula Palmer quotes Selles Johnson, descendant of the original turtle-hunters, on the pirate activity on these shores:

…them pirate boats was on the sea and the English gunboats was somewhere out in the ocean, square rigger, I know that. I see them come to Bocas, square rigger. They depend on breeze. So the pirate boats goes in at Puerto Vargas or at Old Harbour where calm sea, and the Englishmen can't attack them because they in Costa Rican water…so those two ships that wreck at Punta Cahuita, I tell you what I believes did happen. Them was hiding in Puerto Vargas and leave from there and come around the reef, and they must have stopped because in those days the British ship did have coal. You could see the smoke steaming in the air. So the pirate see it out in the sea and they comes in here to hide.

Where you find pirates you also find pirate ghosts, it seems, doomed to guard their ill-gotten treasure for eternity. Treasure from the wrecks near Old Harbour, just south of Cahuita, is said to be buried in secret caches on land. One particular spot, supposedly guarded by a fearsome headless spirit dressed in a white suit, has attracted a fair share of treasure hunters. No one has yet succeeded in exhuming the booty, however; all of them have fainted, fallen sick or become mysteriously paralysed in the attempt.

ARRIVAL AND DEPARTURE
CAHUITA AND AROUND

By bus The easiest way to get to Cahuita from San José is by bus on the comfortable direct Transportes MEPE (☎ 2257 8129) service from the Atlántico Norte terminal that continues on to Puerto Viejo. Taking a bus from San José to Puerto Limón and then changing for Cahuita is only marginally less expensive than taking the direct bus and increases travel time by at least an hour. In Cahuita, buses arrive at the bus station on the main road into the village centre, about 150m northwest of the park.

Destinations Bribrí (18 daily; 30–50min); Puerto Limón (22 daily; 1hr); Puerto Viejo de Talamanca (22 daily; 30min); San José (5 daily; 4hr); Sixaola (9 daily; 1hr 30min).

By car Cahuita is 43km southeast of Limón on Hwy-36. Pay attention, as the turn-off sign is by no means obvious.

INFORMATION

Tourist information The website ⓦ cahuita.cr is the best locally generated resource for information on Cahuita, with comprehensive accommodation, restaurant and tour listings. The tour companies provide the only visitor information in the village itself.

ACCOMMODATION

Though popular with budget travellers, Cahuita is not especially cheap. If you're travelling in a group, however, you can keep costs to a minimum because most *cabinas* charge per room and have space for at least three or four people. Upstairs rooms are slightly more expensive, due to the sea breezes and occasional ocean views. The **centre of the village** has scores of options, the best of which are listed below; staying here is convenient for restaurants, bars and the national park. There's also accommodation in all price ranges on the long (3km or so) road that runs by the sea north along **Playa Negra**. It's quieter here, and the beach is not bad, though women (even if travelling in groups) and those without their own car are better off staying in town; a number of rapes and muggings have been committed along this road at night. You'll find several camping options in the vicinity; the nicest is at the Puerto Vargas ranger station in the national park (see p.191).

IN THE VILLAGE

Alby Lodge Down the signposted path behind Hotel Kelly Creek at the south end of the village ☎ 2755 0031, ⓦ albylodge.com. Built and run by its Austrian owners, this well-equipped lodge, set in pleasant grounds, has individual thatched wooden cabins with porch, hammock and private bathroom. There's an open-air common kitchen and dining *cabina* and wi-fi, too. $\overline{\$60}$

Cabinas Arrecife On the seafront next to Edith's restaurant ☏ 2755 0081, ⓦ cabinasarrecife.com. This relaxed, backpacker-style accommodation has cheap, simply furnished rooms (some with sea views), hammocks slung on the porch and snorkelling gear and bikes to hire. The Spanish classes and sustainable-agriculture workshops taught on-site set it apart from other options in the area. $\overline{\$30}$

Cabinas Jenny On the beach ☏ 2755 0256, ⓦ cabinasjenny.com. Beautiful rooms (especially the more expensive ones upstairs) have high wooden ceilings, sturdy bunks, mosquito nets, fans and wonderful sea views. Deckchairs and hammocks are provided, there's on-site parking and stout locks on all doors. $\overline{\$31}$

★ El Encanto Inn Past the police station in the north of the village ☏ 2755 0113, ⓦ elencanto cahuita.com. Bright and pleasantly furnished B&B, with a gorgeous garden, pool, spa, seven beautifully decorated doubles and a delicious breakfast included in the room rate. There's also a self-contained house that sleeps up to six. Double $\overline{\$96}$, house $\overline{\$260}$

Hotel Kelly Creek Beside the national park beach at Kelly Creek ☏ 2755 0007, ⓦ hotelkellycreek.com. Four vast, wood-panelled rooms right by the park entrance, each with two double beds and mosquito nets, and there's a good Spanish restaurant on-site (open daily from 6.30pm). $\overline{\$62}$

Secret Garden Diagonally opposite Alby Lodge ☏ 2755 0581. Set in a charming rock garden, this popular budget choice has cosy rooms with private bathrooms. Movies from their library shown on request and there's free wi-fi. $\overline{\$33}$

PLAYA NEGRA

Atlantida Lodge Next to the football field on the road to Playa Negra, about 1km from the village ☏ 2755 0115, ⓦ atlantida.cr. This friendly spot is one of the village's pricier options with pretty grounds, good security, and a pool, jacuzzi and poolside bar. The cool rooms are decorated in tropical yellows and pinks, with heated water, and there's free coffee and bananas all day. $\overline{\$97}$

Bungalows Malu Beyond the football field ☏ 2755 0114, ⓔ bungalow-malu@cahuita.cr. Six natural-wood octagonal-shaped *cabinas* with intricate stone and terracotta work set in a large tropical garden facing the sea, decorated with the owner's paintings. Each is spotless and comfortably furnished; all have a/c and some have cable TVs and kitchenettes. $\overline{\$72}$

Cabinas Algebra 2km or so up the Playa Negra Rd ☏ 2755 0057, ⓦ cabinasalgebra.com. Run by a

CAHUITA VILLAGE

Tree of Life (500m)

0   200
metres

● CAFÉS AND RESTAURANTS	
Bananas	1
Café Chocolatte	8
Café del Parquecito	6
Cha Cha Cha	4
La French Riviera	7
Miss Edith's	3
Palenque Luisa	5
Sobre Las Olas	2
Vista del Mar	9

■ BARS AND CLUBS	
Coco's	3
Reggae Bar	1
Ricky's Bar	2

■ ACCOMMODATION	
Alby Lodge	13
Atlantida Lodge	7
Bungalows Malu	5
Cabinas Algebra	1
Cabinas Arrecife	10
Cabinas Iguana	8
Cabinas Jenny	11
Cabinas Nirvana	6
Chalet Hibiscus	4
El Encanto Inn	9
Hotel Kelly Creek	14
Magellan Inn	3
Secret Garden	12
Suizo Loco Lodge	2

3

Sloth Sanctuary (11km) & Puerto Limón (44km)

PLAZA VIQUEZ

Playa Negra

Brigette Tours

CARIBBEAN SEA

Football Field

LA UNION

Pastry shop/ Bakery

Puerto Limón (45km)

Police

Cahuita Tours

CALLE PRINCIPAL

36

School

Supermercado Safari

Banco de Costa Rica

Brisas del Mar

CyberNet

Mr Big J's

Terminal Cahuita

Puerto Viejo (15km)

Kelly Creek Entrance

PARQUE NACIONAL CAHUITA

3

TOURS AND ACTIVITIES AROUND CAHUITA

The principal daylight activity in Cahuita involves taking a boat trip out to the Parque Nacional Cahuita's coral reef to **snorkel** – any of the town's tour companies or local guides can take you ($20). You can **surf** at Cahuita – Cahuita Tours and Turística Cahuita both rent out boards – though Puerto Viejo (see p.192) has better waves. Wherever you swim, either in the park itself or on Playa Negra, don't leave possessions unattended, as even your grubby T-shirt and old shorts may be stolen. All the major tour operators in Cahuita offer combined jeep trips to local villages and the beach ($50). Exploradores Outdoors in Puerto Viejo (see box, p.194) can pick up from Cahuita for their whitewater rafting trips on the Río Pacuare.

★**Brigitte Tours** Playa Negra ☎2755 0053, ⓦ brigittecahuita.com. Leads a variety of enjoyable horseriding tours around Cahuita, including a 6hr trip through the jungle to a farm and waterfall ($85).

Mr Big J's Towards the Parque Nacional Cahuita ranger station ☎2755 0328. Long-running friendly company that offers a variety of tours and acts as the unofficial village information centre. It also has a book exchange, laundry facilities ($5 for a big bag) and bike rentals ($7).

Cahuita Tours 50m south of the police station in the village centre ☎2755 0000, ⓦ cahuitatours .com. Specializes in group snorkelling outings to the national park ($50), but also combines them with hikes and offers day-trips to KéköLdi ($65).

friendly Austrian couple, these funky, attractive *cabinas* are some distance from town, but the owners offer free pick-up from the village, as well as haircuts and laundry service. Good long-term rates. The tasty meals at its on-site restaurant *Bananas* (see p.190) are enough to keep you from wandering far for other options. $23

★**Cabinas Iguana** On the first side-road past the football field ☎2755 0005, ⓦ cabinas-iguana.com. One of the best budget spots in town, with dorm beds and lovely wood-panelled *cabinas* on stilts set back from the beach, a large screened veranda, laundry service, book exchange and a swimming pool with adorable waterfall and sundeck. The friendly Swiss owners also rent out two apartments and a three-bedroom house with kitchen. Dorm $25, *cabinas* $45, apartment $55, house $110

★**Cabinas Nirvana** About 100m back along the road adjacent to Reggae Bar ☎2755 0110, ⓦ cabinas nirvana.com. There are four attractive *cabinas*, one airy bungalow and one basic room to choose from at this pretty and inviting property; all have mosquito nets and free wi-fi, while the bungalow also has a/c. The affable owners are exceedingly helpful and there's a pool and on-site parking. The owners can arrange snorkelling tours to the national park with one of the best guides in the area. Double $30, *cabinas* $45, bungalow $75

Chalet Hibiscus 2.5km north of village on the right ☎2755 0021, ⓔ hibiscus@ice.co.cr. Three chalets and four cabins sit on a small point by the sea with beautiful views, good security and friendly owners. The larger chalet is open and breezy, with a veranda and hammock, rustic wooden decor, an unusual wood-and-rope spiral staircase and comfortable rooms. There's also a swimming pool, wi-fi, games room and a garden sloping down to the sea. $55

★**Magellan Inn** 3km up Playa Negra, on a small signposted road leading off to the left ☎2755 0035, ⓦ magellaninn.com. Run by a friendly Canadian woman, this comfortable, quiet hotel has beautiful gardens dotted with pre-Columbian sculptures and a small pool. The hacienda-style rooms have rattan furniture and hot water; some also have a/c and TVs. Rates include continental breakfast, and there's also wi-fi, a bar and an excellent French Creole restaurant, though it's only open in high season and then only to guests. Secure on-site parking. $68

★**Suizo Loco Lodge** 200m down approach road to Playa Negra ☎2755 0349, ⓦ suizolocolodge.com. Immaculate, Swiss-run, stylish hotel built with great attention to detail and an ecofriendly focus. The staff are particularly helpful and knowledgeable about local activities. There's a good restaurant and a great pool with whirlpool. All rooms have a TV, phone, fridge and hairdryer, and there's wi-fi throughout. $115

EATING

Cahuita has plenty of places to eat fresh local food, with a surprisingly cosmopolitan selection. As with accommodation, prices can be higher elsewhere in Costa Rica, though the quality in general more than makes up for it. As you might expect, the expat and Creole impact is strong and restaurants tend to be creative with their influences.

FROM TOP PUERTO VIEJO DE TALAMANCA (P.192); SLOTH SANCTUARY (P.191) >

Bananas Cabinas Algebra, Playa Negra. Inviting, family-run restaurant serving superb Creole-Caribbean cuisine, such as roasted vegetables with rice and beans ($6). The portions are ample and there is live music some nights. Daily 8am–1pm & 5–8pm.

Café Chocolatte On the principal cross-street where it intersects the main road ☎2755 0010. Using natural ingredients this cute café makes inventive breakfasts, such as a country-style tortilla – eggs and vegetables wrapped inside a pancake ($3.50). They serve freshly baked, crispy cheese bread with good coffee to wash it down. Mon–Fri 6.30am–2pm.

Café del Parquecito Behind the village park ☎2755 0279. This excellent breakfast spot in the village dishes up fresh juices, pancakes and French toast ($4). In the evening, the menu features lighter fare; the vegetarian wrap ($7) is divine. Thurs–Sat 6am–2pm & 5pm–late.

★**Cha Cha Cha** Next door to Cahuita Tours. Fantastic, reasonably priced gourmet cuisine – exotic salads, grilled squid ($11), seafood and Tex-Mex – prepared by a French-Canadian chef and served in a pretty setting with fresh flowers on the tables and fairy lights at night. Tues–Sun noon–10pm.

La French Riviera On the main road into the village across from the Banco Costa Rica ☎2755 0050. Friendly pizza and crêpe joint with a few outdoor tables near the village entrance. Most of the twenty or so pizzas on offer, such as a four-cheese, go for around $9 while the savoury crêpes cost $4–5. Mon–Sat 10am–9pm.

★**Miss Edith's** Northern end of the village ☎8782 4192. Justifiably popular among tourists, *Miss Edith's* dishes up Cahuita's best Creole food. Dig into tasty rice-and-beans, *rundown* (coconut stew with vegetables, fish or meat; $10), *pan bon* (sweet bread) and a wide range of vegetarian dishes. Top off the meal with home-made ice cream and herbal teas. The service is notoriously slow, especially at dinner, and no alcohol is served. Daily 7am–9pm.

Palenque Luisa In the middle of the village opposite the grocery store. This popular restaurant offers an extensive menu of *casados* ($9) and fish and Creole dishes. Enjoy live calypso music on Saturday nights. Tues–Sun noon–8pm.

★**Sobre Las Olas** Northern end of the village, right on the beach. Atmospheric, classy hangout serving first-rate seafood – the lobster is particularly succulent – with the sound of lapping waves in the background. It's easily one of the more expensive spots in the village (most mains are around $15–20) but it rarely disappoints. Wed–Sun noon–10pm.

Vista del Mar Near Kelly Creek. Known by locals as "El Chines", this barn-sized backpackers' favourite has a vast menu featuring Chinese food, as well as inexpensive rice-and-bean combos ($5–8) and fish dishes. Daily noon–9pm.

DRINKING AND NIGHTLIFE

Coco's The centre of the village. *The* place to party in Cahuita, with a pleasant balcony over the main street, a dancefloor inside, nonstop reggae tunes and gaggles of young backpackers soaking up the atmosphere. If you're a single woman you'll inevitably be chatted up by the resident dreadlocked hustlers, though they're harmless enough. Friday is Reggae Night, though it seems like every night is reggae night. Daily noon–late.

Reggae Bar Playa Negra. Local Rasta hangout directly opposite the beach with a refreshingly downbeat vibe and filling Caribbean cuisine. More inviting than some of the spots in the village and made more alluring by the sight of crashing waves. Daily noon–midnight.

Ricky's Bar At the intersection of the main road into the village and the principal cross-street. If you've tired of *Coco's*, this place, with its large, rather dark interior and powerful sound system, operates somewhat erratic opening times but it gets heaving with live music on Wednesday and Saturday nights. Daily 1pm–midnight.

DIRECTORY

Internet Most cafés offer free wi-fi; *Café Chocolatte* (see above) is one of the more inviting spots where you can settle in.

Money and exchange There's a bank at the strip mall attached to the bus station.

Petrol station The nearest petrol station is about 7km south of Cahuita on the road to Puerto Viejo.

Police The small police station is on the last beach-bound road at the north end of the village.

Post office Next door to the police station. It keeps erratic hours, though is theoretically open Mon–Fri 8am–noon & 1.30–5.30pm.

Parque Nacional Cahuita

On the southern edge of the Cahuita • Mon–Fri 8am–4pm, Sat & Sun 7am–5pm • $10 • ☎2755 0302

One of Costa Rica's smallest national parks, 10.7-square-kilometre **PARQUE NACIONAL CAHUITA** covers a wedge-shaped piece of land that encompasses the area between Punta Cahuita and the main highway and, most importantly, the **coral reef** (*arrecife*) about 500m offshore. On land, Cahuita protects the coastal rainforest, a lowland habitat of semi-mangroves and tall canopy cover that backs the gently curving white-sand beaches of Playa Vargas to the south and Playa Cahuita to the north. Resident **birds** include ibis and kingfisher, along with white-faced capuchin monkeys, sloths and snakes, but the only animals you're likely to see are howler monkeys and, perhaps, coati, who scavenge around the northern section of the park, where bins overflow with rubbish left by day-trippers.

Note that **snorkelling** is not permitted on your own; you must make arrangements with a guide or go on a tour (see box, p.188).

The beach trail

The park's one **trail** begins at the Kelly Creek entrance and continues on to the Puerto Vargas ranger station 7km away. It skirts the beach for most of its length, with a gentle path so wide it feels like a road, covered with leaves and other brush and marked by segments of boardwalk. Stick to the trail, as snakes abound here. The Río Perzoso, about 2km from Kelly Creek, or 5km from the Puerto Vargas trailhead, is not always fordable, unless you like wading through chest-high water when you can't actually see how deep it is. Similarly, at high tide the beach is impassable in places: ask the ranger at the Puerto Vargas entrance about the tide schedules. Walking this trail can be unpleasantly humid and buggy: it's best to go in the morning. Despite the dense cover of tall trees, when it rains, you'll still get wet.

ARRIVAL AND INFORMATION   PARQUE NACIONAL CAHUITA

Park entry There are two entrances to the park, one at Kelly Creek at the southern end of Cahuita village (open during daylight hours) and another at Puerto Vargas (Mon–Fri 8am–4pm, Sat & Sun 7am–5pm), 4km south-east of Cahuita along the Limón–Sixaola Road.

ACCOMMODATION

Puerto Vargas campsite You'll find good camping facilities at the Puerto Vargas entrance, complete with barbecue grill, pit toilets and showers, but you'll need to bring your own drinking water, insect repellent and a torch. Be careful, too, not to pitch your tent too close to the high-tide line; check with the rangers first. Theft is also a problem: don't leave anything unattended and ask the rangers for advice – they may be able to look after your belongings. $3

Sloth Sanctuary

11km north of Cahuita and 1km north of the Puente Río Estrella • Open year-round, first tour at 7am, last one departs at 2.30pm • $25; $125 with canoe ride and breakfast or lunch • ☎ 2750 0775, ⓦ slothsanctuary.com

The small **Sloth Sanctuary** sits on a small island at the mouth of the Río Estrella. The sanctuary functions as an important rehabilitation and research centre for injured and orphaned sloths, and, not surprisingly, is the best place in Costa Rica to see them up close. Several walking trails traverse the grounds and there's an observation platform for **birdwatching** (an incredible 312 species have been sighted here – bring binoculars). You may also spot white-faced, howler and spider monkeys. On the one-hour-thirty-minute **canoe tour** through the delta you can catch a glimpse of caimans, river otters and all kinds of birds.

CAHUITA CORAL

Arcing around Punta Cahuita, the *arrecife de Cahuita*, or **Cahuita reef**, comprises six square kilometres of coral, and is one of just two snorkelling reefs on this side of Costa Rica – the other is further south at the Refugio Nacional de Vida Silvestre Gandoca-Manzanillo (see p.201). **Corals** are actually tiny animals, single-celled polyps, that secrete limestone, building their houses around themselves. Over centuries the limestone binds together to form a multilayered coral reef. The coral thrives on algae, which, like land plants, transform light into energy to survive; reefs always grow close to the surface in transparent waters where they can get plenty of sun. The white-sand beaches along this part of the coast were formed by shards of excreted coral.

Unfortunately, Cahuita's once-splendid reef is dying, soured by agricultural chemicals from the rivers that run into the sea (the fault of the banana plantations), and from the silting up of these same rivers caused by topsoil runoff from logging, and the upheaval of the 1991 earthquake. The species that survive are common **brain coral**, grey and mushy like its namesake; **moose horn coral**, which is slightly red; and sallow-grey **deer horn coral**. In water deeper than 2m, you might also spot fan coral wafting elegantly back and forth.

This delicate **ecosystem** shelters more than 120 species of fish and the occasional green turtle. Lobsters, particularly the fearsome-looking spiny lobster, used to be common but are also falling victim to the reef's environmental problems. Less frail, and thus more common, is the blue parrotfish, so called because of its "beak": actually teeth soldered together. Unfortunately, the parrotfish is causing a few environmental problems of its own as it uses its powerful jaws to gnaw away at the coral's filigree-like structures and spines.

3

ARRIVAL AND DEPARTURE — SLOTH SANCTUARY

By bus To reach the Sloth Sanctuary by bus from Cahuita, take the Limón service and ask to be dropped off at the entrance, just before the Puente Río Estrella.

ACCOMMODATION

Sloth Sanctuary Lodge ⓣ2750 0775, ⓦslothsanctuary.com. The sanctuary's lodge has comfortable B&B accommodation in six spacious rooms with either a/c or fans; all have bathrooms and hot water. It's often full, so book ahead. **$113**

Puerto Viejo de Talamanca

The languorous village of **PUERTO VIEJO DE TALAMANCA** has become a byword for backpacker and surf-party culture, with a vibrant nightlife and an attendant drugs scene, though this is fairly low-key. Nevertheless, make sure your room is well secured at night and avoid wandering alone through the village in the small hours.

The village lies between the thickly forested hills of the Talamanca Mountains and the sea, where locals bathe and kids frolic with surfboards in the waves. It's a dusty little place in daylight hours but reasonably well cared for, with bright hand-painted signs pointing the way to *cabinas*, bars and restaurants. The main drag through the centre, potholed and rough, is crisscrossed by a few dirt streets and an offshoot road that follows the shore. As in Cahuita, many Europeans have been drawn to Puerto Viejo, and have set up their own businesses; you'll find lots of places offering health foods and New Age remedies. Most locals, however, are of Afro-Caribbean descent and signs of **indigenous culture** are more evident here than in Cahuita, with the **Reserva Indígena KéköLdi**, inhabited by about two hundred Bribrí and Cabécar peoples, skirting the southern end of the town.

It's **surfing**, however, that really pulls in the crowds; the stretch south of *Stanford's* restaurant at the southern end of Puerto Viejo offers some of the most challenging waves in the country and certainly the best on the Caribbean coast. Puerto Viejo's famous twenty-foot wave "**La Salsa Brava**" crashes ashore between December and March and from June to July; September and October, when La Salsa Brava disappears, are the quietest months of the year. Then there's the **South Caribbean Music and Arts Festival** (ⓣ2750

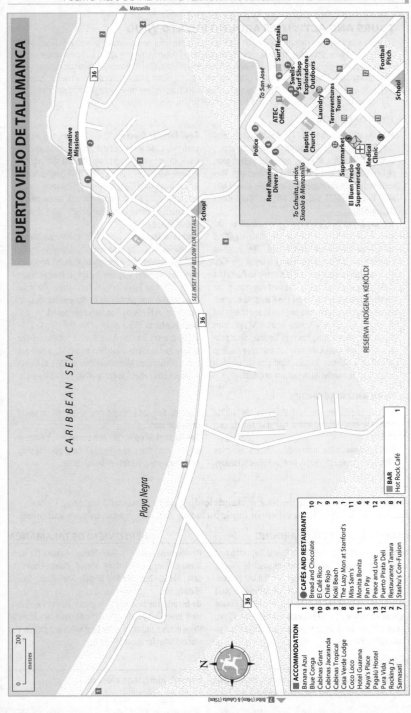

PUERTO VIEJO DE TALAMANCA

CARIBBEAN SEA

Playa Negra

RESERVA INDÍGENA KÉKÖLDI

Manzanillo

To San José

To Cahuita, Limón, Sixaola & Manzanillo

Bribrí (14km) & Cahuita (15km)

■ ACCOMMODATION	
Banana Azul	1
Blue Conga	4
Cabinas Grant	10
Cabinas Jacaranda	9
Cabinas Tropical	3
Casa Verde Lodge	8
Coco Loco	6
Hotel Guarana	11
Kaya's Place	5
Pagalú Hostel	13
Pura Vida	12
Rocking J's	2
Samasati	7

● CAFÉS AND RESTAURANTS	
Bread and Chocolate	10
El Café Rico	7
Chile Rojo	9
Koki Beach	3
The Lazy Mon at Stanford's	1
Miss Sam's	11
Monita Bonita	6
Pan Pay	4
Peace and Love	13
Puerto Pirata Deli	12
Restaurante Tamara	5
Stashu's Con-Fusion	2

■ BAR	
Hot Rock Café	1

SEE INSET MAP BELOW FOR DETAILS

School

Alternative Missions

Surf Rentals

Swells

Surf Shop
Exploradores
Outdoors

Football
Pitch

Police

ATEC
Office

Laundry

Terraventuras
Tours

School

Baptist
Church

Reef Runner
Divers

Supermarket

El Buen Precio
Supermercado

Medical
Clinic

0   200
metres

3

3

TOURS AND ACTIVITIES AROUND PUERTO VIEJO

Though a languorous day on the beach is the biggest draw for most visitors, there's no shortage of tours and activities on offer, from surfing, diving and kayaking along the coast to whitewater rafting and day-trips to indigenous reserves. **Skaters** can drop by Alternative Missions, where Bible study and skateboarding make odd bedfellows. The skate park – complete with a fun box, half pipe and bowl – is free and can provide boards and protective gear: known locally as the "Concrete Jungle", it also serves as a meeting place for the youth of Puerto Viejo.

TOUR OPERATORS

ATEC On the main road ☎ 2750 0398, ⓦ ateccr.org. The ATEC (Asociación Talamanqueña de Ecoturismo y Conservación) office arranges not-to-be-missed tours of KéköLdi ($25) and local Bribrí communities. They exclusively use local guides and also offer guided bike rides to Bribrí ($55) and even Afro-Caribbean dance classes ($35).

Exploradores Outdoors In the mini-mall on the main road on the east edge of the village ☎ 2750 2020, ⓦ exploradoresoutdoors.com. The excellent Exploradores Outdoors runs several tours of the local area, including a kayaking and hiking trip to Punta Uva ($49). They also lead one of the best day-trips in the country, whitewater rafting on the Río Pacuare, which includes four hours of rafting on Class III and IV sections of the river – a total of 38 rapids – and lunch ($99). Tours depart from their rafting centre in Siquirres, with pick-ups from Puerto Viejo, Cahuita or San José: they can drop you off at a different location than pick-up, which is handy if you're moving on to San José or Cahuita.

Reef Runner Divers In the village centre, on the seafront, a block west of the police station ☎ 2750 0480, ⓦ reefrunnerdivers.com. The best dive outfitter in town, Reef Runner Divers offers PADI certification as well as snorkelling ($35) and diving ($55) tours around Puerto Viejo; they also run a hedonistic sunset booze-and-beach-barbecue cruise that includes time to swim and unlimited alcohol ($25).

Seahorse Stables ☎ 2750 0468, ⓦ horsebackriding incostarica.com. The long-running, Argentine-owned Seahorse Stables lead a variety of tours on horseback along the coast and deep into the jungle. The beach tour (2.5hr; $75) from Playa Cocles to Punta Uva is one of the more popular trips, particularly for those with little to no experience, as the riding is on fairly even ground.

Terraventuras 100m south of the bus stop ☎ 2750 0750, ⓦ terraventuras.com. Runs a popular zip-line canopy tour ($55), birdwatching tour ($49), a half-day trip to the Gandoca-Manzanillo reserve ($55), as well as outings further afield, to destinations such as Arenal.

SURF AND BIKE SHOPS

Lessons offered by the surf shops in the village generally cost $20/hr, while half-day rentals cost around $25.

Surf Rentals On the main road at the eastern edge of the village ☎ 2750 1909. Hires out bikes ($15/day),

scooters, surf- and boogie boards and can organize surfing lessons.

Swells Surf Shop On the main road at the eastern edge of the village ☎ 8356 9947. Long-running shop that offers group classes and board rentals.

0062) held every year for the four weekends leading up to Easter, and featuring Costa Rican musicians playing a variety of music including ska, jazz, reggae, calypso and more.

ARRIVAL AND GETTING AROUND PUERTO VIEJO DE TALAMANCA

By bus All buses from San José to Puerto Viejo stop first in Limón and Cahuita and then continue south to Sixaola; the first bus leaves San José at 6am and the last at 4pm. The bus stop is on the beach road at Puerto Viejo's second cross-street. The last bus back to San José leaves Puerto Viejo at 4pm, while six daily buses (earliest at 6.45am, last at 7.15pm) head south from here along the coast to Manzanillo (30min).

Destinations Bribrí (18 daily; 20min); Cahuita (22 daily; 30min); Manzanillo (6 daily; 30min); Puerto Limón (10 daily; 1hr 30–2hr); San José (5 daily; 4hr 30min); Sixaola (9 daily; 1hr).

By bicycle The best way to negotiate Puerto Viejo's dirt-track streets is by cycling. You'll find several bicycle rental shops in town and many of the local hotels and *cabinas* also rent out bikes for about $5–7 a day.

INFORMATION

Tourist information There's no tourist information office but the village's tour operators (see box above) can

help with advice, maps and so on.

ACCOMMODATION

You shouldn't have any problem finding accommodation in Puerto Viejo, although it's still best to reserve a room in advance during high-season and surfing-season weekends (Dec–March, June & July). The majority of places in the village are simple *cabinas*, some without hot water, while more upmarket establishments line the coast south of the village. You can camp on the beaches, but budget travellers should forsake their tents for the excellent *Pagalú Hostel*.

IN THE VILLAGE

★ **Blue Conga** On the eastern edge of town ☎ 2750 0681, ⓦ hotelblueconga.com. One of the better choices in the village, this brightly painted hotel has breezy, pleasantly understated rooms. Breakfast is included, there's wi-fi and you can rent bikes and snorkelling gear. $75

Cabinas Grant On the main road, one block east from the Banco de Costa Rica ☎ 2750 0292. Spotless, locally run hotel with basic but serviceable rooms and dorm beds. Private rooms on the first floor have balconies and cost slightly more. Dorm $11, double $34

Cabinas Jacaranda Just north of the football field ☎ 2750 0069, ⓦ cabinasjacaranda.net. Basic but very clean option, with *cabinas* decorated in lively Guatemalan fabrics and set amid a lush tropical garden. $35

Cabinas Tropical On the eastern edge of the village ☎ 2750 0283, ⓦ cabinastropical.com. Small, quiet and clean hotel with ten large, comfortable rooms, and pet birds in the garden. Owned by a local ecologist couple who offer guided jungle hikes and birdwatching tours. $38

Casa Verde Lodge One block south of the main drag ☎ 2750 00015, ⓦ cabinascasaverde.com. Seventeen comfortable *cabinas*, decorated with shell mobiles and washed-up coral, with sparkling clean showers, ceiling fans, mosquito nets and space to sling hammocks. Get a poolside massage or lounge in the whirlpool near the frog garden. Owner Carolina sells art to benefit local indigenous tribes and those across the border in Panama. Bike rental and parking available. $80

★ **Coco Loco** Two blocks inland at the southern end of the village ☎ 2750 0281, ⓦ cocolocolodge.com. Just 150m from the beach, this lodge is one of the better options if you want to be in the village but a little apart from the attendant late-night revelry. The charming, well-kept bungalows are spread across four acres of attractive landscaped grounds and feature mosquito nets, cable TV and wi-fi. Discounts are offered for paying in cash. $75

Hotel Guarana South of the main drag on the way to the football field ☎ 2750 0244, ⓦ hotelguarana.com. Run by a friendly Italian couple, this lovely small hotel has attractive rooms, tiled bathrooms, hammocks and a communal kitchen. Climb up the treehouse in the garden for great views over the village. Internet access and parking available. $43

★ **Pagalú Hostel** One block back from the main street, across from the MegaSuper supermarket ☎ 2750 1930, ⓦ pagalu.com. By a wide margin the more sedate of the Puerto Viejo area's two hostels (*Rocking J's* being the other), immaculate and cosy *Pagalú* offers spacious doubles and dorms with lockers and wi-fi access. There's a shared kitchen area and the staff are quick to share their local knowledge. First come, first served and cash only. Dorm $12, double $26

Pura Vida Near the football field ☎ 2750 0002, ⓦ hotel-puravida.com. This popular budget hotel has ten pleasant rooms (with both private and shared baths), ceiling fans, mosquito nets, a pleasant veranda and garden. It tends to fill quickly. Breakfast is included. $32

Rocking J's On the southern edge of the village on Hwy-36 ☎ 2750 0665, ⓦ rockingjs.com. To say that *Rocking J's* has contributed its fair share to Puerto Viejo's reputation as a beachside backpacker's party paradise is an understatement, but it's a fun and friendly hostel nonetheless and not always as hedonistic as you may think. Accommodation includes dorm rooms with hammocks, cabins and a "king" suite, which has a double and single bed and a private bathroom and yard. There's wi-fi, bike and surfboard rental, a communal kitchen and the staff can provide information on the village and local activities. Dorm $11, cabin $26, king suite $60

PLAYA NEGRA AND AROUND

★ **Banana Azul** Playa Negra ☎ 2750 2035, ⓦ banana azul.com. Colourful and creatively designed lodge set in gorgeous grounds a short walk from the beach. Each room is spacious with a unique style; those on the top floor have particularly impressive views, and there's also a secluded two-bedroom apartment. The open-air lounge, restaurant and bar area look onto a pool punctuated by thatched-roof shades and vibrant flora. The on-site tour operator, Gecko Travel Adventures (☎ 2756 8412, ⓦ geckotrail.com), can book a variety of outings, including rafting trips, zip-lining and snorkelling. $118

Kaya's Place On the black volcanic sand beach 200m north of town ☎ 2750 0690, ⓦ kayasplace.com. Artistic and unique 26-room lodge built in Afro-Caribbean rustic style, using recycled driftwood from the beach and local materials; there's also a *cabina* and small *casita*, each of which can hold four people. It's run in an ecologically sensitive manner, though there have been complaints about the dust from the road. Parking available. $31

★ **Samasati** About 4 miles north of Puerto Viejo, ☎ 1 880 563 9643, ⓦ samasati.com. If you're looking to combine a stay in Puerto Viejo with yoga classes, *Samasati* is one of the best health-focused and ecologically-minded retreats in the country. The accommodation, ranging from bungalows to a large guesthouse, is impeccably designed and furnished and blends in well with the surroundings:

verandas provide spectacular views. The restaurant serves creatively prepared, mostly vegetarian dishes, and there's a full-service spa. A variety of packages are offered, including daily yoga classes and spa treatments. **$180**

EATING AND DRINKING

Puerto Viejo offers a surprisingly cosmopolitan range of places to eat or, for something more authentic, ATEC (see box, p.194) can put you in touch with village women who cook typical regional meals on request. Although relatively quiet during the day, Puerto Viejo thumps at night.

CAFÉS

★ **Bread and Chocolate** 50m south of the post office ☎2750 0723. People queue before this bakery opens – which, in a village of late risers, says something. A definite must-eat, run by cool expats, offering hearty breakfast in the form of cinnamon-oatmeal pancakes ($5.50), French toast, and creamy scrambled eggs. Lunch involves jerk chicken, tomato hummus, and roasted red peppers. Everything is home-made, even the mayo. No credit cards. Tues–Sat 6.30am–6.30pm, Sun 6.30am–2.30pm.

El Café Rico Opposite Cabinas Casa Verde ☎2750 0510. Englishman Roger knows everything about the locality and can hook you up with anything you need. His legendary café serves some of the best coffee in town, made with Café Britt Arabica, as well as great fruit plates, tasty sandwiches and crêpes ($3.50). Fri–Wed 6am–2pm.

Peace and Love On the seafront near the police station ☎2750 0758. An attractive hippy café specializing in Italian breads, with a nice mix of fresh seafood and salads (from $5), too. Daily 8am–8pm.

BARS AND RESTAURANTS

Chile Rojo On the main road in the mini-mall ☎2750 0025. Old standby serving tasty Thai-style food, with main courses from $5–9. A popular place for a sundowner, with 2-for-1 drinks at happy hour (from 5pm). Thurs–Tues noon–11pm.

Hot Rock Café At the junction of the main street and the road leading to the police station ☎2750 0525. One of the town's more openly touristy places, this lively café-bar shows a movie (7pm nightly), usually followed by live Latin or reggae music. Daily 11am–2am.

★ **Koki Beach** In the centre opposite the beach ☎2750 0902. Hip open-air restaurant and lounge adorned with recycled furnishings and built around an almond tree. Serves mostly Caribbean cuisine with some international dishes (mains $15–25). Tues–Sun 5–11pm.

The Lazy Mon at Stanford's Just east of the main street ☎2750 2116. Very popular at weekends, this sports bar serves a small range of snacks and has a large outdoor disco where you can dance to the sounds of reggae and waves crashing on the shore. Daily 10am–10pm.

Miss Sam Three blocks back from the seafront ☎2750 0108. Tuck into wonderful Caribbean home-cooking including rice-and-beans and *rondon* ($7) – at very reasonable prices. Daily 9am–9pm.

Monita Bonita On the main road, one block east of the post office. Split-level reggae-tinged restaurant serving mostly grilled dishes, such as chicken with mango sauce, and fish tacos. The upstairs bar is a good place to start a night out. Daily 11am–midnight.

Pan Pay On the seafront near the police station ☎2750 0081. This popular breakfast spot and bakery serves up croissants, cakes and delicious Spanish tortillas ($4). Daily 7am–5pm.

Pizzeria Coral Just south of the main street, near the post office. Succulent, if pricey, pizzas (most around $10) and filling breakfast staples served on a lively outdoor terrace. Tues–Sun 8–11am & 5–9pm.

★ **Puerto Pirata Deli** In the centre, across from the beach ☎2750 0459. Cosy local hangout serving Fair Trade coffee, chocolate, pastries ($2) and vegan-friendly sandwiches ($6). There's wi-fi too, and an enviable setting across from the beach. Cash only. Daily 9am–6pm.

Restaurante Tamara On the main road. No-frills lunch and dinner spot serving tasty Caribbean cuisine, such as house shrimp with fried plantains ($9.50). Daily 8am–10pm.

★ **Stashu's Con-Fusion** On the main road leading out of town to Playa Cocoles ☎2750 0530. *Stashu's* devoted following is due to its consistently stellar execution of its far-reaching menu, which includes curries, jerk chicken and tandoori dishes, all well prepared and colourful (most mains $12–22). It's a lively spot with frequent evening music performances, when the inventive cocktails are particularly popular. Mon, Tues & Thurs–Sun 5–10pm.

DIRECTORY

Internet/telephones The ATEC office and has internet access, telephones for international calls and a fax; there's also internet access around the corner at *Jungle Café* (☎8835 9928).
Medical facilities The medical clinic, Sunimedica (☎2750 0079), is on the main road past the first cross-street as you enter town.

Petrol There is a large petrol station about 5km north of Puerto Viejo on Hwy-36.
Post office The post office (Mon–Fri 7.30am–6pm, Sat 7.30am–noon) sits in the small commercial centre two blocks back from the seafront. On the same block is a bank, pharmacy and supermarket.

The southern Caribbean beaches and Manzanillo

The fifteen-kilometre stretch of coast south of Puerto Viejo features some of the most appealing **beaches** on the entire Caribbean coast. **Playa Chiquita**, **Playa Cocles**, **Punta Uva** and **Manzanillo** collectively hold all the trappings of a pristine tropical paradise, with palm trees leaning over calm sands, purples, mauves, oranges and reds fading into the sea at sunset and a milky twilight mist wafting in from the Talamancas. You'll find excellent accommodation along the Puerto Viejo–Manzanillo Road, but public transport is infrequent, so it's much easier with a car, especially if you want to explore the **Refugio Nacional de Vida Silvestre Gandoca-Manzanillo**, which borders the area.

Despite the profusion of foreign-run hotels and *cabinas*, local life around here remains much the same as ever, with subsistence householders fishing for still-abundant lobster and supplementing their income with tourism-oriented activities.

3

THE RESERVA INDÍGENA KÉKÖLDI AND ATEC

About two hundred Bribrí and Cabécar peoples live in the **Reserva Indígena KéköLdi**, which begins just south of Puerto Viejo and extends inland into the Talamanca Mountains. The reserve was established in 1976 to protect the indigenous culture and ecological resources of the area, but the communities and land remain under constant threat from logging, squatters, tourism and banana plantations. The worst problems arise from lax government checks on construction in the area, which, inhabitants claim, have led to several hotels being built illegally on their land. The main obstacle between the indigenous peoples and their neighbours has been, historically, their irreconcilable views of land. The Bribrí and Cabécar see the forest as an interrelated system of cohabitants all created by and belonging to Sibö, their god of creation, while the typical *campesino* view is that of a pioneer – the forest is an obstacle to cultivation, to be tamed, conquered and effectively destroyed.

The best way to visit the reserve is on one of the **tours** ($25 for a half-day, $60 for a full day with meal) organized by **ATEC** (see box, p.194), a grassroots organization set up by members of the local community – Afro-Caribbeans, Bribrí indigenous peoples and Spanish-descended inhabitants. If you're spending even just a couple of days in the Talamanca region, an ATEC-sponsored trip is a must; to reserve a tour, go to their Puerto Viejo office on the main road at least one day in advance. The organization's main goal is to give local people a chance to demonstrate their pride in and knowledge of their home territory, and to teach them how to make a living from tourism without selling their land or entering into more exploitative business arrangements. In this spirit, ATEC has trained about fifteen local people as **guides**, who get about ninety percent of the individual tour price. Whereas many of the hotel-organized excursions use cars, ATEC promotes **horseback and hiking** tours. They also visit places on a rotating roster, so that local hamlets don't deteriorate from foreigners traipsing through daily.

The tour does not take you, as you might expect, to villages where indigenous peoples live in "primitive" conditions. The Bribrí speak Spanish (as well as Bribrí) and wear Western clothes. But underneath this layer of assimilation lie the vital remains of their culture and traditional way of life. Although the area has seen some strife between the reserve dwellers, their neighbours and foreign hotel developments, these altercations remain largely on the level of policy. As a visitor, you won't see any overt ill-feeling between the groups. Treks usually last about four hours, traversing dense rainforest and the Talamanca Mountains. They start near the road to Puerto Viejo – where **Bribrí crafts**, including woven baskets and coconut shell carvings, are on sale – and pass cleared areas, cocoa plantings and small homesteads, and then into secondary, and finally primary, cover. In this ancient forest the guide may take you along the same trails that have been used for centuries by Bribrís on trips from their mountain homes down to the sea, pointing out the traditional medicinal plants that cure everything from malaria to skin irritations. A tour may also involve discussions about the permanent reforestation programme or a visit to the iguana breeding farm established by the local community. However, they conveniently neglect to mention one of the reasons they breed the iguanas is to eat them – especially when the females are pregnant – a major reason they are on the verge of extinction.

Playas Cocles and Chiquita

The first two hamlets heading south from Puerto Viejo, are **Playa Cocles** (2km south) and **Playa Chiquita** (4km south) which, owing to ongoing development, now more or less blend into one another. Patrolled by lifeguards, Playa Cocles offers perhaps the best **surfing** in the entire region and Playa Chiquita has a couple of interesting attractions nearby, plus a good selection of bars and cafés.

Jaguar Centro de Rescate

Guided tours Mon–Sat 9.30am & 11.30am • $15 • ☎ 2750 0710, ⓦ jaguarrescue.com • The centre, signposted from the road, is about a 30min walk from Puerto Viejo or a 5min drive

Founded in 2008 by Spanish expats, Playa Chiquita's **Jaguar Centro de Rescate** has quickly blossomed into one of Costa Rica's most successful conservation initiatives. The aim of the small sanctuary is to eventually release the rescued animals – which include howler monkeys, margays, sloths, owls, snakes and caimans (though no jaguars) – back into the wild once they reach maturity. In the meantime, the informative guided tour allows you to interact with some of the monkeys and parrots that can't be released.

Chocorart

Call for opening times • Tours $20 • ☎ 2750 0075 • Set at the end of a 400m gravel road in Playa Chiquita, and signed off the main road

The Swiss-owned **Chocorart** is a chocolate lover's delight. On a two-hour tour round the cacao plantation, you'll see various stages of the chocolate-making process, as well as have a chance to spot wildlife that live in the surrounding rainforest. The real treat, of course, is sampling the chocolate, which is predictably decadent, some even infused with fruit grown on the land.

Reserva Natural La Ceiba

Guided hikes $45 for solo hikers, $35 for 2 or more people; morning tour starts at 7am, last evening tour at 6pm • ☎ 8401 1169 or ☎ 8889 9184, ⓦ rpceiba.com • The road to the reserve should only be attempted in a 4WD, preferably with high clearance; pick-up can be arranged if necessary

A private reserve that falls within the Gandoca-Manzanillo refuge (see p.201), and is accessed from Playa Chiquita, **Reserva Natural La Ceiba** protects a dense 111-acre swatch of humid tropical forest. The reserve, run by an enthusiastic Spanish couple, is crisscrossed by several trails and occasionally hosts visiting biologists who come to study the thriving flora and fauna. At the heart of it is its namesake, the Ceiba, a massive tree that can live for over five hundred years and reach 50m in height.

After a spectacular survey of the surrounding forest from the elevated deck of the reserve's headquarters, the guided day-hike (2–3hr) winds through the immediate

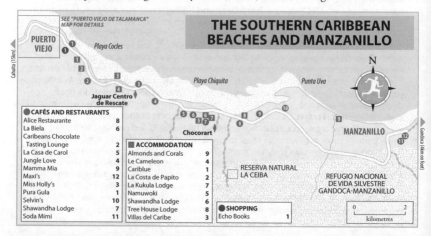

THE SOUTHERN CARIBBEAN BEACHES AND MANZANILLO

CAFÉS AND RESTAURANTS	
Alice Restaurante	8
La Biela	6
Caribeans Chocolate Tasting Lounge	2
La Casa de Carol	5
Jungle Love	4
Mamma Mia	9
Maxi's	12
Miss Holly's	3
Pura Gula	1
Selvin's	10
Shawandha Lodge	7
Soda Mimi	11

ACCOMMODATION	
Almonds and Corals	9
Le Cameleon	4
Cariblue	1
La Costa de Papito	2
La Kukula Lodge	7
Namuwoki	5
Shawandha Lodge	6
Tree House Lodge	8
Villas del Caribe	3

SHOPPING	
Echo Books	1

vicinity, eventually bringing you to a massive hollowed-out tree where you can gaze up at slumbering bats. It's the night tour (same prices as day-tour; 3–4hr), however – when you can spot frogs, nocturnal insects and snakes, and hear the forest come alive – that should not be missed.

Punta Uva

Serene **Punta Uva**, 5km beyond Playa Chiquita, has a pristine white-sand beach set in a protected cove making it particularly good for swimming. Development here hasn't yet reached the pace evident at *playas* Cocles and Chiquita, which gives the hamlet a more unhurried air – relatively speaking, of course.

Manzanillo

Manzanillo, the end of the coastal road, has a large shelf of coral reef just offshore that teems with marine life and offers some of the best **snorkelling** in Costa Rica. The village itself is small and charming, with laidback locals and a couple of great places to eat and hang out.

ARRIVAL AND GETTING AROUND

By car Public transport along the Puerto Viejo–Manzanillo Road is infrequent, so it's much easier with a car, especially if you want to explore the Refugio Nacional de Vida Silvestre Gandoca-Manzanillo, which borders the area. If you're driving, however, be aware that there are no petrol stations south of Puerto Viejo and the coast road is sporadically paved and very bumpy.

By bus The Puerto Viejo–Manzanillo bus (6 daily; 30min) is the only reliable public transportation that plies this route; sometimes the driver will stop on request at one of the three beaches along the way.

TOURS AND ACTIVITIES

Aquamor Adventures Manzanillo ☎2759 9012, ⓦgreencoast.com/aquamor.htm. Although principally a scuba-diving outfit, the friendly and excellent Aquamor also offers a wide range of marine activities including dolphin tours ($50) and kayak outings to Punta Mona ($60) and they can put you in touch with knowledgeable local guides who lead hikes through the Gandoca-Manzanillo refuge.

ACCOMMODATION

PLAYAS COCLES AND CHIQUITA

★**Le Cameleon** Playa Cocles ☎2750 0501, ⓦlecameleonhotel.com. There's nothing on the Caribbean coast quite like *Le Cameleon*, which wouldn't feel at all out of place in Miami. This brilliant white and exceedingly chic boutique hotel has 23 luxurious rooms occupying two storeys around a tempting pool. The range of amenities and service doesn't disappoint and there's a first-rate restaurant on-site, while across the street is its own private beach club. **$215**

Cariblue Playa Cocles ☎2750 0035, ⓦcariblue.com. *Cariblue* has luxurious individual *cabinas*, all with balconies and hammocks, in a well-maintained jungle setting with a top-notch Italian restaurant, a swimming pool (with pool bar) and souvenir shop. **$124**

★**La Costa de Papito** Playa Cocles ☎2750 0704, ⓦlacostadepapito.com. Run by an effusive New Yorker and an extremely friendly staff, *La Costa de Papito* offers "bungalows for the noble savage". Its pretty gardens are home to thirteen bungalows – all with bamboo beds, pink mosquito nets and balconies. There's a lovely spa, bike rental, internet access and an included breakfast buffet. **$107**

La Kukula Lodge Playa Chiquita ☎2750 0653, ⓦlakukulalodge.com. One of the newer lodges along this stretch, *La Kukula* has smartly designed rooms and bungalows powered by a hybrid solar/electric grid. There's a pool, bar, library and wi-fi, and the staff go out of their way to help you with local activities. **$130**

Namuwoki Playa Chiquita ☎2750 0278, ⓦnamuwoki.com. Peaceful, Spanish-owned property with nine spacious bungalows nestled amid thickly-wooded grounds. Popular with families and groups, the bungalows are all handsomely furnished and each has its own deck. There's a small pool and breakfast is included. **$158**

Shawandha Lodge Playa Chiquita ☎2750 0018, ⓦshawandhalodge.com. The long-running *Shawandha* was one of the original lodges built along the Puerto Viejo–Manzanillo stretch and it still has a style entirely its own. Each spacious palm-roofed bungalow combines a Bali-esque look with comfortable furnishings; the unique tile-work in each bathroom is exquisite. The open-air restaurant (see below) is a real gem. Breakfast is included. **$147**

Villas del Caribe Between playas Chiquita and Cocles ☎ 2750 0202, ⓦ villasdelcaribe.com. Actually within the Reserva Indígena KéköLdi, this beachside complex has standard rooms plus comfortable two-storey self-catering villas, with a terrace, hot water, fans and organic rubbish disposal. The grounds are right on the beach, with great sunset views. Double **$80**, villa **$120**

PUNTA UVA

Almonds and Corals 200m off the main road and 100m from the beach in Punta Uva ☎ 2759 9056, ⓦ almondsandcorals.com. The *Almonds and Corals* luxury tent lodge lies amid a lush rainforest setting in the Gandoca-Manzanillo refuge. Jacuzzi aside, the lodge does not aspire to be a luxury resort – more like an adventure. You sleep in a screened-in hut on stilts within the jungle. Wildlife is everywhere and deafening at night. Each of the stilt-set tents has comfortable furniture and an adjoining bathroom. The pathways are raised wooden boardwalks and one must stay on them to avoid the undergrowth. Howler monkeys live in the canopy above and wake you every morning around dawn. Truly a primitive, revitalizing experience. **$283**

Tree House Lodge Set back from the beach ☎ 2750 0706, ⓦ costaricatreehouse.com. Marked by a giant iguana sculpture at the gates on the main road, this creative hotel consists of four separate houses built around six enormous trees, connected by a steel suspension bridge. There's no TV or restaurant on the property, though there is a/c and wi-fi in the bedrooms. The Beach Suite bathroom resembles a colourful UFO – with a seahorse jacuzzi – and claims to be the largest in the country. Free tours of the admirable on-site iguana conservation project. **$300**

EATING AND DRINKING

PLAYAS COCLES AND CHIQUITA

Alice Restaurante Playa Chiquita. Colourful, open-air spot run by Americans that's earned a reputation for its massive fish tacos ($10), organic ingredients and home-made ice cream ($3). Cash only. Hours vary, though generally Tues–Sun noon–9pm.

La Biela Playa Chiquita ☎ 2750 0896. Friendly and intimate café with wi-fi serving pizzas, spaghetti Bolognese ($11) and fish with rice-and-beans. Mon, Tues & Thurs–Sun 9am–9pm.

★**Caribeans Chocolate Tasting Lounge** Playa Cocles ☎ 8836 8930, ⓦ caribeanschocolate.com. Friendly, open-air café serving a variety of decadent home-made chocolate offerings, including bars, brownies ($3.50) and drinks. The iced coffee ($3), made from beans grown on their land, is a real treat. A great spot to people-watch along the Puerto Viejo–Manzanillo Road, and there's free wi-fi, too. Mon–Sat 9am–6pm.

La Casa de Carol Playa Chiquita. Breezy French restaurant that makes the best quiche on the Caribbean coast. They offer freshly baked bread, sandwiches and pizzas, too, though prices aren't exactly cheap. Open Mon, Wed & Fri.

Jungle Love Playa Chiquita ☎ 2750 0162. Restaurant and bar known for its great menu (go for the wraps), fresh ingredients and wonderful garden setting. All recipes are the loving creations of owners Yamu and Poppy, with notable favourites such as mango chicken ($13), Tokyo Tuna ($12) and home-made ravioli specials. Tues–Sat 5–9.30pm, Sun 5–9pm.

Miss Holly's Playa Chiquita ☎ 2750 0131. Hearty omelettes ($6) and an assortment of sandwiches ($7) are served at this cute breakfast and lunch spot with free wi-fi and some outside eating. Wed–Mon 8am–4pm.

★**Pura Gula** Playa Cocles ☎ 8634 6404. Italian-run candlelit restaurant with deceptively simple and exceedingly tasty dishes, like fish burritos ($6), ham and cheese crêpes ($5) and Margarita pizza ($11). Hands down one of the best values on the coast. Daily 11am–10pm.

★**Shawandha Lodge** Playa Chiquita (see p.199). The most elegant night out in the area, this striking open-air restaurant serves an inventive mix of delicious French and Caribbean dishes, with fresh fish and tender beef a speciality; the heart-of-palm salad is a treat, too (mains $18–32). Daily 7.30–10am & 6–10pm.

PUNTA UVA

Mamma Mia Punta Uva ☎ 2750 0628. An enormous selection of pizzas are doled out at this local favourite. Choose from topping-laden choices like the Atómica (tomato, mozzarella, Italian sausage, onion, peppers, pepperoni and olives; $10) or more basic ones such as the Romana (tomato and garlic; $8). Also serves calzones and a few select pasta dishes. Mon, Tues & Thurs–Sun noon–8pm.

Selvin's 25m from the beach ☎ 2750 0664. You can feast on locally caught fish served with coconut-flavoured rice-and-beans ($7) at this perennially popular restaurant-bar. Cash only. Hours can be erratic, so it's good to call ahead. Wed–Sun 8am–2pm & 5–8pm.

MANZANILLO

Maxi's At the end of the paved road from Puerto Viejo, in the village centre ☎ 2759 9073. Split-level restaurant and bar with great views over the beach. It's renowned for its seafood (mains from $8), notably lobster, and gets packed at the weekend. Daily 11.30am–10pm.

Soda Mimi 25m behind Maxi's, set about 100m back from the beach. Simple *soda* with veranda seating serving heaps of Caribbean specialities, like shrimp with rice and Tico staples such as steak with rice-and-beans ($7). Daily 11am–8pm.

SHOPPING

Echo Books Playa Cocles ☎ 8703 8525. While the jungle locale is a bit unexpected, Echo Books has an impressive selection of reading matter and serves excellent coffee and chocolates. Wed–Sun 11am–5pm.

Refugio Nacional de Vida Silvestre Gandoca-Manzanillo

Ranger station and entrance 200 metres south of Manzanillo village • Daily 7am–5pm • Free • ☎ 2750 0398

Covering over fifty square kilometres of land and a similar area of sea, the little-visited but fascinating **REFUGIO NACIONAL DE VIDA SILVESTRE GANDOCA-MANZANILLO** sits in the southeast corner of the country. The refuge, which includes the small hamlets of Gandoca and Manzanillo, borders Río Sixaola and the frontier with Panama. It was established to protect some of Costa Rica's last few **coral reefs**, of which **Punta Uva** is the most accessible and offers great snorkelling. There's also a protected **turtle-nesting beach** south of the village of Manzanillo, along with tracts of mangrove forests and the last *orey* **swamp** in the country. More than 350 **bird** species have been identified, many of them rare – ten years ago there were sightings of the endangered harpy eagle, believed to be extinct in the rest of the country due to deforestation. Other species found in the refuge include the *manatee*, tapir and American crocodile, who hang out along the river estuary, though you're unlikely to see them.

Four kilometres from Manzanillo down a rough track, **Gandoca** provides access to the estuary of the Río Gandoca, a bird-spotter's delight with boat trips organized from the village. You can get here by walking from Manzanillo, or there's access from the Sixaola Road – if you have a 4WD – via the banana *fincas* of Daytonia, Virginia and Finca 96.

Puerto Viejo's tour companies (see box, p.194) offer guided hikes and snorkelling; Aquamor Adventures (see p.199) are a good local option. **Camping** is permitted, but is really only feasible on the beach, due to the mosquitoes, snakes and other biting creatures inland.

3

The trail to Punta Mona

Gandoca-Manzanillo has one fairly demanding but rewarding **trail** (5.5km each way), that passes primary and secondary forest as well as some pretty, secluded beaches on its way from Manzanillo to **Punta Mona** (Monkey Point). It can get extremely hot, and mosquitoes are usually out in force, so carry plenty of water, sunscreen and repellent. Beginning at the northeast end of Manzanillo village, the trail proceeds along the beach for 1km. After crossing a small creek and entering a grove of coconut trees, it becomes poorly marked and easy to lose, but should be just about visible as it climbs up a small bluff. The trail then drops to lower ground and skirts a few small beaches with shark infested waters, before heading inland. Some of these up-and-down sections are quite steep, and if it has been raining (as it invariably has) then mud and mosquitoes can make the trip unpleasant. However, the trail does offer great opportunities for spotting birds and wildlife; you're almost guaranteed a sight of chestnut-mandibled and keel-billed **toucans**. The tiny flashes of colour darting about on the ground in front of you are **poison dart frogs**; watch where you're stepping, and avoid touching them. Punta Mona, at the end of the trail, is flanked by a shady beach, from where you can see across to Panama, only about 8km to the south. From here you return to Manzanillo the same way.

Bribrí and around

From Puerto Viejo, the paved road (Hwy-36) continues inland to **BRIBRÍ**, about 10km southwest, arching over the Talamancan foothills to reveal the green valleys stretching ahead to Panama. This is banana country, with little to see even in Bribrí itself, which is largely devoted to administering the affairs of indigenous reserves in the Talamanca Mountains. Bribrí has a couple of basic places to stay, a few *sodas* and a bank, the Banco Nacional, which changes money and travellers' cheques.

The indigenous reserves

There are several **indigenous reserves** near Bribrí. You can't visit them without special permission both from the communities themselves and from the government. If you're interested, it's possible to make arrangements with local and national tour companies that work in collaboration with villagers. One of the more respected options is Galería Namu (see p.115), in San José, who lead a variety of intimate package tours (from $65) that include village visits and, typically, canoe rides and jungle hikes.

ARRIVAL AND DEPARTURE   BRIBRÍ AND AROUND

By bus Buses stop at the small terminal in the centre of Bribrí.
Destinations Puerto Viejo (18 daily; 20min); San José

(1–2 daily; 3hr 30min).
By taxi From Puerto Viejo it's possible to arrange a taxi to Bribrí for around $3.

ACCOMMODATION AND EATING

Hotel Mango In the village centre. Centrally located spot with clean rooms. Though they lack a/c, the rooms are

airy and comfortable. The on-site restaurant serves pizza (around $10) as well as *comida típica*. $22

Sixaola and into Panama

From Bribrí, a dusty gravel road winds for 34km through solid banana *fincas* to gritty **Sixaola**. Locals cross the border here to do their shopping in Panama, where most things are less expensive. The majority of foreigners who cross into Panama do so simply because their tourist visa for Costa Rica has expired and they have to leave the country for 72 hours, though the pristine Panamanian island of **Bocas del Toro** (see opposite) just over the border offers an inviting prospect even for those who don't need an extension.

The Sixaola–Guabito crossing

The torpid **Sixaola–Guabito** crossing doesn't see much foreign traffic, and for the most part formalities are simple, but you should still arrive as early in the morning as possible. Just walking across the rusty old bridge that looks like it's about to collapse into the river at any moment (yet somehow they are still running tractor-trailers over on lumber boards) is a life-defining experience. There's nowhere to stay in Guabito, the tiny hamlet on the Panamanian side of Río Sixaola, and bus connections in Panama can be tricky, though many locals will be making the same connections as you.

ARRIVAL AND INFORMATION   THE SIXAOLA–GUABITO CROSSING

By bus Transporte Mepes (☎2758 1572) buses arrive at Sixaola regularly from Bribrí and Puerto Viejo. To get further into Panama from Guabito, your best option is to catch a bus to the banana town of Changuinola from where there are connections to the rest of the country as well as a bus service across the Cordillera Central to Chiriquí on the Interamericana, where you can get bus connections to Panama City and back to San José. If you're planning to visit Bocas del Toro, take a bus to Changuinola and transfer to a bus to Almirante (30min) from there. Once in Almirante,

catch a water taxi to Bocas del Toro.
Departures from Sixaola Bribrí (hourly 6am–7am; 40min); Puerto Viejo (10–12 daily; 1hr).
Departures from Guabito Changuinola (every 30min; 30min).
By taxi Taxis (ask at the border post) make the 30min trip to Changuinola for about $15.
Crossing the border The Sixaola–Guabito border is open daily from 8am to 5pm Panama time (one hour ahead of Costa Rica). Tourists leaving Costa Rica need to buy a Red Cross exit stamp (about $2 from the pharmacy in Sixaola);

THE PUNTA MONA CENTER FOR SUSTAINABLE LIVING

If you are looking for an alternative to conventional tourism and even backpacking, and want to settle in a remote spot, Punta Mona is worth a visit. The **Punta Mona Center for Sustainable Living** (W puntamona.org) is an 85-acre organic farm and retreat centre located inside the Refugio National Gondoca-Manzanillo. The only way to get there is on horseback or a two- to three-hour hike from Manzanillo, where the coastal road ends and the rainforest begins. The café and convenience store in the village are the last opportunity to purchase provisions until your return. If you'd like to arrive on horseback, Seahorse Stables in Puerto Viejo (see box, p.194) can lead a tour to the centre.

If you are feeling adventurous, there is a **trail** (see p.201) that goes south along the beach, crosses a stream and on toward Punta Mona. Bear in mind this trail is usually very muddy and can be slow going. There are also paths leading off from there that go to distant indigenous villages; take care not to take a wrong turn and drop in uninvited. The centre will provide detailed directions from the segment from Punta Mora.

The gardeners who give life to Punta Mona are dedicated to teaching environmental awareness, and they welcome visitors for any length of time. Promoting a sustainable way of living through example, they grow their own food organically, recycle and manage all waste, use eco-technologies such as solar power, and create an amazing sense of community. You learn about the fruit and vegetables trees, gather the food, and participate in the cooking. Their architecturally impressive houses are built from fallen trees, they've constructed a complex irrigation system, solar panels provide the electricity, and they've planted a wide variety of tropical fruits, nuts, spices and herbs.

When you're not doing your share to keep the place running, you can laze on a hammock, take Spanish lessons, snorkel, kayak, hike, look for dolphins or nesting turtles (in season), play dominoes or simply surf the internet in your own pocket of paradise.

3

citizens of some nationalities may require a tourist card to enter Panama (valid for 30 days); the Panamanian Consulate in San José issues them, as does the San José office of Copa, the Panamanian airline (see p.104). Immigration requirements often change; check with the Panamanian Consulate (see p.117).

Bocas del Toro

Bocas del Toro, 65km southeast of Guabito on Isla Colón, is the main settlement in a small archipelago of little-inhabited islands, with beautifully clear water, great for snorkelling and swimming. The days of Bocas being a sleepy hamlet off the radar of most travellers have long since passed; these days it's understandably one of Panama's most popular destinations. It can at times feel a bit overrun, but with so many possibilities to get on or in the breath-taking azure waters, it's easy enough to find an idyllic spot away from the crowds.

ARRIVAL AND DEPARTURE   BOCAS DEL TORO

By bus and water taxi From the border town of Guabito take a bus to Changuinola and switch to a bus to Almirante. Once in Almirante you can take one of the regular water taxis to Bocas del Toro (30min; $4).

By plane NatureAir (T 757 9390) flies from San José to the small airport on Isla Colón just to the west of the town centre.
Destination San José (daily Tues–Sun; 1hr).

ACCOMMODATION

Bear in mind there's nowhere decent to stay between the border and Bocas del Toro – and you should leave time in the day to look for a hotel once here.

Hotel Angela On the waterfront, Bocas del Toro T 507 757 9813, W hotelangela.com. The friendly *Hotel Angela* has twelve cheerful rooms and a suite, all with a/c and private bathrooms. The on-site restaurant and bar faces the sea. Double $50, suite $149
Swan's Cay C Principal, Bocas del Toro T 507 757 9090, W swanscayhotel.com. On the main street, this swanky option has sizeable rooms with a nice range of amenities, including flat-screen TVs and wi-fi. The views are a bit pedestrian, but the rooms are among the more comfortable choices in Bocas. $85

The Zona Norte

HOT SPRINGS AT BALNEARIO TABACÓN

The Zona Norte

Vast by Costa Rican standards, the Zona Norte (Northern Zone) spans the hundred-odd kilometres from the base of the Cordillera Central to just short of the mauve-blue mountains of southern Nicaragua. Historically cut off from the rest of the country, the Zona Norte has developed a distinct character, with large segments of the population consisting of independent-minded farmers and Nicaraguan refugees. Neither group journeys to the Valle Central very often, and many here have a special allegiance to, and pride in, their region; indeed, the far north, which for years was mauled by fighting in the Nicaraguan civil war, feels more like Nicaragua than Costa Rica.

Topographically, the Zona Norte separates neatly into two broad, river-drained plains (*llanuras*) stretching all the way to the Río San Juan on the Nicaragua–Costa Rica border: in the west, the **Llanura de Guatusos** is dominated by Volcán Arenal, while to the east the **Llanura de San Carlos** features the tropical jungles of the **Sarapiquí** region. Less obviously picturesque than many parts of the country, it nonetheless has a distinctive appeal, with rivers snaking across steaming plains, and flop-eared cattle languishing beneath riverside trees.

Most visitors use the flourishing town of **La Fortuna** as a gateway to the active **Volcán Arenal**, which looms over the eastern end of **Laguna de Arenal**. The multitude of activities on offer here makes it the most popular destination in the Zona Norte, though the Sarapiquí region, with its tropical-forest ecolodges and the research stations of **La Selva** and **Rara Avis**, also draws significant numbers of visitors. The regional capital, **San Carlos**, lies between the two; though devoid of actual sights, its easy-going nature – and the fact that it's a transport hub – make it a decent place to stop off en route. In the north, the remote flatlands are home to the increasingly accessible wetlands of the **Refugio Nacional de Vida Silvestre Caño Negro**, home to an extraordinary number of birds. Few visitors venture any further, though a steady trickle passes through the border town of **Los Chiles** en route to Nicaragua.

One of the prime agricultural areas in the country, the Zona Norte is carpeted with vast banana, pineapple and sugar-cane plantations and expansive dairy-cattle farms. The worst excesses of slash-and-burn **deforestation** are all too visible from the roadsides and riverbanks, with the matchstick corpses of once-tall hardwoods scattered over stump-scarred fields patrolled by a few cattle.

Legal and illegal logging over the last two decades has cleared more than seventy percent of the region's original forest, though the creation of the **Refugio Nacional de Vida Silvestre Mixto Maquenque** in 2005 helps link protected areas in Nicaragua with the Valle Central.

VOLCÁN ARENAL

Highlights

❶ Volcán Arenal Even though the lava flows are a thing of the past, the volcano remains a stunning sight during the daytime, and the surrounding area is packed with activities. See p.217

❷ Rancho Margot Take a riverside yoga class or help milk the cows at this groundbreaking eco-retreat and organic farm. See p.219

❸ Laguna de Arenal Relax in an intimate lodge on the shores of this serene lake, or get out onto its sparkling waters, to fish or to try your hand at windsurfing. See p.220

❹ Refugio Nacional de Vida Silvestre Caño Negro This spectacular seasonal floodland near the border with Nicaragua offers some of the best wildlife-watching in Central America. See p.228

❺ Birdwatching at La Selva Explore the vast network of trails at this renowned research station – home to nearly 500 species of bird – with some of the most informative guides in the country. See p.234

❻ Reserva Rara Avis The dense rainforest of the Sarapiquí region provides the perfect setting for some excellent private reserves, most notably the wonderfully remote, wildlife-rich Reserva Rara Avis. See p.235

HIGHLIGHTS ARE MARKED ON THE MAP ON P.208

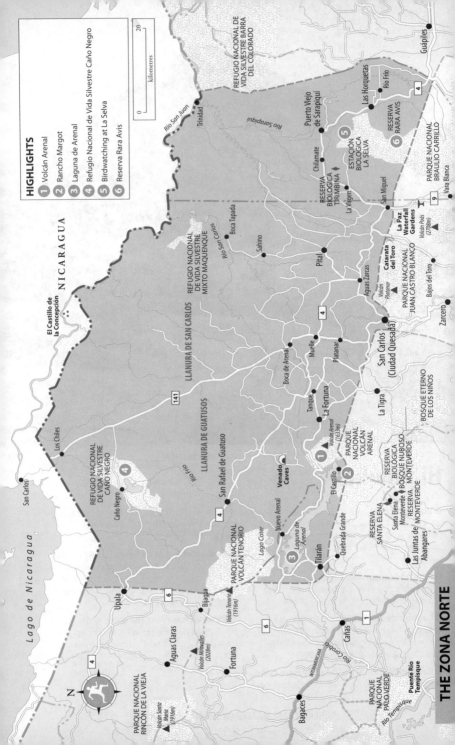

THE ZONA NORTE

HIGHLIGHTS

1. Volcán Arenal
2. Rancho Margot
3. Laguna de Arenal
4. Refugio Nacional de Vida Silvestre Caño Negro
5. Birdwatching at La Selva
6. Reserva Rara Avis

NICARAGUA

El Castillo de la Concepción

Lago de Nicaragua

REFUGIO NACIONAL DE VIDA SILVESTRE BARRA DEL COLORADO

Río San Juan

Río Sarapiquí

Trinidad

Puerto Viejo de Sarapiquí

Las Horquetas

Río Frío

Guápiles

Chilamate

ESTACIÓN BIOLÓGICA LA SELVA

RESERVA RARA AVIS

RESERVA BIOLÓGICA TIRIMBINA

La Virgen

San Miguel

PARQUE NACIONAL BRAULIO CARRILLO

Vara Blanca

La Paz Waterfall Gardens

Volcán Poás (2708m)

Boca Tapada

Río San Carlos

Sahino

REFUGIO NACIONAL DE VIDA SILVESTRE MIXTO MAQUENQUE

Pital

Aguas Zarcas

Catarata del Toro

Volcán Platanar

PARQUE NACIONAL JUAN CASTRO BLANCO

Bajos del Toro

Zarcero

LLANURA DE SAN CARLOS

Boca de Arenal

Muelle

Platanar

San Carlos (Ciudad Quesada)

Tanque

La Fortuna

La Tigra

BOSQUE ETERNO DE LOS NIÑOS

LLANURA DE GUATUSOS

Los Chiles

REFUGIO NACIONAL DE VIDA SILVESTRE CAÑO NEGRO

Caño Negro

Río Frío

LLANURA DE GUATUSO

San Rafael de Guatuso

Venado Caves

Volcán Arenal (1633m)

PARQUE NACIONAL VOLCÁN ARENAL

El Castillo

PARQUE NACIONAL VOLCÁN TENORIO

Lago Coter

Nuevo Arenal

Laguna de Arenal

Tilarán

Quebrada Grande

RESERVA BIOLÓGICA MONTEVERDE

BOSQUE NUBOSO MONTEVERDE

RESERVA MONTEVERDE

Santa Elena

RESERVA SANTA ELENA

Las Juntas de Abangares

San Carlos

Upala

Bijagua

Volcán Tenorio (1916m)

Aguas Claras

Fortuna

Volcán Miravalles (2028m)

PARQUE NACIONAL RINCÓN DE LA VIEJA

Volcán Santa María (1916m)

Bagaces

Cañas

PARQUE NACIONAL PALO VERDE

Puente Río Tempisque

Río Tempisque

Río Corobicí

INTERAMERICANA

N

kilometres

0   20

Brief history

For thousands of years before the Conquest, the original inhabitants of the Zona Norte were tribal groups – chief among them the **Corobicí** and **Maleku** – who made contact with one another via the great rivers. The **Spanish presence** was first felt in the early sixteenth century, when galleons meandered up the Río San Juan and into Lago de Nicaragua, looking for a route to the east. Pirates (mainly British) soon followed, wreaking havoc on the riverside communities. It was another two hundred years before the Spanish made a **settlement** of any size, the Quesada family coming down from San Ramón in the nineteenth century to found a village at present-day San Carlos, or Ciudad Quesada as it's also known. In the meantime, cross-border commerce carried on as it had for thousands of years via the San Juan, Frío, Sarapiquí and San Carlos rivers – the **Río Sarapiquí** in particular remained a more important highway than any road well into the eighteenth century, carrying coffee for export from Heredia out to the Caribbean ports of Matina and Limón.

INFORMATION

Getting around Although many roads in the region are seriously potholed, getting around is easy enough, and there's a good bus network linking La Fortuna and Puerto Viejo de Sarapiquí; if you plan on travelling outside these areas, however, you're better off with a car.

Climate The Zona Norte's climate is hot and wet, more so in the east than in the west near Guanacaste, where there is a dry season. You'll be drenched by regular downpours, but the rain always makes for an enjoyable respite from the heat.

La Fortuna and around

4

LA FORTUNA (or La Fortuna de San Carlos, as it's officially named) was once a simple agricultural town dominated by the majestic conical form of Arenal, just 6km away. True to its name, La Fortuna is now booming as a thriving base for the area's sports, activities and tours. Despite all the tour buses whizzing through town, however, it remains a pleasant, inviting community. There's nothing specific to see, as most of the streets are taken up by agencies selling tours, and visitors wander between them comparing prices, while gazing keenly towards the volcano and popping into *sodas* for much-needed *refrescos* to cope with the heat.

Looming at 1633m, **Volcán Arenal** seems to emerge directly from the town's fringes. Although still considered to be active, the volcano has been slumbering since 2010 and the famous evening lava tours are now a thing of the past. On a clear day it remains a majestic sight, but when it's rainy and foggy – which is more often than not – the volcano is almost totally obscured, its summit hidden behind a sombrero of cloud; indeed, locals estimate that one in two visitors never actually gets a glimpse of the summit.

The picturesque **La Catarata de La Fortuna**, the waterfalls southwest of town, are a popular half-day diversion, while the area to the northwest offers a variety of outdoor activities, from hiking forested trails to zip-lining to bathing in steaming **hot springs** – the perfect relaxing vantage-point for observing the pyrotechnics with drink in hand.

The hot springs

A number of **hot springs** line the road from La Fortuna to Arenal, all set around a variety of pools fed by thermally heated underground streams. The majority of agencies in town sell tickets and transportation to the springs, but you can easily visit them independently. A couple of the newer **hotels**, including *The Springs* (see p.216), have worked hot springs into their landscaped grounds, which are also open (for a fee) to non-guests.

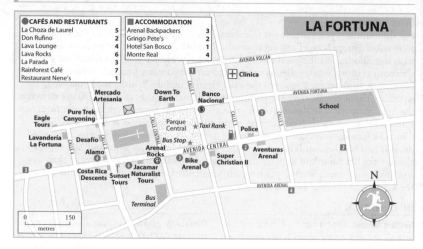

CAFÉS AND RESTAURANTS
La Choza de Laurel	5
Don Rufino	2
Lava Lounge	4
Lava Rocks	6
La Parada	3
Rainforest Café	7
Restaurant Nene's	1

ACCOMMODATION
Arenal Backpackers	3
Gringo Pete's	2
Hotel San Bosco	1
Monte Real	4

For years, locals in the know have been enjoying a natural – and **free** – hot soak in small ponds nestled within the fast-flowing river near the bridge just after Tabacón. If you decide to take the plunge, keep in mind that the rocks here can be slippery and the river treacherous, especially during the rainy season.

Balneario Tabacón

10km west of La Fortuna **Hot springs** Daily 10am–10pm • Day-pass with lunch/dinner $85, night-pass with buffet dinner $70 • **Grand Spa** Daily 8am–9pm **Restaurant** Daily 11am–4pm & 5–9pm • ☎ 2460 2020, ⓦ tabacon.com

The glitziest of the main hot springs and the destination for most tourists is **Balneario Tabacón**. Fed by a magma-boiled underground thermal river originating in the nether parts of Volcán Arenal – the water temperature ranges from 27°C (80°F) to about 42°C (108°F) – the complex comprises fifteen mineral-rich pools, most of which are secluded among rich vegetation. Several are set beneath waterfalls, so you can manoeuvre yourself under the cascades for a pummelling hot-water "massage". The atmosphere, with cocktail bar and bikini-clad tourists, makes you feel like you've just stepped into a 1970s James Bond film. The action-flick excitement is enhanced by the fact that Tabacón lies smack bang in the eruptive path of the volatile volcano and evacuations are not uncommon.

Given the steep admission, many people make a day of it and take lunch at Tabacón's on-site **restaurant**; you can choose between à la carte (think octopus carpaccio), a tandoori menu or a daily-changing buffet.

Grand Spa

Tabacón's award-winning **Grand Spa** offers massages and therapies in a cluster of treatment bungalows, tucked away at the top of the gardens and surrounded by lush foliage. If you really want to push the boat out, opt for their signature Temazcal treatment, a purifying Aztec ritual conducted by a shaman in the spa's sweat lodge.

Baldi Hot Springs

4km west of La Fortuna • Daily 10am–10pm • Day-pass $31, day-pass with dinner $51; $5 for lockers, $10 deposit for a towel • ☎ 2479 2190, ⓦ baldihotsprings.cr

Baldi Hot Springs is more accessible than Tabacón for those without transport. While it lacks the classy touches of its rival, it's significantly cheaper and offers many of the same facilities, including three wet bars. Baldi boasts 25 steaming pools, including Roman-style baths and waterfall-fed pools, and – for younger soakers – has three waterslides.

Ecotermales Fortuna

4km west of La Fortuna • Daily 10am–9pm, split into three allotted sessions of 10am–1pm, 1–5pm & 5–9pm • $34 • ☎ 2479 8787, Ⓦ ecotermalesfortuna.cr

Fronted by imposing wooden gates, the exclusive-looking **Ecotermales Fortuna** has five cascading thermal pools of varying temperatures set in idyllic forested surrounds. It's stylishly low-key, and only 100 people are allowed in during any of the allotted times, so be sure to book ahead in high season. While there's no volcano view from the pools, the rainforest setting more than makes up for it. The price includes towel, locker and access to two bars and a restaurant.

ACTIVITIES AROUND LA FORTUNA

You could spend weeks in La Fortuna rafting, horseriding, mountain biking and zip-lining and still not sample all the activities on offer. The below should keep you busy for awhile, at least.

CANOPY TOURS, AERIAL TRAMS AND HANGING BRIDGES

Arenal Canopy Tour Montaña de Fuego Inn, 9km west of La Fortuna ☎ 2479 9769, Ⓦ canopy.co.cr. La Fortuna's original zip-lining operation, with nine cables ($45), and also offering a 40m rappel and horseriding ($55 for all three activities).

Arenal Hanging Bridges 20km west of La Fortuna ☎ 2479 0469, Ⓦ hangingbridges.com. Sixteen bridges – up to 100m in length – on a 3km-long trail through tropical forest. You can walk the trail alone ($24) or hire a naturalist guide (recommended) to pick out the local flora and fauna ($36).

Canopy Los Cañones Los Lagos, 6km west of La Fortuna ☎ 2479 1047. A top-end hotel with a dozen cables running across its grounds ($50).

Ecoglide Arenal Park 3.5km west of La Fortuna ☎ 2479 7472, Ⓦ arenalecoglide.com. Fifteen cables and a Tarzan swing ($45 for both) in a park beneath the volcano. There's also a mini cable for practice.

Sky Adventures 23km from La Fortuna, on the road to El Castillo ☎ 2479 9944, Ⓦ skyadventures .travel. Aerial tram ($44), hanging bridges and a canopy tour (eight cables). One of only a few places where you can go zip-lining at sunset. Also offers rafting trips.

WHITEWATER RAFTING, CANOEING AND CANYONING

Canoa Aventura 1.5km west of La Fortuna ☎ 2479 8200, Ⓦ canoa-aventura.com. Canoe specialists, with half-day trips on Laguna de Arenal ($72), a full-day paddle in Caño Negro ($113) and a family-friendly "safari float" down the forest-fringed Río Peñas Blancas.

Costa Rica Descents Av Central, opposite the southwest corner of the church, La Fortuna ☎ 2479 9419, Ⓦ costaricadescents.com. Run by two brothers who got their whitewater wings rafting in the Rockies, this is La Fortuna's only Class V outfitter, with full-day trips on the Upper Balsa ($120). They also run the Class III–IV rapids of the Río Toro ($100), plus more

gentle trips on the Class II–III Río Sarapiquí and Río Balsa ($85 each).

Desafío Opposite the west side of the church, La Fortuna ☎ 2479 9464, Ⓦ desafiocostarica.com. Friendly, efficient rafting specialist running tours on the Class II–III Balsa (from $69) and the Class III–IV Sarapiquí (from $85). You can also combine rafting with rappelling or a rainforest canopy tour (from $135).

Pure Trek Canyoning Opposite the northwest corner of the church, La Fortuna ☎ 2461 2110, Ⓦ pure trekcostarica.com. Five rappels (four down a series of waterfalls) in a canyon near town ($98).

HORSERIDING

Desafío (see above). In addition to their recommended rafting trips, Desafío run horseriding tours to the Catarata de La Fortuna ($45); their transfer to Monteverde includes a lakeside ride on well-cared-for horses ($85; 5hr).

Don Tobias Arenal Springs Resort, 7km west of La Fortuna, then 450m down a signed turn-off to the right ☎ 2479 1212, Ⓦ cabalgatadontobias.com.

2hr 30min tours ($65) in the fields and forests around Volcán Arenal, with some creek-crossing involved. Safety-conscious, experienced guides.

Rancho Arenal Paraíso Arenal Paraíso Resort & Spa, 8km west of La Fortuna ☎ 2460 5333, Ⓦ arenal paraiso.com. The hotel's ranch runs similar trips (from $49) to Don Tobias, mostly on mountain trails on the slopes of Arenal.

4

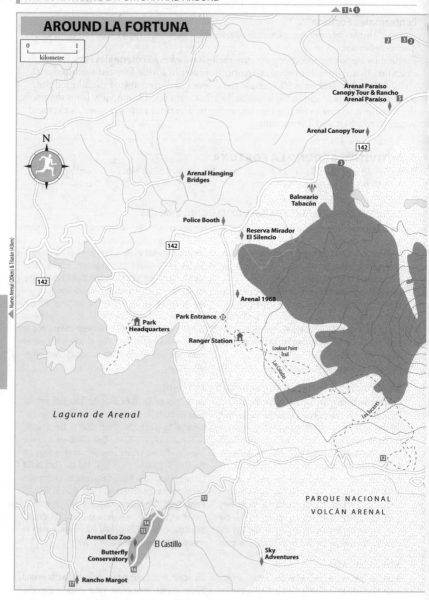

AROUND LA FORTUNA

0   1
kilometre

N

Nuevo Arenal (20km) & Tilarán (43km)

Arenal Paraíso
Canopy Tour & Rancho
Arenal Paraíso   5

Arenal Canopy Tour

142

Arenal Hanging
Bridges

Balneario
Tabacón

Police Booth

Reserva Mirador
El Silencio

142

142

Arenal 1968

Park
Headquarters

Park Entrance

Ranger Station

Lookout Point
Trail

La Colada

Los Tucanes

12

Laguna de Arenal

13

PARQUE NACIONAL
VOLCÁN ARENAL

14
15
Arenal Eco Zoo

Butterfly
Conservatory

El Castillo

16

17   Rancho Margot

Sky
Adventures

Termales Los Laureles

5.5km west of La Fortuna • Daily 9am–9pm • $12 • ☎ 2479 1431, ⓦ termalesloslaureles.com

Termales Los Laureles is the least expensive official hot springs in the Arenal area and is popular with Ticos. Four simple pools (one with slides) are set around a very ordinary garden, but the volcano views are sensational. Bring your own food and booze and make a night of it.

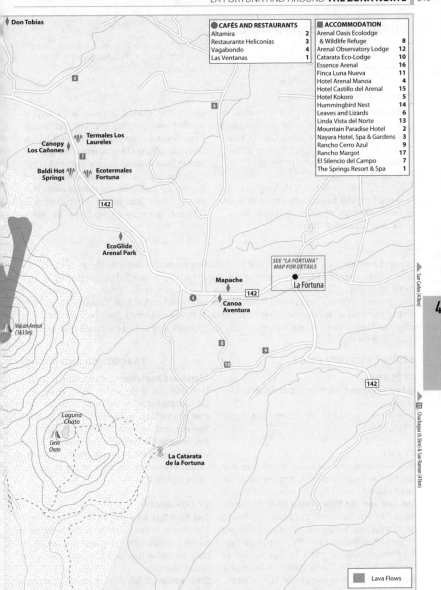

CAFÉS AND RESTAURANTS

Altamira	2
Restaurante Heliconias	3
Vagabondo	4
Las Ventanas	1

ACCOMMODATION

Arenal Oasis Ecolodge & Wildlife Refuge	8
Arenal Observatory Lodge	12
Catarata Eco-Lodge	10
Essence Arenal	16
Finca Luna Nueva	11
Hotel Arenal Manoa	4
Hotel Castillo del Arenal	15
Hotel Kokoro	5
Hummingbird Nest	14
Leaves and Lizards	6
Linda Vista del Norte	13
Mountain Paradise Hotel	2
Nayara Hotel, Spa & Gardens	3
Rancho Cerro Azul	9
Rancho Margot	17
El Silencio del Campo	7
The Springs Resort & Spa	1

La Catarata de La Fortuna

4km southwest of La Fortuna • Daily 8am–5pm • $10 • Most agencies run tours (see box, p.214) to the waterfall, but it's cheaper to get there by taxi (around $8) and more fun by horseriding across the fields; Desafío (see box, p.211) runs 4hr trips ($45) that take in the waterfalls

The dramatically sited **La Catarata de La Fortuna** is the epitome of the picture-book cascade – a tall, thin stream plunging prettily from a narrow aperture in the rocky heights 75m above, and forming a foaming pool among rocks and rainforest vegetation

TOURS AROUND LA FORTUNA

Even though the sunset lava tours are a thing of the past, La Fortuna remains a prime setting-off point for trips to the **Venado Caves** and the remote wildlife refuge of **Caño Negro**; shorter tours to the latter will just take you on a scenic cruise down the Río Frío from Los Chiles, so make sure that you'll actually be visiting the refuge itself.

TOUR OPERATORS

Aventuras Arenal 150m east of the Parque Central ☎ 2479 9133, ⓦ aventurasarenal.com. Professional setup offering tours to the Venado Caves (7.30am & 1pm; 4hr; $65) and the Maleku Indigenous Reserve at Gautuso (8am; $99, minimum 4 people; 4hr).

Eagle Tours 325m west of the Parque Central, in front of La Choza Inn ☎ 2479 9091, ⓦ eagletours.net. Budget backpacker favourite with a trip to the Venado Caves that's dubbed "the darkest tour in town" ($65).

Jacamar Naturalist Tours Next to Lava Rocks

☎ 2479 9767, ⓦ arenaltours.com. Runs a range of naturalist tours, including a walking tour through Parque Nacional Volcán Arenal ($55), kayak trips to Caño Negro ($48), and hiking up Cerro Chato ($91).

Sunset Tours Av Central, by the southwest corner of the church ☎ 2479 9800. Pricier than the rest but they only use professional, well-qualified guides. They run trips to Cerro Chato and the La Fortuna waterfall ($80) and hikes along the Río Celeste near Volcán Tenorio ($105).

below. From the ticket booth, a path leads 600m vertically down to the base of the falls, where a series of pools provide a tempting spot for a quick dip; swimming is not recommended, due to flash floods, although a lot of people do. There's a *mirador* (signposted) 200m along the trail for those who would rather look from a distance, giving great views across the steep valley and its heavily forested floor to the thin finger of the cascade. Make sure you wear waterproof shoes, and be aware that the paths can be slippery.

ARRIVAL AND DEPARTURE

LA FORTUNA AND AROUND

BY PLANE

La Fortuna Airport 7km to the east of town (around $15 by taxi).

Destinations San José (1 daily; 25min) and Quepos (2 daily; 40min).

BY BUS

Most buses terminate at the station, though some drop passengers at the bus stop on the southern side of the Parque Central.

San José and the Valle Central Three direct buses depart daily from San José for La Fortuna (4hr), leaving the Atlántico Norte bus terminal at 6.15am, 8.40am and 11.30am; two daily services make the return run (12.45pm & 2.45pm). Alternatively, take a bus from San José to San Carlos (hourly; 2hr 30min), where there are frequent connections to La Fortuna (every 1–2hr; 1hr–1hr 30min). There are also daily buses from San Ramón (4 daily; 2hr 30min).

Tilarán and Monteverde Daily buses depart for Tilarán (2–3 daily; 3hr), at the head of Laguna de Arenal – if you catch the first one to Tilarán (8am), you can connect there with the Santa Elena service (12.30pm; 2hr 30min); otherwise, you'll have to spend the night in Tilarán.

San Carlos and Puerto Viejo de Sarapiquí For Puerto Viejo de Sarapiquí and the Sarapiquí region, catch a bus to San Carlos (see p.225), where you can pick up an onward service (12 daily; 2hr 30min).

BY COMBINATION

Taxi-Boat-Taxi Many people opt for the "Taxi-Boat-Taxi" transfer to Monteverde (daily departures around 8.30am & 2.30pm; $32; 3hr); it saves time and the boat trip across the lake is spectacular. Trips are also run in the opposite direction.

Other options Slightly different alternatives offered by some agencies, including Desafío (see box, p.211), are a horse or bike ride on the final leg (both $85).

INFORMATION AND GETTING AROUND

Security Theft is on the rise in La Fortuna; never leave anything unattended, especially in a car, and be careful about walking around alone late at night. Note, too, that there have also been a number of serious complaints (credit-card fraud and scams) from travellers about the

agencies that operate out of the bus station. Also keep a close eye (and indeed a firm hand) on your bags when travelling by bus to/from La Fortuna.

By taxi There's a taxi rank on the eastern side of the Parque Central; expect to pay around $8 to La Catarata de La Fortuna.

ACCOMMODATION

Budget travellers usually stay in or around **La Fortuna** itself, while people with their own transport and/or a bit of money tend to head to the lodges that surround town; some of these are quite remote and local public transport is erratic, but many offer a free shuttle service into town. The nearby communities of **Chachagua**, 10km southeast of La Fortuna, and **El Castillo** (see p.219) are more relaxed alternatives to the main town but still close enough to the action.

LA FORTUNA

Arenal Backpackers 300m west of the church ☎ 2479 7000, ⓦ arenalbackpackersresort.com; map p.210. Great if you're a young American who wants to party, this sparkling hostel has a swanky pool with volcano views, a restaurant and double rooms with a/c, TVs and private bathrooms. There are also mixed dorms that are rather dark but have a/c and shared bathrooms, as well as a squadron of permanent dome tents if you'd prefer to camp. Dorm $\overline{\$15}$, tent $\overline{\$35}$, double $\overline{\$45}$

Gringo Pete's 300m east and 100m south of Parque Central ☎ 2479 8521, ⓦ gringopetes.com; map p.210. Classic, chilled-out hostel whose super-basic dorm beds and cell-like private rooms are an absolute steal. There's a nice communal lounge, outdoor patio with garden and barbecue area, and the best information board in town. There are only five rooms, so if it's full, there's a sister establishment 225m west of the bus station. Dorm $\overline{\$5}$, double $\overline{\$7}$

Hotel San Bosco 100m northeast of the Parque Central ☎ 2479 9050, ⓦ hotelsanbosco.com; map p.210. Quiet hotel built around a garden on the north side of town. Rooms, which come with a/c and spacious bathrooms, vary in price and size, so ask to see a few. Enjoy lovely views of Arenal from the pool and hot tub as well as from the upper-level terrace. $\overline{\$82}$

★**Monte Real** 100m south and 300m east of the Parque Central ☎ 2479 9357, ⓦ monterealhotel.com; map p.210. Possibly the best deal in town, this friendly, central hotel is set in tranquil garden surrounds alongside a gurgling river. Stylish rooms – some with dead-on volcano views – are well equipped with a/c, fridge and private bathrooms; superior ones ($90) benefit from a balcony. There's a small pool and wi-fi. $\overline{\$62}$

AROUND LA FORTUNA

Arenal Oasis Ecolodge & Wildlife Refuge 1km west of La Fortuna, then 800m down a signed turn-off to the left ☎ 2479 9526, ⓦ arenaloasis.com; map pp.212–213. Rustic Hansel-and-Gretel-style *cabañas* (which feature carved wooden beds) set in its own reserve just outside of town – once grazed by cattle, it is now home to sloths, tamanduas (anteaters) and around 200 species of bird. Various tours are available. $\overline{\$78}$

Catarata Eco-Lodge 2km southwest of La Fortuna on the road to the waterfall ☎ 2479 9522, ⓦ cataratalodge.com; map pp.212–213. Sitting on fertile farmland

between La Fortuna and the waterfall, this ecolodge offers a swimming pool and cosy and comfortable rooms, all with fan and hot-water bathroom. The restaurant serves tasty local food made with organic produce from its garden, and a hearty breakfast is included. $\overline{\$77}$

★**Finca Luna Nueva** 3.5km south of Chachagua, then 2.5km down a gravel road to the right ☎ 2468 4006, ⓦ fincalunanuevalodge.com; map pp.212–213. Adjoining the Bosque Eterno de los Niños (see p.312), this ecolodge and organic farm is a destination in itself. Good-value rooms and bungalows, made from recycled timber, provide a relaxing base for learning about its sustainable practices or indulging in a number of activities, from waterfall hikes to tours of the farm (included in the rates). A range of treatments are available at the Rainforest Spa, including the soothing "Arenal Volcanic Stone Massage" (massages from $35/30min). Double $\overline{\$115}$, bungalow $\overline{\$127}$

Hotel Arenal Manoa 7km west of La Fortuna, then 800m down a signed turn-off to the right ☎ 2479 1111, ⓦ arenalmanoa.com; map pp.212–213. The welcome cocktails set the tone at this beautifully done hotel, whose brightly decorated rooms boast a/c, TVs, fridges and private patios, complete with rocking chairs. There's a sparkling pool, and the rate includes a guided tour of the hotel's nearby dairy farm. $\overline{£180}$

Hotel Kokoro 8.5km west of La Fortuna ☎ 2479 1222, ⓦ arenalkokoro.com; map pp.212–213. Run by a friendly family from Taiwan who emigrated to the area 30 years ago, *Hotel Kokoro* has fifteen acres of grounds crisscrossed by trails, as well as a hot tub fed by hot springs, spa, and fine restaurant. Accommodation options range from simple rooms to smarter cabins (some of them big enough to host a family). Double $\overline{£130}$, cabin $\overline{£164}$

Leaves and Lizards 7.5km north of La Fortuna ☎ 2478 0023, ⓦ leavesandlizards.com; map pp.212–213. Located high in the mountains above La Fortuna, this incredibly relaxing retreat has a range of cabins (with terraces and hammocks), a great restaurant (lunch $10, dinner from $17) that takes advantage of home-grown, organic produce, and a range of tours (the horseriding is particularly good). Check the website for info on how to get there. Minimum three-night stay. $\overline{£130}$

Mountain Paradise Hotel 7km west of La Fortuna, then 500m down a signed turn-off to the right ☎ 2479 1414, ⓦ hotelmountainparadise.com; map pp.212–213. Spacious hacienda-style *casitas* dotted in pairs among beautiful grounds that are a haven for hummingbirds.

4

Large rooms easily accommodate two big wooden beds and come with flat-screen TV, a/c and huge bathrooms, complete with dramatic-looking "waterfall" showers. Friendly staff, a hot-water pool with wet bar, and an on-site spa complete the package. **$170**

★ **Nayara Hotel, Spa & Gardens** 7km west of La Fortuna, then 500m down a signed turn-off to the right ☎ 2479 1600, ⓦ arenalnayara.com; map pp.212–213. The beautiful en suites at this world-class resort feature super-comfy four-posters – think quality linens and feather duvets – plasma TVs and private gardens with outdoor showers; suites ($441) come with stunning balconies with jacuzzis overlooking the volcano. It also has an excellent wine bar, a Peruvian-Japanese fusion restaurant, and a quality main restaurant, *Altamira*, which is an excellent spot for dinner (see below). The nearby sister hotel *Nayara Springs* has similarly stylish villas ($667), each with their own pool fed by mineral springs. **$316**

Rancho Cerro Azul 1.5km southwest of La Fortuna, on the road to the waterfall ☎ 2479 7360, ⓦ ranchocerroazul.com; map pp.212–213. Economical hotel, with five spacious wooden cabins set amid bucolic grounds

close to the river; each cabin has a/c, TV, attached bathroom, and great volcano views from the private terraces out front. **$72**

El Silencio del Campo 5km west of La Fortuna ☎ 2479 7055, ⓦ hotelsilenciodelcampo.com; map pp.212–213. Though quite clustered together, these tranquil villas with volcano views are perfect for families: there are two swimming pools (one for children only), a restaurant and a small hot spring. The hotel is just 300m from Ecotermales Fortuna (see p.211), and guests get discounted entry. **$195**

The Springs Resort & Spa 9km west of La Fortuna, then 4km down a side road to the right ☎ 2401 3313, ⓦ springscostarica.com; map pp.212–213. Lavish five-star whose multimillion-dollar budget didn't quite stretch to an exterior designer. The dozen different types of room all offer private terraces, sumptuous bathrooms, flat-screen TVs and wi-fi. The spa is vast, and its hot springs (18 pools) are also open to non-guests (daily 8am–11pm; $50). Numerous on-site restaurants include *Las Ventanas*, with stellar volcano views (see opposite). Breakfast costs extra, which is rather miserly considering the rates. **$525**

EATING AND DRINKING

In addition to low-cost joints serving *casados*, *platos del día* and *arroz cons*, La Fortuna has a growing number of restaurants serving imaginative international cuisine, with several fine-dining options on the road west of town.

LA FORTUNA

La Choza de Laurel 400m west of the Parque Central, on the main road ☎ 2479 7063, ⓦ lachozadelaurel .com; map p.210. Very much on the tourist-bus circuit, but atmospheric nevertheless, with hefty slabs of tender steak (around $15) and crispy, wood-roasted chicken ($8.50 for a quarter with sides, $26 for the whole bird). Daily 6.30am–10pm.

Don Rufino 100m east of the Parque Central ☎ 2479 9997, ⓦ donrufino.com; map p.210. The wide-ranging, rather pricey menu (mains $16–35) trots around Latin America and Asia, but steaks are the speciality: from a ribeye for two up to a 20oz Chateaubriand carved at your table. The bar stays open until 11.30pm to keep willing patrons sufficiently lubricated. Daily 11am–10.30pm.

★ **Lava Lounge** 200m west of the Parque Central ☎ 2479 7365, ⓦ lavaloungecostarica.com; map p.210. This funky, reggae-style restaurant-bar serves a mouth-watering mixture of burritos ($10), wraps, organic salads and grilled sandwiches. There's live music on Sunday and Wednesday evenings. Daily 11am–11.30pm.

Lava Rocks 115m west of the Parque Central ☎ 2479 8039, ⓦ lavarockscr.com; map p.210. Shady breakfast hangout (until 11am) that's a good place to grab a snack or a blackberry *batido* at any time of the day. Mains from $9. Daily 8am–10.30pm, bar until 1am.

La Parada Directly opposite the bus stop on the Parque Central ☎ 2479 9098, ⓦ restaurantlaparada .com; map p.210. This popular *soda* is perfect for people-watching while you fill up on *casados* (from $4.50) or one of the variety of pizzas (from $8) – all served up by an enthusiastic staff. Daily 24hr.

Rainforest Café 75m southeast of the Parque Central ☎ 2479 7239; map p.210. Take your time over a cup of Costa Rica's finest in this airy café that hums along to mellow tunes. Smiling waitresses serve up good breakfasts (from $3.50), *casados* (from $6) and cakes too. Daily 7am–8pm.

Restaurant Nene's 250m east and 50m south of the Parque Central ☎ 2479 9192; map p.210. This highly regarded restaurant adorned with a mural of tropical birds is known for its ceviche but people also come from far and wide to enjoy its varied menu of sea bass, steak and pastas (mains $8–32) and a range of cocktails. Daily 10am–11pm.

ON THE ROAD TO ARENAL

★ **Altamira** Nayara Hotel, Spa & Gardens ☎ 2479 1600, ⓦ arenalnayara.com; map pp.212–213. Top-notch, softly lit restaurant with excellent food and charming old-school service (crêpes suzette, for example, are prepared table-side). The menu features delights such as ceviche ($15) and juicy steaks in an Argentine-style chimichurri sauce ($28). Daily 10am–10pm.

Restaurante Heliconias Arenal Kioro Suites & Spa ☎2479 1700, �ⓦhotelarenalkioro.com; map pp.212–213. The main restaurant at this suite-only hotel makes the most of its position at the foot of Volcán Arenal, with huge floor-to-ceiling windows (which open up) perfectly framing its smoking cone. The food (which runs along the lines of sea bass in caper sauce) is top drawer, too. Mains around $20–25. Daily 6.30–10pm.

Vagabondo 2km west of La Fortuna ☎2479 8087, ⍵vagabondocr.com; map pp.212–213. This attractive, open-air restaurant serves up authentic Italian wood-fired

pizzas, pasta dishes and salads ($8–15). In the back, a large convivial bar with pool tables stays open late. Daily noon–11pm.

★**Las Ventanas** The Springs Resort & Spa, 9km west of La Fortuna, then 4km down a side road to the right ☎2401 3313, ⍵springscostarica.com; map pp.212–213. Hanging 300m over the Río Arenal, this fine-dining restaurant (mains $20–30) is as much about what's going on outside as what's going on your plate – seared yellow-fin tuna, organic vegetables and delicate French desserts vie for attention with some of the area's most spectacular volcano views. Daily noon–3pm & 6–10pm.

SHOPPING

Coco Loco Arts & Crafts Gallery 3.5km south of Chachagua ☎2468 0990, ⍵arenalbyowner.com. This excellent art and craft shop/gallery has beautiful masks, mirrors, wall-hangings, ceramics, and paintings produced by the owner and other local artists. Mon, Thurs & Sat 8am–5pm.

Down to Earth Opposite the north side of the Parque Central ☎2479 7061, ⍵godowntoearth.org; map p.210. One-stop shop for your gourmet caffeine needs, specializing in coffee chocolates and liqueurs; there's a café attached if you want to sample anything. Daily 10am–6pm.

DIRECTORY

Bike rental Bike Arenal (☎2479 9454, ⍵bikearenal .com), on Av Central, rents mountain bikes for $20/day; one-day tours from $96.

Car rental Alamo, 200m west of the church ☎2479 9090, ⍵alamocostarica.com; Mapache, 800m west of the church ☎2479 0010, ⍵mapache.com.

Health care Clinica, 125m east and 50m north of the Parque Central (☎2479 9501; Mon 8am–8pm, Tues–Thurs 8am–10pm, Fri–Sun 24hr).

Internet Arenal Rocks, on Av Central, opposite the church (daily 8am–11pm).

Laundry Lavandería La Fortuna, 125m west and 125m north of the Parque Central (Mon–Sat 8am–9pm).

Money and exchange The Banco Nacional on the northeastern side of the Parque Central has an ATM and changes travellers' cheques.

Police On Av Central, 125m east of the Parque Central ☎2479 9501; also a booth at the turning to Parque Nacional Volcán Arenal west of town.

Post office Opposite the north side of the church (Mon–Fri 8am–5.30pm, Sat 7.30am–noon).

Scooter rental *Gringo Pete's Too* (see p.215) rents out scooters for around $50/day.

Supermarkets Super Christian II, diagonally opposite the southeast corner of the Parque Central (Mon–Sat 7am–10pm, Sun 8am–8pm), is a good place to stock up on goods.

Parque Nacional Volcán Arenal

Daily 8am–4pm • $10 • ☎2461 8499

Volcán Arenal was afforded protected status in 1995, becoming part of the national parks system as the **PARQUE NACIONAL VOLCÁN ARENAL**. Though Arenal is still technically active, it has been quiet since 2010, with no lava or explosions and only the occasional release of gas. It remains a spectacular sight, however, and the park has several good walking trails.

The trails

The park contains a few good **trails**, all accessed from the main park entrance, including the **Lookout Point Trail** (1.3km) and the **Las Coladas Trail** (2.8km), which heads southeast to a lava flow from 1992. The **Los Tucanes Trail** (4km), also accessed off the road up to the *Arenal Observatory Lodge* (see p.219), takes you to the part of the forest that was flattened by the 1968 eruption. You may see some wildlife on these hikes; birds (including oropendolas and tanagers) and agoutis are particularly common. Although the park has a simple café, it's best to take a picnic lunch and plenty of water if you intend to walk extensively.

Reserva Mirador El Silencio

5km north of the park entrance • Daily 7am–7pm • $8 • ☎ 2479 9900, ⓦ miradorelsilencio.com

A number of hikes on the fringes of Parque Nacional Volcán Arenal are worth exploring, including those at the **Reserva Mirador El Silencio**. The four trails at this reserve lead through primary forest sheltering peccaries and spider monkeys to a lookout at the foot of the volcano.

Arenal 1968

1.2km north of the park entrance • Daily 8am–8pm • $10 • ☎ 2462 1212, ⓦ arenal1968.com

Arenal 1968 offers taxing but highly worthwhile hikes up to the original 1968 lava flow, including a 3km loop that takes you past a shrine to the victims of the eruption and a longer 4.5km trail that takes you through bird-filled forested areas.

ARRIVAL AND INFORMATION | VOLCÁN ARENAL

By car The entrance to Parque Nacional Volcán Arenal is 14km west of La Fortuna; look for the well-signed driveway off to the left.

By taxi Taxis head from La Fortuna to the west side of the volcano for around $15, though you'll need to negotiate the rate if you want them to wait. Unless you're in a large group, it's cheaper – and easier – to take a tour.

By bus Buses from La Fortuna to Tilarán (2–3 daily; 15min) can drop passengers off 2km from the park entrance, though the return journey can be tricky, as you'll need to connect with the bus coming from Tilarán or Nuevo Arenal.

Tours Although the lava-spotting night tours no longer run, many operators in La Fortuna (see box, p.214) still run day-trips ($50–65).

VOLCÁN ARENAL: EXPLOSIONS AND ERUPTIONS

Volcán Arenal is the youngest and most active **stratovolcano** – the term for a steep, conical volcano created by the eruption of thick lava flows – in Costa Rica. Geologists have determined that Arenal is no more than 2900 years old; by comparison, Cerro Chato, which flanks Arenal to the south, last erupted in the late Holocene period, around 10,000 years ago. Geologists speculate that Arenal directly taps a magma chamber located on a fault about 22km below the surface.

Arenal's growth over the ages has been characterized by massive **eruptions** every few centuries: it is thought to have erupted around 1750, 1525 and 1080 AD, and 220 and 900 BC. At the time of its most recent eruption in the late 1960s, Arenal seemed to be nothing but an unthreatening mountain, and locals had built small farms up its forested sides (take a look at Cerro Chato and you get the idea). But on **July 29, 1968**, an earthquake shook the area, blasting the top off Arenal and creating the majestic, lethal volcano seen today. Arenal killed 78 people that day, with fatalities caused by a combination of shockwaves, hot rocks and poisonous gases. The explosion created three craters, and Arenal has been active ever since, though is currently in a quiet period.

While history would suggest that it's not due another major blowout for a few hundred years yet, and despite the recent years of slumber, Arenal is still very much an active volcano, so a few safety tips are worth bearing in mind: **never veer from trails** or guided tours, and do not attempt to hike anywhere near the crater, since lethal gases, ballistic boulders and molten rock, all of which occurred regularly until relatively recently, can appear or change direction without warning. Indeed, technically everything between the volcano and the roads that run from La Fortuna to Laguna de Arenal and El Castillo lie in a **high-risk area** – a guide and a young girl were killed by a pyroclastic flow while walking "safe" trails (now closed) in the *Los Lagos* complex in August 2000 – so choose your trip with care.

ACCOMMODATION

★ **Arenal Observatory Lodge** 5km beyond the park entrance ☎ 2479 1070, ⓦ arenalobservatorylodge.com; map pp.212–213. You can spend the night in the shadow of the volcano, just 1.8km from the crater. Standard rooms ($133) are rustic but comfortable, while the superior "Smithsonian" rooms ($171) have big beds and huge windows looking out at Arenal, which seems awesomely close; cheaper rooms ($97) are in *La Casona* farmhouse. Families renting the *White Hawk Villa* (sleeps 8; $510), 800m from the main lodge, can soak up the finest views of the lot. The extensive grounds include primary rainforest with trails, a small museum, pool and spa. There's a $4 charge for non-guests to enter the grounds, even if coming to eat at the overpriced restaurant (daily 11.30am–4.30pm & 6–8.30pm) – but you're really paying for the vista. **$97**

El Castillo

Just 23km southwest of La Fortuna but a world away in ambience, the idyllic mountain village of **EL CASTILLO** is all undulating hillsides covered with farmland and rainforest, with dead-on volcano views. The turn-off for El Castillo is 15km west of La Fortuna, on the road to Nuevo Arenal; the (currently) unpaved, bumpy road which heads 8km east from here has for years kept the village off the traditional tourist trail, making it a welcome retreat from the buzzing commercial circus that is La Fortuna.

There's not much to the village itself, just one main street with a school, church, small supermarket and the Arenal Eco Zoo.

Arenal Eco Zoo

Main St • Daily 8am–7pm • $16 • ☎ 2479 1059, ⓦ arenalecozoo.com

Principally a serpentarium housing more than eighty species of snake, including a monster Burmese python that's knocking on for 4m long, the **Arenal Eco Zoo** is also home to an array of rather smaller amphibians, butterflies and insects.

Butterfly Conservatory

About 800m up the road from El Castillo's school • Daily 8.30am–4.30pm • $14 with tour • ☎ 2479 1149, ⓦ butterflyconservatory.org

The enchanting **Butterfly Conservatory**, is a regeneration project occupying a former cattle ranch, with six well-tended butterfly atriums, a small insect museum, medicinal herb garden and riverside trails that weave through lush regenerating rainforest.

Rancho Margot

5km west of El Castillo • Tours 8.30am, 10.30am, 1.30pm & 3.30pm; book in advance • $25; 2hr • ☎ 2479 7259, ⓦ ranchomargot.org • A free shuttle bus runs four times daily to/from La Fortuna

The main reason for coming to El Castillo is to visit the extraordinary **Rancho Margot**, an organic farm, wildlife rescue centre and scenic accommodation (see p.220) that is well on the way to becoming the poster child for ecotourism in Costa Rica. The expansive property, set in a valley of the Río Caño Negro, is a byword for sustainability: a water-powered micro-turbine generates the ranch's electricity, the outdoor hot pool is heated using a biodigester that converts animal waste into energy, and most of the food served in the excellent buffet-style restaurant is grown or raised on the property.

ACCOMMODATION   EL CASTILLO

Essence Arenal 2km outside the village ☎ 2479 1131, ⓦ essencedelarenal.com; map pp.212–213. Ecofriendly hostel set amid 22 acres of farmland, forest and jungle with a peaceful, New Age feel. There are spots to pitch your tent (it also has permanent tents) and rooms, plus a vegetarian restaurant, cooking classes, yoga sessions, jacuzzi and even a trampoline. Camping/person **$5**, tent **$32**, double **$32**

4

Hotel Castillo del Arenal In the centre of the village ☎2479 1146, ⓦhotelelcastilloarenal.com; map pp.212–213. A string of compact *cabinas* (opt for one of the trio of standalone ones; $96) staggered along a ridge directly opposite Arenal, simply attired but with huge windows that make the most of the panorama. There's also a low-key restaurant on site. $85

Hummingbird Nest In the centre of the village ☎2479 1144, ⓦhummingbirdnestbb.com; map pp.212–213. This delightful American-run B&B has a couple of sparkling rooms and an outdoor hot tub – all with spectacular views of the volcano. There's even a beauty therapist on hand offering pedicures and the like. $96

★**Linda Vista del Norte** On the road into El Castillo ☎2479 1551, ⓦhotellindavista.com; map pp.212–213. Perched on a hillside with gobsmacking lake and volcano views from the pool, hot tub or restaurant. The top-notch rooms have picture windows, attractive wood panelling and princely bathrooms. $78

★**Rancho Margot** 5km west of El Castillo ☎2479 7259 or ☎8302 7318, ⓦranchomargot.org; map pp.212–213. This terrific self-sufficient eco-retreat encourages a hands-on stay: you can milk the cows; make cheese, wine or marmalade; or help till the organic gardens. There's a riverside yoga and meditation studio, or you might opt for canyoning, kayaking, horseriding or one of the other activities on offer; adventurous types can even hike to Reserva Santa Elena, 8km away. Accommodation ranges from the basic dorm-style bunkhouse to honeymoon-worthy hilltop bungalows with piping-hot showers, gigantic windows and wraparound terraces. Rates include full-board, daily yoga classes and a guided tour. A free shuttle bus runs four times daily between La Fortuna and the ranch. Dorm $75, bungalow $165

Laguna de Arenal

The waters of **LAGUNA DE ARENAL** make what would otherwise have been a pretty area into a very beautiful one – a fact exploited by the tourist board's promotional posters showing a serene Volcán Arenal rising preternaturally out of the lake. Pretty as it is, it's actually a man-made body of water created when the far smaller original lake was dammed in 1973; the resulting Arenal Dam now generates much of the country's hydroelectricity. The lake is an excellent spot for **fishing** rainbow bass (*guapote*), an iridescent fish found only in freshwater lakes and rivers in Costa Rica, Nicaragua and Honduras, and for **windsurfing**; several schools operate out of **Tilarán**, on the southwest corner of the lake. Tourism has brought with it a sizeable colony of foreign residents, many of them Germans or Austrians attracted by the combination of a rather European-looking landscape with year-round tropical temperatures.

LAGUNA DE ARENAL ACTIVITIES

The area's activities unsurprisingly revolve around the lake. Laguna de Arenal is the country's prime spot for windsurfing (see box, p.223), though this is done mainly out of Tilarán, on the other side of the lake. Many visitors come hoping to hook the hard-fighting *guapote*, while here are also a range of cruises and kayak trips. The agencies below can be contacted by phone/online or via your accommodation.

FISHING

Captain Ron ☎2694 4678 or ☎8339 3345, ⓦarenalfishing.com. Equipped for conventional and fly-fishing trips; expect to pay $225 for a 5hr trip and $325 for a full day.

Enchanted Tours ☎2694 4731, ⓦworldviewsintl.com. Offers a variety of lake tours in a pontoon boat, including half-day catch-and-release fishing expeditions ($225).

BOAT TRIPS

Enchanted Tours ☎2694 4731, ⓦworldviewsintl.com. Runs nature and birdwatching cruises, including a 2hr sunset trip ($75 including snacks and soft drinks).

KAYAKING

Arenal Kayaks ☎2694 4336, ⓦarenalkayaks.com. Offers guided kayak tours (from $30 for 2hr; longer trips available too), which can be tailored depending on how energetic you're feeling.

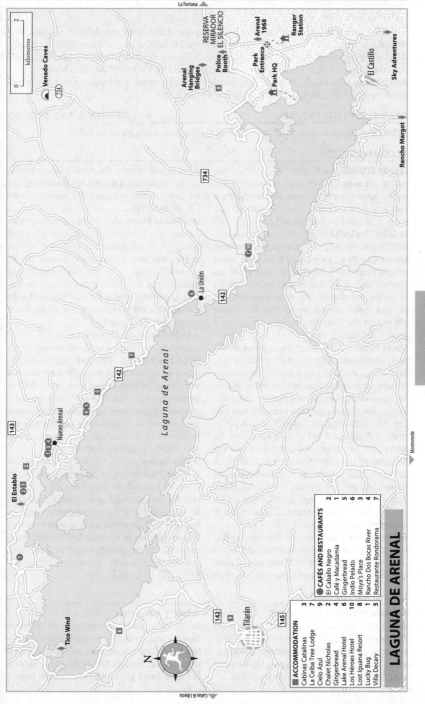

LAGUNA DE ARENAL

ACCOMMODATION	
Cabinas Catalinas	3
La Ceiba Tree Lodge	7
Cielo Azul	9
Chalet Nicholas	2
Gingerbread	4
Lake Arenal Hotel	6
Los Héroes Hotel	10
Lost Iguana Resort	8
Lucky Bug	1
Villa Decary	5

CAFÉS AND RESTAURANTS	
El Caballo Negro	2
Café y Macadamia	1
Gingerbread	5
Indio Pelado	6
Moya's Place	3
Rancho Dos Bocas River	4
Restaurante Rondorama	7

Nuevo Arenal

The road that winds its way from La Fortuna around the northern shore of Laguna de Arenal has beautiful views of the volcano and gentle hills, some of them given over to wind-farming – look for the giant white windmills on the hills above the north edge of the lake. About 40km from La Fortuna, lies lakeside **NUEVO ARENAL**, also known as **Arenal Town** (the original Arenal was flooded when the dam was built), which has a good range of accommodation and dining options.

ARRIVAL AND DEPARTURE

NUEVO ARENAL AND AROUND

By bus Nuevo Arenal is served by Tilarán-bound buses from La Fortuna (2–3 daily; around 1hr 30min).

ACCOMMODATION

Cabinas Catalinas Nuevo Arenal, opposite the petrol station and behind Moya's Place ☎ 2694 4001. This no-frills option is one of the better places to stay if you want to be in the town itself. The simple rooms are light and clean, and you'll get a hot shower. $20

La Ceiba Tree Lodge 4km from Nuevo Arenal ☎ 2692 8050, ⊛ ceibatree-lodge.com. This romantic and relaxing German-run lodge just above Laguna de Arenal has *cabinas* with private bathrooms, fridges, carved wooden doors and tasteful artwork, as well as an excellent apartment perfect for a couple. Best of all is the big, shady communal terrace for great sunset viewing. Named after the massive 500-year-old tree in the grounds, the lodge also has a couple of walking trails. *Cabinas* $71

Chalet Nicholas 2km west of Nuevo Arenal ☎ 2694 4041, ⊛ chaletnicholas.com. Small, beautifully kept hotel with just three rooms, all with private bathroom and hot water, looking out to the lake and distant volcano. You'll get a warm welcome from the charming hosts, not to mention their three massive Great Danes who have their own suite. Horseriding and birdwatching tours can be arranged, though you'll spot plenty of birds within the hotel grounds. Great breakfasts (included in rates) too. $85

Gingerbread 1km east of Nuevo Arenal ☎ 2694 0039, ⊛ gingerbreadarenal.com. Sleep off your meal at the excellent restaurant (see opposite) in one of five themed rooms – Butterfly, Cupid, Jungle, Garden of Eden and the new Wine Cellar – all boasting spacious, locally made beds and adorned with enchanting murals. $100

Los Héroes Hotel 15km east of Nuevo Arenal ☎ 2692 8012, ⊛ pequenahelvecia.com. This small hotel perched above the lake looks transported straight from an alpine meadow. Rooms – decked out with gingerbread woodwork and some with balconies ($10 extra) – are comfortable, and there are spacious apartments too, plus a hot tub, pool and quirky revolving restaurant (see opposite). Double $55, apartment $115

Lost Iguana Resort 18km west of La Fortuna, across the dam, then 1.5km down a signed road to the right ☎ 2461 0122, ⊛ lostiguanaresort.com. This peaceful, upscale jungle lodge has rooms with balconies offering volcano vistas, large, comfortable beds and a/c, TVs and private hot tubs, plus *Las Casitas*, two-bedroom suites set in a separate hilltop building. The resort has several jungle trails and a spa, and they can also arrange any sort of local activity. Double $277, suite $560

★ **Lucky Bug** 3km west of Nuevo Arenal ☎ 2694 4515, ⊛ luckybugcr.net. This bed and breakfast overlooking a pond is truly fantastical – think Alice in Wonderland goes tropical and you're on the right track. Owned by a German artist whose rainforest-inspired work graces the four themed rooms, you'll have a fine night's sleep sprawled in the king-sized beds. There's an inviting communal lounge area and breakfast is served in the adjoining *El Caballo Negro* restaurant (see below). Non-guests should be sure to visit the on-site art gallery and gift shop. $100

★ **Villa Decary** 2km east of Nuevo Arenal ☎ 2694 4330, ⊛ villadecary.com. Set just metres from Laguna de Arenal, the beautifully furnished rooms and *casitas* here have big beds decorated with colourful Guatemalan fabrics, and balconies with lovely forest and lake views. The hospitable hosts can provide a wealth of information on the area, and serve up a delicious breakfast with home-made jams. The lush grounds, planted with rare palms, make this a haven for birds – and, of course, birdwatchers. Double $123, *casitas* $160

EATING AND DRINKING

El Caballo Negro Lucky Bug, 3km west of Nuevo Arenal ☎ 2694 4757, ⊛ luckybugcr.net. Outstanding spot, part of the lovely *Lucky Bug* B&B (see above), dishing up delicious sandwiches (including a Reuben), vegetarian fare such as aubergine parmigiana and schnitzels (mains $15–20) served on a patio overlooking the hotel's lake. Daily 7am–5pm.

★ **Café y Macadamia** 6km west of Nuevo Arenal ☎ 2692 2000. Enormous sandwiches (around $10; try the Capresa – turkey, mozzarella, avocado and pesto on home-baked bread), organic salads, soups and a great selection of cakes make this an essential pit stop en route to Tilarán or La Fortuna. Even if you're not hungry, it's worth stopping for a portion of local macadamia nuts – covered with chocolate, coconut, cinnamon and the like – and to take in the gorgeous lake views from out the back. Daily 7.30am–5pm.

★ **Gingerbread** 1km east of Nuevo Arenal ☎ 2694 0039, ⊚ gingerbreadarenal.com. Fine dining in the expert hands of a French-taught Israeli chef, whose fusion cuisine is among the most creative in the country. The menu (mains $15–20) changes daily, in accordance with whatever's freshest at the time, but has a big Mediterranean influence; the fish and seafood is particularly good. Dishes are large enough to share. The lengthy wine list is stocked with Latin imports. Tues–Sat 5–9pm.

Indio Pelado La Unión, 9km east of Nuevo Arenal ☎ 2692 8036. Bad name – it means "Bald Indian" – but great pizzas: thin-crust, Italian-style pies (from $5) including a meat-lover's "Argentina" number that's topped with steak, chicken, bacon, ham and pepperoni. Tues–Sun 11am–11pm.

Moya's Place Nuevo Arenal, opposite the petrol station ☎ 2694 4001. This cool little café has a laidback vibe, serving snacks and meals ($8–10) such as beef wrap with sweet potato coleslaw, basil chicken curry salad, and pizzas. Daily 11.30am–9.30pm.

Rancho Dos Bocas River 500m west of Nuevo Arenal. A warm welcome awaits at this Tico eatery, which is run by a local women's co-operative; they'll cook a whole fish for you, and also make a fine *chimichanga* ($5). Daily 9am–9pm.

Restaurante Rondorama Los Héroes Hotel, 15km east of Nuevo Arenal ☎ 2692 8012, ⊚ pequenahelvetia .com. It's just as much fun getting to the kitsch revolving restaurant at this alpine-esque hotel (see opposite) as it is eating there – it's reached on a miniature railway ($10; reservations required), which whisks visitors 3km through tunnels, over bridges and up a hill, where you can feast on both the food (mains around $10–20) and the panoramic valley views. Daily 11am–3pm.

Tilarán and around

Unhurried **TILARÁN** lies 40km northwest of Monteverde and roughly 60km west of La Fortuna. The town's wide streets channel the vigorous breezes that breathe life into an otherwise lazy tropical hamlet – these same winds create the best **windsurfing and kitesurfing** conditions in the country at nearby Laguna de Arenal, 5km away. On the last weekend in April, Tilarán celebrates its ranching roots with a well-attended rodeo festival.

ARRIVAL AND DEPARTURE

TILARÁN

By bus Buses from La Fortuna (2–3 daily; 3hr), Santa Elena (2 daily; 2hr 30min) and San José (5–7 daily; 4hr) arrive at and depart from 100m north of the Parque Central. There are also connections west to Cañas and the Interamericana (6 daily; 30min), from where you can head north to Liberia and the Guanacaste beaches.

ACCOMMODATION AND EATING

Cielo Azul 500m northeast of town ☎ 2695 4000, ⊚ cieloazulresort.com. A 10min-walk from the centre of Tilarán, "Blue Sky" has en suites that are comfortable and well-equipped (TVs, fridges, microwaves, etc) if a little

---

WINDSURFING AND KITESURFING

Thanks to its unusually consistent conditions, Laguna de Arenal is the best place in Costa Rica for **windsurfing and kitesurfing** – the strong winds that buffet the surface of the lake from December to April can reach speeds of up to 25mph, drawing experienced riders from around the world. The wind peaks between mid-December and February, so aim for the late-season months if you're looking to learn.

OPERATORS

Ticowind About halfway between Nuevo Arenal and Tilarán ☎ 2692 2002 or ☎ 8383 2694, ⊚ ticowind .com. Well-respected outfit with over twenty years' experience. They rent quality equipment (from $50/ $58 for windsurfing/kitesurfing for a half-day), while windsurfing classes cater for first-timers ($120/3hr) and those looking to improve their technique ($120/3hr). Their comprehensive beginner's kitesurfing course includes 9hr on the water ($530).

dated. There's also a pool and a small gym. **$100**

Lake Arenal Hotel On the lakeshore north of town ☎ 2695 5050, ⓦ hotelminoa.com. After a series of name changes (including *Tilawa* and *Minoa*) in recent years, this place seems to have settled on *Lake Arenal Hotel*. It has large rooms and apartments, a great swimming pool and a hot tub, as well as a microbrewery and a restaurant. Double **$78**, apartment **$118**

North of La Fortuna

The area north of La Fortuna, on the western fringes of the Llanura de Guatusos, is a world away from the activity-driven hubbub of town. The long road that runs from La Fortuna via Tanque sees little traffic, and peters out beyond the village of **San Rafael de Guatuso** into seemingly endless bumpy tracks that head northeast to Caño Negro or northwest to the border with Nicaragua. This is, however, one of the few places outside the Caribbean where you can interact with the country's indigenous peoples: San Rafael is the modern-day home of the **Maleku**, and visitors are welcome to call in at the **Reserva Indígena Maleku**, just south of the village. On the way here – though more often visited on a tour – the **Venado Caves** provide a rare opportunity to head underground, their labyrinthine system of bat-filled caverns proving an interesting alternative to the ubiquitous canopy tours.

Venado Caves

Around 30km northwest of La Fortuna • Nov–April dawn to dusk • $15 • ☎ 2478 8008 • Several travel agencies in La Fortuna (see box, p.214) run tours

Near the tiny mountain town of **Venado** ("Deer"), the **Venado Caves** are a small network of subterranean caverns. They're quite accessible, provided you aren't afraid of bats and don't mind getting wet, as you'll need to walk through waist-high water to get to some of them. Inside is a spooky and unique tangle of stalactites and smoothed-out rock formations; look out for the Papagayo Rock, shaped (with a little imagination) like a parrot. Using the services of a **guide** is a very good idea – the caves are linked by a labyrinth of narrow passages (check that you can fit before you begin the crawl) – and you should bring a flashlight and rubber boots; you may be able to rent them from your hotel if you're staying locally.

Reserva Indígena Maleku

10km north of Venado • Several daily buses travel to Guatuso from La Fortuna (1hr–1hr 30min) and San Carlos (2hr–2hr 30min)

The village of **SAN RAFAEL DE GUATUSO** (known locally as Guatuso) lies at the heart of Costa Rica's few remaining **Maleku communities**, who live in *palenques* (straw huts) on the **Reserva Indígena Maleku**, established by the government in the 1960s. Historically part of the Corobicí tribal group, the present-day Maleku (also known as Guatuso) are a group of interrelated clans that have inhabited northwestern Costa Rica and southern Nicaragua for thousands of years. Now numbering about six hundred, their history and the story of their steady decline is a familiar one for tribal peoples in the area. Victims of disease, intertribal kidnapping and slavery to Spanish settlers in Nicaragua, they were dealt further blows in the 1700s and 1800s by the efforts of the Nicaraguan and Costa Rican Catholic churches to convert them to Christianity.

Though the Maleku speak their own language – broadcast by Radio Sistema Cultural Maleku and taught in schools – you won't see native dress or any outward signs of tribal identity around Guatuso. The best place to get a sense of traditional indigenous culture is at the reserve itself, set in bucolic countryside 7km south of the village.

Centro Ecológico Maleku Araraf

Daily 8am–4pm • 4hr tours $35; ask for Luis Denis • ☏ 8839 0540, ✉ centroecologicomalekuararaf@yahoo.es

On the excellent guided tours at the **Centro Ecológico Maleku Araraf** you'll learn about medicinal plants, get insight into local religious beliefs and burial practices (for example, they bury their dead directly beneath their homes), hike a rainforest trail and eat traditional food. There's also an on-site museum with a modest selection of artefacts and handicrafts.

Centro Ecocultura Maleku TAFA

Daily 7am–8pm • $30 • ☏ 2464 0443 or 8838 1320, ✉ eco_cultura_maleku_tafa@yahoo.ca

The **Centro Ecocultura Maleku TAFA**, run by the family of former Maleku leader Wilson Morera Elizondo ("TAFA"), gives demonstrations of religious ceremonies and organizes language classes; some of the handmade crafts you can buy here include masks and drums constructed out of iguana skin. Tours are also on offer.

San Carlos and around

Perched on the northern slopes of the Cordillera Central, 650m above sea level, **SAN CARLOS** (also known as **Ciudad Quesada**, or simply Quesada) has a decidedly rural atmosphere – fresh produce overflows from market stalls onto the streets, and *campesinos* with weathered faces hang out in the main square in front of the church. You're likely to pass through here on the way from or to La Fortuna; there's little to actually do – though therein lies its charm. Strolling about town, you get a real feel for what drives Costa Rica's economy: much of the nation's milk, beef, citrus fruit and rice come from the large-scale agricultural holdings in these parts. Positioned at the heart of cattle country, San Carlos is also something of a **saddlery** centre; it's well worth dropping by one of the expert saddlers, if only to watch them skilfully working the supple leather.

4

La Marina Wildlife Rescue Center

9km northeast of San Carlos • Daily 8am–4pm • $10, children $8 • ☏ 2474 2202, 🌐 zoocostarica.com

The family-run **La Marina Wildlife Rescue Center** houses some five hundred animals (over eighty species) that have been saved from illegal owners or areas where their habitat has been destroyed. Though acting on a very tight budget – the centre relies completely on donations from its visitors – it has established a successful breeding programme, including tapirs, spider monkeys and the endangered great green macaw, releasing a number of these into the wild.

Muelle

The sleepy village of **Muelle** 22km north of San Carlos is a useful stop-off on the road between La Fortuna, Puerto Viejo de Sarapiquí and Los Chiles (there's a petrol station here); it's worth stretching your legs by the bridge across the Río San Carlos, the trees around which are a favoured basking spot for a large group of **iguanas**.

ARRIVAL AND DEPARTURE   **SAN CARLOS AND AROUND**

By bus There are frequent buses from San José's La Coca-Cola terminal (hourly; 2hr 30min), stopping in the centre of town before heading to the bus station, 1km north of the Parque Central. There are also services to/from La Fortuna (every 1–2hr; 1hr 30min), Los Chiles (12 daily; 2hr 30min) and Puerto Viejo de Sarapiquí (12 daily; 2hr 30min).

INFORMATION

Tourist information The Zona Norte's tourist information centre (Mon–Fri 8am–4pm; ☎ 2461 1112) lies at the far southern end of Calle Central, though the sparsity of information on offer hardly warrants the hike out here.

ACCOMMODATION

You'll find plenty of budget options in San Carlos, but if you're looking for more luxurious accommodation, try the nearby villages of Muelle, Platanar and Aguas Zarcas, set in the beautiful countryside around town.

IN TOWN

Hotel Don Goyo C 2, Av 4 ☎ 2460 1780, ✉ hoteldongoyo @hotmail.com. One of the most pleasing options in town, these clean, quiet, brightly painted rooms, all with private bathrooms and fans, are in a modern building near the centre. There's also a reputable restaurant downstairs. $40

AROUND TOWN

La Garza Opposite the sports field in Platanar, 15km northeast of San Carlos ☎ 2475 5222, ⊛ hotellagarza .com. Named for the herons (*garzas*) that nest in the grounds, this hotel is part of a working dairy farm. Rustic, comfortable polished-floor bungalows have fans or a/c and are decorated in Guatemalan fabrics. Hammock-laden verandas look out onto the river, home to a variety of frogs. There's also a restaurant (reached via a hanging bridge) and pool. $107

Tilajari Resort Hotel 800m west of Muelle, 22km north of San Carlos ☎ 2469 1212, ⊛ tilajari.com. This quiet, beautifully situated resort hotel sits on an out-of-the-way cattle ranch by the croc-populated Río San Carlos (which many of the rooms overlook). Double rooms have private bathrooms, a/c, terraces and TVs, and there's a restaurant, pool, and tennis and basketball courts. Iguanas roam the landscaped grounds, and horseriding and rainforest walks can be arranged. $122

Tree Houses Hotel Santa Clara, 17km northwest of San Carlos ☎ 2475 6507, ⊛ treehouseshotelcostarica .com. Three cute treehouses – or rather wooden cabins raised on stilts and with private bathrooms – surrounded by an 80-acre wildlife refuge filled with birdlife. There's a spa (massages $50/1hr), and plenty of guided tours on offer (including a free night hike). $98

EATING AND DRINKING

Coca Loca C 2, Av 0/2 ☎ 2460 3916. San Carlos is firmly in cattle country, and has several good steakhouses. Among the best value is *Coca Loca*, overlooking the Parque Central, which serves hearty portions of steak and fries (mains from $10) that will set you up for the day. Daily 11am–10.30pm.

La Terraza C 0, Av 5/7 ☎ 2460 5287. Airy first-floor restaurant with a balcony overlooking Calle Central. Meat, of course, tops the list – try the Argentinian steak served with chimichurri sauce – but the bar's varied *boca* menu (ceviche, *papas a la francesa*, etc) takes some beating. Mains around $15. Daily 11am–11pm.

SHOPPING

Talabartería La Moderna Av 3, C0/1, two blocks north of the Parque Central ☎ 2460 1761, ⊛ talabarteria lamoderna.com. One of the best saddlers' stores (*talabarterías*) of those dotted around town, selling a good range of cowboy paraphernalia. While you may not have room in your luggage for a full-sized saddle, they can normally fashion you something smaller while you wait. Mon–Fri 7am–7pm, Sat 7am–6pm.

DIRECTORY

Banks You can change cash and travellers' cheques at the Banco de Costa Rica on the southwestern corner of the Parque Central.
Events As befits its setting, San Carlos hosts various horseriding shows throughout the year – the biggest is the San Carlos International Expo, a ten-day event at the end of April featuring horse parades, rodeos and cattle auctions.
Hospital For medical emergencies, the Hospital de San Carlos (☎ 2460 1176), 750m south of the town centre, is the best in the Zona Norte.

The far north

The **far north** of the Zona Norte is an isolated region, culturally as well as geographically, closer in spirit to Nicaragua than to the rest of the country and mostly devoted to sugar cane, oranges and cattle. Years of conflict during the Nicaraguan civil war made the region more familiar with CIA men and arms-runners than with tourists, but it's all quiet now.

   Most visitors are here to see the **Refugio Nacional de Vida Silvestre Caño Negro**, a vast wetland that makes up one of the most remote wildlife refuges in the country. Located at a key point on the migratory route between North and South America, it acts as the resting place for hundreds of migrant bird species and is considered by the Ramsar Convention on Wetlands to be the third most important wetland reserve in the world.

   Caño Negro is accessed from **Los Chiles**, near the Nicaraguan border, and the only village of any size in the far north. The drive up here, along an unnervingly straight stretch of road from San Carlos, takes you through a flat landscape of rust-red soil and open pasture, broken only by roadside shacks, with the Llanura de Guatusos stretching hot and interminably to the west. During the Nicaraguan civil war, Los Chiles was a Contra supply line. Nowadays, there's a climate of international cooperation, helped by the fact that many of the residents are of Nicaraguan extraction, and **crossing the border** is straightforward, as long as your documents are in order. Incidentally, the **Río San Juan** is technically Nicaraguan territory – the border is on the Costa Rican bank – though Costa Rica is allowed free use of the river.

Los Chiles

The only reason tourists make it to **LOS CHILES**, a border settlement just 3km from the Nicaraguan frontier, is to break their journey on the way to **Caño Negro**, 25km downstream on the Río Frío (see p.228), or to cross the Nicaraguan border –

(see p.228)

4

INTO NICARAGUA

The **border at Los Chiles** has a turbulent history: during the Nicaraguan civil war, US-sponsored Contras were supplied through here, and it was not unusual to see camouflaged planes sitting on the airstrip on the edge of town, disgorging guns. In the past, the border was closed to foreigners, and for a period also to Nicaraguans and Costa Ricans, though it's now possible for anyone to **enter Nicaragua** from here.

CROSSING THE BORDER

The proposed road crossing at Tabillas, 7km north of Los Chiles, is continually plagued by delays, and for the time being the only way to reach Nicaragua is **by boat on the Río Frío**: daily services leave the docks in Los Chiles (generally at noon and around 3.30pm). From the border control point, it's a 14km trip up the Río Frío to the small town of **San Carlos de Nicaragua** ($14; 45min) on the southeast lip of huge Lago de Nicaragua. The Los Chiles *migración* officials are relatively friendly, and you may be able to confirm boat times with the groups of Nicas or Ticos who hang around the office. Make sure that the **Nicaraguan border patrol**, 3km upriver from Los Chiles, stamps your passport, as you will need proof of entry when leaving Nicaragua. Few nationalities require a **visa** (see box, p.77) for Nicaragua.

   You'll need some **local currency** upon arrival in San Carlos de Nicaragua; change a few colones for córdobas at the bank in Los Chiles. From San Carlos de Nicaragua, it's possible to cross the lake to **Granada** and on to **Managua**, but check with the consulate in San José because this is an infrequent boat service: without forward planning you could end up stuck in San Carlos for longer than you'd hoped.

DAY-TRIPS

In the current atmosphere of relative political stability in Nicaragua, you can go on **organized day-trips** from Los Chiles to Nicaraguan **San Carlos**, **Lago de Nicaragua** and even the **Islas Solentiname**. Visitors may even be able to see the fortress **San Juan** (also called the Castillo de la Concepción or Fortaleza) on Lago de Nicaragua, one of the oldest Spanish structures (1675) in the Americas, built as a defence against the English and pirates (often one and the same) plying the Río San Juan, though note that these trips can be very expensive (from $250). For more details, contact *Rancho Tulipán* in Los Chiles (see p.228).

although the majority of travellers still cross at Peñas Blancas, further west on the Interamericana. There's little to do in town other than soak up its end-of-the-world atmosphere – the highway peters out just beyond Los Chiles in the direction of the Río San Juan, leaving nowhere to go but the river – though you can while away some time wandering down to the docks, where the tumbledown houses evoke a forlorn, France-in-the-tropics feel.

ARRIVAL AND DEPARTURE · LOS CHILES

By bus Buses arrive and depart from the small station just west of where the main road turns left down to the port. Two buses do the daily run from San José (C 12, Av 7/9) to Los Chiles (5.30am & 3.30pm, returning 5am and 3pm; 5hr). More frequent buses run to/from San Carlos (hourly; 2hr 30min). For Caño Negro, you'll need to take one of the daily buses signed "Upala" (3 daily; 1hr 15min).

By car Driving from San Carlos, Hwy-141 heads north along a reasonable road through the tiny settlements of Florencia and Muelle, and then along the 66km stretch of virtually empty highway, potholed in places, from Boca de Arenal to Los Chiles. There are few service stations north of Muelle, so make sure you have plenty of petrol.

INFORMATION AND TOURS

Heliconia Tours & Restaurant 100m east of the docks ☎ 2471 2096 or ☎ 8307 8585, ✉ cocas34@hotmail .com. The best source of information in town, where you can check the bus schedules and the times of the *colectivo* boat to Nicaragua, and get details of travelling on to

Granada; they also organize early-morning trips up the Río Frío, spotting birds, reptiles (iguanas and turtles) and monkeys en route ($30; 3hr), and can arrange transportation to San Carlos de Nicaragua should you want to leave earlier than the public boat. Daily 7am–8pm.

ACCOMMODATION AND EATING

Cabinas Jabirú Half a block north of the bus station ☎ 2471 1496, ✉ jcarlos0829@hotmail.com. The best budget lodging in town (not a hotly contested title it must be said), a 5min walk from the bus station, *Cabinas Jabirú* offers a/c rooms with TVs, fridges and private bathrooms. **$30**
Heliconia Tours and Restaurant 100m south of the docks ☎ 2471 2096 or ☎ 8307 8585. *Heliconia Tours and Restaurant* cooks up a fine rainbow bass, plucked

straight from the murky waters meandering just metres from the restaurant entrance. Mains cost around $8–10. Daily 7am–10pm.
Rancho Tulipán Opposite the migración ☎ 2471 1414, ✉ sergioca7@hotmail.com. More comfortable than *Cabinas Jabirú*, though far from plush, *Rancho Tulipán* has large a/c en-suite rooms, as well as an on-site restaurant (daily 6am–10pm) and internet café. Staff can arrange tours to Caño Negro and Nicaragua. **$50**

DIRECTORY

Money and exchange You can change dollars and travellers' cheques, and pick up Nicaraguan córdobas at the Banco Nacional on the north side of the football field (Mon–Fri 8am–3.30pm), which also has an ATM.

Post office The post office (Mon–Fri 8am–noon & 1–5.30pm) is opposite the bus station.
Shopping For supplies, head to Supermercado Carranzo, on the western side of the football field (daily 7am–8pm).

Refugio Nacional de Vida Silvestre Caño Negro

Daily 8am–4pm • $10, payable at the MINAE office, 250m east and 300m north of the Real Tour Association (daily 8am–4pm; ☎ 2471 1309)

The largely pristine **REFUGIO NACIONAL DE VIDA SILVESTRE CAÑO NEGRO**, 25km southwest of Los Chiles, is one of *the* places in the Americas to view enormous concentrations of both migratory and indigenous **birds**, along with mammalian and reptilian **river wildlife**. Until recently, its isolation kept it well off the beaten tourist track, though access has improved and nowadays numerous tours are offered from San José, La Fortuna and – best of all – the adjacent village of **Caño Negro**.

The refuge is created by the seasonal flooding of the Río Frío, so depending on the time of year you may find yourself whizzing around a huge 1980-acre lagoon in a motorboat or walking along mud-caked riverbeds. There's a 3m difference in the water level between the rainy season, when Caño Negro is at its fullest, and the

WATCHING WILDLIFE IN CAÑO NEGRO

The wildlife that calls Caño Negro home includes a staggering variety of **birds** such as **storks**, **cormorants**, **kingfishers** and **egrets**. You should be able to tick off a number of the **heron** species that inhabit the riverbanks (including green, boat-billed and rufescent tiger herons), along with **northern jacana** and **purple gallinule**. The lagoon itself is a good place to spot the elegant, long-limbed **white ibis**; its shimmering dark-green cousin, the **glossy ibis**; and perhaps the most striking of all the reserve's avifauna, the **roseate spoonbill**, a pastel-pink bird that is usually seen filtering the water with its distinctive flattened beak. The most common species are the sinuous-necked **anhingas** (sometimes called "snakebirds" in English), who impale their prey with the knife-point of their beaks before swallowing, though Caño Negro is also home to the world's largest – and Costa Rica's only – colony of **Nicaraguan grackle** (*zanate*), a dark, crow-like bird.

Reptiles are abundant, particularly the large **caimans** that lounge along the river and on the fringes of the lagoon, though you'll also spot plenty of pot-bellied **iguanas**. Look out, too, for the strikingly green **emerald basilisk lizard**; **swimming snakes**, heads held aloft like periscopes, bodies whipping out behind; and the various **turtles** (yellow, river and sliding) that can be seen resting on logs at the water's edge.

Large **mammals** living in Caño Negro include pumas, jaguars and tapirs, but these shy creatures are rarely spotted. **Howler monkeys** are at least heard if not seen – it helps to have binoculars to distinguish their black hairy shapes from the surrounding leaves in the riverside trees – though it takes a good guide to pick out a **sloth**, camouflaged by the green algae often covering their brown hair. The rows of small grey triangles you might see on tree trunks are **bats**, literally hanging out during the day.

Perhaps the reserve's most unusual inhabitant (in the wet season, at least) is the **tropical garfish**, a kind of in-between creature straddling fish and reptile. This so-called living fossil is a fish with lungs, gills and a nose, and looks oddest while it sleeps, drifting along in the water.

4

dry season; while the mammalian population of the area stays more or less constant, the birds vary widely.

Caño Negro village

The tiny village of Caño Negro is a loose collection of ramshackle houses and *sodas* set around a sweltering, dusty grid. Few people here speak English, but the locals are a patient and welcoming bunch. Aside from tours in the refuge, the town has a couple of other attractions to keep visitors lingering for a few hours. **Criadero de Tortugas** (daily 8am–4pm; free; ☎ 2876 1181), 600m west of the football field, is a turtle conservation project run by local volunteers, where turtle eggs are collected and hatchlings looked after for a year and a half before being released into the wild. Fifty metres south of the refuge entrance, **Mariposa La Reinita** (daily 8am–4pm; $4) is a lovingly tended butterfly garden behind the home of the Avalos Jiménez family.

ARRIVAL AND DEPARTURE   CAÑO NEGRO

By bus Daily buses leave Los Chiles for the village of Caño Negro (signed "Upala") at 5am, noon and 4.30pm, stopping outside *Soda La Palmera*, opposite the Parque Central, and the Coopecane Cooperativa; they return at 4.50am, 11am and 4pm (1hr 15min each way).

By car It's nineteen bone-shuddering kilometres from the turn-off south of Los Chiles.

Tours You can take a tour from San José, La Fortuna (see box, p.214), Los Chiles (from where most tour boats leave) or some of the smarter Zona Norte hotels, but

bear in mind that the first 25km of the trip down the Río Frío (taking an hour or more by *lancha*) does not take you through the wildlife refuge, which begins at the mouth of the large flooded area and is marked by a sign poking out of a small islet. Make sure your boatman takes you into Caño Negro – some operators will skimp on the time, petrol and refuge entrance fee and take you nowhere near the real thing – or better still, that your tour company drives all the way to Caño Negro village and starts the boat tour from there.

INFORMATION AND TOURS

Guides Unless you're an expert in identifying wildlife, the most rewarding way to enjoy Caño Negro is to use the services of a local guide who knows the area and can point out animals and other features of river life. The Real Tour Association (daily 8am–4pm; ☎2471 1621, ⊚realtourcanonegro.com), on the southwest corner of the *parque*, near the refuge entrance, represents all official tour operators in the community and charges set rates: $40–63/1hr, depending on the number of people in the group; $60–80/2hr (if you want to visit the main lagoon, you'll need to take a 2hr – or longer – tour); the $10 entrance fee is sometimes included. They can also arrange guided canoeing, horseriding and hiking. If the office is closed,

your hotel or just about anyone in Caño Negro can hook you up with a local guide.
Fishing permits The reserve is also hugely popular with anglers, who trawl the murky waters during the fishing season (Aug–May) for snook, tarpon and rainbow bass; you'll need a permit ($30) from Incopesca (⊚incopesca .go.cr) – the bigger lodges and travel agencies can sort them out for you.
When to visit The best time to visit Caño Negro is between January and March, when the most migratory bird species are in residence and you'll see scores of caiman basking on the riverbanks.

ACCOMMODATION

There are a handful of options in the village of Caño Negro, including a couple of **homestays**, and all can help arrange tours in the wildlife refuge.

Caño Negro Natural Lodge 200m east and 100m north of the Parque Central ☎2471 1000, ⊚canonegro lodge.com. Surprisingly smart, given the modesty of the village, *Caño Negro Natural Lodge*'s elegant en suites are set in manicured gardens and come with a/c. Facilities include a good restaurant (see below) and a swanky swimming pool with wet bar. $141
Hotel de Campo Caño Negro Near the entrance to the village, about 100m from the Los Chiles/Upala junction ☎2471 1012 or ☎8877 1212, ⊚hotelde campo.wix.com/hotel-de-campo. Occupying fruit-tree-filled grounds on the edge of a large lagoon, the bungalow

rooms at *Hotel de Campo Caño Negro* have big beds, a/c and private bathrooms. There's a pool, and the kitchen serves up mostly organic produce – the proprietor might even cook you fresh fish reeled in from the Río Frío. $95
Kingfisher Lodge 100m east and 400m north of the Parque Central; reception at Casa Sequera, 100m east of the Parque Central ☎2471 1116 or ☎8870 0458, ⊚kingfisherlodgecr.com. Five tasteful cabins that sleep up to five surrounded by groomed gardens; you can pay $10 more for a/c. Cheaper, more basic digs ($25) are offered at *Casa Sequera*, under the same management. $55

EATING AND DRINKING

Restaurant Jabiru Caño Negro Natural Lodge ☎2471 1000, ⊚canonegrolodge.com. The best place to eat in town is at the airy *Restaurant Jabiru*, which has a

good-value menu (dishes $8–15) that runs the gamut from burger and fries to tilapia in a mushroom sauce. Daily 1–3pm & 6–10pm.

The Sarapiquí region

Costa Rica's **Sarapiquí region** stretches around the top of Parque Nacional Braulio Carrillo and west to the village of San Miguel, from where Volcán Arenal and the western lowlands are easily accessible by road. Tropical and carpeted with fruit plantations, the area bears more resemblance to the hot and dense Caribbean lowlands than the plains of the north and, despite large-scale deforestation, still shelters some of the best-preserved **premontane rainforest** in the country.

The largest settlement in the area, sleepy **Puerto Viejo de Sarapiquí**, attracts few visitors and is primarily a river transport hub and a place for the plantation workers to stock up on supplies, though it can make a good base for exploring the superb **Estación Biológica La Selva**. The region's chief tourist attractions, however, are the rainforest lodges of **Rara Avis** and **Selva Verde**, which offer access to some of the last primary rainforest in Costa Rica.

Unsurprisingly, the region receives a lot of rain, though these heavy downpours help create a variety of whitewater thrills for kayakers and rafters who flock to the area around **La Virgen** for runs on the **Río Sarapiquí**.

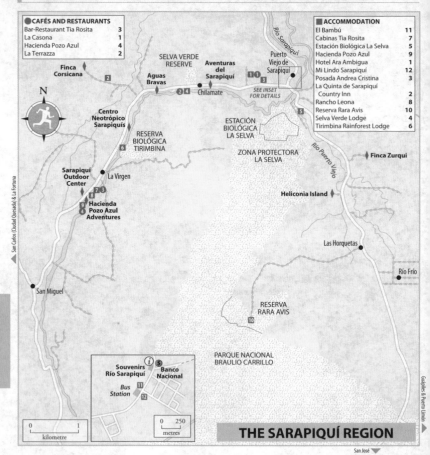

CAFÉS AND RESTAURANTS

Bar-Restaurant Tia Rosita	3
La Casona	1
Hacienda Pozo Azul	4
La Terrazza	2

ACCOMMODATION

El Bambú	11
Cabinas Tia Rosita	5
Estación Biológica La Selva	7
Hacienda Pozo Azul	9
Hotel Ara Ambigua	1
Mi Lindo Sarapiquí	12
Posada Andrea Cristina	3
La Quinta de Sarapiquí Country Inn	2
Rancho Leona	8
Reserva Rara Avis	10
Selva Verde Lodge	4
Tirimbina Rainforest Lodge	6

THE SARAPIQUÍ REGION

INFORMATION

Getting there The road between San José and the region via Vara Blanca has now been largely repaired, following the damage done to it by the Cinchona Earthquake (see box, p.138). An alternate route from San José or the Valle Central is via the Guápiles Highway through Parque Nacional Braulio

Carrillo, heading left at the Las Horquetas/Puerto Viejo de Sarapiquí turn-off at the base of the mountain pass.

When to visit The Sarapiquí receives as much as 4500mm annually, and there's no real dry season (although less rain is recorded Jan–May), so rain gear is essential.

Puerto Viejo de Sarapiquí and around

Just short of 100km northeast of San José, **PUERTO VIEJO DE SARAPIQUÍ** (not to be confused with Puerto Viejo de Talamanca on the Caribbean) is an important hub for banana plantation workers and those who live in the isolated settlements between here and the coast. Life in Puerto Viejo is inextricably linked with the Río Sarapiquí, and most cargo, both human and inanimate, is still carried by river to the Río San Juan and the Nicaraguan border to the north, and to the canals of Tortuguero and Barra del Colorado in the east.

A humid jungle outpost, Puerto Viejo serves as a jumping-off point for visiting the nearby **rainforest reserves**, and the research station at **La Selva**; everything in town itself

FRUITS OF THEIR LABOUR

Despite harbouring some of the largest remaining tracts of primary rainforest in the country, the Sarapiquí region is also home to a frightening number of **banana and pineapple farms**, while south of Puerto Viejo de Sarapiquí, the land around the small town of Las Horquetas is the sight of the biggest **palmito** (heart-of-palm) plantations in the world. As in the rest of Costa Rica, it's a difficult balance between preserving the rainforest (land rendered useless by monobiotic methods employed in the cultivation of pineapples, for example, can take up to fifty years to recover), and appeasing the needs of the local workers – *palmitos*, along with bananas and pineapples, form the core of the regional economy.

For a closer look into the everyday lives of these workers (many of them Nicaraguan migrants), you can take a tour of the organic pineapple plantation at **Finca Corsicana** (tours daily at 8am, 10am & 2pm; $24; 2hr; reserve in advance on ☎2761 1700, ⓦfincacorsicana .com), 8km northeast of La Virgen, or the Dole banana plantation at **Finca Zurqui** (phone for tour times; $15; 1hr 30min; ☎2768 8683, ⓦbananatourcostarica.com), 5km southeast of Puerto Viejo de Sarapiquí.

focuses on the main street, lined with coconut trees, and the small docks at its eastern end. Puerto Viejo plods along during the week, though things can get a bit lively on Friday evenings when the plantation workers are paid.

ARRIVAL AND DEPARTURE   PUERTO VIEJO DE SARAPIQUÍ

By bus Numerous buses leave San José's Gran Terminal del Caribe for Puerto Viejo de Sarapiquí (those marked "Río Frío" also serve Puerto Viejo), running via the Guápiles Highway and Las Horquetas (10 daily; 2hr). There are also a dozen daily services to/from La Fortuna (3–4hr 15min, depending on connection), via San Carlos (2hr 30min). Local buses for La Virgen (hourly; 30min) and attractions in between run on the hour, and can be

hailed from any roadside bus stop.
By boat It's possible to continue by boat north along the Río Sarapiquí to the Nicaraguan border and then east along the Río San Juan to Barra Colorado and Parque Nacional Tortuguero, though it'll be a pricey trip – you'll have to rent a private *lancha*, which can take anywhere between 4 and 5hr (you're going upstream) and will cost around $700 for up to ten people; ask at your hotel.

INFORMATION AND TOURS

Souvenirs Río Sarapiquí Diagonally across from the Banco Nacional on the main road ☎2766 6727. The best source of general information, this place is run by the knowledgeable Luis Alberto Sánchez, who can make reservations for the area's lodges and arrange tours to the Tortuguero/Barra del Colorado area as well as

riverboat rides on the Río Sarapiquí ($30; 2hr) to see caimans, crocodiles, sloths and monkeys lounging around in the heat – note, though, that the river is heavily populated by Costa Rican standards and its wildlife suffered following the Cinchona Earthquake (see box, p.138). Daily 8am–5.15pm.

ACCOMMODATION

Puerto Viejo de Sarapiquí's **accommodation** is quite varied considering the town's size, though Friday and Sunday nights can get booked up with plantation workers. To experience the region's dense rainforest, however, you may prefer to stay at one of the nearby **jungle lodges**, such as *Selva Verde Lodge* (see p.237) and *Reserva Rara Avis* (see p.235).

El Bambú On the main street opposite the football field ☎2766 6005, ⓦelbambu.com. The swishest accommodation in the town centre, this hotel has nicely decorated rooms (all with a/c and TVs), a bar and restaurant set around the massive stand of bamboo that gives the place its name, as well as a good-sized pool and a gym. A range of tours can be arranged, including boat trips along the Río Sarapiquí. Breakfast costs extra. $88

★**Hotel Ara Ambigua** 1.5km west of Puerto Viejo, 400m down a signed gravel road to the right ☎2766 7101, ⓦhotelaraambigua.com. Lovely rustic cottages, nicely furnished and impeccably clean. Beautifully decorated with pastel shades and pictures of birds, the rooms come with private bathrooms and a/c. There's a swimming pool, sauna and a frog garden. It's worth a visit alone for the tasty food dished up in the hotel's rustic restaurant (see p.234). $86

Mi Lindo Sarapiquí On the main street by the football field ☎ 2766 6281. The best budget accommodation in town features well-scrubbed rooms with fans and private bathrooms beside a good restaurant. Ask for one of the quieter rooms at the back. $15

Posada Andrea Cristina 1km west of Puerto Viejo ☎ 2766 6265, ⓦ andreacristina.com. This family-owned operation has simple rooms with fan and private bathroom, some in A-frame cabins with high wooden ceilings, plus a new tree house – all with top-notch breakfasts and coffee. One of the owners, Alex Martínez, is a qualified nature guide and can offer good advice on what to do in the local area. $55

EATING AND DRINKING

There are several inexpensive *sodas* in town, with smarter restaurants attached to the hotels. For a snack, a few fruit stalls on the main street sell seasonal treats like *mamones chinos*, the spiky lychees that look like sea anemones.

La Casona Hotel Ara Ambigua, 1.5km west of Puerto Viejo, 400m down a signed gravel road to the right ☎ 2766 7101, ⓦ hotelaraambigua.com. If you have transport or don't mind the walk, it's worth venturing 2km west of town to *La Casona*, attached to *Hotel Ara Ambigua*, where you can sample Costa Rican standards (from $10) and some mighty fine pizza in a laidback, rustic barn (call in advance to let them know you're coming). Daily noon–10pm.

Estación Biológica La Selva

☎ 2766 6565 or ☎ 2524 0607, ⓦ ots.ac.cr or ⓦ threepaths.co.cr • Guided walks daily 8am & 1.30pm • $30 half-day, $40 full-day (book well in advance)

The fully equipped research station of **ESTACIÓN BIOLÓGICA LA SELVA**, 4km southwest of Puerto Viejo de Sarapiquí, is one of the best **birdwatching** destinations in the Sarapiquí, if not the country. You can spot over half of Costa Rica's bird species here (489 in total), including the red-capped manakin – La Selva is a regular port of call for documentary makers looking to capture their energetic mating displays. An equally staggering number of tree species (some 350) have been identified, as well as 113 species of mammal, including anteaters, sloths (both two- and three-toed) and monkeys.

Leading biologists from around the world have studied here, and its facilities are extensive: a large swath of premontane rainforest shouldering the northern part of Parque Nacional Braulio Carrillo forms the natural laboratory, while the research facilities include lecture halls and accommodation for scientists and students.

Note that you cannot explore the reserve on your own – you must take a guided walk.

Trails and tours

The terrain at La Selva extends from **primary forest** (sixty percent of the reserve's total area) through abandoned plantations to pastureland and brush, and is crossed by an extensive network of about 25 **trails** totalling just over 60km. The trails vary in length from short to more than 5km long, and some are accessible to pushchairs and travellers with disabilities. Tourists tend to stick to the main routes within the part of La Selva designated as the **ecological reserve**, next to the Río Puerto Viejo; these radiate from the river research station and lead through dense primary growth, the close, tightly knotted type of tropical forest that the Sarapiquí area is famous for. Most trails are in very good condition and clearly marked, but only visitors staying at the complex are allowed to walk them unsupervised; day-trippers have to take one of two daily **guided walks**, though when the guides are as good as they are at La Selva, that's hardly a drawback.

Twitchers may prefer to take a private **birdwatching tour**, recommended for both the quality of the guiding and the birding – you've a good chance of seeing slaty-tailed trogon and rufous motmot. For beginner birders, the full-day **birdwatching workshop** is a detailed introduction to habitats and behaviour that includes a guided walk on which you'll learn how to look for birds and then identify them. You can also join a **night tour** in search of porcupines and kinkajou, or, for a glimpse of what life is like for the 350 or so researchers who study in the reserve each year, sign up for the **Scientist for a Day** workshop, where you'll be taught how to use scientific methodology to help record the station's flora and fauna.

ARRIVAL AND TOURS LA SELVA

By bus Local buses from Puerto Viejo de Sarapiquí (every 30min; 15min) run past the turn-off to La Selva on their way to Las Horquetas and Guápiles; it's a 15min walk from the road. Buses from San José to Puerto Viejo can also drop you off at the entrance. The station also runs shuttle buses to/from San José; book when you make your reservations.

By taxi A taxi from Puerto Viejo costs about $10.
Tours Birdwatching tour daily 5.45am (2hr; from $48); birdwatching workshop (1 day; $70); night tour daily 7pm (2hr; from $48); Scientist for a Day workshop (1 day; $80). Tours and workshops should be booked well in advance.

ACCOMMODATION

Estación Biológica La Selva ☎ 2766 6565 or ☎ 2524 0607, ⊛ ots.ac.cr or ⊛ threepaths.co.cr. The cabin accommodation at La Selva includes private bathrooms, three buffet-style meals a day served in the communal dining hall, and one half-day guided walk (additional guided walks from $30/person). It's impossible to overstate the reserve's popularity – if you want to stay you need to reserve months in advance (particularly Nov–April). **$93**

Heliconia Island

8km south of Puerto Viejo • Daily 8am–5pm • $12, $18 with tour • ☎ 2764 5220, ⊛ heliconiaisland.com • Local buses for Las Horquetas and Guápiles run every 30min or so from Puerto Viejo (ask to be let off at the turn-off on the main highway, then follow the signs down a dirt track before crossing a metal bridge to the island); a taxi from Puerto Viejo costs around $15

Set on a five-acre island on the Río Puerto Viejo, the immaculately landscaped gardens of **HELICONIA ISLAND** boast over 400 varieties of heliconia, and as the island's microclimate makes it blissfully cooler than Puerto Viejo, it has become a refuge for sloths, howler monkeys, river otters and more than 300 species of **bird**, including various hummingbirds (the exclusive pollinator of the heliconia). Plant-lovers will get a kick out of the fragrant ylang ylang tree, torch gingers and Phenomenal sperm – a flowering Guyana native.

Reserva Rara Avis

17km south of Puerto Viejo and about 80km northeast of San José

Remote **RESERVA RARA AVIS** offers one of the most thrilling and authentic ecotourism experiences in Costa Rica. Bordering the northeastern tip of pristine Parque Nacional Braulio Carrillo, the reserve features both primary rainforest and some secondary cover dating from about 35 years ago and boasts an incredibly diverse rainforest **flora**. The area is home to a number of unique **palm species**, including the stained-glass palm tree, a rare specimen much in demand for its ornamental beauty, and the walking palm, whose tentacle-like roots can propel it over a metre of ground in its lifetime as it "walks" in search of sunlight. **Orchids** are also numerous, as are non-flowering bromeliads, heliconias, huge ancient hardwood trees smothered by lianas, primitive ferns and other plants typically associated with dense rainforest cover.

Established in 1983 by American Amos Bien (a former administrator of the Estación Biológica La Selva), forest ranger Robert Villalobos and biologist Carlos Gómez, Rara Avis combines the functions of a tourist lodge and a private rainforest reserve, and is dedicated to both the conservation and farming of the area. A pioneer in the country's ecotourism movement, its ultimate objective is to show that the rainforest can be profitable, giving local smallholders a viable alternative to clearing the land for cattle. Another significant part of the reserve's mandate is to provide alternative sources of

WATCHING WILDLIFE AT RARA AVIS

A mind-boggling number of **bird species** have been identified at Rara Avis, and it's likely that more are yet to be discovered. As well as the fearsome black, turkey and king vultures and the majestic osprey, you might see nine species of parrot, over twenty types of antbird, thirty different species of hummingbird, both chestnut-mandibled and keel-billed toucans, and the unlikely named great potoo. The endangered great green macaw also nests here, and trogons, bare-necked umbrellabirds and the distinctive-looking three-wattled bellbird can also be spotted.

Among the more common **mammals** are opossums, monkeys, armadillos, anteaters, sloths and bats (eleven species in total). The reserve harbours five of the country's six cat species, though the closest you'll probably come to an ocelot or jaguar is discovering their tracks on a muddy trail. You may also encounter the Watson's climbing rat that frequents the *Waterfall Lodge* and has a voracious appetite for hand soap.

Amphibians and reptiles are abundant, ranging from the tree-climbing salamander to the white-lipped mud turtle, and including eight species of tree frog alone. Along with other vipers, the fer-de-lance and bushmaster **snakes**, two of the most venomous in the world, may lie in wait, so take extra care on the trails by looking everywhere you step and put your hand. Boa constrictors also hang out here; if you do see one, be careful as the generally torpid boa can get aggressive when bothered.

employment in nearby Las Horquetas, where most people work for the big fruit companies or as day-labourers on local farms.

Rara Avis also functions as a **research station**, accommodating student groups and volunteers whose aims include development of rainforest products – orchids, palms and so forth – as crops, as well as the silk of the golden orb spider. It also hosts travellers in the *Waterfall Lodge* and *Las Casitas* (see opposite).

Trails

Rara Avis has a 30km network of excellent **trails**, which are well marked and offer walks of thirty minutes to several hours. The informative **guided walks** are a great opportunity for spotting some of the 386 species in the reserve (see box above); they are run by knowledgeable guides, most of whom have lived at or around the reserve for some time. Guests are also welcome to go it alone: you'll be given a map at the lodge reception, but you should always let the staff know which trail you are following and about how long you intend to be. After dark you see a different side of the rainforest, and night walks offer the chance to spot a variety of insects, amphibians and nocturnal mammals, such as the arboreal four-eyed opossum.

Other activities

A short walk below the *Waterfall Lodge*, the main accommodation complex in the reserve, a 50m-high waterfall plummets into a deep pool – **swimming** in the ice-cold pool, shrouded in a fine mist, is a wonderful experience, but keep an eye on the weather and check with the staff regarding approaching floodwaters, an occasional but deadly hazard up here. Within 50m of the *Waterfall Lodge*, guests are free to wander around the small **butterfly garden**, home to the exquisite Blue Morpho butterfly. Also nearby is the wooden "**Spider House**", where golden orb spiders are studied and their shimmering golden silk – supposedly stronger than steel – is harvested for research purposes.

ARRIVAL AND DEPARTURE   RARA AVIS

Rara Avis is extremely isolated – it's what makes the place so special – and getting here is something of an endurance test. The reserve's office is in the village of Las Horquetas, just off the Guápiles Highway; here guests are kitted out with rubber boots before making the arduous 15km journey (3hr) to the reserve itself.

GETTING TO LAS HORQUETAS

By bus Local buses from Puerto Viejo run to the school in Las Horquetas (hourly; 20min), 100m from the reserve's office; Puerto Viejo-bound buses from San José (10 daily; 1hr 30min) can drop you at the turn-off to the village, a 5min walk away.

By taxi Taxis from Puerto Viejo cost around $20 to Las Horquetas; the lodge can also arrange a transfer from San José ($95 for up to four people) and Puerto Viejo ($50).

By car The reserve's office is signed off the Guápiles Highway; you can leave your car here.

GETTING TO THE RESERVE

By cart A truck-pulled cart (departs 9am; if coming direct from San José, you'll need to catch the 6.30am bus via the Guápiles Highway to make this connection; $200/vehicle for up to 14 people) laboriously ascends the first 12km (2hr). Remarkably, the road gets even worse after this, and it's necessary to complete the final 3km in a tractor-pulled cart (1hr), which slithers and slides down pitted hills – though visitors have the option of hiking this final leg on a rainforest trail (1hr 30min).

On horse and foot Horses are available to hire for the first section of the journey (until 2pm; $35; 3–4hr), but doing so means you will need to complete the final 3km to the reserve on foot (1hr 30min).

LEAVING THE RESERVE

By cart The tractor departs for Las Horquetas at 2pm, in time to connect with the last bus for San José that passes the village around 6pm.

ACCOMMODATION AND EATING

Rara Avis has a couple of accommodation options (neither of which have electricity): *Waterfall Lodge*, the main accommodation complex, and the slightly more rustic, dorm-like *Las Casitas*. Rates are fully inclusive, with all meals served in the *Waterfall Lodge*'s communal dining area (which has electricity for 3-4 hours in the evenings), home to a small naturalist library and board games; two guided tours/day are also included in the rates. Given the arduous journey here, it's worth staying at least a couple of nights.

Las Casitas Reserva Rara Avis ☎ 2764 1111, ⓦ rara -avis.com. Five minutes from the main lodge, *Las Casitas* consists of six rooms each sleeping four people in bunk beds. Facilities are comfortable enough, with shared bathrooms, although you'll have to hike from the dining area through dense forest at night. Dorm $\overline{\$73}$

★**Waterfall Lodge** Reserva Rara Avis ☎ 2764 1111, ⓦ rara-avis.com. Set 200m from a picture-perfect cascade, *Waterfall Lodge* has simple rooms with hot water, private bathrooms, kerosene lamps and spacious wrap-around balconies with hammocks and fantastic views of pristine rainforest and the hot lowland plains stretching towards the Caribbean. Less than 50m from the dining area, it's an idyllic place to stay: the only sounds heard at 5 or 6 in the morning are the echoing shrieks of birds and howler monkeys, and the light, especially first thing, is sheer and unfiltered, giving everything a wonderfully shimmering effect. $\overline{\$181}$

Selva Verde

☎ 2766 6800, in the US ☎ 1 800 451 7111, ⓦ selvaverde.com

A paradise for birdwatchers, **SELVA VERDE** has two square kilometres of preserved primary rainforest alongside the Río Sarapiquí. You can visit the reserve for the day, but for the full experience you need to stay at the luxurious *Selva Verde Lodge*, which comprises an impressive complex of rooms, bungalows, lecture halls and a lovely riverside restaurant-bar where monkeys chatter above and the Sarapiquí bubbles below. It's set in tropical gardens rather than dense overgrowth, though the vegetation around the lodge is still home to toucans, sloths and howler monkeys, while iguanas and basilisk lizards are frequent poolside visitors. Wilder, primary rainforest stretches off into the distance the other side of the river, accessed on a guided tour, and provides habitat for one of the region's most endangered species, the **great green macaw** (see box, p.238).

Trails and tours

Selva Verde's expanse offers an excellent variety of walks along well-marked trails through primary and secondary forest, riverside, swamps and pastureland. The **guided walks** through the denser section of premontane forest across the Río Sarapiquí are a must – the informative guides are top-notch and can make uncannily authentic bird

THE GREAT GREEN MACAW: BACK FROM THE BRINK?

The Sarapiquí region harbours the country's last flocks of **great green macaw** (*lapa verde*), the largest parrot in Central America. Globally endangered, it is estimated that fewer than 200 birds remain in Costa Rica (with fewer than 30 breeding pairs), but the fact that they survive here at all – in what constitutes just ten percent of their original home range – is only due to some sterling conservation work. Continued deforestation across the Zona Norte has caused a dramatic decrease in the population of the great green macaw, whose unfortunate fate is to rely on the **almendro tree** (a popular tropical hardwood) its their existence, nesting in its boughs and feeding on the large nuts it produces.

The almendro is now, belatedly, protected, but the first major step in the fight to save this beautiful bird was the creation of the **San Juan–La Selva Biological Corridor**, which ecologically links the Reserva Biológica Indio-Maíz in Nicaragua with the Cordillera Central – great green macaws require a wide area for breeding and foraging, and the corridor acts as a vital migratory pathway. Its conservational focus is the **Refugio Nacional de Vida Silvestre Mixto Maquenque** (see p.240), which plays a vital role in sustaining Costa Rica's great green macaw population, though the bird's future depends as much on the continuity of the corridor, which can only really be achieved through the creation of private eco-reserves that provide a financial incentive for conserving their habitat.

The first of these initiatives, the **Costa Rican Bird Route** – which includes Reserva Biológica Tirimbina (see opposite), *Selva Verde Lodge* (see p.237) and Estación Biológica La Selva (see p.234) – was set up to improve bird tourism in the region, thus delivering greater economic opportunities to local communities. The development of the Bird Route (see p.73) has resulted in another fifteen square kilometres of forest being newly protected as official private reserves.

4

calls to get the attention of trogons and toucans as well as pointing out poison-dart frogs, primitive ferns and complex lianas.

You can take a **self-guided walk** in the section of secondary rainforest across the road from the lodge – ask for a map at the reception – which is explored in greater detail on one of the free **birdwatching tours** (ask at the reception for details). If you're staying at the lodge, staff can also organize whitewater rafting, horseriding and boat trips on the Río Sarapiquí.

Sarapiquí Conservation Learning Center

School/community visits from $20 • ☎ 2766 6482, ⓦ learningcentercostarica.org

Selva Verde is heavily involved in the local community and is home to the nonprofit **Sarapiquí Conservation Learning Center**, which can arrange visits to local communities and schools, as well as tree-planting activities and dance classes.

ARRIVAL   SELVA VERDE

By bus Buses (10 daily; around 20min) running westwards from Puerto Viejo de Sarapiquí can drop you at the entrance to Selva Verde.

By taxi Taxis from Puerto Viejo cost around $12; the lodge

can arrange transport from most parts of Costa Rica.

By car Selva Verde is signed off the road near the village of Chilamate, which is 8km west of Puerto Viejo and 9km east of La Virgen.

TOURS AND ACTIVITIES

Tours Early-morning guided bird walks (daily 6am; $24); guided nature walk (daily 9am & 2pm; 2hr; $22); guided

birdwatching tours (daily 8am & 1pm; 4–8hr; $85–165); self-guided walks (daily 8.30am–5pm; 1.5hr; $20).

ACCOMMODATION AND EATING

Bungalows Selva Verde Lodge ☎ 2766 6800, in the US ☎ 1 800 451 7111, ⓦ selvaverde.com. A scenic 10–15min walk from the reception, these secluded bungalows are the most comfortable accommodation option at the lodge, with a/c, private bathrooms, tea/coffee-making facilities, and

screened balconies. Rates include breakfast but not lunch or dinner ($16–17 for buffet, more if taken at *La Terrazza*). **$163**

★ **River Lodge** Selva Verde Lodge ☎ 2766 6800, in the US ☎ 1 800 451 7111, ⓦ selvaverde.com. The comfortable rooms at the *River Lodge*, from which the Sarapiquí's gentle gurglings can be heard, are connected to each other by a walkway and have dark-wood floorboards contrasting with bright walls. You can lounge on hammocks and there's electric light after dark, so night owls have the option of reading (everybody seems to go to bed early – the bar empties out by 9pm). Rates include breakfasts but not lunch or dinner ($16–17 for a buffet, more if taken at *La Terrazza*). **$134**

La Terrazza Selva Verde Lodge ☎2766 6800, ⓦselvaverde.com. Arguably the best restaurant in the area, *La Terrazza* overlooks the Sarapiquí, with an Italian-influenced menu that includes home-made spinach and ricotta ravioli ($10) and lemon tilapia with capers, as well as half-a-dozen varieties of pizza baked to perfection in the wood-fired oven (from $10). Daily 6–10pm.

La Virgen and around

Lying on a bend in the Río Sarapiquí, the rafting hub of **LA VIRGEN** sprawls for 5km along the busy road between San Miguel and Puerto Viejo de Sarapiquí, the latter 17km to the east. The town is second only to Turrialba as Costa Rica's prime **rafting and kayaking centre**, and between July and December, outdoor types with well-toned arms come here by the busload to brave the variety of nearby runs.

Reserva Biológica Tirimbina

2km east of La Virgen • Daily 7am–5pm • $15 • ☎2761 1579, ⓦtirimbina.org

The thrilling **RESERVA BIOLÓGICA TIRIMBINA** is a small private reserve with 9km of trails weaving through primal rainforest and across a couple of suspension bridges, one of which is 272m long and straddles the gurgling Río Sarapiquí. While the trails here are well marked and maintained, this is no sanitized rainforest experience: hidden cameras have captured jaguars, margay, ocelots and Baird's tapir going about their business.

A variety of **guided walks** (advanced bookings are required for all) are offered, including night hikes, frog tours, bird-spotting strolls and even a chocolate tour explaining the cacao fruit's journey from tree to chocolate bar. Perhaps the most interesting, though, is the **bat programme**, one of only two activities in the country

4

WHITEWATER THRILLS: THE PUERTO VIEJO AND THE SARAPIQUÍ

The wild Río Pacuare near Turrialba may lure adrenaline junkies to Costa Rica, but the churning waters around La Virgen also offer plenty of thrilling whitewater action. The relaxing **Class I–II** run that puts in on the **Río Puerto Viejo** is essentially a scenic float along a jungle-lined river, suitable for wildlife-watchers and small children (from 3). Moving up a grade, the **Class III** runs, which start on the **Río Sarapiquí** around La Virgen, require good physical fitness but can be ridden by anyone over 8. If you want to tackle the ferocious and technically more demanding **Class IV** runs on the Upper Sarapiquí, you must be over 16 and have plenty of experience wielding a paddle.

TOUR OPERATORS

A number of companies in and around La Virgen offer guided whitewater rafting and kayaking tours, most of which include lunch and transportation.

Aventuras del Sarapiquí 12km east of La Virgen ☎2766 5101, ⓦsarapiqui.com. Offers a range of rafting, canoeing and tubing trips, as well as private full- and four-day kayaking courses ($150/600). They also run mountain-biking and hiking trips and have a zip-line canopy tour that shoots strapped-in victims across two rivers.

Hacienda Pozo Azul Adventures 2km west of La Virgen ☎2761 1360, ⓦpozoazul.com. Rafting Class I, II–III and IV rapids ($58–84; 2–3hr) is just part of the package at this one-stop-shop for outdoor adventure sports; other activities include rappelling ($40),

horseriding ($44/2hr) and a nine-cable canopy tour ($53).
Rafting Aguas Bravas Roble, 12km east of La Virgen ☎2766 6524 or ☎2992 2072, ⓦcostarica raftingvacation.com. Perhaps the largest rafting company in the country, with runs on Class I–II, III (both from $80/2–3hr) and IV (from $85/3hr) rapids. Prices include transport from La Fortuna; pick-ups from San José cost $14 extra.
Sarapiquí Outdoor Center 1.5km west of La Virgen ☎2761 1123, ⓦcostaricaraft.com. Established rafting and kayaking company offering trips on the Puerto Viejo and Sarapiquí ($55–89).

dedicated to this misunderstood mammal (the other is in Monteverde); part of an ongoing research project, the programme uses bats caught in drift nets that evening to explain their physiology and feeding habits.

Centro Neotrópico Sarapiquís

1km north of La Virgen • Daily 8am–6pm • $20 • ☎ 2761 1004, ⓦ sarapiquis.org

Part-funded by the Belgian government and set up as both a hotel and nonprofit educational centre, the various parts of the **CENTRO NEOTRÓPICO SARAPIQUÍS** seem to be pulling in different directions, giving the place a rather disjointed feel. Essentially an archeological park built on the site of a six-hundred-year-old pre-Columbian tomb, it also features a museum that explores the relationship between indigenous cultures and the rainforest, plus botanical gardens and a hotel.

ARRIVAL AND TOURS

By bus Buses from San José travel via the Guápiles Highway and Las Horquetas (12 daily; 2hr) and terminate in Puerto Viejo (see p.233), from where you can hop on one of the hourly local buses for the 30min journey to La Virgen.

LA VIRGEN AND AROUND

Tours Nature walk (daily 8am, 10am, 1.30pm & 3pm; 2.5hr; $25); Night walk (daily 7.30pm; 2hr; $25); Frog tour (daily 7.30pm; 2hr; $25); Bird tour (daily 6am; 2hr 30min; $25); Chocolate tour (daily 8am & 1.30pm; 2hr 30min; $27); Bat tour (daily 7.30pm; 2hr; $22).

ACCOMMODATION

In addition to the accommodation listed below, there is also local lodging at the Centro Neotrópico Sarapiquís (see above) and *Selva Verde Lodge* (see p.237).

Cabinas Tia Rosita 1km west of La Virgen ☎ 2761 1125. Although somewhat lacking in atmosphere, these four clean and basic cabins – attached to the *soda* of the same name (see below) – are good value. Each comes with TV and private bathroom. $22

Hacienda Pozo Azul 2km west of La Virgen ☎ 2761 1360, ⓦ pozoazul.com. Large tourist centre offering 30 luxury tents (with shared bathrooms) set in the forest just metres from the bubbling Río Sarapiquí. Facilities include TV and reading rooms and a decent restaurant (see below). A range of tours are also on offer. $92

La Quinta de Sarapiquí Country Inn 5km east of La Virgen, then 1.5km up a side road on the left ☎ 2761 1052, ⓦ laquintasarapiqui.com. On the banks of the Río Sardinal, this comfortable lodge has spacious a/c *casitas* set amid heliconia plants, so there's plenty of hummingbird activity to watch from the rocking chair or

hammock on your veranda. Activities include swimming in the pool, tubing down the river and exploring the lodge's butterfly house and frog pond. $124

Rancho Leona 1km west of La Virgen ☎ 2761 1019, ⓦ rancholeona.com. This tired-looking riverside lodge has some of the cheapest lodgings in the area: dorm beds, well liked by backpackers, and very rustic rooms with shared bathrooms. There's a communal kitchen, laundry facilities and internet access. Dorm $12, double $24

Tirimbina Rainforest Lodge Reserva Biológica Tirimbina ☎ 2761 1579, ⓦ tirimbina.org. The Tirimbina reserve has comfortable flagstone-floored rooms, equipped with a/c; smarter options ($105) come with more space and private terraces. Rates include entry to the reserve, valid for three consecutive days. Buffet-style lunches and dinners available ($15). $85

EATING AND DRINKING

Bar-Restaurant Tia Rosita 1km west of La Virgen ☎ 2761 1125. The most popular *soda* around these parts, *Bar-Restaurant Tia Rosita* serves above-average Tico specialities for around $5. Mon–Fri 7am–9pm, Sat 8am–9pm, Sun 8am–4pm.

Hacienda Pozo Azul 2km west of La Virgen ☎ 2761

1360, ⓦ pozoazul.com. The adventure centre at *Hacienda Pozo Azul* has a decent restaurant where you can munch on everything from delicious *enyucados* (filled cassava patties) to juicy steaks while taking in the view over the Río Sarapiquí from its outdoor deck. Mains from $10. Daily 7am–10pm.

Refugio Nacional de Vida Silvestre Mixto Maquenque

Just beyond the town of Boca Tapada, and separated from Nicaragua by the San Juan River, the **Refugio Nacional de Vida Silvestre Mixto Maquenque** is a multiuse wildlife refuge encompassing more than 500 square kilometres of wetlands, lagoons and lowland Atlantic forest. This remote reserve, established in 2005, after ten years of hard lobbying, is home to an array of birdlife, and is one of the very few places in Costa Rica where you might still see the highly endangered **great green macaw** (see box, p.238), as well as a large resident colony of more common oropendolas.

ARRIVAL AND DEPARTURE

Both lodges (see below) will pick you up from Boca Tapada, or you can arrange transfers from San José, La Fortuna or Puerto Viejo de Sarapiquí.

By car To reach the reserve by car from San José or San Carlos, head east through Aguas Zarcas to Pital and then – on good gravel roads – to Boca Tapada. It's possible to drive 7.5km east to *Laguna del Lagarto Lodge*; it's a reasonable road, although a 4WD is recommended.

By bus There are daily buses from San José (Av 9, C 12; 2 daily; 4hr 30min) and San Carlos (every 30min; 1hr 15min) to Pital, from where you can connect with buses north to Boca Tapada (9.30am & 4.30pm, returns 5.30am & 12.30pm; 2hr–2hr 30min).

ACCOMMODATION

Laguna del Lagarto Lodge Inside Refugio Nacional de Vida Silvestre Mixto Maquenque ☎ 2289 8163, ⊚ lagarto -lodge-costa-rica.com. One of the most remote lodges in the country – and only 16km from the Nicaraguan border – this ecolodge is home to an incredible variety of trees, plants and animals, and offers some of the best birdwatching in the country. Rooms are rustic but comfortable, with private bathrooms and peaceful views from their balconies. There are 10km of well-marked rainforest trails to explore, as well as canoeing (included in the rates) and boat trips ($27; 4hr) on the San Carlos and San Juan rivers. Breakfast costs extra ($7; lunch $9, dinner $16). **$75**

Maquenque Ecolodge Inside Refugio Nacional de Vida Silvestre Mixto Maquenque ☎ 2479 8200, ⊚ maquenqueecolodge.com. Inside Mixto Maquenque, bordering the San Carlos River, this lodge has a cluster of attractive bungalows, a good restaurant and a range of activities – from boat trips to visits to local schools. Rates include a rainforest walk and the chance to plant a tree in the rainforest. Lunch/dinner ($16/20). **$131**

4

Guanacaste

OLIVE RIDLEY TURTLES

5

Guanacaste

For the majority of the Tico population, Guanacaste Province, hemmed in by mountains to the east and the Pacific to the west, and bordered on the north by Nicaragua, is distinctly apart. Guanacastecos still sometimes refer to Valle Central inhabitants as "Cartagos", an archaic term dating back to the eighteenth century when Cartago was Costa Rica's capital. Though little tangible remains of the dance, music and folklore for which the region is distinct, there is undeniably something special about the place. Granted, much of the landscape has come about through the slaughter of tropical dry forest, but it's still some of the prettiest you'll see in the country, especially in the wet season, when wide-open spaces, stretching from the ocean across savannah grasses to the brooding humps of volcanoes, are awash in earth tones, blues, yellows and mauves.

The dry heat, relatively accessible terrain and panoramic views make Guanacaste the best place in the country for **walking** and **horseriding**, especially around the mud pots and stewing sulphur waters of the spectacular **Parque Nacional Rincón de la Vieja** and through the tropical dry forest cover of **Parque Nacional Santa Rosa**. Beyond Cañas, protected areas administered by the **Area de Conservación Tempisque (ACT)** encompass **Parque Nacional Palo Verde**, an important site for migratory birds, **Reserva Biológica Lomas Barbudal**, and the deep underground caves of **Parque Nacional Barra Honda** on the Nicoya Peninsula, just across the Río Tempisque.

For many travellers, however, Guanacaste means only one thing: **beaches**. Most are found where the **Nicoya Peninsula** joins the mainland. Roughly two-thirds of this mountainous peninsula is in Guanacaste, while the lower third belongs to the Puntarenas Province, covered in Chapter 6 (see p.327). Beaches range from simple hideaways such as quiet Nosara to large resorts aimed at the North American winter market. Several beaches are also nesting grounds for marine turtles – giant leatherbacks haul themselves up onto Playa Grande, near Tamarindo, while Parque Nacional Santa Rosa is the destination for olive ridley turtles. The only **towns** of any significance for travellers are the provincial capital of **Liberia**, and **Nicoya**, the main town on the peninsula. If you are overnighting on the way to **Nicaragua**, La Cruz makes a useful base.

These days, Guanacaste is changing fast. An enormous number of hotels, some all-inclusive resorts, are being built on the Pacific coast. Inland, mass tourism is less

PLAYA SÁMARA

Highlights

❶ Parque Nacional Rincón de la Vieja The beautiful landscapes of Volcán Rincón de la Vieja encompass terrains varying from rock-strewn savannah to patches of tropical dry forest, culminating in the blasted-out vistas of the volcano crater itself. **See p.256**

❷ Fiestas Lively community fiestas celebrate Guanacaste's livestock heritage with bullfights, rodeos, processions and traditional dancing. **See p.264, p.289 & p.292**

❸ Parque Nacional Santa Rosa Costa Rica's oldest national park, and also one of its most popular, with good trails, great surfing and plenty of turtle-spotting opportunities. **See p.265**

❹ Leatherback turtles Playa Grande is the annual destination for hundreds of leatherback turtles, the largest of the four species of marine turtle that lay their eggs along Costa Rica's shores. **See p.281**

❺ Cowboys Skilful and self-reliant, Guanacaste's cowboys – or *sabaneros* – encapsulate the history of Costa Rica's vibrant rural communities. **See p.289**

❻ Parque Nacional Barra Honda Explore subterranean limestone caves filled with eerie formations, stalagmites and stalactites. **See p.292**

❼ Playa Sámara One of the Pacific coast's finest beaches, with excellent swimming, spectacular sunsets and good waves for beginner surfers. **See p.294**

HIGHLIGHTS ARE MARKED ON THE MAP ON P.246

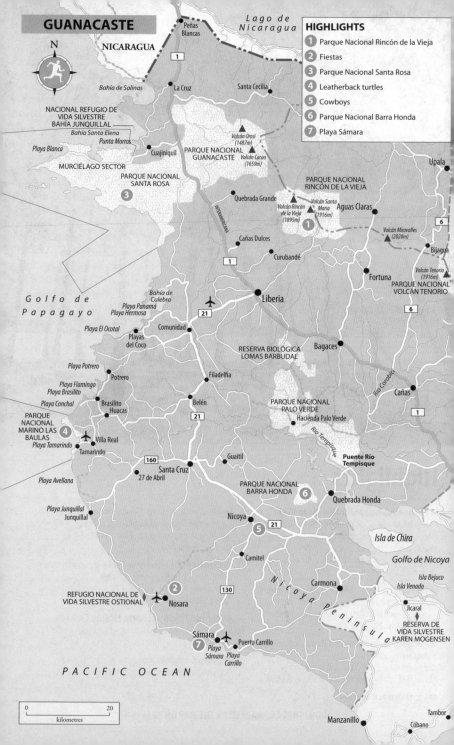

evident, and, despite the presence of *McDonald's* in its dignified streets, Liberia itself remains one of the most charming towns in the country. There seems to be no getting away from "progress", however, and the province may become many tourists' first, and perhaps only, glimpse of the country.

Brief history

Due to significant excavations in the area and some contemporaneous Spanish accounts, Guanacaste's **pre-Columbian** history is better documented than that of the rest of Costa Rica. Archeologists have long been interested in the **Chorotegas**, considered to have been the most highly developed of all Costa Rica's scattered and isolated pre-Columbian peoples, but whose culture predictably went into swift decline after the Conquest. In archeological terms it belongs to the **Greater Nicoya Subarea**, a pre-Columbian designation that includes some of western Nicaragua, and which continues to yield buried clues to the extent of communication between the Maya and Aztec cultures to the north and smaller groups inhabiting Mesoamerica from the fifth to the fifteenth centuries.

Following the Conquest, the region became part of the administrative entity known as the **Capitanía General de Guatemala**. Guanacaste was annexed by Nicaragua in 1787, but in 1812 the Spanish rulers about-turned and donated the province to Costa Rica, so that its territory became large enough for it to be officially represented in the Captaincy. When the modern-day Central American nations declared independence from Spain, and the Captaincy was dissolved in 1821, Guanacaste found itself in the sensitive position of being claimed by both Costa Rica and Nicaragua. In an 1824 vote the province's inhabitants made their allegiances clear: the Guanacastecos in the north, traditionally cattle ranchers with familial ties to Nicaragua, voted to join that country, while the inhabitants of the Nicoya Peninsula wished to maintain links with Costa Rica. The peninsular vote won out, by a slim margin.

As the nineteenth century progressed, **cattle ranching** began to dominate the landscape, providing the mainstay of the economy until well into the twentieth century. Despite the continuing presence of the cattle culture and the *sabanero* (see box, p.289) in Guanacaste, however, beef prices have been dropping in Costa Rica for some years now, after the boom years of the 1960s and 1970s when deforestation was rife. In contrast, as in the rest of the country, the **tourist industry** is becoming increasingly important to the local economy.

ARRIVAL AND DEPARTURE

By car Access to most of Guanacaste from San José is easy via the Autopista General Cañas (Hwy-27) to the Puntarenas turn-off, then the Interamericana (Hwy-1), which runs right through to the Nicaraguan border at Peñas Blancas. Follow the road rules, particularly on the Interamericana, which is heavily patrolled by traffic cops.

By bus Modern, comfortable buses ply the highway, with good services to Cañas, Liberia and the border. The national parks of Rincón de la Vieja and Santa Rosa are trickier to reach, however, and bus travellers may have to walk, hitch or take a taxi for part of the journey. All the beaches are accessible by bus and car, though the roads are not in fantastic shape, and journeys from San José can take several hours.

GUANACASTE'S CLIMATE

Highland Ticos tend to describe Guanacaste as a virtual desert, liberally applying the words *caliente* (hot) and *seco* (dry). Certainly it is dry, in comparison to the rest of the country: parts of it receive only 500mm of rain a year, ten times less than the Caribbean coast. To some extent irrigation has helped, but in summer (Dec–April), Guanacaste still experiences some drought. This is when you'll see an eerie landscape of bare, silver-limbed trees glinting in the sun, as many shed their leaves in order to conserve water. The province is significantly greener, and prettier, in the wet season (May–Nov), which is generally agreed to be the **best time** to come, with the added benefit of fewer travellers and lighter rainfall than the rest of the country receives during these months.

5

INFORMATION

Tourist information In Bagaces, opposite the Interamericana turn-off to Parque Nacional Palo Verde (Mon–Fri 8am–4pm; ☎ 2671 1455). This ACT regional office is not geared up for tourists, though staff can advise on current road conditions to Palo Verde and provide information on parks in Guanacaste. For general information, it's best to stop by the ICT offices in Liberia (see p.261) or Nicoya (see p.291).

Cañas

Sleepy, arid **CAÑAS**, 168km northwest of San José, is the heart of agricultural commerce for the surrounding area. While a pleasant morning or afternoon can be spent **rafting** the nearby **Río Corobicí**, it's only really worth staying overnight in Cañas if you arrive late or are planning to use it as a base for a trip into Palo Verde or Tenorio.

In town, activity is decidedly at a minimum; what there is of it mostly takes place within a few blocks of the unremarkable grassy and concrete **central square**. It's a pleasant town of single- and two-storey traditional buildings with only one real sight to speak of, the incongruous modernist **church**, on the east side of the square. The barn-like structure is replete with colourful, Gaudí-esque mosaics that reach a bright blue crescendo in the steeple, capped by an understated cross. Its interior is significantly more subdued, marked by a ceiling covered with stained wood blocks and a minimalist altar backed by a wall patterned with limestone rectangles.

Las Pumas Rescue Shelter

5km west of Cañas on Hwy-1 • Daily 8am–4pm • $10 • ☎ 2669 6044, ⓦ centrorescatelaspumas.org • It is 500m up a side road from Safaris Corobicí

For about forty years, **Las Pumas Rescue Shelter** has provided a refuge for native wildlife once kept as pets or orphaned due to human activity. Although its enclosures are not huge, the centre cares for over sixty species of animal, including five of Costa Rica's six native cats: jaguars, pumas, margays, jaguarundi and ocelots, who cannot be released back into the wild.

ARRIVAL AND INFORMATION   CAÑAS

By bus Buses arrive at the terminal at Av 11, C 1, four blocks north of the central square.
Destinations Bagaces (every 15–30min; 1hr); Bijagua (9 daily; 1hr 5min); Liberia (9 daily; 50min); Nicoya (12 daily; 2hr 15min); San José (11 daily; 3hr 30min); Upala (1hr 45min).

Tourist information The town has no tourist office; the staff at *Hotel Cañas* (see opposite) are a good source of area information.

ACCOMMODATION AND EATING

Cafetería Sol Café Av 3, C 5 ☎ 8627 9558. Cute café and one of the few places in town that seems to have a constant buzz about it, particularly at lunchtime when you can order salads ($5–8), sandwiches ($6–10) and heftier fare. It's a good place to linger over a cup of coffee, which is first-rate. Daily 7am–6pm.

RAFTING THE RÍO COROBICÍ

Five kilometres west of Cañas on the Interamericana, the long-established **Safaris Corobicí** (trips depart daily from 7am–3.30pm; ☎ 2669 6191, ⓦ safaricorobici.com) specializes in gentle floating trips on the Río Corobicí (2hr to half a day; $52–65, snacks included). Knowledgeable guides row while you observe the local mammals and reptiles, including howler and spider monkeys, surprisingly large crocodiles, iguanas and caimans. The trip also provides a prime opportunity for birdwatching, as several species, including motmots, cuckoos, falcons, ospreys, herons and the endangered jabiru stork, can all be spotted along the river's length.

Hacienda La Pacifica 5km northeast of town on the Interamericana ☎2669 9393, Ⓦpacificacr.com. Set in the grounds of a large cattle ranch, this hotel has country-style *cabinas* furnished with wi-fi, sleek bathrooms and comfortable, ornate beds. The most refined meal in the area can be had at the restaurant here, where most of the ingredients are grown or raised on the ranch's land (most mains around $14–20). **$86**

Hotel Cañas C 2, Av 3 ☎2669 0039, Ⓦhotelcanascr.com. A couple of blocks from the main square, this central option has 36 bland, but clean rooms with wi-fi; some have cable TV and a/c. The restaurant is not exactly memorable but serves straightforward good-value food, such as rice-and-beans with chicken ($7). **$33**

DIRECTORY

Money and exchange The most central bank is the Banco Nacional branch on C Central at Av 1.

Petrol station There's a petrol station on the Interamericana at Avenida 2, on the western edge of town.

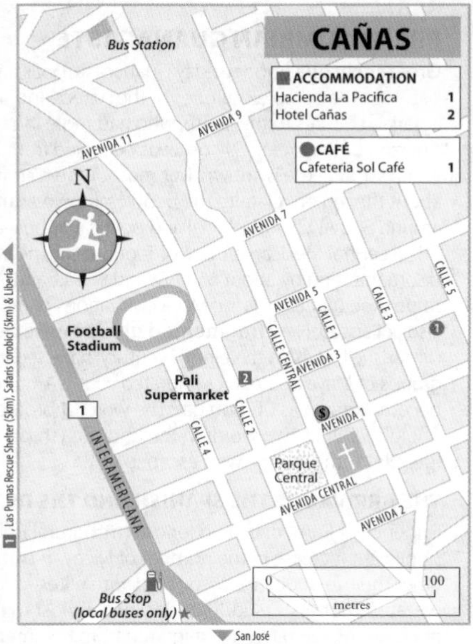

Parque Nacional Palo Verde and around

23km southwest of Bagaces • Daily 8am–4pm • $10

The **PARQUE NACIONAL PALO VERDE**, on the northern bank of the Río Tempisque, was created in 1982 to preserve the habitat of the **migratory birds** that nest in the estuary of the Tempisque and a large patch of relatively undisturbed lowland dry forest. With a distinctive topography featuring ridged limestone hills – unique to this part of the country, and attesting to the fact that certain parts of Guanacaste were once under water – the park shelters about fifteen separate ecological habitats. From December to May, Palo Verde can dry out into baked mudflats, while in the wet season, extensive flooding gives rise to saltwater and freshwater lakes and swamps. Following the wet season, the great floodplain drains slowly, creating marshes, mangroves and other habitats favoured by migratory birds. Little visited by tourists, the park is mainly of interest to serious **birders**, but what you see depends on the time of year – by far the **best months** are at the height of the dry season (Jan–March), when most of the 250 or so migratory species are in residence. In the wet season, flooding makes parts of the park inaccessible.

The park is home to one of the largest concentrations of **waterfowl** in Central America, both indigenous and migratory, with more than three hundred species of bird, among them the endangered jabiru stork and black-crowned night heron. Further from the riverbank, in the tree cover along the bottom and ridges of the limestone hills, you may spot toucans, and perhaps even one of the increasingly rare scarlet macaws. At evening during the dry season, many birds and other species – monkeys, coatis and even deer – congregate around the few remaining waterholes; bring binoculars and a torch. Note, though, that you shouldn't swim in the Río Tempisque (or anywhere else), as it's home to particularly huge crocodiles – some, according to the park rangers, are as much as 5m long.

5

PRE-COLUMBIAN GUANACASTE

Greater Nicoya (modern-day Guanacaste) was an archeological and cultural buffer zone between the complex cultures of the Aztecs and the Maya to the north, and the simpler agrarian cultures to the south, who had more in common with the prehistoric peoples of the Amazon basin. Greater Nicoya was occupied from an indeterminate date by the **Nicoyans**, about whom little is known, but most of the historical and archeological facts discovered about the region relate to the peoples known as the **Chorotegas**, who arrived in Nicoya around 800 AD, fleeing social and political upheavals far to the north.

The central Mexican empire of Teotihuacán, near the Mexico City of today, had fallen into disorganization by about 650 AD, and was abandoned about one hundred years later, at the same time that the Classic Maya civilizations of modern-day Yucatán and northern Guatemala also collapsed. New **fragmented groups** were created, some of whom forged migratory, militaristic bands. In the eighth century, harassed by their territorial enemies the Olmecs, groups of Maya and Aztecs migrated south. Among them were the people who would become known as Chorotegas. The word Chorotega derives from either their place of origin, Cholula, or from two words in the Chorotegan language: *cholol* (to run or escape) and *teca* (people) – "the people who escaped".

THE ARRIVAL OF THE SPANISH AND THE DEMISE OF THE CHOROTEGAS

Evidence of immediate and long-term cultural upheaval in the area after 800 AD includes a significant increase in the number of Nicoyan **burial sites** found dating from around this time. The use of objects associated with elites – like ceremonial skulls, jades and elaborate metates (mortars) – suddenly declined almost to the point of disappearing completely, and populations seem to have migrated from the interior toward the coasts. While this evidence could suggest a natural disaster (a volcanic eruption, perhaps) it also bears the hallmarks of what could be termed an invasion.

The Chorotegas' first contact with the **Spanish** was calamitous. The 1522 Spanish expedition from Panama up the Pacific coast to Nicaragua brought smallpox, the plague and influenza to the indigenous people of Greater Nicoya. Imprisonment and slavery followed, with coastal peoples raided, branded and sold into slavery in Panama and Peru. The demise of the Chorotegas from the sixteenth century was rapid and unreversed.

BELIEF SYSTEMS AND RITUALS

Excavations in Guanacaste and the Nicoya Peninsula reveal something of the Chorotegas' **belief systems** and social arrangements. Near Bahía Culebra, anthropologists

The trails

From the Hacienda Palo Verde Research Station two **trails** lead up to the top of hills, from where you can see the expansive mouth of the Río Tempisque to the west and the broad plains of Guanacaste to the east. A number of other **loop trails**, none more than 4km long, run through the park. The shortest of the trails, at just 300m, is **Las Calizas**; others include **El Manigordo** ("ocelot"; 1.5km), **El Mapache** ("raccoon"; 2km) and **El Venado** ("deer"; 2km), all of which give you a good idea of the landscape and a chance of viewing the animals after which they're named. You've also got a good chance of seeing collared peccaries, abundant in this area, or a coati, which you may see or hear foraging in the undergrowth. White-tailed deer also live here, but they're very shy and likely to dart off at the sound of your approach.

For longer treks, try the **Bosque Primario** trail (about 7km), through, as the name suggests, primary forest cover. You can also walk the 6km (dry season only) to the edge of the Río Tempisque from where you'll see the aptly named **Isla de los Pájaros** (Bird Island). Square in the mouth of the river, the island is chock-full of our feathered friends all year, with black-crowned night herons swirling above in thick dark clouds. Many hotels and tour agencies in the province offer boat trips around the island, but landings are not permitted, so you have to content yourself with bird-spotting and taking photographs from the boat.

unearthed pottery shards, utensils and the remains of hearths, along with a burial ground holding twenty females, children and infants. Chorotega villages were made up of longhouse-type structures – common to many indigenous cultures of the Americas – inhabited by entire extended families, and centred on a large square, site of religious ceremonies and meetings.

Like the Maya and Aztecs, the Chorotegas had a belief system built around **blood-letting** and the **sacrifice** of animals and humans. Although it is not known if beating hearts were ripped from chests, virgins were definitely thrown into volcano craters to appease their gods, about whom little is known. Chorotegas also believed in **yulios**, the spirit alter ego that escaped from their mouths at the moment of death to roam the world forever. Although pagan, Chorotega priests shared a number of duties and functions with the Catholic priests who worked to destroy their culture. Celibate, they may also have heard confessions and meted out punishments for sins.

Few Chorotega **rituals** are documented. One known practice was the formation of a kind of human maypole, consisting of *voladores*, or men suspended "flying" (actually roped) from a post, twirling themselves round and round while descending to the ground. Originating with the Aztecs, the ritual was dedicated to the Morning Star, considered to be a deity; the four *voladores* represented the cardinal points. While no longer displayed in Costa Rica, it is still performed in the Mexican state of Veracruz and in certain villages in Guatemala.

SOCIETAL AND CULTURAL MARKERS

The Chorotega **economy** was based on maize (corn). They also cultivated tobacco, fruit, beans and cotton, using cacao beans as currency, and the marketplace was run by women. All land was held communally, as was everything that was cultivated and harvested, which was then distributed throughout the settlement. This plurality did not extend to social prestige, however. Three strata characterized Chorotega society: at the upper echelon were chieftains (*caciques*), warriors and priests; in the middle were the commoners, and at the bottom were the slaves and prisoners of war. The Chorotegas were the only indigenous peoples in Costa Rica to have a written **language**, comprising hieroglyphs similar to those used by the Maya. They were also skilled artisans, producing ornamental jewellery and jade, and colouring cotton fabrics with animal and vegetable dyes. It was the Chorotegas who made the bulk of the distinctive **ceramics** so celebrated in the country today, many of which can be seen in San José's Museo Nacional (see p.96).

Check with rangers regarding **conditions** before walking on any of the trails: access is constantly subject to change, due to flooding and sometimes bee colonies. The Río Tempisque walk in particular can be muddy and unpleasantly insect-ridden in all but the driest months. You should bring plenty of water, as the heat and humidity are considerable.

ARRIVAL AND INFORMATION

PARQUE NACIONAL PALO VERDE

By car Getting to Palo Verde takes a while, though it is theoretically possible year-round with a regular non-4WD vehicle. From the well-signed turn-off from the Interamericana at Bagaces (opposite the Área de Conservación Tempisque regional office), it's a 23km drive to the entrance hut, and a further 7km to the Organization for Tropical Studies (OTS) Research Station. There are signs all along the road to the park, but at long intervals, and the road forks unnervingly from time to time without indicating which way to go. If in doubt, follow the tyre tracks made by the rangers.

Tourist information The ACT office (see p.248) is the most complete source of information on the park; the ranger station at the park entrance can also advise on the trails and where to spot wildlife.

ACCOMMODATION

Ranger Station Campsite ☎ 2671 1290 or ☎ 2671 1062. It's possible to camp at the small site next to the ranger station at the park entrance, where there are lavatories, but it's best to call ahead to check that there's space. $$

Hwy-1 (8km)   Bagaces (11km) & Ortega (98km)

PARQUE NACIONAL PALO VERDE AND RESERVA BIOLÓGICA LOMAS BARBUDAL

Entrance

Visitor Centre

RESERVA BIOLÓGICA
LOMAS BARBUDAL

922

N

Entrance
1

Research
Station 1 2

Sendero Isla Pájaros

PARQUE NACIONAL
PALO VERDE

Sendero Bosque Primario

Isla de
los Pájaros

Laguna Nicaragua

ACCOMMODATION
Hacienda Palo Verde
  Research Station   2
Ranger Station Campsite   1

RESTAURANT
Hacienda Palo Verde
  Research Station   1

0   4
      kilometres

Río Tempisque

- - - - - Trail

Hacienda Palo Verde Research Station About 7km south of the park entrance ☎ 2524 0607, ⊛ ots.ac.cr. The OTS has a rustic field station at Palo Verde, originally set up for comparative ecosystem study and research into the dry forest habitat. If it's not full of scientific researchers, you can stay there. Accommodation is in clean dormitories, and all meals are included in the rate. ̄$93

TOURS

While it's possible from the trails to see some of the bird species for which Palo Verde is noted, travelling along the Río Tempisque offers far more opportunities. In addition to the tour operator listed below, some of the tour operators based in Liberia (see p.261) offer boat tours in the park.

Palo Verde Boat Tours Ortega ☎ 2651 8001, ⊛ palo verdeboattours.com. With its main office in a small community just west of the national park, this locally owned and operated company leads friendly and informative 2hr tours on the Tempisque. Pick-ups can be arranged from several points throughout Guanacaste, with prices varying depending on the distance from the national park. If you make your own way to the national park, the rate is $50.

5

> ### BEWARE THE KILLER BEES
>
> In recent years swarms of **Africanized bees** – sometimes sensationally termed "killer bees" – have taken to colonizing Palo Verde. Africanized bees are aggressive, and may pursue – in packs – anyone who unwittingly disturbs one of their large, quite obvious, nests. They are known to attack dark colours, so if attacked remove all dark clothing and cover dark hair. The conventional technique is to cover your head and run in a zigzag pattern so that you can dodge the cloud of pursuing bees. Although, luckily, this occurs very rarely, you should take special care if you are sensitive to stings, and ask the rangers about the presence of nests on or around trails. Bees are also found in the Reserva Biológica Lomas Barbudal (see below).

Reserva Biológica Lomas Barbudal

7km north of Parque Nacional Palo Verde • Daily 8am–4pm • $10

The **RESERVA BIOLÓGICA LOMAS BARBUDAL** is an impressive, though small-scale, initiative just north of Parque Nacional Palo Verde. Home to some of the last vestiges of true **tropical dry forest** in the region, Lomas Barbudal means "bearded hills" and that's just what they look like, with relatively bare pates surrounded by sideburns of bushy deciduous trees. Stretches of savannah-like open grassland are punctuated by the thorny-looking **shoemaker's tree** and crisscrossed by rivers and the strips of deciduous woods that hug their banks. The reserve also features isolated examples of the majestic **mahogany** and **rosewood** trees, whose deep-blood-red timber is coveted as material for furniture.

Lomas Barbudal is also rich in **wildlife**. If you don't spot a howler monkey, you'll at least likely hear one. And, this is practically the only place in Guanacaste where you have a reasonable chance of seeing the **scarlet macaw**. Like Parque Nacional Santa Rosa to the north, Lomas Barbudal hosts an abundance of **insects** – over 200 **bee species** alone, around 25 percent of the species of bees in the entire world. Those allergic to stings or otherwise intolerant of insects might want to give Lomas Barbudal a miss; they're everywhere, including the aggressive Africanized bees (see box above).

The visitor centre and around

The visitor centre (called the Casa de Patrimonio) has a small museum with a few displays on the flora and fauna; from here a **short trail** (2km roundtrip) leads to a sizeable watering hole equally popular with wildlife (particularly in the dry season) which come to cool off and swimmers who do the same. There are also two swimmable rivers and a small network of unmarked trails designed and cleared by local volunteers.

ARRIVAL AND INFORMATION	RESERVA BIOLÓGICA LOMAS BARBUDAL
By car Lomas Barbudal is 14km from Bagaces and is best reached with your own transport. Take Hwy-1 northwest from Bagaces, and after about 8km follow the road off to the left; note that it's in pretty bad condition. It's also possible to reach the reserve from Palo Verde via a very rough 7km track from the national park's entrance; ask at the ranger station if the road is passable before trying this route.	**By taxi** It's possible to arrange a taxi from Bagaces, which costs about $30 round-trip. **Tourist information** The visitor centre (at the park entrance 6km from the Interamericana turn-off; ☎ 2659 9194) is on the scenic banks of the Río Cabuyo, and can provide information about the reserve.

Cordillera de Guanacaste

The rugged Cordillera de Guanacaste cuts a large diagonal swath through the region's uppermost reaches, stretching from Volcán Arenal (see p.217) in the southeast to Volcán Orosi in the northwest in Parque Nacional Guanacaste (see p.268). At its heart, **VOLCÁN MIRAVALLES** and **VOLCÁN TENORIO** loom large over the hot Guanacaste lowlands. Miravalles, at 2028m the highest volcano in Guanacaste, is home to an

5

TROPICAL DRY FOREST

With its mainly deciduous cover, Guanacaste's **tropical dry forest**, created by the combination of a Pacific lowland topography and arid conditions, looks startlingly different depending upon the time of year. In the height of the dry season, almost no rain falls on lowland Guanacaste, the trees are bare, having shed their leaves in an effort to conserve water, and the landscape takes on a melancholy, burnt-sienna hue. In April or May, when the rains come, the whole of Guanacaste perks up and begins to look comparatively green, although the dry forest never takes on the lush look of the rainforest.

The story of the demise of the tropical dry forests in Mesoamerica is one of nearly wholesale destruction. In all, only about two percent of the region's pre-Columbian dry forest survives, and what was once a carpet stretching the length of the Pacific side of the isthmus from southern Mexico to Panama now exists only in besieged pockets. Today, dry forests cover just 518 square kilometres of Costa Rica, almost all in Guanacaste, concentrated around the Río Tempisque and, more significantly, north in the Parque Nacional Santa Rosa. Due to deforestation and climatic change, tropical dry forests are considered a rare life-zone. Their relative dryness means they are easily overrun by field fires, which ranchers light in order to burn off old pasture. Hardy grasses spring up in their wake, such as the imported African jaragua, which gives much of Guanacaste its African savannah-like appearance.

TREE SPECIES

Along with the leafy trees, tropical dry forest features **palms** and even a few **evergreens**. At the very top of a good thick patch of dry forest you see the umbrella form of **canopy trees**, although these are much shorter than in the tropical rainforest. Dry forest is a far less complex ecosystem than the humid rainforest, which has about three or four layers of vegetation. Like temperate-zone deciduous forests, the tropical dry forest has only two strata. The ground shrub layer is fleshed out by thorn bushes and tree ferns, primitive plants that have been with us since the time of the dinosaurs. Unlike rainforest, dry forest has very few epiphytes (plants growing on the trees), except for bromeliads (the ones that look something like upside-down pineapple leaves). The most biologically diverse examples of tropical dry forest are in the lower elevations of Parque Nacional Santa Rosa, where the canopy trees are a good height, with many different species of deciduous tree. There are also some pockets of mangroves and even a few evergreens in the wetter parts of the park.

WILDLIFE

Tropical dry forests can support a large variety of **mammal life**, as in the Parque Nacional Santa Rosa–Parque Nacional Guanacaste corridor. Deer and smaller mammals, such as the coati and paca, are most common, along with large cats, from the jaguar to the ocelot, provided they have enough room to hunt. You may see the endangered **scarlet macaw**, which likes to feed on the seeds of the sandbox tree, in a few remaining pockets of Pacific dry forest, including Lomas Barbudal and, further south, around Río Tárcoles and Parque Nacional Carara (see p.341), itself a transition zone between the dry forests of the north and the wetter tropical cover of the southern Pacific coast. In addition, the staggering number and diversity of **insects** are of great interest to biologists and entomologists: there are more than two hundred types of bee in Lomas Barbudal, for example, and a large number of butterflies and moths in Parque Nacional Santa Rosa.

important forest reserve with abundant wildlife and birds, though it's not open to the public, while Tenorio forms the centrepiece of an increasingly popular national park. From **Hwy-6**, a reasonably maintained fifty-eight-kilometre stretch that runs between the two volcanoes, you can contemplate the spectacular colour changes and cloud shadows on their flanks.

Parque Nacional Volcán Tenorio

Daily 8am–5pm • $10

An active volcano (1916m), although so far without spectacular eruptive displays, **TENORIO** was designated a national park in 1995. Though most people come to the park to glimpse the surreal turquoise waters of the **Río Celeste**, wildlife also thrives within the park's borders, and you may be lucky enough to spot tapirs, agoutis, armadillos, long-tailed manakins and howler monkeys.

A **trail** (6km; 4hr round-trip) departs from the ranger station at the park entrance and enters the forest where it eventually splits into a few well-marked loops. Don't wander from the trails, for the area is geothermically active; there are fumaroles (little columns of hot vapour escaping from the ground) and mud pots – one false move and you could step into skin-stripping superheated volcanic soil. The main trail climbs steadily and opens up to a spectacular view of Volcán Miravalles, before eventually leading to a striking waterfall of the Río Celeste where you can take a dip. The highlights of the park, though, are a stunningly blue lagoon, the **Laguna Azul**, and similarly coloured (bright blue) sections of the river that flow alongside the trail – all created by a rare mix of sulphur, copper sulphate and calcium carbonate.

ARRIVAL	PARQUE NACIONAL VOLCÁN TENORIO

By car From the Reserva Biológica Privada La Pacífica, 7km north of Cañas, turn north off the Interamericana onto the paved road to Upala (Hwy-6). In Bijagua, there's a sign by the supermarket for the turn-off to the park.

ACCOMMODATION AND EATING

Restaurante Los Pilones Opposite the ranger station ☏ 8866 8088. The only place to eat in the national park is the friendly *Restaurante Los Pilones* in a whitewashed building with outside seating and a pleasant overlook. It serves reasonably priced, well-made *comida típica*, such as chicken with rice-and-beans ($6). Daily 10am–8pm.

Rio Celeste Hideaway 2km south of the entrance to Parque Nacional Volcán Tenorio on Hwy-4 ☏ 2206 5114, ⓦ riocelestehideaway.com. Within walking distance of the national park entrance, this striking property has several comfortable garden- and forest-side earth-toned *casitas*, each adorned with handsome dark-wood furnishings. Amenities include huge canopy beds, outdoor showers, and flat-screen TVs. There's also a pretty pool with its own bar as well as an upscale restaurant and sleek lounge. **$215**

Bijagua

About thirty minutes north from the Interamericana turn-off and located roughly equidistant between the two volcanoes is the small hamlet of **BIJAGUA**, an impressively enterprising community that is home to a number of ecotourism projects, including an ecology centre, organic farms and a collective of female artisans. Though there's not much to detain you, it's a good spot to stock up on picnic supplies before venturing into the national park, or to take a tour to Refugio Nacional de Vida Silvestre Caño Negro (see p.228), travelling via the spectacular road north to Upala, from where you can glimpse the shimmering blue waters of Lago Nicaragua and the Islas Solentiname.

ARRIVAL AND DEPARTURE	BIJAGUA

By bus There's a small bus stop on the main road in the centre of the village. Destinations Cañas (8–10 daily; 50min); Upala (8–10 daily; 40min).

ACCOMMODATION AND EATING

Albergue Ecoturística Heliconia 3km north of Bijagua on the road to Upala ☏ 2466 8483. At 750m elevation in a private forest reserve right between the volcanoes, this beautifully sited lodge holds several hiking trails, waterfalls and natural hot springs. The accommodation consists of six cabins with private bath, and four smartly designed spacious cottages; there's also a restaurant and stunning views from around the grounds. The lodge can arrange walking tours of Parque Nacional Volcán Tenorio as well as trips to the Refugio Nacional de Vida Silvestre Caño Negro. Breakfast is included. *Cabinas* **$55**, cottage **$74**

La Carolina Lodge 7km northeast from Bijagua, in the hamlet of San Miguel ☏ 2466 6393, ⓦ lacarolinalodge .com. The rustic *La Carolina Lodge* is set on a working farm well off the beaten path amid tranquil surroundings and has *cabinas* (all meals included) as well as a house off the grounds (sleeping up to seven people; meals not included). By the lodge is a (swimmable) river where toucans, green parrots and hummingbirds nest, and where you might also catch a glimpse of sloths and anteaters. Included in the very reasonable price are delicious home-style meals, a guided walk and a horseriding tour. Trips to Parque Nacional Tenorio

5

can be arranged ($65/person includes three meals and a guide), and the owners offer transport from Liberia ($75/carload); alternatively, a taxi from Bijagua to the lodge costs about $12. *Cabinas* $75, house $75

Casitas Tenorio About 3km east of Bijagua ☎ 8312 1248, ⓦ casitastenorio.com. Two charming and comfortable *casitas* set on a farm with views of Volcán Miravalles. There is an outdoor kitchen, and camping is possible on-site. The friendly owners can arrange guided hikes and tours of the area as well as homestays. Camping $10, *casitas* $70

The Miravalles hot springs

Over 26,000 acres encircling **Volcán Miravalles** are given over to the Miravalles Protected Zone, a diverse mix of cloudforest and dry savannah home to a wide variety of species, including peccaries, coyotes and capuchin and howler monkeys. While the Protected Zone lacks tourist facilities, the surrounding area holds numerous enticing **hot springs** and mud pools, by-products of the extensive underground geothermal activity. A handful of complexes have been erected around the more accessible hot springs, all of which are within easy reach of Bijagua, making an afternoon or evening visit ideal after a hike in Parque Nacional Volcán Tenorio.

Las Hornillas Volcanic Activity Center

4km northeast of Bagaces • Daily 8am–5pm • $35; waterfall $40; combo $55; all rates include lunch • ☎ 8839 9769, ⓦ hornillas.com

One of the first operators in the area to capitalize on Miravalles' geothermic activity, **Las Hornillas Volcanic Activity Center** offers dips in large mud pools, soothing hot springs, swimming pools, walks to and around an active crater, a sauna, a torpedo-like ride down a never-ending water slide and a pretty hike through the forest to two nearby waterfalls. The facilities are not as well maintained as they could be, but the owners are friendly and the views – drifting clouds permitting – can be spectacular.

Yökö Termales

3km northeast of Bagaces • Daily 7am–10pm • $10 • ☎ 2673 0410, ⓦ yokotermales.com

If you're mainly interested in a therapeutic soak, inexpensive **Yökö Termales** is a good bet with its five hot springs surrounded by a manicured lawn near the base of Miravalles. The sterile feel aside – you can order food and drinks from a poolside bar and the layout is reminiscent of a water park – it's not usually as crowded as some of the other area options.

Parque Nacional Rincón de la Vieja

About 25km northeast of Liberia • Daily 8am–4pm • $10 • ☎ 2661 8139, ⓦ acguanacaste.ac.cr

Arguably Guanacaste's most memorable national park, the entirety of **PARQUE NACIONAL RINCÓN DE LA VIEJA** is utterly dominated by its massive and majestic

---

THE FLOWERING TREES OF GUANACASTE

Guanacaste's many flowering trees dot the landscape with pastel puffs of colour. Trees blossom in a strange way in the dry lands of Guanacaste, flowering literally overnight and then, just as suddenly, shedding their petals to the ground, covering it in a carpet of confetti colours. The **corteza amarilla** bursts into a wild Van Gogh-like blaze in March, April and May, and is all the more dramatic being set against a landscape of burnt siennas, muted mauves and sallow yellows. The **guanacaste** tree itself, also called the "elephant ear", is a majestic wide-canopied specimen and an emblem of the nation. Its cream-coloured flowers appear in May, and its curious seed pods feed the cattle and horses.

In November the deciduous **guachipelín** tree blooms, with its delicate fern-like leaves; in January it's time for the pastel-pink floss of the **poui**, followed in March by the equally pretty **tabebuia rosea**. By the end of the dry season, the red flowers of the **malinche** explode into colour.

namesake volcano, a perfectly proportioned conical-shaped peak. In the park's eastern sector, the crater of Volcán Santa María is impressive in its own right, even if it's not quite as visually arresting. The beautifully dry landscape encompasses terrains varying from rock-strewn savannah to patches of tropical dry forest and it's undeniably an enchanting place, with quite simply the best **hiking** and **horseriding** in the country. A variety of elevations and habitats reveals hot springs, sulphur pools, bubbling **mud pots** (*pilas de barro*), fields of *guaria morada* (purple orchids) – the national flower – plus a great smoking volcano at the top to reward you for your efforts. **Animals** in the area include all the big cats (just don't expect to see them), the shy tapir, red deer, collared peccary, two-toed sloth, and howler, white-faced and spider monkeys. There's a good chance you will see a brilliant flash of fluttering blue – this is the **Blue Morpho** butterfly, famous for its electric colours. **Birders** will enjoy the profusion of over two hundred species in residence and may spot the weird-looking three-wattled bellbird, the Montezuma oropendola, the trogon and the spectacled owl, among others.

The local dry season (Dec–March especially) is the **ideal time** to visit the park, when the hiking trails and visibility are at their best and the heat is fairly comfortable.

The trails

From the Las Pailas ranger station (see p.258), you have several walking options, with trails leading west to the *cataratas escondidas* (hidden waterfalls) and east to the Santa María station, along an 8km path. **Sendero Las Pailas**, the most popular and least demanding trail, heads east on a very satisfying 6km circuit past many of the highly unusual natural features with which the park abounds, including a mini-volcano and "Pilas de Barro" **mud pots**; listen out for strange bubbling sounds, like a large pot of water boiling over. Mud pots, which should be treated with respect, are formed when mud, thermally heated by subterranean rivers of magma, seeks vents in the ground, sometimes actually forcing itself out through the surface in great thick gloops. It's a surreal sight: grey-brown muck blurping out of the ground like slowly thickening gravy. Another feature is the geothermal **hornillas** (literally, "stoves"), mystical-looking holes in the ground exhaling elegant puffs of steam. You almost expect to stumble upon the witches of *Macbeth*, brewing spite over them. Make sure not to go nearer than a metre or so, or you'll be steamed in no time. The combined effect of all these boiling holes is to

5

SAFETY IN RINCÓN DE LA VIEJA

The land here is actually alive and breathing: Rincón de la Vieja's last major eruptions took place in 1995 and 1998, and were serious enough to evacuate local residents. The danger has always been to the northern side of the volcano, facing Nicaragua (the opposite side from the two entrance points), and the most pressing **safety** issue for tourists is to be aware that rivers of lava and hot mud still boil beneath the thin epidermis of ground. While danger areas are clearly marked with signs and fences, you still have to watch your step: walkers have been seriously burned from crashing through this crust and stepping into mud and water at above-boiling temperatures.

If you stay at one of the lodges and take their summit tours, either by horseback or on foot, you may pass through areas not covered in this section. Also, bear in mind that Rincón de la Vieja is an active volcano, and the trails described may be altered due to periodic **lava flows**. Before setting out, you should always check current conditions at one of the ranger stations, or call the Area de Conservación de Guanacaste (ACG) headquarters at the Parque Nacional Santa Rosa. It's also advisable to carry all your **drinking water** – streams might look inviting, but often carry high concentrations of minerals (like sulphur) that can lead to extreme stomach upset if drunk.

make the landscape a bit like brittle Swiss cheese – tread gingerly and look carefully where you're going to avoid the ground crumbling underneath you. Many hikers have been scalded by blithely strolling too close to the holes. The trail also takes you through forest with abundant fauna and flora, and be prepared to ford a couple of streams.

The hike to the summit

The most direct approach to the crater and summit of the Rincón de la Vieja volcano is via the Las Pailas entrance, along a marked trail. **Warning**: the trail to the summit is often closed due to low visibility or high winds, so it's definitely worth ringing ahead to check conditions. It's hard to get lost, but the top is 7.7km away, so you should start early to get up and down without hurrying too much.

The hike to the summit is definitely the highlight of the park; it takes you through forest similar to lower montane rainforest, densely packed, and lushly covered with epiphytes and mosses. Cool mist and rain often plague this section of the trail: if you are anywhere near the top and lose visibility, which can happen very suddenly, you're advised to stay away from the crater, whose brittle and ill-defined edges become more difficult to see, and consequently more dangerous, in cloudy weather.

At the **summit**, Rincón de la Vieja presents a barren lunar landscape, a smoking hole surrounded by black ash, with a pretty freshwater **lake**, Lago los Jilgueros, to the south. Quetzals are said to live in the forest that surrounds the lake, though you're unlikely to see them. When clear, the **views** up here are ample reward for the uphill sweating, with Lago de Nicaragua shimmering silver-blue to the north, the hump of the Cordillera Central to the southeast and the Pacific Ocean and spiny profile of the Nicoya Peninsula to the west. You can get hammered by wind at the top; bring a sweater and windbreaker.

Bosque Encantado trail

From the Santa María entrance, it's a more difficult and longer walk to the crater, but there are a number of other worthwhile trails, including the three-kilometre **Bosque Encantado** (Enchanted Forest) trail. It leads to a small forest and some hot springs next to a creek, which hikers love to leap into after a wallow in the springs, imitating a sauna effect. The temperature is usually just about right for soaking, but you should never jump into any thermal water without first checking current temperatures at the ranger station.

ARRIVAL AND INFORMATION	PARQUE NACIONAL RINCÓN DE LA VIEJA

Park entrances The park is split into two sectors: Sector Las Pailas ("cauldrons") and Sector Santa María, each with its own entrance and nearby ranger station. The two are linked by an 8km walking trail. From Liberia most people travel through the hamlet of Curubandé, about 16km northeast, to the Las Pailas sector. The other ranger station, Santa María, lies about 25km northeast of Liberia.

By private transfer Getting here from Liberia is an easy prospect – transfers run by hotels such as *La Posada del Tope* (see p.262) are convenient and good value.

By car To get to the Las Pailas sector by car (you'll almost certainly need a 4WD), where most of the lodges are, take the Interamericana north of Liberia for 6km, then turn right to the hamlet of Curubandé. Here you'll see signs for the *Guachipelín* and *Rincón de la Vieja* lodges. A couple of kilometres before *Guachipelín* there's a barrier and

tollbooth, where you'll be charged $1.75 to use the road. The Santa María sector and the *Rinconcito Lodge* are reached by driving through Liberia's Barrio La Victoria in the northeast of the town; ask for the *estadio* – the football stadium – from where it's a signed 24km drive to the park.

Hitching Hitching is also an option if you can find a truck driver making a delivery, possibly at the petrol station at La Esquina de las Bombas on the Interamericana at Liberia.

On foot Both routes to the park are along stony roads, not at all suitable for walking. People do, but it's tough, uninteresting terrain, and it's really more advisable to save your energy for the trails within the park itself.

ACCOMMODATION

Borinquen Mountain Resort About 3km northwest of the Las Pailas park entrance ☎ 2690 1900, ⓦ borinquenresort.com. Upmarket, expensive lodge with its own spa centre, mudpools and sauna, set in a stunning landscape at the skirts of Volcán Rincón de la Vieja. Accommodation is in luxurious and fully-equipped villas and bungalows. There's a classy restaurant, disabled access and facilities for kids. They also organize horseriding and ATV (all-terrain vehicle) excursions to the volcano. Villa $219, bungalow $244

Buena Vista Lodge 2km north of Cañas Dulces and 20km west of the Las Pailas park entrance ☎ 2665 7759, ⓦ buenavistalodgecr.com. A working cattle ranch – you can even ride with the cowhands if your horsemanship is up to it – with stupendous views over Guanacaste and some great trails through pockets of rainforest on the flanks of the volcano and up to the crater. Double rooms are housed in individual bungalows, many set around a small lake in which you can swim. A restaurant serves up wholesome meals, and there are reasonably priced horseriding and hiking tours available – the place even has its very own canopy tour. If you're driving here, a 4WD is recommended; alternatively, you can arrange to be picked up from Cañas Dulces (accessible from Liberia by bus). $89

Hacienda Guachipelín 5km beyond Curubandé on the edge of the park ☎ 2666 8075, ⓦ guachipelin.com. A working ranch, the *Guachipelín* looks every inch the old cattle hacienda, with comfortable doubles in the main house. There's a fantastic swimming pool, and breakfast is included in the price. Attractions include a nearby waterfall, mud pots and some well-marked trails; guides are available for several tours, including riding and hiking

to the volcano. Pick-ups from Liberia can be arranged for a fee. $112

Rincón de la Vieja Lodge 5km northwest of Guachipelín and 3.5km from the Las Pailas park entrance; follow the signs ☎ 2200 0238, ⓦ hotelrincondelaviejacr.com. Popular lodge with simple, rustic accommodation, including doubles with private bathroom and hot water, and bungalows decorated in attractive *sabanero* style. There's a pool and reading area and the restaurant serves tasty, filling meals. Horseriding, mountain biking, a canopy tour and swimming at nearby waterfalls can all be arranged. Pick-ups from Liberia can be arranged for a fee. $78

Rinconcito Lodge In San Jorge, 3km south of the Santa María park entrance ☎ 2666 2764, ⓦ rinconcito lodge.com. The cheapest option close to the park, this farm is owned by a friendly family and has plain but good-value *cabinas* with cold-water shared or private bathrooms. The owners are a good source of advice on local transport, guides and directions, and can also arrange horseriding, guided tours and pick-ups from Liberia. All meals are available at an additional cost. $39

Santa María and Las Pailas campsites Adjacent to both ranger stations. There's a basic campsite near the Las Pailas ranger station, and another slightly better equipped one at the Santa María ranger station, where there are lavatories and water, though you should take your own cooking utensils, food and water. $3

Santa María ranger station At the Santa María entrance ☎ 2666 5051. If you have a sleeping bag, and ask in advance, you can stay inside the musty bunk rooms in the Santa María ranger station (phone the ACG office at Santa Rosa for permission). $5

Liberia and around

True to its name, the spirited provincial capital of **LIBERIA** (from *libertad*, meaning liberty) is distinctively friendly and progressive, its wide streets the legacy of the pioneering farmers and cattle ranchers who founded it. Known colloquially as the "Ciudad Blanca" (White City) due to its whitewashed houses, Liberia is the only town

5

in Costa Rica that seems truly colonial in style and character. Many of the white houses still have their **puerta del sol** – corner doors that were used, ingeniously, to let the sun in during the morning and out in the late afternoon, thus heating and then cooling the interior throughout the day – an architectural feature left over from the colonial era and particular to this region.

Most travellers use Liberia simply as a jumping-off point for the national parks of **Rincón de la Vieja** and **Santa Rosa**, an overnight stop to or from the **beaches** of Guanacaste, or a break on the way to Nicaragua. However, Liberia is an appealing town, particularly to explore on foot in the shade of its numerous mango strees. The nearby international airport delivers busloads of visitors to the western beaches, but Liberia happily remains unchanged: it's still the epitome of dignified (if somewhat static) provincialism, with a strong identity and atmosphere all its own.

Parque Central

Av Central/1, C Central/2

The town is arranged around a large **Parque Central**, officially called Parque Mario Cañas Ruiz, named after a twentieth-century poet and musician whose songs paid tribute to *sabanero* culture. The *parque* is dedicated to *el mes del anexión*, the month of the annexation (July), celebrating the fact that Guanacaste is not in Nicaragua. Liberia's Parque Central is one of the loveliest central plazas in the whole country, ringed by benches and tall palms that shade gossiping locals. On the eastern edge of the *parque* is the town **church**, a contemporary structure whose startlingly modernist – some would say downright ugly – form looks a little out of place in this very traditional town.

Iglesia de la Agonía

Av Central, C 11 • Irregular hours • Free

The colonial, gleaming white **Iglesia de la Agonía** on the eastern end of town was long on the verge of collapse – it had a hard time from successive earthquakes – but a recent renovation has infused it with new life. It's still almost never open, but try

LIBERIA

ACCOMMODATION	
El Bramadero	5
Guanacaste	3
Hostal Ciudad Blanca	4
Hotel Liberia	1
Hotel Rincón del Llanó	6
La Posada del Tope	2
El Punto	7

CAFÉS AND RESTAURANTS	
Café Liberia	5
Cantarranas Tacos	8
Casa Verde	9
Los Comales	1
Jauja	6
Pan y Miel	7
Paso Real	3
Pizza Pronto	4
Restaurante Kleaver	2

BARS, CLUBS AND LIVE MUSIC	
Ciros Bar	3
Kurú	1
Las Tinajas	2

San José, Liberia Central Mall & Africa Mía

shoving the heavy wooden door. If it gives way, inside you'll see numerous remnants of the church's storied history, including ecclesiastical paintings hanging from the pillars and imposing statues.

Calle Real

The most historic street in town is the **Calle Real** (marked as Calle Central on some maps). In the nineteenth century this street was the entrance to Liberia, and practically the whole road has been restored to its original colonial simplicity. Stately white adobe homes feature large windows with ornate wooden frames and wide overhanging eaves under which locals pass the evenings in cane armchairs.

ARRIVAL AND DEPARTURE   LIBERIA

By plane 12km west of the town, Liberia's international airport is connected to San José by regular Sansa and NatureAir flights; you can take a taxi from here into town ($10) unless you fancy a 15min walk from the terminal to the main road, where any eastbound bus will take you to town.
Destinations via Sansa Nosara (1 daily; 1hr 10min); Playa Sámara (Mon–Sat 1 daily; 1hr); San José (1 daily; 1hr 15min); Tamarindo (3 daily; 50min).
Destinations via NatureAir Nosara (3 daily; 1hr 10min); Playa Sámara (4 daily; 1hr); San José (4 daily; 1hr 45min).
By bus Liberia is a main regional transport hub, providing easy access to Guanacaste's parks and beaches, the Nicaraguan border and San José. The city's clean and efficient bus terminal is on the western edge of town near the exit for the Interamericana – it's a 10min walk at most from here to the centre of town – and serves all destinations except San José. At the bus station is an elaborate list of departure times; these are pure fiction, so you must check with the ticket office. San José buses arrive at and depart from the Pulmitan terminal, a block southeast of the main bus terminal.
Destinations Bagaces (11 daily; 40min); Cañas (11 daily; 50min); Cuajiniquil (1 daily; 1hr 30min); La Cruz (14 daily; 1hr); Nicoya (10 daily; 2hr); Parque Nacional Santa Rosa (5 daily; 1hr); Peñas Blancas (6 daily; 2hr); Playa del Coco (12 daily; 1hr); Playa Hermosa (8 daily; 1hr 20min);

Playa Panamá (8 daily; 1hr 20min); Puntarenas (5 daily; 3hr); San José (11 daily; 4hr 30min); Santa Cruz (14 daily; 1hr); Tamarindo (6 daily; 1hr 30min–2hr).
To the border If you're heading for the border, take one of the hourly buses to La Cruz or Peñas Blancas, the border's official name (1hr). Through-buses from San José to Managua stop at the main bus terminal in Liberia, although it can be tricky to get a seat. The bus station sells tickets for this route (as does *Hotel Guanacaste*) if there is a vacant seat; otherwise it's a question of jumping on the bus, paying the driver and hoping you can grab a seat.
By car If you're coming by car, the exit off the Inter-americana is at an intersection with traffic lights and three petrol stations – known as La Esquina de las Bombas (Gas Station Corner). Turning left (if coming from the south) takes you to the beaches, while a right takes you along the town's Avenida Central, lined with floppy mango trees.
Car rental Liberia is a useful place to rent a car, with many operators, mostly along the road to the beaches; 5km east of the airport on Hwy-21, Vamos Rent-A-Car (☎ 2665 7650, ⊚ vamos4x4.com) is a great choice with a fleet of 4WDs. Most hotels can also arrange car rental, with *La Posada del Tope* consistently offering the best deals. It's definitely worth considering a 4WD, as the potholed roads can easily cause a flat tyre in a smaller car.

INFORMATION AND TOURS

Tourist information There's an ICT office 50m west of the *guardia rural* (☎ 2666 2976, ⊚ ictliberia@ict.go.cr), a few kilometres north of Liberia on the Interamericana. In town, the best source of local and regional info is *La Posada del Tope* (see p.262).
Offi Tours ☎ 8899 8149, ⊚ offitours.com. The best independent operator in town, Offi Tours, run by the affable José Mario Quesada, leads fun and knowledgeable excurions

to the nearby national parks and the Guanacaste beaches as well as day-trips to Parque Nacional Volcán Tenorio ($120), Monteverde ($125) and Granada, Nicaragua ($140). Except for the Nicaragua tour, prices are per car, so it makes sense to go with a group.
La Posada del Tope (see p.262). Run tours to attractions in the surrounding area, including Rincón de la Vieja ($15– 20), Palo Verde ($25–35) and the Guanacaste beaches.

ACCOMMODATION

El Bramadero Av 1, Interamericana ☎ 2666 0371, ⊚ hotelbramadero.com. The setting, beside the fuel pumps on the Interamericana on the western edge of town, isn't the loveliest, but it's convenient for the beaches

and popular with Ticos. The rooms are fairly nondescript, but surprisingly quiet (try to get one at the back), and there's a decent open-air restaurant and a pool. A good bet if everything else is full. **$55**

5

VISITING SANTA ROSA AND RINCÓN DE LA VIEJA

For **Parque Nacional Santa Rosa** (40min), take a La Cruz or Peñas Blancas bus. You should take the earliest bus possible to give yourself time for walking; ask the driver to let you off at Santa Rosa – it takes about an hour to walk from here to the park's administration centre. You can also reach the park by *colectivo* taxi ($15 per car), shared between four or five people. Catch one at the northwestern corner of Parque Central. *Colectivo* taxis are also good value if you're heading to **Parque Nacional Rincón de la Vieja** or the lodges near Las Pailas ranger station (roughly $25 for four people). Pretty much the best way to get to Rincón de la Vieja is to travel with one of the Liberia hotels – *La Posada del Tope*, *Hotel Liberia* and *Hotel Guanacaste* can all arrange transport to the park. All services are open to non-guests, though hotel guests get first option.

Guanacaste Av 1, 300m south of the bus station ☎2666 0085, ⊛higuanacaste.com. Popular, HI-affiliated hostel, with a traveller-friendly cafeteria-restaurant. The rooms are simple, clean and dark; the doubles aren't great value compared to the town's other options, but there are a few dorm places available. The hostel fills up quickly, so book ahead. With an HI card you get a 15 percent discount, and you might wangle a further 10 percent with a student ID. The management organizes a daily transfer ($16) to Rincón de la Vieja and Santa Rosa ($16) and offers car rentals as well. Dorm **$8**, double **$26**

Hostal Ciudad Blanca Av 4, 200m south and 150m east of the Gobernación ☎2666 3962. Spotless hotel in a stately rancher's mansion with a small breakfast terrace/bar, and twelve modern, a/c rooms with TV, private bathroom and ceiling fans. Popular with American travellers bedding down before heading out to the beach. Breakfast included. **$59**

Hotel Liberia C 0, 75m south of Parque Central ☎2666 0161. Well-established, friendly youth-hostel-type hotel with a jolly papaya-orange exterior. The bare and basic rooms with shared cold-water bathroom are set around a sunny courtyard. The newer rooms in an annexe to the rear are better and have their own bath, though they cost an extra $4. The hotel staff can organize transport to Rincón de la Vieja. The hotel is popular, so a reservation and deposit are required in the high season: Visa accepted. **$14**

Hotel Rincón del Llanó 3 miles west of the airport ☎8493 1424. Spotless hotel that's convenient to the airport. The rooms are unimaginatively designed and have a chain hotel feel, but they're comfortable and come with a good range of amenities, including large TVs, a/c and wi-fi. There's a decent restaurant, pool and adjacent bar, and the hotel runs an airport shuttle. **$62**

★**La Posada del Tope** C 0, 150m south of the Gobernación ☎2666 3876, ⊛laposadadeltope.com. Popular, cheap budget hotel in a beautiful historic house. The six basic rooms with fan and shared showers in the old part of the hotel are a bit stuffy, but clean; the more modern rooms across the street in the annexe Casa Real cost only slightly more and are set around a charming courtyard; all come with cable TV, wi-fi and fans. The shared bathrooms aren't great, but there's plenty of character here, as well as a friendly staff, parking and a rooftop telescope for stargazing. The manager runs transport to Rincón de la Vieja for $10/person round-trip, as well as trips to Palo Verde. **$15**

★**El Punto** ☎2665 2986, ⊛elpuntohotel.com. Vibrantly coloured B&B in a converted school run by an enthusiastic local artist. Set in leafy landscaped grounds, it has six colour-themed rooms, each with an unfussy layout, high ceilings, a/c, wi-fi, mini-fridge and a loft that can accommodate additional guests. A well-prepared breakfast is included and Liberia's finest restaurant, *Casa Verde*, is just a few metres away. Easily the best deal in town. **$55**

EATING AND DRINKING

Liberia has a surprisingly strong dining scene in its favour with stellar international cuisine and several restaurants that serve local dishes such as **natilla** (soured cream) eaten with eggs or *gallo pinto* and tortillas. For a real feast, try **desayuno guanacasteco**, a hearty local breakfast of tortillas, sour cream, eggs, rice-and-beans, and sometimes meat. For rock-bottom cheap lunches, try the **stalls** at the bus terminal or head to one of the numerous fried-chicken places. You can pick up Guanacastecan **corn snacks** from stalls all over town.

★**Café Liberia** C Real, Av 2/4 ☎2665 1660. Wonderful café and arts centre set in a historic house that screens films and hosts occasional live performances. It's always been the best place in town to relax with a cup of coffee and hear locals discuss the region's latest political and arts developments and now it also serves some of the area's more inspired meals. Choose from dishes such as ceviche ($9), paella ($22) and several satisfying salads ($9–11). Mon–Sat 7am–10pm.

Cantarranas Tacos 5km down the road towards the beaches, 50m back from the road on the right. Non-descript Mexican restaurant on the road from Liberia to the beaches – a bit of a local secret. Delicious tacos ($4) served inside or alfresco. Great atmosphere and staff. Mon–Sat 9am–6pm.

★ **Casa Verde** Next door to El Punto ☎ 2665 5037. Hip, stylish restaurant and lounge with startlingly good food and exemplary service. The menu features a wide range of well-executed dishes, from surf 'n' turf to Thai specialities, with main courses costing $15–20. There's also an extensive selection of sushi on offer, some using an inventive mix of ingredients. Tues–Sun 11am–11pm.

Los Comales C Real, Av 5/7, 200m north of the northeast corner of Parque Central. A typical Costa Rican *soda*, very popular with locals for its generous portions of tasty rustic food, with *gallos* and *pintos* costing a mere $2, and *casados* $3; there are also several rice dishes on offer. Daily 7am–9pm.

Jauja Av Central, C 8/10 ☎ 2665 2061. One of the better restaurants in town, though very touristy. Large and tasty pasta dishes and pizzas cost around $8, and there are also typical steaks and fish dishes. It's all served in a pleasant, outdoor garden setting, although the big-screen TV can be off-putting. Daily 11am–11pm.

Pan y Miel Av Central, C 8/10. Order straightforward Tico specialities in this frequently packed *soda*, where locals visit in droves for the large portions at great prices ($5–7 for lunch). Daily 6am–6pm.

Paso Real Av 0 on the south side of the plaza ☎ 2666 3455. Popular second-floor restaurant looking out over the Parque Central and church. Its extensive menu includes moderately priced *comida típica* dishes, as well as fish entrées and straightforward international fare like burgers ($8). Daily 10am–10pm.

★ **Pizza Pronto** C 1, Av 4 ☎ 2666 2098. Rustic-chic local favourite where dark-wood tables are covered with Guanacaste topographical maps. Select from over twenty kinds of pizza (most $9–15), all baked in an adobe clay oven. Daily 11am–11pm.

Restaurante Kleaver Av 1, C 0. Basic *soda* with counter seating and small tables churning out staples like grilled chicken with rice-and-beans and fried plantains ($6.50). Though it lacks atmosphere, it's one of the few places in town where you can get a late-night meal. Daily 24hr.

Las Tinajas West side of Parque Central. Liberia's best bar, with regular live music, also serves basic *casados* and excellent hamburgers ($3.50). The outdoor tables on the veranda of this old house are a pleasant spot to watch the goings-on in the *parque* while enjoying a *refresco* or beer, the latter available on tap and served in chilled glasses. Daily 11am–11pm.

NIGHTLIFE AND ENTERTAINMENT

The main Saturday evening activity – especially on weekends – involves watching the locals parading around the Parque Central in their finery, having an ice cream, and maybe going to the movies at the Cine Liberia, located in the shopping mall 1km south of the main Interamericana intersection. Beyond that, there are a couple of clubs that regularly teem with action.

Ciros Bar C2, Av 1/Central ☎ 2665 3022. Always packed, thanks in large part to its central location, *Ciros* draws the crowds with its sleek design and outside seating. The atmosphere can be a little raucous at times, but usually not too far out of control. Daily 4pm–2am.

Kurú About 200m west of the Interamericana down the road to the beaches. The town's main disco gets lively with young locals showing off their best salsa and merengue moves, especially on weekends and holidays. $4 cover fee. Tues–Sat 6pm–late.

LA COCINA GUANACASTECA: CORN COOKING

Corn is still integral to the regional cuisine of Guanacaste, thanks to the Chorotegas, who cultivated maize (corn) to use in many inventive ways. One pre-Columbian corn concoction involved roasting and grinding the maize, and then combining the meal-like paste with water and chocolate to make the drink *chicha*. Although you can't find this version of *chicha* any more you can still get **grain-based drinks** in Guanacaste, such as *horchata* (made with rice or corn and spiced with cinnamon), or *pinolillo* (made with roasted corn), both milky and sweet, with an unmistakeably grainy texture.

Corn also shows up in traditional Guanacastecan snacks such as **tanelas** (like a cheese scone, but made with cornflour) and **rosquillas**, small rings of cornflour that taste like a combination between tortillas and doughnuts. You can buy these at roadside stalls and small shops in Liberia. Served throughout the country, **chorreados** crop up most often on menus in Guanacaste: they're a kind of pancake made (again) with cornflour and served with *natilla*, the local version of sour cream.

5

FIESTAS IN LIBERIA

Liberia boasts several lively local **festivals**, including the **Fiestas Cívicas de Liberia** in early March. The festival has its origins as an annual livestock fair and is now celebrated over ten days with parades, bands, fireworks and bulls wreaking havoc on daring but alcohol-addled young locals. Most of the action takes place in the fairgrounds in the northwest corner of town. On July 25, **El Día de la Independencia** celebrates Guanacaste's independence from Nicaragua with parades, horseshows, cattle auctions, rodeos, fiestas and roving marimba bands. If you want to attend, make bus and hotel reservations as far in advance as possible.

DIRECTORY

Bookshop Librería Universitaria on Av 1, 100m east of Parque Central sells the *Miami Herald* and *New York Times* newspapers.

Hospital Just off C 13, east of the football stadium ☎ 2666 0011.

Internet Cybermania (daily 8am–10pm), in a small business centre on the north side of Parque Central, is efficient, friendly, air-conditioned and cheap, as is the handy Planet Internet (daily 8am–10pm) on C Real just off

Parque Central: both cost about $2/hr.

Money and exchange There are plenty of banks, many on Av Central, leading into town, several with ATMs. The Banco de Costa Rica, across from Parque Central, will change travellers' cheques.

Post office Av 3, C 8 (Mon–Fri 7.30am–6pm, Sat 7.30am–noon). The efficient post office is a bit hard to find: it's between Av 3 and Av 5 in the low-slung white house across from an empty, square field bordered by mango trees.

Africa Mía

10km southeast of Liberia on the Interamericana, outside the town of El Salto • 9am–6pm, last entry at 5pm • $18 for hike and ride around the perimeter of some sections; $65 for 2hr ride inside the park in a 4WD • ☎ 2666 1111

Africa Mía is one of Guanacaste's most curious and highly touted attractions. Eight years in the making, the preserve has taken the region's resemblance to the African savannah one step further by populating several hundred acres with animals endemic to the continent, such as giraffes, zebras, giant elands, ostriches and warthogs; for good measure you can spot native wildlife too, including monkeys and various bird species. All of the animals roam free (there are no predators), and your best chance of seeing a good number of them is on one of the safari vehicle tours. The somewhat curious decision to import exotic animals into a country already teeming with wildlife aside, the preserve is exceedingly well run and there's no denying the thrill of seeing animals galloping about you that you might have only previously glimpsed in the confines of a zoo. There are two cafés, a restaurant and several shops on-site.

Northwestern Guanacaste

Densely forested and comparatively little-developed, **northwestern Guanacaste** feels much more isolated than its proximity to Liberia would indicate. Much of it is given over to a triumverate of striking protected areas: **Parque Nacional Santa Rosa**, **Parque Nacional Guanacaste** and **Refugio Nacional de Vida Silvestre Bahía Junquillal**. Together

BORDER CHECKS IN GUANACASTE

Driving along the Interamericana north of Liberia, don't be surprised to see a blue-suited *policía de tránsito* (traffic cop) or a light-brown-suited *guardia rural* (border police officer) leap out, kamikaze-like, into the highway directly in front of you – you'll need to stop and show your driver's licence and passport (which you must have on you at all times). These are routine checks, mainly to deter undocumented Nicaraguans from entering Costa Rica. The nearer the **border** you get, the more frequent the checks become. Make sure you drive carefully: knocking over a policeman is not a good move.

they form a large part of the ecologically significant Area de Conservación Guanacaste (ⓦacguanacaste.ac.cr), which provides an uninterrupted wildlife corridor extending from the Pacific to the Caribbean lowlands. Not surprisingly, conservation research takes precedence over tourism in this corner of the province, but there are still plenty of trails to explore and remote beaches to savour. Much of the coast along here sees few visitors, in fact, with one notable exception: **Bahía Salinas**, whose powerful winds draw kitesurfers from around the world.

Parque Nacional Santa Rosa

35km north of Liberia • Daily 8am–4pm; a maximum of twenty visitors are allowed access to the nesting area each day (ask at the administration centre or call the number listed) • $10, which includes access to the Murciélago sector; guides $10/person • ☎ 2666 5051, ⓦ acguanacaste.ac.cr/turismo/sector-santa-rosa

Established in 1971 to protect a stretch of increasingly rare dry tropical forest, **PARQUE NACIONAL SANTA ROSA** (also known as the Santa Rosa sector), is Costa Rica's oldest national park. Today it's also one of the most popular in the country, thanks to its good trails, great surfing (though poor swimming) and prolific turtle-spotting opportunities. It's also, given a few official restrictions, a great destination for **campers**, with a couple of sites on the beach.

Santa Rosa has an amazingly diverse topography for its size of 387 square kilometres, ranging from mangrove swamp to deciduous forest and savannah. Home to 115 species of mammal (half of them bats), 250 species of **bird** and 100 of **amphibian** and **reptile** (not to mention 3800 species of **moth**), Santa Rosa is a rich biological repository, attracting researchers from all over the world. Jaguars and pumas prowl the park, though you're unlikely to see them; what you may spot – at least in the dry season – are coati, coyotes and peccaries, often snuffling around watering holes.

The appearance of the park changes drastically between the **dry season**, when the many streams and small lakes dry up, trees lose their leaves, and thirsty animals can be seen at known waterholes, and the **wet months**, which are greener, but afford fewer animal-viewing opportunities. From July to November however, you may be able to witness hundreds of **olive ridley turtles** (*lloras*) dragging themselves out of the surf and nesting on Playa Nancite by moonlight; September and October are the months on which you are most likely to see them. Though too rough for swimming, the picturesque **beaches** of Naranjo and Nancite, about 12km down a bad road from the administration centre (see p.267), are popular with serious **surfers**. They're also great places to hang out for a while, or do a little camping and walking on the nearby trails.

La Casona

About 400m from the administration building • Daily 8–11.30am & 1–4pm • Free

The formidable wooden and red-tiled homestead **La Casona** (Big House), one of Costa Rica's most famous historical sites, was for many years the centre of a working hacienda until the land was expropriated for the national park in 1972. In 2001, it was burned down by poachers who were retaliating against arrests by park rangers. However, phoenix-like, it stands again after being lovingly (and painstakingly) reconstructed in less than a year – this time, with the addition of smoke alarms.

Information panels recount the various instances of derring-do which have occurred at La Casona, with resumés of the battles of March 20, 1856 – the confrontation between William Walker's filibusters and the Costa Rican forces (see box, p.269) – of 1919 (against the Nicaraguans), and of 1955, against another Nicaraguan, the dictator Anastasio Somoza García, who ruled the country from 1936 until his assassination in 1956. His hulk of a tank can still be seen, rusting and abandoned, along a signed road just beyond the entrance hut.

La Casona, set around a flowering courtyard, is full of rustic character. It's now entirely given over to **exhibitions**, and you are free to clamber up and down the steps

5

and wander around the dark rooms, which have a significant population of resident bats. Many of the exhibits were destroyed in the fire, but there's some information on the life of the notorious William Walker (see box, p.269), remnants of dead animals and archeological remains. At one side of La Casona, a stair path leads up to a viewpoint with a magnificent perspective of the twin volcanoes of Parque Nacional Rincón de la Vieja.

The trails

Many of Santa Rosa's **trails** are intended for scientific researchers rather than tourists, and so are not well signed. If you do set off to walk, it's a good idea to hire a guide. If you walk only one trail in the entire park, make it the very short (1km) and undemanding *sendero natural*, which provides an introduction to the unique features of the tropical dry forest. Curving around from the road just before La Casona, it's signed as the **Sendero "Indio Desnudo"**, after the peeling-bark trees of the same name (also tongue-in-cheekily called "sunburned-tourist trees"). Along the trail you'll see acacia and **guapinol** trees, whose colloquial name is "stinking toe" on account of its smelly seed pods. Look out for monster iguanas hiding innocuously in tree branches, and for the ubiquitous bats.

From the administration centre a rough (but signposted) track leads past La Casona camping area, with several trails branching off along the way. Some of these may be

restricted at any one time for research purposes; check first at the administration centre, however, as you can usually walk where you want as long as you let someone know. After about 5km you come to a fork, bearing left to Playa Naranjo, and right to Playa Nancite, both of them about 3km further on.

Playa Nancite

Playa Nancite is a lovely grey-sand beach and when the tide has just gone out, it's as lustrous as a wet seal's skin. It is also the nesting home of the **olive ridley turtles**, a species which nests only here and at Ostional near Nosara on the Nicoya Peninsula (see p.301). With none of the large tour groups you find at other Costa Rican turtle beaches, it's a great place to watch the **arribadas** (see box, p.34), during which up to eight thousand turtles – weighing on average around 40kg each – come ashore on any given evening, virtually covering the beach. According to estimates, more than eleven million eggs can be deposited by the turtles during a single *arribada*.

Due to riptides, Playa Nancite is no good for swimming but, as is usually the case, it's good for **surfers**, with huge, rolling, tubular waves.

Playa Naranjo

For the best surf you should head for **Playa Naranjo** (also known as Witch's Rock). Theoretically you can hike between the two (2hr) on a narrow trail across the rocky headland, which opens out on top into hot, dry scrub cover, but you have to watch the tide, since the trail crosses the deep Estero Real, the drainage point for two rivers. Ask for the *marea* (tidal times) from the administration centre before setting out.

ARRIVAL AND INFORMATION — PARQUE NACIONAL SANTA ROSA

By car Santa Rosa's entrance hut is 35km north of Liberia, signed from the Interamericana.

Maps and information After paying the park fee at the entrance hut, pick up a map and proceed some 6km or so, taking the right fork to the administration centre (daily 8am–4pm; ☎2666 5051), which can provide further information and also runs Guanacaste and Rincón de la Vieja national parks. You can check road conditions and get your camping/turtle-watching permits here.

GETTING AROUND

By car From the administration centre a rough road leads to the beaches; to drive to these, even in the height of the dry season, you need a sturdy 4WD. The administration discourages any driving at all beyond the main park road; nevertheless, people – surfers, mainly – insist on doing so, and survive. Most park their vehicle at the administration centre and walk. One thing is for sure: don't try to drive anywhere in the park (including the road to Cuajiniquil and the Murciélago sector to the north) in the rainy season without asking rangers about the state of the roads. You could get bogged down in mud or stopped by a swollen creek. Before setting off, you can always phone the Area de Conservación de Guanacaste (ACG) headquarters (☎2666 5051, Spanish only) to check the current state of the roads in the park.

On foot If you're walking down to the beach (8km), a ranger or fellow tourist will probably give you a ride, but on no account set out without water – you'll need a couple of litres per person, at least.

ACCOMMODATION AND EATING

You can also buy snacks and drinks, including small bottles of water, at the administration centre. Alternatively, the petrol stations on the road from Liberia stock easy-to-carry bottles of water with plastic handles.

La Casona and Playa Naranjo campgrounds. Camping facilities at Santa Rosa are some of the best in the country. There are two sites; the shady *La Casona* campground has bathrooms and grill pits, while *Playa Naranjo*, on the beach (and only open outside the turtle-nesting season), has picnic tables and grill pits, and a ranger's hut with outhouses and showers plus, apparently, a boa constrictor in the roof. Wherever you camp, watch your fires (the area is a tinderbox in the dry season), take plastic bags for your food, do not leave anything edible in your tent (it will be stolen by scavenging coati) and, of course, carry plenty of water. The fee is per person; payable as you arrive at the administration centre, it is valid for the length of your stay. $2

5

Comedor Adjacent to the administration centre. Make reservations at the administration centre (at least 3hr in advance) for a simple lunch in the basic comedor. The food – *casados* with fish, chicken or meat and salad ($6) – is good, and this is a great place to get talking to rangers and other tourists. Daily 11am–4pm.

Murciélago sector

9km west of Cuajiniquil • Daily 8am–4pm • $10, which includes access to the Santa Rosa sector; surfing $5 extra • ☎ 2666 5051, ⓦ acguanacaste.ac.cr/turismo/sector-murcielago

Few tourists go to ACG's **MURCIÉLAGO SECTOR**, an area of reserve to the northwest of – and entirely separate from – the Santa Rosa sector. It's a kind of reforestation laboratory in which former cattle pasture is slowly being regenerated, though there's also a campsite and a beach that's safe for swimming. Dirt roads lead from the Murciélago ranger station to a series of fine swimming beaches (this part is known as the **Area Recreativa Junquillal**), accessible by walking or by 4WD. The westernmost of these, **Playa Blanca**, a small white stretch of sand, is the prettiest and one of the most isolated and least visited in the country.

Just 30km from the border, Murciélago is home to the remains of the training grounds used by the CIA-backed **Contras** during the Nicaraguan civil war. They're overgrown and scrubby today, with no sign that anything was ever there. It was also the location of the famous "secret" airstrip built, on US National Security Council member Oliver North's orders, in direct violation of Costa Rica's declared neutrality in the conflict. Originally given the go-ahead by President Alberto Monge, the airstrip was eventually destroyed under President Oscar Arias's subsequent administration – a unilateral action that led to the US reducing its financial and political support for Costa Rica.

ARRIVAL AND INFORMATION   MURCIÉLAGO SECTOR

Border checks Officials are particularly vigilant in this area (see box, p.264). As usual, have your passport and all other documents in order.
By car Drive along the Interamericana from the main Santa Rosa entrance about 10km north then take the left turn 8km to the hamlet of Cuajiniquil. A poor road

continues here another 9km to the ranger station. Be sure to take the dirt road, not the paved one. You'll almost certainly need a 4WD, at least in the wet season, when there are two creeks to ford.
Ranger station 9km from Cuajiniquil (open daily 8am–7pm).

ACCOMMODATION

Murciélago Sector Campsite At the ranger station you can camp and arrange meals (at the Santa Rosa administration centre) with prior notification. Limited water and simple toilet facilities. $\overline{\underline{\$3}}$

Parque Nacional Guanacaste

36km north of Liberia on the Interamericana • Daily 8am–4pm • $10 • ☎ 2666 5051, ⓦ acguanacaste.ac.cr

Much of **PARQUE NACIONAL GUANACASTE** was not long ago anything more than cattle pasture. Influential biologist D.H. Janzen, editor of the seminal *Costa Rican Natural History*, who had been involved in field study for many years in nearby Santa Rosa, was instrumental in creating the park virtually from scratch in 1991. Raising over $11 million, mainly from foreign sources, he envisioned creating a kind of biological corridor in which animals, mainly mammals, would have a large enough tract of undisturbed habitat in which to hunt and reproduce.

The **Santa Rosa–Guanacaste** (and, to an extent, Rincón de la Vieja) **corridor** is the result of his work, representing one of the most important efforts to conserve and regenerate tropical **dry forest** in the Americas. Containing tropical wet and dry forests and a smattering of cloudforest, Parque Nacional Guanacaste also protects the **springwell of the Río Tempisque**, as well as the ríos Ahogados and Colorado. More than three hundred species of **bird**, including the orange-fronted parakeet and the white-throated magpie jay, have been recorded, while mammals lurking behind the

5

THE GREAT PRETENDER: WILLIAM WALKER

Born in Tennessee in 1824, **William Walker** was something of a child prodigy. By the age of 14 he had a degree from the University of Nashville, notching up further degrees in law and medicine just five years later before setting off to study at various illustrious European universities. However, upon his return to the US, Walker failed in his chosen professions of doctor and lawyer and, somewhat at a loose end, landed up in California in 1849 at the height of the Gold Rush. Here he became involved with the **pro-slavery** organization Knights of the Golden Circle, who financed an expedition, in which Walker took part, to invade Baja California and Mexico to secure more land for the United States. Undeterred by the expedition's failure, Walker soon put his mind to another plan. Intending to make himself overlord of a Central American nation of five slave-owning states, and then to sell the territory to the US, Walker invaded Nicaragua in June 1855 with mercenary troops. The next logical step was to secure territory for the planned eleven-kilometre canal between Lago de Nicaragua and the Pacific. Gaining much of his financial backing from Nicaraguan get-rich-quick militarists and North American capitalists who promptly saw the benefits of a waterway along the Río San Juan from the Pacific to the Atlantic, in 1856 William Walker, and several hundred mercenary troops, invaded Costa Rica from the north.

Meanwhile, Costa Rican president **Juan Rafael Mora** had been watching Walker's progress with increasing alarm and, in February 1856, declared war on the usurper. Lacking military hardware, Costa Rica was ill-prepared for battle, and Mora's rapidly gathered army of nine thousand men was a largely peasant-and-bourgeois band, armed with machetes, farm tools and the occasional rusty rifle. Marching them out of San José through the Valle Central, over the Cordillera de Tilarán and on to the hot plains of Guanacaste, Mora got wind that Walker and his band of three hundred buccaneers were entrenched at the **Santa Rosa Casona**, the largest and best-fortified edifice in the area. Although by now Mora's force was reduced to only 2500 (we can only guess that, in the two weeks that it took them to march from San José, heat exhaustion had left many scattered by the wayside), on March 20, 1856, they routed the filibusters, fighting with their *campesino* tools. Mora then followed Walker and his men on their retreat, engaging them in battle again in Nicaraguan territory, at **Rivas**, some 15km north of the border, where Walker's troops eventually barricaded themselves in another wooden *casona*. It was here – and not, as is commonly thought, at Santa Rosa – that **Juan Santamaría**, a 19-year-old drummer boy, volunteered to set fire to the building in which Walker and his men were barricaded, flushing them out, and dying in the process. Walker, however, survived the fire, and carried on filibustering, until in 1857 a US warship was dispatched to put an end to his antics which were increasingly embarrassing for the US government, who had covertly backed him. Undeterred after a three-year spell in a Nicaraguan jail, he continued his adventuring until he was shot dead by the Honduran authorities in September 1860.

Later, Mora, no devotee of democracy himself, rigged the 1859 Costa Rican presidential election so that he could serve a second term – despite his military victories against Walker, there was strong popular opposition to his domestic policies – but he was deposed later that year. He attempted a coup d'état, but was subsequently shot in 1860, the same year that his former adversary met his Waterloo in Honduras.

undergrowth include jaguar, puma, tapir, coati, armadillo, two-toed sloth and deer. It's also thought that there are about five thousand species of moth and **butterfly**, including the giant owl butterfly.

The park is devoted to research rather than tourism, and the administration staff at Santa Rosa (see p.265) discourage casual visitors. There are three main research stations, and it is sometimes possible to stay at two of them if you show enough interest and contact the Santa Rosa administration centre well in advance. Apart from the primary rainforest that exists at the upper elevations, the park's highlight is an astonishing collection of **pre-Columbian petroglyphs** at El Pedregal on the lower flanks of **Volcán Orosi**. The Sendero de los Indios leads up to the site from the Maritza field station. In addition to the path to the petroglyphs, the Sendero Cacao connects Maritza with the Cacao station on the southwestern slope of **Volcán Cacao**.

5

PARQUE NACIONAL GUANACASTE

ACCOMMODATION
Cacao Field Station Lodge	2
Maritza Field Station Lodge	1

ARRIVAL AND DEPARTURE

PARQUE NACIONAL GUANACASTE

By car Access is very difficult, unless (as usual) you've got a Range Rover or some other tank of a vehicle; if you don't have one, it's not worth the risk of being stranded along the road.

To the Cacao station The road to the Cacao field station leaves the Interamericana 10km south of the Santa Rosa turn-off. It leads to the hamlet of Potrerillos; once there, head for Quebrada Grande (on some maps called García

Flamenco) and continue for about 8km. It's passable most of the way, but the suspension-rattling boulders begin to appear 3km from the entrance; at this point you have to ditch non-4WD vehicles and walk.

To the Maritza station To reach the Maritza station from the Interamericana, take a right turn opposite the left turn-off to Cuajiniquil (see p.268), and continue along the poor road for about 15km.

ACCOMMODATION

Cacao and Maritza field station lodges ☎ 2666 5051. There's very basic lodge accommodation of four rooms with a capacity of 32 people max at Cacao and

Maritza field stations (see above). Call the Santa Rosa sector administration centre to check if it's open. They'll try to discourage you, but make your interest clear. $20

Refugio Nacional de Vida Silvestre Bahía Junquillal

5km north of Cuajiniquil • Daily 7am–5.30pm • $13 • ☎ 2666 5051, ⓦ acguanacaste.ac.cr/turismo/sector-junquillal

Occupying five square kilometres that fan out from its namesake bay, **REFUGIO NACIONAL DE VIDA SILVESTRE BAHÍA JUNQUILLAL** holds particular significance for the variety of coastal ecosystems it protects. Thanks to its relatively remote location, it sees fewer visitors than the nearby national parks and is an idyllic spot to spend a day or two and glimpse a surprising variety of wildlife in the process, from sea urchins to spider monkeys. A few short, mostly flat **trails** depart from near the ranger station by the entrance, all of which can together be walked in under an hour. The shortest of these, **Sendero El Carao**, passes briefly through a mangrove forest before reaching an overlook, while the slightly longer **Sendero La Laguna** parallels 2km-long **Playa Junquillal** and provides a good opportunity to spot hermit crabs, sea stars and several seabirds, including frigate birds, which typically only land to breed or nest.

Most people, though, come to soak up the sun on the picturesque beach and to cool off in the calm, clear waters, which are ideal for **swimming** and **snorkelling**. *Santa Elena Lodge* (see below) in the village of Cuajiniquil can help arrange tours.

ARRIVAL AND INFORMATION

RN DE VIDA SILVESTRE BAHÍA JUNQUILLAL

By car Take the Interamericana turn-off to Cuajiniquil (Hwy-914) for 8km. Near the western edge of the village, turn north along the dirt road to the refuge entrance.
By bus It's possible to take a bus to Cuajiniquil, 5km to the south of the refuge. From there you can hire a taxi for the 15min drive to the entrance.

Destinations from Cuajiniquil La Cruz (daily; 45min); Liberia (2 daily; 1hr).
Tourist information The ranger station (daily 7am–5.30pm) can provide the current tide conditions and information on where to see the refuge's wildlife.

ACCOMMODATION

Santa Elena Lodge On Hwy-914 in Cuajiniquil ☎ 2679 1038, ⓦ santaelenalodge.com. On the left side of the main road just before the turn-off to the national refuge, this welcoming lodge offers eight simple rooms with a/c, hot water and private bathrooms. There's an attached restaurant that features tasty dishes of freshly caught fish, and the gregarious owner can arrange tours (including

whale watching in the Bahía Junquillal in season) with local guides. Breakfast included. $70
Sector Junquillal Campsite Just west of the ranger station. This large campsite with striking views is set back a few metres from Playa Junquillal. Several of the sites have shade and there are basic services, including showers. $3

La Cruz

Set on a plateau north of Parque Nacional Guanacaste, overlooking Bahía de Salinas and the Pacific Ocean to the west, the tiny, sleepy town of **LA CRUZ** is the last settlement of any size before the border, just 20km away. For this reason alone it makes a reasonable stopover if you're heading up to Nicaragua, though the striking vista afforded at **sunset** certainly warrants lingering as well. There's not much else to see, though the town is pleasant enough and there are a few nice places to stay in the area.

ARRIVAL AND DEPARTURE

LA CRUZ

By bus Buses pull in at the station two blocks north of the Parque Central.

Destinations Liberia (every 45min; 1hr); Peñas Blancas (every 45min; 30min); San José (8 daily; 5hr 10min).

ACCOMMODATION AND EATING

Amalia's Inn About 100m south of the town's Parque Central ☎ 2679 9618. The quirky *Amalia's Inn* has spacious rooms with a/c, a pool and a spectacular view over the bay. It's well worth paying extra for a room with a view. $44
Cabinas Santa Rita Across from the courthouse ☎ 2679 9062. Casual, friendly *Cabinas Santa Rita* offers clean, simple rooms with shared or private bathrooms, along with more upmarket, a/c doubles in an annexe at the back ($8 surcharge); there's also secure parking. Shared

bath $12, private bath $17
Finca Cañas Castilla About 7km north of La Cruz, near the hamlet of Sonzapote ☎ 8381 4030, ⓦ canas-castilla .com. A Swiss-run ranch on 150 acres alongside the Río Sapoa. The farm has several groves of fruit trees, including orange and bananas, while free-range chickens produce fresh eggs daily for guests and the local market. Mainly hilly terrain with thick forests as well as expansive grassland for grazing, the ranch can be explored on horseback – in

5

addition to the livestock you might catch a glimpse of sloths and anteaters. To get to the farm from La Cruz, head north on the Interamericana and turn right after 5km onto an unpaved road which leads to the village of Sonzapote; continue for another 2km from here and you'll see signs to the *finca*. $63

Hotel Bella Vista On Hwy-935, one block west of the Parque Central ☎ 2679 8050. Near the square, this pretty hotel perched on a hill has decent rooms, a few of which enjoy some of the best views in town, and a pool, restaurant and bar. $33

DIRECTORY

Money and exchange There's a Banco Nacional at the turn-off (Hwy-935) into town off the Interamericana, where there's an ATM.

Petrol station You can fill up at the petrol station opposite Banco Nacional.

Bahía de Salinas

To the west of La Cruz, Hwy-935 descends for about 12km to the windswept kitesurfing mecca of **BAHÍA DE SALINAS**. Prevailing conditions produce gusts throughout the year, but they tend to intensify from November to July, which is when the bay sees the most visitors. While the reliable (and often quite forceful) winds attract professional kitesurfers from around the world, it's also a good place for beginners to try their hand at the sport.

Though most of the pretty bay's **beaches** are predictably windy throughout the year, if you're looking to rest on the sand without having it blown in your face, the most sheltered spot is at **Playa Jobo**, on the bay's southern arm. Just 1.5km offshore is rocky and rugged **Isla Bolaños**, an important nesting site for numerous seabirds – including the frigate bird, which rarely sets foot on land. While the island has no facilities, a number of the bay's hotels lead day-trips to it and, at low tide you can walk around the island on the beach; dense vegetation makes it just about impossible to trek into the interior.

ARRIVAL AND DEPARTURE

BAHÍA DE SALINAS

By car Much of Hwy-935 to Bahía de Salinas is prone to being mud-laden at certain times of the year; check about the road's condition in La Cruz before setting out.
By taxi It's also possible to arrange a taxi from La Cruz ($8).

By bus Buses from La Cruz stop in the hamlet of El Jobo, on the southern edge of the bay.
Destination La Cruz (5 daily; 40min).

ACCOMMODATION AND EATING

Blue Dream On the left of the approach road to Bahía de Salinas ☎ 8826 5221, ⓦ bluedreamhotel.com. *Blue Dream* has some of the most comfortable accommodation on the bay, with nine pleasant rooms, four wooden bungalows with balconies and a dorm room. Its lively on-site restaurant serves mostly Mediterranean fare (mains around $8–15) and wood-oven pizzas. Dorm $12, double $45, bungalow $52
Eco Playa On the right of the approach road to Bahía

de Salinas, Playa La Coyotera ☎ 2676 1010, ⓦ ecoplaya .com. Sprawling and attractive resort with a combination of rooms and more spacious villas. All have satellite TV and a/c; the villas also have kitchenettes. The resort has its own private beach, leads a variety of tours, including day-trips to Nicaragua and snorkelling outings to Isla Bolaños. The Eco-Wind kitesurfing school (see box below) is based here. Double $103, villa $126

KITESURFING IN BAHÍA DE SALINAS

There are several places lining the bay where you can take **kitesurfing lessons** for as short as an hour as part of a multi-day package. Most of these spots all rent gear as well.

Blue Dream Kitesurfing School Blue Dream Hotel. The best choice in the bay, Blue Dream Kitesurfing School is the longest-running school of its kind in the country. It rents all the gear you'll need to get up on the water and provides lessons ranging from hourly ($30; minimum of two people) to a four-day package for $230.

Eco-Wind Eco Playa. Offers hour-long introductory windsurfing and kitesurfing lessons (both $30; minimum of two people), full-day lessons (windsurfing $180; kitesurfing $150), as well as rentals as short as an hour ($25) to as long as a week ($315).

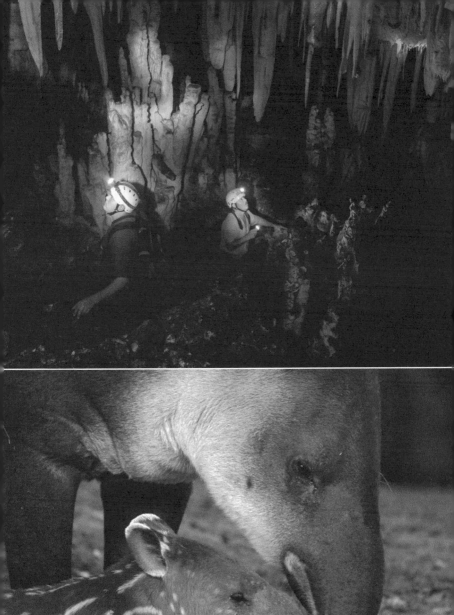

5

Peñas Blancas

Peñas Blancas, the main crossing point into Nicaragua, is emphatically a border post and not a town, with just one or two basic *sodas* and no hotels. Aim to get here as **early** as possible, as procedures are ponderous and you'll be lucky to get through the whole deal in less than ninety minutes. Costa Rican and Nicaraguan border officials are quite strict, and there are many checks to see that your paperwork is in order.

CROSSING THE NICARAGUAN BORDER   PEÑAS BLANCAS

Information The border crossing is 20km north of La Cruz (open daily 7am–8pm); few nationalities require a visa (see box, p.77) to cross into Nicaragua. Exit stamps are given on the Costa Rican side, where there is a restaurant and a helpful, well-organized Costa Rican tourist office (daily 6am–noon & 1–8pm). Money-changers are always on hand and can change colones, córdobas and dollars. After getting your Costa Rican exit stamp it's a short walk north to the barrier from where you can get one of the regular shuttle buses ($2), 4km north to the Nicaraguan shantytown of Sapoa, where

you go through Nicaraguan *migración*. There's a $13 entry fee for foreigners charged on the Nicaraguan side; re-entering Costa Rica costs $3 for foreigners.
By bus Buses on both sides of the border are far more frequent in the morning. If you're arriving from Nicaragua, the last San José-bound bus (Transportes Deldú; ☎ 2677 0091) leaves at 5.30pm, and the last Liberia bus (Tranbasa; ☎ 2677 0157) at 6.30pm. After that, the only alternative is to take a costly taxi.
Destinations Liberia (roughly every hour; 2hr); San José (11 daily; 5hr 30min).

Northern Nicoya Peninsula

The impressive expanses of playas Flamingo and Tamarindo aside, few of the **beaches** along the rocky coastline of the **northern Nicoya Peninsula** could truthfully be called beautiful and most are actually quite small. Often located in coves or sheltered bays, they are generally ideal for swimming. Getting around can take time, as the beaches tend to be separated by rocky headlands or otherwise impassable formations, with barren hilly outcroppings coming right down to the sea, carving out little coves and bays, but necessitating considerable backtracking inland to get from one to the other.

The landscape of the Nicoya Peninsula is changing rapidly and many of the northern beaches, such as Tamarindo and Playa Panamá, are being aggressively developed for mass tourism. The nearby airport in Liberia exists mainly to service the package and charter market along this coast. Within easy reach of the airport are the calm waters in the **Bahía Culebra** (marked on some maps as Playa Panamá), some of the clearest and most sheltered in the country, with good snorkelling. Sprawling across nearly the entire Bahía Culebra is the **Papagayo Project**, the country's largest tourist development consisting of hotels, condos, a mall and a golf course.

The signs of mass tourism lessen as you head further south towards **Parque Nacional Marino Las Baulas**, where droves of **leatherback turtles** come ashore to lay their eggs between October and February. The beaches here have drawn foreign expatriates in pursuit of paradise, and these cosmopolitan enclaves are in sharp contrast to the rest of the region, with resorty **Tamarindo** being the top spot for surfing.

ARRIVAL AND DEPARTURE   NORTHERN NICOYA PENINSULA

It can take a long time to get to the Guanacaste coast from San José by bus or car (4–5.5hr) and in some places you feel very remote indeed. From Liberia, the coast is more easily within reach, with most beaches 45min–2hr away.

By plane Another possibility is travel by air from San José, both NatureAir and Sansa offering regular flights to Tamarindo (see p.282).
By bus Travelling from beach to beach on the peninsula by bus is tricky, and you'll have to ask locals to figure out

the peninsular services, whose schedules are not formally published, but which locals will know.
By car By far the most popular option is to rent a car, which allows you to beach-hop with relative ease. Roads are not bad, if somewhat potholed –

you'll do best with a 4WD, though this can prove expensive. Another possibility for couples or small groups is to hitch, as there's a fair amount of tourist traffic around here.

Bahía Culebra

Sheltered from the full force of the Pacific, the clear blue waters around **Bahía Culebra** boast some of the best beaches in the country for swimming and snorkelling. The calm waters quietly lap at the grey volcanic sands of **Playa Panamá**, the northernmost beach of the bay. Unusually for this dry, hot zone of Guanacaste, **Playa Hermosa**, on the southern edge of the bay at the mouth of the Golfo de Papagayo, is blessed with soothing shade, calm waters and gorgeous sunset views of the Pacific and offshore islets (be aware that there are two beaches named Playa Hermosa in Costa Rica – the other is farther south in Puntarenas). The waters off Playa Hermosa are also a popular spot for diving (see below). Development in the bay is proceeding at a brisk pace and while upscale shops are becoming more commonplace, the whole area still has an appealingly laidback feel to it.

ARRIVAL AND DEPARTURE   BAHÍA CULEBRA

By car Both Panamá and Hermosa beaches are easily accessible by car from Liberia. Take the turn-off to the right just after the hamlet of Comunidad – signposted to Playas Hermosa, Panamá and Coco – and continue for several kilometres over the good paved road. There's another turn-off to Hermosa and Panamá on the right.
By bus There's a bus stop on the main road at the northern edge of Playa Hermosa.
Destinations Liberia (8 daily; 50min); San José (1 daily; 5hr 30min).

ACTIVITIES AND TOURS

Aqua Sport On the beach in Playa Hermosa ☎ 2672 0050. A good spot to pick up gear for getting on and in the water, including snorkelling gear, kayaks and canoes.
Diving Safaris On a side road toward the beach at the north end of Playa Hermosa ☎ 2672 1259, ⍟ costaricadiving.net. The family-run Diving Safaris offers expert trips and lessons as well as PADI courses; they also lead snorkelling tours and rent equipment.
The Rock Water Sports On the northern end of the beach in Playa Hermosa ☎ 2672 0056. Named for the solitary rocky outcrop offshore, this beachfront bar offers jet-ski rentals ($20/hr) and sunset boat trips in the bay.

ACCOMMODATION

La Finisterra Up a steep dirt road off the southern access road to Playa Hermosa ☎ 2672 0227, ⍟ lafinisterra.com. A charming, small hotel with a superb setting on the cliff at the southern end of the beach. Enjoy stunning sunset views, a swimming pool and warm hospitality. The excellent restaurant offers tasty international dishes (see p.276) and breakfast is included in the price. $170
Hilton Papagayo Resort At the end of the Playa Panamá beach road ☎ 2672 0000, ⍟ hiltonpapagayoresort.com. Plush all-inclusive complex that has just about everything you might need plus quite a bit more, including an infinity pool, spa, fitness centre and several restaurants and bars. The rooms and bungalows are elegantly furnished with a minimalist design and have a wide range of amenities. $458
★**Hotel Bosque del Mar** On Playa Hermosa ☎ 2672 0046, ⍟ hotelplayahermosa.com. Situated in a great spot right on the beach, with lush gardens featuring hundred-year-old trees near a large swimming pool with jacuzzi. This hotel is owned and managed by Ticos offering old-fashioned hospitality, with a stellar beachfront open-air restaurant that's also open to non-residents. Rooms have hot water, a/c and cable TV. $220
Hotel Giardini di Papagayo On a plateau overlooking Playa Panamá ☎ 2672 0067. Well-located hotel offering immaculate rooms decorated in the Californian-Spanish colonial style favoured by upmarket hoteliers hereabouts. Rates include all meals, but you pay extra for sea views. Free snorkelling and kayaking trips are included. $146
Iguana Inn On the northern access road to Playa Hermosa ☎ 2672 0065. A stone's throw from the beach, this pleasant budget option has simple, colourful rooms with fan and small hot-water bathrooms. There's also a swimming pool and a well-equipped shared kitchen. $25
Occidental Grand Papagayo Off the northern access road to Playa Hermosa ☎ 2690 8000. An all-inclusive gated property with two lovely pools, a handful of posh restaurants and bars and a fitness centre. The rooms, some of which have ocean views, are decorated with muted colours and dark-wood furniture and have a/c, cable TV and safes; all have balconies. Adults only. $540

5

El Velero Off the northern access road to Playa Hermosa ☎2672 1017, ⓦcostaricahotel.net. Friendly hotel with split-level rooms with balconies. Enjoy sea views from the lovely gardens that are filled with birds and lizards; a short path leads from the hotel down to the beach. There's also a good restaurant, a small pool and they offer guests sunrise, sunset and full-day tours on their 38ft sailboat. $89

EATING

Bistro Restaurant La Finisterra. Creatively prepared dishes like ceviche ($14) and beef tenderloin, several tapas ($5–8) and an impressive wine list in an elegant setting. It's less expensive than you might expect, and the views of the Pacific are spectacular. Daily 7am–10pm.

★**Ginger** On the main road, 2km inland from Playa Hermosa ☎2672 0041. Chrome, glass and sharp angles cantilevered in the hills, *Ginger* is popular with the trendy expat community. The menu consists of a diverse range of Asian-fusion/Mediterranean-inspired small plates ($5–7) designed for sharing; don't look for *comida típica* here. Tues–Sun 5–10pm.

★**Mario's Cuisine** On the left side of Playa Hermosa's principal side road ☎5705 1645. It's not too often when you can dine on the front porch of a trained chef's home, let alone hope for such exquisite food and warm Costa Rican welcome. The menu changes regularly, but count on Guanacaste beef, fresh seafood options caught offshore (by one of the owners) and local fruits and vegetables. The mains, inspired mixes of a variety of cuisines, are around $9–15; don't leave without dessert. Reservations required. Daily breakfast and dinner only.

Pescado Loco Opposite El Velero. For appealing cheap eats, head to this low-key restaurant where freshly caught fish costs $8–10 and roast chicken is $7. Daily 11am–9pm.

Playas del Coco

Some 35km west of Liberia, booming **PLAYAS DEL COCO** was the first Pacific beach to hit it big with weekending Costa Ricans from the Valle Central. These days it's particularly popular with North American expats, who have helped give it an unmistakeable, and decidedly laidback, international feel. The beach itself is nice enough and is kept clean by rubbish-collecting brigades organized by local residents. The town's accessibility and wide range of budget accommodation make it a useful base to explore the more photogenic beaches nearby. It also has a thriving restaurant scene with more variety than you can find elsewhere along this stretch of the coast, and is a good place from which to take a **snorkelling** or **diving** tour (see below). El Coco town spreads out right in front of the beach, with a tiny **parquecito** and the adjacent unmissable lime-green **Iglesia Católica** as the focal point.

ARRIVAL AND GETTING AROUND

By car Playas del Coco is a 35min drive west of Liberia, with good road conditions along the entire route.

By bus Buses stop next door to the Banco Nacional on the main road leading to the beach.

Destinations Liberia (hourly from 6am–7pm; 1hr); San José (3 daily; 5hr 30min).

By taxi Taxis gather by the *parquecito* on the beach; trips to the nearby neaches of Playa Hermosa and Playa Ocotal cost around $7–10.

DIVING

Deep Blue Diving On the main road diagonally across from the Banco Nacional ☎2670 1004, ⓦdeepblue-diving.com. Excellent dive shop with a full slate of trips on offer, including two tank dives in the Gulfo de Papagayo ($79) or more technical excursions around the Islas Catalinas (from $110).

Rich Coast Diving On the main road about 300m from the beach ☎2670 0176, ⓦrichcoastdiving.com. This venerable dive shop organize snorkelling and scuba trips ($50–80 for a two-tank dive) and offer PADI certification.

ACCOMMODATION

Coco has plenty of fairly basic *cabinas*, catering to weekending nationals and tourists. In the **high season** you should **reserve at weekends**, when the village often sees a large influx of visitors. You can probably get away with turning up on spec midweek, when rooms may also be a little cheaper. In the **low season** bargains abound.

B&B Villa del Sol 1km north of the village; turn right off the main road 150m before the beach ☎2670 0085, ⓦvilladelsol.com. Small, welcoming B&B in a quiet location with rooms set around a large grassy space – all have private bathroom with hot water and ocean views. Pleasantly decorated by the friendly French-Canadian owners, the hotel also has a large pool and tasty meals. $65

Cabinas Coco Azul A few blocks back from the beach, northeast of the main road ☎2670 0431, ⓦcabinas cocoazul.co. One of the better budget options and a short walk from the beach. The rooms are decidedly basic, but are pleasant enough and clean; some have a/c and it's worth paying a few dollars more for one that does. $33

Hotel Chantel On a hill about 4km from the beach ☎2670 0389, ⓦhotelchantel.com. Small boutique hotel with eleven rooms that have a/c, ceiling fans, wi-fi, safe-deposit boxes, private bathrooms and a magnificent ocean view. Breakfast included. $89

Hotel Coco Palms On the beach, next to the football pitch ☎2670 0367, ⓦhotelcocopalms.com. Like a motel in style, with nice and clean rooms with a/c and wi-fi. There's a pool as well as Coco's only sushi spot and the *Lazy Frog* sports bar. Rooms away from the pool are usually quieter. $27

Pato Loco Inn On the road coming into town, about 300m before the village ☎2670 0145, ⓦcosta-rica-beach-hotel-patoloco.com. The "Crazy Duck" offers nice

airy rooms with private bath and fan or a/c. Cordial, personal treatment is the standard, which explains the steady stream of returning regulars. There are a couple of long-stay apartments with kitchen, as well as internet access for guests. $59

La Puerta del Sol Off the road leading to the right 100m before you reach the beach ☎2670 0195, ⓦlapuertadelsolcostarica.com. Friendly Italian-run retreat set in quiet gardens; rooms have a/c, phone and cable TV and a small terrace and lounge area. The thoughtfully arranged complex has a pool, gym and the *Sol y Luna* restaurant (see below) serving top-notch Italian food. Breakfast is included in the price. $113

★**Rancho Armadillo** On a hill about 5km from the beach ☎2670 0108, ⓦranchoarmadillo.com. Run by an easy-going American former chef, this stunning hilltop estate with centuries-old sculptures spread throughout the grounds is quite unlike anything else in the area. The rooms are exceedingly comfortable, well appointed and decorated with striking wood furnishings, the communal areas invite extended lingering, the pool is beautiful and the views of the Pacific are unmatched. That said, what truly makes the place memorable is the care and attention of the staff, who make you feel right at home. $204

EATING AND DRINKING

Coco has two very distinct types of places to eat and drink: those catering to Ticos and those that attempt a cosmopolitan vibe to hook the gringos. There's a lively nightlife – over two dozen bars and nightclubs rock through the night. Much of it emanates from the *Lizard Lounge*, *La Vida Loca* and *Zouk Santana* on the main street, three bars with plenty of cocktails, shooters and moody bass beats.

Andre's Beach Bar On the beach just northeast of the main road ☎2670 2052. A low-key spot favoured by expats and worth a stop for filling, Chicago-style hot dogs ($6) and decent pizzas ($11–15). Daily 7am–late.

Coconutz On the main road, a block and a half from the beach ☎2670 1982. Popular sports bar with plenty of outside seating where you can watch Costa Rican club football matches and American NFL football games. There's also standard bar fare, free wi-fi and a lovely little pond where turtles swim. Daily 11am–midnight.

Lizard Lounge On the main road, 100m before the beach, on the right ☎2670 0181. Relaxing bar and restaurant serving Tico fare and Western burgers ($7) and steaks ($13) – all at reasonable prices. It's a pleasant spot to grab a snack, chill out listening to music or catch the latest sporting events and news on the big screen. Daily 4pm–2am.

Las Olas On the main road, about 100km before the beach, on the right ☎2670 2003. Stylish *soda* serving some of the best food in town, including salads and chicken and pasta dishes (most mains $6.50–12). The speciality is fish and seafood – don't miss the stuffed red snapper ($15). Daily 11am–10pm.

Papagayo On the main drag, 100m before the beach ☎2670 0298. If it's fresh and available, you'll find it on the menu at Coco's best seafood restaurant, run by the family of the big shot of the local fishing fleet. The "catch of the day" will set you back $7, while a delectable mixed seafood platter comes in at $15. The fish is prepared in a wide variety of styles, but the quality is consistently excellent. Daily noon–11pm.

★**Sol y Luna** La Puerta del Sol hotel. An attractive and intimate setting where you can sample expertly prepared Italian food, including home-made pasta seasoned with herbs. The owners make a big effort to import authentic ingredients, and there's also a decent wine selection. Mains dishes are $8–10. Wed–Mon 5–10pm.

Tequila Bar On the main road, near the parquecito ☎2670 0741. Although the building looks a little ramshackle, the Mexican food here is high quality. Filling plates, such as chicken fajitas, start at $5 and the Mexican owner extends a warm welcome to diners. As the name suggests, there's a solid selection of tequilas and the best margaritas in Coco. Tues–Thurs noon–10pm.

La Vida Loca On the beach south of the main road just past the wooden pedestrian bridge ☎2670 0181. Popular with expats, this American-owned beachfront bar

5

with a buxom mermaid out front is a good spot for an afternoon drink and can get pretty lively when most other places close for the night. Daily 11am–1am.

★**Zouk Santana** On the main road, near the parquecito ☎ 2670 0191. With a fresh vibe and chic style,

Zouk is the rare spot that merits a visit both for breakfast and for settling in at the cigar bar for a late-night aperitif. That said, its dinner meals, which feature tasty dishes (mains around $9–17) made from locally sourced ingredients, don't disappoint either. Tues–Sun 7am–2am.

DIRECTORY

Internet There's internet access at Leslie's (daily 10am–6pm), next door to *Zouk Santana*.

Money and exchange The Banco Nacional, on the main road as you enter town, will change dollars and travellers' cheques and has an ATM.

Post office There's a miniscule post office (Mon–Fri 7.30am–5pm) across from the *parquecito*.

Supermarket The biggest supermarket within walking distance of the beach is Luperón (☎ 2670 0950), next to the Banco Nacional.

Playa Ocotal

Past the rocky headland south of Coco, the upmarket enclave of **PLAYA OCOTAL** is reached by taking the signed turn-off to the left 200m before reaching the beach at Coco. Ocotal and its surroundings have lovely views over the ocean and across to the Papagayo Gulf from the top of the headland, and the small beach is better for swimming than Coco. But the real attractions are the marlin and other "big game" fish that glide through these waters: many of Ocotal's **hotels** are often tied in with sportfishing packages.

ACCOMMODATION AND EATING   PLAYA OCOTAL

Bahía Pez Vela Follow the sign to Ocotal Beach Resort off the main road, and after 1km you'll see another sign for Bahía Pez Vela ☎ 2670 0129, ⓦ bahiapezvela.com. Upmarket resort with forty two-storey villas, in beautiful grounds with two pools, a wading pool, and a gorgeous lawn area above a nice private beach ideal for swimming. If you want to be near the beach, ask for a villa on the grounds' lower end. The bar and restaurant *Picante* is open-air, casual and by the pool, but pricey by local standards. $339

Father Rooster Bar and Grill Take the road past Ocotal Beach Resort's gate, then take the first right and continue to the end ☎ 2670 1246. This beachfront locals' favourite has gorgeous views and some of the best seafood around. Tempting dishes such as fish tacos ($11.50) and shrimp kebabs ($13) are all reasonably priced and served by fun staff. Daily 11.30am–10pm.

Ocotal Beach Resort Signposted on the turn-off from the road to Playa del Coco ☎ 2670 0321, ⓦ ocotalresort .com. Set on top of a hill, this top-end hotel has stunning views over the Pacific and elegantly furnished rooms with TV, hammocks, a/c and fridges. In addition to sportfishing packages, it also offers tennis, swimming and scuba-diving packages. $209

★**Villa Casa Blanca** Signposted off the road to Ocotal Beach Resort ☎ 2670 0448, ⓦ hotelvillacasablanca .com. A small, quiet and very accommodating B&B that offers boat tours, deep-sea fishing, scuba diving to the Islas Murciélagos near Santa Rosa, and horseriding trips. The Spanish-style villas feature colourful and bright canopy beds. There's a charming bridged pool, a tennis court in the grounds and rates include breakfast. No restaurant, however. $105

Playa Flamingo and around

Despite its name, there are no flamingoes at the upmarket and expensive gringo enclave of **PLAYA FLAMINGO**, a place that feels more Cancún than Costa Rica – some of the big beach houses lining the white sands are owned by the odd movie star. It does, however, have the best beach on this section of the coast, with white sand, gentle breakers and picturesque rocky islets offshore. There's also great **sportfishing**: almost all the resort-style hotels in the area cater to fishing enthusiasts or sun-worshippers on packages. It's approached via the road to the small, unappealing **PLAYA BRASILITO**, a scruffy beach with darkish sand, which lies about 5km before Playa Flamingo's marina.

To escape the rather static and standoffish atmosphere of Flamingo, head 3km north to **PLAYA POTRERO**, a small cove that opens onto a decent crescent-shaped beach with secluded camping and calm waters good for swimming.

The most southerly of the four beaches, **PLAYA CONCHAL** ("Shell Beach") is set in a steep broad bay a couple of kilometres south of Playa Brasilito. Protected by a rocky headland, it has appealing pink-coloured sand, with mounds of tiny shells and quiet waters that are good for swimming and snorkelling.

ARRIVAL AND DEPARTURE

By car To reach the beaches by car, take the Liberia–Nicoya road to Belén, then turn right off the main road and follow a side road to the hamlet of Huacas, 25km beyond Belén, from where the beaches are signposted. To get to Conchal from Flamingo, you have to backtrack inland, turning right at the village of Matapalo. It's quicker to drive along the sand from Brasilito, but you'll need a 4WD or a tug-of-war team.

By bus Buses arrive in Playa Flamingo on the main road at

PLAYA FLAMINGO AND AROUND

the stop diagonally opposite *Mariner Inn*; those to Playa Brasilito pull in at the stop on the main road next to the Super Brasilito; Playa Concha's stop is on the main road next to the Banco Costa Rica and Playa Potrero's stop is by the plaza set back from the beach. Note that the destinations below reflect times from Playa Flamingo; add 5–15min to the times for the other beaches.

Destinations San José (3 daily; 6hr); Santa Cruz (13 daily; 1hr 40min).

ACCOMMODATION AND EATING

Bahía Esmeralda Playa Flamingo ☎ 2654 4480, ⓦ hotelbahiaesmeralda.com. Friendly and tranquil Italian-run option with colourful rooms, apartments, villas and newer suites; all have a/c, cable TV and wi-fi. There's a pool in the centre of the grounds and a small restaurant, though the hours can be erratic. Double $76, apartment $95, villa $123

Cabinas Cristina Playa Potrero ☎ 2654 4006, ⓦ cabinascristina.com. Bright, comfortable rooms and apartments with kitchenettes, cable TV, a/c and wi-fi. There's a pool, and the helpful owners rent boats and can arrange tours. Double $56, apartment $90

Camping y Cabinas Mayra's Playa Potrero ☎ 2654 4213. You can camp under palm trees at the relaxed and very basic *Mayra's* right on the seashore in Playa Potrero. $5

Flamingo Beach Resort Playa Flamingo ☎ 2654 4444, ⓦ resortflamingobeach.com. Large, fairly characterless hotel though it boasts a pretty setting across from the beach, a large pool, a restaurant and bar, a casino, spa and spacious rooms. The hotel can arrange charter flights and will pick you up from the nearby airstrip. $175

Flamingo Marina Resort Playa Flamingo ☎ 2654 4141, ⓦ flamingomarina.com. A popular resort that has modern rooms – some of which have fantastic views – as well as enormous suites with jacuzzis. There are

several pools, a tennis court, restaurant, lively bar and tour service. $146

Hotel Brasilito Playa Brasilito ☎ 2654 4237, ⓦ brasilito.com. The best budget option in the area and right on the beach. The seventeen spacious rooms are sparsely furnished but with large beds, fans and hot-water bathrooms; some have a/c ($5 surcharge). The hotel rents kayaks for $10/day, and there's a pleasant restaurant on-site. $50

Mariner Inn Playa Flamingo ☎ 2654 4081, ⓦ marinerinn.com. On the marina, this is one of the cheaper options in Playa Flamingo with twelve clean a/c rooms and wi-fi. It's a pleasant spot to hang out, especially at the appealing bar *Spreader*, where fishermen's tall tales are swapped over cold beers and tasty burgers. $33

El Oasis Hotel Brasilito. Reasonably priced restaurant that serves typical regional fare such as shrimp with rice and red snapper as well as more international choices (most mains $9–14). Daily 7.30am–9pm.

Westin Golf Resort & Spa Playa Conchal ☎ 2654 3500, ⓦ starwoodhotels.com. Set back from the beach between playas Brasilito and Conchal is this plush mega complex, whose arrival dramatically changed the character of an area that was once a sleepy low-key beach community. The exclusive resort is nothing if not brash, boasting hundreds of suites, tennis courts, a golf course and a gorgeous pool. $480

Parque Nacional Marino Las Baulas

4km west of Matapalo • Daily 9am–4pm; open for guided night tours in nesting season • $10, including tour • ☎ 2653 0470

On the Río Matapalo estuary between Conchal and Tamarindo, **PARQUE NACIONAL MARINO LAS BAULAS** is less a national park than a reserve, created in 1995 to protect the nesting grounds of the critically endangered **leatherback turtles**, which come ashore here to nest from November to February. Leatherbacks have probably laid their eggs at **Playa Grande** for millions of years, and it's now one of the few remaining such nesting sites in the world. The beach itself offers a beautiful sweep of light-coloured sand, and outside laying season you can surf and splash around in

5

the waves, though swimming is rough, plagued by crashing waves and riptides. Despite its proximity to an officially protected area, developers have been given carte blanche to build: the *Rancho Las Colinas Golf and Country Club*, which includes an eighteen-hole golf course and over two hundred separate villas, is symptomatic of the lack of planning, the short-termism and the plain daftness (the golf course is located in an area with a long, hot dry season and a history of water shortages) that characterizes so much recent tourist development in Costa Rica. What effect the development will have on the ancient nesting ground of the turtles remains to be seen.

Playa Grande has in the past been a magnet for tour groups from upmarket Guanacaste hotels as well as day-trippers from Tamarindo and Coco. Nowadays, however, visitor numbers are regulated and you are no longer allowed to walk on the beach during nesting season (get the rangers to tell you stories of what people used to do to harass the turtles and you'll see why).

Turtle-watching tours

Turtle nesting takes place only in season and at **night**, with moonlit nights at high tide being the preferred moment. Note that you are not guaranteed to see a nesting turtle on any given night, and it's definitely worth calling in at El Mundo de la Tortuga (see below) before your visit, both to see the informative exhibition and to ask if tides and weather are favourable for nesting – alternatively you could ask the rangers at the entrance hut.

Those who see a nesting are often moved both by the sight of the turtles' imposing bulk, and also by their vulnerability, as they lever themselves up on to the beach. Each female can nest up to twelve times per season, laying a hundred or so eggs at a time, before finally returning to the sea – after which she won't touch land again for another year. Eggs take about sixty days to hatch, and the female turtle **hatchlings** that make the journey from their eggs to the ocean down this beach will (if they survive) return here ten to fifteen years later to nest themselves.

While it's worth seeing a nesting, it's difficult not to feel like an intruder. Groups of up to fifteen people are led to each turtle by guides (some of them "rehabilitated" former poachers), who communicate via walkie-talkie – and if it's a busy night there might be several tour groups after the same turtle. When the guide locates a turtle ready to lay her eggs you trudge in a group along the beach and then stand around watching the leatherback go through her procreative duty, while from time to time the turtle will cast a world-weary glance in the direction of her fans. It's hard not to think it would be better for the turtle if everyone just stayed away and bought the video, although the viewing is well managed and fairly considerate, and the revenue does help to protect the turtles' habitat.

El Mundo de la Tortuga

Around 200m from the park entrance • Daily 8am–1pm & 2–4pm, or until much later when turtles are nesting • Free with entrance fee • ☎ 2653 0471

The impressive and educational **El Mundo de la Tortuga** exhibition includes an audio-guided tour in English and some stunning photographs of the turtles. You'll gain an insight into the leatherbacks' habitats and reproductive cycles, along with the threats they face, and current conservation efforts. There's also a souvenir shop and a small café where groups on turtle tours are often asked to wait while a nesting turtle is located. It's open late at night – often past midnight – depending on demand and nesting times.

ARRIVAL AND INFORMATAION   **PARQUE NACIONAL MARINO LAS BAULAS**

There are two official entrances to Playa Grande, though tickets to enter the reserve can only be bought at the southern entrance, where the road enters the park near the *Villa Baula*. There are no bus services to the park.

THE LEATHERBACK TURTLE

Leatherback turtles (in Spanish, *baulas*) are giant creatures. Often described as a relic from the age of the dinosaurs, they're also one of the oldest animals on earth, having existed largely unchanged for 120 million years. The leatherback's most arresting characteristic is its sheer size, reaching a length of about 2.4m and a weight of 500kg. Its front flippers are similarly huge – as much as 2.7m long – and it's these which propel the leatherback on its long-distance migrations (they're known to breed off the West Indies, Florida, the northeastern coast of South America, Senegal, Madagascar, Sri Lanka and Malaysia). Leatherbacks are also unique among turtles in having a skeleton that is not firmly attached to a shell, but which consists of a **carapace** made up of hundreds of irregular bony plates, covered with a leathery skin. It's also the only turtle that can regulate its own body temperature, maintaining a constant 18°C even in the freezing ocean depths, and withstanding immense pressures of over 1500 pounds per square inch as it dives to depths of up to 1200m.

Since the 1973 Convention on the International Trade of Endangered Species, it is illegal to harvest green, hawksbill, leatherback and loggerhead turtles. Unlike olive ridleys or hawksbills, leatherbacks are not hunted by humans for food – their flesh has an unpleasantly oily taste – though poachers still steal eggs for their alleged aphrodisiac powers. Even so, leatherbacks still face many human-created hazards. They can choke on discarded plastic bags left floating in the ocean (which they mistake for jellyfish, on which they feed), and often get caught in longline fishing nets or wounded by boat propellers – all added to a loss of nesting habitats caused by beachfront development and the fact that, even in normal conditions, only one in every 2500 leatherback hatchlings makes it to maturity.

The number of nesting females at Las Baulas alone dropped from 1646 in 1988 to 215 in 1997, although numbers have since increased to over 800. At Las Baulas, authorities have established a hatchling "farm" to allow hatchlings to be born and make their trip to the ocean under less perilous conditions than would normally prevail, though this will not affect adult mortality, which is believed to be the root cause of the drop in leatherback numbers. While the population is healthier than it was fifteen years ago, it continues to be plagued by longline fishing, large-scale rubbish dumping, ocean contamination and other factors contributing to fertility problems.

If you're interested in **volunteering**, Earthwatch (w earthwatch.org) have run conservation holidays on playas Grande and Langosta for a number of years, documenting numbers of nesting turtles and their activity patterns.

By car To drive to Las Baulas, take the road from Huacas to Matapalo, and turn left at the football field (a 4WD is recommended for this stretch during the wet season).

By boat Most people visit the park by boat with a Tamarindo tour operator (see p.283), entering at the southern end rather than from the Matapalo road.

ACCOMMODATION AND EATING

Bula Bula At the southern end of the Playa Grande ☎ 2653 0975, w hotelbulabula.com. In a splendid setting between Playa Grande and the river that runs behind the beach, this brightly coloured hotel offers ten rooms, plus some bungalows (sleeping 4–6), all with wi-fi, a/c and cable TV. Excursions include kayaking, sportfishing, horseriding and mountain biking. The restaurant serves fantastic food, particularly the large continental and Costa Rican breakfasts (included in the room rate). $141

Las Tortugas Hotel Centre of Playa Grande ☎ 2653 0423, w lastortugashotel.com. The area's longest established hotel with a pool, restaurant and a combination of eleven standard and more luxurious rooms and suites. The conscientious owners have kept the light the hotel reflects onto the beach to a minimum (turtle hatchlings are confused by light coming from land), and designed the building so that it will block light from any future developments to the north. They also rent surfboards, can advise on turtle tours and horseriding and have hillside apartments available for extended stays. $56

Villa Baula South end of Playa Grande ☎ 2653 0493. Nestled among the trees on the beach, *Villa Baula* has comfortable (though dark) seaside rooms with ceiling fans, plus some attractive private bungalows, all with private bathrooms and hot water (some also have a fridge). There are two lovely pools in the grounds and a good restaurant serving Indonesian and international dishes. Double $44, bungalow $61

5

Playa Tamarindo and around

Sprawling and perennially popular, **TAMARINDO** village boasts a decent selection of restaurants, a lively beach culture (think beautiful young things parading up and down) and a healthy nightlife, at least during high season. Many come here to learn to surf – indeed, the gentle breakers are an ideal training ground – or simply to laze on the beach, which is undeniably gorgeous. Tamarindo is, however, the least Costa Rican of places, with locals completely outnumbered by tourists and expats. Even by its own trendy terms, the village is booming, with small complexes of shops springing up in the concrete-mini-mall style favoured hereabouts, while internet cafés, flashy restaurants

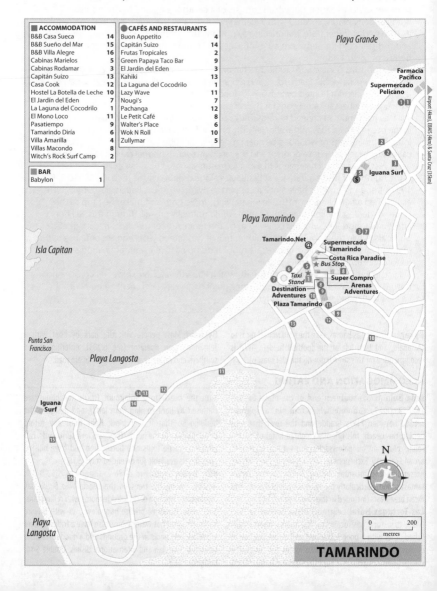

■ ACCOMMODATION	
B&B Casa Sueca	14
B&B Sueño del Mar	15
B&B Villa Alegre	16
Cabinas Marielos	5
Cabinas Rodamar	3
Capitán Suizo	13
Casa Cook	12
Hostel La Botella de Leche	10
El Jardín del Eden	7
La Laguna del Cocodrilo	1
El Mono Loco	11
Pasatiempo	9
Tamarindo Diría	6
Villa Amarilla	4
Villas Macondo	8
Witch's Rock Surf Camp	2

● CAFÉS AND RESTAURANTS	
Buon Appetito	4
Capitán Suizo	14
Frutas Tropicales	2
Green Papaya Taco Bar	9
El Jardín del Eden	3
Kahiki	13
La Laguna del Cocodrilo	1
Lazy Wave	11
Nougi's	7
Pachanga	12
Le Petit Café	8
Walter's Place	6
Wok N Roll	10
Zullymar	5

■ BAR	
Babylon	1

Playa Grande

Farmacia Pacífico
Supermercado Pelicano

Airport (4km), EBAIS (4km) & Santa Cruz (35km)

Iguana Surf

Playa Tamarindo

Tamarindo.Net
Supermercado Tamarindo
Costa Rica Paradise
Bus Stop
Taxi Stand
Super Compro
Destination Adventures
Arenas Adventures
Plaza Tamarindo

Isla Capitan

Punta San Francisco

Playa Langosta

Iguana Surf

N

Playa Langosta

0   200
metres

TAMARINDO

and estate agents colonize the centre of the village, as foreigners rush in to snap up their plots in paradise. The constant development gives the area an unsettled air and it can all feel a bit characterless at times.

Though fishing still plays a small part in the local economy, Tamarindo's transformation from village to beach resort has been rapid, with the usual associated worries about drugs and the loss of community. The village loop at the end of the main road effectively constitutes Tamarindo's small centre and is lined by restaurants, New-Age jewellery stalls and surf shops. **Swimming** isn't great around Tamarindo, because of choppy waters and occasional riptides. Most people are content to paddle in the rocky coves and tide pools south of the town. Tamarindo is, however, an ideal **surf** spot because of the reliable, but relatively gentle, waves and the beach attracts a combination of enthusiastic surfers and well-to-do Costa Ricans, who own holiday houses in the vicinity.

In the evening, the main activity here is watching the typically opulent **sunsets**, as the sun disappears into the Pacific just beyond the rocky headland that marks the southern end of the beach, but attention soon shifts to the bar with the cheapest drinks specials.

North of the Tamarindo river estuary begins the long sweep of Playa Grande (see p.279), where the **leatherback turtles** lay their eggs. Turtles also come ashore at Tamarindo, but in much smaller numbers. Officially, Tamarindo is within the boundaries of Parque Nacional Marino Las Baulas, in so far as the ocean covered by the protected area extends out in an arc, encompassing Tamarindo beach. SINAC has bought up the beach south of Tamarindo to Playa Langosta, too, preventing further hotel development and allowing turtles to continue coming ashore along this entire stretch.

ARRIVAL AND DEPARTURE
PLAYA TAMARINDO AND AROUND

By plane NatureAir (☎2653 1452) and Sansa (☎2653 0012) fly to the small airport 4km north of the village off Hwy-152. Both companies have offices in town.
Destinations via NatureAir Liberia (daily; 15min); San José (2 daily; 50min).
Destinations via Sansa San José (2 daily; 50min).

By bus Buses arrive by the village loop. Interbus (Centro Comercial Plaza Conchal; ☎2653 4374) is a another useful option to and from Tamarindo, with pick-up at your hotel and daily departures all over the country.
Destinations Liberia (9 daily; 2hr); San José (4 daily; 6hr); Santa Cruz (9 daily; 1hr).

GETTING AROUND

By car, scooter or bike For getting around the area, and out to Playa Langosta, the beach just south of the village, you can rent a scooter or mountain bike from Costa Rica Paradise (see below), among other places. Several places rent cars, including Economy and Alamo, both on the main road at the northern entrance to the village.
By taxi Taxis congregate on the loop across from the bus stop. Trips to Las Baulas and Playa Avellanas each cost $15–25.

TOURS AND ACTIVITIES

Many operators in town run a popular 2hr boat excursion ($40/person) that takes you around the **river estuary** where you might spot monkeys, birds and crocodiles. In **leatherback nesting season** (Nov to mid-Feb), you can head out on a turtle tour ($30/person; about 2hr); trips leave in the evening, the exact hour depending on the tide. During the rest of the year, turtles also nest further south at Refugio Nacional de Vida Silvestre Ostional (see p.301), usually only on a couple of days each month, depending on the moon. A trip there and back costs around $40. Numerous Tamarindo operators run these and other trips.

Costa Rica Paradise Centro Comercial Plaza Conchal ☎2653 2251, ☯crparadise.com. One of the most professional and helpful options in the village, this operator offers all the usual tours as well as day-trips to Palo Verde ($90), horseriding into dry tropical forest (2hr; $35) and short, but exhilarating gyrocopter flights ($120).
Destination Adventures On the village loop ☎2653 3842, ☯destinationadventures.net. A well-run operator that leads snorkelling trips around Tamarindo ($55; 3hr),

horseriding along the beach ($45; 2hr 30min) and day-trips further afield, including a popular trip to Parque Nacional Rincón de la Vieja which includes climbing, rappelling and zip lines ($125; 12hr).
Ser Yoga Studio Plaza Tamarindo, second floor ☎8346 8005, ☯seryogastudio.com. Daily Vinyasa, Hatha and Ashtanga yoga classes (1hr 15min–1 hr 45min; $10) and pilates classes are offered at the welcoming Argentinian-owned Ser Yoga Studio.

5

SURF SCHOOLS

The Tamarindo area has always been a **surfing paradise**, and its credibility was upped several notches when Bruce Brown's seminal surfing docudrama *Endless Summer II* was partly filmed here. Most surfers ride the waves at Tamarindo, Playa Grande and adjacent Playa Langosta, an excellent surf beach a couple of kilometres south. All schools rent surfboards; typical prices are $25 for a day's rental of a long board, or $100 for a week. You can also rent boogie boards, windsurfing equipment, and masks and snorkels.

Arenas Adventures On the village loop ☎ 2653 0108. Arenas Adventures in a popular school in an unmistakable round building with a huge sign reading "hightide." They also rent out ATVs, dirt bikes and kayaks.

Iguana Surf On the main road about 100m north of Plaza Conchal; also along the road to Playa Langosta ☎ 2653 0613, ⓦ iguanasurf.net. The friendly and professional Iguana Surf will almost certainly have you standing on a board by the end of your first two-hour class; cost is around $45 including board rental.

Witch's Rock Surf Camp See opposite. Witch's Rock Surf Camp, named after one of the best breaks in the area, offers non-guests a full slate of lessons ($45/2hr) and board rentals ($20/day).

Xplore Costa Rica Plaza Tamarindo ☎ 2653 4130, ⓦ xplorecostarica.com. Though one of the newer tour operators in the village, this wildy popular company has quickly earned a strong reputation based on reliable service and knowledgeable guides. They offer a long list of local and long-distance tours, from snorkelling and kayaking combo tours off nearby beaches (2.5hr; $50) to day-trips to Granada, Nicaragua (13hr; $170).

ACCOMMODATION

Many of Tamarindo's hotels are very good, if expensive, with plenty of options for all budgets. While staying in the **village** places you steps from the heart of the action, **Playa Langosta**'s upmarket B&Bs and hotels offer an often-necessary retreat from the hectic Tamarindo beachside scene, and are a quiet 15–20min walk away.

IN THE VILLAGE

Cabinas Marielos ☎ 2653 0141, ⓦ cabinasmarieloscr .com. Basic rooms, light and clean, with fan, cold water and the use of a small kitchen, in pleasant and colourful grounds set back from the main road. There are also rooms available with a/c ($10 surcharge), and a handful with hot-water bathrooms and fridge. The owner is helpful and professional. $45

Cabinas Rodamar ☎ 2653 0109. A very basic, friendly budget traveller's hangout, this motel-style compound set back from the main road has dark *cabinas* with cold-water bathrooms, big beds and fans. The cheaper rooms with shared bathroom are a bit more spartan, and there's a communal kitchen. $27

★**Hostel La Botella de Leche** ☎ 2653 2061, ⓦ labotelladeleche.com. Excellent backpacker hostel with comfortable bunk-bed accommodation in dorms. It has a/c, wi-fi, a small pool and a well-equipped communal kitchen as well as spick-and-span shared cold-water bathrooms. It's designed with surfers in mind – you can rent and repair boards here, as well as arrange classes. It's very popular, and although the super-friendly owner will do her utmost to squeeze you in, you'd be wise to reserve ahead. Dorm $15, double $52

★**El Jardín del Eden** On the hilltop behind the main road through town ☎ 2653 0137, ⓦ jardindeleden.com. Discreet, upmarket hotel in an exclusive hilltop position, with fine views over Tamarindo. Villas have all the usual amenities – a/c, fans, satellite TV, telephone and fridge – plus nice touches like tiled bathrooms and wicker chairs on the large private balconies. There's also a landscaped pool, jacuzzi, bar and an excellent French restaurant. Breakfast included. $140

La Laguna del Cocodrilo ☎ 2653 0255, ⓦ lalaguna delcocodrilo.com. With a prime beachfront spot at the northern end of the village, *Laguna del Cocodrilo* offers a more tranquil stay than the more central spots and has ten bright and spacious rooms and two suites with views of the ocean and a pretty garden, each with a/c, cable TV and wi-fi. The excellent on-site French bakery and restaurant (see p.286) will likely keep you from wandering at mealtime. Double $79, suite $138

Pasatiempo ☎ 2653 0096 ⓦ hotelpasatiempo.com. Popular hotel with a relaxed and friendly atmosphere. The spotless rooms have a/c, wi-fi, hot water and CD players. The larger rooms sleep five and are a good deal for groups. The atmosphere is homely, with hammocks strung outside the rooms and around the pool. There's also a lively restaurant and bar (that can get loud in high season). $99

Tamarindo Diría ☎ 2653 0032, ⓦ tamarindodiria .com. One of Tamarindo's oldest hotels, set in shady palm groves on the beach. Arranged around two swimming pools looking out to the ocean, the large rooms all have a/c, cable TV, telephone and private bathroom. Sea-view rooms are worth the additional cost ($65 surcharge). There's a great seaside bar/restaurant on-site. Breakfast included. **$198**

Villa Amarilla ☎ 2653 0038, ⓦ hotelvillaamarilla .com. A favourite spot for a quick beer on the beach between catching waves, *Villa Amarilla* also has seven *cabinas* and a communal kitchen. Rooms are decked out in wood; the simpler ones have fridge, fan and shared bathroom, while the en-suite rooms have a/c and cable TV. There's a cheap and cheerful restaurant. **$113**

★ **Villas Macondo** ☎ 2653 0812, ⓦ villasmacondo .com. Tamarindo is sometimes overpriced, but this quiet, welcoming spot is a refreshing exception. The colourful *cabinas*, set around an enticing swimming pool, have comfortable beds, wooden ceilings and a little terrace strung with hammocks; the more expensive ones include cable TV, a/c and fridge ($25 surcharge). There are also apartments with one or two bedrooms. Guests have access to a kitchenette with gas stove. *Cabinas* **$42**, apartment **$110**

Witch's Rock Surf Camp ☎ 2653 1262, ⓦ witchs rocksurfcamp.com. The best choice in the village for all-in daily surf lessons, unlimited board rentals and accommodation. The breezy, brightly coloured rooms vary in size, though all have a/c, private bathrooms, ocean views and wi-fi; some also have balconies. Packages typically start at seven nights though shorter stays can be arranged. Breakfast is included at the open-air restaurant, *Eat at Joe's*, and there's an on-site surf shop. Seven nights from **$980**

PLAYA LANGOSTA

B&B Casa Sueca On the road to Playa Langosta ☎ 8876 6675, ⓦ tamarindocs.com. Beautifully appointed, cosy apartments, all artistically decorated, with private bathroom, hot water, fans and breezy balconies. You can rent surfboards and get advice on local surf hotspots. Good weekly discounts. **$168**

B&B Sueño del Mar Playa Langosta ☎ 2653 0284, ⓦ sueno-del-mar.com. Swing in a hammock on the ocean-facing veranda of this beautiful Spanish hacienda-style house, with tiled roofs and adobe walls. The charming and luxurious rooms and *casitas* all come with pretty tiled showers. Rates include a tasty and filling breakfast. Double **$220**, *casitas* **$249**

B&B Villa Alegre Playa Langosta ☎ 2653 0270, ⓦ villaalegrecostarica.com. Relaxing, Californian-owned B&B in a quiet location on the beach. The five rooms, with large, comfortable beds, are bright and tastefully decorated. The generous breakfast is served on the veranda by the pool. Also available are a pair of villas (accommodating 2–5 people) with kitchen facilities. Double **$192**, villa **$260**

Capitán Suizo On the road to Playa Langosta ☎ 2653 0075, ⓦ hotelcapitansuizo.com. Popular, upmarket Swiss-run hotel set in spacious, landscaped grounds on the beach. The *cabina*-style rooms all have a balcony or terrace, fridge, ceiling fans or a/c, bathtub, hot water and an outside shower. The palm-shaded pool is bigger than most, and the atmosphere friendly and relaxed. There's also a cocktail bar, restaurant (see p.286), beautiful beach views and a buffet breakfast. **$254**

★ **Casa Cook** On the road to Playa Langosta ☎ 2653 0125, ⓦ casacook.net. Small, beautiful hotel with beachfront *cabinas*, a *casita* and a studio apartment, each pleasantly furnished and with a full range of amenities, including a/c, wi-fi and cable TV. There's a pool, and the affable staff are an excellent source of information on the area. Apartment **$175**, *cabinas* and *casitas* **$237**

El Mono Loco About 300m up the road to Playa Langosta ☎ 2653 0238, ⓦ hotelmonoloco.com. Run by a relaxed Tico family, this clean little hotel is set around a tranquil garden with a small plunge pool. There are dorm beds as well as large simple rooms with a/c and hot water – try and get room 1, which receives considerably more sunlight than the others. Some rooms sleep up to seven, so it's good value for groups. The owners also rent bikes and prepare meals. Dorm **$19**, double **$33**

EATING AND DRINKING

IN THE VILLAGE

Babylon In the centre about 100m from the beach ☎ 8939 3588. Spacious reggae bar that is the place to be on Thursday and Friday evenings ($3 including first drink). There's frequent live music, particularly on the weekends and though it's often packed, it never feels sweltering thanks to ocean breezes. Daily 11am–3am.

Buon Appetito Across from Zullymar ☎ 2653 0598. Italian-owned café serving sandwiches ($5–7) on fresh ciabatta bread as well as filling breakfasts and fruit shakes. Daily 7am–10pm.

Frutas Tropicales On the main road, at the north end of town. One of the few genuinely cheap places in Tamarindo. The name says it all: all kinds of tropical fruit are on offer, including delicious fruit *refrescos*. They also serve good *casados* ($4) and hamburgers ($4). Daily 8am–10pm.

★ **Green Papaya Taco Bar** 50m down the road from Pasatiempo hotel ☎ 2653 0863. Attractive café and taco bar with reclaimed wood furnishings, terrace seating and plenty of natural light. There's a nice selection of coffee drinks and teas, and the tacos ($7) and burritos ($8.50) are

5

full of flavour and made from organic ingredients. Daily 7am–9pm.

El Jardín del Eden El Jardín del Eden hotel. Romantic, upmarket (but reasonably priced) restaurant in tropical gardens that serves high-quality French and Italian cuisine made with top-notch ingredients. The lobster, seafood brochettes and *pargo* (snapper) are all recommended. Count on spending around $30/person. Daily 6.30am–10pm.

Kahiki South of the loop on the road to Playa Langosta ☎ 2653 4263. Sip exotic tropical fruit Kahikiritas while enjoying a Polynesian-themed dining experience beneath an open-air traditional thatched roof rancho. The New York-trained chef's menu features creative dishes from Hawaiian coconut shrimp ($15) to Thai curry ($13). Daily 7am–2pm & 5–10pm.

La Laguna del Cocodrilo La Laguna del Cocodrilo hotel. Classy Mediterranean restaurant in a palm-fringed garden (with resident crocodile) right on the beach. Starters include an exquisite tuna carpaccio ($7); for main course, try the seafood, steak and other exotic offerings such as fried camembert in honey sauce or chicken stewed in a spicy beer sauce, all for $10–15. Stock up on picnic fare at the on-site French bakery. Daily 6am–10pm.

★ Lazy Wave Opposite the entrance to Tamarindo resort, 100m up the Playa Langosta turn-off from the beach road ☎ 2653 0737. This outdoor restaurant may look casual, but it dishes up some of the best cooking in the region, if not the country. The very fairly priced menu (changes daily; mains can be upwards of $40) is distinguished by the delicacy and inventiveness of its ingredients and flavours, and includes sushi, seared tuna steaks and beef Wellington in giant portions. The bakery-patisserie is worth a visit, too. Sat–Thurs 6–10pm.

Nougi's On the Tamarindo loop ☎ 2653 0059. Long-running favourite where you can dine on smoked pork chops with fruit salsa ($14), sandwiches and local fish dishes. Save room for the divine coconut cream pie ($4). Mon, Tues & Thurs–Sun 6am–10pm.

Pachanga Near the Pasatiempo hotel; turn left up towards Playa Langosta; as the road bends right, go straight ahead ☎ 2653 0406. Intimate, candlelit restaurant, tastefully decorated and with a French-influenced gourmet menu. The fish tartar ($6) is exquisite, as is the snapper fillet ($12), but it's also worth considering the enticing daily specials. Cash only. Mon–Sat 11am–10pm.

Le Petit Café Plaza Tamarindo ☎ 2653 4285. Those in need of a coffee fix should make a stop at this cute café a priority. As well as some of the best coffee drinks in the village and free wi-fi, *Le Petit* serves homemade pastries, oversized bagels, sandwiches ($5.50–8) and salads ($6–10.50). Mon–Sat 8am–5pm.

Walter's Place On the beachfront about 25m north of the loop. One of the few places in the village where you're likely to encounter more locals than foreigners, this relaxed and reasonably priced open-air spot serves *comida típica*, shrimp specialities and filling breakfasts, like rice, beans, eggs and coffee for $7. Daily 7am–10pm.

Wok N Roll Right in the centre of town, next to Essence Day Spa and across from the Tamarindo Plaza ☎ 2653 0156. As its name suggests, it serves stir-fries (you choose ingredients; from $11) and sushi (with fresh fish caught daily). Service isn't exactly hurried but the food is enticing. Mon–Sat 7.30am–10pm.

Zullymar On the Tamarindo loop ☎ 2653 0140. Unbeatable beachfront location – everybody seems to come here for a drink while watching the sun go down – and good food, with main dishes for $7–10. Service is slow, so plan on sitting and watching the crabs scuttling across the sand while waiting. All will be forgiven, however, once your tasty corvina or dorado arrives. Inexpensive pizzas are served during the day only. Daily 11am–10pm.

PLAYA LANGOSTA

Capitán Suizo Capitán Suizo hotel. Popular, inviting open-air restaurant fronted by the hotel's gorgeous pool and with views of the ocean. Though the menu changes regularly, it features creative and reasonably priced healthy dishes prepared with sustainable ingredients. The fish and seafood in particular is worth sampling, as it typically includes fresh, home-made sauces. Mains around $13–25. Daily 11am–9pm.

DIRECTORY

Internet *Le Petit Café* (see above) is the best spot in the village to go online.

Medical services EBAIS (☎ 2653 0736), the nearest public health clinic, is located 4km away in the hamlet of Villareal. There's a pharmacy, Farmacia Pacífico, on the beach side of the main road as you enter the village.

Money and exchange There are many banks in town, several with ATMs, and you'll be hard-pressed to find anywhere that doesn't accept dollars as currency.

Petrol The nearest petrol station to the village is Servicentro in El Llano, about 8km north of Tamarindo on Hwy-155.

Supermarket There's a Super Compro on a side street next to Plaza Conchal.

5

Playa Avellanas

The waves at the **surfing** hotspot of **PLAYA AVELLANAS**, 11km south of Tamarindo, can be, at times, every bit as enticing as those in Tamarindo; that you won't be threading through crowds to get on them makes them that much more appealing. The **beach** itself is wide and long with a pleasantly isolated feel to it. There are a few surfers' hangouts where you can stay at Avellanas, with spartan but good-value accommodation, though if you're not a surfer, you might feel a bit out of it.

ARRIVAL AND DEPARTURE   PLAYA AVELLANAS

By car It's not possible to continue straight down the coast from Tamarindo: to pick up the road south you have to return a couple of kilometres inland to the hamlet of Villareal. Don't head south in the rainy season without a 4WD, and not at all unless you like crossing creeks – there are plenty on this stretch, and they can swell worryingly fast in the rain.

ACCOMMODATION AND EATING

Cabinas Las Olas Set back from the beach ☎ 2652 9315, ⓦ cabinaslasolas.co.cr. A more upmarket option than some of the places catering to surfers, *Cabinas Las Olas* has pleasant light bungalows and swinging hammocks among mangroves. It also has wi-fi and a surf shop where you can rent equipment as well as kayaks and mountain bikes. $\overline{\underline{\$100}}$

★ **Lola's** On the beach ☎ 2652 9097. Revered up and down the coast, *Lola's* draws a devoted crowd with its Asian-Californian fusion dishes that use fresh local ingredients. The chicken satay ($9) and mahi mahi tacos ($9) are both delicious, though it's hard to make a bad choice. It's also a popular spot to relax with a few cocktails and take in the action out on the waves. Arrive early for lunchtime and dinner tables. Tues–Sun 8am–6pm.

Playa Junquillal

Ten kilometres beyond Avellanas, lovely **PLAYA JUNQUILLAL** has a long, relatively straight beach. It's ideal for **surfing**, pounded by breakers crashing in at the end of their thousand-kilometre journeys, but far too rough for swimming. If you're looking for seclusion and quiet, however, it's a great place to hang out for a few days – there's precious little to do, and nothing at all in the way of nightlife.

ARRIVAL AND DEPARTURE   PLAYA JUNQUILLAL

By bus Buses arrive at the centre of the hamlet on the side road off Hwy-160 from Santa Cruz.

Destinations San José (2 daily; 6–7hr); Santa Cruz (3 daily; 1hr 30min).

ACCOMMODATION AND EATING

El Castillo Divertido On a hillside about a third of a mile from the beach ☎ 2658 8428, ⓦ castillodivertido.com. Enchanting, small white turreted "castle" run by entertaining hosts. The rooms have fans, some have an ocean view and there's a bar, restaurant and rooftop terrace. $\overline{\underline{\$45}}$

Guacamaya Lodge 2km south of Junquillal ☎ 2658 8431, ⓦ guacamayalodge.com. Swiss-run hotel in a serene setting with comfortable, semicircular rooms, lovely views, wi-fi, friendly management and a pool. There's also an on-site bar and restaurant serving Swiss specialities and a few Tico staples. $\overline{\underline{\$73}}$

Hotel Iguanazul 3km north of Playa Junquillal ☎ 2658 8123, ⓦ hoteliguanazul.com. Friendly hotel in a great setting overlooking the sea: it has bright rooms decorated with indigenous art (those with a/c have a $28 surcharge), plus a pool, bar and restaurant with a lovely view of the beach. It offers fishing, diving and horseriding tours, as well as excursions to Las Baulas. $\overline{\underline{\$78}}$

Los Malinches About 5km south of Hotel Iguanazul ☎ 8628 5920. Nice campground with shaded sites steps from the beach. Services include water, showers and electricity. $\overline{\underline{\$5}}$

Santa Cruz

Generally regarded by travellers as little more than somewhere to pass through on the way from Liberia or San José to the beach, the sprawling town of **SANTA CRUZ**, some 30km inland from Tamarindo and 57km south of Liberia, is actually "National Folklore City". Much of the music and dance considered quintessentially Guanacastecan originates here, like the various complex, stylized local dances,

5

COWBOY CULTURE IN GUANACASTE

Much of Guanacaste has long been turned into pasture for cattle ranching, and a huge part of the region's appeal is its **sabanero** (cowboy) culture. As in the US, the *sabanero* has acquired a mythical aura – industrious, free-spirited, monosyllabic, and a skilful handler of animals and the environment – and his rough, tough body, clad in jeans with leather accoutrements symbolizes "authenticity" (women get assigned a somewhat less exciting role in this rural mythology: the *cocinera*, or cook). In reality, however, the life of the *sabaneros* is hard; they often work in their own smallholdings or as *peones* (farmworkers) on large haciendas owned by relatively well-off ranchers.

To witness the often extraordinary skills of the *sabaneros*, head for the smaller towns – particularly on the Nicoya Peninsula – where during the months of January and February weekend **fiestas** are held in the local *redondel de toros* (bullring). More a rodeo than a bullfight, unlike in Spain, no gory kills are made: the spectacle comes from amazing feats of bull riding and roping. You'll see cowboys riding their horses alongside the Interamericana highway, too, often towing two or three horses behind them as big transport trucks steamroll past on their way to Nicaragua.

This dependence on cattle culture has its downside. Much of Guanacaste is degraded pastureland, abandoned either because of its exhaustion by grazing or as a result of continually poor domestic and foreign markets for Costa Rican meat. Although impressive efforts to regenerate former tropical dry forest are ongoing – at Parque Nacional Santa Rosa and Parque Nacional Guanacaste, for example – it is unlikely that this rare habitat will recover its original profile.

including the "Punto Guanacasteco" ("*el punto*"), which rivals Scottish country dancing for its complexity and has been adopted as the national dance. That said, however, they're not exactly dancing in the streets of Santa Cruz; life is actually rather slow, much of it lived out in contemplative fashion on the wide verandas of the town's old houses.

Unless you arrive during the **Fiesta Santa Cruz** (mid-Jan), when the town comes alive with bullfights and fireworks and the streets overflow with revellers, Santa Cruz offers little reason to linger longer than it takes to catch the bus out. There are few facilities too, apart from the **Banco Nacional** on the way into town.

ARRIVAL AND DEPARTURE
SANTA CRUZ

By bus Santa Cruz is a regional transport hub, with good connections inland and to the coast. Tralapa (☎ 2221 7202) and Alfaro (☎ 2222 2666) run daily buses to San José which depart more or less hourly from the bus terminal on the west side of the central plaza. There are also numerous local bus services to Liberia. A number of buses leave for Tamarindo including a direct

service. You can also get to playas Flamingo and Brasilito, via Tamarindo.
Destinations Liberia (14 daily; 1hr); Nicoya (18 daily; 30min); Playa Brasilito (2 daily; 1hr 30min); Playa Flamingo (8 daily; 1hr 40min); Playa Junquillal (3 daily; 1hr 30min); San José (9 daily; 4.5hr); Tamarindo (6 direct daily; 1hr).

ACCOMMODATION AND EATING

★**Coope-Tortillas** Just off the central plaza. For food, join the locals at this popular barn-sized tortilla-making co-operative with its own restaurant that serves chicken, Guanacastecan *empanadas* ($3) and sweet cheese bread, as well, of course, as tortillas ($4.50). Cash only. Daily 8am–6pm.
Hotel La Estancia One block west of the central plaza

☎ 2680 0476. A decent budget option in the centre whose rooms have TV, wi-fi, private bathroom (though no hot water) and fans; note that they can be stuffy. $34
Paraje del Diriá 3km north of town ☎ 2680 1826. A little outside town, *Paraje del Diriá* makes a decent choice with its two pools and 50 a/c rooms with TV and wi-fi. $40

DIRECTORY

Money and exchange Banco Nacional, on Hwy-21 at C Central, has an ATM.

Petrol There's a Total petrol station on Hwy-21 on the northern edge of the town centre.

5

Guaitíl

The one town in Guanacaste where you can still see crafts being made in the traditional way is **GUAITÍL**, 12km east of Santa Cruz, well known throughout Costa Rica for its **ceramics**. On the site of a major Chorotega potters' community, the present-day artisans' co-operative (*cooperativo artesanía*) was founded more than twenty years ago by three local women whose goal was to use regional traditions and their own abilities as potters and decorators for commercial gain. Today the artisans are still mainly women, keeping customs alive at the distinctive, large, dome-shaped kilns, while the men work in agricultural smallholdings.

Every house in Guaitíl seems to be in on the trade, with pottery on sale in front of people's homes, on little roadside stalls and in the Artesanía Cooperativa on the edge of the football field. Some of the houses are open for you to wander inside and watch the women at work. Wherever you buy, don't haggle and don't expect it to be dirt cheap, either. A large vase can easily cost $20 or $25. Bear in mind, too, that this is decorative rather than functional pottery, and may not be that durable.

ARRIVAL AND DEPARTURE   GUAITÍL

By car Guaitíl is on the old road to Nicoya; to get there from Santa Cruz, head east on the smaller road instead of south on the new road; turn off to the left where you see the sign for Guaitíl.

By taxi Taxis from Santa Cruz cost about $15.
By bus The main bus stop is in the centre, adjacent to the church.
Destination Santa Cruz (2 daily; 20min).

Central Nicoya Peninsula

The **central Nicoya Peninsula** is marked by the contrast behind the traditional Tico character of the pastoral interior and the expat-favoured coast. Though they are easier to reach than they once were, the laidback surfing towns of **Sámara** and **Nosara** feel far removed from the glitz and encroaching resorts along the coast to the north. The peninsula's principal town, **Nicoya**, remains little changed and is still a quiet base from which to make forays into the otherworldly caverns of nearby **Parque Nacional Barra Honda**.

CHOROTEGA POTTERY

The chief characteristics of **Chorotega pottery** are the striking black and red on white **colouring**, called *pataky*, and a preponderance of panels, decorated with intricate anthropomorphic snake, jaguar and alligator motifs. Archeologists believe that pieces coloured and designed in this way were associated with the elite, possibly as mortuary furniture for *caciques* (chiefs) or other high-ranking individuals. In the Period VI (an archeological term for the years between 1000 BC and 500 AD) the *murillo appliqué* style emerged, an entirely new, glossy, black or red pottery with no parallel anywhere else in the region, but curiously similar to pottery found on Marajó Island at the mouth of the Amazon in modern-day Brazil, thousands of kilometres away.

After the Conquest, predictably, pottery-making declined sharply. The traditional anthropomorphic images were judged to be pagan by the Catholic Church and subsequently suppressed. Today you can see some of the best specimens in San José's Museo Nacional (see p.96) or watch them being faithfully reproduced in Guaitíl, where potters use local resources and traditional methods little-changed since the days of the Chorotegas. To make the clay, local rock is ground on ancient *metates*, which the Chorotegas used for grinding corn. The pigment used on many of the pieces, *curiol*, comes from a porous stone that has to be collected from a natural source, a four-hour walk away, and the ceramic piece is shaped using a special stone, also local, called *zukia*. Zukias were used by Chorotega potters to mould the lips and bases of plates and pots; treasured examples have been found in Chorotega graves.

Nicoya

Bus travellers journeying between San José and the beach towns of Sámara (see p.294) and Nosara (see p.297) need to make connections at the country town of **NICOYA**, inland and northeast of the beaches. Set in a dip surrounded by low mountains, Nicoya is the peninsula's major travel and agricultural centre. It's also Costa Rica's oldest city and one that retains a strong indigenous presence alongside a considerable Chinese comminity, with many of the town's restaurants, hotels and stores owned by descendants of Chinese immigrants.

The town is permeated by an air of infinite stasis but is undeniably pretty, with a lovely **Parque Central**, cascading bougainvillea, colourful plants and the white adobe church, the **Parroquis San Blas**. Founded in 1644, the church is the oldest in the country; it's survived multiple earthquakes and has recently undergone extensive renovation.

ACCOMMODATION
Hotel Jenny	2
Hotel Las Tinajas	1

CAFÉ AND RESTAURANT
Bobo's Burger House	2
Café Daniela	1

ARRIVAL AND INFORMATION

NICOYA

By bus Most buses arrive at Nicoya's spotless bus station on the southern edge of town, a short walk from the centre; the Liberia service pulls in across from the *Hotel Las Tinajas*.

Destinations Liberia (every 30min from 6.30am–10pm; 1hr 40min); Nosara (6 daily; 1hr 30min); Playa Sámara (8–12 daily; 1hr); San José (8 daily; 4hr); Santa Cruz (18 daily; 30min).

By taxi Taxis line up by the Parque Central (or call Coopetico on ☎ 2658 6226).

Tourist information The ICT office (☎ 2685 3260, ✉ ictnicoya@ict.go.cr), a few blocks south of the centre on Hwy-150 across from the national university, provides a wealth of information and maps on the peninsula as well as most of Guanacaste.

ACCOMMODATION AND EATING

Bobo's Burger House C Central, Av Central/2 ☎ 8757 7777. For a quick, if unadventurous, bite *Bobo's* serves juicy burgers ($4.50–7) and a fine selection of wraps ($5–7) across from Parque Central. Daily 10am–8pm.

Café Daniela 100m east of Parque Central ☎ 2686 6148. A pleasant *soda* that doles out straightforward *comida típica* all day long; their chicken *casados* are a very good deal at $6. Daily 7am–9pm.

Hotel Jenny C 1, Av 4 ☎ 2685 5050, ✆ hoteljenny

.com. Friendly spot near the Parque Central and a good deal for what you're getting, with 36 old, basic rooms with TV, a/c and phone. They can help arrange tours and are a great source of area information. $24

Hotel Las Tinajas Av 1, C 3 ☎ 2285 5081. *Hotel Las Tinajas* is clean and modern, with dark, if dreary rooms inside the main building and lighter *cabinas* around the back. $17

DIRECTORY

Hospital Seven blocks north of Parque Central is Hospital La Anexion (☎ 2685 8400), C 3, Av 11/15.

Money and exchange There's a Banco Nacional with an ATM at C3, Av 1/3.

Petrol The most central petrol station is Gasolinera Barrantes on Hwy-150, just north of Av 27.

Supermarket Pali is the most central of the numerous supermarkets in town, at C 3, Av 11.

5

DANCE AND MUSIC IN GUANACASTE

In their book *A Year of Costa Rican Natural History*, Amelia Smith Calvert and Philip Powell Calvert describe their month on Guanacaste's **fiesta** circuit in 1910, starting in January in Filadelfia, a small town between Liberia and Santa Cruz, and ending in Santa Cruz. They were fascinated by the formal nature of the functions they attended, observing: "The dances were all round **dances**, mostly of familiar figures, waltzes and polkas, but one, called '*el punto*' was peculiar in that the partners do not hold one another but walk side by side, turn around each other and so on."

At Santa Cruz, "All the ladies sat in a row on one side of the room when not dancing, the men elsewhere. When a lady arrived somewhat late, then the rest of the guests of the company, if seated, arose in recognition of her presence. The **music** was furnished by three fiddles and an accordion. The uninvited part of the community stood outside the house looking into the room through the open doors, which as usual were not separated from the street by any vestibule or passage." The Calverts were also delighted to come across **La giganta**, the figure of a woman about 4m high; actually a man on stilts "with a face rather crudely moulded and painted". What exactly *La giganta* represented isn't known, but she promenaded around the streets of Santa Cruz in her finery, long white lace trailing, while her scurrying minders frantically worked to keep her from keeling over. *La giganta*, along with other oversized personalities, still features in nearly every large village fiesta, usually held on the local saint's day.

Parque Nacional Barra Honda

3km northeast of the hamlet of Santa Ana • Dec–April daily 7am–4pm • $10

PARQUE NACIONAL BARRA HONDA, about 13km west of the Río Tempisque, is popular with spelunkers for its forty-odd subterranean **caves**. A visit to Barra Honda is not for claustrophobes, people afraid of heights (some of the caves are more than 200m deep) or anyone with an aversion to creepy-crawlies.

The landscape around here is dominated by the **limestone plateau** of the Cerro Barra Honda, which rises out of the flat lowlands of the eastern Nicoya Peninsula. About seventy million years ago this whole area – along with Palo Verde, across the Río Tempisque – was under water. Over the millennia, the porous limestone was gradually hollowed out, by rainfall and weathering, to create caves and weird karstic formations.

The caves

The caves form a catacomb-like interconnecting network beneath the limestone ridge, but you can't necessarily pass from one to the other. Kitted out with a rope harness and a helmet with a lamp on it, you descend with a guide, who will normally take you down into just one. The **main caves**, all within 2km of each other and of the ranger station, are the Terciopelo, the Trampa, Santa Ana, Pozo Hediondo and Nicoa, where the remains of pre-Columbian peoples were recently found, along with burial ornaments and utensils thought to be over two thousand years old. Most people come wanting to view the huge needle-like **stalagmites** and **stalactites** at Terciopelo, or to see subterranean wildlife such as bats, blind salamanders, insects and even birds.

Down in the depths, you're faced with a sight reminiscent of old etchings of Moby Dick's stomach, with sleek, moist walls, jutting rib-like ridges and strangely smooth protuberances. Some caves are big enough – almost cathedral-like, in fact, with their vaulted ceilings – to allow breathing room for those who don't like enclosed spaces, but it's still an eerie experience, like descending into a ruined subterranean Notre Dame inhabited by crawling things you can barely see. There's even an "organ" of fluted stalagmites in the Terciopelo cave; if knocked, each gives off a slightly different musical note.

The trails

Above ground, three short **trails**, not well marked, lead around the caves. It's easy to get lost, and you should walk them with your guide or with a ranger if there is one free, and take water with you. Some time ago, two German hikers attempted to walk the trails independently, got lost and, because they were not carrying water, died of dehydration and heat exhaustion.

The endangered **scarlet macaw** sometimes nests here, and there are a variety of ground mammals about, including anteaters and deer. As usual, you'll be lucky to see any, though you'll certainly hear howler monkeys. Note that anyone who wants to follow the trails at Barra Honda has to tell the rangers where they are intending to walk and how long they intend to be gone for.

ARRIVAL AND INFORMATION

By bus Buses from Nicoya arrive at 11.30am and 4.30pm in Santa Ana, 3km from the park entrance. From there it's sometimes possible to find a ride to the park; if you go on foot, the walk is pleasant and not taxing.
Destination Nicoya (2 daily; 35min).

By car Driving to Barra Honda is possible even with a regular car. From the Nicoya–Tempisque road, the turn-off, 13km before the bridge, is well signed. It's then 4km along a good gravel road to the hamlet of Nacaome (also called

PARQUE NACIONAL BARRA HONDA

Barra Honda), from where the park is, again, signed. Continue about 6km further, passing the hamlet of Santa Ana until you reach the ranger station, where most people arrange to meet their guide.

By taxi It's possible to arrange a taxi in Nicoya to drive you to the entrance; the cost is usually around $15.

Information The ranger station at the entrance (7am–4pm; ☎ 2659 1551) can provide information and maps.

TOURS AND ACTIVITIES

Spelunking You need to be pretty serious about caves to go spelunking in Barra Honda. Quite apart from all the planning, what with the entrance fee, the payment to the guide and the price of renting equipment ($25), costs can add up. It's obligatory to go with a guide, who will also provide equipment; to do otherwise would be foolhardy, not to mention illegal. Sometimes the ranger station can supply a guide, but to save a trip, it's worth checking conditions and availability of guides first,

either at the ACT regional headquarters (see p.248) on the Interamericana or in Nicoya.

Bat tour Witnessing the mass exodus at dusk of the thousands of bats who reside in the Pozo Hediondo cave and hearing the flapping of their wings in the air is one of the park's clear highlights. Guided tours ($8) to the cave depart from the ranger station daily at 4pm and return by 8pm.

ACCOMMODATION AND EATING

★**Café Kura** On the road to the park in Santa Ana ☎ 2659 2115. Cute little spot run by a friendly German woman who makes some of the best home-made ice cream ($3–4) you're ever likely to try; that you can savour it after a day in the national park is truly a treat. There are also filling *empanadas* ($3–5) and *lasagne* to help you

recharge. Mon–Sat 11am–4pm.

Camping Park entrance. There's a campsite inside the park to the left, with picnic tables and drinking water, but most people who come to Barra Honda stay in Nicoya (see p.291), or across the Río Tempisque on the mainland. Cost is per person $̲2̲

CAVE ARCHITECTURE

Created by the interaction of water, calcium bicarbonate and limestone, the distinctive cave formations of stalagmites and stalactites are often mistaken for each other. **Stalagmites** grow upwards from the floor of a cave, formed by drips of water saturated with calcium bicarbonate. **Stalactites**, made of a similar deposit of crystalline calcium bicarbonate, grow downwards, like icicles. Both are formed by water and calcium bicarbonate filtering through limestone and partially dissolving it. In limestone caves, stalagmites and stalactites are usually white (from the limestone) or brown; in caves where copper deposits are present colours might be more psychedelic, with iridescent greens and blues. They often become united, over time, in a single column.

5

Playa Sámara

SÁMARA is one of the peninsula's most peaceful and least developed beachside villages. It's a great place to relax, and its distance from the capital makes it much quieter than the more accessible Pacific beaches. Even at the busiest times, there's little action other than weekenders tottering by on stout *criollo* **horses** (available for rent on the beach at around $10 per hour) and the occasional dune buggy racing up the sand. On Sundays, the town turns out in force to watch the local **football** teams who play on the village field as if they're Brazil and Argentina battling it out for the World Cup – even weekending Ticos shun the beach for the sidelines.

Sámara boasts some of the calmest waters, making it ideal for **swimming**. The long, gorgeous stretch of sand is protected by a reef about a kilometre out, which takes the brunt of the Pacific's power out of the waves. The effect also makes the beach one of the best spots on the Pacific coast to learn to **surf**; the waves are strong enough without being too unforgiving on beginners.

ARRIVAL AND DEPARTURE
PLAYA SÁMARA

By plane Sansa (☎2656 0765) planes from San José arrive at the airstrip 6km east of town at Carrillo, from where 4WD taxis make the trip to Sámara for about $6.
By car Hwy-150 runs the 35km between Nicoya and the coast at Sámara.
By bus Buses stop at the village's northern edge, where

the roads to Nicoya and Nosara meet. You can buy tickets for some bus services from the Transporte Alfaro office (daily 7am–5pm) in the centre of the village.
Destinations Nicoya (8–12 daily; 1hr); Nosara (3 daily; 40min); San José (1 daily; 4hr 45min).

ACTIVITIES AND TOURS

Alexis Boat Tours On the beach at the north end of town ☎8358 0793. Runs a variety of fishing and water-sports excursions, as well as wildlife-spotting trips to the Refugio Ostional (see p.301).
C & C Surf Shop At the south end of the beach ☎2656 0628, ⓦticoadventurelodge.com/lesson.html. C & C Surf Shop offers expert surfing instruction ($40/1hr lesson)

plus surf board ($20/day) and boogie board ($12/day) rentals.
Sámara Adventure Company In the middle of the beach ☎2656 0920, ⓦsamara-tours.com. Choose from a host of tours at this enthusiastic operator, including stand-up paddle boarding (3hr; $65), snorkelling to see dolphins (3hr; $60) and mountain biking (3hr 30min; $60).

ACCOMMODATION

Aparthotel Mirador de Sámara First left as you come into Sámara and 100m up the hill from the Marbella ☎2656 0044, ⓦmiradordesamara.com. Huge apartments (5–7 people) with large bathrooms, bedrooms, living room, kitchen and terrace, all with panoramic views of the town and beach. The bar is in an impressive tower with spectacular sunset views, and there's a small pool with wooden sundecks. Good low-season and extended-stay discounts. Better value for four or more people, rather than couples. $119

Belvedere 100m down the road to Carrillo ☎2656 0213, ⓦbelvederesamara.net. This wonderfully pleasant hotel has ten rooms and two apartments with either a/c or fan, and all are brightly furnished in light wood, with mosquito nets and solar-heated water. There's also a jacuzzi, two swimming pools, and a good German breakfast is included. Double $70, apartment $75
Cabinas El Ancla On the beachfront road 200m south of the centre ☎2656 0254. Simply furnished rooms, with cold-water bathroom and fan, right on the beach. The

---

THE FRIENDSHIP BRIDGE

Opened in 2003, the 780m **Puente Tempisque** connects the mainland with the Nicoya Peninsula, spanning from near Puerto Moreno (17km east of the Nicoya–Carmona road) on the peninsula to a point 25km west of the Interamericana on the mainland. The bridge replaced a time-consuming ferry connection and saves at least two hours on the journey between San José and Sámara. The $26 million bridge was financed by Taiwan in exchange for commercial fishing rights in Costa Rican waters, which were quickly rescinded due to abuse. It's partly held up by suspension cables connected to towers that, at 80m, make it the tallest structure in Costa Rica.

upstairs rooms are a bit hotter but still better than the dark and oppressive downstairs rooms. There's a friendly *dueña* and good beachfront seafood restaurant. **$40**

Camping Los Cocos ☎ 2656 0496. The best spot in the village to pitch a tent is *Camping Los Cocos*, on the beach under the shade of coconut trees. It's clean and well run, with cooking grills. **$7**

Casa del Mar 50m north of the entrance to beach on the left ☎ 2656 0264, ⓦ casadelmarsamara.net. Large, good-value rooms (although a bit sparsely furnished) close to the beach. The downstairs rooms are clean and white, but rather dark; ask for an upstairs room with shared bath and palm-fringed sea view. The price includes breakfast; private bathroom and a/c costs extra. **$45**

Giada About 100m before you come to the beach, on the left ☎ 2656 0132, ⓦ hotelgiada.net. Small hotel set around a compact pool, with spotless banana-yellow rooms, good beds, overhead fans, private bathrooms and tiled showers – the upstairs rooms are better for views and breeze. There's also a friendly Italian restaurant. **$90**

★ **Sámara Treehouse Inn** On the beach ☎ 2656 0733, ⓦ samaratreehouse.com. Five units on tree-trunk stilts, with hammocks beneath; four face the beach while the other faces the pool. They have modern ceramic-tiled bathrooms, and there's a shady open patio with barbecue as well as wi-fi throughout. Includes breakfast. **$147**

★ **Tico Adventure Lodge** On the third road back from the beach ☎ 2656 0628, ⓦ ticoadventurelodge.com. A fantastic deal, this smartly designed American-run hotel has nine cheerful rooms with a/c and balconies, a house set alongside the pool and an upstairs apartment for larger groups. There's wi-fi throughout and the personable owner is a great source of local information. They can also arrange surfing lessons with C & C Surf Shop (see opposite). **$57**

Villas Kalimba On the road to Carillo ☎ 2656 0929, ⓦ villaskalimba.com. The six earth-toned villas are set around a pool and jacuzzi and have handcrafted wooden windows and furniture, kitchenettes, a/c and wi-fi. **$168**

Villas Playa Sámara On the road to Carrillo ☎ 2656 1111, ⓦ villasplayasamara.com. Upmarket resort, wildly popular among wealthy Costa Rican families, with both all-inclusive and accommodation-only tariffs. The well-built villas come with large, spacious kitchens and sitting rooms, plus outside terrace and hammock. The whole effect (golf carts for your luggage; see-your-neighbour proximity) is a bit suburban, and the management could be more efficient – although the beachside setting at the quiet, south end of the beach is lovely. **$360**

EATING AND DRINKING

El Ancla Cabinas El Ancla. Brightly-painted waterside restaurant with an extensive menu of fish dishes ($7–11) that attracts plenty of holidaying Ticos who know good seafood when they smell it. Mon–Wed & Fri–Sun 11am–11pm.

Las Brasas On the main road in the town centre ☎ 2656 0546. Split-level restaurant serving Spanish dishes such as paella or an entire suckling pig (with advance notice). The fillet steaks ($14) are tasty, as is the guacamole, but the pasta dishes are nothing special. Daily noon–10pm.

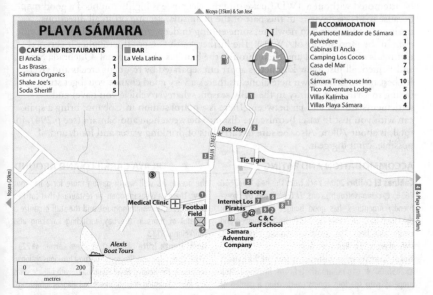

PLAYA SÁMARA

▲ Nicoya (35km) & San José

N

● CAFÉS AND RESTAURANTS
El Ancla — 2
Las Brasas — 1
Sámara Organics — 3
Shake Joe's — 4
Soda Sheriff — 5

■ BAR
La Vela Latina — 1

■ ACCOMMODATION
Aparthotel Mirador de Sámara — 2
Belvedere — 1
Cabinas El Ancla — 9
Camping Los Cocos — 8
Casa del Mar — 7
Giada — 3
Sámara Treehouse Inn — 10
Tico Adventure Lodge — 5
Villas Kalimba — 6
Villas Playa Sámara — 4

Bus Stop

MAIN STREET

Tío Tigre

Grocery

Medical Clinic
Football Field

Internet Los Piratas

C & C Surf School

Samara Adventure Company

Alexis Boat Tours

Nicoya (29km)

& Playa Carrillo (5km)

0 — 200 metres

5

Sámara Organics On the main road in the centre of the village ☎ 2656 3056. Run by a Californian couple, this cheerful café attached to a health food market offers guilt-free breakfasts and lunches, like potatoes, eggs and toast ($5.50) and home-made veggie burgers ($7). Mon–Sat 7.30am–4.30pm.

★ **Shake Joe's** On the beach ☎ 2656 0252. Low-key restaurant that attracts a lot of students from the language school up the beach. A good spot for a burger ($6–10) and a shake, and they also do a couple of refreshing salads.

Tues–Sun 11am–10pm.
Soda Sheriff On the beach. Pleasant, no-frills *soda* serving *comida típica* including noteworthy *casados* in the $6–9 range. Daily 8am–10pm.
La Vela Latina South of the centre on the beach ☎ 2656 2286. By some margin the most peaceful and stylish spot for a drink, where you can sip a daiquiri while relaxing on a rocking chair inside or on the beach. They also serve decent food, including sandwiches ($8–11) and sushi. Daily 11am–midnight.

DIRECTORY

Internet Internet Los Piratas (Mon–Fri 9am–9pm; ☎ 2656 2123) offers cheap internet access across from *Sámara Treehouse Inn*.
Medical services For non-emergency medical attention, visit the medical clinic (Mon–Fri 8am–4pm; ☎ 2656 0166) a few blocks north of the main street near the beach; for emergencies contact the Red Cross on ☎ 2685 5458.

Money and exchange There's a Banco Nacional (with an ATM) located down the first road to the right off the main street as you enter the village.
Petrol The nearest petrol station is La Bomba, 6km west of Sámara.
Post office Sámara's small shack of a post office (☎ 2656 0368), 50m before the entrance to the beach, offers minimal services.

Playa Carrillo and around

Aficionados of Pacific sunsets will want to head 6km east of Sámara to **PLAYA CARRILLO**, a ninety-minute walk along flat sands. Known for its beautiful evening light and colours, beautiful palm-fringed Carrillo is also safe for swimming, though the fact that more and more people are setting up hotels and restaurants means the beach no longer has the sleepy, end-of-the-line feel it once had.

Hwy-160 east of Carillo

The stretch of **Hwy-160 east of Carrillo** is for off-road driving nuts only, and should not be attempted without a 4WD (make sure the clearance is high). You need a good **map**, because roads go haywire in this part of the peninsula, veering off in all directions, unsigned and heading to nowhere, some ending in deep creeks (unpassable at high tide even in the most sturdy of 4WDs). The further south you go, the tougher it gets, as dirt roads switch inland and then through the hamlets of Camaronal, Quebrada Seca and Bejuco, all just a few kilometres apart but separated by frequent creeks and rivers. It's best not to drive down here alone, as there's a very good chance you'll get stuck (rising to a virtual certainty in the rainy season, whatever vehicle you have) and settlements are few and far between. There is a **petrol station** in Cóbano: bring a spare can with you just in case, because the distance between here and Sámara (see p.294), in total, is about 70km. Also, be sure to carry lots of drinking water and food, and, if possible, camping gear.

ACCOMMODATION AND EATING

PLAYA CARRILLO AND AROUND

Cabinas El Colibrí 200m back from the beach ☎ 2656 0656, ⓦ cabinaselcolibri.com. *El Colibrí*, run by super-friendly Argentines, has good budget accommodation: the rooms have a/c, cable TV, tiled floors, hot showers and comfortable beds. The steakhouse on-site serves huge slabs of expertly grilled meat. **$60**
Hotel Guanamar On the beach in front of the hamlet ☎ 2656 0054, ⓦ guanamarhotel.com. Inviting hilltop property with spacious rooms overlooking a garden or

the ocean; it's well worth paying more for a bayfront view. There's a pleasant open-air restaurant that catches nice breezes, a swimming pool, and the staff organize a handful of tours in the bay, including kayaking and snorkelling. **$113**
Hotel Punta Islita 8km east of Playa Carrillo ☎ 2231 6122, ⓦ hotelpuntaislita.com. The most luxurious option in the area is the isolated *Hotel Punta Islita*, with hillside villas and rooms boasting majestic views and elegant furnishings.

The atmosphere is exclusive and facilities include a driving range, tennis courts, pools, restaurants and a canopy tour, while snorkelling, mountain-biking and fishing trips can also be arranged. Double $260, villa $509

Nosara and around

The pretty drive from Sámara 25km northwest to the village of **NOSARA** runs along shady, secluded dirt and gravel roads punctuated by a few creeks. It's passable with a

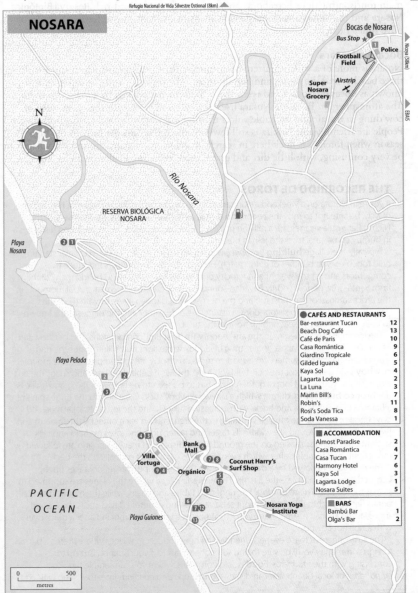

Refugio Nacional de Vida Silvestre Ostional (8km)

NOSARA

Bocas de Nosara
Bus Stop
Police
Football Field
Airstrip
Super Nosara Grocery

Nicoya (50km)
EBAIS

Río Nosara

RESERVA BIOLÓGICA NOSARA

Playa Nosara

N

Playa Pelada

PACIFIC OCEAN

Villa Tortuga
Bank Mall
Coconut Harry's Surf Shop
Orgánico
Nosara Yoga Institute
Playa Guiones

● CAFÉS AND RESTAURANTS	
Bar-restaurant Tucan	12
Beach Dog Café	13
Café de Paris	10
Casa Romántica	9
Giardino Tropicale	6
Gilded Iguana	5
Kaya Sol	4
Lagarta Lodge	2
La Luna	3
Marlin Bill's	7
Robin's	11
Rosi's Soda Tica	8
Soda Vanessa	1

■ ACCOMMODATION	
Almost Paradise	2
Casa Romántica	4
Casa Tucan	7
Harmony Hotel	6
Kaya Sol	3
Lagarta Lodge	1
Nosara Suites	5

■ BARS	
Bambú Bar	1
Olga's Bar	2

0   500
metres

Garza (6km) & Sámara (25km)

5

regular car (low clearance) in the dry season (though you'll still have to ford two creeks except at the very driest times of year), but you'll need a 4WD or high clearance in the wet. The road follows a slightly inland route; you can't see the coast except where you meet the beach at **Garza**, about ten minutes before Nosara. This little hamlet is a good place to stop for a *refresco* at the *pulpería*, and perhaps take a dip in the sea.

In contrast to Sámara, the vast majority of people who come to Nosara are North Americans and Europeans in search of quiet and natural surroundings. Indeed, the two main tourist attractions hereabouts are nature reserves: the bird-rich **Reserva Biológica Nosara** and the **Refugio Nacional de Vida Silvestre Ostional**, famed for its *arribadas* of olive ridley turtles.

Bocas de Nosara

Nosara is more of a widely scattered community than a village as such; it spreads along three beaches and the hinterland behind them. The centre, if you can call it that, is known as **Bocas de Nosara** and is set about 5km inland, backed by a low ridge of hills. The atmosphere in Bocas de Nosara itself is shady and slow, with the sweet smell of cow dung in the air and excitable voices drifting out from the local Evangelical church. People are friendly, and Nosara is still low-key, though it does get busy in the high season when foreigners flock here in search of seclusion. The area around the village can be very confusing, with little dirt and gravel roads radiating in all directions. To

---

THE RECORRIDO DE TOROS

If you're in Nosara on a weekend in January or February, or on a public holiday such as the first of May, be sure not to miss the **recorrido de toros** (rodeo). *Recorridos*, held in many of the Nicoya Peninsula villages, are a rallying point for local communities, who travel long distances in bumpy communal trucks to join in the fun.

Typically, the village **bullring** (*redondel*) is no more than a rickety wooden circular stadium, held together with bundles of palm thatch. Here local radio announcers introduce the competitors and list the weight and ferocity of the bulls, while travelling bands, many of them from Santa Cruz, perform oddly Bavarian-sounding oom-pah-pah music at crucial moments in the proceedings. For the most fun and the best-seasoned rodeo jokes, sit with the band – usually comprising two saxophones, a clarinettist, a drummer and the biggest tuba known to man – but avoid the seat right in front of the tuba.

The *recorrido* usually begins in the afternoon, with "Best Bull" competitions, and gets rowdier as evening falls – after dark, a single string of cloudy white light bulbs illuminates the ring – and more beer is consumed. The *sabanero* tricks on display are truly impressive: the mounted **cowboy** who gallops past the bull, twirls his rope, throws it behind his back and snags the bull as casually as you would loop a garden hose, has to be seen to be believed. The grand finale is the **bronco bull-riding**, during which a sinewy cowboy sticks like a burr to the huge spine of a Brahma bull who leaps and bucks with increasing fury. During the intervals, local men and boys engage in a strange ritual of wrestling in the arena, taking each other by the forearm and twirling each other round like windmills, faster and faster, until one loses his hold and flies straight out to land sprawling on the ground. These displays of macho bravado are followed by mock fights and tumbles, after which everyone slaps each other cordially on the back.

The *recorrido* is followed by a **dance**: in Nosara the impromptu dancefloor takes up the largest flat space available – the airstrip. The white-line area where the planes are supposed to stop is turned into a giant outdoor bar, ringed by tables and chairs, while the mobile disco rolls out its flashing lightballs and blasts out salsa, reggae and countrified two-steps. Wear good shoes, as the asphalt is super-hard: you can almost see your soles smoking after a quick twirl with a hotshot cowboy.

The atmosphere at these events is friendly and beer-sodden: in villages where there's a big foreign community you'll be sure to find someone to talk to if your Spanish isn't up to conversing with the *sabaneros*. **Food** is sold from stalls, where you can sample the usual *empanadas* or local Guanacastecan dishes such as *sopa de albóndigas* (meatball soup with egg).

counter the lost-tourist effect locals have erected copious signs – though there are so many at certain intersections that they simply add to the confusion. Resign yourself to driving around looking lost at least some of the time.

The beaches
The three beaches in the area – **Guiones**, **Pelada** and **Nosara** – are fine for **swimming**, although you can be buffeted by the crashing waves, and there are some rocky outcrops. Playa Guiones is the most impressive of the beaches: nearly 5km in length, populated by pelicans, and with probably the best swimming, though there's precious little shade. It's also popular for **surfing**, though not so suitable for beginners as Sámara (see p.294). One of the favourite local pastimes is watching the mass of surfers at sunrise and sunset – that is, if you're not among those out on the waves. The whole area is a great place to beachcomb for shells and driftwood, and the vegetation, even in the dry season, is greener than further north. Some attempts have been made to limit development, and a good deal of the land around the Río Nosara has been designated a wildlife refuge.

ARRIVAL AND GETTING AROUND — NOSARA AND AROUND

By bus There's a daily direct bus from San José as well as five daily buses from Nicoya and two from Playa Sámara: all pull in at the stop adjacent to the Super Nosara Grocery.
Destinations Nicoya (5 daily; 1hr 30min); Playa Sámara (3 daily; 40min); San José (1 daily; 5hr 30min).
By plane NatureAir (🕿 2682 0181) and Sansa (🕿 2682 0856) fly daily to Nosara from San José, landing at the small airstrip by the village centre and the namesake river.
By bike It's well worth paying a visit to The Frog Pod (🕿 2682 4039, 🖰 thefrogpod.com), in the Villa Tortuga complex about 150m back from Playa Guiones, where you can rent a bike ($15/day).

ACCOMMODATION

Nosara has some **excellent beachside accommodation** if you've money to spend, and the owners and managers tend to be more **environmentally conscious** than at many other places on the peninsula. Indeed, a local civic association keeps a hawkish eye on development in the area, with the aim of retaining Nosara's natural charms and preventing it from becoming another Tamarindo or Montezuma. The cheaper accommodation options are in or near the village, but you'll need to rent a bike or count on doing a lot of walking to get to the ocean.

PLAYA GUIONES
Casa Romántica On a side road near the beach 🕿 2682 0272, 🖰 casa-romantica.net. Clean, well-kept family-run hacienda-style hotel right on the beach. The bright rooms have hot water, fridge and terrace; some have a/c. There's also a pool and a fantastic restaurant. If you fly or take the bus, the owners will pick you up if you let them know in advance. $119
Casa Tucan On the eastern end of the beach 🕿 2682 0113. Small, eight-room hotel, with brightly decorated rooms (some with kitchen), sleeping up to five people; all have private bathrooms, hot water, fridge, and fan or a/c. There's a good restaurant and bar, a juice bar and a pool. In peak period you have to book a package deal including surf lessons, yoga classes and full meals; these are also available throughout the year. $69
★**Harmony Hotel** About 150m from the beach 🕿 2682 4114, 🖰 harmonynosara.com. A model of sustainability, this luxurious hotel is integrated seamlessly within a tropical garden and lies a short walk from the beach. The rooms are supremely comfortable with king-size beds, a/c, ceiling fans, wi-fi, and inside and outside showers. The service is attentive but not obtrusive and there is a juice bar

and beautifully understated yoga studio. The striking pool is just a few steps from the open-air restaurant, which serves some of the best food in Nosara. $339
KayaSol Playa Guiones, about 100m back from the beach 🕿 2682 1459, 🖰 kayasolsurfhotel.com. One of the better budget choices in Nosara, this relaxing spot has simply furnished, brightly painted dorm rooms, double and suites. There's a nice pool, kitchen access and an excellent restaurant serving healthy dishes (see p.300). Dorm $20, double $57, suite $79
★**Nosara Suites** At the entrance to Playa Guiones 🕿 2682 1036, 🖰 nosarasuites.com. Five immaculate and positively enormous themed suites with a/c, wi-fi, cable TV and fridge. There's also a fine restaurant and bakery attached (see p.300). $107

PLAYA NOSARA
★**Lagarta Lodge** Signposted from the village near the mouth of the Río Nosara 🕿 2682 0035, 🖰 lagarta .com. Set on the edge of the Reserva Biológica Nosara (see p.301) southwest of the village, this lodge has excellent birdwatching and stunning coastal views. The rooms above

5

the pool overlooking the ocean boast one of the best panoramas in the country. Rooms have private bathroom, hot water and fridges. A healthy buffet breakfast (not included), as well as other meals, is also available. **$90**

PLAYA PELADA

Almost Paradise 150m back from the beach ☏ 2682

0172, ⊛ almostparadise2012.com. One of the better budget options in Nosara, this friendly hostel has two basic dorms (opt for the ocean-facing one, which has more light), a couple of private rooms (one with an ocean-facing terrace) and a few camp sites. It's clean and well-organized and there's a decent restaurant and bar on-site. Camping **$5**, dorm **$12**, double **$30**

EATING AND DRINKING

The Nosara area has a profusion of very good restaurants, and prices are not as high as you might expect, given the area's relative isolation. There are a number of places in the village, most of them on and around the road leading to the beach or on the road into town, though many of the better restaurants are huddled together near **Playa Guiones**, where the majority of tourists eat.

IN THE VILLAGE

Bambú Bar Next to the Abastecedor general store ☏ 2682 0262. A bit dark, and with pounding music, though it's still a decent place to have a beer and watch the kids kick balls around the football field across the road. There's occasional live music, too. Daily 4pm–late.

Soda Vanessa Near the airstrip. A nondescript typical *soda* with filling *casados* for under $3, as well as lighter snacks. Daily 7am–9pm.

PLAYA GUIONES

Bar-restaurant Tucan Next to the Casa Tucan hotel. The menu features seafood in adventurous fruit-based sauces, chicken, pasta and steaks (all $9–15), served in a pleasant rancho strung with inviting hammocks and coloured lights. Daily 11am–10pm.

Beach Dog Café About 25m from the beach. An expat favourite, this open-air café is the closest spot to the beach for a meal. American-style breakfasts, such as waffles and *huevos rancheros*, are served along with fruit smoothies and a nice selection of coffee. Free wi-fi. Breakfast and lunch only.

★ **Café de Paris** At the southern entrance to the beach ☏ 2682 1036. The brioche and *pain au chocolat* confirm this bakery as a bona fide overseas *département* of France, while the pleasant poolside restaurant serves sandwiches and pizzas for lunch ($4.50–9). Daily 7am–9pm.

★ **Casa Romántica** Casa Romántica hotel. Some of the most ambitious food in town, featuring a changing menu of fish, steak and pasta dishes ($9–12). There's a great wine list, too. Dining is in a small outdoor area, lit with candles at night. Daily 11am–11pm.

Giardino Tropicale South end of Nosara, on the road towards Sámara ☏ 2682 4000. Superior-quality real Italian pizza cooked in a wood oven and served in a pretty plant-festooned dining area ($6–12). Other well-crafted Italian dishes are also on offer, and there's takeaway. Daily 5–11pm.

Gilded Iguana Set back from the beach ☏ 2682 0259. Upmarket gringo bar with Mexican food that

attracts the local expats. Aside from dishes you'd expect such as a chicken *quesadilla* ($10), there are plenty of sandwiches and burgers to choose from, including fillet of dorado sandwich ($10) and a veggie burger ($9). Daily 7.30am–10.30pm.

KayaSol KayaSol hotel. Inventive and cheerful restaurant serving some of the best health food in Nosara. Standouts include a flavourful beet burger ($8.50) and a dragon bowl that includes tofu, steamed vegetables, rice and a tantalizing chipotle cashew sauce ($12). There are plenty of daily specials to choose from, too. Daily 7am–10pm.

Marlin Bill's On the main road ☏ 2682 0458. Fairly pricey but well-prepared grilled seafood such as broiled dorado ($16) and fried jumbo shrimp ($25) served on a terrace at the entrance to Playa Guiones. Daily 11am–2pm & 6–11pm.

Robin's On the main road towards the beach ☏ 2682 0617. Cute café where you can munch on feel-good wraps ($6) and gorge on decadent crêpes ($3) stuffed with chocolate and other savouries. The main draw for many, though, is the selection of sorbet and ice cream and the home-made cones ($4.50–7) it's served in. Mon–Fri 7.30am–7pm, Sat & Sun 7.30am–5pm.

★ **Rosi's Soda Tica** On a small hill above the road leading into Playa Guiones ☏ 2682 0728. Small, friendly, family-run restaurant (one of the few in the area run by locals) serving excellent *comida típica*, including *casados* ($4–6) for lunch and *gallo pinto* ($3–5) for breakfast. Mon–Sat 8am–3pm.

PLAYA NOSARA

Lagarta Lodge Lagarta Lodge. Although the changing menu is perfectly fine – and the breakfast buffet ($6.50) makes for a filling start to the day – it's the setting rather than the food that makes this place special, as you dine to the sound of the Pacific crashing gently below. The sociable seating arrangement has all guests sitting around a big mahogany table – a good way to meet people. Mon & Wed–Sun 7.30–9.30am, noon–2pm & 4.30–8pm.

PLAYA PELADA

★ La Luna On the beach ☎ 2682 0122. A loveable spot right on Playa Pelada, with tranquil terrace tables overlooking the sea. The constantly changing menu features lip-smacking international dishes and seafood, with mains $7–15. Highlights include salads, home-made bread as well as Thai soups and curries. The cheerful owners dream up some sinful desserts, including vanilla toffee pudding and chocolate fudge cake. Daily 11am–11pm.

Olga's Bar On the beach. Cold beer, good *casados* ($7–9.50) and fish, and ocean views, but watch the bill – they don't itemize your food and drinks. One of the best spots to watch the setting sun. Daily 10am–10pm.

DIRECTORY

Food markets There are a couple of small grocery stores in the village, while at the entrance to Playa Guiones there's Orgánico (daily 7.30am–7pm; ☎ 2682 1434), a natural food market.

Internet You can go online at NosaraNet (10¢/min) in the Villa Tortuga complex in Playa Guiones.

Medical services There's an EBAIS public health clinic (☎ 2682 0266) a block east of the airstrip.

Money and exchange Banco Popular (☎ 2682 0011) is on the left side of the main road to Playa Guiones.

Post office There's a small post office (usually Mon–Fri 8am–4pm) next to the airstrip.

Reserva Biológica Nosara

Behind *Lagarta Lodge* on the northern edge of Playa Nosara • Daily 8am–4pm • $6 • Guides available ($5)

Accessed through the *Lagarta Lodge* (see p.299), the **RESERVA BIOLÓGICA NOSARA** protects nearly 100 acres of mangroves and dense forests that are home to a bewildering number of bird species, such as blue-footed boobies, ospreys and peregrine falcons. There is quite a bit of terrestrial wildlife too, including crocodiles and caimans. An **elevated walkway** (2hr round-trip) passes through a beautiful section of mangrove swamp where the calls of birds and frogs seem jarring against the often ghostly silence. Consider hiring a guide at the *Lagarta Lodge* for the chance to learn more about the fascinating reserve; you're likely to spot far more animals than you would on your own.

Refugio Nacional de Vida Silvestre Ostional

8km northwest of Nosara • $10; guide required for an additional fee of around $8 • ☎ 2682 0400

The tiny community of **Ostional** and its chocolate-coloured beach make up the **REFUGIO NACIONAL DE VIDA SILVESTRE OSTIONAL**, one of the most important nesting grounds in the country for **olive ridley turtles** who come ashore to lay their eggs en masse from July to December. If you're in town during the first few days of the *arribadas* (see box, p.34), you'll see local villagers with horses, carefully stuffing their big, thick bags full of eggs and slinging them over their shoulders. This is quite legal: villagers of Ostional and Nosara are allowed to harvest eggs, for sale or consumption, during the first three days of the season only. Don't be surprised to see them barefoot, rocking back and forth on their heels as if they were crushing grapes in a winery; this is the surest way to pick up the telltale signs of eggs beneath the sand. You can't swim comfortably at Ostional though, since the water's very rough and is plagued by sharks, for whom turtle-nesting points are like all-you-can-eat buffets.

ARRIVAL AND INFORMATION   REFUGIO NACIONAL DE VIDA SILVESTRE OSTIONAL

By car It takes about 15min to drive the bumpy gravel-and-stone road from Nosara to the refuge.

By taxi There is no local taxi service, but if you ask at your hotel, they will arrange for a local to drive you for about $8–10.

Tourist information There's a ranger station at the southern end of the village. To arrange a guide you can enquire here or stop by the Asociación de Guías Locales (☎ 2682 0428), in the centre of Ostinal, who can make arrangements for you.

The Central Pacific and southern Nicoya

PARQUE NACIONAL MANUEL ANTONIO

The Central Pacific and southern Nicoya

6

Costa Rica's Central Pacific region boasts several of the country's most popular tourist spots, including the number-one attraction, the Reserva Biológica Bosque Nuboso Monteverde (the Monteverde Cloudforest Biological Reserve), draped over the ridge of the Cordillera de Tilarán. Along with nearby Reserva Santa Elena, Monteverde protects some of the last remaining pristine cloudforest in the Americas. Southern Nicoya, effectively cut off by bad roads and a provincial boundary from the north of the peninsula (covered in Chapter 5), is part of Puntarenas Province, whose eponymous capital, a steamy tropical port across the Gulf of Nicoya on the mainland, is the only town of any size in the entire area.

The area is home to some of Costa Rica's best-known **beaches**, several of which are easily accessed from San José on the Caldera Highway. Each offers a distinct experience, from the coves of chilled-out **Montezuma**, a former fishing village that has been transformed into a traveller hub, to the forest-flanked coastline of **Mal País** and **Santa Teresa**, to the huge waves of **Jacó** and **Playa Hermosa**, two of the country's most popular places to surf. Further south, **Parque Nacional Manuel Antonio** has several extraordinary beaches, with white sands and azure waters, while the surrounding area is packed with hotels, restaurants and tourist services.

ARRIVAL AND INFORMATION

GETTING THERE

Monteverde The journey from the capital to Monteverde (4hr 30min by bus, quicker by car) can be quite an expedition – although it's only 180km from San José, the final 35km is along a poor and unpaved road. There is, however, a scenic "taxi-boat-taxi" route from La Fortuna (see p.214).

The Pacific coast Three routes connect San José with the Central Pacific coast (45min–2hr). The Interamericana climbs over the Cordillera Central before dropping precipitously into the Pacific lowlands and the town of Esparza, a few kilometres before the turn-off for Puntarenas. A more direct route for Jacó and Manuel Antonio is the Caldera Highway, a fast toll road that shadows Hwy-3 as far as Orotina, where it continues on to Puerto Caldera; the older (more pleasant) Hwy-3 heads south from Orotina to Jacó, a stretch that is in very good condition for most of the way and offers some of the least stressful driving in the country.

The southern Nicoya The majority of visitors cross over to the southern Nicoya Peninsula from Puntarenas on the ferries to Naranjo (for Nicoya) or Paquera (for Tambor, Mal País and Santa Teresa, and Montezuma), though the bridge across the mouth of the Río Tempisque is an alternative route for drivers.

SANTA TERESA

Highlights

❶ Monteverde night walk The jungle comes alive after dark – take an eerie hike through Monteverde's dense rainforest on the lookout for bats, frogs and tarantulas. **See p.319**

❷ Reserva Santa Elena Search for the elusive quetzal in this lush reserve that protects one of Costa Rica's most perfect cloudforests. **See p.320**

❸ Reserva de Vida Silvestre Karen Mogensen Follow puma tracks to waterfall pools on the Nicoya Peninsula's most ecologically important nature reserve. See p.328

❹ Reserva Natural Absoluta Cabo Blanco Costa Rica's oldest piece of protected land features unique Pacific lowland tropical forest and is home to howler monkeys, white-tailed deer and flocks of pelicans. **See p.335**

❺ Mal País and Santa Teresa Ride the waves at these popular surfing hangouts on the southwest Nicoya Peninsula. **See p.336**

❻ Parque Nacional Manuel Antonio Relax on palm-fringed beaches and explore tangled tropical forests and mangroves abundant with wildlife, from sloths to rare squirrel monkeys. See p.357

HIGHLIGHTS ARE MARKED ON THE MAP ON PP.306–307

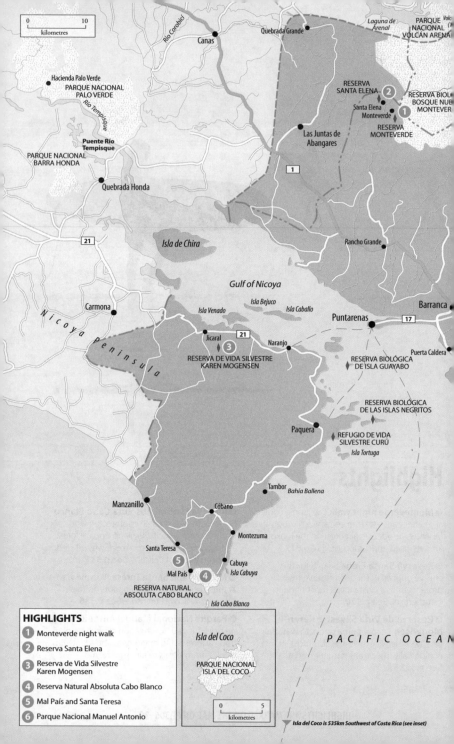

0
10
kilometres

Río Corobicí

Canas

Quebrada Grande

Laguna de Arenal

PARQUE NACIONAL VOLCÁN ARENA

Hacienda Palo Verde

PARQUE NACIONAL PALO VERDE

Río Tempisque

RESERVA SANTA ELENA

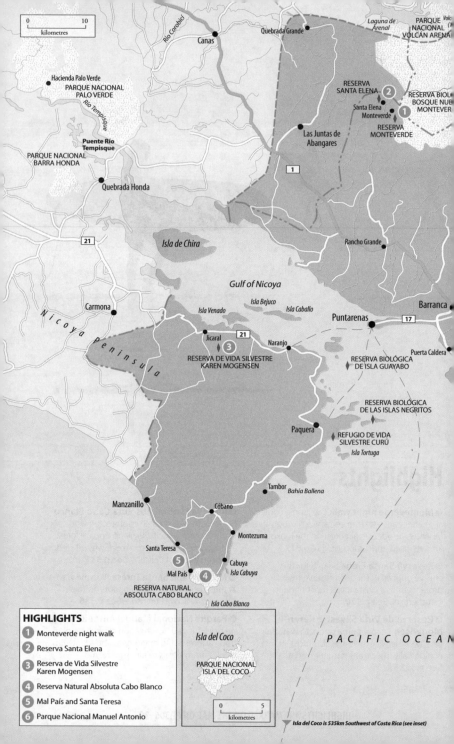2

RESERVA BIOL BOSQUE NUB MONTEVER

Santa Elena
Monteverde

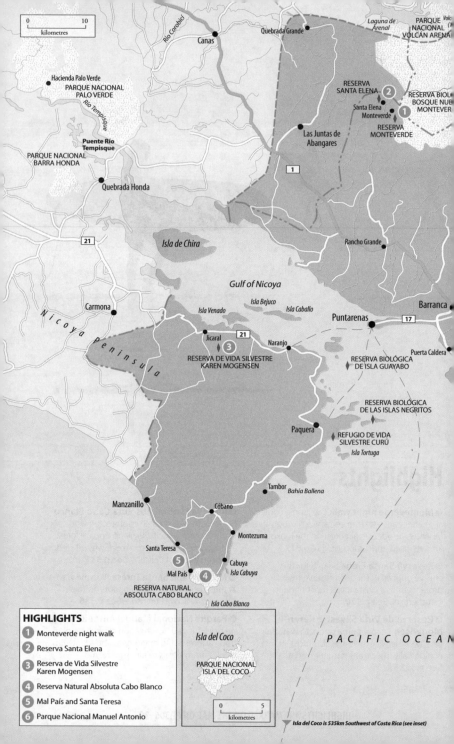1

Las Juntas de Abangares

RESERVA MONTEVERDE

Puente Río Tempisque

PARQUE NACIONAL BARRA HONDA

Quebrada Honda

1

21

Isla de Chira

Rancho Grande

Gulf of Nicoya

Carmona

Isla Bejuco

Isla Caballo

Barranca

N i c o y a   P e n i n s u l a

Isla Venado

Jicaral

21

3

RESERVA DE VIDA SILVESTRE KAREN MOGENSEN

Naranjo

Puntarenas

17

Puerta Caldera

RESERVA BIOLÓGICA DE ISLA GUAYABO

RESERVA BIOLÓGICA DE LAS ISLAS NEGRITOS

Paquera

REFUGIO DE VIDA SILVESTRE CURÚ

Isla Tortuga

Tambor

Bahía Ballena

Manzanillo

Cóbano

Montezuma

Santa Teresa

5

Cabuya

Isla Cabuya

Mal País

4

RESERVA NATURAL ABSOLUTA CABO BLANCO

Isla Cabo Blanco

PACIFIC OCEAN

HIGHLIGHTS

1 Monteverde night walk

2 Reserva Santa Elena

3 Reserva de Vida Silvestre Karen Mogensen

4 Reserva Natural Absoluta Cabo Blanco

5 Mal País and Santa Teresa

6 Parque Nacional Manuel Antonio

Isla del Coco

PARQUE NACIONAL ISLA DEL COCO

0
5
kilometres

Isla del Coco is 535km Southwest of Costa Rica (see inset)

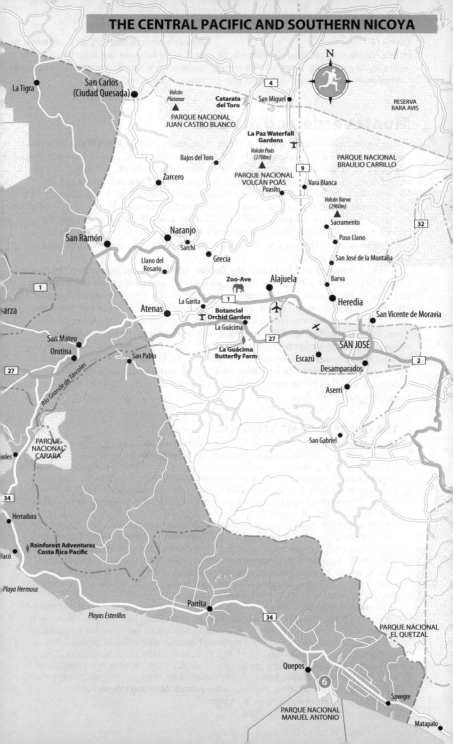

N

RESERVA
RARA AVIS

La Tigra

San Carlos
(Ciudad Quesada)

Volcán
Platanar

Catarata
del Toro

4

San Miguel

Parque Nacional
Juan Castro Blanco

La Paz Waterfall
Gardens

PARQUE NACIONAL
BRAULIO CARRILLO

Bajos del Toro

Volcán Poás
(2708m)

9

Vara Blanca

32

Zarcero

PARQUE NACIONAL
VOLCÁN POÁS

Poasito

Volcán Barva
(2960m)

San Ramón

Naranjo

Sacramento

Sarchí

Paso Llano

Grecia

San José de la Montaña

Llano del
Rosario

Barva

Zoo-Ave

Alajuela

1

Heredia

La Garita

1

San Vicente de Moravia

Atenas

Botanical
Orchid Garden

La Guácima

27

arza

San Mateo

Orotina

La Guácima
Butterfly Farm

SAN JOSÉ

2

27

San Pablo

Escazú

Desamparados

Río Grande de Tárcoles

Aserrí

PARQUE
NACIONAL
CARARA

oles

San Gabriel

34

Herradura

Rainforest Adventures
Costa Rica Pacific

acó

Playa Hermosa

Playas Esterillos

Parrita

PARQUE NACIONAL
EL QUETZAL

34

Quepos

6

Savegre

PARQUE NACIONAL
MANUEL ANTONIO

Matapalo

CLIMATE

With the exception of the cool climate of Monteverde, the region is tropical and drier than in the south of the country – temperatures can be uncomfortably high, with a dry-season average of about 30°C (86°F), and even in the much quieter wet season (Quepos and Manuel Antonio, in particular, receive torrential afternoon rains) temperatures don't cool down by much.

Monteverde and around

Though generally associated only with its cloudforest reserve, **MONTEVERDE** actually covers a larger area, straddling the hump of the Cordillera de Tilarán between Volcán Arenal and Laguna de Arenal to the northeast and the low hills of Guanacaste to the west. Along with the reserve, you'll find the spread-out Quaker community of Monteverde village; the neighbouring town of **Santa Elena** – with the majority of the area's amenities and budget accommodation – and, further afield, its own cloudforest reserve; as well as several small hamlets, including **Cerro Plano**. Throughout the region, the enchantment of the cloudforests is magnified by a combination of tranquil beauty, invigorating weather and the odd mix of Swiss-style farms and tropical botanical gardens.

Seeking autonomy and seclusion, the **Quaker** families living here arrived from the United States in the 1950s. The climate and terrain proved ideal for **dairy farming**, which soon became the mainstay of the economy – the region is famed domestically for its dairy products, and you'll see a variety of its cheeses in most *supermercados*. Abroad, however, Monteverde is known for its pioneering private nature reserves. Of these, the **Reserva Biológica Bosque Nuboso Monteverde** is the most popular, although the **Reserva Santa Elena** offers equally pristine cloudforest cover and, because it receives fewer visitors, may prove the more fruitful for spotting wildlife. The huge **Bosque Eterno de los Niños**, established with funds raised by school children from all over the world, surrounds Monteverde; the Bajo del Tigre section is the easiest part to explore.

THE QUAKERS OF MONTEVERDE

Quakerism (*cuáquerismo*), also called the Society of Friends (Ⓦquaker.org), is an altruistic, optimistic belief system founded by an Englishman, **George Fox** (1624–91), who instilled in his followers the importance of seeing God in everybody. From the beginning, Quakers placed themselves in opposition to many of the coercive instruments employed by the state and society – a philosophy that subjected them to severe discrimination when they first arrived in the New World in 1656 – and they continue to embody a blend of the conservative with an absolute resistance to state control.

In the early 1950s, a group of Quakers from Alabama fled the US, having been harassed to the point of imprisonment for refusing the draft (**pacifism** is a cornerstone of Quaker beliefs). Attracted by the fact that Costa Rica had abolished its army a few years earlier in 1948, they settled in Monteverde. At the time, the remote village was home to only a few Costa Rican farming families; there was no road, only an ox-cart track, and the journey to San José took several days. The Quakers bought and settled some twelve square kilometres of mountainside, dividing the land and building their houses and a school.

Quakerism doesn't impose any obvious standards of dress or appearance upon its followers – you're not going to see the jolly old man from the oatmeal box sauntering by – nor does it manifest itself in any way that is immediately obvious to visitors, except for the area's relative lack of bars. The Quakers manage their **meeting houses** individually, with no officiating minister and purely local agendas. Gatherings focus on meditation, but anyone who is moved to say a few words or read simply speaks up – all verbal offerings in context are considered valid. The meeting houses welcome outsiders, who are never subject to being converted. In Monteverde, visitors can attend meetings at the **Friends Meeting House**, held on Wednesdays at 9.30am and Sundays at 10.30am.

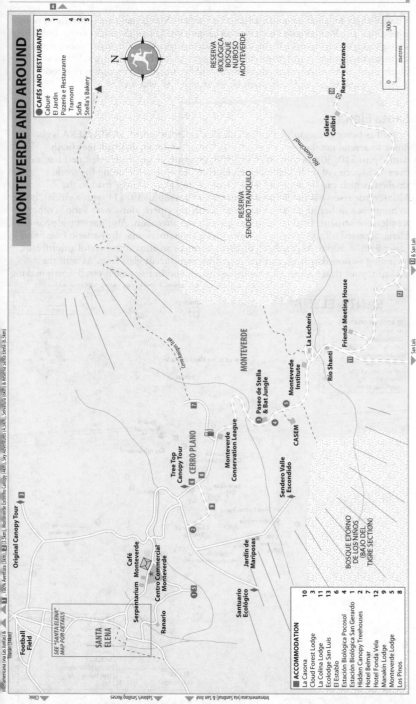

MONTEVERDE AND AROUND

RESERVA BIOLÓGICA BOSQUE NUBOSO MONTEVERDE

Reserve Entrance

Galería Colibrí

RESERVA SENDERO TRANQUILO

Río Guacimal

MONTEVERDE

La Lechería

Friends Meeting House

Paseo de Stella & Bat Jungle

Monteverde Institute

Río Shanti

San Luis

CASEM

Sendero Valle Escondido

BOSQUE ETERNO DE LOS NIÑOS (BAJO DEL TIGRE SECTION)

Monteverde Conservation League

Tree Top Canopy Tour

CERRO PLANO

Cerro Amigos Trail

Original Canopy Tour

Café Monteverde

Centro Commercial Monteverde

Serpentarium

Ranario

SANTA ELENA

SEE "SANTA ELENA" MAP FOR DETAILS

Football Field

Santuario Ecológico

Jardín de Mariposas

0 — 300 metres

Interamericana (via Las Juntas) & Tilarán (34km)

100% Aventura (3km), (13.5km), Monteverde Extremo Canopy (4km), Sky Adventures (4.5km), Sevillana (6km) & Reserva Santa Elena (6.5km)

Clinic

Sabine's Smiling Horses

Interamericana (via Sardinal) & San José

& San Luis

San Luis

6

Surprisingly for such a popular place, the roads to Monteverde are generally in poor condition. The **Monteverde Conservation League (MCL)** and the wider community have resisted suggestions to pave them, arguing easier access would increase visitor numbers to unsustainable levels and threaten the integrity of local communities. Whatever the future holds, it's unlikely that Monteverde will be ruined: the community is too outspoken and organized to let itself be overrun by its own success.

Santa Elena

As well as being the region's transport and commercial centre, **SANTA ELENA** is also home to several good nature museums. In town, the **Jardín de Orquídeas** (daily 8am–5pm; $10; 30min tour; ⓣ2645 5308, ⓦmonteverdeorchidgarden.net) has more than 425 species of orchid, all of them local to the region, including the world's smallest, which can be observed with a magnifying glass. On the road to the Monteverde reserve is the **Serpentarium** (daily 9am–8pm; $9, $11 with a guide), home to numerous slithering snakes, including deadly pit vipers, along with various other reptiles; the serpents tend to be more active in the afternoon. Also just outside Santa Elena, accessed off the main road down to the Interamericana, the **Ranario** frog pond (daily 9am–8.30pm; $12; ⓣ2645 6320) is home to an array of colourful amphibians, including poison-dart frogs and the incredible translucent glass frog. As with the snakepit, your ticket is valid for multiple entries, and in this case it's well worth making

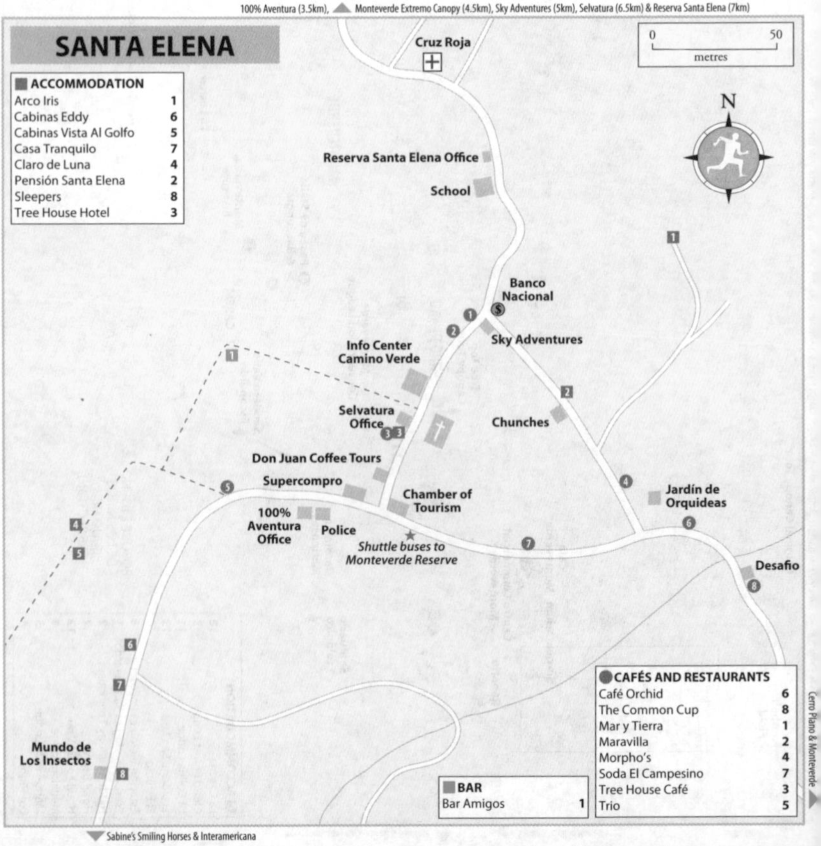
100% Aventura (3.5km), Monteverde Extremo Canopy (4.5km), Sky Adventures (5km), Selvatura (6.5km) & Reserva Santa Elena (7km)
SANTA ELENA
ACCOMMODATION
Arco Iris 1
Cabinas Eddy 6
Cabinas Vista Al Golfo 5
Casa Tranquilo 7
Claro de Luna 4
Pensión Santa Elena 2
Sleepers 8
Tree House Hotel 3
Cruz Roja
0 50 metres
N
Reserva Santa Elena Office
School
Banco Nacional
Sky Adventures
Info Center Camino Verde
Selvatura Office
Chunches
Don Juan Coffee Tours
Supercompro
Chamber of Tourism
Jardín de Orquideas
100% Aventura Office
Police
Shuttle buses to Monteverde Reserve
Desafio
Mundo de Los Insectos
BAR
Bar Amigos 1
CAFÉS AND RESTAURANTS
Café Orchid 6
The Common Cup 8
Mar y Tierra 1
Maravilla 2
Morpho's 4
Soda El Campesino 7
Tree House Café 3
Trio 5
Cerro Plano & Monteverde
Sabine's Smiling Horses & Interamericana

COFFEE IN THE CLOUDFOREST

Monteverde is probably the best place outside the Valle Central (see box, p.125) to learn about Costa Rica's golden beans. Two companies here offer **tours** of their coffee fields and processing plants, enabling you to follow the journey from bush to bag. The co-operative **Café Monteverde** (☎ 2645 5901) was the country's first sustainable coffee producer and offers a hands-on tour of an organic plantation in San Luis ($30; 3hr), where you can visit their water-powered coffee mill, as well as a shorter trip to an agro-ecological, organic farm just north of Santa Elena ($22; 1hr 30min); you can sample their beans without leaving town, at the *Casa del Café Monteverde* (daily 8am–5pm), near the post office on the road to Cerro Plano. **Don Juan Coffee Tour** (☎ 2645 7100, ⓦdonjuancoffeetour.com), with an office on the Santa Elena triangle, runs similar trips to a small farm 2km north of the village ($30; 1hr 30min), as well as chocolate- and sugar-cane-themed trips.

a visit during the day and one at night, when different species emerge from beneath their lily pads.

If you haven't yet been (un)lucky enough to get intimate with Costa Rican insects in the privacy of your hotel room, you may want to check out the **Mundo de los Insectos** (daily 9am–7pm; $10; ☎ 2645 6859), just beyond the turning to the Ranario; it's home to a collection of 25 species of live creepy-crawlies from Costa Rica, united by an alarmingly short life span.

Cerro Plano

The village of **CERRO PLANO**, up the road from Santa Elena, has several attractions. A signposted side road leads to the **Jardín de Mariposas** (daily 8.30am–4pm; $15; ☎ 2645 5512, ⓦmonteverdebutterflygarden.com), the oldest butterfly farm in the country, with four individual butterfly gardens and a leafcutter ant colony; the butterflies are at their most active on sunny mornings. The entry fee includes a guided tour, which begins in the on-site natural history museum.

Several private reserves in Cerro Plano offer walks along well-maintained trails in search of sloths, monkeys and birds. Signposted down a right-hand turn in the village centre, the **Santuario Ecológico** (daily 7am–6pm; $12; ☎ 2645 5869, ⓦsantuarioecologico.com) encompasses a swath of transition forest and can be a good place to spot a diverse range of species; night walks (daily 5.30pm; $20 includes transport from your hotel; 2hr) head out each evening to spot porcupines, kinkajous and bats. Trails on the nearby **Sendero Valle Escondido** (daily 7am–4pm; $40 with guided tour; ☎ 2645 6601, ⓦmonteverdenighttour.com), 27 acres of former farming land, run past a cascading waterfall and afford panoramas of the Pacific; their night walk (daily 5.30pm; $25 includes transport from your hotel; 2hr) allows free access to the reserve during the day. In the **Reserva Sendero Tranquilo** you can take guided walks (daily 7.30am & 1.30pm; $35; 3hr; with transport from your hotel; ☎ 2645 5010, ⓦsapodorado.com) around a 210-acre reserve bordering the Reserva Biológica Bosque Nuboso Monteverde, as well as a night walk that leaves later than most (daily 6pm; 2hr).

Monteverde village

Just off the main road east of Santa Elena sprawls the settlement of **MONTEVERDE**, a timeless place where modest houses perch above splendid forested views, and farmers trudge along the muddy roads in sturdy rubber boots. Established in 1954 by the original Quaker settlers (see box, p.308), **La Lechería** forms the heart of the community and, along with ecotourism, is its economic mainstay. The cheese factory produces a range of European-style cheeses, of which Monte is the best known, along with yoghurts and cream. You can buy fresh cheese at La Lechería's shop (daily 6.30am–5pm) or take an informative tour, which is as much about the area's history as it is about the cheese-making process (Mon–Sat 9am & 2pm; $12; reservations on ☎2645 7090, ⓦcrstudytours.com).

A few hundred metres northwest along the same road, the arts and crafts collective **CASEM** (Mon–Sat 8am–5pm, Sun 10am–4pm) holds exhibits and sells the work of local artists. Founded thirty years ago by eight women, CASEM has long played an important role in this small community and supports over a hundred local artisans. Just up the road towards Santa Elena is the distinctive Paseo de Stella, a hilltop colonial-style complex housing the **Bat Jungle** (daily 9am–7.30pm, feeding times 9am, noon & 3pm; $11; ☎2645 6566, ⓦbatjungle.com). The first of its kind in the world, this worthy little attraction aims to dispel stereotypes of bats as bloodthirsty, disease-ridden creatures of the night. The exhibit and 45-minute guided tour takes visitors through a simulated tropical rainforest to view cute little Monteverde bats (eight of the region's sixty species) going about their business – roosting, munching on bananas and flying about in their bat cave.

Bosque Eterno de los Niños

Southwest of Monteverde village **Bajo del Tigre** Daily 8am–4pm · $12 · **Birdwatching** Daily 5.30am, 8am & 2pm · $28 **Night walks** Daily 5.30pm · $20 **Trek to Pocosol** Around $300 · ☎ 2645 5003, ⓦ acmcr.org

Central America's largest private reserve, the vast **Bosque Eterno de los Niños** (Children's Eternal Rainforest), known colloquially as the "BEN", stretches over 210 square kilometres and accounts for half of the Zona Protectora de Monteverde. Initiated in 1987 by Swedish school children, the reserve is run by the **Monteverde Conservation League** – their information office is opposite the petrol station in Cerro Plano – and encompasses cloudforest, rainforest and montane evergreen forest, harbouring over fifty percent of Costa Rica's known vertebrate species. The most accessible section is at **Bajo del Tigre**, between CASEM and La Lechería, which has 3.5km of easy-going trails and offers birdwatching tours and guided day and night walks, the latter a memorable trek through transition forest, with a good chance of spotting tarantulas, frogs and roosting birds.

You can stay at the reserve's two **field stations** (see p.316): *Estación Biológica San Gerardo*, 7.5km north of Santa Elena, has access to 5km of trails and is a good spot for birdwatching, while *Estación Biológica Pocosol* is on the far eastern fringes of the BEN, with 10km of trails leading to a natural lagoon and bubbling mud pots. *San Gerardo* is a 3.5km hike from the Reserva Santa Elena, but to get to *Pocosol* – which is actually easier to reach from La Tigra, on the road between San Ramón and La Fortuna – you'll need to embark on a two-day trek from the Monteverde reserve, overnighting at a refuge along the way. This is real bushwhacking stuff, on unmarked trails (pumas have been spotted around the refuge), and each trip is escorted by two fully equipped rangers trained in first aid; you'll need to carry all your food in, plus a sleeping bag.

ARRIVAL AND DEPARTURE   MONTEVERDE AND AROUND

BY BUS

Buses arrive at and depart from the Centro Commerical Monteverde complex, near the MegaSuper supermarket, just east of Santa Elena. It's worth buying tickets for the more popular routes (especially if you're heading to San José) in advance but be aware that the timetable changes periodically. Watch your bags on all buses as thefts are common.

San José Most people coming by bus from San José (C12, Av 7/9) arrive on one of the two direct services (6.30am & 2.30pm; 4hr 30min); demand is high, so book your tickets a few days in advance in high season. Buses for San José

leave daily also at 6.30am & 2.30pm.

La Fortuna Buses from La Fortuna travel via Tilarán, on the shores of Laguna de Arenal (daily 8am, 12.15pm & 5.30pm; 3hr), from where two daily buses run on to Santa Elena (4.30am & 12.30pm; 2hr 30min); if you don't catch the first service from La Fortuna, you'll need to spend the night in Tilarán (see p.223). Buses run in the opposite direction twice a day (7am & 4pm; 2hr 30min to Tilarán).

Puntarenas Three daily buses travel between Puntarenas and Santa Elena (from Puntarenas 7.50am, 1.50pm & 2.15pm, to Puntarenas 4.20am, 6am & 3pm; 3hr).

Guanacaste The 4.20am Santa Elena–Puntarenas service stops in Las Juntas de Abangares (2hr), from where you can travel on to Liberia and points north in Guanacaste; otherwise, take any San José-bound bus and get off just after the bus turns onto the Interamericana, at the intersection for Chomes, from where you can hail northbound buses to Liberia and elsewhere.

BY COMBINATION

Taxi–Boat–Taxi These immensely popular transfers to/from La Fortuna are a superb (and time-saving) way to travel between two of the country's major attractions. They depart La Fortuna daily around 8.30am and 2.30pm, returning around 8am and 2pm ($32; 3hr), and include a spectacular ride across Laguna de Arenal, with Volcán Arenal looming above.

Horse–Boat–Taxi For a slightly different journey to/from La Fortuna, Desafío Expeditions and Sabine's Smiling Horses (see below) can arrange a horse–boat–taxi trip ($85; 5hr), riding along the shores of Laguna de Arenal or, in the dry season (Dec–July), via El Castillo or the old trade route down the Río Chiquito.

BY CAR

Regardless of what route you take here, a 4WD is highly recommended during the rainy season – some agencies even refuse to rent regular cars for Monteverde at this time – and you should check that your hotel has parking, as it's impossible to park on the street once you arrive.

From San José Driving from San José takes about 4hr via the Interamericana. The quickest route branches off at Rancho Grande and heads up to Monteverde via Sardinal (it's paved as far as Guacimal), though local taxistas argue a better route is the one through Las Juntas de Abangares, a tiny town reached via a small road (labelled "145" on some maps) off the Interamericana; the first 7km of this 37km road, via Candelaria, are paved, but beware some spectacular hairpin bends.

From Tilarán You can also reach Monteverde from Tilarán, near Laguna de Arenal, a 40km uphill judder along often very rough roads (2hr).

TOURS

From San José tours to Monteverde average around $350–400 for two nights and usually include accommodation, return transport and sometimes meals. The main difference is the type of hotel used and whether or not the reserve entrance fee is covered in the price.

ON FOOT

Trekking to La Fortuna Adventurous types with a bit of stamina can hike to La Fortuna, or at least to El Castillo, just west of Volcán Arenal, trekking through the Bosque Eterno de los Niños and Parque Nacional Volcán Arenal en route with the Monteverde Conservation League (see opposite); the 8hr trip (Feb to late May only) departs from the Estación Biológica San Gerardo and emerges, after several river crossings and some exciting jungle trekking, near the town of El Castillo, on the shores of Laguna de Arenal ($140 plus entrance fees; reserve at least two weeks in advance).

INFORMATION

Tourist information For information in Santa Elena, try the Chamber of Tourism (daily 8am–8pm; ☎ 2645 6565, ✉ turismomv@racsa.co.cr) and the *Pensión Santa Elena* (see p.315), a few steps downhill from the Banco Nacional, whose friendly staff offer excellent impartial advice to everyone, non-guests included.

Website For a preview of the area, ⓦ monteverdeinfo.com has details on the cloudforest's flora and fauna, tours and nearby hotels.

TOURS AND ACTIVITIES

Horseriding Tours with Desafío, below *The Common Cup* in Santa Elena (☎ 2645 5874 or ☎ 8379 9827, ⓦ monteverdetours.com), come in a variety of forms, including "mountains and farmland" ($45; sunset tour at 3pm; 2hr 30min); there's also an all-day "cowboy tour" ($120). Sabine's Smiling Horses (☎ 2645 6894 or ☎ 8385 2424, ⓦ smilinghorses.com) arrange trips that stop at various panoramic views of the Pacific and the Nicoya Peninsula ($57; sunset tour at 3.30pm; 3hr) as well as monthly full-moon rides ($57; 3hr).

Yoga Río Shanti, near La Lechería (☎ 2645 6121, ⓦ rioshanti.com), holds various classes (Mon–Sat), from meditation (1hr; free) to rigorous Ashtanga (1hr 30min; $10) in a mellow sixty-year-old building in Monteverde village; massages cost $70/1hr.

GETTING AROUND

By bus Shuttle buses run from near Santa Elena's Chamber of Tourism to the Monteverde reserve (daily 6.15am, 7.30am, 1.20pm & 3pm, returning 6.45am, 11.30am, 2pm & 4pm; 30min; $1 each way); shuttle buses to the Santa Elena reserve (daily 6.30am, 8.30am, 10.30am & 12.30pm, returning 11am, 1pm, 3pm & 4pm; 30min; $2 each way) must be booked in advance; you'll then be picked-up and dropped-off at your hotel.

By taxi Jeep-taxis charge around $10–12 one-way from in and around Santa Elena to the Monteverde reserve or the Santa Elena reserve.

6

CANOPY TOURS AND HANGING BRIDGES

The ever-popular **canopy tours** that now seem an obligatory part of any activities centre in Costa Rica were pioneered in Monteverde, using techniques developed by cavers and canyon rappellers to let visitors experience the rainforest from a bird's-eye view. For a different – but no less exhilarating – forest adventure, take a hike along one of the **hanging bridges**, which thread through the treetops for several kilometres; bring binoculars, for here's your chance to spot birds and howler monkeys at their own level.

100% Aventura Office near the police station, park 3.5km north of Santa Elena ☎ 2645 6959, ⓦ monteverdeadventure.com. A dozen cables interspersed with a Tarzan swing and rappelling ($45), plus 2.5km of hanging bridges ($35).

Monteverde Extremo Canopy 4.5km north of Santa Elena ☎ 2645 6058, ⓦ monteverdeextremo.com. The newest company on the block, with adrenaline-fuelled tours of fifteen cables through secondary forest ($40); the Superman ($5 extra) requires adopting an arms-out, legs-up pose down a kilometre-long wire hanging 180m above the trees.

Original Canopy Tour Near Cloud Forest Lodge ☎ 2645 5243, ⓦ canopytour.com. They're not fibbing: the first canopy tour in Monteverde (and therefore the world) may be smaller than its competitors, but it's more in harmony with its surroundings – stepladders run up the trees themselves (and even through one old fig tree), and the platforms barely get beyond poking out from their boughs. Tours ($45) include a rappel and a Tarzan swing, and there's also the option of a night

ride (daily 5.30–8pm).

Selvatura Office opposite the church in Santa Elena, reserve located 6.5km north of Santa Elena ☎ 2645 5929, ⓦ selvatura.com. Similar setup to Sky Adventures, with sixteen-cable canopy tours ($65) and a network of hanging bridges ($90 combined with a canopy tour), plus a number of wildlife exhibits, the most interesting of which is the Jewels of the Rainforest, one of the largest collections of insects in the world.

Sky Adventures Office on the northern corner of the Santa Elena triangle, reserve located 5km north of Santa Elena ☎ 2645 5238, ⓦ skyadventures .travel. After a tram ride up above the trees, zip along ten high-tension cables, including one that's a whopping kilometre in length ($65).

Tree Top Canopy Tour El Establo, 1.3km east of Santa Elena ☎ 2645 5110, ⓦ elestablo.com. The sixteen cables on this luxury-hotel canopy tour ($40) enjoy great views of the Gulf of Nicoya; there are also rope bridges and a Tarzan swing to try out.

ACCOMMODATION

Santa Elena has the area's lowest-priced accommodation – it's generally simple but you'll get heated water to go with a warm welcome, and the owners usually offer an array of services, from home-cooking and laundry to horse hire. In contrast, hotels in and around the **Monteverde** community aspire to European mountain-resort facilities – large rooms, orthopedic mattresses and even saunas and hot tubs are the norm –and tend to be expensive, appealing to those who like their wilderness deluxe. These hotels often have a restaurant and meals may be included. Aside from illustrated nature talks, nightlife within the hotels is low-key to nonexistent – some have a small bar, and that's about it.

SANTA ELENA AND AROUND

★ **Arco Iris** Up a side street just east of the town centre ☎ 2645 5067, ⓦ arcoirislodge.com; map p.310. Relax in spacious, well-appointed cabins amid quiet landscaped gardens near the town centre. You can also stay in cheaper rooms with double or bunk beds. The delicious breakfast ($7.50) of hearty German bread, granola, fresh fruit, eggs and toast is also available to non-guests (daily 7–9am). Double $42, cabin $88

Cabinas Eddy 100m southwest of the supermarket ☎ 2645 6618, ⓦ cabinas-eddy.com; map p.310. The well-scrubbed rooms here (some with private bath) can accommodate up to seven people and are a cut above most of the other budget options in town. Combine this with friendly owners, free tea, coffee and internet, and

mountain views from the wraparound balcony, and you're onto a winner. Breakfast is $5 extra. $30

Cabinas Vista Al Golfo 300m southwest of the church ☎ 2645 6682, ⓦ cabinasvistaalgolfo.com; map p.310. One of the best budget options in Santa Elena, *Cabinas Vista Al Golfo* boasts bright, clean dorms and rooms, some with bathroom, plus fully equipped apartments with private balconies. Enjoy fantastic views of the Gulf of Nicoya and hang out with fellow travellers in the sociable shared kitchen. The cheery owners can organize tours. Dorm $10, double $20, apartment $50

Casa Tranquilo 100m downhill from the supermarket ☎ 2645 6782; map p.310. This cheerful terracotta-coloured hangout buzzing with seasoned travellers has seven clean, bright rooms (some with private bathrooms) and comfortable mattresses to boot. The on-site laundry service is a bonus. **$30**

Claro de Luna 300m southwest of the church, opposite Cabinas Vista Al Golfo ☎ 2645 5269, ⓦ clarodelunahotel .com; map p.310. *Claro de Luna* has a small collection of pretty rooms, each with blissfully comfortable beds (deluxe rooms have four-posters) and luxurious bathrooms occupying an exquisite wooden house with a dramatically sloped roof. **$71**

Cloud Forest Lodge 500m northeast of Santa Elena ☎ 2645 5058, ⓦ cloudforestlodge.com; map p.309. Set in seventy acres of primary and secondary forest high above Santa Elena, this secluded, surprisingly low-priced hotel is one of the classiest in the area. The well-appointed wood-panelled cabins have cable TV, large private bathroom and terraces with dizzying views, and the hotel has its own 5km system of trails. **$113**

★ **Hidden Canopy Treehouses** 4km north of Santa Elena, on the road to the reserve ☎ 2645 5447, ⓦ hidden canopy.com; map p.309. Fantastic treehouses, the sort you dreamed of as a child, perched up in the canopy, with oversized beds and huge windows that make the most of the superb views down to the Gulf of Nicoya. Bathrooms have exotic waterfall showers, and two (split-level) treehouses even have jacuzzis on their balconies. There are also rooms in the main house if you haven't got a head for heights. Two-night minimum stay. Double **$255**, treehouse **$322**

Pensión Santa Elena 25m downhill from the Banco Nacional ☎ 2645 5051, ⓦ pensionsantaelena.com; map p.310. Perennially popular central hostel – the helpful staff are a wealth of information – offering spots to pitch your tent, four- and six-bed dorms with shared hot-water bathrooms, some decent doubles with private bathroom out back and attractive *cabinas*. Amenities include a kitchen, cheap internet and large communal area where you can yap the night away with fellow backpackers. Camping/person **$7**, dorm **$12**, double **$24**, cabin **$47**

Sleepers 200m southwest of Santa Elena ☎ 2645 7133, ⓦ www.sleepersleepcheaperhostels.com; map p.310. Simple accommodation in a variety of clean (mixed) dorms and rooms (sleeping up to four people) that ticks all the boxes for backpackers: inexpensive lodgings, communal atmosphere, shared kitchen and free tea, coffee, pancakes and internet. Dorm **$9**, double **$25**

Tree House Hotel On the main street ☎ 2645 5004, ⓦ monteverdeinfo.com/tree-house-hotel; map p.310. Built around a fifty-year-old strangler fig, this central hotel offers superb value for money. The rooms (try to get one with a balcony) are fresh and light and can sleep up to seven people; good-value singles ($24) too. They've done their best with sound insulation, but bear in mind that the hotel is next door to rowdy *Bar Amigos*. It's a good source of local knowledge – the owners run ⓦ monteverdeinfo.com – and the *Treehouse Café* is downstairs (see p.316). **$48**

CERRO PLANO

El Establo 1.3km east of Santa Elena ☎ 2645 5110, ⓦ elestablo.com; map p.309. Large-scale luxury lodgings with copious facilities (heated swimming pools, tennis and basketball courts and a canopy tour), should you still have energy to burn after a hike in the reserve – and a spa for those who don't. Carpeted rooms are a decent size given the layout and come with two queen beds and large bathrooms. **$216**

Hotel Belmar 2km east of Santa Elena ☎ 2645 5201, ⓦ hotelbelmar.net; map p.309. The oldest of the area's many Swiss-style hotels, the perennially popular and very ecofriendly *Belmar* sits on a hillside above Cerro Plano, with sweeping views of the gulf. Pricier rooms are somewhat larger and equipped with a fan, rarely a necessity in blustery Monteverde. **$170**

Manakín Lodge 1.3km east of Santa Elena ☎ 2645 5080, ⓦ manakin.hostel.com; map p.309. This family-run lodge with the forest as its backyard offers some of the friendliest budget accommodation in the area, including family rooms that almost disappear into the trees. Guests also have access to laundry service and internet. The owner can whip up traditional or vegetarian food on demand. **$49**

★ **Monteverde Lodge** 400m southeast of Santa Elena ☎ 2521 6099, ⓦ monteverdelodge.com; map p.309. The Monteverde outpost of well-regarded tour operator Costa Rica Expeditions has tasteful rooms with super-comfy beds and corner windows overlooking thick forest, plus three cheaper garden lodgings. After a walk in the reserve, settle down in the cosy bar (with open fire) for afternoon tea and cake. Staff are exceedingly helpful, and the on-site restaurant is superb (see p.317). **$224**

Los Pinos 1.5km east of Santa Elena ☎ 2645 5252, ⓦ lospinos.net; map p.309. A terrific family hideaway, these great-value self-catering cabins set amid forested gardens are far enough from each other to guarantee privacy. The six-bed, three-bathroom cabins are a good deal ($140) and come with large kitchens and lounge area. Guests can pick their own dinner from the hydroponic greenhouse. **$70**

MONTEVERDE

La Casona Reserva Biológica Bosque Nuboso Monteverde ☎ 2645 5122, ⓦ reservamonteverde.com/lodging.html; map p.309. Accommodation is in basic dorms and private en suites and this lodge, which is located just inside the reserve and has an infectious environmental buzz. It's often packed with researchers and students (who get cheaper rates); tourists are second priority, so advance reservations are essential. Rates include entrance to the reserve and three meals a day, including dinner at *Pizzeria e Restaurante Tramonti* (see p.317). Dorm **$62**, double **$73**

La Colina Lodge About 2km before the entrance to the Monteverde reserve ☎ 2645 5009, ⓦ lacolinalodge .com; map p.309. This handy, rustic spot near the reserve

6

has cute, country-cottage-style rooms with homely wooden furnishings. Rooms have private or shared bathrooms, and some have a balcony. There are also low-cost dorms or you can camp in the grounds (if you have your own tent). Camping/person $5, dorm $10, double $25

Ecolodge San Luis San Luis town, a 15min drive south of Monteverde village ☎ 2645 7363, ⊛ external affairs.uga.edu/costa_rica; map p.309. Located on a reserve owned by the University of Georgia, this ecolodge offers accommodation in dorm-like "bunkhouses" and more comfortable bungalows and cabins. Rates for all include three daily meals and a variety of activities ranging from cow-milking to birdwatching. The reserve has an extensive network of wildlife-filled trails, as well as a botanical garden. Dorm $49, bungalow $144, cabin $192

Estación Biológica Pocosol and Estación Biológica San Gerardo Bosque Eterno de los Niños ☎ 2645 5003, ⊛ acmcr.org; map p.309. You'll be vying for space with scientists and researchers at these two lodges in the heart of the Bosque Eterno de los Niños. Both provide simple, dorm-style accommodation (each has space for 32 people), and rates include three meals a day. Dorm $52

Hotel Fonda Vela About 1.5km before the entrance to the Monteverde reserve ☎ 2645 5125, ⊛ fondavela .com; map p.309. Near the reserve amid quiet grounds, this old-fashioned family-run hotel is expertly managed by attentive staff. Newer suites ($180) aim for deluxe, with huge bathrooms and beautiful furniture, while the older, rustic rooms have attractive wood-panelled walls and huge windows – the better to enjoy the astonishing views, particularly at sunset. Breakfast costs extra. $135

EATING AND DRINKING

Santa Elena and neighbouring Cerro Plano are home to a number of inexpensive *soda*-style **eateries** as well as a number of classier options; several of these are hotel restaurants that are open to non-guests. You can pick up fresh fruit and vegetables, home-baked bread, cheese and pickles from the **Farmers' Market** (Sat 6am–noon) at the Colegio Santa Elena. **Drinking** is kept to a minimum in the Quaker community of Monteverde – and even in gringo-packed Santa Elena, bars aren't all that prevalent; *Bar Amigos* sees most of what little action there is. In February and March, *Bromelia's Café and Amphitheatre*, up a driveway opposite CASEM, is the setting for the **Monteverde Music Fest**, which showcases top Costa Rican artists.

SANTA ELENA

Bar Amigos Down a side street opposite the church in Santa Elena ☎ 2645 5071, ⊛ baramigos.com; map p.310. Most of Santa Elena's nightlife centres on *Bar Amigos*, which has live bands (every Fri night), DJs, big-screen sports events and locals and visitors slinging back beers (from $2). Daily noon–2/3am.

Café Orchid Next to the Jardín de Orquídeas ☎ 2645 6850; map p.310. Charming café with a breezy terrace out front that's good at any time of the day. The menu features no fewer than 28 types of coffee ($2–6), plus teas, crêpes (sweet and savoury; $4–12), panini and salads. Daily 7am–7pm.

★**The Common Cup** Near the Jardín de Orquídeas ☎ 2645 6247; map p.310. Ignore the disingenuous name, the coffee ($2–4) at this cabin-like café and roastery, just above the Desafío office, is anything but average. It also serves a good range of breakfasts and cakes too. Daily 7am–6pm.

Mar y Tierra Opposite the Banco Nacional ☎ 2645 6111; map p.310. As the name suggests, *Mar y Tierra* has a good range of tempting meat and fish dishes, including shrimp ceviche and sesame-breaded mahi-mahi, served with organic vegetables from their garden. Mains $10–15. Daily 11am–10pm.

Maravilla Opposite the bus stop ☎ 2645 6623; map p.310. This bustling, no-frills *soda* is typically packed and for good reason: the food is tasty and the portions generous. For lunch or dinner, you can't go wrong with one

of the *arroz cons* ($6–8); the strawberry milkshake is good too. Daily 7am–9pm.

Morpho's Next to the Jardín de Orquídeas ☎ 2645 5607; map p.310. This stylish split-level restaurant decorated with unusual hanging butterflies and an extravagant wraparound mural serves inventive (sometimes a little too inventive) mains ($9–21) like passion fruit chicken and Monteverde blue-cheese-tenderloin, as well as less expensive soups and subs. Daily 11.30am–9.30pm.

Soda El Campesino On the southern side of the Santa Elena triangle ☎ 8704 1867; map p.310. The menu at this unassuming *soda* holds few surprises (the usual *casados*, *arroz cons*, etc), but everything is well-prepared, portions are sizeable, and the service is friendly. Mains $6–12. Daily 6am–8pm.

Tree House Café Next to the Tree House Hotel ☎ 2645 5004, ⊛ treehouse.cr; map p.310. The eclectic menu includes huge platters, but you're better off opting for something simpler – pancakes and granola for breakfast, a creamy *batido* (around $4) or a cocktail ($5–11) – as you're really here for the huge fig tree that grows right through the centre of the restaurant. Daily 7am–10pm.

Trio 50m west of the supermarket ☎ 2645 7254; map p.310. Cool restaurant from the Karen Nielsen stable (the brains behind Cerro Plano's *Sofia*) with an unusual menu (mains $11–18) – ribs with sugarcane syrup and beer, sea bass with spiced watermelon sauce – served on an attractive terrace. Daily 6–9pm.

CERRO PLANO

★**El Jardín** Monteverde Lodge, 400m southeast of Santa Elena ☎ 2645 5214, ⓦ costaricaexpeditions.com; map p.309. Beautifully presented dishes such as succulent *bife de chorizo* steak and tuna with garlic and macadamia flakes (mains 13–20) hit the spot every time. Considering the quality, prices aren't too high and the imaginative salads are tremendous value. The wine (glass from $7) list is strong too, with especially good Argentine options, and the first-rate service manages to combine efficiency with friendliness. Daily 11am–10pm.

Sofía Near the bullring in Cerro Plano ☎ 2645 7017; map p.309. The creative "Nuevo Latin" cuisine (mains $15–25) at this stylish restaurant with a candlelit interior won't disappoint. Sweet-and-sour fig-roasted pork loin is a real hit, and the cocktail list is top-notch. Daily except Sun 11.30am–9.30pm.

MONTEVERDE

Caburé In the Paseo de Stella complex on the road to the Monteverde reserve ☎ 2645 5020, ⓦ cabure.net; map p.309. Relish the coastal sunset views from the lofty balcony over a glass of Malbec at this great little Argentine restaurant and *chocolatería*. There's a range of mains (from $15) on offer, but the highlights are the sweet treats, which include *alfajores* (*dulce de leche*-filled biscuits), green mango strudel, and sumptuous home-made truffles and chocolates. Daily except Sun 9am–9pm.

★**Pizzeria e Restaurante Tramonti** Opposite the Paseo de Stella complex on the road to the reserve ☎ 2645 6120; map p.309. Don't leave Monteverde without dining at this divine Italian restaurant. Many of the ingredients are sourced from Italy and you can taste the Mediterranean in everything from the Caprese salad to the wood-fired pizzas ($10–18), which are the highlights. Daily 11.30am–9.45pm.

Stella's Bakery Opposite CASEM ☎ 2645 5560, ⓦ stellasbakery.webs.com; map p.309. Pleasant little coffee shop whose walls are adorned with said Stella's artwork; the freshly-baked bread, cakes and pastries (from $2) are delicious – keep an eye out for the coffee cake and the blackberry pie. Daily 6am–10pm.

DIRECTORY

Bookshops *Chunches* (Mon–Sat 8am–6pm; ☎ 2645 5147) book and coffee shop, south of the bank, sells espresso, snacks and secondhand paperbacks.

Internet access There are several cybercafés in Santa Elena, and virtually all the hotels and restaurants offer free wi-fi.

Laundry *Chunches* (see above) charges $5/load.

Medical care The clinic on the road that runs past the football field north of Santa Elena is open 24hr (☎ 2645 7778).

Money and exchange The Banco Nacional (with an ATM) sits at the northern apex of the triangle in Santa Elena.

Post office Just east of *Casa del Café Monteverde*, on the road from Santa Elena to Cerro Plano (Mon–Fri 8am–noon & 1–4.30pm).

Reserva Biológica Bosque Nuboso Monteverde

Daily 7am–4pm • $18 • ☎ 2645 5122, ⓦ reservamonteverde.com

Attracting visitors in their droves, the **RESERVA BIOLÓGICA BOSQUE NUBOSO MONTEVERDE** (Monteverde Cloudforest Biological Reserve) is one of the last sizeable pockets of primary cloudforest in Mesoamerica. At an altitude of 1440m and straddling the Continental Divide, the reserve was established in 1972 by George Powell (an American biologist) and Wilford Guindon (a local Quaker) to protect the country's rapidly dwindling pristine cloudforest. Today, it encompasses ten square kilometres of protected land and is administered by the nonprofit Centro Científico Tropical (Tropical Science Centre), based in San José.

VOLUNTEERING IN THE RESERVES

Both the Santa Elena and Monteverde reserves depend significantly on **volunteer labour**. Volunteers are assigned tasks according to their experience – activities include trail maintenance, teaching English and helping with conservation projects. At **Monteverde**, volunteers are expected to work Monday to Friday from 7am to 4pm and Saturday from 7am to 11.30am, for a minimum of two weeks. The reserve charges $20 per day, which includes accommodation with a local family, three meals a day and laundry. For more information on volunteering at **Santa Elena**, email ❸ reservaciones@reservasanta elena.org.

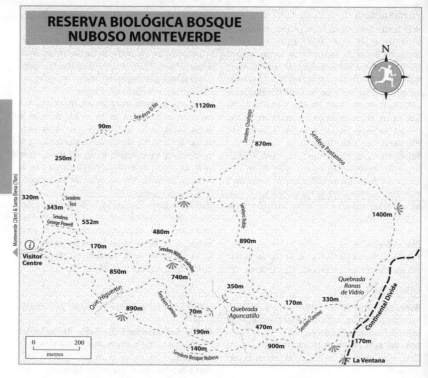

RESERVA BIOLÓGICA BOSQUE NUBOSO MONTEVERDE

The reserve's sheer diversity of **terrain** – from semi-dwarf stunted forest on the wind-exposed areas to thick, bearded cloudforest vegetation elsewhere – supports six different **life zones**, or eco-communities, hosting an estimated 3000 species of plant, more than 100 types of mammal, some 490 species of butterfly and over 400 species of bird, including the resplendent quetzal and the three-wattled bellbird. The cloudforest cover – dense, low-lit and heavy – can make it difficult to spot wildlife, though the amazing diversity of tropical plants and insects more than makes up for this, with guided walks leading past thick mosses, epiphytes, bromeliads, primitive ferns, leaf-cutter ants and poison-dart frogs.

The trails

Nine **trails** wind through 13km of the reserve and most are contained in a roughly triangular pocket known as **El Triángulo**. They're clearly marked and easily walkable (at least in the dry season), and many of them are along wooden or concrete pathways that help prevent slipping and sliding on seas of mud.

If you're keen to plunge straight into the cloudforest, make for the **Sendero Bosque Nuboso** (1.8km). The forest canopy along this trail is literally dripping with moisture, each tree thickly encrusted with moss and epiphytes. You'll probably hear howler monkeys and the unmistakeable "boink" of the three-wattled bellbird, but it's difficult to spot either in this dense cover – your best bet for birdwatching is at the beginning of the trail. The spongy terrain efficiently preserves animal tracks, and in the morning especially you may see tracks from agouti or coati. One creature that you will see on this trail is the clearwing butterfly, whose transparent wings are as fragile as the thinnest parchment.

At the end of the trail, a small *mirador*, **La Ventana**, has vistas of the thickly forested hills on the other side of the Continental Divide. It's reached via a staircase of cement-laid steps that lead to a lookout point suspended over an amazingly green expanse of hills – a surreal place, with only the sound of wind as company.

The **Sendero Camino** (2km), higher in elevation than the others, is stony, deeply rutted in spots and often muddy, but as this trail (which also leads to La Ventana) is wider than the others, it gets more sunlight, attracting greater numbers of birds and butterflies. Often quite steep, the **Sendero Pantanoso** (1.4km) passes through sun-dappled swamp forests and leads past magnolias and the rare podocarpus – the reserve's only conifer. It links with **Sendero El Río** (1.1km) to bring you, in a long arch, back to the park's entrance. The **Sendero Wilford Guindon** features a 100m suspension bridge that takes you high up into the trees for great bird's-eye views of the cloudforest canopy.

The tours

Guided tours Daily 7.30am, noon & 1.30pm • 2–3hr • $32 • Book a day in advance through your hotel or the reserve office **Birdwatching** Daily 5.45pm • $64 • 6hr **Night walk** Daily 6.15pm • 2hr • $17 • Transport to the reserve visitor centre for the night walk ($5) leaves from Santa Elena at 5.40pm • ☎ 2645 5122, ⊚ reservamonteverde.com

The reserve runs excellent **guided tours**, with knowledgeable guides who have a knack for spotting wildlife you'd never see on your own, as well as early-morning **birdwatching tours** and a fascinating if eerie **night walk**. Many of the reserve's animals are nocturnal, and your chances of seeing one, albeit only as two brilliant eyes shining out of the night, are vastly increased after dark – you may spot tarantulas, toucans with their beaks tucked between their feathers, and some guides will even catch bats. Although the guides carry a powerful flashlight, it's useful to bring your own, as well as rain gear.

ARRIVAL AND DEPARTURE

BOSQUE NUBOSO MONTEVERDE

By bus Several buses make the 6km run from Santa Elena to the reserve (daily 6.15am, 7.30am, 1.20pm & 3pm, returning 6.45am, 11.30am, 2pm & 4pm; $1 each way; 30min); they depart from the southern road of the triangle in Santa Elena.

By taxi A taxi from Santa Elena costs about $10.

THE CLOUDFOREST

The most obvious property of the cloudforest is its dense, dripping **wetness**. Cloudforests are formed by a constant, near-one-hundred-percent humidity created by mists, produced here when northeasterly trade winds from the Caribbean drift across the high ridge of the Continental Divide to cool and become dense clouds settling over this high-altitude forest.

The cloudforest environment can be rather eerie, due to the sheer layering of vegetation, and the preponderance of **epiphytes** – plants that grow on other living plants for physical rather than nutritional support. Everything seems to be stacked on top of each other, and when walking the Monteverde and Santa Elena trails you'll notice that green mosses wholly carpet many trees, while others seem to be choked by multiple layers of strangler vines, small plants, ferns and drooping lianas.

The **leaves** of cloudforest plants are often dotted with scores of tiny holes, as though they were gnawed by insects that soon gave up – which is, in effect, exactly the case. Many cloudforest plants produce toxins to deter insects from eating an entire leaf or plant. The plants are able to produce these poisons because they harbour excess energy that would otherwise be used to protect themselves against adverse weather conditions, such as a prolonged dry season or heavy winds and rain. The insects, in turn, guard themselves by eating only a little of a leaf, and by sampling a wide variety, so that they are not overwhelmed by one powerful toxin.

For an in-depth look into cloudforests, check out *An Introduction to Cloudforest Trees*, by William Haber, Willow Zuchowski and Erick Bello, available at the reserve visitor centre and in bookshops in San José.

INFORMATION

Guides In addition to the official tours, which depart from the visitors' centre at the entrance, a number of experienced local guides can lead you through the reserve; try AGUINAMON (☎ 2645 6282, ⍟ aguinamon.webs.com; tours from $17), the Association of Naturalist Guides of Monteverde.

What to bring Temperatures are cool at this altitude (15°C or 16°C is not uncommon, though in the sun it often feels more like 22°C to 25°C), and the average rainfall is 3000mm per year, so dress in layers and carry an umbrella and light rain gear. You should also bring binoculars and insect repellent; you might get away without rubber boots in the dry season, but you'll most definitely need them in the wet – the reserve office rents out both boots and binoculars.

When to go The reserve imposes a quota on the number of people allowed in the cloudforest at any given time (220), so it's a good idea to arrive early. Serious birders, wildlife spotters and those who would prefer to walk the trails in peace should avoid the peak hours of 8–11am, when tour groups pour in.

Reserva Santa Elena

7km northeast of Santa Elena • Daily 7am–4pm • $14 • ☎ 2645 5390, ⍟ reservasantaelena.org • Daily buses run from Santa Elena at 6.30am, 8.30am, 10.30am & 12.30pm, returning at 11am, 1pm, 3pm & 4pm ($2 each way; 30min; book in advance via ☎ 2645 6332) • A taxi costs about $12

Less touristed than Monteverde, the **RESERVA SANTA ELENA**, 7km northeast of Santa Elena, offers an equally memorable cloudforest experience. Poised at an elevation of 1650m, the three-square-kilometre reserve is higher than Monteverde and boasts steeper, more challenging trails and a slightly better chance of seeing quetzals (and three-wattled bellbirds) in season. Established in 1992, the self-funded reserve is

---

WATCHING WILDLIFE IN MONTEVERDE AND SANTA ELENA

WHAT YOU MIGHT SEE...

Ever since **National Geographic** declared that Monteverde might just be the best place in all of Central America to see the **resplendent quetzal**, spotting one has become almost a rite of passage, and many zealous, binocular-toting birders come here with this express purpose in mind. This slim bird, with a sweet face and tiny beak, is extraordinarily colourful, with shimmering green feathers on the back and head, and a rich, carmine stomach. The male quetzal is the more spectacular, with a long, picturesque tail and fuzzy crown. About a hundred pairs of quetzals mate at Monteverde, in monogamous pairs, between March and June. During this period, they descend to slightly lower altitudes than their usual stratospheric heights, coming down to about 1000m to nest in dead or dying trees, hollowing out a niche in which to lay their blue eggs. Your best chance of seeing one is on a guided tour; alternatively arrive on your own just after dawn, the most fruitful time to spot birds.

Another bird to look out for, particularly in Santa Elena (and from March to August), is the bizarre-looking **three-wattled bellbird**, whose three black "wattles", or skin pockets, hang down from its beak; even if you don't see one, you'll almost certainly hear its distinctive metallic call, which has been likened to a pinball machine. The far rarer **bare-necked umbrella bird** can only be seen in Santa Elena, and not very often at that, but those lucky enough to witness its spectacular mating routine will never forget it.

Several types of endangered **cat**, including puma, jaguar, ocelot, jaguarundi and margay, live in the reserve, which provides ample space for hunting. You're unlikely to come face to face with a jaguar, but if you're lucky, you may hear the growl of a big cat coming out of the dense forest – usually unnerving enough to cure you of your desire to actually see one.

AND WHAT YOU DEFINITELY WON'T...

Another famous resident (now thought to be extinct) of the Monteverde area is the vibrant red-orange *sapo dorado*, or **golden toad**. First discovered here in 1964, the golden toad hasn't been spotted in many years and is thought to have either been killed off by global warming – the mean minimum temperature in Monteverde has risen from 15°C in 1988 to around 17°C today – or to have succumbed to the chytrid fungus that has decimated amphibian populations worldwide over the last few decades.

supported by entrance fees and donations and depends largely on volunteers, particularly foreign university students. It's run by the local high school board, whose students help maintain the trails year-round.

The **visitor centre** at the reserve entrance has a small interpretive display documenting the life of the cloudforest ecosystem and the history of the reserve itself, and hands out a helpful leaflet on cloudforests, epiphytes and some of the mammals you might see here. It also rents out rubber boots and has a **cafeteria** that provides coffee, cold drinks and sandwiches.

The trails

Guided walks daily 7.30am, 9am & 11.30am • $15 • 3hr

Santa Elena's 12km network of **trails** is confined to an area just east of the entrance – cut wood and mesh cover some trails, while others are rough tracks. The easiest is the hour-long **Youth Challenge Trail** (1.4km) with an observation tower halfway along, from where it's possible to see Volcán Arenal on clear days; for the best chance of viewing the volcano, arrive early before cloud, mist and fog roll in to obliterate vistas. The longest, the **Caño Negro Trail** (4.5km), named after the river that flows from here north to the border with Nicaragua, takes about four hours to complete and crosses two streams en route. There's also a **wheelchair-accessible trail** that loops from the visitors' centre, passing a couple of lookouts and a small orchid garden.

You'll see plenty of hummingbirds – strung along the entrance path is a line of feeders that draw many of the multicoloured birds – but for a better chance of viewing all the wildlife that lives here, sign up for one of the highly recommended **guided walks**.

Puntarenas and around

Heat-stunned **PUNTARENAS**, a thin, island-like finger of sand pointing out into the Gulf of Nicoya 115km west of San José, has the look of raffish abandonment that haunts so many tropical port cities. It's hard to believe now, but in the seventeenth century this was a prosperous port – the export point for much of Costa Rica's coffee to England – and a popular resort for holidaying Ticos. Today, most vacationing Costa Ricans have abandoned its dodgy beaches, and foreign tourists, who never spent much time here anyway, come only to catch a ferry across to southern Nicoya. More importantly, this working port remains a jumping-off point for pristine **Isla Tortuga** (see p.327) and two of Costa Rica's least-explored islands: **Isla de Chira** (see p.325) and **Isla del Coco** (see box, p.326).

Puntarenas's decaying streets exude a certain melancholy charm. The southerly promenade is optimistically called **Paseo de los Turistas**, from the eastern end of which the old dock crooks out into the gulf. This is where bananas and coffee were loaded, before all the big shipping traffic shifted 18km down the coast to Puerto Caldera; it's now used by giant cruise ships. The docks on the northern, **estuary** side, are a jungle of ketches and sturdy mini-trawlers testifying to a thriving fishing industry. Despite the aura of hot lassitude, plenty of business is conducted in the few blocks surrounding the docks, especially in the hectic **mercado**. Though safe enough during the day, it's best to avoid the docks at night.

Casa de la Cultura and Museo Histórico Marino

Av Central, C 5 **Casa de la Cultura** Mon–Fri 8am–4pm • Free **Museo Histórico Marino** Tues–Sun 9.45am–noon & 1–5.15pm • Free • ☎ 2661 1394

In the centre of town, the orange colonial-style **Casa de la Cultura** exhibits evocative *fin-de-siècle* photographs documenting Puntarenas' lost prosperity. Sepia images of tough fishermen hang alongside photos of white-clad ladies whose husbands made their wealth from coffee exports. The Casa's **Museo Histórico Marino** has a rundown of the region's archeology, biology and history, focusing on the town's relationship with the sea that virtually surrounds it.

Parque Marino del Pacífico

Paseo de los Turistas, C 4 • Tues–Sun 9am–5pm • $7, children $4 • ☎ 2661 5272, ⊕ parquemarino.org

Two blocks east of the bus station, **Parque Marino del Pacífico** is a small aquarium and rescue centre dedicated to Costa Rica's marine life. Among the species here are clown fish, nurse sharks, seahorses, eels and anemones. There's also a (marine life-free) swimming pool for children (Fri–Sun).

ARRIVAL AND DEPARTURE   **PUNTARENAS**

Puntarenas is something of a transport hub, with several daily buses to San José, Liberia, Monteverde, Jacó and Quepos. While the bridge across the Río Tempisque north of town has made access to the **Nicoya Peninsula** easier, **ferries** are still popular, particularly if you're heading to Montezuma and other destinations around the peninsula's southern tip.

BY BUS

Services to and from San José use the bus station on the corner of C 2 and Paseo de los Turistas, just southeast of the Casa de la Cultura, as do services from Liberia. Buses from Santa Elena/Monteverde (3 daily from Puntarenas: 7.50am, 1.50pm & 2.15pm) pull in at the bus stop on the opposite side of the *paseo*. If you're heading south along the coast to Manuel Antonio, you'll need to take the Quepos service from the bus station; the bus runs via Jacó (1hr 30min).
Destinations Liberia (9 daily; 3hr); Puntarenas (4.20am, 6am & 3pm; 3hr 30min); Quepos (8 daily; 3hr); San José (hourly; 2hr).

BY FERRY

Ferries dock at the northwestern end of Puntarenas, a 15min

walk from the city centre; buses (labelled "FERRY") run up and down Av Central. It can be a slow process buying a car ticket, so in high season arrive at least an hour before departure and park in the queue before purchasing your ticket.
Paquera Navieras Tambor (☎ 2661 2084, ⊕ naviera tambor.com) travels to Paquera (6 daily; $1.50; 1hr 15min), from where buses run on to Montezuma (2hr), via Tambor (50min) and Cóbano (1hr 30min); the 5pm ferry is the last one that connects with this service. You'll need to change buses in Cóbano for Mal País and Santa Teresa (daily 10.30am & 2.30pm; 30min).
Playa Naranjo COONATRAMAR (☎ 2661 1069) travels to Playa Naranjo (6.30am, 10am, 2.20pm & 7.30pm, returning 8am, 12.30pm, 5.30pm & 9pm; 1hr), from where buses travel on to Nicoya (4 daily; 2hr).

INFORMATION

Tourist information You can pick up maps and brochures from the tourist office on the second floor of the Plaza del Pacífico, the large white building opposite the Capitanía

de Puerto (Mon–Fri 8am–5.30pm, Sat 8am–12.30pm; ☎ 2661 2980).

ACCOMMODATION

If you're catching an early ferry to Paquera, you may find the **budget hotels** around the north-shore docks quite handy, though be warned that at night this area can be seedy, and at some of the more dismal hotels the clientele may not be there for sleeping. Even considering Costa Rica's tropical climate, Puntarenas stands out as an exceptionally hot town – wherever you stay, make sure your room has a **fan** (or even better a/c) that works, otherwise you'll be as baked as a ceramic pot by morning.

CANOPY TOUR SANTA ELENA (P.314)) >

6

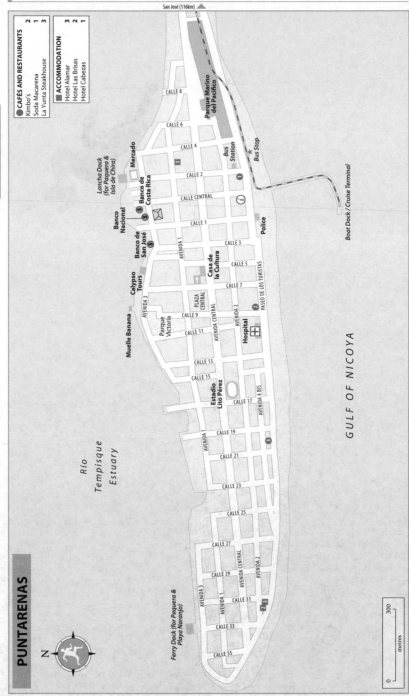

PUNTARENAS

● CAFÉS AND RESTAURANTS
Kimbo's   2
Soda Macarena   1
La Yunta Steakhouse   3

■ ACCOMMODATION
Hotel Alamar   3
Hotel Las Brisas   2
Hotel Cabezas   1

San José (116km)

Parque Marino del Pacífico

CALLE 8
CALLE 6
CALLE 4
CALLE 2
Bus Station
Bus Stop
Mercado
Lancha Dock (for Paquera & Isla de Chira)
Banco de Costa Rica
CALLE CENTRAL
Banco Nacional
Banco de San José
CALLE 1
Police
Boat Dock / Cruise Terminal
AVENIDA 1
CALLE 3
CALLE 5
Casa de la Cultura
Calypso Tours
CALLE 7
PASEO DE LOS TURISTAS
AVENIDA 3
Muelle Banana
AVENIDA 2
PLAZA CENTRAL
CALLE 9
AVENIDA CENTRAL
Parque Victoria
CALLE 11
Hospital
GULF OF NICOYA
CALLE 13
CALLE 15
Estadio Lito Pérez
CALLE 17
AVENIDA 4 BIS
AVENIDA 1
CALLE 19
CALLE 21
CALLE 23
Río Tempisque Estuary
CALLE 25
CALLE 27
CALLE 29
AVENIDA 3
AVENIDA CENTRAL
AVENIDA 2
AVENIDA 1
CALLE 31
Ferry Dock (for Paquera & Playa Naranjo)
CALLE 33
CALLE 35

N

0   300
     metres

Hotel Alamar Paseo de los Turistas, C 31/33 ☎ 2661 4343, ⓦ alamarcr.com. One of the better options on the seafront strip, the spacious rooms in this family-friendly hotel have a/c, cable TV and private bathrooms. There are two pools, a hot tub, secure parking and a restaurant. $72

Hotel Las Brisas Corner of Paseo de los Turistas & C 33 ☎ 2661 4040, ⓦ lasbrisashotelcr.com. Relax at this cheerful, clean waterfront hotel on the peninsula's southwestern tip. Rooms come with TVs, phones and a/c; some also have balconies overlooking the Gulf of Nicoya. Splash about in the swimming pool and enjoy Greek fare at the breezy café. $80

Hotel Cabezas Av 1, C 2/4 ☎ 2661 1045. A couple of blocks from the dock, this airy budget option – the best low-cost hotel in town – is painted in pink and yellow tones and has a number of clean, basic rooms with fans, TVs and either shared or private bathrooms. $25

EATING, DRINKING AND NIGHTLIFE

Perhaps because of its history as a bona fide resort, eating out in Puntarenas tends to be expensive; even fish – probably caught no more than a couple of hundred metres away – can be pricey. Pick up an inexpensive meal in the **mercado**, on Av 3, but avoid drinking anything made with the local water. Or, linger over a quiet drink or a seafood lunch at the beachside *sodas* near the **old dock**. For **nightlife**, the Casa de la Cultura hosts concerts on summer weekends (Dec–April). Some of the larger hotels have nightclubs that draw crowds on Saturday nights and holiday weekends, and you can always enjoy drinks at the open-air **bars** along the Paseo de los Turistas.

Kimbo's Paseo de los Turistas, C 7/9 ☎ 2661 2923. This lively restaurant and bar serves fried fish, grilled prawns and the like (around $15). Tico tourists pop in for drinks at night, when the music, from salsa and merengue to Costa Rican karaoke classics, cranks up. Daily 7am–2.30am.

Soda Macarena Opposite the bus station. This small *soda* with ocean views serves up cheap, delicious fare (from $5), from fruit plates to toasted sandwiches; try their "Churchills", similar to a crushed-ice *granizado* but made with ice cream. Daily 10am–midnight.

La Yunta Steakhouse Paseo de los Turistas, C 19/21 ☎ 2661 3216. Carnivores can enjoy superb ocean vistas while tucking into succulent slices of meat (around $15–20), and there's plenty on offer for fish fanatics, from sea-food risotto to octopus ceviche. Daily 10am–midnight.

DIRECTORY

Money and exchange The Banco de Costa Rica, Banco de San José and Banco Nacional, virtually next to each other on Av 3, have ATMs and currency exchange.

Post office In the town centre, just a few blocks northwest of the bus station (Mon–Fri 8am–5pm, Sat 8am–noon).

Isla de Chira

Shaped like a dinosaur skull and surrounded by crocodile-infested mangrove swamps, untouristed **ISLA DE CHIRA** is like stepping back in time to Costa Rica three decades ago. At 42 square kilometres, it is the largest island in the Gulf of Nicoya, home to three thousand Ticos who eke out a simple existence through small-scale fishing and subsistence farming. Inhabited since pre-Columbian times, more than a third of the island is mangroves, the remainder essentially farmland and tropical dry forest. Running water and the first car didn't arrive until the early 1990s, and you can still count on one hand the number of vehicles that pass daily along the island's rough main road.

On the surface it seems there would be little to entice visitors, but one of Costa Rica's most inspiring rural ecotourism projects is under way here. In 2000, with overfishing impacting on the island's traditional economy, a group of local women resolved to generate an alternative income based on promoting the responsible use of Isla de Chira's natural resources. Their decision to establish the island's first proper tourism initiative (consisting of a small hotel, restaurant and nature tours) was met with scepticism by the community – many feared tourism would bring prostitution, and some of the husbands felt threatened by their wives' entrepreneurship, accusing them of visiting San José to find new boyfriends rather than attend business meetings. But with international funding, the **Asociación de Damas de la Isla de Chira** soldiered on, buying a small plot of forested land and the materials to build a lodge, restaurant and small fibreglass boat.

Hiking trails lead from *La Amistad Lodge* (see opposite) to lookout points, and bikes can be borrowed to explore the island. Boat tours are offered to mangrove swamps and to Isla Paloma, a tiny aquatic bird sanctuary that is an important nesting site for pelican, frigate, great egret and cormorant. About 2km east of the lodge an association of female artisans have a shop where they make and sell locally produced jewellery and crafts.

6

PARQUE NACIONAL ISLA DEL COCO

Rising dramatically out of the Pacific Ocean 535km southwest of the Costa Rican mainland, **PARQUE NACIONAL ISLA DEL COCO** is revered among divers, biologists and treasure-hunters. Gigantic waterfalls plunge off jungle-strewn cliffs straight into an underwater world that has made this national park a veritable "Costa Rican Galapagos". It's the only island in this part of the Pacific that receives enough rain to support the growth of rainforest and is home to 150 endemic species that are found nowhere else in the world, including the Cocos flycatcher and the Cocos gecko. In addition, more than 250 species of fish – including one of the world's largest concentrations of hammerhead and white-tipped reef **sharks** – patrol the surrounding waters. The rugged, mist-shrouded volcanic island itself appeared as "Dinosaur Island" in **Jurassic Park**: in the opening frames of the film, a helicopter swoops over azure seas to a remote, emerald-green isle – that's Coco.

Nearly 25 square kilometres in size, Isla del Coco is one of the world's largest uninhabited islands, yet few would be able to locate it on a map. Perhaps that's why pirates found it such a perfect hideout during the seventeenth and eighteenth centuries. Legend has it the golden spoils from fruitful church-looting expeditions to Lima were buried here; known as the "Lima Booty", the stories sparked a frenzy of treasure-seeking missions. More than 500 tried their luck (and failed) before Isla del Coco was declared a national park in 1978, ending all gold-digging expeditions. Though evidence suggests that the island was known by pre-Columbian seagoing peoples from Ecuador and Colombia, in the modern age it was "discovered" by the navigator and sea captain Joan Cabezas in 1526. Attempts were made to establish a colony here in the early twentieth century, and nowadays wild descendants of the would-be settlers' pigs and coffee plants have upset the island's ecosystem.

Today, however, conservation is the order of the day on this **UNESCO World Heritage Site**, although illegal fishing, shark-finning in particular, within the 15km restriction zone is rife, and park rangers and marine organizations lack the resources to bring it under control. Despite this, Isla del Coco remains an increasingly coveted destination for experienced **scuba divers**. More than a thousand a year brave the gut-wrenching **32-hour boat journey** from Puntarenas to spend a week or so moored in the island's sheltered harbour on liveaboard boats. The subterranean treasures range from underwater caves and technicolour coral reefs to schools of manta rays and, off the northeastern side of the island, the occasional whale shark. The real danger here, however, is not sharks but **strong currents**, and divers often wear gloves to grip onto rocks to stop themselves from drifting away. Water temperatures are a balmy 22–26°C and the best time of year for seeing sharks is the rainy season (May–Nov). Two sheltered bays provide access to the island itself, and during the day visitors can venture onshore to hike the steaming tropical forests.

INFORMATION AND DIVING COMPANIES

Tourist information Contact the national park itself on ☎ 2258 8570 or ☎ 2250 7295 or Fundación Amigos de La Isla del Coco (☎ 2256 7476, ⓦ cocosisland.org), which was founded in 1994 to help preserve the unique terrestrial and marine biodiversity of Coco. **Aggressor** ☎ 2289 2261 or US ☎ 1 800 438 2628,

ⓦ aggressor.com. This diving and liveaboard operator runs 10-day trips (packages from $4735) from Puntarenas. **Undersea Hunter** ☎ 2228 6613 or US ☎ 1 800 203 2120, ⓦ underseahunter.com. Runs similar expeditions to Aggressor, also departing Puntarenas, with ten- to twelve-day trips ($4595–6295).

ARRIVAL AND TOURS

By lancha The easiest way to get to Isla de Chira is from Puntarenas: a *lancha* leaves daily from the dock near the *mercado* (1.30pm, returning 6am; 2hr), and is met by a public bus, which can stop on request at *La Amistad Lodge*, 10km east.

By ferry Ferries run between Costa de Pájoros, 33km northwest of Puntarenas (3 daily; 45min), reached by taking any bus heading towards Cañas and transferring in Chomes, and Isla de Chira.

Tours Tours can be arranged through ACTUAR (☎2248

ISLA DE CHIRA

9470, ⓦactuarcostarica.com), whose overnight package (around $130) includes full-board accommodation at *La Amistad Lodge* with bike trips, a birdwatching tour and a boat ride through the mangroves, plus the ferry from Costa de Pájaros; they also offer a day-trip departing from San Pablo, southwest of the Río Tempisque Bridge. ACTUAR can arrange direct transfers from Isla de Chira to the Reserva de Vida Silvestre Karen Mogensen (see p.328) on the southern Nicoya Peninsula.

ACCOMMODATION AND EATING

La Amistad Lodge ☎2248 9470, ⓦactuarcostarica .com. This lodge is the fruit of the labour of Asociación de Damas de la Isla de Chira, consisting of partially-open basic

bungalows (bring a mosquito net) and a dorm with private hot-water bathrooms. Rates include three delicious home-cooked meals. Homestays can also be organized. **$60**

The southern Nicoya Peninsula

Most visitors' first sight of the **southern Nicoya Peninsula** is from the slow-paced ferry from Puntarenas: you'll see its low brown hills rising up in the distance, ringed by a rugged coastline and pockets of intense jungly green. Much of the region, though, has been cleared for farming or cattle grazing, or, in the case of the surf towns on its far southwestern tip, given over to tourism.

The area's main town is **Cóbano**, a dull transport hub with a petrol station, a post office and a Banco Nacional with an ATM, a rare convenience in these parts. Most tourists pass straight through on their way to the thriving coastal towns of **Mal País**, **Santa Teresa** or **Montezuma**, one of Costa Rica's most popular beach hangouts. The partly paved road to Montezuma, lined by acres of cattle pasture, offers a startling – and disconcerting – vision of the future of the deforested tropics. Once covered with dense, primary Pacific lowland forest, today only stumps dot the fields. Still, heroic efforts are being made by local conservationists to create a biological corridor throughout the peninsula, with the wildlife refuges of **Reserva Karen Mogensen** and **Curú** proving that nature can – and is – making a comeback.

Isla Tortuga

One of the most popular day-trip destinations in Costa Rica, **ISLA TORTUGA** is actually two large uninhabited islands (over three square kilometres in total), just off the coast of the Nicoya Peninsula near Paquera. Characterized by its poster-perfect white sands, palm-lined beaches and lush, tropical deciduous vegetation, it's certainly a picturesque place, offering quiet – during the week, at least – sheltered swimming and snorkelling. At the weekend, however, boatloads of passengers come ashore roughly at the same time, somewhat marring the islands' image as an isolated pristine tropical paradise.

There's plenty of opportunity for spotting **marine animals**, including large whale sharks, depending upon the season. You also pass by Negritos and Guayabo island

---

GETTING TO/FROM THE NICOYA PENINSULA

The quickest way to get to the southern Nicoya Peninsula is on one of the daily ferries from Puntarenas to Paquera or Playa Naranjo (see p.322). Buses generally meet these ferries and travel on to Montezuma (from Paquera) and Nicoya (from Playa Naranjo).

sanctuaries, where swarms of **sea birds** nest, including brown pelicans and magnificent frigatebirds. On the island, there's time for lunch (usually included in the tour price) and **snorkelling**, followed by sunbathing or a little walking.

ARRIVAL AND TOURS

One-day cruises (2hr each way; $115–139 including from San José, Jacó or Quepos) are offered by **Calypso Tours** (☏ 2256 2727, ⊛ calypsotours.com) and **Bay Island Cruises** (☏ 2258 3536, ⊛ bayislandcruises.com); slower-paced, cheaper tours run from Curú (see p.331), Montezuma (see p.333), and Mal País and Santa Teresa (see p.338).

Reserva de Vida Silvestre Karen Mogensen

20km southwest of Playa Naranjo • Daily 8am-4pm • $7 • ASEPALECO ☏ 2650 0607, ⊛ asepaleco.com

The wildlife-rich **RESERVA DE VIDA SILVESTRE KAREN MOGENSEN** offers the most rewarding ecotourism experience on the southern Nicoya Peninsula. This nine-square-kilometre patch of primary and secondary dry-humid tropical forest functions as both a private reserve and tourist lodge, and has become the most crucial link in an expanding biological corridor that runs between the Reserva Natural Absoluta Cabo Blanco, 85km south at the end of the peninsula, and Parque Nacional Barra Honda, 50km north in Guanacaste. Named after the late Karen Mogensen, the Danish conservationist who was instrumental in creating Cabo Blanco (see p.335), the reserve was established in 1996 by the local not-for-profit ASEPALECO – a name that references the peninsula's three main towns, Paquerea, Lepanto and Cóbano.

Fence removal, tree planting and natural regeneration has returned this former patch of farmland into a fully functioning jungle ecosystem. Endangered **plant species** such as rónrón, mahogany, teak and ebony grow in the reserve, while white-faced and howler **monkeys** abound, and deer roam the forest, preyed on by elusive pumas. More than 240 species of **bird** have been spotted, including great curassow, motmot, long-tailed manakin, spectacled owl and three-wattled bellbird.

Five kilometres of well-maintained **hiking trails** run through the reserve, leading to lookouts with jaw-dropping views of the Gulf of Nicoya as well as to one of the most breathtaking waterfalls in the country – the 18m **Catarata Velo de Novia** (Bridal Veil Falls), which cascades down a rounded cliffside before dropping to a deep, turquoise swimming hole.

ARRIVAL AND DEPARTURE

RESERVA KAREN MOGENSEN

To/from Jicaral The reserve is best accessed from the village of San Ramón de Río Blanco, 16km southwest of Jicaral by rough road; buses for Jicaral meet the ferry at Playa Naranjo (4 daily; 30min), or you can get here from San José, on one of the two daily buses that leave from C 12, Av 7/9 (6am & 3.30pm).

Destinations San José (4.45am & 2.30pm; 4hr); Nicoya (4 daily; 1hr 30min).
To/from the reserve Once in Jicaral, take a taxi (around $25) or 4WD vehicle (organized via ASEPALECO; similar price) to the reserve entrance.

INFORMATION

Left luggage ASEPALECO can store excess luggage in their office in the town of Jicaral.
What to bring The temperature drops a few degrees on the mountain at night, so pack something warm and

waterproof. Rubber boots are essential, as you'll be crossing five rivers on the hike up to the lodge; the reserve office can supply them for average sizes.

ACCOMMODATION

★**Cerro Escondido Posada Rural** ☏ 2650 0607 or ☏ 2248 9470 for English, ⊛ actuarcostarica.com. Remote but comfortable, featuring four solar-powered

cabins with private bathrooms and wide balconies; the adjacent open-air restaurant serves delicious buffet-style meals, and at night local musicians provide entertainment.

FROM TOP RESERVA KAREN MOGENSEN; VARIEGATED SQUIRREL, RESERVA NATURAL ABSOLUTA CABO BLANCO (SEE P.335) >

Rates include three meals and the services of a local guide, and profits are reinvested in purchasing more land and planting trees. Due to the effort involved in getting here (it's a 3km uphill hike from San Ramón de Río Blanco, or a 1hr horse ride from the town of Montaña Grande, 6km northeast), visitors are encouraged to stay at least two nights. $71

Tambor

Since 1992, when Spanish hotel group Barceló unveiled its four-hundred-room *Hotel de Playa Tambor*, the small village of **TAMBOR** has become synonymous with large-scale tourist-resort development (see box below). Despite the presence of the mega-hotel – set off by itself, with its own road, grounds and guards – the whole area remains rather remote, and the village, surrounded on two sides by thickly forested hills, exudes a friendly, laidback vibe missing in some of the peninsula's more touristed resorts. Its sandy beach stretches along a narrow horseshoe strip at the western end of the sheltered **Bahía Ballena** where, true to its name, you can sometimes spot *ballenas* (whales).

ARRIVAL AND DEPARTURE   TAMBOR

By plane NatureAir (⊕ natureair.com) and Sansa (⊕ flysansa.com) flights from San José to Tambor (8 daily; 25min) land at the small airstrip about 4.5km out of town.

By bus The bus that runs between Montezuma and Paquera (6 daily; 50min) stops in Tambor.

ACCOMMODATION AND EATING

Cabinas Cristina A block back from the beach ☎ 2683 0028, ✉ cabinascristina@ice.co.cr. This chilled-out place is the best budget accommodation in Tambor, with basic but clean rooms, most with private bathrooms and one with kitchen. The Tico owners dish up lovingly prepared meals at the popular on-site restaurant and can arrange tours. $35

Hotel Costa Coral Near the bus stop ☎ 2683 0105, ⊕ hotelcostacoral.com. Friendly owners run this boutique hotel, where rooms have a/c and TVs with DVD players; most also have a private terrace overlooking the pretty pool area

and tropical gardens. There's a restaurant (mains $18–34) and spa too (massages from $60). Rates drop by $30 Sun–Thurs. $225

Hotel Tambor Tropical Facing Playa Tambor ☎ 2683 0011, ⊕ tambortropical.com. The best place to stay in town, *Tambor Tropical* is set in palm gardens facing languid Playa Tambor, with an inviting pool, hot tub and beautiful wooden *cabinas* with large kitchens; no children under 16 are allowed. It's also the base for Seascape Kayak Tours, which runs recommended trips to nearby Curú (see opposite). $160

Refugio de Vida Silvestre Curú

16km northeast of Tambor • Daily 7am–3pm • $10 • ☎ 2641 0100, ⊕ curuwildliferefuge.com

The small, semi-privately owned **REFUGIO DE VIDA SILVESTRE CURÚ** protects a wide variety of flora, including deciduous forest and many endangered mangrove species.

HOTEL DE PLAYA TAMBOR: PARADISE LOST?

The building of the **Hotel de Playa Tambor** is a textbook example of the type of development environmental agencies are increasingly struggling to prevent from tarnishing Costa Rica's well-earned eco credentials. The hotel has been plagued by controversy since before it even opened, and throughout its construction the backers at times seemed willfully bent on acting out every environmental and social gaffe possible. Barceló was convicted of both **illegally draining and filling mangrove swamps**, an ecologically valuable resource similar to those protected by the nearby Refugio de Vida Silvestre Curú. They were also accused of **violating Costa Rican law** dictating that the first 50m of any beach is public property, with no development or habitation allowed. Despite an order ruling that the project be stopped, the government, in the end, appeared unwilling to close them down. Grupo Barceló now owns several other hotels throughout Costa Rica.

Pretty white-sand beaches, dotted with rocky coves and backed by exuberantly chaotic palm fronds, unfold along the reserve's coasts where, at low tide, rocky pools yield crabs and assorted shellfish.

A network of **trails** fans out through the reserve (you can pick up a map from the office): the long Sendero Quesara and Sendero Posa Colorado trails lead down to picturesque beaches, while the shorter Sendero Finca de los Monos passes through mangroves and is a good place to spot some of the reserve's great variety of **wildlife**, including northern tamanduas, iguanas and agoutis. You're also likely to see or hear monkeys – white-faced capuchin, howler and squirrel, who were reintroduced a few years ago after being driven to extinction on the Nicoya Peninsula. Of the many bird species in evidence, the most exciting to spot are the **scarlet macaws**, which can sometimes be seen foraging for almonds along the coast. Extinct locally since the late 1960s, they were reintroduced to Curú in 1999 and have successfully bred in the years since.

ARRIVAL AND TOURS

CURÚ

By bus Buses from Tambor to Paquera (6 daily; 15min) pass by the reserve entrance, from where it's a 2km walk to the administration office.

★**Seascape Kayak Tours** Based at Hotel Tambor Tropical (see opposite) ☎ 8314 8605, ⓦ seascape kayaktours.com. Runs excellent small-group kayak trips in the waters off Curú, with an emphasis on wildlife-watching and learning about the local environment; you're likely to see dolphins, turtles and spotted eagle rays en route. The half-day ($85) or full-day ($150, including gourmet lunch and snorkelling) tours run from November to April and include entrance to the reserve.

It also runs multiday trips, camping overnight on white-sand beaches.

Turismo Curú By the administration office ☎ 2641 0004, ⓦ curutourism.com. Organizes guided walks ($15/person; 1hr 30min) and horseriding tours ($10/hour) around the reserve, as well as night walks ($20/person; 1hr 30min) for overnight visitors, which can help pick out some of the wildlife that you might otherwise miss. It also offers boat trips to nearby Isla Tortuga (daily 9am; $50 including BBQ lunch, snorkel rental and entrance to the refuge; 3hr 30min), as well as kayaking, sportfishing and scuba diving.

ACCOMMODATION

Cabinas On the beach ☎ 2641 0100, ⓦ curuwildlife refuge.com. You can stay in the reserve at some very basic cold-water *cabinas*, which are located on the beach;

they're popular with students and researchers, so you'll need to book in advance. Meals ($10 each) are available at the on-site comedor. **$60**

Montezuma

The popular beach resort of **MONTEZUMA** lies about 40km southwest of Paquera, near the southern tip of the Nicoya Peninsula. Some three decades ago, a handful of foreigners seeking solitude fell in love with Montezuma and decided to stay. In those days, it was just a sleepy fishing village, largely cut off from the rest of the country, but today Montezuma draws tourists galore, and virtually every establishment in town offers gringo-friendly food and accommodation and sells tours. Nevertheless, it still feels like a village because large-scale development has been kept to a minimum – and it's still a bit of an effort to get here.

Montezuma and the area south to the Reserva Absoluta Cabo Blanco features some of Costa Rica's loveliest coastline: leaning palms and jutting rocks dot the white-sand beaches. Here you can enjoy uninterrupted views of the Pacific, especially arresting when the occasional lightning storm illuminates the horizon and silky waters. Inland, thickly forested hills, including rare Pacific lowland tropical forest, dominate the landscape.

The beaches

It's Montezuma's atmosphere, rather than its activities, that draws visitors, and other than hanging out and sipping smoothies, there's not much to do in the village itself.

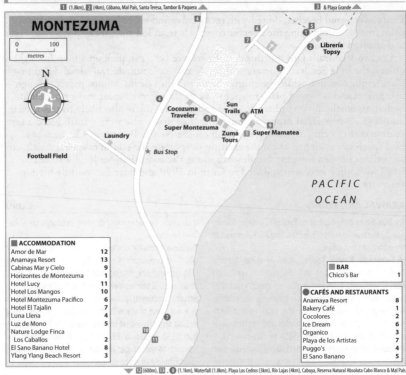

MONTEZUMA

ACCOMMODATION
Amor de Mar	12
Anamaya Resort	13
Cabinas Mar y Cielo	9
Horizontes de Montezuma	1
Hotel Lucy	11
Hotel Los Mangos	10
Hotel Montezuma Pacífico	6
Hotel El Tajalin	7
Luna Llena	4
Luz de Mono	5
Nature Lodge Finca Los Caballos	2
El Sano Banano Hotel	8
Ylang Ylang Beach Resort	3

BAR
Chico's Bar	1

CAFÉS AND RESTAURANTS
Anamaya Resort	8
Bakery Café	1
Cocolores	2
Ice Dream	6
Organico	3
Playa de los Artistas	7
Puggo's	4
El Sano Banano	5

Despite the palm-fringed, white-sand **beaches**, swimming isn't very good immediately north of Montezuma – there are lots of rocky outcroppings, some hidden at high tide, and the waves are rough and currents strong. Your best bet is to head further north along a lovely **trail** (1.5km) that dips in and out of several coves before ending at **Playa Grande** (olive ridley turtles nest along this stretch). Here, you'll find reasonable swimming, decent surfing and a small waterfall at the beach's eastern edge. Experienced surfers head in the other direction, to **Playa Los Cedros**, a left-hand reef break 3km south of Montezuma, and, a kilometre further on, the right-hand point break at the mouth of the **Río Lajas**, a very rocky spot best surfed at high tide.

The waterfalls

A number of **waterfalls** lace Montezuma and its environs; the closest lies about a kilometre south down the road towards Cabo Blanco and then another 800m on a path (signposted to the *catarata*) through dense vegetation. Bring your swimsuit if you want to bathe, but always take care, especially in the wet season when flash floods may strike. Under no circumstances should you try to climb the waterfalls; many people have been injured – sometimes fatally – in the attempt.

ARRIVAL AND DEPARTURE   MONTEZUMA

By bus Buses stop behind *El Sano Banano Hotel* in the centre of Montezuma; the Paquera bus passes the airstrip near Tambor, for flights to San José.
Destinations Paquera (for the ferry; 6 daily; 2hr); San José (2 daily; 5hr). For Mal País and Santa Teresa take the 10am

or 2pm Paquera bus and change in Cóbano (30min) to connect with onward services there (daily 10.30am & 2.30pm).
By taxi A taxi to/from Mal País/Santa Teresa costs around $45.

By taxi-boat The taxi-boat from Playa Herradura, 7km north of Jacó (10.45am; $40; 1hr), is by far the quickest way of getting here from the Central Pacific. The return journey (9.30am; $40; 1hr) is useful for connections south to Manuel Antonio.

INFORMATION AND TOURS

Cocozuma Traveler In the centre of town, next door to El Sano Banano Hotel ☎ 2642 0911, ⓦ cocozumacr .com. Offers a similar range of excursions as Zuma Tours.

Sun Trails ☎ 2642 0808, ⓦ montezumatraveladventures .com. Offers a canopy tour (750m southwest of Montezuma; daily 9am, 1pm & 3pm; $40) that also stops at the waterfalls for a quick dip.

Zuma Tours In the centre of town, near El Sano Banano Hotel ☎ 2642 0024, ⓦ zumatours.net. The helpful multi-lingual folks at Zuma Tours offer information and the largest range of tours in town, such as day-trips to Isla Tortuga ($55, including lunch and snorkelling tour), horseriding to the Florida Waterfall ($45) and trips to Refugio de Vida Silvestre Curú ($75).

ACCOMMODATION

Accommodation prices are rising in Montezuma, though the village remains significantly cheaper than Manuel Antonio, for example. While convenient, staying in the **village** can be noisy due to traffic and the shenanigans at *Chico's Bar*. Elsewhere, you'll find it peaceful, with choices out on the **beach**, on the road that heads southwest to the Reserva Natural Absoluta Cabo Blanco, and on the sides of the steep hill about 1km above the village. **Camping** is prohibited on the beach, but there are a couple of campsites on the edge of town.

IN THE VILLAGE

Cabinas Mar y Cielo By the beach, down a lane behind Super Mamatea ☎ 2642 0261. The clean rooms in this rambling wooden house come with fridge, private bath-room – and if you're upstairs – a balcony with ocean views and sea breezes. The hammock-filled garden is a great place to relax, though nearby *Chico's Bar* can be noisy. $40

Hotel Montezuma Pacífico Just north of the church ☎ 2642 0204, ⓦ montezumapacifico.com. The rooms at this hotch-potch hotel are rather characterless but clean and quiet, and come with a/c, fridge, good-sized beds and hot water. Try to get one of the front rooms with decent views or a room with a balcony. $40

Hotel El Tajalin Just west of Hotel Montezuma Pacífico ☎ 2642 0061, ⓦ tajalin.com. In a quiet location just northwest of the centre, this hotel – named after the purple-clawed crabs that frequent the hillside behind the village – has attractively simple wood-floored rooms with a/c; the airier ones on the top floor have sea views. They also have a communal lounge with television, books and coffee. $50

★ **Luna Llena** 200m north of the village, on the road to Paquera ☎ 2642 0390, ⓦ lunallenahotel.com. This surfer-friendly hostel sits peacefully on a forested hillside, with a regular troupe of monkeys as visitors. Attractive rooms (one is en suite) have fans and sleep up to five; most are a combination of double beds and bunks (extra guests $10 each). There are two shared kitchens, a BBQ and a sociable TV lounge. Dorm $15, double $38

Luz de Mono At the eastern end of the village, 50m from the beach ☎ 2642 0090, ⓦ luzdemono.com. Set between the jungle and the beach, with en-suite rooms (queen beds, satellite TV) or *casitas* (jacuzzis, terraces). There are two pools (one for children), a restaurant and a bar (serving wine from their Playa Grande vineyard). $85

El Sano Banano Hotel In the centre of town above the restaurant of the same name ☎ 2642 0638, ⓦ ylangylangresort.com. This is a good central option if you manage to score a room without a brick-wall view. Mexican bedspreads brighten up the small and clean rooms, all with private hot-water bathrooms, a/c and a TV. The price includes breakfast at the on-site restaurant and guests can use the pool at *Ylang Ylang Beach Resort* (see p.334). $85

AROUND THE VILLAGE

Amor de Mar 600m southwest of the village on the beach, just across the bridge ☎ 2642 0262, ⓦ amordemar.com. Rustic seafront hotel with its own tide pool sitting in pretty landscaped gardens on a rocky promontory. Hammocks hang between giant palm trees, and a nice selection of rooms come with and without bathroom; those upstairs and facing the sea are best, most of which have a veranda and ocean views. The two villas ($283) can sleep up to six people and are a great deal for families. $102

★ **Anamaya Resort** 500m up the hill, accessed on the road next to Amor de Mar ☎ 2642 1289, ⓦ anamaya resort.com. Yoga-centric wellness hotel set high up on the cliffs behind Montezuma, and offering a stylish women-only dorm and individually designed *cabinas*, most with superb ocean views, and a gorgeous saltwater infinity pool where it feels like you're swimming out into the Pacific. The mostly organic, mostly local restaurant (see p.334) is also open to non-guests. Rates include three daily meals, but not activities (you can buy week-long packages of classes and activities, which include everything from aerial

6

6

yoga to tantric sex, from $299/person). Dorm/week/person **$1011**, *cabinas*/week/person **$463**

Horizontes de Montezuma 1.8km before Montezuma, on the road from Paquera ☎ 2642 0534, ⦿ horizontes -montezuma.com. Perched in the hills above Montezuma, this small, distinctive, tropical-Victorian-style hotel has spacious, airy rooms with hot-water private bathroom and balcony looking over the jungle. There's a nicely lit pool and the owners offer intensive Spanish lessons (see opposite). Breakfast (which features home-made German wheatbread and jams) costs extra. **$73**

Hotel Lucy 500m south of the village ☎ 2642 0273. This Montezuma stalwart, still operating even though the government once attempted to have it torn down because it violates the *zona maritime* prohibiting building on the first 50m of beach (the same can't be said for their restaurant, which has had to move to Santa Teresa), offers adequate accommodation with cold-water showers on a small stretch of grey-sand beach; a couple of the private rooms have attached bathrooms. Dorm **$15**, double **$30**

Hotel Los Mangos 500m south of the village ☎ 2642 0384, ⦿ hotellosmangos.com. Split-level hotel set amid mango trees, with brightly decorated rooms, plus expensive-looking but slightly dark bungalows; some have their own verandas and rocking chairs. There's also a pool and hot tub, and regular yoga classes are held in an airy wooden pavilion. **$40**

Nature Lodge Finca Los Caballos 4km before Montezuma, on the road from Paquera ☎ 2642 0124, ⦿ naturelodge.net. Set in tropical gardens with a small pool, this casual lodge has twelve good-value rooms with hot-water private bath and a restaurant serving gourmet international cuisine – the more romantic rooms come with huge beds, views of the ocean and either a balcony or an outdoor shower ($165). The owners offer highly recommended horse tours to Playa Grande. **$97**

★**Ylang Ylang Beach Resort** A 10min walk along the beach from the village (your bags will be taken care of) ☎ 2642 0638, ⦿ ylangylangresort.com. This truly romantic retreat offers secluded circular bungalows ($316) all with beachfront verandas and outside showers. The newer split-level apartment rooms, perfect for families, boast beach views, and there are also luxury tents ($203) in the dry season. There's a lovely freeform swimming pool with a waterfall, beautifully landscaped gardens and an on-site spa. Rates include breakfast and candlelit dinner at the seafront restaurant. **$237**

EATING, DRINKING AND NIGHTLIFE

Just a few years ago, all you could eat in Montezuma was fresh **fish**, served practically straight off the hook. Nowadays, varied menus offer not just *comida típica* but a slew of tourist favourites, though you can still find a couple of (relatively) low-cost *sodas* too. Self-caterers can stock up at Super Montezuma on the main street (daily 7am–10pm) or sample the organic produce at the Saturday morning market in the park opposite (10am–noon).

Anamaya Resort Anamaya Resort ☎ 2642 1289, ⦿ anamayaresort.com. Three-course ultra-healthy set menu ($35), changing daily but including such dishes as raw Thai coconut soup and oyster mushroom, fig and quinoa stir-fry. Non-guests (reserve by 1pm) can arrive at 3pm to walk the waterfall trail and take a dip in the infinity pool. Tues–Sat 7–10pm.

Bakery Café Opposite Luz de Mono ☎ 2642 0458. Stop by for the tasty home-made sandwiches, cakes and pastries served on a soothing, shady terrace – perfect for lunch (*casados* around $7) after a morning spent on the nearby beach. Mon–Sat 6am–10pm.

Chico's Bar Near Super Mamatea. Nightlife in Montezuma centres on *Chico's Bar*, where a heady mix of local kids – who arrive packed in the back of pick-ups – and tourists guzzle from a wide choice of alcohol (beer from $2). At closing time people tend to adjourn to the beach for some alfresco drinking. Daily 11am–2am.

★**Cocolores** Diagonally opposite Bakery Café ☎ 2642 0348. This intimate restaurant in a garden by the beach serves generous portions of fajitas, kebabs and fish dishes (mains $8–24), plus some good vegetarian options and a selection of beers, ales and porters from a local microbrewery

($5.50). There's a happy hour (5–6pm), but you'll have to arrive early to secure one of the prime beachfront tables. Tues–Sun noon–10pm.

Ice Dream Opposite Chico's ☎ 2640 1005. Tiny *heladería* serving tip-top gelato (from $3) – the *dulce de leche*, peanut butter and Nutella flavours are among the highlights – as well as frappes, plus fine espressos, if you need something to cut through the sweetness. Daily 10am–8pm.

★**Organico** Just east of the church ☎ 2642 1322, ⦿ facebook.com/organicocostarica. Wholesomeness doesn't come at the expense of taste at this charming restaurant, with appealing salads, snacks, mains ($12–16.50) like veggie lasagne, and treats such as chilli, rum and chocolate gelato; vegans are particularly well catered for. There's live music most nights, including an open-mike session on Mondays. Mon–Sat 11am–9pm.

★**Playa de los Artistas** 500m south of the village ☎ 2642 0920. Beachside dining doesn't get any better – an unhurried candlelit dinner of fresh fish and lobster, vegetable dishes and delectable sushi (Fri) at hewn-wood tables or on cushions on the sand. Main courses hover around $15–20 – the tuna and snapper are particularly recommended. Mon–Sat 10.30am–9.30pm.

Puggo's Just beyond the main turning down into the village ☎2642 0325, ⓦfacebook.com/Puggos Restaurant. This mellow place with substantial tables fashioned from tree trunks serves up excellent Middle Eastern-inspired fare, including hummus and falafel, and a top Moroccan fish stew, plus home-baked focaccia. Daily except Tues 8am–9.30pm.

El Sano Banano El Sano Banano Hotel. Although the food's a little pricey, this is a good spot for a smoothie or something alcoholic, especially if you catch the daily happy hour (4–7pm), when you can expect to pay around $5 for a cocktail or $2 for a beer. Films are screened every evening (free with dinner or a $6 food order; arrive early to get a seat), and there's always sport from around the world on the TVs. Daily 7am–11pm.

DIRECTORY

Bookshops Librería Topsy on the beachfront road sells newspapers and books (Mon–Fri 8am–1pm & 3–5pm, Sat 8am–noon).

Laundry There's a *lavandaría* up the road opposite the bus stop (daily 7am–5pm; $2/kg).

Medical care The nearest clinic is in Cóbano (☎2642 0208).

Money and exchange Montezuma has an ATM, but the nearest bank is in Cóbano, 7km away. Dollars are accepted everywhere.

Spanish lessons Horizontes de Montezuma (see opposite) has a language school (group classes and accommodation $390/week).

Cabuya

Laidback **CABUYA**, 7km south of Montezuma, is a pleasant village that draws a growing community of permanent foreign residents who enjoy the slow pace of life, relative isolation and unspoiled scenery. It's everything its neighbour isn't, so if you're looking to escape the crowds and loll on secluded beaches, this is the place to come; it's also just a twenty-minute walk from the nearby Reserva Natural Absoluta Cabo Blanco. When the tide is low, it's possible to walk on a stony trail out to the village **cemetery** located on the otherwise uninhabited **Isla Cabuya**; it's a great spot for snorkelling but bear in mind that the path is covered by the ocean during high tide. To get there, walk west of the main intersection and follow the first road south of town.

ARRIVAL AND DEPARTURE
CABUYA

By bus The bus from Montezuma to Cabo Blanco (see below) runs past Cabuya.

By car The road from Montezuma is rough, so you'll need a 4WD if driving yourself. Another rough, and hilly, road links Cabuya with Mal País; it's only driveable in a 4WD, and a water crossing often makes the road impassable in the rainy season.

ACCOMMODATION AND EATING

El Ancla de Oro 2km southwest of the bridge, before the turning to Mal País ☎2642 0369, ⓦhotelelancla deoro.com. Surrounded by greenery, this is a welcoming place of rustic rooms with mosquito nets and fans; there are also some self-catering "jungalows": atmospheric, fan-cooled cabins raised up on stilts, with private bathrooms below. Double $28, jungalow $40

Hotel Cabo Blanco On the beach ☎2642 0332, ⓦcaboblancohotelresort.com. Set on a gentle beach with good swimming; the rooms come with fan or a/c and TV, and there's a swimming pool if you just can't face the short walk to the beach. $75

Hotel Celaje Near the entrance to the village ☎2642 0372, ⓦcelaje.com. Belgian-owned beachside beauty with A-frame, palm-roofed bungalows that come with two beds with mosquito nets and small bathrooms. There's an inviting swimming pool, a bar and restaurant. Closed Sept–mid-Nov. $90

Reserva Natural Absoluta Cabo Blanco

9km south of Montezuma • Wed–Sun 8am–4pm • $8 • ☎2642 0093, ⓦcaboblancopark.com

RESERVA NATURAL ABSOLUTA CABO BLANCO is Costa Rica's oldest protected piece of land, established in 1963 by Karen Mogensen, a Danish immigrant to Costa Rica, and her Swedish husband Olof Wessberg. Until 1989, no visitors were allowed into the twelve square kilometres of reserve, which covers nearly the entire southwestern tip of the Nicoya Peninsula. Though hard to believe today, most of the reserve was pasture

6

WATCHING WILDLIFE IN CABO BLANCO

The best time for animal spotting is around 8am, or on Wednesday mornings, after the reserve has been closed for two days. The heat chases a lot of the wildlife into the more heavily forested sections of the reserve, which are off-limits to visitors, but you're still likely to see **howler monkeys**, **white-faced capuchin monkeys** and **white-tailed deer**; **agoutis** and **coati** are also common. Harder-to-spot mammals include the **margay**, **northern tamandua** and **collared peccary** – Cabo Blanco has what is thought to be the last herd of these boar-like creatures on the Nicoya Peninsula. Birdlife is astonishingly plentiful, in the forest itself (where you might catch a glimpse of a **long-tailed manakin** or a **sulphur-winged parakeet**) but particularly down by the shore – you'll often see scores of **pelicans** and clouds of **magnificent frigatebirds**, while Costa Rica's largest community of **brown boobies** nests on Isla Cabo Blanco, the guano-encrusted island that lies 2km offshore.

and farmland until the early 1960s. Since its inauguration, Cabo Blanco has been allowed to regenerate naturally; a small area of original forest that had escaped destruction served as a "genetic bank" for the re-establishment of the complex tropical forest that now fills the reserve.

The trails

You can pick up a trail map (there are only two) at the ranger hut, which outlines the history of the reserve and the species living here. The **Sendero Sueco** (5km; 2hr) leads from the entrance through tropical deciduous forest to **Playa Cabo Blanco**, a lovely, lonely spot (in low season, anyway). Swimming, however, isn't great around here; due to the high tide (*marea alta*), you'll need to walk back along the trail rather than the coast. Ask the ranger at the entrance when and where you'll likely get cut off if you want to venture along the beach. Note that it's very hot: 30°C is not uncommon, so, if possible, hike the trails early, and bring a hat, suncream and plenty of water.

ARRIVAL AND DEPARTURE   **CABO BLANCO**

By bus An old, road-hardened bus runs along the rough road from Montezuma to the reserve (30min), leaving the village's *parque* daily at 8am, 10am, 2pm, 4pm and 6pm, returning from Cabo Blanco at 1pm, 3pm and 5.30pm, although it may not always run in the rainy season.

By jeep-taxi Jeeps make the trip for around $10–15/ person.

By car You'll need a 4WD to get there yourself, except in the very driest time of year, and even then you'll need to keep an eye out for the two creeks, which are deep at high tide.

Mal País and Santa Teresa

Just over a decade ago, the long grey-sand surf beaches fronting the virtually seamless towns of **MAL PAÍS** ("Bad Land") and **SANTA TERESA**, 12km southwest of Cóbano and also accessible via a steep and very bumpy road from Cabuya, began luring an increasing number of travellers. First came the surfers, then the hippies, and not long after, curious hipsters, celebrities and families started trickling in. A building boom over the past decade, particularly in Santa Teresa, has transformed this formerly sleepy stretch of Pacific coast into a trendy beach resort, and foreigners now outnumber Tico residents. The developers, banks and car rental chains show no signs of leaving town, and the fear on these dusty, rutted streets is that the neighbouring towns are well on their way to becoming "the next Jacó". But as long as the roads here remain appalling, the area seems certain to retain its laidback charm; and in the rainy season at least, you can still walk along jungle-flanked surf beaches for hours and see few other people.

The straggly oceanfront communities spread along 8km of rough road and three separate **beaches** – Mal País, Carmen and Santa Teresa. The intersection by the hotel *Frank's Place*, known as "**El Cruce**", is the traditional boundary between the three.

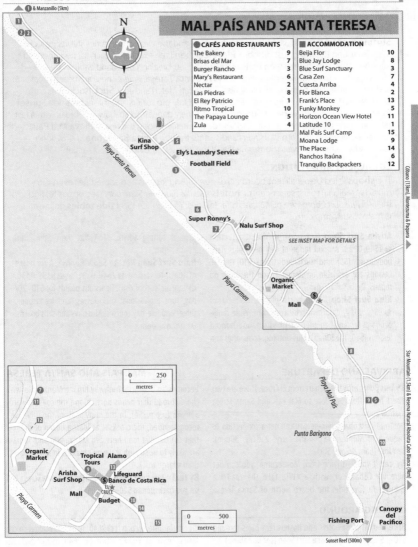

MAL PAÍS AND SANTA TERESA

CAFÉS AND RESTAURANTS		ACCOMMODATION	
The Bakery	9	Beija Flor	10
Brisas del Mar	7	Blue Jay Lodge	8
Burger Rancho	3	Blue Surf Sanctuary	3
Mary's Restaurant	6	Casa Zen	7
Nectar	2	Cuesta Arriba	4
Las Piedras	8	Flor Blanca	2
El Rey Patricio	1	Frank's Place	13
Ritmo Tropical	10	Funky Monkey	5
The Papaya Lounge	5	Horizon Ocean View Hotel	11
Zula	4	Latitude 10	1
		Mal País Surf Camp	15
		Moana Lodge	9
		The Place	14
		Ranchos Itaúna	6
		Tranquilo Backpackers	12

The beaches

Turning south at El Cruce takes you along the **Mal País** section of the beach strip, which is quieter and more peaceful than Santa Teresa; straight over the intersection lies **Playa Carmen**, while turning north leads quickly into **Santa Teresa**. Beyond Santa Teresa lies **Manzanillo**, a rocky beach with a couple of point breaks on the western side of the peninsula; while there were few facilities here at the time of writing, the Manzanillo coastal strip looks set to experience the next development boom.

Despite the long stretches of sand, all the beaches here are prone to riptides and not ideal for **swimming**, though there are often good tidal pools for splashing about in. They are, however, excellent for **surfing** (see box, p.338).

6

SURF'S UP

Surfing put Mal País and Santa Teresa on the map, and the two communities still very much revolve around the rollers just offshore. **Playa Carmen** is an excellent beach for beginner and intermediate surfers, with a long right and a shorter left breaking over sand. More experienced types head north to the steeper waves at **Playa Santa Teresa**, where there are beach breaks and point breaks; on high swells, particularly between March and July, **Suck Rock**, at its northern end, peels into long, right-handed tubes. Only pro surfers and masochists ride **Sunset Reef** (also known as Playa de los Suecos), an extremely dangerous shallow reef-break with a fast take-off at the far southern end of Mal País; rocky outcrops along the rest of **Playa Mal País** render it uninviting for both swimmers and surfers, though **Punta Barrigona**, a slow, long left-hander halfway between Sunset Reef and the intersection, works well on a high-tide swell.

EQUIPMENT AND TUITION

The **shops** listed below all rent boards, organize surfing lessons and sometimes even run multiday regional tours; surfer-centric **hotels** such as Blue Surf Sanctuary (see opposite) and the Mal País Surf Camp (see p.340) also offer lessons. You can get local **tide tables** online at ⓦ malpaissurfcamp.com.

Arisha Surf Shop Just north of the intersection ☎ 2640 0228. A good range of surf gear, plus daily bodyboard ($5) and surfboard (from $10) rental. Lessons are available on demand, and they also do repairs. Daily 9am–7pm.

Kina Surf Shop 2.2km north of the intersection ☎ 2640 0627, ⓦ kinasurfcostarica.com. Wide range of boards for rent; beginner, intermediate and advanced lessons ($50; 1hr 30min); plus clothing, accessories and

general surfing advice. Mon–Sat 9am–5pm, Sun 10am–4pm.

Nalu Surf Shop Next to Super Ronny's, 1km north of the intersection ☎ 2640 0391 or ☎ 8358 4436, ⓦ nalusurfschool.com. Rents out boards for $10–20/ day, runs professional surf classes, and leads one-, three- and five-day courses. Also buys and sells boards. Daily 9am–6pm.

ARRIVAL AND DEPARTURE

MAL PAÍS AND SANTA TERESA

By bus Buses arrive at/depart from El Cruce. There are two direct buses from San José to Mal País and Santa Teresa (6am & 2pm).

DestinationsCóbano (where you can get a connection to Paquera or Montezuma for the ferry; 2 daily; 30min); San José (6am & 2pm; 5hr).

By car If you're driving from Montezuma, you can get here via Cóbano or, with a 4WD, take the road via Cabuya. At low tide, the beach north of Santa Teresa

becomes an unofficial highway linking Manzanillo with the dirt road that heads north along the coast towards Sámara (see p.294). In the rainy season, the drive isn't recommended; the creeks – at least a dozen of them – that cut the dirt road between Manzanillo and Sámara are likely to be so high you won't make it in anything less than a large truck.

By taxi A taxi from Cóbano to Mal País or Santa Teresa will set you back around $20–30.

GETTING AROUND

Bike rental Most hotels and hostels rent bikes (around $10–15/day), as does Arisha Surf Shop (see box above).

Car rental Budget, housed in the white strip mall at

the main intersection (☎ 2640 0500, ⓦ budget.co.cr); Alamo, east of Frank's Place (☎ 2640 0526, ⓦ alamo costarica.com).

TOURS AND ACTIVITIES

Canopy del Pacífico ☎ 2640 0071. A canopy tour ($40) that affords blurry Pacific views as you whizz through tree-tops adjoining the Reserva Natural Absoluta Cabo Blanco.

Star Mountain ☎ 2640 0101, ⓦ starmountaineco.com. If you fancy horseriding along the beach or in the surrounding jungle, try Star Mountain who will take you for a 2hr trot through the waves at Playa Carmen ($40).

Tropical Tours Opposite Budget ☎ 2640 0811, ⓦ tropical tourshuttles.com. Arranges a variety of tours, including

day-trips to Isla Tortuga ($55), plus 5hr guided tours of the Reserva Natural Absoluta Cabo Blanco ($75).

Yoga and pilates Daily classes (Mon–Sat 9am, Sun 5pm, $12; ☎ 2640 0524, ⓦ horizon-yogahotel.com) are held on the panoramic deck at Horizon Ocean View Hotel (see opposite); Casa Zen (see opposite) also offers yoga classes (daily 9.30am and 3.30pm, plus Tues & Thurs 6.30pm; $9); as does Beija Flor (see p.340; Mon, Wed & Fri 9am; $15; 2hr).

ACCOMMODATION

The recent construction boom has brought with it a smorgasbord of boutique **hotels** and even the budget options here are surprisingly modern. The majority of the accommodation is set along the shores of Playa Carmen and Playa Santa Teresa, and most places are equipped with kitchens to suit the long-term surfer clientele; as it can be hot day and night, it's well worth splashing out on a/c. **Camping** is officially prohibited on the beach, but you can pitch a tent at *Tranquilo Backpackers* and the *Mal País Surf Camp*, both listed below. Most places, like the towns themselves, shut down during September and October.

SANTA TERESA

The following places are listed in the order you encounter them heading north from the intersection.

Frank's Place El Cruce ☎ 2640 0096, ⓦ franksplacecr .com. A local landmark and one of the area's most established hotels, the central location makes this a popular place to bed down, especially with holidaying Ticos. Although a bit underwhelming, all the rooms come with a/c, private bathrooms, kitchens and fridges: the more expensive ones are considerably bigger. You can hang out on hammocks around the pool, framed on one side by a decent restaurant. $75

Tranquilo Backpackers Around 650m north of the intersection ☎ 2640 0546, ⓦ tranquilobackpackers .com. This popular hostel attracts a boisterous gringo crowd, making it anything but "tranquilo". Set in a stylish two-storey ranch flanked by plenty of hammocks, the loft-style dorms can pack in six people and some have private bathrooms; doubles are also either shared bathroom or en suite; the hostel's not always as clean as it could be, so ask to see a few rooms first. A communal kitchen, DVD movie room, pool table and ping pong complete the picture. Camping $7, dorm $13, double $30

Horizon Ocean View Hotel Around 750m north of the intersection ☎ 2640 0524, ⓦ horizon-yogahotel .com. Staggered up the hillside overlooking jungle and Playa Carmen, these romantic bungalows are small but have expansive views that make up for it. Rooms come with a/c, firm mattresses, hot-water bathrooms and balconies adorned with hammocks and bamboo wind chimes; there are also two villas, one with a private pool ($210). You can munch vegetarian food, bliss out in the intimate triangular pool, stretch yourself in an outdoor yoga class or settle down for a massage (from $70). Breakfast costs extra. $120

★Casa Zen Around 1.1km north of the intersection ☎ 2640 8523, ⓦ zencostarica.com. The pick of the area's hostels, *Casa Zen* is a stylish wooden house featuring Asian-inspired trimmings and plenty of space. Just 50m from the beach, accommodation options include well-maintained dorm rooms, doubles and apartments. There are morning yoga classes, movie nights and a professional kitchen for guests to use. Dorm $15, double $34, apartment $55

Ranchos Itaúna Around 1.3km north of the inter-section ☎ 2640 0095, ⓦ ranchos-itauna.com. This beachfront property lies smack bang between the surf breaks of Playa Carmen and Playa Santa Teresa. With just four comfortable octagonal rooms (two have kitchens and all have one double bed, a bunk bed, a/c, fridge and private hot-water bath), this place oozes tranquillity. The owners can arrange massage and surf lessons, and Brazilian fare is served in the restaurant (closed Sun). The lively bar hosts regular DJ sets, live music and full-moon beach parties. $100

Funky Monkey Around 1.9km north of the intersection ☎ 2640 0272, ⓦ funky-monkey-lodge.com. This hillside lodge with a swish pool and sushi restaurant is part boutique hotel, part swish backpacker hangout. Whether staying in a bamboo bungalow with outdoor shower, a self-contained apartment with ocean views or bunking down in a dorm with cold-water bathroom, you can enjoy the lodge's excellent facilities and mingle with other travellers in the bar-side communal area. There's also a yoga and dance studio. Dorm $17, bungalow $93, apartment $135

Cuesta Arriba Around 2.8km north of the intersection ☎ 2640 0607, ⓦ santateresacostarica.com. Mixed dorm beds are arranged six to a room in this sparkling hostel, ideally located for the Playa Santa Teresa breakers. Rooms are cleaned daily and come with lockers, fan and a bathroom with hot shower. There are also a range of private doubles, including a cute, split-level one ($60). There's plenty of space in the upstairs TV lounge or downstairs communal kitchen. Free coffee and toast in the morning, but no breakfast per se. Dorm $15, double $30

Blue Surf Sanctuary Around 3.6km north of the intersection ☎ 2640 1001, ⓦ bluesurfsanctuary.com. Top-end surf camp, sponsored by Billabong and appealing to boardriders with bigger budgets – the swanky bungalows (there are just four) have luxurious bathrooms and treetop views from their balconies. Surf lessons ($60/2.5hr) and board rental are available of course. $149

Flor Blanca Around 4.2km north of the intersection ☎ 2640 0232, ⓦ florblanca.com. Positioned on a small beach between playas Santa Teresa and Hermosa, this beachside haven is fit for honeymooning Hollywood celebrities, and their wallets – the Honeymoon Suite costs $1045. Its Balinese-style villas set in groomed grounds come with large open-air lounge areas and outdoor "jungle" bathrooms with sunken baths. There's also a pool, spa, yoga studio, bar and snazzy restaurant (see p.340). $452

★ Latitude 10 Around 4.4km north of the intersection ☎ 2640 0396, ⊛ latitude10resort.com. Set amid wildlife-rich forest, this ultra-exclusive boutique hotel manages to retain a relaxed and welcoming ambience. The five suites are beautifully furnished and completely open, allowing them to benefit from the sea breezes; the Master Suite ($610), with four-poster bed (and foot-high mattress) and spacious outdoor bathroom, must be among the finest in the country. There's a lovely little chemical-free pool, excellent restaurant (guests only), and surf- and bodyboards for use on the secluded stretch of beach out front. **$271**

MAL PAÍS

The following places are listed in the order you encounter them heading south from the intersection.

The Place Around 200m south of the intersection ☎ 2640 0001, ⊛ theplacemalpais.com. Crisply furnished rooms, chic beach-hut-style bungalows and spacious villas set around a chill-out lounge and garden pool. Movies are played on a big screen hanging over the pool on Tues & Fri at 7pm. Double **$78**, bungalow **$153**, villa **$250**

★ Mal País Surf Camp Around 350m south of the intersection ☎ 2640 0061, ⊛ malpaissurfcamp.com. There's a good community vibe at this surfer centre near the top of Mal País, thanks to its mix of guests – accommodation ranges from dorms through to *cabinas*, dotted around a nice pool – and chilled-out restaurant area. Stacks of magazines and on-loop surfing films should get you in the mood. Daily lessons and surf-and-accommodation packages (from $60/

day/person for the latter) available too. Camping **$11**, dorm **$17**, *cabinas* **$40**

Blue Jay Lodge Around 750m south of the intersection ☎ 2640 0089, ⊛ bluejaylodgecostarica.com. The intimate, widely spaced bungalows at this easy-going place sleep two to three people. Head up the hillside for the best bungalows, with ocean views and plenty of nearby wildlife; to relax, cool off in their swimming pool. **$83**

★ Moana Lodge Around 1.25km south of the intersection ☎ 2640 0230, ⊛ moanalodge.com. Run by a chatty Irishman and his Tica wife, this boutique hotel is one of the area's most romantic and stylish. Set on a forested slope, the lovely rooms have been tastefully decorated with African-inspired trimmings and come with a/c, hot-water bathrooms and large beds draped with silk throws. Try to score one of the higher ones with a balcony for nice ocean breezes, or – if your budget allows – the superb honeymoon suite ($260), right at the top of the hill, with panoramic views from the jacuzzi and a private deck. You can while away the day in suspended beds by the pool before taking sunset drinks in *The Papaya Lounge* (see opposite). **$99**

Beija Flor Around 1.75km south of the intersection ☎ 2640 1007, ⊛ beijaflorresort.com. Line of thatched-roof rooms minimally furnished in a design hotel kind of way, with partial outdoor showers. There are also garden-view doubles and a master suite that can accommodate five. The on-site restaurant fronts an attractive kidney-shaped pool and a popular yoga deck. **$80**

EATING AND DRINKING

Mal País and Santa Teresa's large expat population translates into a wide range of **restaurants**, though the municipal government's decision to shut down the beachfront establishments has diluted the scene a bit, which fluctuates at the best of times (restaurants come and go with alarming frequency). **Nightlife** isn't the area's strong point, and bars pop up and disappear even more often than restaurants, so ask around to find out the current hotspot during your visit.

SANTA TERESA

The following places are listed in the order you encounter them heading north from the intersection.

★ The Bakery 150m north of the intersection ☎ 2640 0560. An appealing stop-off at any time of the day, with delicious pastries for breakfast, light meals like soups, pasta, quiches and salads for lunch, and top pizza for dinner (from 6pm). Picnic baskets and a delivery service are also available, and on Mon evenings there's an all-you-can-eat pizza session (6–8pm; $10). Daily 7am–10pm.

Las Piedras 250m north of the intersection ☎ 02640 0453. Delicious wood-fired chicken, grilled steak, fresh tuna and succulent pork ribs, prepared by a beaming Argentinian chef who knows he's onto a winner. Most mains around $15–20. Mon–Sat 8.30am–2pm & 6–10pm, Sun 6–10pm.

★ Brisas del Mar Hotel Buenos Aires, 700m north of the intersection ☎ 2640 0941, ⊛ buenosairesmalpais .com. It's a long way to the top of a very steep hill, but fish

restaurants don't come much better than this – fresh, creative and with generous portions. Sample the spread of seafood tapas or tuck into tuna in port or delicious shrimp with bourbon-spiked Cajun cream (most mains $15–20). Daily except Mon 8–11am & 4–10pm.

Zula Around 1.1km north of the intersection ☎ 2640 0614. A buzzing local eatery that serves up Israeli favourites (mains around $10–12) like falafel, *shakshuka*, kebabs, and creamy bowls of hummus to dunk your pitta in. Daily except Sat 9am–10pm.

Burger Rancho Around 2km north of the intersection ☎ 2640 0583. Head here for the best burgers (from $5) in the area – including a delicious one made from fresh tuna – as well as sandwiches, salads and tacos. Great milkshakes and smoothies too. Daily 5–10pm.

Nectar Flor Blanca, 4.2km north of the intersection. Artistic, Asian-influenced cuisine, heavily focused on seafood: dishes range from ginger, coconut and coriander ceviche to sugarcane skewered jumbo prawns (mains $15–25). The strong sushi menu is matched by some high-quality sakes. Daily noon–3pm & 6–9.30pm.

El Rey Patricio 5km north of the intersection ☎ 2640 0248, ⊛ elreypatricio.com. Welcoming, Catalan-run restaurant specializing in tapas ($4–18): highlights include a zingy gazpacho and *botifarra* (a Catalan sausage) cooked with beans. There's paella ($28 for two people) too, plus several good Catalan *vinos tintos* and, of course, *sangría*, ideal for a sundowner. Daily 5.30–10pm.

MAL PAÍS

The following places are listed in the order you encounter them heading south from the intersection.

Rítmo Tropical Around 150m south of the intersection ☎ 2640 0174, ⊛ hotelritmotropical.net. Soak up your antipasti with five types of focaccia; the real draw is the tasty thin-crust pizzas that dominate the menu (around $10). Daily 5.30–10.30pm.

The Papaya Lounge Moana Lodge, 1.25km south of the intersection ☎ 2640 0230, ⊛ moanalodge.com. The home-made Latin food changes daily but usually includes some mouthwatering fish dishes (think sea bass in coconut broth or peanut-encrusted mahi-mahi in ginger) as well as meaty mains like tamarind BBQ ribs. The great views – as far as Punta Islita – can also be enjoyed over sunset drinks and *bocas* (from 5pm). Mains around $15–20. Daily except Tues 5–10pm.

Mary's Restaurant 2km south of the intersection ☎ 2640 0153, ⊛ maryscostarica.com. Locals pack the tables and booths at this buzzing restaurant to tuck into a wide variety of Mexican dishes (nachos, tacos and burritos) and wood-fired pizzas ($10–14). Daily except Wed 5–10pm.

DIRECTORY

Internet access Virtually every hotel and restaurant offers free wi-fi access; Tropical Tours, opposite Budget, has a few computers too.

Laundry Ely's Laundry Service, 2.4km north of the intersection (Mon–Sat 8am–6pm).

Markets An organic fruit and vegetable market is held beachside every Saturday near the intersection (3–5pm).

Medical care Paradise Medical Services, in the mall at the intersection (☎ 2640 1010; open 24hr).

Money and exchange Both the Banco Nacional (Mon–Sat 1–7pm), next door to Budget, and the Banco de Costa Rica (Mon–Fri 9am–4pm) change travellers' cheques and have ATMs.

Supermarkets Self-caterers will find several well-stocked supermarkets, including Super Ronny's (daily 7am–10pm), near *Casa Zen*.

South of Puntarenas

On the mainland south of Puntarenas, the coast road (sometimes signposted as the **Costanera Sur**) leads down to Quepos and continues, in various states of paving, south to Dominical (covered in Chapter 7). At first, the landscape is sparse and hilly, with the coast coming into view only intermittently, but things improve considerably once you're past the huge trucks heading to the container port and refineries at hideous **Puerto Caldera**, the terminus of the new toll road linking San José and the Pacific. About 30km southeast of Puerto Caldera, just across the wide crocodile-ridden mouth of the Río Tárcoles, **Parque Nacional Carara** encompasses a range of habitats and is known for its rich birdlife. Beyond Carara, and a different beast altogether, is the resort of **Jacó**, which thanks to its relative proximity to San José is more popular than it might otherwise be. Better beaches (and surf) lie further south, particularly at **Playa Hermosa** and **Playas Esterillos**. From here, it's an uneventful 45km to Quepos and Parque Nacional Manuel Antonio, the last stretch along the coast from the hamlet of Parrita comprising a long corridor of African oil-palm plantations, a moody landscape of stout, brooding tree sentinels.

Parque Nacional Carara

90km west of San José • Daily: Dec–April 7am–4pm, May–Nov 8am–4pm • $10 • ☎ 2637 1054

Ecologically vital **PARQUE NACIONAL CARARA** occupies a transition area between the hot tropical lowlands of the north and the humid, more verdant climate of the southern Pacific coast. Consequently, the park teems with **wildlife**, from monkeys to margays and motmots to manakins.

6

WATCHING WILDLIFE IN CARARA

Much of Carara's bounty of wildlife is of the unnerving sort: huge **crocodiles** lounge in the bankside mud of the Río Tárcoles ("carara" means "crocodile" in the language of the pre-Columbian inhabitants, the Huetar), while **snakes** (19 out of Costa Rica's 22 poisonous species) slither about. Mammals include **monkeys** (mantled howler and white-faced capuchin), **armadillos**, **agoutis** (commonly seen), aggressive **collared peccaries** and most of the large cats, including **jaguars** and **ocelots**. Birding is excellent, and this is one of the best places in the country to see the brightly coloured **scarlet macaw** in its natural habitat – at dawn and dusk, they migrate between the lowland tropical forest areas and the swampy mangroves, soaring over in a burst of red and blue against the darkened sky. Other birds that frequent the treetops include trogons (five species), toucans (both chestnut-mandibled and keel-billed) and **guans**, while riverside birds include **anhingas** (or snake birds), the coot-like **purple gallinule** and **storks**.

Carara's well-maintained **trails** are split between the heavily canopied area near the park's ranger station and the more open terrain around Laguna Meándrica, an oxbow lake that is home to crocodiles; the ranger station is accessed from a trailhead 2km north along the highway, towards the Río Tárcoles Bridge (see below). From here, the loop trails of **Sendero Las Aráceas** (1.2km; 1hr) and **Sendero Quebrada Bonita** (1.5km; 1hr 30min) take in primary and transitionary forest and are reliable places to spot agouti and other small rodents; you can also often see great tinamou on the paths here, and sometimes even catch the spectacular leks of orange-collared manikins. Both routes are reached via the **Sendero Encuentro de Ecosistemas**, a 1.2km loop near the ranger station that is accessible to wheelchair users. Birdwatching is perhaps even better along the rivers and in the clearings on the **Sendero Laguna Meándrica** (4.3km; 2–4hr), where the wide range of avifauna includes boat-billed herons.

ARRIVAL AND TOURS   CARARA

By bus Buses between Puntarenas and Jacó pass by the trailhead for Parque Nacional Carara (8 daily; around 1hr from Puntarenas, 30min from Jacó).

By car To get to Carara from San José, take either the Caldera Highway or Hwy-3, following the latter over the long bridge that crosses the Río Tárcoles; the park entrance is 3km after the bridge.

Tours Several agencies offer tours (around $200–250) from San José; try Costa Rica Expeditions (☎ 2257 0766, ⓦ costaricaexpeditions.com).

INFORMATION

Information Staff at the ranger station (see above) have basic maps and answer questions about the reserve's wildlife.

Guides It's worth hiring a guide (around $20/person/2hr) from the ranger station, as they can also take you into areas where tourists aren't allowed on their own.

Security There have been thefts and robberies in the area, so leave your vehicle in sight of the guards at the ranger station (even if walking the Laguna Meándrica trail), and check the latest situation before setting off.

When to visit Note that it's extremely hot in Carara, so hit the trails early (the wildlife will be much less evident by 10am); if you want to stay overnight to get an early start, there are a number of accommodation options in nearby Tárcoles and the surrounding area (see opposite).

Tárcoles and around

The village of **Tárcoles**, 2km south of Parque Nacional Carara and a further 1km west along a rough road, sprawls along a dusty street and parallels a beach that is too polluted for even the briefest of toe-dippings. The main attraction here – apart from visiting the nearby national park – is the **Río Tárcoles**, or more correctly the huge **crocodiles** that bask on its muddy banks. You can spot them at the estuary just northwest of town and from the **Río Tárcoles Bridge** – it's one of the best free attractions in Costa Rica, although there have been robberies on the bridge and a police booth is now positioned on the southern side for added security – or take to the water and view them from the comfort of a boat.

Catarata Manatial de Agua Vida

About 5km east of the turn-off to Tárcoles village • Daily 8am–3pm • $20 • ☎ 2645 1017

Set amid a pristine rainforest valley is the **Catarata Manatial de Agua Viva**; at 200m high, this cascading waterfall, also known as Bijagual Waterfall, is supposedly the highest in the country, and it's a difficult 2km climb downhill to reach its base. While there's no designated place for swimming, there's nothing stopping you from cooling off in the river.

Pura Vida Gardens and Waterfalls

1km up the road from Catarata Manatial de Agua Vida, just before the village of Bijagual • Daily 8am–5pm • $20 • ☎ 2645 1001, Ⓦ puravidagarden.com

The jungle has been tamed into submission at the **Pura Vida Garden and Waterfalls**, but as Parque Nacional Carara is next door, visitors are very likely to see scarlet macaw and poison-dart frogs while strolling the manicured nature trails at this private botanical gardens. Only avid hikers can get close to the Catarata Manatial de Agua Vida from here, although a lookout point does provide dead-on views of the falls as well as the surrounding valley and Pacific coast; there are also four smaller waterfalls on the grounds.

ACTIVITIES AND TOURS

Costa Rica Birding Journeys ☎ 8889 8815, Ⓦ costaricabirdingjourneys.org. Birdwatching tours explore the mangroves at the mouth of the river in search of herons, egrets and the endemic mangrove hummingbird; the price includes transfer from local hotels (4 daily; $65; 3hr).

Jungle Crocodile Safari ☎ 2236 6473, Ⓦ junglecrocodilesafari.com. Two local companies run crocodile tours on the river, complete with crocodile-feeding antics straight out of the Steve Irwin school of shameless wildlife harassment; this is the less brazen of the two (4 daily; $35; 2hr).

ACCOMMODATION   TÁRCOLES AND AROUND

There are a number of decent accommodation options around Tárcoles. Most lodges can meet you off the bus from San José; some also offer transport from the capital, or from nearby Jacó or Quepos.

Cerro Lodge 3km down a side road, signed off the road 3km north of the Río Tárcoles Bridge ☎ 2427 9910 or ☎ 8871 3523, Ⓦ hotelcerrolodge.com. This lodge offers good-value rooms and *cabinas* on a quiet working farm (trails run through the property): it's set in lush surrounds, with a pool to cool off in after a walk in Carara. Start the day watching scarlet macaws feeding in the trees opposite the on-site restaurant. Double **$90**, *cabina* **$115**

Los Cocodrillos Just north of the Río Tárcoles Bridge ☎ 2200 5623. These three basic *cabinas* are old, musty and depressingly bare, but are the only real choice round these parts for budget travellers; they come with a/c, TV and private cold-water bathrooms. It's next door to a popular restaurant of the same name. **$40**

Hotel Carara In Tárcoles ☎ 2637 0178, Ⓦ hotelcarara.com. On the beach, this much-improved hotel has clean, modest rooms with TVs and private bathrooms set around a small pool; $15 more buys you more space, a/c and sea views. It's on the flight path between Carara and the coastal mangroves, so sightings of macaws are almost guaranteed in the early morning and late afternoon. **$59**

Villa Lapas 500m east of the turn-off to Tárcoles, signed from the road just past the Río Tárcoles Bridge ☎ 2203 3553, Ⓦ villalapas.com. Set in landscaped gardens near the river, this well-equipped hotel has large a/c rooms, a pool and – rather oddly – a replica of an old Costa Rican "town", complete with church, *cantina*, large restaurant and even larger souvenir shop. There's also a Sky Walk, canopy tour and small network of trails in their nearby private reserve. **$139**

Jacó and around

Just over two hours from San José, **Jacó** sits in a hot coastal plain behind the broad **Playa Jacó**, the closest beach to the capital. An established seaside attraction, the

6

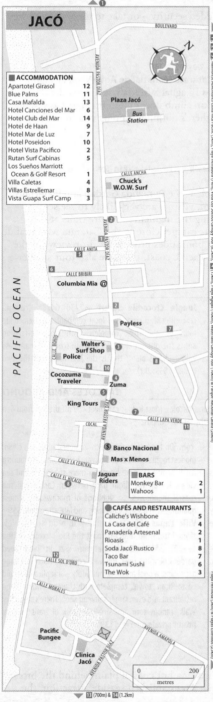

JACÓ

■ ACCOMMODATION

Apartotel Girasol	12
Blue Palms	11
Casa Mafalda	13
Hotel Canciones del Mar	6
Hotel Club del Mar	14
Hotel de Haan	9
Hotel Mar de Luz	7
Hotel Poseidon	10
Hotel Vista Pacifico	2
Rutan Surf Cabinas	5
Los Sueños Marriott Ocean & Golf Resort	1
Villa Caletas	4
Villas Estrellemar	8
Vista Guapa Surf Camp	3

■ BARS

Monkey Bar	2
Wahoos	1

● CAFÉS AND RESTAURANTS

Caliche's Wishbone	5
La Casa del Café	4
Panadería Artesenal	2
Rioasis	1
Soda Jacó Rustico	8
Taco Bar	7
Tsunami Sushi	6
The Wok	3

resort draws a mix of surfers, package tourists, holidaying Ticos and retired North American baby-boomers, along with a less savoury selection of drug dealers and prostitutes. Jacó has seen some of the most excessive development along the Pacific, but the partying crowd don't seem to mind too much. And as a base from which to explore the surf beaches along this stretch of coast, its multitude of amenities takes some beating.

The beaches

Jacó's appeal is its long, spacious **beach** – when covered in mist and backed by a spectacular Pacific sunset, the wide sands look quite attractive. It's popular with novice surfers (though the water isn't the cleanest and you do have to watch out for riptides), while more advanced riders head for the beaches nearby, including **Playa Herradura**, 7km north, a calm spot in front of the *Los Sueños Marriot Ocean and Golf Resort* complex (see p.346) and frequented by Ticos, and **Playa Hermosa** (see p.347) and **Playas Esterillos** (see p.349), wild, untamed stretches to the south of town.

Rainforest Adventures Costa Rica Pacific

3km northeast of Jacó • Daily 6.30am–4pm, Mon from 9am • Tram $60, children $30; Tranopy Tour $75; birdwatching tour $99; various multi-activity packages available • ☎ 2257 5961, ⓦ rainforestadventure.com

Sister operation of the groundbreaking aerial tram just outside Parque Nacional Braulio Carrillo (see p.143), the catchily titled **Rainforest Adventures Costa Rica Pacific** lets you view the rainforest canopy from the surrounds of a slow-moving gondola; the price includes access to nature trails and a serpentarium. You can combine the ride with a ten-cable canopy tour – the "**Tranopy Tour**" – to pick up the pace a little, or hit the trails with a naturalist guide on an early-morning birdwatching tour before taking a closer look at the canopy dwellers from the comfort of the tram.

TOURS AND ACTIVITIES IN AND AROUND JACÓ

Although **surfing** is the be-all-and-end-all for many visitors, there are plenty of other activities on offer, from **kayaking** to zip-lining, as well as tours to nearby **Parque Nacional Carara** or **Isla Tortuga** (see p.327).

SURFING AND KAYAKING

You can rent boards at a number of competing places in Jacó. Staff at **Walter's Surf Shop** (☎ 2643 1056, ⓦ waltersurfshop.com), opposite Budget on Avenida Pastor Diaz, can match you with the right board and offer rentals for $10–20 a day and two-hour lessons for $40. Drop into **Chuck's W.O.W. Surf** (☎ 2643 3844, ⓦ wowsurf.net), on Plaza Palma, at the northern end of town, for tide tables and an excellent free "surf treasure map": board hire here is pricier at $15–40 a day, and a three-hour lesson will set you back $65.

For a less-extreme water workout, **Kayak Jacó** (☎ 2643 1233, ⓦ kayakjaco.com) runs daily excursions (8.15am & 2.30pm; $70; 2hr) from its base in nearby Playa Agujas, which can include snorkelling and fishing if you like; it can also organize tailor-made multiday itineraries.

CANOPY TOURS AND BUNGEE JUMPING

The canopy craze is alive and well here, with **Waterfalls Canopy Tour** (tours from $99; ☎ 2643 3322, ⓦ adventureparkcostarica.com) offering a zip-line rush that includes a rappel, suspension bridges and Tarzan swing (you can also whizz through the air under the cover of darkness on their night canopy tour), and **Vista Los Sueños Canopy Tour** (tours from $80; ☎ 2637 6020, ⓦ canopyvistalossuenos.com), whose thirteen cables (including the longest in the area) are accessed by tractor-pulled cart.

The daredevils at **Pacific Bungee** (☎ 2643 6682, ⓦ facebook.com/pacificbungeecostarica) can send you plunging off a 40m crane towering above the Pacific, with the option of a "water touchdown", plus a Big Swing and a Rocket Launcher (all $50; multi-activity packages available).

TOURS

King Tours (☎ 2643 2441, ⓦ kingtours.com) runs numerous excursions, including rafting on the Class II–III Río Savegre (daily 7am; $130), half-day tours of Parque Nacional Carara (daily 7am & 2.30pm; $79) and full-day whale-watching trips to Parque Nacional Marino Ballena (Wed, Sat & Sun; $139) for the chance to spot humpbacks (mid-July to mid-Nov & mid-Nov to March). **Cocozuma Traveler**, on Calle Bohío (☎ 2643 5196, ⓦ cocozumacr.com), has a similar list of tours.

ARRIVAL AND INFORMATION

JACÓ AND AROUND

By bus Buses to and from San José, Puntarenas and Quepos stop at Plaza Jacó at the north end of Av Pastor Diaz, the 3km road that constitutes the town's main drag. If you're travelling at a weekend in high season, buy your ticket at least 3 days in advance.

Destinations Puntarenas (8 daily; 1hr 30min); Quepos (8 daily; 1hr 30min); San José (7 daily; 2hr 30min).

By taxi-boat A taxi-boat from Montezuma runs to Playa Herradura, 7km north of Jacó at 9.30am each day (1hr; $42, including transfer to or from town), returning at

10.45am; it's a fast-paced trip that offers the possibility of spotting dolphins, turtles and other marine life, but note that the outward leg is a beach landing, so wear shorts and water shoes.

Security Locals advise against walking on the beach at night: hold-ups have been reported. Although bike-riding police officers patrol the streets, it is worth taking care around town at night. Part of the police's mandate is to crack down on the use of recreational drugs, and stop-and-searches are not uncommon.

GETTING AROUND

Bike and scooter rental Many places rent out bikes (about $10/day); try Jaguar Riders on Av Pastor Diaz (☎ 2643 0180, ⓦ jaguariders.com) for scooters (around $40–50/day).

Car rental Agencies include Zuma (☎ 2643 1528, ⓦ zumarentacar.com) and Payless (☎ 2643 5409), both on Av Pastor Diaz.

ACCOMMODATION

Jacó's cheapest *cabinas* generally cater to weekending Josefinos or surfers; much of the mid-range accommodation is self-catering, useful if you're in town for more than a couple of days, and there are also a number of smarter places. In general, be prepared to pay more than either the town or, in some cases, the accommodation, merits. Staying on the main road can mean traffic noise, particularly on busy weekends.

NORTH OF JACÓ

★ **Hotel Vista Pacífico** On the hill at the far north end of town, signed off the Boulevard ☎ 2643 3261, ⊛ vistapacifico.com. An intimate hideaway, this tranquil hotel has it all: sweeping coastal views, mountaintop breezes and an attractive garden setting. Clustered around a sparkling blue pool, the studios and suites are bright and spotless and come with private bathrooms, a/c and TVs. **$77**

Los Sueños Marriott Ocean & Golf Resort Playa Herradura, 7km north of Jacó ☎ 2630 9000, ⊛ marriott .com. Overlooking Playa Herradura, *Los Sueños* is an expansive resort set amid 4.5 square kilometres of neatly-tended grounds. Many of the spacious en suites come with sea views, and some have private terraces and hammocks. Among the attractions are a beautiful series of inter-connected pools, plenty of activities for children and families, no fewer than six restaurants and bars, a spa and gym, and a world-class 18-hole golf course, plus highly professional service. It's an $8–10 taxi ride from Jacó. **$214**

Villa Caletas 15km north of Jacó, signed off the Costanera Sur ☎ 2637 0505, ⊛ hotelvillacaletas.com. Perched on a clifftop above the Pacific, this is one of Costa Rica's most extravagant boutique hotels. Beautifully decorated villas sit amid landscaped grounds that resemble a film set, with a small Greek theatre and Doric columns surrounding the pool; there are stunning views all round, especially at sunset. The restaurant serves gourmet cuisine with prices to match. A shuttle takes guests down the precipitous 1km trail to the private beach. **$220**

Vista Guapa Surf Camp At the far north end of town, signed 500m off the Boulevard ☎ 2643 2830 or ☎ 8364 3155, ⊛ vistaguapa.com. As the name implies, this surf hangout located high on the hill overlooking Jacó enjoys handsome views, so you can check out the breaks over breakfast. It's run by a former national champion – the staff are always on hand for surfing advice – while the smart bungalows themselves have a/c and hot-water bathrooms. Week-long packages (based on two people sharing) including lessons, board hire and food start at (per person) **$1100**

CENTRAL JACÓ

Blue Palms 350m east of Pops Heladería, on a street just south of C Bohío ☎ 2643 0099, ⊛ bphotel.com. This bright two-storey hotel with pool and wraparound balcony is good value for money. The crisp and comfortable rooms are equipped with telephones, a/c, cable TV, safe deposit and hot-water bathrooms. One room, sleeping up to six, has a kitchen ($94). **$81**

Hotel Canciones del Mar On the beach, at the end of C Bri Bri ☎ 2643 3273, ⊛ cancionesdelmar.com. The

colourful apartments in this appealing, bamboo-framed beachfront hotel come with large beds, patio and modern kitchen. Other pluses include an ample pool and worthwhile discounts for weekly and monthly stays. **$115**

Hotel de Haan C Bohío ☎ 2643 1795, ⊛ hoteldehaan .com. Run by a Dutch-Tico couple, this budget spot is popular with surfers. It has simple dorms and private rooms, a pool, and a lively atmosphere. Surf lessons are available too. Dorm **$19**, double **$45**

Hotel Mar de Luz Av Pastor Diaz ☎ 2643 3000, ⊛ mardeluz.com. This well-kept, family-friendly hotel sits amid soothing, landscaped grounds. Colourful modern apartments (sleeping up to five) surround two large pools and a garden. Large rooms are crammed with furniture and come with TV, a/c, microwave and kitchenette, plus there's a lounge and small library. The Dutch owners speak English, Spanish, Italian, German and French. **$92**

Hotel Poseidon C Bohío ☎ 2643 1642, ⊛ hotel -poseidon.com. The recently refurbished rooms at this two-storey, white stucco hotel are elegantly decorated and come with smart bathrooms and all modern conveniences, including TV and DVD player. There's a tiny pool if you can't face the 30m walk to the beach. Rates dip a bit Sun–Thurs. **$130**

Rutan Surf Cabinas C Anita ☎ 2643 3328, ⊛ rutan surfcabinas.com. A relaxed surfing vibe pervades this unpretentious little spot (also known as *Chuck's Cabinas*) with dorms and simple rooms with battle-weary mattresses and cold-water bathrooms. The BBQ area increases the social element. Dorm **$10**, double **$20**

Villas Estrellemar C Las Olas ☎ 2643 3102, ⊛ estrellamar.com. Set in landscaped gardens around a 25m pool, this unpretentious holiday complex is a terrific family option. Rooms come with private hot-water bath-rooms, a/c, TV and safes; villas (one to three bedrooms) also have a kitchen and private terrace (from $106). There's a bar and restaurant, table tennis, bike rental and palm-roofed chill-out area. **$89**

SOUTH JACÓ

Apartotel Girasol C Los Almendros ☎ 2643 1591, ⊛ girasol.com. Relax right on the beach in these spacious tiled apartments (sleeping up to four) with fan, a/c, a full kitchen and a cane-furnished lounge area. There's a lovely swimming pool and garden, plus secure parking. **$129**

★ **Casa Mafalda** C Hidalgo, off Av Pastor Diaz ☎ 2643 1687, ✉ casamafalda@live.com. Cute rooms and friendly service define this arty little beachfront hotel with just five rooms (some a/c, some fan, all with private bathrooms) and a funky thatched-roof breakfast bar overlooking the beach. **$105**

Hotel Club del Mar 1.5km south of Jacó, off the Costanera Sur ☎ 2643 3194, ☏ clubdelmarcostarica.com. Set on a quiet stretch of beach, these British-owned, luxury rooms and apartments (from $338) have a family-friendly atmosphere and a huge range of amenities, including pool, restaurant, spa, small library and games room. **$180**

EATING AND DRINKING

Caliche's Wishbone Av Pastor Diaz ☎ 2643 3406. Running the gamut from sushi to Mexican, stuffed pitta sandwiches to *casados* and pizzas to potato salads, this recommended restaurant has just about all your cravings covered (mains $11–30). Daily noon–10pm.

La Casa del Café Av Pastor Diaz ☎ 2643 5915. Cute little coffee shop that roasts its own beans and serves some of the best espressos, cappuccinos and frappes in town ($2–6; drink in or take away), as well as tempting cakes and filled panini. Daily 8am–6pm.

Panadería Artesenal Av Pastor Diaz ☎ 2643 6413. This little bakery and café near *Chuck's* serves a good range of breads, pastries and cakes (including croissants and baguettes), as well as *empanadas* ($2) and light meals to eat in or take away. Daily 6.30am–6pm.

Rioasis Av Pastor Diaz ☎ 2643 3354. Wood-fired pizzas and Mexican favourites (around $8–16) are dished up with fervour at this cavernous eatery by the *Best Western*: there's a relaxed outdoor area and an indoor bar that throbs with loud music. Daily 11.30am–10pm.

Soda Jacó Rústico C Hicaco. Join the queue of hungry locals and load your plate with Tico standards at this inexpensive, buffet-style *soda*, where you can have a good feed for around $5. Ask for takeaway and eat your feast on the beach just 50m away. Mon–Sat 7am–7pm, Thurs till 5pm.

★**Taco Bar** Off Av Pastor Diaz, at the start of the road out towards the Costanera Sur ☎ 2643 0222. Top lunch spot, and very novel: order your taco (from $7.50) – fish (mahi-mahi, wahoo, snapper, tuna) is the speciality – get it grilled or fried, and then smother it in BBQ, spicy or coconut sauce before scoffing it in one of the bar-side swings. Also huge burritos and hummus combos; a good all-you-can-eat salad bar is included with most dishes. Daily 7.30am–10pm, Mon from noon.

★**Tsunami Sushi** Upstairs in the Il Galeone Mall, Av Pastor Diaz ☎ 2643 3678. Stick your chopsticks into sushi, sashimi, tempura rolls and chicken teriyaki from the a/c confines of a curved leather chair. It's not cheap (expect to pay around $15–20), but the produce is top-notch – and there are daily specials (including half-price sushi rolls on Wed and Fri). Daily 11am–10pm.

The Wok Av Pastor Diaz ☎ 2654 6168. Popular pit stop for a quick Chinese-, Thai- or Indian-inspired stir-fry featuring roasted pork, chicken and tofu with rice or noodles (around $10); the pad thai here is particularly good. Mon–Sat 11.30am–10pm.

NIGHTLIFE

Nightlife is predictably hedonistic, with young holidaymakers jostling for bar space with prostitutes and their clientele; clubs are definitely of the meat-market variety.

Monkey Bar Av Pastor Diaz ☎ 2643 2357. Big a/c bar that draws a boisterous young crowd with pop and dance tracks. There are plenty of promotions and theme nights, including two-for-one drinks on Sunday nights. Daily 9pm–late.

Wahoos Av Pastor Diaz ☎ 2643 1876. This restaurant-bar draws in tourists and expats with its long cocktail list, karaoke nights (in English and Spanish), live music, and big-screen sports. The food's pretty good too. Daily noon–10/11pm.

DIRECTORY

Internet access Columbia Mía, just south of C Bri Bri (daily 9am–9pm).

Laundry Lava Max, Av Pastor Diaz.

Medical care Clínica Jacó, opposite the post office (☎ 2643 1767).

Money and exchange Several on Av Pastor Diaz, the main drag, including a Banco Nacional that accepts foreign-issued credit cards and changes travellers' cheques.

Post office At the southern end of town (Mon–Fri 8am–4.30pm, Sat 8am–noon).

Supermarkets Mas x Menos, Av Pastor Diaz, is smack in the centre of Jacó (daily 8am–10pm).

Playa Hermosa

Grey-sand **Playa Hermosa**, 5km south of Jacó, has long been a playground for hotshot surfers. Pummelled by powerful waves, the 10km-long strip rivals Dominical for having the most consistent **beach breaks** on Costa Rica's Pacific coast. Given its proximity to Jacó, it was inevitable the development craze would reach here, too, and condos are now going up along the beachfront at a rapid pace. The area is being sold as

6

a smarter version of Jacó: a coastal getaway without the noise, pollution, drugs and prostitution plaguing its neighbour – at least for now.

Hermosa is definitely not a beach for a casual dip (the riptides here are formidable), nor for novice surfers. Steep sand bars cause waves to break hard, fast and close to the shore, most impressively during the rainy season between May and August – with the best breakers in front of *Terraza del Pacífico* and the *Backyard Hotel*. On Saturday afternoons, you can watch how it should be done, when local surfers and gung-ho visitors tackle the waves as part of the Backyard Surf Series competition (4pm; free to enter; $300 top prize).

Refugio Nacional de Vida Silvestre Playa Hermosa y Punta Mala

South of the hotel strip, the **Refugio Nacional de Vida Silvestre Playa Hermosa y Punta Mala** protects a nesting site for olive ridley turtles, which come ashore to lay their eggs between August and December. It's off-limits to the public, but you can visit the turtle hatchery at the ranger station, a gridded block of beach being used to monitor the species' reproduction rates in this part of the Pacific.

ARRIVAL AND DEPARTURE   PLAYA HERMOSA

By bus You can get to Playa Hermosa from Jacó by catching a Quepos-bound bus (8 daily; 15min from Jacó) and asking to be let off at the relevant stop.

By taxi Taxis from Jacó cost around $8–10.

ACCOMMODATION

Condos and luxury hotels rising up along the beachfront are starting to bulldoze or overshadow Hermosa's more humble dwellings, although for the moment there are still plenty of budget options for thrifty surfers.

Backyard Hotel 500m south of the football field ☎ 2643 7011, ⓦ backyardhotel.com. The top choice for surfers with money, the sprightly rooms in this beachfront hotel have a/c, TVs and attached bathrooms. You can do laps in the swimming pool, just outside your balcony, party at the popular bar and restaurant next door and enjoy one of Hermosa's best surf breaks on your doorstep. **$150**

Cabinas Playa Hermosa 400m north of the football field ☎ 2643 2640, ⓦ fbsurfboards.com/surfcamp/. When there's a surfboard factory on-site, you know the place is the real deal. A crash-pad for pro surfers, each of the well-appointed *cabinas* sleep up to four people and have walk-in wardrobes and private bathrooms with hot water. Hang out in the communal kitchen and small TV lounge. **$57**

Cabinas Rancho Grande Just south of the football field ☎ 2643 7023, ⓦ cabinasranchogrande.com. The cheapest option on the strip, this sprucely renovated hostel buzzes with friendly surfers who congregate in the outdoor communal kitchen to cook after a hard day battling Hermosa's tubes. The private en-suite doubles have good facilities for the price – a/c, TV, etc – and there are low-cost bunks in the dorm. Dorm **$15**, double **$40**

Las Olas Hotel 300m south of the football field ☎ 2643 7021, ⓦ lasolashotel.com. Hang surfside with a sociable crowd at these rustic two-storey teak wood ranchos (sleeping up to seven; $100) or in the two-room main house. There's a modest swimming pool and beachfront restaurant with jaw-dropping views that dishes up hearty portions all day long. The laidback owner also arranges "stormchaser surf tours" around Costa Rica. **$50**

Terraza del Pacífico 500m north of the football field ☎ 2440 6862, ⓦ terrazadelpacifico.com. One of the most established hotels on the beach, but now overpriced, light-filled rooms here come with cable TV, wi-fi and a/c, and most have private balconies. The spacious grounds have two pools, a bar and restaurant virtually on the sand. **$165**

EATING AND DRINKING

Backyard Bar and Restaurant Next to the Backyard Hotel ☎ 2643 7011, ⓦ backyardhotel.com. A great spot to watch the sun melt into the horizon over sunset happy-hour drinks (4.30–7.30pm; frozen cocktails $5; there's also a second happy hour 9–11pm); at weekends, live music livens up the joint, while ladies' night (Wed) draws a large and boisterous crowd. Daily 8am–11pm; bar often stays open later.

Bistro Las Olas Las Olas Hotel, 300m south of the football field ☎ 2643 7021, ⓦ lasolashotel.com. At lunchtime, a young surfer crowd congregates beneath the palm-fringed roof of *Las Olas Hotel's* beachfront restaurant to scoff enormous portions of burgers and fries (around $7–10) while watching their fellow surfers get barrelled just metres away. Two-for-one tuna steak dinners on Wed. Daily 7am–9pm, closed Mon morning.

Jungle Surf Café Just off the Costanera Sur. Marked by a striking mural, the *Jungle Surf Café* is the stomach-filling spot of choice for hungry surfers and does a roaring trade in banana pancakes and seared tuna (mains around $8–12). Daily 7am–9pm.

Playas Esterillos

South of Playa Hermosa, some 25km from Jacó, palm-fringed **Playas Esterillos** fulfils the archetypal image of a tropical paradise beach: a long wedge of chocolate-brown sands, backed by jungle and stretching into the spray-shrouded distance. Rocks and river split the coastline here into three sections, each accessed by a different side road off the Costanera Sur; the most attractive beaches are **Esterillos Centro** and **Esterillos Este**, 3km apart by road, the latter home to one of the coolest hotels on the Central Pacific. The waves that pummel Esterillos' shores break further out than at Jacó and Playa Hermosa, and will appeal to more advanced **surfers** than those who ride the rollers further north.

ARRIVAL AND DEPARTURE   PLAYAS ESTERILLOS

By bus Quepos–Jacó buses (6–7 daily; around 25min from Jacó, 55min from Quepos) can drop you off on the highway, from where it's just under a kilometre to Playas Esterillos.

ACCOMMODATION

★**Alma de Pacífico** Esterillos Este ☏ 2778 7070, ⓦ legendarylodging.com/costarica. This fantastic beachfront boutique hotel put Esterillos on the map. It has an array of classy touches – unique architecture, artworks by the owner – along with personal plunge-pools in the swankier deluxe beachfront villas ($605). There's also a top-notch spa (massages from $90/1hr) and the on-site restaurant is superb. $214

Hotel Monterey del Mar Esterillos Este ☏ 2778 8787, ⓦ montereydelmar.com. This relaxing spot, just metres from the beach and with hammocks strung around its grounds, has a variety of rooms and garden- or ocean-view bungalows, let down slightly by their dated furnishings. The beachfront pool has a wet bar, and there's a romantic ambience to the softly lit restaurant. $94

Hotel Pelican Esterillos Este ☏ 2778 8105, ⓦ pelicanbeachfronthotel.com. Small beachfront hotel with tiled-floor rooms featuring a/c and attached bathrooms. Guests have free use of bodyboards, and the hotel also rents out surfboards and runs lessons; after tackling the waves, hit the on-site restaurant for sandwiches or ceviche. $96

Parque Nacional Manuel Antonio and around

Small but perfectly formed, **Parque Nacional Manuel Antonio** ranks among the top tourist destinations in the country – visitors descend in droves to experience its stunning, picture-postcard setting, with spectacular white-grey sand beaches fringed by thickly forested hills. The striking *tómbolo* formation of **Punta Catedral**, jutting out into the Pacific, accounts for much of the region's allure, and as you watch a lavish sunset flower and die over the ocean, it does seem as though Manuel Antonio may be one of the more charmed places on earth.

That said, the huge tourist boom has undeniably taken its toll on the area, and the small corridor of land between the old banana-exporting town of **Quepos** and the little community of **Manuel Antonio** is one of the most crowded pieces of real estate in the country, featuring an unbroken line of hotels and restaurants that run right down to the park's perimeter.

Quepos and around

Arriving in **QUEPOS** from San José, Puntarenas or Jacó, it's immediately apparent that you've crossed into the lush, wetter, southern Pacific region. The vegetation grows thicker and greener than further north, and more often than not it has just started or finished raining. Backed up against a thick hill, with a polluted beach in front (obscured by the seaside road out to the old dock), Quepos can look pretty ramshackle, though the **Marina Pez Vela**, a newish dock built on reclaimed land southwest of town, adds a glossier sheen. What Quepos does enjoy is close proximity to **Parque Nacional Manuel Antonio** and its beaches, as well as the very different, and much more low-key, **Reserva Los Campesinos**; Quepos' range of (affordable) hotels, bars and restaurants and frequent bus services to the park make it the most useful base.

Once a banana-exporting town, Quepos (the name is derived from the indigenous language of the Quepoa people, who occupied this area before the arrival of the Spanish in 1563) was severely hit by the Panama disease, a devastating banana virus, which prompted United Fruit to pull out in the 1950s. With the establishment of the nearby African oil-palm plantations, though, the area has gone through something of a resurgence in recent decades, and thanks to the bounty of big fish (sailfish, marlin and wahoo) occupying its waters offshore, has also developed into one of the country's prime **sportfishing** destinations.

Reserva Los Campesinos

25km east of Quepos • Day-tours $44.50 • ☎ 2248 9470, ⓦ actuarcostarica.com

If you want to experience an authentic Costa Rican peasant lifestyle, **Reserva Los Campesinos**, set in a small mountain community 25km east of Quepos along a rough road, offers a memorable day-long eco-adventure. The reserve is managed by the Quebrada Aroyo community, an association of local vanilla producers who are creating a biological corridor to Parque Nacional Manuel Antonio, and activities involve guided hikes to waterfall pools and a ride on an old-school aerial tram; additional tours include trips to local organic farms, horseriding and whitewater rafting on the Río Savegre.

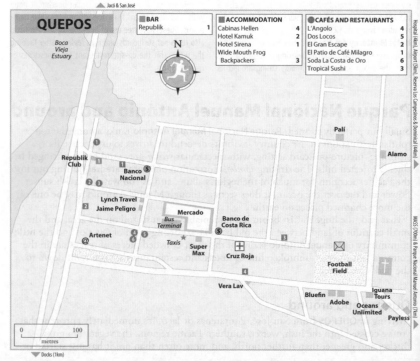

■ BAR	
Republik	1

■ ACCOMMODATION	
Cabinas Hellen	4
Hotel Kamuk	2
Hotel Sirena	1
Wide Mouth Frog Backpackers	3

● CAFÉS AND RESTAURANTS	
L'Angolo	4
Dos Locos	5
El Gran Escape	2
El Patio de Café Milagro	1
Soda La Costa de Oro	6
Tropical Sushi	3

ARRIVAL AND GETTING AROUND

By plane Due to the long drive, many people fly from San José; the flights tend to be heavily booked, so reserve early. Lynch Travel (see below) can book tickets. A minibus ($10) runs from the airstrip, 5km north of town, into Quepos and on to Manuel Antonio; a taxi costs around $10 to Quepos and $20 to Manuel Antonio.

Destinations La Fortuna (2 daily; 40min); San José (7 daily; 25min).

By bus All buses stop at Quepos's busy terminal, which doubles as the *mercado*, one block east of the town centre. Of the buses that run from San José's La Coca-Cola bus station, only the five (four on Sun) slower regular buses continue on to Manuel Antonio, dropping off at hotels on

QUEPOS AND AROUND

request. On weekends, holidays and any time during the dry season, buy your bus ticket at least three days in advance, and your return ticket as soon as you arrive.

Destinations Dominical (6 daily; 1hr 30min); Manuel Antonio (every 30min from 7am to 7pm; 20min); Puntarenas (8 daily; 3hr) via Jacó (1hr 30min); Uvita (3 daily; 1hr 30min); San José (9–11 daily; 3hr 30min–4hr 30min).

By car If you're driving, you can get to San Isidro, Golfito, the Osa Peninsula and other points in the Zona Sur via Dominical, 44km south of Quepos.

By taxi Taxis line up at the rank at the south end of the *mercado*; the journey to Manuel Antonio costs around $15.

6

INFORMATION

Tourist information There's no official tourist office, although you can get unbiased information at Lynch Travel (see below). For up-to-date town info (including bus schedules), pick up *Quepolandia* (w quepolandia.com), a free bi-monthly English newsletter found at many local businesses.

Security Take the usual precautions against theft and bear in mind that it's unwise to walk around at night in Quepos, as the sea-wall area is a hangout for local drug users – drugs have become a problem in the area and are blamed for many of the robberies from hotel rooms and cars.

TOURS AND ACTIVITIES

Amigos del Río Just outside Quepos, on the road to Manuel Antonio ☎ 2777 0082, w amigosdelrio.net. Runs whitewater-rafting tours on the Class II–III Río Savegre ($89/6hr) and Class III–IV Río Naranjo ($70/4hr).

Bluefin On the south side of the football field ☎ 2777 0000, w bluefinsportfishing.com. One of several agencies in the Quepos area running sportfishing trips (from $500).

Dreamforest Canopy 3km northeast of Quepos ☎ 2777 4567, w dreamforestcanopy.com. Dreamforest is the canopy tour company of choice for adrenaline junkies (tours $69).

Iguana Tours Just south of the church ☎ 2777 2052, w iguanatours.com. Iguana Tours offers horseriding and whitewater rafting, plus hiking in Parque Nacional Manuel Antonio ($48, includes entrance fee) and boat and kayak trips around Isla Damas, a wildlife-rich mangrove estuary just north of Quepos (both $65).

Luna Tours In the lobby of Hotel Kamuk ☎ 2777 0725, w lunatours.net. Luna Tours offers a range of sportfishing trips (from $450).

Lynch Travel Just west of the bus terminal ☎ 2777 1170, w lynchtravel.com. The biggest operator in Quepos. You can book whitewater-rafting and canopy tours through them, and their many local tours include horse rides to a waterfall ($65) and daytime or sunset cruises, some specifically to see dolphins (both $75). They also run trips to Dominical, Corcovado and Bahía Drake, and can organize transfers to Panama.

MASS Just south of Quepos, on the road to Manuel Antonio ☎ 2777 4842, w masurfschool.com. MASS offers surfing lessons ($65/3hr) on Playa Espadilla in Manuel Antonio.

Oceans Unlimited Just southeast of the church ☎ 2777 3171, w scubadivingcostarica.com. If you'd rather see the fish than catch them, Oceans Unlimited runs scuba-diving excursions (around $150) and multi-day PADI courses.

Titi Canopy Tour 5km northeast of Quepos ☎ 2777 3130, w titicanopytour.com. Slower and more suitable for families than Dreamforest (day tours $65, night tours $80).

ACCOMMODATION

Cabinas Hellen A block south and east of the bus station ☎ 2777 0504. These secure *cabinas* at the back of a family home are equipped with private bathroom, fridge and fans. They offer decent single rates ($20), and there's also a small patio and parking. $30

Hotel Kamuk On the western avenue ☎ 2777 0811, w kamuk.co.cr. Part of the Best Western chain, *Kamuk*

offers rooms around a small pool, with a/c and TVs and – in the pricier ones – balconies with sea views. The restaurant centres on seafood – they'll cook up the fish you catch. $79

★**Hotel Sirena** On first road to the left as you enter Quepos ☎ 2777 0572, w lasirenahotel.com. Pretty little hotel, whose charming blue-and-white rooms – those upstairs receive more light – come with private bathrooms and a/c. The small pool is flanked by a bar and restaurant; the bountiful breakfast served here is all either home-made or locally sourced. $94

Wide Mouth Frog Backpackers 150m east of the bus station ☎ 2777 2798, ⊛ widemouthfrog.org. The best place to stay on a budget. The efficient Kiwi–British owners

at this sociable hostel offer a swimming pool, TV lounge, breakfast, internet and tight security. The dorms though are a bit institutional, and the rooms could do with a bit of a freshen-up (en-suite bathrooms cost $10 extra). Rules pasted everywhere can get a bit tedious, but they don't detract from the relaxed vibe. Dorm $12, double $40

EATING AND DRINKING

The **restaurants** in Quepos fall into two categories: gringo-owned and -geared eateries and cheaper ones owned by locals and frequented by Ticos. **Fish** is predictably good – order grilled *pargo* (dorado) and you can't go wrong. Midweek, **nightlife** is more or less limited to excited fishermen debating the merits of different tackle; at the weekends, several bars in the centre get lively with a mix of tourists, expats and locals who hang out until fairly late at night.

L'Angolo 25m west of the bus station ☎ 2777 4129. Make up your own panini (from $3) using the range of Italian meats and cheeses on offer at this deli, or try one of the salads or fresh pasta dishes from an extensive list. Mon–Sat 10am–10pm.

Dos Locos Just southwest of the bus station ☎ 2777 1526. Enjoy the usual range of fajitas, burritos and tacos, plus Mexican pizza (mains $7–17), while taking in street views from the open-air dining area. Wash it all down with a margarita or two. Mon–Sat 7am–11pm, Sun noon–4pm.

El Gran Escape On the sea wall ☎ 2777 0395, ⊛ elgranescape.com. Decent, if fairly pricey, salads, burgers (from $11) and seafood ($6.50–25; no marlin, despite the statue) and a good selection of drinks at the bar (happy hour 5–7pm) draws an overwhelmingly American fishing crowd. The pleasant, plant-filled seating area opens to the street – and weekend nights can get rowdy. Daily except Tues and Sun 8am–10pm.

★**El Patio de Café Milagro** Facing the sea wall ☎ 2777 0794, ⊛ cafemilagro.com. The coffee ($2–4) here is among the best in the country; try the delicious Queppuccino or buy a bag of roasted beans to take home from the shop two doors down. They also serve

refrescos (in flavours like vanilla nut chill or iced raspberry mocha) and cakes, as well as selling English-language newspapers and magazines. The breakfasts are creative and hearty, and by night it turns into a quality restaurant serving Latin-influenced cuisine, from pulled-pork corn cakes to coconut rum shrimp. There's also a branch on the road to Manuel Antonio (see p.356). Mon–Sat 7am–5pm.

Republik On the western avenue ☎ 2777 2120. Quepos's premier nightclub, *Republik* is a little smarter than the others in town (though not as cool as the owners, who have installed a so-called "VIP section", seem to think) and draws a fun mix of locals and visitors. Expect dance, Latin and reggaeton. Tues–Sat 7pm–4.30am.

Soda La Costa de Oro Next to Banco Popular. The best and cheapest *soda* in town, *Soda La Costa de Oro* serves up tasty chicken *casados* ($5) to a busy lunchtime (or early evening) crowd of locals and tourists. Daily 6am–7pm.

Tropical Sushi Near El Gran Escape ☎ 2777 1710. Brightly coloured sushi shack serving fresh tuna hauled out of the Pacific that morning – as well as maki rolls and sashimi ($6–8) – in an all-you-can-eat sushi extravaganza, eaten either in the cramped interior or on the patio out back. Daily 4–11pm.

DIRECTORY

Bookshop Jaime Peligro, next to Lynch Travel, sells new and secondhand books and CDs, and is a good source of information (Mon–Fri 9.30am–6pm, Sat 11am–5pm; ☎ 2777 7106, ⊛ queposbooks.com).

Car rental Adobe (☎ 2777 4242, ⊛ adobecar.com), opposite the football field; Alamo (☎ 2777 3344, ⊛ alamo costarica.com), near the Palí supermarket; and Payless (☎ 2777 0115), on the road towards Manuel Antonio.

Internet access Many places, including Artenet, opposite the park (Mon–Sat 9am–7pm).

Laundry Vera Lav, 100m west of the football field (Mon–Sat 8am–5pm).

Markets The *mercado* sells fish and fresh fruit and veg (Mon–Sat 6.30am–5pm); there's also a weekend *fería*

(Fri 6–9pm, Sat 6am–2pm) offering fruit, veg and home-made bread.

Medical care Hospital Dr Max Teran (☎ 2777 0922) near the airport, or the Red Cross (Cruz Roja; ☎ 2777 0116) between the bus station and the football field.

Money and exchange Banco Nacional, just northwest of the bus station, changes money and travellers' cheques and has an ATM; also Banco de Costa Rica, opposite the bus station. Most businesses in town accept and change dollars.

Post office The post office (Mon–Fri 8am–noon & 1–4.30pm, Sat 8am–noon) is near the football field, at the eastern end of town.

Manuel Antonio village

Southeast of Quepos, a 7km stretch of road winds over the surrounding hills, pitching up at the entrance to the village of **MANUEL ANTONIO** and Parque Nacional Manuel Antonio. Manuel Antonio was one of the first places in the country to feel the effects of the 1990s tourist explosion – drawn by its lavish beauty, hoteliers and businesses rushed to the area, and these days the entire road from Quepos is lined with some sort of hotel or restaurant.

Playa Espadilla

Just north of the park entrance, lies **Playa Espadilla** (also sometimes called Playa Primera or Playa Numero Uno), one of the most popular beaches in Costa Rica, and boasting wide, smooth, light-grey sands and stunning sunsets; MASS (see p.351) has an outlet here, offering surf lessons. The beach is plagued by **riptides** (travelling up to 10kph), however, though lots of people do also swim here – or rather, paddle and wade – and live to tell the tale. Lifeguards now patrol in high season, so it's considerably safer.

ARRIVAL AND DEPARTURE

MANUEL ANTONIO VILLAGE

By bus The Manuel Antonio bus from San José (5–6 daily; 5hr) drops people off at their hotel along the road between the town and park entrance; local services from Quepos to Manuel Antonio village (every 30min; 20min) depart from the terminal between 7am and 7pm and also at 5.45am, 6.45am & 10pm (Sat & Sun also 9.30am).

ACCOMMODATION

The most exclusive – and expensive – hotels are hidden away in the surrounding hills, with lovely ocean and sunset views. Though you'll find some affordable places in Manual Antonio village, and the occasional low-season discount, prices are high compared to the rest of the country. Reserve well in advance – as much as four months if visiting in the peak season (Dec 1–Jan 15).

THE ROAD TO MANUEL ANTONIO
The following places are listed in the order you encounter them from Quepos.

El Mono Azul Quepos–Manuel Antonio road ☎ 2777 2572, ⊛ monoazul.com. Small but bright rooms come with a fan or a/c and a terrace, centred round lovely swimming pools; across the road, villas sleep up to five. The on-site restaurant is popular for its down-to-earth, good honest grub. Double $62, villa $96

★ **Gaia Hotel and Reserve** Just off the Quepos–Manuel Antonio road ☎ 2777 9797, ⊛ gaiahr.com. Beloved by the glossy-brochure brigade, this ultra-chic boutique hotel takes style and service to the next level. Well-appointed terraced suites and villas, decked with natural flooring, come with huge, cloud-soft beds, flat-screen TVs and rainforest views – the hotel is set on a former wildlife rehabilitation centre and its reserve takes up 85 percent of the property (rates include guided tours). There are two pools, one cascading into the other, and you could quite easily eat all your meals at the fine restaurant, with its varied menu and globetrotting wine list. Room rates include a free treatment at the on-site spa. No children. $328

Didi's B&B Quepos–Manuel Antonio road ☎ 2777 0069, ⊛ didiscr.com. Thoughtful Italian hosts run this B&B, which has three colourfully decorated rooms including TVs and either fans or a/c ($17 extra). By prior request, the owner can whip up a three-course Italian dinner using produce bought at the market that day. $62

Hotel Las Tres Banderas Quepos–Manuel Antonio road ☎ 2777 1871, ⊛ hoteltresbanderas.com. Set in a quiet wooded area, this welcoming hotel has large double rooms that open onto a terrace or balcony overlooking the forest. Spacious suites have a kitchenette and sofa bed, while the "tropical hideaways" feature two deluxe rooms – if you can find them amid the foliage. There's a swimming pool and a restaurant that sometimes serves tasty Polish specialities. Double $90, suite $113

Hotel La Colina Quepos–Manuel Antonio road ☎ 2777 0231, ⊛ lacolina.com. Set on an incline locals call "Cardiac Hill", this lovely hotel offers comfortable rooms with private bath and a/c; if your legs are up to it, the rooms higher up boast a fantastic 180-degree view of the jungle and sea. A sparkling pool flows over two levels, and there's also an on-site restaurant. $79

★ **Vista Serena Hostel** Quepos–Manuel Antonio road ☎ 2777 5162, ⊛ vistaserena.com. Clean, welcoming hostel offering million-dollar views and plenty of dorm beds full of gringo students looking for a good time; the private ocean-view bungalows with shared bathroom can sleep three people. Watch the sunset from the hammock-strung balcony or cook with fellow travellers in the

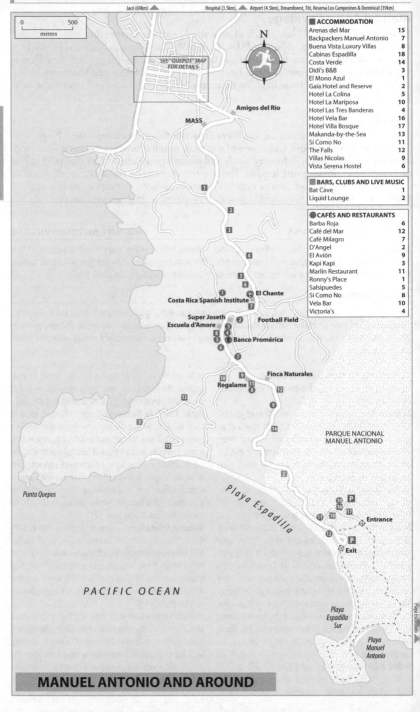

Jacó (69km), Hospital (3.5km), Airport (4.5km), Dreamforest, Titi, Reserva Los Campesinos & Dominical (39km)

0 500 metres

N

SEE "QUEPOS" MAP FOR DETAILS

Amigos del Rio

MASS

Costa Rica Spanish Institute
@ El Chante

Super Joseth
Escuela d'Amore
Football Field
Banco Promérica

Finca Naturales

Regalame

Punta Quepos

Playa Espadilla

PARQUE NACIONAL MANUEL ANTONIO

P
Entrance

P
Exit

PACIFIC OCEAN

Playa Espadilla Sur

Playa Manuel Antonio

Playa Escondido

ACCOMMODATION

Arenas del Mar	15
Backpackers Manuel Antonio	7
Buena Vista Luxury Villas	8
Cabinas Espadilla	18
Costa Verde	14
Didi's B&B	3
El Mono Azul	1
Gaia Hotel and Reserve	2
Hotel La Colina	5
Hotel La Mariposa	10
Hotel Las Tres Banderas	4
Hotel Vela Bar	16
Hotel Villa Bosque	17
Makanda-by-the-Sea	13
Sí Como No	11
The Falls	12
Villas Nicolas	9
Vista Serena Hostel	6

BARS, CLUBS AND LIVE MUSIC

Bat Cave	1
Liquid Lounge	2

CAFÉS AND RESTAURANTS

Barba Roja	6
Café del Mar	12
Café Milagro	7
D'Angel	2
El Avión	9
Kapi Kapi	3
Marlin Restaurant	11
Ronny's Place	1
Salsipuedes	5
Si Como No	8
Vela Bar	10
Victoria's	4

MANUEL ANTONIO AND AROUND

6

communal kitchen. Extras include BBQ nights and a TV/DVD lounge. Dorm $10, bungalow $45

Backpackers Manuel Antonio Quepos–Manuel Antonio road ☎ 2777 2507, ⓦ backpackersmanuelantonio.com. This family-run hostel is one of the cheapest options on the road to the park, offering a mix of cell-like dorms and private rooms, all with shared hot-water bathrooms. It's also one of the most sociable, whether you're teaming up on the table football or grilling meat on the patio out back (there's a good butcher's just across the road). Dorm $12, double $35

★**Buena Vista Luxury Villas** Quepos–Manuel Antonio road ☎ 2777 0580, ⓦ buenavistaluxuryvillas.com. High-spec suites and villas, perched among the treetops, enjoy sweeping views down over the Pacific. Villas, in particular, are beautifully furnished and kitted out with just about anything you could ever need – the open kitchens are chock-full of designer goods; bedrooms in the stunning "premium villas" ($527) have their own private terraces in addition to the jacuzzi-toting main balcony, plus outdoor rainwater showers. If you can drag yourself away, there are three pools (one for families) and an exclusive beach complete with (free) bodyboards and kayaks. $316

Hotel La Mariposa Just off the Quepos–Manuel Antonio road ☎ 2777 0355, ⓦ lamariposa.com. Manuel Antonio's original luxury hotel offers villas set in lovely gardens around a pair of swimming pools. Take in Punta Catedral views from many of the luxurious rooms or treat yourself to the unsurpassed views from the penthouse suite, complete with floor-to-ceiling glass walls and private hot tub. Enjoy excellent meals at the prestigious (though overpriced) Mediterranean restaurant or settle for a sunset cocktail. $182

Makanda-by-the-Sea Off the Quepos–Manuel Antonio road ☎ 2777 0442, ⓦ makanda.com. Surrounded by quiet gardens with ocean views, these elegant luxury studios and villas feature beautiful hardwood ceilings and long wraparound sofas. The many amenities include fully equipped kitchenettes and CD players and iPod docks in the lounge. No children under 16. Studio $299, villa $452

★**Arenas del Mar** Off the Quepos–Manuel Antonio road ☎ 2777 2777, ⓦ arenasdelmar.com. Set over large grounds on the headland at the northern end of Playa Espadilla (golf carts whizz you about), this sumptuous resort has spacious en suites, with huge bathrooms, flat-screen TVs and tasteful design; some also have outdoor jacuzzis and great views down over Punta Catedral. It's strong on sustainability – the hotel incorporates everything from solar-powered hot water to recycled roof tiles – and the owners spent twenty years replanting the area (it was formerly a plantain farm) before it opened in 2008, so there's plenty of wildlife on-site, from howler monkeys to black iguanas. There's also an excellent restaurant, plus two pools, and direct access to secluded sections of beach. $350

Villas Nicolas Quepos–Manuel Antonio road ☎ 2777 0481, ⓦ villasnicolas.com. Set high above the surrounding greenery, these classy villas come with hot-water private bathroom and ceiling fans; some have kitchens, and there's also a small pool. Villas with full sea views go for $40 more. No children under 6. $141

★**Sí Como No** Quepos–Manuel Antonio road ☎ 2777 0777, ⓦ sicomono.com. Enjoy beautiful views of the Pacific and Punta Catedral from this award-winning complex set high on a hill. Lovely, brightly furnished rooms vary from well-appointed doubles to fully equipped villas; extensive facilities include a hot tub, two pools, swim-up bar, spa and a small cinema with nightly screenings. The two restaurants (see p.356) serve excellent food. The hotel also runs a small forest reserve, Fincas Naturales, with a butterfly garden and wildlife refuge/zoo. $283

The Falls Quepos–Manuel Antonio road ☎ 2777 1332, ⓦ fallsresortcr.com. Individually designed suites offering comfortable four-poster beds, large bathrooms and a pleasant patio with views of the tropical gardens – plenty of animals, including toucans and sloths, can be spotted in the waterfall-laced grounds. There's also a small infinity pool that seems to "hang" out over the foliage. $168

Costa Verde Quepos–Manuel Antonio road ☎ 2777 0584, ⓦ costaverde.com. Spacious rooms and studio apartments, all constructed out of beautiful hardwood, with ocean-view balconies and lovely details like decorative tiles, plus arguably the most distinctive suite in the country: a salvaged Boeing 727, furnished with teak, which appears to be launching right out of the hillside. Choose from three swimming pools with stupendous vistas, and cap off the day with a fine meal in the restaurant. $130

MANUEL ANTONIO VILLAGE

Cabinas Espadilla Off the Quepos–Manuel Antonio road ☎ 2777 2113, ⓦ espadilla.com. Set in attractive gardens with a pool, these pleasant, airy cabins have large beds, hot-water private bathrooms, a kitchen and fan or a/c, though are better value for groups of three to four people. Guests have use of the tennis court at the nearby sister hotel, and there's easy access to Playa Espadilla. $120

Hotel Vela Bar Near the park entrance ☎ 2777 0413, ⓦ velabar.com. This small hotel near the beach and surrounded by tropical gardens, has basic, pleasant rooms with private bathrooms and fan or a/c. Apartments come with lounge, kitchenette and terrace. Good restaurant (see p.356) too. $57

Hotel Villa Bosque Near the park entrance ☎ 2777 0463, ⓦ hotelvillabosque.com. Light, bright rooms in a whitewashed, terracotta-tile-topped villa with wicker chairs, private hot-water bathrooms and a/c. There's also a pleasant outdoor reading and TV area, a decent restaurant and bar, and a small oval swimming pool. $177

6

EATING AND DRINKING

Eating in Manuel Antonio is notoriously expensive, and the area's few reasonably priced restaurants are understandably popular. For nightlife, there's live music and/or dancing at *Barba Roja*, *Liquid Lounge* and *Salsipuedes* (see below).

THE ROAD TO MANUEL ANTONIO

The following places are listed in the order you encounter them from Quepos.

Ronny's Place Off the Quepos–Manuel Antonio road ☎ 2777 5120, ⓦ ronnysplace.com. Simple food – grilled chicken, steaks and pricey seafood specials ($12.50–25) – but sensational sunsets, the real reason you've come to this rustic place perched on the edge of the coast. Order a jug of headachingly strong *sangría* and plop yourself down at the tables lined up along the ridge. Daily noon–10pm.

★ D'Angel Quepos–Manuel Antonio road. Fill up with the cheapest and best *casados* on the hill – five types are on offer, including liver (from $5) – at this charming and unpretentious *soda*, home to just a few tree-trunk tables. Daily 9am–9pm.

Kapi Kapi Quepos–Manuel Antonio road ☎ 2777 5049, ⓦ restaurantekapikapi.com. The select menu at this fine-dining restaurant specializes in seafood and also offers meat dishes, such as grilled chicken with miso and honey and macadamia-encrusted mahi-mahi (mains from $20). Sinful desserts include a one-is-not-enough chocolate soufflé. Tues–Sun 4–10pm.

Victoria's Quepos–Manuel Antonio road ☎ 2777 5143, ⓦ victoriasgourmet.com. Upscale Italian restaurant with delicious, though pricey, pizzas (from $15) with ingredients such as home-made pesto and house mozzarella, as well as similarly priced American-Italian-style pasta dishes such as spaghetti and meatballs. Daily 4–11pm.

Salsipuedes Quepos–Manuel Antonio road ☎ 2777 5019. Lively restaurant serving tapas-style dishes (from $8–10) – so little portions of fajitas, grilled mahi-mahi, white-bean stew and the like – which you can upgrade to mains. Soak up the great balcony vistas with a (*guaro* sour) cocktail in hand. Wed–Mon 7am–10pm.

Barba Roja Quepos–Manuel Antonio road ☎ 2777 5159, ⓦ barbarojarestaurant.com. This friendly, popular restaurant dishes up quality American cuisine ($14.50–20), including grilled fish, tenderloin steaks, chunky burgers and lip-smacking BBQ ribs. Come and nurse a quiet drink while watching the sunset (happy hour 4.30–6.30pm), or crank things up a gear on Saturday nights, when live music is on the menu (from 8pm). Tues–Sun 3–10.30pm, Sat 3–11pm.

Café Milagro Quepos–Manuel Antonio road ☎ 2777 2272, ⓦ cafemilagro.com. Pop by for one of the best breakfasts around, or drop in any time to enjoy delicious home-made pastries washed down with excellent locally roasted coffee ($2–4) or a perfect cappuccino. The main branch in nearby Quepos (see p.352) doubles as a great little evening bistro. Daily 7am–10pm.

Bat Cave La Mansion Hotel, off the Quepos–Manuel Antonio road ☎ 2777 3489, ⓦ lamansioninn.com. For something different, if a little claustrophobic, head down a winding staircase to the *Bat Cave*, an underground bar housed in a natural grotto that has bats flittering around the ceiling. Daily 7pm–midnight.

Sí Como No Quepos–Manuel Antonio road ☎ 2777 0777, ⓦ sicomono.com. Succulent fish brochettes and other grilled treats at the *Rico Tico Grill* (daily 6.30am–9.30pm), which has a good children's menu and features nightly live music, or more upmarket dining at the poolside *Claro Que Sí* (daily 5–10pm), a Caribbean-influenced seafood restaurant dishing coconut shrimps ($25) and the like; both overlook forest that is home to squirrel monkeys and coati. Diners at *Claro Que Sí* can also catch a complimentary film afterwards in the hotel's private cinema.

El Avión Quepos–Manuel Antonio road ☎ 2777 0584. Dine or drink inside a US aircraft used in the 1980s for arms-trafficking at this appropriately named restaurant. In truth, dining is more enjoyable in the open-air section, with sensational views, but the whole place exudes character. The menu includes average burgers, pastas and fajitas (dishes from $10). Daily noon–11pm (low season 1–10pm).

Liquid Lounge Quepos–Manuel Antonio road ☎ 2777 5158, ⓦ facebook.com/Liquid.Lounge.Manuel.Antonio. Cool gay and lesbian (though hetro-friendly) lounge bar-club with anything from pop tunes to electro tracks on the sound system. It's a good opportunity to dress up. Thursdays are big nights. Daily except Mon 9pm–2.30am.

MANUEL ANTONIO VILLAGE

Café del Mar On the beach ☎ 2777 1035. This popular thatched *chiringuito* (snack bar) kiosk serves up burgers, sandwiches and salads (from $6), as well as cold beers to thirsty beach-goers; the relaxing music adds to the vibe. Daily 9am–8.30pm.

Marlin Restaurant 5min from the park entrance ☎ 2777 1035. One of the cheaper places to eat in Manuel Antonio, this cheerful terrace restaurant serves up fresh seafood, Tex-Mex sandwiches and salads (mains from $8–10) to crowds of hungry tourists. Daily 7am–9pm.

Vela Bar Near the park entrance ☎ 2777 0413, ⓦ velabar.com. Dine on grilled fish, paella and an assortment of vegetarian dishes (from around $15) in this dark, thatched restaurant, the swankiest in the village, or push the boat out and go for the seafood platter. Daily 7am–9.30pm.

DIRECTORY

Bookshop Regalame (daily 7am–10pm), *Sí Como No's* *artesanía* shop, next to the hotel, sells glossy coffee-table books and also stocks the work of local painters and craftsmen.

Internet access In *La Cantina's* restored carriage (daily from 4pm), brought all the way from Chile; otherwise, El Chante (Mon–Sat 9am–9pm).

Language schools Several including reputable Escuela d'Amore (☎ 2777 1143, ⓦ escueladamore.com) and the

Costa Rica Spanish Institute (☎ 2234 1001, ⓦ cosi.co.cr); from $340 for a week of classes.

Medical care The nearest hospital is in Quepos (see p.352).

Money and exchange Banco Promérica, 400m south of the football field, opposite *Barba Roja*, has an ATM.

Supermarket Super Joseth: 150m southwest of the football field (daily 7.30am–9.30pm, Sun from 8am); and at Playa Espadilla (daily 8am–9pm).

Parque Nacional Manuel Antonio

150km southwest of San José as the crow flies • Tues–Sun 7am–4pm • $10 • ☎ 2777 5185

PARQUE NACIONAL MANUEL ANTONIO may be Costa Rica's smallest national park, but it's also its most popular. Considering the number of hotels and restaurants sidling up to the park's borders, one can easily imagine the fate that might have overtaken its limestone-white sands had it not been designated a national park in 1972. Even so, the park suffers from a high number of visitors (over 300,000 in 2010), and came within days of being closed down by the Ministry of Health in January 2009, after its then-inadequate facilities (much improved since) caused the pollution of local rivers and coastline. The park does close on Mondays, however, to give the animals a rest and the rangers and trail maintenance staff a chance to work.

Covering an area of only 6.8 square kilometres, Manuel Antonio preserves not only the lovely **beaches** and the unique *tómbolo* formation of Punta Catedral

PARQUE NACIONAL MANUEL ANTONIO

(Cathedral Point), but also **mangroves** and humid tropical **forest**. Visitors can only visit the part of the park that faces the sea – the eastern mountain section, off-limits to the public, is regularly patrolled by rangers to deter poaching, which is rife in the area, and incursions into the park from surrounding farmers and *campesinos*.

The trails

Manuel Antonio has a tiny system of short **trails**, all easy, except in rainy conditions, when they can get slippery. From the park entrance, the main trail, **Sendero El Perezoso**, runs for 1.3km down to Playa Manuel Antonio, providing, as the name suggests, a fair chance of spotting sloths in the guarumo trees along the way, as well as squirrel and howler monkeys. About 400m in, the short **Sendero La Catarata** (900m) leads to the pretty little waterfall after which it's named.

At the end of the trail, most people continue straight down to Playa Manuel Antonio, but for more rainforest hiking you can either head inland on the **Sendero Mirador** (1.3km), which ends at a viewpoint overlooking Playa Puerto Escondido, or take the beachside **Sendero Playas Gemelas y Puerto Escondido** (1.6km), which heads through relatively dense, humid tropical forest cover, crossing a small creek before eventually reaching the rocky beach itself; a turn-off halfway along leads to Playas Gemelas. You can clamber across Playa Puerto Escondido at low tide – but check tide times with the rangers before leaving to avoid getting cut off.

Playa Manuel Antonio is the park's best swimming beach and, predictably, its most crowded – both with people and with white-faced capuchin monkeys, who seem to be running a competition with the local racoon population as to who can steal the most backpack snacks. At the southern end of the beach, low tide reveals a pile of stones believed to have been used as **turtle traps** by the area's indigenous peoples – green turtles have probably nested in Manuel Antonio for thousands of years. Beyond here, it's worth embarking on the **Sendero Punta Catedral** (1.4km), an energetic loop offering wonderful views of the Pacific, dotted with jagged-edged little islands; like all *tómbolos*, Punta Catedral was once an island that, over millennia, has been joined to the mainland through accumulated sand deposits.

MANUEL ANTONIO BEACHES

The **beaches** around Parque Nacional Manuel Antonio can be confusing, since they're called by a variety of different names. It's important to know which beach you're on, however, because some are unsafe for swimming; check with the rangers about conditions. From north to south, the beaches are as follows:

Playa Espadilla (also called Playa Primera or Playa Numero Uno). This long, popular curve of sand fronting Manuel Antonio village runs down to the park exit, just outside the park itself (see p.353).

Playa Espadilla Sur (also called Playa Dos or Playa Segunda). Espadilla Sur is the last beach you come to inside the park – the main trail towards the exit runs along the back of the beach. It's on the north side of Punta Catedral, and while usually fairly calm, it's also the most dangerous in rough conditions – beware the currents.

Playa Manuel Antonio (also called Playa Tres or Playa Blanca). Immediately south of Punta Catedral, and in a deeper and more protected bay than the others, Manuel Antonio is by far the best swimming beach, though you can still get clobbered by the deceptively gentle-looking waves as they hit the shore. Unfortunately, it's quite narrow and can get crowded (the best time to come is before 10am).

Playa Puerto Escondido (also called Playa Cuatro). Reached along the Sendero Puerto Escondido, this is a pretty, white horseshoe-shaped beach. Don't set out without first checking with the rangers about the *marea* (tide), because at high tide you can't get across the beach, nor can you cross it from the dense forest behind. At best, it'll be a waste of time; at worst, you'll get cut off on the other side for a few hours. Rangers advise against swimming here, as the currents can be dangerous.

WATCHING WILDLIFE IN MANUEL ANTONIO

Manuel Antonio is one of the few remaining natural habitats of the **squirrel monkey**, the smallest of Costa Rica's primates, with close-set bright eyes and a delicate, white-haired face – their cuteness is their own nemesis, and they were once a prime target for poachers. You might spot them springing through the canopy above the park trails or outside the park in the Manuel Antonio area in general – local schoolchildren have set up a project to build overhead wooden "bridges" for the monkeys to cross the increasingly busy road from Manuel Antonio to Quepos; ask at *El Mono Azul* for details (see p.353).

You also have a good chance of seeing other smaller **mammals**, such as coati, agouti, two- and three-toed sloths and white-faced capuchin monkeys. The abundant **birdlife** includes the shimmering green kingfisher, the brown pelican, which can often be seen fishing off the rocks, and the laughing falcon. Big **iguanas** hang out near the beaches, often keeping stock-still for ten minutes at a time, providing good photo opportunities, though beware the **snakes** that drape themselves over the trails and look like vines – be careful what you grab onto.

Due to the park's high visitor numbers, some of the wildlife is unnervingly familiar with humans, and white-faced capuchin monkeys in particular have no qualms raiding backpacks in the hope of finding a bite to eat. You can **help the animals** by not feeding them (for which you can be fined), being quiet as you walk the trails and by not leaving any litter.

The trail out of Manuel Antonio, the **Sendero Principal** (2.2km), runs along the back of the long **Playa Espadilla Sur**. It's usually calm and less crowded than Playa Manuel Antonio, but isn't often supervised, so be careful of currents. Hit the trails early, as much to avoid the influx of visitors that flood in mid-morning as the searing heat.

ARRIVAL AND DEPARTURE PARQUE NACIONAL MANUEL ANTONIO

By bus Buses from Quepos (every 30min from 7am to 7pm; 20min) and San José (5–6 daily; 5hr) drop passengers off 200m before the park entrance.

By taxi If you're staying at a hotel on the road to the park and want to travel by taxi, it's cheaper to flag one down on the road rather than calling from the hotel.

By car If you're driving, note that you'll be charged ($4–6) to leave your car at one of the supervised car parks on the road loop at the end of Manuel Antonio village, or anywhere on the main street.

INFORMATION

Guides You can take informative tours with guides at the park entrance ($25 per person; 2hr). You may be approached by "guides" offering their services in the village, so check their ICT (Costa Rican Institute of Tourism) photo ID first.

What to bring Whether you walk the trails guided or not, make sure you take plenty of water – the climate is hot, humid and wet, all year round, with temperatures easily climbing to 30°C and above.

Security Note that there have been problems with theft in Manuel Antonio, usually as a result of people leaving valuables (like cameras) on the beach; take care also if walking the trails alone, as there have been a number of robberies, most significantly when armed robbers stole $20,000 from rangers (the day's takings) as they left the park one evening in January 2009.

Tours Iguana Tours (see p.351) offer a range of day-trips in and around the national park, including hiking and kayaking.

The Zona Sur

CERRO CHIRRIPÓ SUMMIT

The Zona Sur

Costa Rica's Zona Sur (southern zone) is the country's least-known area, both for Ticos and for visitors, though tourism is increasing at a steady pace. It's a geographically diverse region encompassing the high mountain peaks of the Cordillera de Talamanca at its northern edge, the agricultural heartland of the Valle de El General, the river-cut lowlands of the Valle de Diquis around Palmar and the coffee-growing Valle de Coto Brus, near the border with Panama.

7

The Zona Sur is particularly popular with hikers, who are spoiled for choice between the cloudforest trails around **San Gerardo de Dota** in the north to the epic multiday jungle treks of Parque Nacional Corcovado in the south. Of course, many come to climb **Cerro Chirripó** in the Talamancas – one of the highest peaks in Central America – set in the chilly, rugged terrain of the **Parque Nacional Chirripó**. Experienced walkers also venture into the giant neighbouring Parque Internacional La Amistad, a UNESCO Biosphere Reserve and World Heritage Site that protects an enormous tract of land along Costa Rica's southern border.

Halfway down the region's Pacific coast, the **Playa Dominical** area was originally a surfing destination, but its tropical beauty now draws an ever-increasing number of visitors (not to mention property developers), especially since the paved **Costanera Sur** has made this entire stretch of coast accessible without a 4WD. Further south down the coast, the **Península de Osa** is the site of the **Parque Nacional Corcovado**, one of the country's prime rainforest hiking destinations, whose soaring canopy trees constitute the last chunk of tropical wet forest on the entire Pacific side of the Central American isthmus. The Península de Osa is also home to the remote and picturesque **Bahía Drake**, from where tours depart to the nearby **Reserva Biológica Isla del Caño**, still home to a few lithic spheres fashioned by the local Diquis. On the opposite side of the Golfo Dulce from the Península de Osa, near the border with Panama, is **Golfito**, the only town of any size in the region, and one that suffered from an unsavoury reputation for years after the pull-out of the United Brands fruit company's banana operations in 1985. It has been attracting more visitors of late since being made a tax-free zone for manufactured goods from Panama, though for foreign visitors it's more useful as a base from which to move on to the Península de Osa and Corcovado. **Golfo Dulce** also holds two of Costa Rica's best surfing beaches, **Playa Zancudo** and **Playa Pavones**, the latter the site of one of the most sought after waves in the world.

Despite the region's profusion of basic, inexpensive **accommodation**, you may find yourself spending more money than you bargained for simply because of the time, distance and planning involved in getting to many of the region's more beautiful spots – this is particularly true if you stay in one of the very comfortable private **rainforest**

RESPLENDENT QUETZAL

Highlights

① San Gerardo de Dota Set off in search of quetzals or try your hand at fly-fishing at this remote mountain village with a jaw-dropping setting. **See p.367**

② Climb Cerro Chirripó The hike up Costa Rica's highest peak is a long but varied ascent through cloudforest and paramo to rocky mountaintop. **See p.371**

③ La Cusinga Lodge Relax in a luxurious, ecofriendly rainforest lodge overlooking the marine splendour of the Parque Nacional Marino Ballena. **See p.379**

④ Bahía Drake Explore the stunning natural scenery and marine life of remote Bahía Drake. **See p.384**

⑤ Isla del Caño Snorkel among coral beds and spot dolphins, manta rays and whales at Costa Rica's premier dive spot. **See p.388**

⑥ Parque Nacional Corcovado Strike out into the heart of the visually and biologically magnificent coastal rainforest at Corcovado and you'll understand why it draws comparison with the Amazon basin. **See p.392**

HIGHLIGHTS ARE MARKED ON THE MAP ON PP.364–365

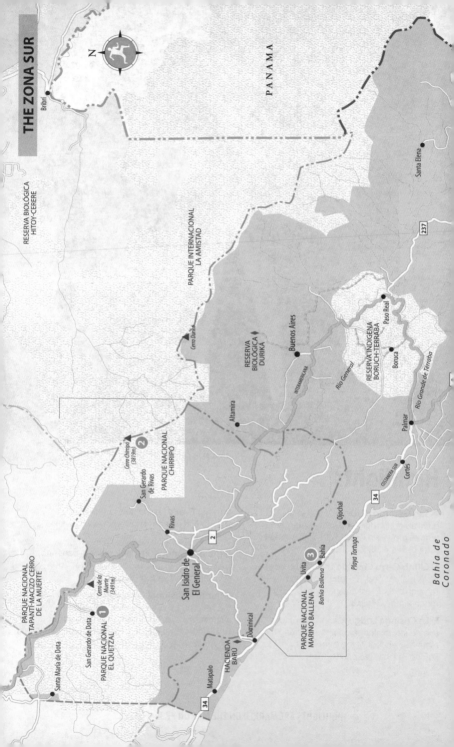

THE ZONA SUR

N

PANAMA

RESERVA BIOLÓGICA
HITOY-CERERE

Bribrí

PARQUE INTERNACIONAL
LA AMISTAD

Santa Elena

[237]

Cerro Dúrika

RESERVA BIOLÓGICA
DÚRIKA

Buenos Aires

Paso Real

RESERVA INDÍGENA
BORUCH-TÉRRABA

Boruca

INTERAMERICANA

Río General

Río Grande de Térraba

Cerro Chirripó
(3819m)

②

Altamira

PARQUE NACIONAL
CHIRRIPÓ

San Gerardo
de Rivas

Palmar

Cortés

COSTANERA SUR

[34]

Rivas

②

PARQUE NACIONAL
TAPANTÍ-MACIZO CERRO
DE LA MUERTE

Cerro de la
Muerte
(3491m)

Santa María de Dota

San Gerardo de Dota

①

PARQUE NACIONAL
EL QUETZAL

San Isidro
de El General

Ojochal

Bahía
③
Uvita

Bahía Ballena

Playa Tortuga

PARQUE NACIONAL
MARINO BALLENA

Dominical

HACIENDA
BARÚ

Matapalo

[34]

*Bahía de
Coronado*

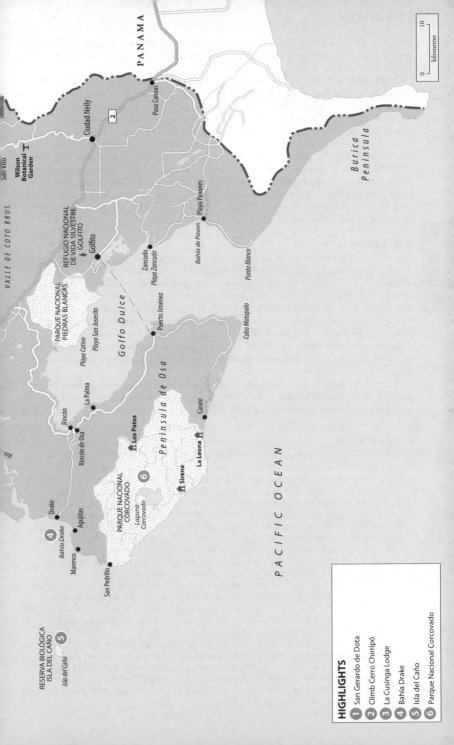

PANAMA

Burica Peninsula

VALLE DE COTO BRUS

Soli Vido

Wilson Botanical Garden

Ciudad Neily

2

Paso Canoas

REFUGIO NACIONAL DE VIDA SILVESTRE GOLFITO

Golfito

Zancado

Playa Zancudo

Playa Pavones

Bahía de Pavón

Punta Blanca

PARQUE NACIONAL PIEDRAS BLANCAS

Playa Cativo

Playa San Josecito

Golfo Dulce

La Palma

Rincón

Rincón de Osa

Puerto Jiménez

Cabo Matapalo

Río

Drake

Bahía Drake

4

Agujitas

Marenco

Los Patos

Península de Osa

PARQUE NACIONAL CORCOVADO

Laguna Corcovado

6

Sirena

La Leona

Carate

San Pedrillo

PACIFIC OCEAN

RESERVA BIOLÓGICA ISLA DEL CAÑO

Isla del Caño

5

0   10
kilometres

HIGHLIGHTS

1. San Gerardo de Dota
2. Climb Cerro Chirripó
3. La Cusinga Lodge
4. Bahía Drake
5. Isla del Caño
6. Parque Nacional Corcovado

lodges in the Osa, Golfo Dulce and Bahía Drake areas. Many people prefer to take a package rather than travel independently, and travellers who stay at the rainforest lodges often choose to fly in.

Climatically the Zona Sur has two distinct regions. The first comprises the Pacific lowlands, from south of Quepos (covered in chapter 6) roughly to the Río Sierpe Delta at the top of the Península de Osa, and the upland Valle de El General and the Talamancas, both of which experience a dry season from December to April. The second region – the Península de Osa, Golfito and Golfo Dulce – does not have so marked a dry season (although the months from December to April are less wet) and, due to localized wind patterns from the Pacific, gets very wet at other times, receiving up to 5000mm of rain a year, with spectacular seasonal thunder and lightning storms cantering in across the Pacific from around October to December. In the rainy season, some parts of Parque Nacional Corcovado become more or less unwalkable, local roads can't be crossed and everything gets more difficult. This makes it a good time to come if you want to avoid the crowds, but you'll need a 4WD.

7

Brief history

The earliest inhabitants of the Zona Sur were the **Diquis**, who lived around modern-day Palmar and Bahía Drake, on the shoulder of the Península de Osa – a region still called Valle de Diquis. They are best known for **goldsmithing**, which the Museo de Oro Precolombino in San José documents in detail (see p.92), and for their crafting of almost perfectly round **lithic spheres**. Less is known of the early history of the Diquis than of any other group in Costa Rica, chiefly because their burial sites have been plundered by *huaqueros* (grave robbers/treasure hunters), who in some cases dynamited tombs in their zeal to get at buried gold. These days the only indigenous group of any size in the area is the Borucas – sometimes called the Bruncas – a subgroup of the Diquis.

The modern history of the Zona Sur has been defined by its isolation. Before the building of the **Interamericana** in the 1950s, transport across the Cerro de la Muerte was by mule only. **Charcoal-burning** was until very recently the main economic activity up in

---

THE DIQUIS

Very little is known about the history of the **Diquis region** before 1000 BC, though culturally it appears to have formed part of the Greater Chiriquí region, which takes its name from the province in southwestern Panama. Archeologists date the famous **lithic spheres** (see box, p.381) from sometime between 1000 BC and 500 AD; between around 700 and 1600 AD the Diquis began fashioning **gold** pendants, breastplates, headbands and chains, becoming master goldsmiths within a hundred years or so. Between 500 and 800 AD drastic changes occurred in the culture of the Diquis. Archeologists attribute them to the impact of the arrival of seagoing peoples from Colombia or possibly the Andes – a theory borne out by their metates and pottery, which show llama or guanaco figures, animals that would have been unknown on the isthmus. In the Diquis' own artisanry, both the ingenious – often cheeky – goldwork and the voluptuous pottery display a unique humour as well as superlative attention to detail.

The Diquis were in a state of constant **warfare** among themselves and with foreign groups. Like the Chorotegas to the north in Greater Nicoya, they seem to have engaged in sacrifice, ritually beheading war captives. Huge metates unearthed at Barilles in Panama show images of these rituals, while smaller crucible-like dishes – in which coca leaves, yucca or maize may have been crushed and fermented – suggest ritual inebriation.

The indigenous peoples of Zona Sur first met the Spaniards in 1522 when the *cacique* of the Térraba group graciously hosted Captain **Gil González** for a fortnight. González was on his way from near the present-day Panama border, where his ship had run aground, to Nicaragua. Despite infirmity (he was in his fifties), he was walking all the way. The Diquis seem to have declined abruptly after this initial contact, most likely felled by influenza, smallpox, the plague and other diseases brought by Spanish settlers.

these heights, using the majestic local oaks, but *campesinos* in the area are now being discouraged from charcoal-burning, due to its deforesting effects. For a glimpse of how the charcoal-burners lived before the building of the Interamericana, read the short story "The Carbonero" by Costa Rican writer Carlos Salazar Herera, translated into English and anthologized in *Costa Rica: A Traveller's Literary Companion* (see p.436).

San Gerardo de Dota

The lovely, sprawling hamlet of **SAN GERARDO DE DOTA** enjoys a spectacular setting along the Río Savegre, with lush valley walls looming on either side of it. Though it has long been known by ornithologists for the staggeringly high number of species found in the area, particularly the striking **resplendent quetzal**, it has a bit of a forgotten feel to it. While the rare opportunity to see the almost mythical bird is for many the main reason to visit San Gerardo de Dota, the village's unhurried charm has an undeniable appeal.

Beyond a preponderance of apple and peach trees, there's not much to the village itself, which spreads 9km down a steep winding road to the valley floor. Other than making guided hikes in and around the village and to the Parque Nacional Los Quetzales to see the bird, the most popular pastime around here is **fishing** (see below).

7

Quetzal Education Research Center Museum
On the main road in the village centre • Mon–Fri 9am–5pm • Free • ☎ 2740 1010

If you have no luck seeing a resplendent quetzal in the wild, try stopping by the **Quetzal Education Research Center Museum** in a yellow building signposted at the base of the village. While the centre is mainly devoted to protecting the Río Savegre it has a stuffed male quetzal (which died of natural causes) on display, as well as examples of other local wildlife, including moths and snakes.

ARRIVAL   SAN GERARDO DE DOTA

By car The turn-off to San Gerardo de Dota is about 80km south of San José; you'll need a 4WD to get here, since the road down from the Interamericana is treacherously steep in parts.
By bus There are no buses to San Gerardo de Dota, though

San José buses bound for San Isidro de El General will stop for you at the turn-off at Km80 on the Interamericana, 8km from the village centre. Make arrangements in advance for your hotel to pick you up from there.

ACTIVITIES

Birdwatching All hotels arrange early morning tours to see the resplendent quetzal, usually for around $25/half-day.
Fishing Lure-fishing is from December to March and

fly-fishing mostly in May and June. Most of the village's lodges can arrange fishing outings on the Savegre with local guides (from $50 for a half-day, including equipment); make arrangements in advance of your stay.

ACCOMMODATION AND EATING

For such a small village, there are some absolutely **wonderful places to stay**, both in San Gerardo de Dota and the surrounding area. Bear in mind that although it's set in a valley, the village lies at over 2000m; it can get **chilly at night**.

Cabinas El Quetzal In the village ☎ 2740 1036, ⓦ cabinaselquetzal.com. A good bargain, these clean and nicely furnished cabins on the main road near the river are a great option if you're on a budget. Includes three meals a day. **$68**
Café Kahawa Near the end of the village road alongside the river ☎ 2740 1081. Wonderful open-air restaurant with scenic river views and friendly owners. The menu features a variety of fish (mostly trout) dishes, such as a smoke trout sandwich ($9) and trout tacos ($6). Daily 11am–7pm.

Comida Típica Miriam About 300m or so uphill from Dantica ☎ 2740 1049. This inviting, family-run *soda* serves hearty Costa Rican staples throughout the day. Highlights include a trout *casado* ($8.50) and linguine with trout ($11). Daily 7am–7.30pm.
★ Dantica Cloud Forest Lodge 4km from the Interamericana on the road to the village centre ☎ 2740 1067, ⓦ dantica.com. Striking modern lodge and art gallery with seven villas and a suite, all of which have south-facing terraces, comfy furnishings, jacuzzi, satellite

7

TV and, most crucially, floor-to-ceiling windows with jaw-dropping views. Breakfast is included and there's a restaurant attached to the gallery where you can dine on creative beef and pork dishes, as well as locally caught trout. As well as organizing tours to see quetzals, the lodge's private reserve abuts the national park and has a network of trails. $189

★ **Mirador de Quetzales** Turn off at Interamericano Km70, 10km north of the San Gerardo exit ☎ 2200 4185, ⓦ quetzalscostarica.com. Sitting on a 100-plus-acre cloudforest reserve run by a local family, the *albergue* itself is cosy and very reasonably priced, with an eight-room lodge (shared bathrooms) and several wooden *cabinas* with private bathrooms overlooking a misty valley. Bedside electric heaters warm you through near-freezing nighttime temperatures. Included in the rate is a guided hike along El Robledal, the *finca*'s 4km trail, which winds past 1500-year-old cypresses and 14-million-year-old

marine fossils, offering good chances to spot the resplendent quetzal. You can also take a horseride past an old plane wreck down to a waterfall. Breakfast and dinner included. Rooms and *cabinas* both $68

Savegre In the village ☎ 2740 1028, ⓦ savegre.com. Long-running ecolodge well known among birdwatchers for the number of quetzals that nest on or near its land. The rooms are straightforward and comfortable, with homely furnishings. The very friendly *dueños* have trail maps, can arrange guides (which cost extra) and offer bird-spotting tips and horseriding on their 400-hectare private reserve. Breakfast included $70, All meals included $136

Trogon Lodge In the village ☎ 2293 8181, ⓦ trogon lodge. The *Trogon Lodge* has comfortable heated cabins (though they can still get chilly at night) and beautifully landscaped grounds, with several trout ponds, marked trails through the woods and a zip-line tour. There are also normally many quetzals to be seen around here. $106

Parque Nacional Los Quetzales

About 4km north of the turn-off to San Gerardo de Dota • Daily 8am–4pm • $10 • ☎ 2514 0403

Opened in 2005 and Costa Rica's newest national park, **Parque Nacional Los Quetzales** covers an area of over 12,000 densely forested acres. Set higher in elevation – between 2000 and 3000m – than many of the other national parks, Los Quetzales consists mostly of cloudforest, an ideal habitat for numerous wildlife, including coyotes, jaguars, Baird's tapirs and, of course, quetzals. The quetzals feed on the reserve's abundant aguacatillo trees, and the best time to spot them is during their nesting season, from March to June.

Currently the park has no facilities for tourists, so is best visited on a tour with one of the lodges in San Gerardo de Dota (see p.367). A couple of poorly maintained **trails** depart from the park entrance, north of the turn-off to San Gerardo de Dota.

ARRIVAL AND INFORMATION

PARQUE NACIONAL LOS QUETZALES

By car The park entrance is just past the Km76 marker on the Interamericana.

Information While the park entrance is rarely staffed, there are displays in English that provide park information.

San Isidro de El General

After a chilly ride over Cerro de la Muerte, a spectacular descent into **SAN ISIDRO DE EL GENERAL**, 702m above sea level, brings you halfway back into tropical climes. In Costa Rica, San Isidro is regarded as an increasingly attractive place to live, with its clean, country-town atmosphere. While the Talamancas are a non-volcanic range – and the Valle de El General therefore lacks the incredibly fertile soils of the Valle Central – there is still considerable local agricultural activity, and pineapples grow particularly well. The town hosts an **agricultural fair** in the first week in February on the Parque Central, when farmers don their finery, put their produce up for competition and sell fresh food in the streets. May is the **month of San Isidro** – patron saint of farmers and animals – and is celebrated by fiestas, ox-cart parades, dog shows and the erection of gaudy Ferris wheels. The town's one museum, the **Museo Regional del Sur** (Tues–Sat 8am–4pm in theory; free), is 75m northwest of the modern church on the Parque Central's eastern side: it's devoted to the *campesino* history of the area and features occasional displays of local artwork.

THE ROAD TO CERRO DE LA MUERTE AND BEYOND

The **Interamericana** south of San José heaves with international transport trucks and other large vehicles. Yellow-topped kilometre markings line the highway, and villages and hamlets are often referred to by these numbers (Briseño, for example, is usually called "kilómetro treinta y siete"). The ease of travel from the capital, via Cartago, to San Isidro de El General depends on the current condition of the highway. The views can be impressive along this stretch, but they're not often easy to appreciate given the need to keep one's eyes glued to the road. It's not a good idea to drive at night – not just because of the chance of robbery, but more crucially because of reduced visibility, particularly on the ride up **Cerro de la Muerte** and the descent that ensues. Fog, mist and rain are a constant threat at all times, and the road lacks shoulder or meridian markings. The biggest problem you'll likely face, though, are the long tailbacks caused by lack of overtaking opportunities. Ticos frequently risk life and limb passing large trucks on blind corners, but don't be tempted to follow suit – Costa Rica has one of the world's highest road-accident rates.

ARRIVAL AND DEPARTURE

SAN ISIDRO DE EL GENERAL

7

By bus San Isidro's main bus terminal is adjacent to the town's central market at Av 6, C 0/2, but most buses from here head to local destinations. To and from San José and most other destinations further afield, TRACOPA (☎ 2221 4214) buses stop at the terminal on the Interamericana and C 2, while Musoc (☎ 2771 0468) buses pick up passengers across the road. If you're travelling south from San Isidro to Palmar, Golfito or Paso Canoas, it's better to get a bus that

originates in San Isidro rather than one that's coming through from San José, as they're often full and you could find yourself standing all the way to Panama.

Destinations Dominical (4 daily; 40min–1hr); Golfito (2 daily; 5hr); Palmar (2 daily; 4hr); Paso Canoas (2 daily; 6hr); Puerto Jiménez (3 daily; 5hr); Quepos (4 daily; 3hr 30min); San Gerardo de Rivas (2 daily; 1hr 40min); San José (every 30min; 3hr); Uvita (2 daily; 1hr 30min).

INFORMATION

Ecotourism Costa Rica On C 4, Av 1/3 are the offices of Ecotourism Costa Rica (Mon–Sat 9am–4pm; ☎ 2772 5911, ⓦ ecotourism.co.cr), a nonprofit organization, with a useful website, that promotes ecotourism mainly in the Zona Sur; its helpful staff can book hotel rooms and answer queries.

National parks information Information about the

Parque Nacional Chirripó and Parque Internacional La Amistad is available from the regional office of the national parks service (Mon–Fri 8am–4pm; ☎ 2771 3155, ⓔ aclap @ns.minae.go.cr) at C 2, Av 4/6, south of the Parque Central. It's worth stopping off here to ask about current conditions and, if possible, to make reservations for Chirripó (see p.370).

ACCOMMODATION

Casa de los Celtas 4km northeast of the city centre ☎ 2770 3524, ⓦ casaceltas.com. Quaint hilltop British-owned B&B with a cottage and a double room. Both are clean and comfortably furnished; the cottage also has a kitchenette. The grounds include an orchid garden, while the views are breathtaking. Lunch and dinner offered at an additional cost. Double and cottage both $\overline{$70}$

Hotel Chirripó C 1, Av 2/4 ☎ 2771 0529, ⓦ hotel chirripo.com. Of the budget choices in town, the best best is the large *Hotel Chirripó*, which has simple rooms with

private bathroom and hot shower; some rooms have a/c (for an $8 surcharge). There's a decent restaurant on-site and free parking. Breakfast included. $\overline{$57}$

Hotel del Sur Country Club and Casino 5km south of the city centre on the Interamericana ☎ 2771 3033, ⓦ hoteldelsur.net. Set in quiet, pleasant grounds, this somewhat bland hotel and casino complex has spacious en-suite rooms, wi-fi, tennis courts, a swimming pool and a decent restaurant. $\overline{$73}$

EATING AND DRINKING

La Casa del Marisco C Central and Av 20. It doesn't look like much, but this central spot serves up some of the best – and freshest – seafood in San Isidro, with ceviche ($14) being one of its specialities. The portions are huge, making this one of the better deals around. Daily 11am–8pm.

★ **Nimbus** About 3km northeast of the city centre off

the Interamericana, 500m west of the Gasotica petrol station ☎ 2771 5685. Homely spot with outdoor seating and consistently top-notch hearty meals, including pasta and seafood, *casados* and burgers (most mains $9–15). Well worth the short detour on the way to or from San José. Daily noon–9pm.

La Terraza Hotel Chirripó. The best place for breakfast is this contemporary-styled café at the *Hotel Chirripó*, which serves heaps of *gallo pinto*, toast and eggs along with excellent local coffee at its buffet ($6). Daily 6am–10pm.

DIRECTORY

Medical services The most central hospital is Hospital Dr Escalante Pradilla (☎ 2771 3122), C 1, Av 12.
Money and exchange The Banco Nacional on the north side of the main square changes travellers' cheques and has an ATM, as does the Banco de Costa Rica on Av 4, C 0.
Internet There are several internet cafés around the main square; Fofo's Center (daily 9am–8pm; ☎ 2770 1186), C 4, Av 1, is a good bet.

Parque Nacional Chirripó

About 20km northeast of San Isidro • $15 for two days, $10 for every day after that • ☎ 2742 5083, ⊛ parquenacionalchirripo.com

PARQUE NACIONAL CHIRRIPÓ is named after Cerro Chirripó, which looms at its centre – at 3819m the highest peak in Central America south of Guatemala. Ever since the conquest of the peak in 1904 by a missionary priest, Father Agustín Blessing (local indigenous peoples may of course have climbed it before), visitors have been flocking to Chirripó to do the same, finding accommodation in the nearby villages of **San Gerardo de Rivas** and **Rivas** (see p.373).

The park's terrain varies widely, according to altitude, from cloudforest to rocky mountaintops. Between the two lies the interesting alpine **paramo** – high moorland, punctuated by rocks, shrubs and hardy clump grasses more usually associated with Andean heights. The colours here are muted yellows and browns, with the occasional deep purple. Below the paramo lie areas of **oak forest**, now much depleted through continued charcoal-burning. Chirripó is also the only place in Costa Rica where you can observe vestiges of the **glaciers** that scraped across here about thirty thousand years ago: narrow, U-shaped valleys, moraines (heaps of rock and soil left behind by

PARQUE NACIONAL CHIRRIPÓ

■ ACCOMMODATION
Cabinas El Descanso	5
Camping Chirripó	1
Los Crestones	3
Hotel y Restaurante Roca Dura	4
Hotel y Restaurante Urán	2
Monte Azul	6
Rancho La Botija	7
Talari Mountain Lodge	8

● RESTAURANT
Restaurante El Bosque	1

CLIMBING CERRO CHIRRIPÓ

Almost everyone who climbs Chirripó goes up to the accommodation huts first, rests there overnight, and then takes another day or two to explore the summit, surrounding peaks and paramo – it's not really feasible to climb Chirripó in one day. During high season, you'll have company on the path up the mountain, and the trail is well marked with signs stating the altitude and the distance to the summit. Watch out for **altitude sickness**, though; if you have made a quick ascent from the lowland beach areas, you could find yourself becoming short of breath, experiencing pins and needles, nausea and exhaustion. If this happens, stop and rest; if symptoms persist, descend immediately. The main thing to keep in mind is **not to go off the trail** or exploring on your own without telling anyone, especially in the higher areas of the park. Off the trail, definite landmarks are few, and it's easy to get confused.

To ensure you have a spot on the trail, make an advance reservation (see p.372) for your hike. It's also worth considering hiring a porter as well as a guide (see p.372), both of which can make your experience that much more enjoyable.

THE HIKE

The **hike** begins at 1219m and ends at 3819m, the summit. It's almost entirely uphill and so exhausting that you may have trouble appreciating the scenery. On the first day most hikers make the extremely strenuous fourteen-kilometre trek to the accommodation huts – reckon on a minimum of seven hours if you're very fit (and the weather is good), up to twelve hours or more if you're not. On the second day you can make the huts your base while you hike to the summit and back, which is easily done in a day, perhaps taking in some of the nearby lagoons.

The trailhead is well marked about 100m uphill from *Hotel y Restaurante Urán*, a little over half a kilometre northeast and on the opposite side of the river from the centre of San Gerardo de Rivas. The walk begins in a cow pasture, before passing through thick, dark cloudforest, a good place to spot **quetzals** (March–May are the best months). After a relatively flat stretch of several kilometres, where you're likely to be plagued by various biting insects, you'll arrive at a **rest station** halfway to the accommodation huts. Some people stay here, splitting the hike into a less-taxing two days, but conditions are extremely rustic, with three sides open to the wind. The **Cuesta de los Arrepentidos** ("Hill of the Repentants", meaning you're sorry at this point that you came) is the real push, all uphill for at least 3km. At **Monte Sin Fé** ("Faithless Mountain"), about 10km into the trail, is another patch of tropical montane forest, more open than the cloudforest. Keep your eye out for the *refugio natural*, a big cave where you can sleep in an emergency, from where it's just 3km to the **accommodation huts**. At the huts, the land looks like a greener version of Scotland: bare moss cover, grasslands and a waterlogged area where the lagoons congregate. There are no trees, and little wildlife in evidence.

THE SUMMIT

The **rangers** based up here are friendly, and in the high season (Jan–April) you can ask to accompany them on walks near the summit to avoid getting lost. Do not expect this, however, as it is not their job to lead guided walks. It's just ninety minutes' walk from the accommodation huts along a well-marked trail to **the summit** – there's a bit of scrambling involved, but no real climbing. You'll need to set off by dawn, as clear weather at the peak is really only guaranteed until 9 or 10am. There's also a little book in a metal box where you can sign your "I did it" message; bring a pen. From the top, if it's clear, you can see right across to the Pacific. However, you're above the cloud line up here, and the surrounding mountains are often obscured by drifting milky clouds.

PREPARING FOR THE HIKE

While Chirripó is hot at midday, it frequently drops to freezing at the higher altitudes at night. You should bring warm clothing (temperatures can fall to –7°C at night) and a proper sleeping bag (though these can be rented on site), a blanket, water, food and a propane gas stove. A short list of clothing and other essentials might include a good pair of boots, socks, long trousers, T-shirt, shirt, sweater, woolly hat and jacket, lots of insect repellent, sunglasses, first aid (for cuts and scratches), gloves (for rocks and the cold), binoculars and a torch – the accommodation huts only have electricity between 6 and 8pm.

retreating glaciers) and glacial lakes, as well as the distinctive **crestones**, or heavily weathered fingers of rock, more reminiscent of Montana than Costa Rica. The land is generally waterlogged, with a few bogs – take care where you step, as sometimes it's so chilly you won't want to get your feet wet.

Many **mammals** live in the park, and you may see spider monkeys as you climb from the lower mountain to the montane rainforest. Your best bet for **bird-spotting** is in the lower elevations: along the oak and cloudforest sections of the trail you may spot hawks, trogons, woodpeckers and even quetzals, though in the cold and inhospitable terrain higher up, you'll only see robins and hawks.

The **weather** in Chirripó is extremely variable and unpredictable. It can be hot, humid and rainy between May and December, but is clearer and drier between January and April (the peak season for climbing the mountain). Even then, clouds may roll in at the top and obscure the view, and rainstorms move in very fast. The only months you can be sure of a dry spell are March and April. **Temperatures** may drop to below 0°C at night and rise to 20°C during the day, though at the summit, it's so cold that it's hard to believe you're just 9° north of the equator. Be advised that it's not possible to climb Chirripó in October or the last two weeks in May, when the trail is closed for maintenance.

ARRIVAL AND INFORMATION   PARQUE NACIONAL CHIRRIPÓ

The park entrance is at the trailhead for the hike up Cerro Chirripó. Though it's a short walk from the village centre along the dirt road that leads east from the centre and over the river; it's also possible to reach the entrance by car via the same route. As for parking, your best bet is *Hotel y Restaurante Urán* (see opposite) or in front of a local's house for a varying fee.

Guides and porters The services of a guide can be useful and interesting in helping to identify local species and interpreting the landscapes you pass through. Ask at the ranger station at the entrance for recommendations or check ⓦ sangerardocostarica.com/activities/hire-a-guide, which has a list of guides currently leading hikes to the summit. In San Gerardo de Rivas you can hire a porter to carry your gear for you (around $60 per 20kg).

Maps The staff at the ranger station (see below) can supply you with an adequate map of the park, showing some altitude markings.

Ranger station By the bus stop in the centre of San Gerardo de Rivas (daily 6.30am–4.30pm; ☎ 2200 5348).

Reservations Visiting the Parque Nacional Chirripó requires advance planning. First you have to reserve a place, since no more than forty hikers are allowed in the park at any one time, and demand far outstrips capacity in the popular travel seasons (around March and April, especially Easter, and Christmas) – although there are sometimes cancellations. When making reservations you should state your preferred dates, bearing in mind that it's not possible to book for the high season (which starts in January) before November 1. Most hikers find two or three nights sufficient. To reserve a place, call SINAC at ☎ 2742 5083. Once you have your reservation you're required to check in at the ranger station – even if you're heading for the camping trail that starts from the nearby village of Herradura de Rivas. If you turn up without a reservation, there's a small chance you may be able to secure one of the ten daily walk-in tickets available from the ranger station.

ACCOMMODATION

Camping Chirripó About 10km from the start of the Herradura trail. You can camp in the park, although this takes some planning. You'll need to make a special reservation through SINAC (see above) and it's compulsory to hire a local guide ($25/day for up to 10 people). To camp at the park's lone site, you'll enter the park from Herradura. Note that the trail to the summit of Chirripó via the campsite is longer and significantly more arduous than the more common trek via the accommodation block at Los Crestones – you'll need a minimum of three days. Keep in mind that no fires are allowed in the park, since forest fires frequently devastate the area. $10

Los Crestones About 5km inside the park entrance ☎ 2742 5083. The only accommodation in the park itself is the block at *Los Crestones*, which has fifteen rooms (each sleeping four people), wi-fi, cold showers, a cooking area and a big sink where you can wash clothes. $10

San Gerardo de Rivas

At the doorstep to the national park, the small community of **SAN GERARDO DE RIVAS** caters to a steady stream of hikers intent on making the trek up Chirripó. Both it and to a lesser extent the village of **Rivas**, eight kilometres to the south, hold a few pleasant places to stay and eat, though there's not much other than the park and a stunning backdrop to detain you.

ARRIVAL AND DEPARTURE

SAN GERARDO DE RIVAS

By car San Gerardo de Rivas, 3km west of the park entrance, can be reached via a well-maintained road that connects with San Isidro de El General, 17km to the west; follow the signs for Rivas. The final stretch from Rivas, about 8km to the south, is unpaved; a 4WD is not necessary at most times, but if in doubt about current road conditions call the ranger station in advance (see opposite).

By bus Buses from San Isidro de El General for San Gerardo de Rivas depart at 5.30am and 2pm and arrive at the stop on the central square., adjacent to the church.
Destinations San Isidro de El General (2 daily; 1hr).
By taxi It's possible to hire a 4WD taxi from the bus terminal in San Isidro de El General to San Gerardo de Rivas for around $20–25.

ACCOMMODATION AND EATING

While it's possible to **stay in the park**, most people choose accommodation in **San Gerardo de Rivas**. It is home to several very reasonably priced, friendly places to stay – try to get somewhere with hot water, though, as it can get very cold at night. There are also a couple of attractive family-run hotels a few kilometres further back down the road towards San Isidro in the village of **Rivas**. Most of the hotels listed below have restaurants serving food well suited to loading up on before starting a hike to the summit.

IN SAN GERARDO DE RIVAS

Cabinas El Descanso 200m beyond the ranger station ☎2742 5061, ⓦsangerardocostarica.com/accommodations/el-descanso. Private house close to the ranger station with basic rooms, some with shared bathrooms others with private bathroom. It also has an excellent restaurant serving Costa Rican comfort food and offers free transport to the park entrance and horseback tours of the Cloudbridge Nature Reserve. $22

Hotel y Restaurante Roca Dura On the central square ☎2742 5071, ⓦsangerardocostarica.com/accommodations/roca-dura-cafe/. Seven smallish but clean rooms – one is built into the large slab of rock after which the hotel is named – four of which have private bathrooms and hot water. The café and restaurant are a hive of activity. It's possible to camp on-site and the hotel offers free transport to the park entrance. Double $28, campsite $5

Hotel y Restaurante Urán 50m from the Chirripó trailhead ☎2742 5003, ⓦhoteluran.com. Thirteen neat, small rooms come with shared bathrooms and eight slightly bigger ones have private bathrooms; all have hot water. They offer a variety of tours – including to the summit – and free pick-up from the ranger station. The on-site restaurant serves up big platefuls of good, solid Tico food – the perfect preparation for a long day's hike. Shared bathroom $18, private bathroom $45

Restaurante El Bosque Diagonally opposite the ranger station ☎2742 5021. The long-established *Restaurante El Bosque* serves tasty *bocas* ($5) and *casados* ($7.50), and has table football and gorgeous views over the river below. Daily 8am–8pm.

IN AND AROUND RIVAS

★ **Monte Azul** Across the bridge to the right of the bus stop in Rivas ☎2742 5222, ⓦmonteazulcr.com. Posh, high-end boutique hotel that exudes a level of artistic style and refined comfort few places in the country can match. Choose from one of four spacious riverside *casitas*, each with bold colours and lines, a private garden and compact kitchen. There's wi-fi throughout, free international calls, a gorgeous restaurant serving organic meals, a spa and a network of trails in its own nature reserve. Not an inexpensive option, but a fantastic deal nonetheless. With breakfast and dinner $208

Rancho La Botija 2km south of the village ☎2770 2146, ⓦrancholabotija.com. Eleven unfussy rooms, plus a freshwater swimming pool, a viewing tower overlooking the farm's coffee and banana plantations and a restaurant. Several large petroglyphs carved with pre-Columbian indigenous patterns have been discovered on the property, including the mysterious "Rock of the Indian", and can be seen on a daily tour. $68

Talari Mountain Lodge 7km off the Interamericana on the road to Rivas ☎2771 0341, ⓦtalari.co.cr. Eight brightly coloured rooms, all of which offer private bathroom with solar-heated shower, mosquito nets, fridge and a small terrace, set in twenty acres of tranquil riverside forest, with walking trails and a pool. An excellent restaurant prepares dishes according to local market availability, with a three-course evening meal costing $15. They also offer guided packages to Chirripó ($475 for three nights) and birdwatching outings. $90

DIRECTORY

Food market There's a *pulpería*, Abastecedor Las Nubes (6.30am–8pm; ☎2742 5045), across from the bus stop, where you can stock up on supplies.

Cloudbridge Nature Reserve

2.5km northeast of San Gerardo de Rivas • Daily 8am–5pm • Donation suggested • No phone, ⓦ cloudbridge.org

Adjoining the national park, the private **Cloudbridge Nature Reserve** protects 450 acres of lush cloudforest on the lower flanks of Cerro Chirripó. Focused on studying reforestation and habitat recovery as well as the numerous mammals that live in the reserve, Cloudbridge offers an excellent primer to the flora and fauna that lies just beyond in the national park. It also holds a few short **trails**, **waterfalls** that cascade into the Río Chirripó Pacífico, and a thriving **botanical garden**.

ARRIVAL	CLOUDBRIDGE NATURE RESERVE
By car You'll need a 4WD to negotiate the rough dirt track that leads from the football field in the centre of San	Gerardo de Rivas to the reserve.

The Costanera Sur

7

The 35km segment of **The Costanera Sur** highway from **Dominical** in the north to **Ojochal** in the south parallels one of the more tranquil and scenic stretches of the central Pacific coast. Among the highlights is the lovely **Bahía Ballena**, 20km south of Dominical, and the bay's twin tiny hamlets of **Bahía** and **Uvita**. Rather than hotels and glitzy shops you'll find a string of gloriously empty beaches washed by lazy breakers, palms swaying on the shore, and a hot, serene and very quiet atmosphere. Offshore is the **Parque Nacional Marino Ballena**, 56 square kilometres of water around Uvita and Bahía created to safeguard the ecological integrity of the local marine life and breeding humpback whales, while 15km south is the lovely shallow bay at **Playa Tortuga**, one of the most pristine in Costa Rica.

Outside of comparatively bustling Dominical, there's not a great deal to do along this portion of the Costanera Sur. That said, if you like hanging out on the beach, **surfing**, walking along rock ledges and spotting **dolphins** frolicking in the water, you'll be happy. You can also take **boat tours** around Bahía Ballena and to the Isla del Caño (see p.388) or, if you have your own equipment, you can **snorkel** to your heart's content directly off the beaches.

Matapalo

Some 15km north of Dominical, **MATAPALO** is a sleepy village stretching for less than a kilometre along a sweeping grey-sand surf beach. Backed by mountains, the straggly seaside community is a blissfully underdeveloped blip on the Pacific coast and provides a rare glimpse hereabouts of the Costa Rica of yesteryear. Sunbathing iguanas share the dusty street with children on bicycles, while a growing community of foreigners lives alongside a small Tico population. The **beach**, which enjoys monster waves and strong currents, has a dedicated team of local lifeguards patrolling.

ARRIVAL AND DEPARTURE	MATAPALO
By bus Buses chugging between Quepos and Dominical can drop you off at the turn-off to the village, marked by Pulpería la Espiral, from where it's a 2km walk to the ocean	and hotel strip. Destinations Dominical (6 daily; 40min); Quepos (5 daily; 1hr 30min–2hr).

INFORMATION AND ACTIVITIES

Jungle House On the beach ☎ 2787 5005, ✉ jungle house@gmail.com. The helpful American owner of the *Jungle House* (see opposite) is the area's unofficial source of tourist information. He can also arrange horseriding on the beach and in the surrounding jungle ($30/2hr), as well as sportfishing, canopy tours, snorkelling and whitewater rafting excursions.

ACCOMMODATION

Albergue Suiza Near the entrance to the village ☎2787 5220. One of the better budget options, and particularly popular with Germans: six of its nine clean and straightforward *cabinas* have a/c for an extra $15. **$33**

Dos Palmas A few hundred metres down the road from Albergue Suiza ☎8762 7673, ✉dospalmascabinas @gmail.com. An intimate beachside bed and breakfast with two of the loveliest, brightest rooms in town. Steps from the beach, and dinner is served at an additional cost. **$62**

Dreamy Contentment On the main strip ☎2787 5223, ⓦdreamycontentment.com. This beachside whitewashed colonial property set in landscaped tropical grounds has two self-contained bungalows with kitchenettes and a/c as well as a spacious main house that can sleep four people and has a kitchen, lounge area, bathtub and laundry. Bungalow **$102**, house **$226**

Hotel El Coquito On the beach ☎2787 5031, ⓦelcoquito.com. Six bungalows with private bathrooms and fan (three have a/c for a $15 surcharge), a bar-restaurant, a swimming pool and direct access to a wide and mostly deserted beach, good for bathing (but ask about currents). **$73**

Jungle House On the beach ☎2787 5005, ✉jungle house@gmail.com. More bachelor pad than nature lodge, *Jungle House* has a number of dark wooden-panelled rooms with leopard-print curtains and a/c. **$67**

EATING

Restaurant Bay Bambú On a side road leading to the beach ☎2787 5013. American-run restaurant that boasts an artery-clogging international menu ranging from pork crackling to chicken and pasta in vodka sauce ($12). Daily 8am–midnight.

Tico Gringo On the beach ☎2787 5023. Those craving a hamburger or perhaps some fried calamari ($8) and buffalo wings should drop by this friendly, surfside spot, where Eddie (the gringo) and his Tica wife Betty will set you up with an ice-cold beer under a thatch roof. Daily 11am–10pm.

7

Dominical and around

The ever-expanding surfing town of **DOMINICAL**, 44km southeast of Quepos and 25km southwest of San Isidro, likely represents the face of things to come along this stretch of the Pacific coast. Previously a secluded fishing village, it has, since the paving of the coastal road and the laying down of electricity and phone lines, expanded dramatically. A glut of new hotels, shops and restaurants have opened in town, while the coastal

ACTIVITIES AND TOURS AROUND DOMINICAL

Dominical offers a good range of tours and is home to half a dozen **surf schools** offering lessons for around $50 per person for a two-hour session.

Bamboo Yoga Play On the right side of the main road towards the beach ☎2787 0229, ⓦdanyasa .com. Highly regarded yoga studio and eco-resort offering some of the finest classes ($14) in the area in an open-air studio space.

★Costa Rica Surf Camp On a side street towards the beach off the main road ☎8812 3625, ⓦcrsurf school.com. Excellent surf school with experienced and patient instructors and a friendly atmosphere. They offer a variety of six-night packages (from $820) that include accommodation, daily lessons, area tours, meals and transportation as well as private instruction for all levels.

★Don Lulo's Cataratas Nauyaca Tour ☎2787 0541, ⓦcataratasnauyaca.com. Away from the water, the best way to pass a half-day is on Don Lulo's horseback waterfall tour ($60/person including break-fast and lunch; Mon–Sat). The tour begins with a 1hr horse ride to Don Lulo's home and small private zoo for breakfast, before continuing on horseback through lush rainforest with knowledgeable guides to the two cascades that make up the Cataratas Nauyaca – the principal one drops 46m into a sparkling pool where you can swim. A *típico* lunch cooked over an open flame on the return trip completes the day.

Green Iguana Surf Camp Just back from the seafront ☎2787 0157, ⓦgreeniguanasurfcamp .com. The longest-running surf school in Dominical and still going strong. As well as lessons and rentals, they offer multi-night packages that include accommodation at a nearby hotel, tours, and airport transfers (6 nights from $835).

Southern Expeditions On the main road into the village ☎2787 0100, ⓦsouthernexpeditionscr .com. Southern Expeditions specialize in kayak and snorkelling trips (from $75/person) to the Parque Nacional Marino Ballena (see p.379) and Isla del Caño (see p.388) and trips further afield to Parque Nacional Corcovado (see p.392).

areas to the south, still largely made up of unspoilt stretches of beach and rainforest, are rapidly being bought up by hungry foreign property developers and hotel chains. It does, however, remain a good place to chill out by the beach and visit the nearby **Hacienda Barú National Wildlife Refuge**.

Dominical consists of a dusty or muddy, unpaved, unnamed main street (where you'll find most of the town's bars and restaurants) and a beachfront road heading south from the Río Barú lined with hotels and surf schools. And that's about it – no park, no main square, no museums.

Whatever the village might be lacking, it more than makes up for it with its main draw: **surfing**. Thousands flock here every year to ride the big waves that crash onto the town's dark-sand beach. As is usual with surfing beaches, the **swimming** varies from not great to downright dangerous, and is plagued by riptides and crashing surf. About twenty minutes' walk south along the beach brings you to a small cove, where the water is calmer and you can paddle and snorkel.

As seasons can often pass in-between major cultural events in Dominical, the collective enthusiasm on display at the excellent **Envision Festival** (ⓦenvisionfestival .com) is that much more pronounced. Held over four days in late February or early March in a field alongside Bamboo Yoga Play, this nascent festival features a compelling slate of concerts, dance, multimedia performances and yoga classes.

ARRIVAL AND DEPARTURE   DOMINICAL

By bus Buses arrive about 50m past the village turn-off. Destinations Matapalo (6 daily; 40min); Quepos (5 daily; 2hr–2hr 40min); San Isidro de El General (8 daily; 1hr 30min); Uvita (6–8 daily; 20min).
By car While you can get to Dominical via San Isidro de

El General or Quepos in any car, it makes sense to have a 4WD if you want to explore the surrounding area.
By taxi Taxis in San Isidro de El General will make the drive to Dominical for about $30; they usually gather around the bus terminal.

INFORMATION

Tourist information The village's small information centre (☎2787 0454; irregular hours) is in the central plaza on the turn-off from the highway just past the

bridge. It has a good deal of information on the area and the beaches further south and offers internet access.

ACCOMMODATION

There's a broad range of good accommodation in the Dominical area. In the **village** itself, most lodgings are basic and cater to the surfing community, but you'll also find a number of more upmarket **places**, usually owned by foreigners. The most expensive hotels include some wonderful hideaways, good for honeymooners, romantics and escapists. There are also a string of increasingly lavish hotels and B&Bs along the coast road (Hwy-34) south towards Uvita, a number of which are in the hamlets of **Dominicalito** and **Escaleras**.

IN DOMINICAL

Cabinas San Clemente Down the main street and on the beach to the right ☎2787 0026. Attractive en-suite rooms plus basic but very clean dormitories with shared bathrooms for the surfer crowd who relax on the hammocks strung up on the balcony facing the sea. Surf- and boogie board rental available. Dorm $11, double $68

Cabinas Sun Dancer On the main street 50m west of the school ☎2787 0189. Twelve budget *cabinas* aimed squarely at the surfing community with basic, dated rooms, a small pool, the ubiquitous hammocks and a garden. They offer very cheap long-term rates. $50

Diuwak Hotel & Beach Resort Just off the main street 50m from the beach in front of the ICE electrical sub-station ☎2787 0087, ⓦdiuwak.com. A glimpse into

Dominical's future, *Diuwak* is an upmarket mini-resort offering eighteen well-equipped *cabinas*, all with private bathrooms (some with a/c) and wi-fi, extensive gardens, a supermarket, a restaurant, a tour service and private parking. $119

Domilocos 150m past the fork on the left ☎2787 0244, ⓦdomilocos.com. Something of a mixed bag, this attractive hotel on the beach has enviable features such as nicely furnished rooms with a/c and an excellent restaurant (see opposite). That said, the rooms are not always as tidy as you might expect; ask to see other rooms if you're not satisfied with what you're shown. $85

Río Lindo On the right as you enter Dominical ☎8857 4937, ⓦriolindoresortcostarica.com. Eight comfortable, plain rooms with private bathroom, a/c, some with satellite

TV. There's also a lovely round pool, bar and whirlpool on the grounds and they offer horseriding, fishing and ATV tours. On Sunday there's a rotisserie BBQ with live music. Price includes breakfast. $89

Tortilla Flats Next to Cabinas San Clemente on the beach ☎ 2787 0033. Popular surfers' hotel with eighteen brightly decorated en-suite rooms (those upstairs get more of a breeze) and a beachfront restaurant and bar (see below) where crowds gather in the evening to watch the sunset. They can arrange a variety of tours as well as spa treatments. $37

Villas Río Mar Down a track to the right as you enter the village ☎ 2787 0052, ☷ villasriomar.com. Comfortable, upmarket rooms in individual chalets with wi-fi and satellite TV; some have a/c. The rooms front extensive terraced gardens with a swimming pool, bar, spa, tennis court and jacuzzi. $101

SOUTH OF DOMINICAL

★ **Costa Paraíso** 2km south of Dominical, Dominicalito ☎ 2787 0025, ☷ costa-paraiso.com. Set in beautifully landscaped grounds spreading down to a rocky coastline, this eye-catching hotel has just five exceedingly comfortable rooms, all with either a queen- or king-size bed, a/c and wi-fi; four also have kitchenettes. Breakfast (not included) is served in the open-air restaurant, with both a pool and the ocean a few steps away. $158

Pacific Edge 3km south of Dominical, Escaleras; follow the signed left-hand fork ☎ 2200 5428, ☷ pacificedge .info. Secluded, simple and comfortable, on a ridge 600m above the sea, with beautiful views of Cerro Chirripó and the beach. The four roomy chalets each have a private shower and hammocks. Delicious breakfasts (for an additional cost) are prepared daily. A 4WD is necessary to reach the property. $70

★ **Roca Verde** 1.5km south of Dominical ☎ 2787 0036, ☷ rocaverde.net. Small, ritzy hotel in a wonderful position right on the beach. All ten rooms have en-suite bathroom, a/c, wi-fi and balcony, and there's also a swimming pool, table tennis and a restaurant serving Tex-Mex and American food. $75

Villa Ambiente About 1km south of Dominical ☎ 2787 8453, ☷ villaambiente.net. Striking whitewashed B&B nestling in the hills south of town and run by a Swiss family. The eight rooms are nicely appointed with a/c, TVs and terraces or balconies with prime views of the ocean below; there's also a suite with a jacuzzi. The alluring large oval pool is almost worth a stay alone and the owners will do their best to make you feel right at home. Double $146, suite $225

EATING AND DRINKING

IN DOMINICAL

Café Delicias At the turn-off into the village ☎ 2787 0097. Small café serving coffee and breakfast as well as inexpensive fruit smoothies ($3–5), healthy sandwiches ($5–7.50) and baked goods throughout the day. Wed–Sun 7am–6pm.

Coconut Spice At the end of the turn-off into the village ☎ 2787 0033, ☷ coconutspice.com. Riverside restaurant serving up bona fide Southeast Asian flavour. The hot-and-sour *tom yan goong* soup ($6) is recommended if you can take the chilli heat. There are also jumbo prawns, satays, curries and other Thai-influenced dishes. The atmosphere is much nicer and temperature much cooler out on the terrace. Tues–Sun 5–10pm.

★ **ConFusione** Inside Domilocos. *ConFusione* would fit in just as well in Milan or Rome. A class act, and the only restaurant in town with linen napkins. Try the *fettuccine* with salmon and shrimp ($9.50) or the seafood risotto ($10) and you'll see why it's an enduring favourite along this stretch of the coast. Daily 3–11.30pm.

★ **Kebab Divina** Across from the tourist office in the central plaza ☎ 8932 2207. Small kebab shack with a few outdoor tables. Though the setup is simple enough and the choices are limited, the friendly owners have clearly decided to focus on what they know best. A juicy chicken kebab with a Persian iced tea comes to about $8 and is the best quick meal in the village. Daily noon–8pm.

San Clemente Bar and Grill On your left as you enter the village, just past the football pitch ☎ 2787 0026. Large, breezy Tex-Mex restaurant that's popular with the surf crowd for its potent hot sauce and cheap prices, with favourites such as shrimp tacos costing around $6–12. There's a pool table and cocktails on Tuesdays are half-price. Daily 9am–midnight.

Soda Nanyoa On the main street opposite Posada del Sol ☎ 2787 0195. This pleasant, airy diner serves a hybrid menu catering to the town's cosmopolitan population: *gallo pinto* and *casados* ($5–7) for the local Ticos; nachos and Philly cheese steak sandwiches ($6) for the US contingent. Daily 6–10pm.

Tortilla Flats Tortilla Flats hotel. The best of the beachfront bars, this expat hangout offers fish tacos ($7) and cocktails to go with fine sunset views over the Pacific. Daily 8am–midnight.

SOUTH OF DOMINICAL

La Parcela 5km south of Dominical; take a signed right fork down to the beach, which then winds up onto the rocky point above ☎ 2787 0016, ☷ laparcelacr.com. Part of a gated luxury community, this fancy oceanfront restaurant has excellent food and spectacular views. The only place in the area where you can follow meals like ceviche and other seafood specialities (most mains $14–20) with a delicious tropical flambé dessert prepared at your table. Daily 11am–9pm.

7

DIRECTORY

Bank There's a Banco Costa Rica in the small plaza on Hwy-34 to the west of the turn-off into the village.

Post office There's a small post office with erratic hours

upstairs in the same commercial centre as *San Clemente Bar and Grill* (see p.377).

Hacienda Barú National Wildlife Refuge

About 1km north of Dominical • Daily 7am–5pm • Self-guided walks $7; canopy and climbing tours each $40; overnight hiking tours $125 • ☎ 2787 0003, ⓦ haciendabaru.com

The private reserve at **Hacienda Barú National Wildlife Refuge** comprises over three square kilometres of rainforest, mangroves and protected beach. There's enough here to occupy the better part of a day, with climbing trips where you winch yourself up extremely tall trees, hiking trails and an exhilarating canopy tour, which involves swooping from platform to platform through primary rainforest on long steel cables, accompanied by guides who impart a wealth of forest folklore; a sixteen-hour overnight hiking tour is also available. A great spot for birders and orchid lovers – 250 varieties grow around the reserve; there's also a butterfly enclosure and observation tower set high in the forest canopy. Take time to chat with the hacienda's owner, Jack Ewing, a committed environmentalist with lots of local knowledge.

ACCOMMODATION AND EATING   HACIENDA BARÚ

Hacienda Barú Lodge By the refuge entrance. You can stay on-site in one of the comfortable self-catering cabins or in one of the lodge's rooms that face the pool. The

attached restaurant serves mostly *comida típica* and a smattering of seafood dishes, with mains $13–21. **$85**

Uvita

Of the two villages on Bahía Ballena, **Uvita**, which winds inland at the crossroads just north of the Río Uvita, is more developed. In the centre of the village, the modern Rincón de Uvita sports complex houses **shops**, a gym, an indoor football field, a small Saturday-morning **farmers' market** (8am–1pm) and a couple of restaurants.

Aside from the sweeping **Playa Bahía Uvita** that juts out into the bay and the offshore national park, the main natural attraction is the **Catarata Uvita** ($1), a nearby waterfall that drops into a deep and thoroughly inviting pool in a pretty jungle setting. To get there, follow the signs from the Banco de Costa Rica in the village centre for about 1.5km.

ARRIVAL AND DEPARTURE   UVITA

By bus From San Isidro de El General, buses leave from the Transportes Blanco bus station, C 1, Av 4/6, twice daily at 9am and 4pm, heading for Uvita via Dominical.

Destinations Dominical (6 daily; 20min); San Isidro (2 daily; 1hr 30min).

INFORMATION, TOURS AND ACTIVITIES

Bahía Aventuras Next to the elementary school in the village ☎ 2743 8362, ⓦ bahiaaventuras.com. Friendly and professional tour operator leading a number of guided outings, from a whale-watching and snorkelling half-day trip ($85) to sea kayaking in the national park ($75) and a boat trip through the labyrinth Térraba-Sierpe mangrove forest ($85).

Uvita 360 100m south of Restaurante Los Delfines ☎ 8586 8745, ⓦ uvitasurfcamp.com. Offers a full range of surfing and stand-up paddle-boarding lessons (from $60/2hr) and six-night packages as well as rentals,

including surf boards ($15/day), kayaks ($50/day) and SUP boards ($50/day).

Uvita Information Center Across from the Banco de Costa Rica on the highway at the northern edge of the village ☎ 8843 7142, ⓦ uvita.info. The extremely helpful staff can book a wide assortment of tours, both on the water and further inland: its boat trips include snorkelling and sportfishing, while on land there are outings on horseback (from $25) and evening hikes ($35).

ACCOMMODATION AND EATING

Cabinas Bahía Uvita To the right of the T-junction ☎2743 8016. The pleasant, no-frills *Cabinas Bahía Uvita* has comfortable *cabinas* with a/c and hot water. $45

★**Cascada Verde** ☎2743 8191, ⓦcascadaverde-costarica.com. Taking a left at the second road north from the bus stop will bring you to *Cascada Verde*, a great place for the nature-loving budget traveller. Five minutes' walk away from beautiful waterfalls and swimming holes, and only a few more minutes from Uvita's coconut-laden beaches, it has rustic private rooms and a dormitory loft. It also offers vegetarian food, organic gardens, a kitchen, an ocean-view yoga deck and classes, body and mind work-shops, tours and wi-fi. Dorm $12, double $21

La Fiore de Bahía At the first intersection on the main road ☎2743 8171, ⓦbahiauvitahotel.com. Welcoming

two-storey hotel with simple, but spacious rooms and two apartments that sleep six. All have a/c, wi-fi and cable TV; the apartments also have kitchenettes. There's a nice pool and a restaurant on-site. Breakfast is included. Double $40, apartment $170

Que Pura Vida 100m from the national park entrance ☎8322 6553. The moderately priced *Que Pura Vida* has open-air seating: it serves home-made *comida típica* such as chicken with rice-and-beans ($7.50) as well as a few seafood dishes. Tues–Sun 10am–9pm.

Tucan Hotel ☎2743 8140, ⓦtucanhotel.com. The budget-oriented *Tucan Hotel* offers backpacker-style dormitories as well as spartan private rooms and campsites. Wi-fi is available throughout and they can arrange surfing lessons ($30; 2hr). Dorm $13, double $33, campsite $6

DIRECTORY

Money and exchange There's a Banco Nacional on Hwy-34 near the turn-off to the village and a Banco de Costa Rica in the centre.

Supermarket Across the street from the Banco Nacional on Hwy-34 is Supermercado BM (☎2743 8031), the best place to stock up on food.

Bahía

A couple of kilometres or so south from Uvita and accessed via two dirt roads branching off from the highway, tiny **Bahía** has a better location, on the lovely beach next to the Parque Nacional Marino Ballena, but a more limited tourist infrastructure.

ACCOMMODATION AND EATING   BAHÍA

★**La Cusinga Lodge** Just past the Puente Uvita ☎2770 2549, ⓦlacusingalodge.com. If you're keen on exploring the area in depth, and have the funds to finance it, your best bet is to book a stay at *La Cusinga Lodge*. One of the country's best ecolodges and one of the few owned and run by Ticos, it occupies a gorgeous rainforest setting overlooking the Parque Nacional Marino Ballena and is an excellent example of how the environment can be preserved for both the benefit of tourists and the local community. Its seven *cabinas* are all made of wood from the lodge's sustainable teak plantation; all the electricity is provided by solar and

hydro power; and there's an education centre where local children can come and learn about the area. It has an excellent restaurant (see below), as well as trails leading down from the lodge through rainforest (inhabited by howler and white-faced monkeys) to a beautiful stretch of quiet beach. $172

Gecko La Cusinga Lodge. First-rate restaurant serving up the most satisfying meals in the area: dishes such as dorado with mango sauce are moderately priced (most mains $11–22) and mostly made from locally grown or caught ingredients. Reservations are required for non-guests. Daily 7am–9pm.

Parque Nacional Marino Ballena

Beach entrances at Uvita, Colonia, Ballena and Pinuela • Dec–March Tues–Sun 6am–6pm; April–Nov Tues–Sun 8am–4pm • $10 • ☎2786 5392, ⓦsinac.go.cr

Created in 1989, the **PARQUE NACIONAL MARINO BALLENA** protects a large area of ocean and coastline south of Uvita that contains one of the biggest chunks of **coral reef** left on the Pacific coast. It's also the habitat of **humpback whales**, who come here from the Arctic and Antarctica to breed – although they are spotted very infrequently (Dec–April is best) – and **dolphins**. The main threats to the ecological survival of these waters is the disturbance caused by shrimp trawling, sedimentation as a result of deforestation (rivers bring silt and pollutants into the sea and kill the coral) and dragnet fishing, which often entraps whales and dolphins.

On land, the sandy and rocky beaches fronting the ocean are also protected, as is **Punta Uvita** – a former island connected to the mainland by a narrow land bridge. At low tide, you can walk from the point along the 1km **Tómbolo of Punta Uvita trail**, which stretches out into the sea and resembles a whale's tail. At certain times of the year (usually May–Oct), olive ridley and hawksbill **turtles** may come ashore to nest, but in nowhere near the same numbers as at other turtle nesting grounds in the country. If you want to see the turtles, talk first to the rangers (see below) and, whatever you do, remember the ground rules of turtle-watching: come at night with a torch, watch where you walk (partly for snakes), keep well back from the beach and don't shine the light right on the turtles.

Other than spotting nesting turtles or dolphins and whales frolicking from the shore, the best way to take in the park's abundant marine life is either **snorkelling**, on a **boat** or in a **kayak**; tours of each type can be arranged in Uvita (see p.378).

INFORMATION   PARQUE NATIONAL MARINO BALLENA

Tourist information The park has four beach entrances and designated sectors to match, from north to south at playas Uvita, Colonia, Ballena and Pinuela, with a ranger station at each entrance. All the ranger stations provide information about the park, nearby picnic areas, as well as basic shower and toilet facilities, except at Uvita. Note that the ranger stations are not always staffed.

ACCOMMODATION

Camping It is possible to camp at sectors Colonia and Ballena, but only at spots well away from the high-tide line; ask a ranger first. $\overline{\$3}$

Ojochal

About halfway between Dominical and Palmar, **OJOCHAL** sees more visitors than it once did, but it's still very much a pleasant and unhurried Tico town. Unlike most settlements along this stretch of the coast, it's on the inland side of Hwy-34. The walk to the town's beach, **Playa Tortuga**, is therefore just a tad further than elsewhere, but you'll be rewarded with one of the cleanest and most idyllic stretches of sand in the country.

ARRIVAL   OJOCHAL

By bus Buses arrive at the dusty stop in the centre of town.

Destinations Dominical (3 daily; 40min); Palmar (3 daily; 50min).

ACCOMMODATION AND EATING

★ **Villas Gaia** Playa Tortuga ☏ 2786 5044, ⓦ villasgaia .com. Proudly sustainably operated, *Villas Gaia* offers twelve brightly coloured *cabinas* – most with a/c – a pool and an inviting restaurant. It also runs a range of tours including snorkelling at Isla del Caño and boat trips around the local mangrove swamps. $\overline{\$84}$

Villas de Oros Playa Tortuga ☏ 2786 5170, ⓦ villasde oros.com. Five attractive and comfortable villas with balconies overlooking the ocean, kitchenettes, and a/c. The villas occupy over 30 lush acres, which are crisscrossed by a small network of trails. $\overline{\$122}$

★ **Ylang Ylang** In the town centre ☏ 2786 5054. The fragrant aromas wafting from this cute open-air restaurant hint that you're in for a different sort of meal, but they still don't quite prepare you for the explosion of flavours soon to follow. Count on mouthwatering Indonesian seafood and vegetarian dishes enlivened by an assortment of spices (most mains $14–32) and be sure you get a reservation – there are only ten seats and they fill up fast. Wed–Sat 5–9pm.

Palmar

Wedged in where Hwy-34 joins the Interamericana, and about 100km north of the Panama border, the small, prefab town of **PALMAR** serves as the hub for the area's banana plantations. This is a good place to see **lithic spheres** (see box opposite), a few of which dot a small park in the centre. Others are scattered on the lands of several nearby

LITHIC SPHERES

Aside from goldworking, the Diquis are known for their precise fashioning of large stone **spheres**, most of them exactly spherical to within a centimetre or two – an astounding feat for a culture without technology. Thousands have been found in southwestern Costa Rica and a few in northern Panama. Some are located in sites of obvious significance, like burial mounds, while others are found in the middle of nowhere; they range in size from that of a tennis ball up to about two metres in diameter.

The spheres' original function and meaning remain obscure, although they sometimes seem to have been arranged in positions mirroring those of the constellations. In many cases the Diquis transported them a considerable distance, rafting them across rivers or the open sea (the only explanation for their presence on Isla del Caño), indicating that their placement was deliberate and significant. (Ironically, some of the posher Valle Central residences now have stone spheres – purchased at a great price – sitting in their front gardens as lawn sculpture.)

You can see lithic spheres in and around **Palmar** (there are a few sizeable ones in the park across from the airport) and also on **Isla del Caño**, which is most easily accessed on a tour run by one of the lodges in Bahía Drake (see p.387).

7

plantations and on the way to Sierpe, 15km south on the Río Sierpe; ask politely for the "*esferas de piedra*". Palmar also makes a useful jumping-off point for visiting the nearby **Reserva Indígena Boruca** (see p.382), where you can buy local crafts from the indigenous population.

Palmar is divided in two by the Río Grande de Térraba: **Palmar Sur** contains the airport, while most of the services, including hotels and buses, are in **Palmar Norte**.

ARRIVAL AND DEPARTURE   PALMAR

By plane The airport in Palmar Sur is undergoing a $42 million dollar expansion to become Costa Rica's third airport to take international flights. As of now it services NatureAir (☎ 8843 3535) and Sansa (☎ 2290 4100), each of which offer daily flights to and from San José.
Destinations Quepos (daily; 25min); San José (2 daily; 1hr).
By bus TRACOPA (☎ 2786 6511) buses from San José and San Isidro run to the station in the centre of Palmar

Norte while Transportes Térraba (☎ 2732 2306) buses for Puerto Jiménez, Sierpe and Costanera Sur destinations leave Palmar Norte from in front of the Panadería Palenquito, Banco Coopealianz or Supermercado Térraba on the main street.
Destinations Dominical (2 daily; 1hr 30min); Golfito (2 daily; 2hr); Puerto Jiménez (3 daily; 3hr); San Isidro (4 daily; 3hr); San José (7 daily; 6hr); Sierpe (6 daily; 1hr).

INFORMATION AND TOURS

Camara de Turismo de Osa Comercial del Norte in Palmar Norte ☎ 2786 6534, ⓦ osacostarica.net. CATUOSA provides tourist information, can help with reservations and transport, and also sells stamps.
Osa Mountain Water Adventures At Km206 on the

Interamericana ☎ 8644 0481, ⓦ osamountainwater adventures.com. Enthusiastic operator leading gentle river floats to more adrenaline-filled whitewater outings along the Costanera Sur and in the Osa Peninsula.

ACCOMMODATION

Brunka Lodge A block and a half south of the Interamericana, just beyond the Banco Nacional ☎ 2786 7489, ⓦ brunkalodge.com. The 25 cabins are pleasantly furnished and have cable TV, a/c and wi-fi, and there are two pools and a restaurant. **$68**
Casa Amarilla 300m east of the TRACOPA bus stop in

front of the Parque Central ☎ 2786 6251. Bland establishment but not a bad choice, with clean rooms that have private bath and a/c; the upstairs ones have balconies and better ventilation. There's also a restaurant that serves *comida típica*. **$50**

DIRECTORY

Hospital Palmar Sur Hospital, about 10km south of the airport (☎ 2786 6204).
Money and exchange Banco Nacional (Mon–Fri

8.30am–3.45pm; ☎ 2786 6263), one block east of where the Costanera Sur and Interamericana intersect.

Buenos Aires and around

BUENOS AIRES, a nondescript town 65km southeast of San Isidro de El General, provides access to two little-visited sites in the area: the remote **Reserva Biológica Dúrika** and **Reserva Indígena Boruca**, home to the Boruca peoples. Beyond the austere concrete angularity of the **San Pedro Apostol church** on the central square, the town itself is not likely to hold your interest longer than the time it takes to drive through it. It is, however, a good place to stock up on supplies or withdraw money before continuing on.

ARRIVAL AND DEPARTURE   BUENOS AIRES

By bus Buses pull into the terminal in Buenos Aires at Av Central, C 6.

Destinations Ciudad Neily (10–14 daily; 2hr 40min); San Isidro de El General (hourly; 1hr 20min).

DIRECTORY

Money and exchange The Banco de Costa Rica, one block east of the central square on C 6, has an ATM.

Supermarket There's a Pali supermarket on Av 5 at C Central.

Reserva Biológica Dúrika

17km northeast of Buenos Aires • ☎ 2730 0657, ⓦ durika.org

Completely off the beaten track, the isolated **RESERVA BIOLÓGICA DÚRIKA** is a compelling mix of an agricultural-based community and private reserve where you can go on hikes and explore a working farm. Nestled within 21,000 acres of largely untouched and unexplored wilderness, it consists of only thirty or so permanent members (though it also is home to over twice as many semipermanent residents and visitors). The community's farm has enabled them to be entirely self-sufficient, and they offer **tours** where you can learn first-hand about their organic approach to farming. Members also lead guided **hikes** to nearby Bribrí and Cabécar villages and into the wildlife-rich reserve, where a variety of habitats are home to several endangered species, including Baird's tapir. Guides also lead multiday treks up one of Costa Rica's highest peaks, Cerro Dúrika (3280m), part of the Cordillera Talamanca that cuts through the reserve.

ARRIVAL AND INFORMATION   RESERVA BIOLÓGICA DÚRIKA

By car The reserve is 17km northeast from Buenos Aires on a gravel road. A 4WD is recommended to navigate the bumps.
By taxi From Buenos Aires it is possible to hire a taxi to the reserve for $25–30.

Information The foundation's office in Buenos Aires (☎ 2730 0657), C 1, Av 6, can make reservations and provide information on the various tours and extended stay possibilities (call well in advance if you're considering the latter).

ACCOMMODATION

Dúrika cabins At the centre of the community. The reserve has nine simple, cosy cabins available for visitor stays, each with private bath, comfortable linens and

sweeping valley views. Vegetarian takes on *comida típica* are served in the centre's restaurant. $48

Reserva Indígena Boruca

Reached via the Interamericana, either 14km south of Buenos Aires and then a further 15km off the Interamericana or 25km east of Palmar and then 8km further north. You will need a 4WD to get here from Palmar • ⓦ boruca.org

About 25km east of Palmar on the Interamericana, and then eight car- and body-rattling kilometres from the Interamericana is the village of **Boruca**, within the **RESERVA INDÍGENA BORUCA**. The village is known for its local **crafts**, with the women making small tablecloths and purses on home-made looms, while the men fashion balsa-wood masks, some of which are expressly intended for the *diablitos* (little devils) ceremony (see box below) and procession that takes place on New Year's Eve. You can buy either from the artisans themselves or from the local women's co-operative, La Flor de Boruca – it'll help if you have at least a working knowledge of Spanish. Local people have little other outlet for their crafts (you won't find them in the San José shops), so a visit can be a good way of contributing to the local economy.

ARRIVAL AND INFORMATION   RESERVA INDÍGENA BORUCA

By bus Buses for Boruca depart Buenos Aires at noon and 3.30pm. As the return buses leave Boruca at 6am and 11am, it's not feasible to visit Boruca as a day-trip if travelling by bus.
Destinations Buenos Aires (2 daily; 1hr 30min).
By car To reach the reserve by car from Palmar, head 25km east on the Interamericana, and then take the signed turn-off 8km further north. You will need a 4WD to get here, and

if it's raining heavily, the road can become impassable. From Buenos Aires, the drive is slightly longer but more manageable in a non-4WD.
Tourist information Mileni González (☎ 2730 5178, ⊜ laflordeboruca@gmail.com), president of the long-running local artisans group La Flor de Boruca, is the best source of information about the village and the reserve, including where to stay.

Península de Osa

In the extreme south of the country, the **Península de Osa** is an area of immense biological diversity, somewhat separate from the mainland, and few will fail to be moved by its beauty. Whether you approach the peninsula by *lancha* from Sierpe or Golfito, on the Jiménez bus, driving in from the mainland, or – especially – by air, you'll see what looks like a floating island – an intricate mesh of blue and green, with tall canopy trees sailing high and flat like elaborate floral hats. A surfeit of natural wonder awaits, from the sweeping arc of **Bahía Drake** in the northwest and the world-class diving and snorkelling spots of nearby **Isla del Caño** to one of the planet's most biologically rich pockets, **Parque Nacional Corcovado**, which covers the bulk of the peninsula. In the early years of the twentieth century, Osa was something of a penal colony; a place to which men were either sent forcibly or went, machete in hand, to forget. Consequently, a violent, frontierlands folklore permeates the whole peninsula, and old-time residents of **Puerto Jiménez** are only too happy to regale you with hosts of gory tales. Some may be apocryphal, but they certainly add colour to the place. The road to **Cabo Matapalo**, at the tip of the peninsula, and further on to sleepy **Carate**, the southeastern gateway to Corcovado, is a pretty one, with the jungle pressing against much of it.

THE FIESTA DE LOS DIABLITOS

Many indigenous peoples throughout the isthmus, and all the way north to Mexico, enact the **Fiesta de los Diablitos**, a resonant spectacle that is both disturbing and humorous. In Costa Rica the Borucas use it to celebrate New Year and to re-enact the Spanish invasion, with Columbus, Cortez and his men reborn every year. The fiesta takes place over three days and is a village affair: foreigners and tourists are not encouraged to come as spectators.

On the first day a village man is appointed to play the bull; others disguise themselves as little devils (*diablitos*), with burlap sacks and masks carved from balsa wood. The *diablitos* taunt the bull, teasing him with sticks, while the bull responds in kind. At midnight on December 30 the *diablitos* congregate on the top of a hill, joined by musicians playing simple flutes and horns fashioned from conch shells. During the whole night and over the next three days, the group proceeds from house to house, visiting everyone in the village and enjoying a drink or two of home brew (*chicha*). On the third day, the "bull" is ritually killed. The symbolism is indirect, but the bull, of course, represents the Spaniard(s), and the *diablitos* the indigenous people. The bull is always vanquished and the *diablitos* always win – which of course is not quite how it turned out, in the end.

You could feasibly explore the whole peninsula in four days, but this would be rushing it, especially if you want to spend time walking the trails and wildlife-spotting at Corcovado. Most people allot five to seven days for the area, taking it at a relaxed pace, and more if they want to stay in and explore Bahía Drake. Hikers and walkers who come to Osa without their own car tend to base themselves in Puerto Jiménez – a place where it's easy to strike up a conversation, and people are relaxed, environmentally conscientious and not yet overwhelmed by tourism.

Brief history

It was on the Península de Osa that the Diquis found **gold** in such abundant supply that they hardly had to pan or dig for it. Indeed, the precious metal can still be found today, as can the odd *orero* (goldminer/panner). When Parque Nacional Corcovado was established in the mid-1970s, substantial numbers of miners were panning within its boundaries, but the heaviest influx of *oreros* stemmed directly from the pull-out of the United Brands Company in 1985. Many were laid-off banana plantation workers with no other means of making a living. They resorted to panning for gold, an activity that posed a threat to the delicate ecosystem of the park – and a clear example of how the departure of a large-scale employer can lead to environmental destruction. In 1986 the *oreros* were forcibly deported from the park by the Costa Rican police. Today, several well-known international conservationist groups are involved in protecting and maintaining Osa's ecological integrity.

A revealing picture of *precarista* (squatter) life on the country's extreme geographical margins persists in the peninsula. Since the 1980s, when the road between Jiménez and Rincón was improved, many families arrived here seeking land. Most have built simple shacks and cultivated a little roadside plot, burning away the forest to do so. They plant a few vegetables and a banana patch and may keep a few cattle. Soil here is classically tropical, with few nutrients, poor absorption and minimal regenerative capacity. In a few years it will have exhausted itself and the smallholders will have to cultivate new areas or move on.

GETTING AROUND   PENÍNSULA DE OSA

Travel around the peninsula is rarely a straightforward prospect. **Bus services** are not extensive and many of the peninsula's roads are best suited for a 4WD, as the bumps can be substantial and water levels can make passage tricky in places. If you **drive** to the peninsula, be sure to arrive with a full tank; the only petrol station in Osa is in Puerto Jiménez.

Bahía Drake and around

BAHÍA DRAKE (pronounced "Dra-kay") is named after Sir Francis Drake, who anchored here in 1579. Today a favourite spot for sailors, the calm waters of the bay are dotted with flotillas of swish-looking yachts. This is one of the most stunning areas in Costa Rica, with the blue wedge of **Isla del Caño** floating just off the coast, and fiery-orange Pacific sunsets. The bay is rich in marine life, and a number of **boat trips** offer opportunities for spotting manta rays, marine turtles, porpoises and even whales. The bay's lone settlement of any size is the sprawling village of **Agujitas**, which acts as the area's main transport hub.

Bahía Drake and Agujitas make a good base to explore Parque Nacional Corcovado (see p.392) as the park's San Pedrillo entrance is within a day's walk. Visitors can combine serious trekking with serious comfort by staying at one of the region's upmarket rainforest ecolodge-type hotels.

FROM TOP PARQUE NACIONAL MARINO BALLENA (P.379); PARQUE NACIONAL CORCOVADO (P.392)>

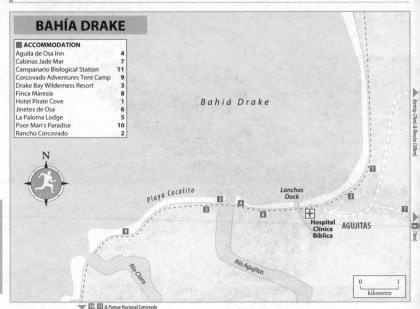

BAHÍA DRAKE

ACCOMMODATION

Aguila de Osa Inn	4
Cabinas Jade Mar	7
Campanario Biological Station	11
Corcovado Adventures Tent Camp	9
Drake Bay Wilderness Resort	3
Finca Maresia	8
Hotel Pirate Cove	1
Jinetes de Osa	6
La Paloma Lodge	5
Poor Man's Paradise	10
Rancho Corcovado	2

ARRIVAL AND DEPARTURE

BAHÍA DRAKE AND AROUND

Like many other places in Zona Sur, getting to Bahía Drake requires some planning. There are four options: the really tough way, **hiking** in from Corcovado; the cheap way, **by bus** from San José and then **by boat** along the Río Sierpe (possible in a day if you leave San José at 5am); the bumpy way, **by 4WD** along the gravel and dirt road between Rincón and Agujitas (which is impassible at various times of the year); and the luxury way, **flying** from San José to Drake, and taking one of the many packages offered by hotels in the area. If you do the latter, transport to your lodge is taken care of.

BY BOAT FROM SIERPE

From Palmar you can get a local bus (see p.381) or taxi to Sierpe (about $12), where there are a few *cabinas*. Once in Sierpe, make your way to the waterfront *Restaurante Las Vegas* (☎ 2788 1082), from which a boatman can take you the 30km downriver on a lancha to Bahía Drake (1hr 30min). The going rate for a one-way trip to Drake is about $15–25 per person or around $60–85 per boatload (maximum usually eight). Some hotel *lanchas* will take independent travellers if there's room, but be sure to arrive early; the first regularly scheduled *lancha* departs at 11am. Note that owing to fierce afternoon tides, the second and

last scheduled *lancha* leaves around 3pm. If you're driving to Sierpe, it's possible to park your car at *Las Vegas* during your stay at Bahía Drake.

BY PLANE

Both NatureAir (☎ 8897 9393) and Sansa (☎ 2815 5191) operate daily flights to Bahía Drake from San José. Be sure to arrange transport to your lodge in advance of your arrival at the tiny airstrip, 7km north of Agujitas. Destinations via NatureAir Quepos (daily; 1hr 50min); San José (2 daily; 45min–1hr 30min).
Destinations via Sansa San José (2 daily; 45min).

THE BOAT RIDE TO BAHÍA DRAKE

The **lancha trip to Bahía Drake** from Sierpe (see above) down the scenic mangrove-lined Río Sierpe is serene and provides plenty of opportunity to spot monkeys, sloths and sometimes kingfishers. The journey's tranquility dissolves abruptly when you see the Pacific rolling in at the mouth of the river. The Sierpe is very wide where it meets the sea, and huge breakers crash in from the ocean, making it a turbulent and treacherous crossing (sharks reportedly wait here for their dinner). If the tide is right and the boatman knows his water, you'll be fine. All the *lanchas* used by the lodges have powerful outboard motors, and there's little chance of an accident; all the same, some find this part of the trip a bit hairy. Once you are out in Bahía Drake the water is calm.

BY CAR AND BUS

Rainfall can make the road into Agujitas impassable at just about any time of year; if you plan on driving to your lodge, call first to find out the latest conditions. There are few bus connections to Agujitas. Your best bet would be to connect with the 11am or 5pm bus that departs from the hamlet of La Palma de Osa on the Golfo Dulce and passes through Rincón de Osa; the bus stops at the end of the road in Agujitas by the beach.

ON FOOT

If you plan on trekking to or from Corcovado, there is a 17km-long beachside trail from Agujitas via Marenco to the San Pedrillo entrance of Parque Nacional Corcovado, a walk of around 8–12hr. You can camp at San Pedrillo ranger station (see p.396), though you should inform SINAC in advance by contacting the Puerto Jiménez office (☎ 2735 5036). If you are staying at any of the Bahía Drake lodges, they should be able to contact the Puerto Jiménez office and make a reservation on your behalf.

INFORMATION AND TOURS

All of the bay's *cabinas* and lodges offer a wide variety of tours, from guided hikes to Corcovado and Isla del Caño (see p.388) to snorkelling and diving trips.

The Night Tour ⓦ thenighttour.com. Beyond trips to Corcovado and Isla del Caño, there is one activity not to be missed in Bahía Drake: the evening insect tour ($35/ person; reservations required; 2hr 30min) led by an enthusiastic American biologist known as "Tracie the Bug Lady". The tour departs from a few of the bay's lodges and explores the fascinating world of nocturnal insects, arachnids and other animals; with luck you might spot a trapdoor spider or a caecilian, an extremely rare and little-known amphibian.

ACCOMMODATION

Accommodation is clustered either in the tiny village of **Agujitas** itself, or on **Punta Agujitas**, the rocky point on the other side of Río Agujitas. Virtually all the ecolodges listed below offer a range of tours, from guided excursions to Corcovado to boat trips around Bahía Drake and out to Isla del Caño. The larger lodges often bring visitors on **packages** from San José and can include transport from the capital, from Palmar or from Sierpe. The packages usually include three meals a day – there are few eating options in Bahía Drake otherwise – and all the prices given below include full-board. Although hoteliers say you can't **camp** in the Drake area, people do – if you want to join them, pitch your tent considerably and be sure to leave no litter.

★**Aguila de Osa Inn** At the end of the village on Río Agujitas ☎ 2296 2190, ⓦ aguiladeosa.com. Very posh sportfishing lodge with a smart restaurant, landscaped gardens and thirteen beautifully decorated rooms nestling into the hillside. All have large Italian-tiled bathrooms and cathedral-style ceilings with fans. The lodge has its own marina. Two nights $565

Cabinas Jade Mar In the village ☎ 8384 6681, ⓦ jademarcr.com. A good place to stay if you want to get a taste of local life on a budget, with pleasant, if basic, *cabinas*, kept very clean by the informative Doña Martha. All cabins have private bathrooms (cold water only), and the meals are hearty. Inexpensive tours to Corcovado and Isla del Caño are also available. $23

Campanario Biological Station About 150m north of the San Pedrillo entrance to Corcovado ☎ 2289 58694, ⓦ campanario.org. Established by ex-Peace Corps volunteers, this remote field station offers courses in tropical ecology and tour "packages" for hardy ecotourists not fazed by its isolation. Tours consist of short walks, long hikes or all-day expeditions to Parque Nacional Corcovado as well as trips to deforested and impacted areas to talk to local communities. They also offer snorkelling and scuba-diving excursions to the Isla del Caño. Three nights $553

Corcovado Adventures Tent Camp Playa Las Caletas, 2km south of Agujitas ☎ 8386 2296, ⓦ corcovado.com. En route to Parque Nacional Corcovado, this collection of well-screened and furnished tents (complete with beds and tables) sits on platforms on an isolated beach facing the sea. Arrange for a boat in Sierpe or Agujitas to take you here. Two nights $299

Drake Bay Wilderness Resort Punta Agujitas ☎ 2775 1715, ⓦ drakebay.com. The most established lodge in the area, providing a buffer zone between tourist and wilderness with rustic, comfortable *cabinas* or, if you want to rough it a bit, well-appointed tents – both options are well screened. There's hearty local food available, and the camp also has its own solar-heated water supply, night-time electricity, plus excellent snorkelling and canoeing. Two nights $590

★**Finca Maresia** 2km south of Agujitas ☎ 2775 0279, ⓦ fincamaresia.com. Seven charming and raised bungalows spread along a hillside in the midst of the jungle. All have open, contemporary designs, attractive furnishings and ceiling fans. The welcoming owner is a wealth of information on Osa Peninsula and the staff lead a full slate of tours in and around the bay. The meals are a revelation and are served in a pleasant communal setting. $40

7

Hotel Pirate Cove About 2km north of Agujitas ☎ 2234 6154, ⓦ piratecovecostarica.com. Seven en-suite tent-style *cabinas* (including three very large family *cabinas*) and newer rooms with a/c in the main building in a lush rainforest overlooking a pristine 2km stretch of beach. The excellent restaurant serves Costa Rican and European cuisine. Tours of Parque Nacional Corcovado and Isla del Caño are offered. All accommodation types $̶1̶05

Jinetes de Osa Between Punta Agujitas and Agujitas ☎ 2231 5806, ⓦ costaricadiving.com. Right on the main beach, this is one of the less expensive options in Bahía Drake. The accommodation is clean, simple and comfortable – you might even hear monkeys hanging out on the roof. There's an on-site PADI dive school run by two American brothers, as well as one of the few canopy tours in the bay. $̶108

★ **La Paloma Lodge** Punta Agujitas ☎ 2293 7502, ⓦ lapalomalodge.com. Beautiful, well-appointed rooms in hilltop bungalows, with king-size beds, private bath, balconies and hammocks. The airy, two-storey bungalows are best, surrounded by forest and boasting spectacular views, particularly at sunset. Kayaks, boogie boards and snorkelling gear are available for guests to explore the Río Agujitas behind the lodge, and there's an attractively tiled swimming pool. Excellent service with friendly and helpful staff. Three nights $̶1119

Poor Man's Paradise About 1km north of the San Pedrillo entrance to Corcovado on the way to Bahía Drake ☎ 2771 9686, ⓦ poormansparadiseresort.com. One of the most secluded lodges in what is, after all, a pretty secluded area. The *cabinas* are set in pretty gardens and have ocean views. A mixture of private and shared bathrooms are available and you can also camp in the tents provided on the grounds. Meals are served in the lodge's lovely indigenous-style thatched-roof restaurant. Campsite $̶58, *cabina* $̶82

Rancho Corcovado On the beach in front of Agujitas ☎ 8869 5701, ⓦ ranchocorcovadocr.com. Set on the best part of the beach for swimming, this family-run hotel has beautiful views over the bay and fourteen simple, clean en-suite rooms. You can camp on the grounds or take one of their camping or horseriding tours. They also have a few boats, and competitive rates for trips to Isla del Caño. Campsite $̶10, double $̶83

DIRECTORY

There are very few facilities at Bahía Drake. As there are **no banks or ATMs** at the bay, bring all the cash you will need with you.

Medical services Hospital Clínica Bíblica (Mon–Thurs 7am–3.45pm, Fri 7am–2.45pm; ☎ 2786 6273) on the beach in Agujitas.

Reserva Biológica Isla del Caño

Daily 8am–4pm • $10 • ☎ 2735 5036 • You can't get there on your own, but a tour is usually included in the package price of the Bahía Drake lodges

The tiny **RESERVA BIOLÓGICA ISLA DEL CAÑO** sits placidly in the ocean some 20km due west of Bahía Drake. Just 3km long by 2km wide, the uninhabited island is the exposed part of an underwater mountain, thrown up by an ancient collision of the two tectonic plates on either side of Costa Rica. It's a pretty sight in the distance, and going there is even better – if you can afford it.

The island is thought to have been a burial ground of the Diquis, who brought their famed **lithic spheres** here from the mainland in large, ocean-going canoes. Your guide can take you hiking into the thick rainforest interior to look for examples near the top of the 110-metre-high crest, and you'll probably see some en route too, as the trail passes a few groups of them. Caño is also a prime **snorkelling** and diving destination; there are six dive sites around the island. Underwater you'll see coral beds and a variety of **marine life**, including spiny lobsters and sea cucumber, snapper, sea urchins, manta rays, octopus and the occasional barracuda. On the surface, porpoises and olive ridley turtles are often spotted, along with less frequent sightings of humpback and even sperm whales.

Puerto Jiménez

The peninsula's biggest town, relaxed **PUERTO JIMÉNEZ** – known locally simply as Jiménez – has plenty of places to stay and eat and good public transport connections. It caters mainly to the budget end of the spectrum, its basic *cabinas* in a whole different class and price range from the luxury lodges (many American-owned) lining the road to Carate, 43km southwest (see p.392). From Jiménez, you can also take a *colectivo* truck, the local transport, to Carate from where it's possible to enter Corcovado.

Despite its small size, lack of big-city facilities and somewhat sleepy, down-at-heel appearance, Puerto Jiménez nonetheless has a distinctly cosmopolitan flavour to it, welcoming a constant flow of visitors by land, sea and air throughout the year. Most are backpackers looking for a cheaper route to Corcovado than that offered via Bahía Drake. It is, however, a transient cosmopolitanism. Puerto Jiménez has no permanent expat community in the manner of Dominical or Puerto Viejo. This is a place to pass through – not to linger. The **main street**, which runs for just a few hundred metres from the football field in the north to the petrol station in the south, represents the rather dusty heart of town. The town is not especially known for its beaches, though if you venture 5km east to **Playa Platanares**, you'll find a pleasantly secluded beach with plenty of empty sand and an ideal spot to recover after a strenuous hike in Corcovado.

ARRIVAL AND DEPARTURE
PUERTO JIMÉNEZ

By plane You can fly in to Puerto Jiménez with Sansa (☎ 2735 5890) or NatureAir (☎ 2735 5428), landing at the sliver of an airstrip a few minutes' walk from the centre. The helpful Osa Tropical (see p.390) books flights.
Destinations via NatureAir Golfito (daily; 10min); San José (3–4 daily; 50min).
Destinations via Sansa San José (3–4 daily; 1hr).

By bus The bus station is one block west of the football field where you can also buy tickets (open daily 7–11am & 1–5pm).
Destinations Ciudad Neily (2 daily; 3hr); San Isidro de El General (2 daily; 5hr); San José (1–2 daily; 8hr).
By boat Regular *lanchas* depart daily for Golfito from the dock on the north side of town. It's also possible to hire a

Jetty for Lancha
to Golfito

N

*Golfo
Dulce*

ACCOMMODATION
Cabinas Jiménez	2
Crocodile Bay Lodge	5
Hotel Agua Luna	1
Hotel Oro Verde	4
Iguana Lodge	6
The Palms	3

CAFÉS AND RESTAURANTS
Cafeteria Monka	2
Il Giardino	1
Juanita's	3
Pearl of the Osa	6
Restaurante Carolina	4
Sarpes	5

Football
Field

Bus
Station

Police
Station

Colectivos ★

CaféNet El Sol &
Osa Corcovado

El Tigre
Supermarket

Osa Wild

Airstrip

Oficina de Área de
Conservación Osa

Osa Tropical

Banco
Nacional

Corcovado
BM Supermercado

PUERTO JIMÉNEZ

0   100
metres

▼ Carate (43km) & Parque Nacional Corcovado (45km)

Playa Platanares, 5, 6 & 6 ▼

ACTIVITIES AND TOURS FROM PUERTO JIMÉNEZ

Puerto Jiménez is increasingly catering to outdoor adventurers, with a growing list of tour operators leading all manner of trips across the peninsula. If you're planning a **trip to Corcovado** you can contact the Oficina de Área de Conservación Osa (see below).

Osa Aventura ☎2735 5670, ⓦosaaventura.com. Knowledgeable tours led by affable biologist Mike Boston with a strong focus on the fauna and flora of Corcovado, including three-day hikes to Sirena (see p.393) and back ($550) and longer, more gruelling treks to San Pedrillo (from $660).

Osa Corcovado On Hwy-245, one block south of the football field in the same building as CafeNet El Sol ☎8632 8150, ⓦsoldeosa.com. One of the newer outfitters in town, Osa Corcovado run a bewildering range of tours; chances are if there's a remote corner of Osa you want to see, they can take you there. Options include birdwatching (4hr; $40), surfing lessons at Cabe Matapalo (2–3hr; $40) and sunset kayak tours to see dolphins (3hr; $40).

Osa Wild On Hwy-245, two blocks south of the football field ☎2735 5848, ⓦosawildtravel.com. With an emphasis on trips that benefit rural communities, this Costa Rican-owned and ecologically-minded operation provides expertly-led and intimate tours. Their informative trips to chocolate *fincas* (2hr; around $25) provide a glimpse of Osa that not many see; they offer more standard tours on the water and into Corcovado as well.

Psychotours/Everyday Adventures ☎8353 8619, ⓦpsychotours.com. Biologist Andy Pruter takes people on high-adrenaline "psycho" tours that include climbing 45m fig trees, rappelling waterfalls and ocean kayaking ($55–75). They also lead short hikes into the rainforest ($45).

water taxi, which is usually quicker. Stop by Osa Corcovado (see box above) for a list of private boat operators.
Destination Golfito (3 daily; 1hr 30min).
By car Note that Puerto Jiménez has the only petrol station on the entire Península de Osa, so be sure to fill up before you leave.
By colectivo The main form of local public transport, the *colectivo* (a truck), departs one block south of the bus station in Jiménez to Carate ($9; in theory 2hr), twice daily (except Sundays in the dry season) at about 6am and 1.30pm. Note that it's an achingly bumpy drive and involves the careful

negotiation of at least half a dozen small (and in the rainy season not so small) rivers. The *colectivo* will drop you off at any of the lodges between Jiménez and Carate, and will also pick you up on its way back to town if you arrange this in advance – ask the driver. The *colectivo* also heads to Bahía Drake on Mondays and Fridays at noon (less frequently in the wet season) but confirm with the times posted at CafeNet El Sol or at the El Tigre supermarket.
By taxi If you don't get a place on the truck, a number of local taxi drivers have 4WDs. The average rate for a ride to Carate is about $80/car.

INFORMATION

There is no tourist office in town, but all of the tour operators (see box above) can provide local information.

Osa Tropical On the main road 50m north of the petrol station (☎2735 5062, ⓦosa-tropical.com). Provides a wealth of information on the area and books both NatureAir and Sansa flights.
Oficina de Área de Conservación Osa Facing the airstrip

(Mon–Fri 8am–noon & 1–4pm; ☎2735 5036). Staffed by friendly rangers who can answer questions and arrange accommodation and meals at Sirena (see p.398). They can also recommend local guides; Ballardo Diaz (✉jaguardman @hotmail.com) is one such guide with a strong reputation.

ACCOMMODATION

Hotels in town are reasonably priced, clean and basic. There are a few comfort-in-the-wilderness places **between Jiménez and Carate** around the lower hump of the peninsula, a couple of which make great retreats or honeymoon spots. These tend to be quite upmarket; backpackers usually stay in Jiménez.

IN PUERTO JIMÉNEZ

Cabinas Jiménez One block north of the football field ☎2735 5090, ⓦcabinasjimenez.com. Quiet *cabinas* next to the waterfront, with simple, nicely furnished and spotlessly clean rooms. They're well screened, with bathroom, fans, a/c and wi-fi, though some can be dark – ask to

see a few before you choose. $\overline{$50}$
Hotel Agua Luna On the waterfront near the lancha pier ☎2735 5393, ✉agualu@racsa.co.cr. A range of comfortable waterfront accommodation, from basic rooms with fans to luxury lodgings with cable TV, a/c and fridge. $\overline{$65}$

Hotel Oro Verde On the main street ☎ 2735 5241. Ten basic, clean second-storey rooms right in the middle of town, with restaurant, laundry service and friendly owners. Ask for one of the five front rooms with streetside terraces. **$38**

The Palms On the waterfront, just east of the football field ☎ 2735 5012. This clean, bright and straightforward complex overlooking the gulf offers newly remodelled and comfortable rooms with a/c and hot water. The popular on-site restaurant and bar serves fresh seafood at moderate prices with sunset views. **$44**

OUTSIDE TOWN

Crocodile Bay Lodge 4km out of town towards Playa Platanares ☎ 2735 5631, ⓦ crocodilebay.com. Luxury sportfishing resort with swimming pool, jacuzzi, landscaped gardens, restaurant and a large pier. Very expensive all-inclusive package deals only. Three nights **$1695**

★**Iguana Lodge** Follow the signs for 5km to Playa Platanares ☎ 8848 0752, ⓦ iguanalodge.com. Wonderful hotel run by very friendly Americans Toby and Lauren, with luxurious club rooms and four two-storey *casitas* in lovely gardens right on the beach – all rooms face the sea and are attractively decorated. Breakfast is included in the club room rate, while breakfast and dinner is included in the *casita* rate. Club room **$150**, *casita* **$186**

EATING AND DRINKING

Cafetería Monka Across from the police station on the main road ☎ 2735 5051. Small pavement café serving piping-hot coffee as well as *comida típica* breakfasts ($5.50), bagels and smoothies. Daily 7am–noon.

★**Il Giardino** On the waterfront road by the jetty ☎ 2735 5129. For the most refined dining in town check out this quaint Italian restaurant which, strangely enough, also boasts the only sushi bar in town. Most people, however, come for the fresh pasta dishes ($8–14) lathered in home-made sauces. Daily 8am–10pm.

Juanita's Around the corner from CafeNet El Sol ☎ 2735 5056. The most popular place in town (particularly with tourists), this funky little restaurant serves up affordable Mexican food like heaping fish fajita plates ($6), including a very hot chilli. It's a great place to hang out with a cool drink even if you're not eating. Daily 7am–midnight.

Pearl of the Osa Iguana Lodge. Lively open-air restaurant and bar serving international fare and solid Costa Rican dishes (most mains $12–19). Their "Pasta Night", when a DJ sets up shop, speakers blare and locals arrive in droves, is well known throughout the area. Daily 11am–10pm.

Restaurante Carolina On the main road one block south of the police station ☎ 2735 5696. A popular spot among locals, this no-frills open-air restaurant has an inexpensive *comida típica* menu ($4–8). Try to find a spot beneath one of the ceiling fans, as it can get absolutely sweltering inside. Daily 7am–10pm.

Sarpes On the main road ☎ 2753 5373. Very popular seafood restaurant and bar, heavy on the sailing motif, with garden seating available. While most of what's on the menu is unfailingly tasty, their specialities are dishes that feature locally sourced food, with ginger and mango sauces and rice (mains around $12). Mon–Sat 11am–11pm, Sun 5–11pm.

DIRECTORY

Health centres The Red Cross (☎ 2735 5109) and medical clinic (☎ 2735 5203) are opposite each other on the side road that leads to the bus station.

Internet At the post office and at CafeNet El Sol, one block south of the football field on the main road.

Money and exchange The Banco Nacional, just north of the petrol station on the southern edge of town, changes travellers' cheques and dollars as does the Banco de Costa Rica, diagonally opposite.

Petrol The peninsula's lone petrol station, Bomba Osa, is at the bend of the main road on the south side of the centre.

Police On the main road, 50m south of the football field.

Post office Opposite the football field on the main road (typically Mon–Fri 8am–2pm, though the hours can be erratic).

Supermarket There's a Corcovado BM supermarket across from the petrol station (Mon–Fri 7am–9pm, Sun 8am–8pm).

Cabo Matapalo

Occupying Osa's southern edge about 17km from Puerto Jiménez, **Cabo Matapalo** was for many years the exclusive domain of surfers, who still come here for some of the country's best breaks. Nowadays, it's become increasingly popular as a place to build holiday homes and for its excellent wilderness lodges hidden in the primary rainforest.

The first beach on the cape, **Pan Dulce** is the best one for swimming and has long breaks for surfers. The most southerly, **Playa Matapalo** provides the hardest tests for surfers and is a great spot to watch if your own skills aren't quite up to the challenge.

Nearby is the largest **waterfall** in the area, 90m King Louis, which can be reached on a short hike from the trailhead off the Playa Matapalo road.

All the local lodges lead **tours** of the area. If you're planning to come to Cabo Matapalo for the day, Everyday Adventures in Puerto Jiménez (see box, p.390) runs several half- and full-day tours of the cape.

ACCOMMODATION   CABO MATAPALO

Bosque del Cabo Above Playa Matapalo, down a private road to the left off the Carate road ☎ 2735 5206, ⓦ bosquedelcabo.com. Run by a friendly American couple, this grand lodge has ten luxurious hardwood and stucco *cabinas* (several with magnificent ocean views) plus two even more luxurious houses that sleep up to six. The lodge sits in landscaped grounds with acres of rainforest and is very ecofriendly; all the electricity is supplied by solar and hydro power. There's also a very good restaurant and several tours are available. All meals are included in the *cabina* rates. Cabina $235, house $495

Lapa Ríos Signposted 20km south of Puerto Jiménez ☎ 2735 5130, ⓦ laparios.com. One of the country's most comfortable and impressive jungle lodges, set in a large private nature reserve with excellent birdwatching and beach access. Rooms have big beds and mosquito nets, and, being built of locally sourced materials (bamboo furniture, hardwood floors, palm thatched roofs), blend nicely with the surrounding forest. There's also a huge thatched restaurant, complete with spiral staircase, and a swimming pool. All meals included. $452

Carate

About 25km west of Cabo Matapalo and 43km from Puerto Jiménez, **CARATE** is literally the end of the road – the beach is just steps away from the road with the Parque Nacional Corcovado to the west, which is the overwhelming reason why people make the journey here. There's nothing in the tiny hamlet to detain you, save for the **mini-grocery** (*pulpería*) just off the beach, where you can stock up on expensive basic foodstuffs before entering the park. You can pitch your **tent** right outside the grocery (a minimal charge of $3 per tent per night covers the use of toilets and showers), but for those requiring more comfort, there are a few idyllic **lodges** in the area that are well worth considering.

ARRIVAL AND DEPARTURE   CARATE

By colectivo The *colectivo* from Puerto Jiménez (see p.390) arrives in Carate twice daily and returns at

8.15am and 3.45pm.

ACCOMMODATION

★ **Lookout Inn** Just north of Carate ☎ 2735 5431, ⓦ lookout-inn.com. Kick off your shoes and relax – there's a barefoot policy and an informal, fun atmosphere at this beach house set on a rainforested hillside with large open-air rooms, secluded bungalows and huts, swimming pool and beautiful ocean views. Birdlife is abundant, with plenty of scarlet macaws and hummingbirds. Several tours are offered, including kayaking, dolphin boat cruises and hiking on area trails. Rates include three wonderful buffet meals daily. Double $130, hut $158, bungalow $170

★ **Luna Lodge** Set in the hills above Carate ☎ 2206 5859, ⓦ lunalodge.com. Remote, tranquil and beautiful lodge with welcoming owners and staggering views over the surrounding virgin rainforest. The eight thatched-roof bungalows each have private gardens, large windows, high ceilings and are handsomely furnished; there are also sturdy, comfortable tents in heavily forested settings. Yoga classes take place on a specially built platform overlooking the jungle and three healthy, home-cooked meals daily are included in the rate. Bungalow $225, tent $130

Parque Nacional Corcovado

Southwestern Osa Peninsula • Daily 8am–4pm • $10 • ☎ 2735 5036

Created in 1975, **PARQUE NACIONAL CORCOVADO** protects an undeniably beautiful and biologically complex area of land, with deserted beaches, some laced with waterfalls, high canopy trees and better-than-average wildlife-spotting opportunities.

Many people come with the sole purpose of spotting a **margay, ocelot, tapir** and other rarely seen animals. Of course, it's all down to luck, but if you walk quietly and there aren't too many other humans around, you should have a better chance of seeing some of these creatures here than elsewhere.

Serious walking in Corcovado is not for the faint-hearted. Quite apart from the distances and the terrain, **hazards** include insects (*lots* of them, especially in the rainy season: take a mosquito net, tons of repellent and all the precautions you can think of), herds of peccaries – who have been known to menace hikers – rivers full of crocodiles (and, in one case, sharks) and nasty snakes, including the terciopelo and bushmaster, which can attack without provocation. That said, most of these are present elsewhere in the country anyway, and everybody seems to make it through Corcovado just fine. But you must at least be prepared to get wet, dirty and incredibly hot – bear in mind that there are **sharks** in the sea here, though everyone swims and no attacks have ever been recorded.

The **terrain** in Corcovado (literally "hunchback") varies from beaches of packed or soft sand, riverways, mangroves and *holillo* (palm) swamps to dense forest, although most of it is at lowland elevations. Hikers can expect to spend most of their time on the beach trails that ring the outer perimeters of the peninsular section of the park. Inland, the broad, alluvial Corcovado plain contains the **Corcovado Lagoon**, and for the most part the cover constitutes the only sizeable chunk of tropical **premontane wet forest** (also called tropical humid forest) on the Pacific side of Central America. The Osa forest is as visually and biologically magnificent as any on the subcontinent: biologists often compare the tree heights and density here with that of the Amazon basin cover – practically the only place in the entire isthmus of which this can still be said.

The coastal areas of the peninsular section of the park receive at least 3800mm of **rain** a year, with precipitation rising to about 5000mm in the higher elevations of the interior. This intense wetness is ideal for the development of the intricate, densely matted cover associated with tropical wet forests; there's also a dry season (Dec–March). The inland lowland areas, especially those around the lagoon, can be amazingly **hot**, even for those accustomed to tropical temperatures.

Trails in the park

It's suggested that you come in a group of at least two people, that you bring your own mosquito net, sleeping bag, food and water – though you can fill up at the beachside waterfalls and at the ranger stations – and be more or less experienced in hiking in this kind of terrain. If you can afford it, your best option is to hire a **guide** (see box, p.395). Not only will doing so ensure you stick to the trails – they sometimes can be tricky to follow after a heavy rain – but it will also improve dramatically your chances of spotting the recalcitrant wildlife.

When you enter the park, make sure you jot down the details of the **marea** (tides) that are posted in prominent positions at all the ranger stations. You'll need to cross most of the rivers at low tide – to do otherwise is dangerous. Rangers can advise on conditions. You should plan to **hike** early in the day – though not before dawn, due to snakes – and take shelter at midday.

The park's three longest **trails** all lead from the four peripheral ranger stations (see p.396) **to Sirena**, where you can stay for a day or two in the simple lodge (see p.398), exploring the local trails around the Río Sirena. Though there is some overlap in the type of flora and fauna you might see along the way on the different trails, each offers a distinct hiking experience. For this reason, and if your schedule permits, it's a good idea to walk into Sirena on one trail and back out via another. If you plan to spend a few days in the park, consider hiking in from Los Patos, spend a night or two in Sirena and then back out to La Leona; it's much easier to move on from La Leona at the end of a hike than from Los Patos.

7

PARQUE NACIONAL CORCOVADO

ACCOMMODATION	
Corcovado Lodge Tent Camp	4
Danta Lodge	1
La Leona Eco Lodge	3
Sirena Ranger Station	2

N

0 ————— 5
kilometres

▲ 1 & La Palma

El Tigre 🏠

Río Tigre

4 Carate (2km) & Puerto Jiménez (41km) ▼

La Leona 🏠

Playa Madrigal

Río Sirena

Los Patos 🏠

Río Rincon

Río Claro

Río Pavo

Sirena 🏠

Playa Sirena

Laguna
Corcovado

Río Sirena

RÍO CORCOVADO

Los Planes ●

Río Llorona

Playa
Corcovado

San Pedrillo 🏠

Punta
Llorona

PACIFIC
OCEAN

▲ Bahía Drake

Río
Piedras Blancas   Claro

Chacarita ●

INTERAMERICANA

PARQUE NACIONAL
PIEDRAS BLANCAS

Golfito ●

Golfo Dulce

REFUGIO
NACIONAL
DE VIDA
SILVESTRE
GOLFITO

Rincón de Osa ●

La Palma ●

Puerto
Jiménez ●

PARQUE
NACIONAL
CORCOVADO

Agujitas ●

Carate ●

LOCAL GUIDES IN OSA

In recent years, a programme to train local men and women between the ages of 18 and 35 as **naturalist guides** has been initiated at Rincón de Osa, a village about 35km northwest of Jiménez, snug in the curve of the Golfo Dulce. The programme is typical in Costa Rica – Rara Avis and Selva Verde in Sarapiquí, among others, have similar schemes – enabling people not only to make a living from their local knowledge, but also to appreciate the many ways in which a rainforest can be sustainable. Guides are taught to identify some of the 367 or more species of bird recorded in the area, the 177 amphibians and reptiles, nearly 6000 insects, 140 mammals and 1000 trees – Corcovado's biodiversity makes for a lot of homework. They are also given lectures in tourism and tutored by working professional guides. If you wish to hire a local guide, ask in Rincón or at the Oficina de Área de Conservación Osa office in Puerto Jiménez (see p.390) for details. This arrangement works best if you are planning to hike around the Los Patos–Sirena Trail, as this has the nearest entrances to Rincón.

Los Patos to Sirena

The reasonably marked 20km inland **trail from Los Patos to Sirena** is, for many, the holy grail of Corcovado hikes, a thoroughly intoxicating jungle adventure with opportunities to glimpse tapirs, peccaries, margay or the tracks of jaguars. This is a trail for experienced rainforest hikers, which is why it is **compulsory to hire a guide** for it. While some people elect to do the hike without a guide, it is not wise as you risk getting lost – not to mention the chances of spotting wildlife along the way decrease markedly. You'll want to start your hike from Los Patos to Sirena early, so plan on arriving at Los Patos soon after dawn or, preferably, the night before.

From Los Patos the trail takes you steeply uphill for some 5km into high, wet and dense rainforest, after which the rest of the walk is flat. It's a gruelling trek, especially with the hot inland temperatures (at least 26°C, with 100 percent humidity) and the lack of sea breezes. Although there are crude shelters en route where you can rest in the shade (but not camp), they're not really suited for anything beyond catching your breath or waiting for torrential downpours to pass.

La Leona to Sirena

A 16km trail runs from **La Leona ranger station to Sirena** just inland from the beach, making it easy to keep your bearings. You can only walk its full length at low tide; if you do get stuck, the only thing to do is wait for the water to recede. If you can avoid problems with the tides, you should be able to do the walk in five to six hours, taking time to look out for birds. The walking can get a bit monotonous, but the beaches are uniformly lovely and deserted, and you may be lucky enough to spot a flock of **scarlet macaws** in the coastal trees – a rare sight. You will probably see (or hear) monkeys, too. Take lots of sunscreen, a big hat and at least five litres of water per person – the trail gets very hot, despite the sea breezes.

San Pedrillo to Sirena

Hikers and tour groups coming from the Bahía Drake area enter the park at the **San Pedrillo** ranger station, from where there are a few well-marked and short trails leading into the forest. The ranger station itself can be a good spot to see foraging wildlife, as there are several fruit trees within close proximity to it.

Corcovado's most heroic walk, all 25km of it, is from **San Pedrillo to Sirena**, the stretch along which you'll see the most impressive trees. It's a two-day trek, so you need a tent, sleeping bag and mosquito net, and you mustn't be worried by having to set up camp in the jungle. Fording the **Río Sirena**, just 1km before the Sirena ranger station, is the biggest obstacle: this is the deepest of all the rivers on the peninsula, with the strongest out-tow current, and has to be crossed with care, and at low tide only – **sharks** come in and out in search of food at high tide. Be sure to get the latest information from the San Pedrillo rangers before you set out.

The first half of the walk – a seven-hour stint – is in the jungle, just inland from the coast. Much of the rest of the hike is spent slogging it out on the beach, where the sand is more tightly packed than along the La Leona–Sirena stretch. Some hikers do the beach section of the walk well before dawn or after dark; there are fewer dangers (like snakes) at night on the beach and as long as you have a good torch with lots of batteries and/or the moon is out, this is a reasonable option.

Around El Tigre

El Tigre ranger station, at the eastern inland entrance to the park, is a decent place to take breakfast or lunch with the ranger(s) before setting off on the local trails. The short walking trails laid out around the ranger station provide a quick introduction to Corcovado without making you slog it out on the marathon trails, and can easily be covered in a morning or afternoon.

ARRIVAL AND INFORMATION
PARQUE NACIONAL CORCOVADO

Entry and reservations Unless you're coming as part of a tour package, in the dry months, at least, you should reserve at least several days in advance – and ideally longer – with SINAC (☎ 2735 5036, ✉ pncorcovado @gmail.com). You'll have to specify in advance your group size and dates, plus any meals you require at Sirena (see p.398); it's possible to do all this at the Oficina de Área de Conservación Osa office in Jiménez (see p.390). Incidentally, it's especially important when coming to Corcovado to brush up on your Spanish. You'll be asking the rangers for a lot of crucial information and few, if any, speak English. Bring a phrase book if you're not fluent.

Ranger stations All the ranger stations (8am–4pm) have camping areas, drinking water, information, toilets and telephone or radio-telephone contact. Corcovado is set up so that the rangers at each station always know how many people are on a given trail, and how long they are expected to be. If you are late getting back, they will go looking for you. This gives a measure of security but, all the same, take precautions. Always check with the rangers or ask around in Jiménez regarding current

conditions. If you plan to bring your own food and utensils, the park rangers will allow you to use the stoves at all the ranger stations.

La Leona It's a 1hr 30min walk along the beach from the village of Carate (see p.392) to the La Leona ranger station: refreshments are available en route at the *Corcovado* or *La Leona* tent camps (see below).

Los Patos The small hamlet of La Palma, 24km northwest of Puerto Jiménez, is the gateway to the Los Patos ranger station. It's a 12km walk from here to the park, much of it through hot lowland terrain. A much more sensible idea, however – given the hike that awaits you in the park – is to try and arrange for a taxi in La Palma to take you as far as water levels on the bumpy dirt track will allow.

San Pedrillo Most people travelling to the San Pedrillo ranger station do so on a boat tour with one of the Bahía Drake lodges (see p.387). From Aguijitas you can also follow the 17km trail to San Pedrillo (see p.387).

El Tigre To get here from Puerto Jiménez, drive 10km north and take the second left, a dirt track, signed to El Tigre and Dos Brazos.

ACCOMMODATION AND EATING

NEAR LA LEONA

Corcovado Lodge Tent Camp About a 45min walk along the beach from Carate ☎ 2257 1665, ✇ costa ricaexpeditions.com. Twenty self-contained and fully screened "tent-camps" elevated on short stilts in an amazing beachside location, with bedrooms and screened verandas, communal bathrooms and good local cooking. Packages are available, some including flights right to Carate, and they also offer guided tours around Corcovado ($45–75) and horseriding. Two nights $394

La Leona Eco Lodge Just south of La Leona ranger station ☎ 2735 5705, ✇ laleonacolodge.com. Striking a balance between comfort and convenience, the *La Leona* complex of rustic-style tent *cabinas* is set right on the beach just a short walk from the entrance to Parque Nacional Corcovado. Though they can get uncomfortably

hot, the tents are well equipped and there's a very good restaurant (the price includes three meals a day). The lodge also offers a range of tours including crocodile-spotting, night hikes and rappelling. $140

NEAR LOS PATOS

★**Danta Lodge** 8km from Los Patos ☎ 2735 1111, ✇ dantalodge.com. If you want to stay near Los Patos and begin the hike early, *Danta Lodge* is an outstanding choice. A friendly, family-run lodge outside La Palma, *Danta* was built entirely from sustainable materials and features intricate woodwork and handmade furniture throughout. Accommodation is in attractive rooms or bungalows, the latter 200m from the main lodge. Rates include breakfast; hearty lunches ($12) and dinners ($15) are served in the communal open-air dining area, where there is wi-fi. They rent out horses for

WHAT TO SEE IN CORCOVADO

Chances are you'll have read much about Corcovado's unparalleled **biodiversity** before your arrival, but that does little to prepare you for the sheer scope of it when you step into the park. Suffice it to say, there is much to feast your eyes on in Corcovado.

PLANTS AND TREES

Walking through Corcovado you'll see many lianas, vines, mosses and spectacularly tall trees – some of them 50 or 60m high, and a few more than 80m high. All in all, Corcovado's area is home to about a quarter of all the tree species in the country, including the **silkwood** (or *ceiba pentandra*), characterized by its height – thought to be the largest tree in Central America – and its smooth grey bark. One silkwood, near the Llorona–San Pedrillo section of the trail, is over 80m high and 3m in diameter. You'll also notice huge **buttresses**: above-ground roots shot out by the silkwoods and other tall canopy species. These are used to help anchor the massive tree in thin tropical soil, where drainage is particularly poor.

MAMMALS

Corcovado supports a higher volume of **large mammals** than most other areas of the country, except perhaps the wild and rugged Talamancas. **Jaguars** need more than 100 square kilometres each for their hunting; if you are a good tracker you may be able to spot their traces within the park, especially in the fresh mud along trails and riverbeds. Initially they look identical to those made by a large dog, but the four toes are of unequal size (the outermost one is the smallest) and the fore footprint should be wider than its length. You might, too, see the **margay**, a spotted wildcat about the size of a large domesticated house cat, which comes down from the forest to sun itself on rocks at midday. The **ocelot**, a larger spotted cat, is even shyer, rarely seen for more than a second, poking its head out of the dense cover and then melting away into the forest immediately.

With a body shape somewhere between a large pig and a cow, the **Baird's tapir** is an odd-looking animal, most immediately recognizable for its funny-looking snout, a truncated elephant-type trunk. Tapirs are very shy – and have been made even more so through large-scale hunting – though you stand a reasonable chance of spotting one crossing the clearing at Sirena's airfield. More threatening are the packs of white-lipped **peccaries**, a type of wild pig, who in Corcovado typically group themselves in packs of about thirty. They are often seen along the trails and should be treated with caution, since they can bite you. The accepted wisdom is to climb a tree if they come at you threateningly, clacking their jaws and growling, though this, of course, means you have to be good at climbing trees, some of which have painful spines.

More common mammals that you'll likely spot are the ubiquitous **agouti**, foraging in the underbrush. Essentially a large rodent with smooth, glossy hair, the agouti looks similar to a large squirrel. The **coati**, a member of the racoon family, with a long ringed tail, is also sure to cross your path. Another mammal found in significant numbers in the park – and all over the peninsula – is the **tayra** (tolumuco), a small and swift mink-like creature. They will in most cases run from you, but should not be approached, as they have teeth and can be aggressive.

BIRDS

Among Corcovado's resident **birds** is the **scarlet macaw**, around 300 of which live in the park – more, in terms of birds per square kilometre, than anywhere else in the country. Macaws are highly prized as caged birds and, despite the efforts of the SPN, poaching is still a problem here, as their (relative) abundance makes them easy prey. Around the Río Sirena estuary, especially, keep an eye out for the **boat-billed heron**, whose wide bill gives it a lopsided quality. The big black **king vulture** can also be found in Corcovado; a forager rather than a hunter, it nevertheless looks quite ominous. There are many other smaller birds in Corcovado including, perhaps, the fluffy-headed **harpy eagle**. Though the harpy is thought to be extinct in Costa Rica, ornithologists reckon there's a chance that a few pairs still live in Corcovado, and in the Parque Internacional La Amistad on the Talamanca coast.

7

the 2hr trip to Los Patos and lead several well-run tours in the area including kayaking in Golfo Dulce and night walks on their 70 hectares. Double $122, bungalow $155

park, Sirena is also a research station, and often full of biologists. Meals are offered at designated times; breakfast costs $20, while lunch and dinner each cost $25. $15

SIRENA

Sirena Ranger Station You can sleep in the no-frills accommodation block at Sirena ranger station, which has hot water; bring bedding. The biggest ranger station in the

CAMPING

Ranger station campsites All the ranger stations have camping areas; Sirena's has the most services, while the other three stations have very basic sites. All have drinking water. $4

Golfo Dulce

One of the deepest gulfs of its size in the world, the **GOLFO DULCE** is no longer passed over so quickly by visitors once drawn to the extreme south almost exclusively by the Osa Peninsula and Parque Nacional Corcovado. Increasingly, the gulf's **eastern shores** are receiving attention and though this is partly due to improved infrastructure, there's little doubt there's plenty here to make a memorable itinerary. The only town of any real size, **Golfito** has a dramatic setting that it's still trying to live up to, but it makes for a good base to explore the nearby **Parque Nacional Piedras Blancas**, whose dense interior is home to many of the country's signature mammals and birds. South of Golfito, well off the road to Panama, are a couple of Costa Rica's most isolated – and most alluring – beaches, **Playa Zancudo** and **Playa Pavones**.

Golfito

The former banana port of **GOLFITO**, 33km north of the Panamanian border, straggles for 2.5km along the water of the same name (*golfito* means "little gulf"). The town's setting is spectacular, backed up against steep, thickly forested hills to the east, and with the glorious Golfo Dulce to the west. The low shadow of the Península de Osa

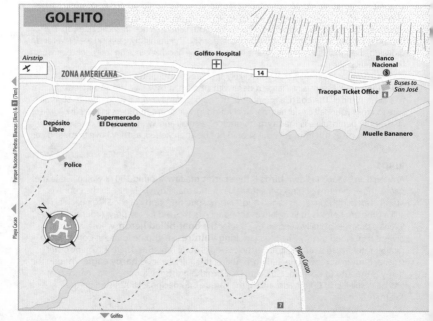

shimmers in the distance, and everywhere the vegetation has the soft, muted look of the undisturbed tropics. It is also very **rainy**; even if you speak no Spanish, you'll certainly pick up the local expression *va a caer baldazos* – "it's gonna pour".

Golfito extends for ages without any clear centre, through stretches where the main road is hemmed in by hills on one side and the lapping waters of the *golfito* on the other. The town is effectively split in two – by a division in wealth as well as architecture. In the north is the **Zona Americana**, where the banana company executives used to live and where better-off residents still reside in beautiful wooden houses shaded by dignified palms. Here you'll find the tax-free **Depósito Libre** (see box, p.400), an unaesthetic outdoor mall ringed by a circular concrete wall. Some 2km to the south of the Depósito, the **Pueblo Civil** (civilian town), is a very small, tight nest of streets – hotter, noisier and more crowded than the *zona*. It's here you'll find the *lancha* across the Golfo Dulce to Puerto Jiménez and the Península de Osa. Although the Pueblo Civil is perfectly civil in the daytime, be careful at night. Be wary of entering any bar with a sign positioned outside so that you can't see in – these are for professional transactions only.

The Zona Americana

There's little to see in Golfito itself, other than the **old homes** of the banana company executives in the **ZONA AMERICANA**, which includes the sprawling Depósito Libre. These are obvious from their grandeur: wide verandas, painted in jolly, if sun-bleached, colours, with huge screens and sun canopies. One row, just east of the main street in the centre of town (near the Banco Nacional) displays a particularly fine series of washed-out tropical hues – lime green blends into faded oyster-yellow, followed by tired pink and metallic orange.

Refugio Nacional de Vida Silvestre Golfito

The most accessible trailhead is the one across from *Samoa del Sur* • Daily 8am–4pm • Free • ☎ 2775 2620

Immediately to the east of town, some **trails** lead up a steep hill, giving fantastic views across the Golfo Dulce in the tiny **REFUGIO NACIONAL DE VIDA SILVESTRE GOLFITO**. It isn't easily explored, however, since the trail entrances tend to be overgrown and

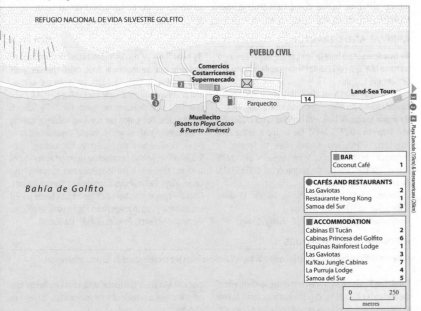

UNITED BRANDS ("LA YUNAI")

Golfito's history is inextricably linked with the giant transnational **United Brands** (later the United Fruit Company and now Chiquita), which first set up in the area in 1938, twenty years before the Interamericana hit town. The company – known locally as "La Yunai" – built schools, recruited doctors and police and brought prosperity to the area, though "problems" with labour union organizers began soon afterwards, and came to characterize the relationship between company and town. What with fluctuating banana prices, a three-month strike by workers and local social unrest, the company eventually decided Golfito was too much trouble and pulled out in a hurry in 1985. The town declined and, in the public eye, became synonymous with rampant unemployment, alcoholism, abandoned children, prostitution and general unruliness.

Today, at the big old *muelle bananero* (banana dock) container ships are still loaded up with bananas to be processed further up towards Palmar. This residual traffic, along with tourism, has combined to help revive the local economy. Many visitors come to Golfito because it's a good base for getting to the Parque Nacional Corcovado by *lancha* or plane, and also a major **sportfishing** centre. The rescue, though, came from the Costa Rican government, who in the early 1990s established a **Depósito Libre** – or tax-free zone – in the town, where Costa Ricans can buy manufactured goods imported from Panama without the 100 percent tax normally levied. Ticos who come to shop here have to buy their tickets for the Depósito 24 hours in advance, obliging them to spend at least one night, and therefore colones, in the town.

difficult to find; in the Pueblo Civil look for the sign by the Plaza Deportes football field or so ask around locally.

Playa Cacao

Less than 1km from town across the bay • Water taxis (around $5) depart to the beach from the *muellecito* (ferry dock) just north of the petrol station. In the dry season, you can drive there along a rough unfinished track from the turn-off right in front of the *guardia*, bearing left

Despite lining Bahía de Golfito, Golfito doesn't exactly have the kinds of beaches you might be hoping for. The one beach worth spending an afternoon on, **PLAYA CACAO**, is across the bay. It has good swimming and a number of decent bars and restaurants nearby, although the beach itself is a little grimy.

ARRIVAL AND DEPARTURE
GOLFITO

By bus Buses leave from in front of the *muelle bananero*, with two TRACOPA (☎ 2258 4214) services daily to San José (at 5am and 1.30pm).
Destinations Ciudad Neily (daily; 1hr); playas Pavones and Zancudo (daily; 2hr 30min–3hr); San José (2 daily; 7hr).
By plane You can fly here with both Sansa (☎ 2775 0303) and NatureAir (☎ 2775 0145); the airstrip is in the Zona Americana. There's also a small plane to Jiménez for Corcovado (about $150 for up to five people) – contact Alfa Romeo Aero Taxi's office at the airstrip, or call ☎ 2755 1515, ✉ corcovadotaxi@racsa.co.cr.
Destinations via NatureAir Puerto Jiménez (1 daily; 10min); San José (1–2 daily; 40min).
Destinations via Sansa San José (2–3 daily; 55min).

By boat There are two ferry piers in Golfito: the old *muelle bananero* and the municipal dock, called the *muellecito*, near the Pueblo Civil. All boats are motorized *lanchas*, and prices are much the same from either pier. Make sure your boat has lifejackets on board: the Golfo Dulce is usually calm, but winds can come up suddenly, causing unexpectedly high waves. A *lancha* departs Golfito to Puerto Jiménez from the *muellecito*. Alternatively, Land-Sea Tours (see below) can organize transport in their boats to almost anywhere in the Golfo Dulce area, including Playa Cacao, Playa Cativo, Playa Zancudo and Puerto Jiménez. Costs are competitive, but you'll get a much better price if you gather a group together (from $50 for up to six people).
Destinations Puerto Jiménez (6 daily; 1hr 30min).

INFORMATION AND TOURS

There is no official tourist information centre in town; Land-Sea Tours is a capable stand-in for area information.

Land-Sea Tours On the waterfront at the southern end of the pueblo (☎ 2775 1614, ⓦ golfitocostarica.com). As well as leading a variety of tours around Golfo Dulce, they also maintain a "cruisers' clubhouse" with a book exchange, film collection and a wealth of local information; there's free wi-fi too.

ACTIVITIES AND TOURS IN GOLFITO

If you're in Golfito to **sportfish**, the larger hotels can help arrange tours and tackle – the area is particularly rich in marlin and sailfish. **Swimming** is no good, however, as the bay is polluted, and you'll see oil in the water and various bits of floating refuse all around Golfito. Your best bet for a swim is to head across to Playa Cacao, or to move south towards the Península Burica.

For activities out of town, the highly recommended Land-Sea Tours (see opposite) lead a variety of tours around Golfo Dulce, including horseriding and boat trips to the beaches at Parque Nacional Piedras Blancas, jungle hikes, panning for gold and cave exploration, as well as *lanchas* to Playa Zancudo (see p.403).

ACCOMMODATION

Much of Golfito's accommodation is **basic and inexpensive**, catering to Costa Ricans visiting the Depósito Libre, though there are a couple of slightly smarter hotels too. Upstairs at Land-Sea Tours (see opposite) there is one bedroom which, if available, is a steal at $20/night. Be warned that the sheer number of people coming to Golfito to shop, especially at Christmas, means that rooms are often booked in advance – if you don't have reservations try to get to town as early in the day as possible. You'll find several **luxurious accommodation** options along the coast north of Golfito; choices are fewer to the south.

IN TOWN

Cabinas El Tucán On the main road, 50m north of the muellecito ☎ 2775 0553. Basic but perfectly serviceable accommodation near the Pueblo Civil. The rooms all have private bathrooms and fans and the owner is a great source of local information (and stories). Free parking available. $33

Cabinas Princesa del Golfito Opposite the Banco Nacional ☎ 2775 0442. Small and friendly with pleasantly decorated, good-value rooms that have a/c and wi-fi. $36

Las Gaviotas At the southern entrance to town ☎ 2775 0062. Well-equipped, if slightly shabby resort with nice views out over the gulf and a swimming pool. The somewhat barrack-like (but very affordable) rooms all have private bathrooms with hot water, a/c and cable TV. The waterside open-air restaurant serves great local seafood, and the weekend buffets are a veritable feast. $67

Samoa del Sur On the main road between the Zona Americana and the Pueblo Civil ☎ 2775 0233, ⓦ samoadelsur.com. Fourteen spacious but slightly gloomy rooms on the waterfront, with a large and rather raucous boat-shaped bar-restaurant. $50

AROUND GOLFITO

★ **Esquinas Rainforest Lodge** La Gamba, about 7km from Km37 on the Interamericana ☎ 2741 8001, ⓦ esquinaslodge.com. Friendly ecolodge, originally funded by Austria's government as part of a project combining development aid, nature conservation and rainforest research – all profits go to the local community. It's set in primary rainforest, with resident wildlife and on-site hiking and horseriding trails leading into Parque Nacional Piedras Blancas. The fourteen pleasantly rustic rooms have ceiling fans and private bathrooms and are adorned with textiles crafted by local indigenous artisans. There's also a roomy jungle villa set off from the main lodge that can accommodate four. A wide range of packages are available, plus a variety of tours, including to Corcovado and the Wilson Botanical Gardens. Three fantastic meals a day are included in the room rate. $145

Ka'Kau Jungle Cabinas Playa Cacao ☎ 8583 2899, ⓦ todocontento.com. Mountain-top indigenous-styled, thatched-roof *cabinas* with pretty views of the bay. Though simply furnished, they're very comfortable with fans and there's a communal dining area. Jungle walks and dolphin-watching boat trips are also available. Breakfast included. $34

La Purruja Lodge La Purruja, 4km south of Golfito towards the Interamericana ☎ 2775 5054, ⓦ purruja .com. Small family-run hotel set in lovely gardens, with spacious rooms and a pool. Several tours are offered, including mangrove-swamp boat trips ($120) and hikes in the *refugio nacional* ($30). Good choice if you have a car. Breakfast is included. $40

EATING AND DRINKING

Golfito has plenty of decent places to eat. For **casados** and **platos del día** there are two groups of simple **sodas**: one near the Depósito Libre, catering to Ticos who have come to Golfito on shopping trips, and another, slightly better-value cluster on the main drag of the Pueblo Civil and in the surrounding streets.

Coconut Café Opposite the main dock ☎ 2775 0518. A nice place for a beer or a simple *casado* ($7) and a great source of local information – the American owner seems to know just about everyone in Golfito. There's free wi-fi, too. Daily 8am–10pm.

Las Gaviotas Las Gaviotas. Good meat dishes, a

reasonable wine list and all-you-can-eat barbecue ($10–15) on Friday and Saturday evenings from 6pm – though its best feature is the waterside location on the *golfito*. Daily 11am–9pm.

Restaurante Hong Kong In the Pueblo Civil ☎ 2775 2383. Renowned for its excellent (and cheap) chow mein dishes ($5.50) and a magnet for expat yachters: despite the completely forgettable interior, it serves up some of the best Chinese food to be found in the south. Daily 11am–10pm.

Samoa del Sur Samoa del Sur. The beachside bar and restaurant at the *Samoa del Sur* hotel is a pleasant spot for an evening beer or meal, with a menu featuring seafood, such as ceviche ($14) and pizza ($6–10). Bear in mind that it can get rowdy later in the evening (it's the bar of choice for US marines on shore leave). Daily 11am–midnight.

DIRECTORY

Hospital Golfito Hospital is in the Zona Americana (☎ 2775 7800).
Internet El Estudiante Bizarre (☎ 2775 2036), across from the Comercios Costarricenses Supermercado, has wi-fi.
Money and exchange The Banco Nacional (Mon–Fri 8.30am–3.30pm; ☎ 2775 1101) opposite the TRACOPA terminal changes travellers' cheques.
Post office Right in the centre of the Pueblo Civil (Mon–Fri 7.30am–5pm, Sat 8am–noon; ☎ 2775 1911).
Supermarket A Comercios Costarricenses Supermercado (☎ 2775 0356) is located on the main street in the Pueblo Civil.

Parque Nacional Piedras Blancas

3km north of Golfito • Daily 8am–4pm • Free • ☎ 2775 2620

Stretching inland from the Golfo Dulce and abutting the village of La Gamba, **PARQUE NACIONAL PIEDRAS BLANCAS** comprises land that was formerly part of Parque Nacional Corcovado as well as parcels purchased and donated by such disparate entities as the international hydroelectric behemoth Tenaska, the Austrian government and The Nature Conservancy. All told, almost 150 square kilometres of mountainous rainforest, beaches and portions of the Piedras Blancas and Esquinas rivers are protected, an area teeming with tropical flora and some of Costa Rica's signature **mammals**, including jaguars, pumas, two-toed sloths, kinkajous, and squirrel and capuchin monkeys. The most prevalent mammals, though, are **bats**: over fifty species have been observed here, among them the vampire bat. The park is also one of the top spots in the country for birdwatching, mainly due to it being a favoured stopover for **migrating birds**. Poaching was a significant problem when the park was formed two decades ago, though efforts throughout the previous decade have been successful in greatly reducing illegal hunting.

The park has a few secluded **beaches**, though the only practical way of reaching them is on a thirty-minute boat ride from Golfito (see p.400). **Playa San Josecito**, ringing a pretty little bay, is the site of a few of the park's ecolodges.

ARRIVAL AND INFORMATION   PARQUE NACIONAL PIEDRAS BLANCAS

The park has a few, somewhat difficult to reach, access points; your best bet is to enter from *Esquinas Rainforest Lodge* (see p.401) in La Gamba, where you can make arrangements for a guide to lead you through the forest. As the park does not yet have any infrastructure for visitors, having a guide with you is a sensible way to explore the thick primary forest. Book any of the accommodation in advance and you'll be picked up by *lancha* from Golfito.

ACCOMMODATION

Dolphin Quest Playa San Josecito ☎ 8811 2099, ⓦ dolphinquestcostarica.com. This secluded ecolodge has a range of accommodation, from spacious dormitory rooms to private *cabinas* to a small house that sleeps five. The lodge's extensive grounds are wedged between the ocean and dense rainforest crisscrossed by a network of trails. Between periods of lazing about in a hammock, you'll find plenty of activities and tours to keep you occupied, from snorkelling and kayaking to horseriding and fishing. Dorm <u>$19</u>, *cabinas* <u>$51</u>, house <u>$247</u>

Golfo Dulce Lodge Playa San Josecito ☎ 8821 5398, ⓦ golfodulcelodge.com. This Swiss-run ecolodge is surrounded by the undisturbed primary rainforest of Parque Nacional Piedras Blancas. There are three standard rooms as well as five posher detached wooden bungalows named after local wildlife, each with private veranda with hammocks. A thatched restaurant, nearby observation platform and a small freshwater pool are also in the grounds. Three-night minimum stay; all meals included. Double <u>$300</u>, bungalow <u>$360</u>

★Playa Nicuesa Rainforest Lodge Playa Nicuesa ☎2258 8250, ⓦ nicuesalodge.com. Owners Michael and Donna go the distance to welcome guests to the jungle at this nature retreat, adventure camp and all-inclusive resort. A model of sustainability, the lodge offers spectacular ocean and forest views from private verandas and the treetop bar. Hit the beach for kayaking, snorkelling, fishing, sailing or let a resident naturalist guide you to a nearby waterfall. All meals included. **$215**

Playa Zancudo

15km southeast of Golfito

Ask anyone in Golfito where you can swim, and they'll direct you to black-sand **PLAYA ZANCUDO**, 15km southeast of Golfito, facing the Golfo Dulce and bordered on one side by the Río Coto Colorado. On summer weekends from December to April, Playa Zancudo fills with Zona Sur Ticos taking a beach break, but otherwise it's fairly low-key, except for a small colony of mainly US expats. There are a couple of professional **sportfishing** outfits, while other local activities include **surfing** and **boat trips** along **the Río Coto.**

7

ARRIVAL AND DEPARTURE   PLAYA ZANCUDO

By boat You can reach Zancudo from Golfito by a *lancha* that departs the *muellecito* at noon or via private water taxi (45min). *Lanchas* arrive at the boat dock at the northern end of the beach.

By bus Zancudo is serviced by buses that depart from in front of the *muelle bananero* in Golfito.

Destination Golfito (2 daily; 1hr 45min).
By car Driving to Zancudo takes about 1hr 30min from Golfito, a trip shortened by the building of a bridge in 2010 over the Río Coto. You need a 4WD, whatever time of year; during the wet season it's worth checking the levels of the creeks and fords that you'll have to pass before you set out.

ACCOMMODATION AND EATING

Cabinas Los Cocos On the northern half of the spit ☎2776 0012, ⓦ loscocos.com. Pretty, well-equipped *cabinas* – each with kitchen, fridge, screens, fans and hammocks – surrounded by dense tropical foliage and steps from the beach. Bikes, kayaks, boogie boards and beach chairs are available for guests. They also lead a few boat tours (from $50), including along the Río Coto. **$79**

Oceano Middle of the spit ☎2776 0921, ⓦ cabinas-costa-rica.com. Two cosy rooms are available at this beachfront B&B. The rooms are nicely appointed with a/c, TVs, ceiling fans, mosquito nets and plenty of hot water. As thoroughly comfortable as the rooms are, the biggest draw is the lively restaurant, where you can feast on succulent fresh seafood, such as jumbo shrimp plates ($15). **$84**

Sol y Mar About 25m from the boat dock ☎2276 0014, ⓦ zancudo.com. Five groovy screened cabins in a garden by a wide section of the beach, each with fans, hot showers and wi-fi. They offer sportfishing outings and boat trips through the mangrove swamps of the Río Coto and serve gourmet French cuisine at their restaurant. The bar is usually a hive of activity and is the site of popular volleyball competitions on Saturday afternoons. **$52**

Playa Pavones

About 12km south of Playa Zancudo is **PLAYA PAVONES**, famed among surfers for having the **longest continuous wave in the world** – exactly how long, they do not divulge. The waves are biggest and best from May to November. Needless to say, the water's too rough for anything else and, though tourism is mushrooming around Pavones, the community here still largely consists of avid surfers. Not surprisingly, most of the services cater to them as well, and there are the requisite surf camps and surf shops and just about every one of the many lodges around the beach offers lessons. Regardless of the pull the waves hold on you, the hamlet has a palpable end-of-the-road charm all its own, with its breezy dirt roads and all-round welcoming air.

ARRIVAL AND DEPARTURE   PLAYA PAVONES

By boat You can hire a private water taxi in Golfito to the beach (about 1hr 15min).

By bus Two buses depart daily for Pavones from in front of the *muelle bananero* in Golfito.

Destination Golfito (2 daily; 1hr 45min).
By car Driving to Pavones takes about 1hr 15min from Golfito; a 4WD is recommended, especially in wet season.

ACCOMMODATION AND EATING

★**Castillo de Pavones** In the hills above Pavones, about a 5min walk to the beach ⓦcastleofcostarica .com. Fashioning itself as a jungle castle, this bold, intimate property is marked by a stunning design throughout and very reasonable rates. The four stately rooms all have attractive furnishings and a full range of high-end amenities, including king-size beds, a/c, wi-fi and hot tubs overlooking the sea. The rooftop split-level restaurant and lounge delivers panoramic views and some of the finest meals in the Zona Sur, all with organic ingredients. There's a long list of tours, such as horseriding and yoga classes to choose from, and surfboards are included in the rate. **$150**

La Manta On the main road ☎2776 2281. Cavernous, thatched-roof restaurant exuding cool and a popular

hangout spot throughout the day, thanks in no small part to its excellent sound system and movie screenings on a massive screen. The menu is full of crowd pleasers like burgers, burritos and fish tacos, all nicely prepared and boosted by home-grown spices (mains $8–15). Daily 10am–midnight.

★**Tiskita Lodge** Punta Banco, 10km south of Playa Pavones ☎2296 8125, ⓦtiskita.com. This extremely comfortable rainforest lodge (which doubles as a biological research station) has sixteen *cabinas* overlooking the beach and a swimming pool on the grounds. Trails weave through the surrounding forest and the birdwatching is good. You can also tour their fruit farm (the owner is an agronomist). They offer good-value packages that include guided hikes and three high-quality meals a day. Three nights **$570**

Towards the Panama border

At Palmar, travellers heading south face a choice: most people intent on the quickest route to Panama stick to the Interamericana, which heads south for the final 100km to Panama. This section of the trip down to the **Paso Canoas** border crossing is through an empty, featureless, frontier region, with the refuelling point of **Ciudad Neily** the only point of minor interest.

The alternative route is to head east along the Interamericana, which switchbacks its way to the small, sleepy town of **Paso Real**, 20km away, following the wide and fast-running **Río Grande de Térraba** as it cuts a giant path through the almost unbearably hot lowland landscape, its banks coloured red with tropical soils. Rainstorms seem to steamroller in with the express purpose of washing everything away, and you can almost see the river rise with each fresh torrent. This stretch is prone to landslides in the rainy season, when you can find yourself stranded by a sea of mud.

At Paso Real, you can pick up the paved **Hwy-237**, which takes you south through some spectacularly scenic country. Steep and winding, with beautiful views, it is little used by tourists except those few heading to the pretty mountain town of **San Vito**, the jumping-off point for the **Wilson Botanical Gardens**, **Parque Internacional La Amistad** and the **Río Serena** border crossing. Even though the roads around here have improved, it's much easier with a 4WD to deal with occasional washouts and landslides, especially from May to November.

San Vito

Settled largely by post-World War II immigrants from Italy, **SAN VITO** is a prosperous agricultural town with a lovely setting in the Talamancas. At nearly 1000m above sea level it has a wonderfully refreshing climate, as well as great views over the Valle de Coto Brus below. The town is growing as more and more Costa Ricans discover its qualities, though there's not much to do in San Vito itself – the nearby **Wilson Botanical Garden** provides the principal diversion in the area.

ARRIVAL   SAN VITO

By bus TRACOPA (☎2221 4214) buses stop 25m east of Hwy-237 in the centre of town.

Destinations Ciudad Neily (8–10 daily; 1hr 40min); Paso Real (4 daily; 1hr 30min); San José (3 daily; 6hr).

ACCOMMODATION

★**Casa Botania** 5km southeast of San Vito ☎ 2773 4217, ⓦ casabotania.com. This eye-catching B&B, run by a young Costa Rican and Belgian couple, is full of individual touches that make a stay here feel like a real treat, from ornate wood furnishings to a superb design that's harmonious with the surrounding countryside. The understated rooms and bungalows, each with private terraces, exude class, and superb meals are served in an open-air dining area with striking valley views. A real bargain for the rate. Room and small bungalow __$73__

Wilson Botanical Garden

6km south of San Vito • Daily 8am–4pm • $10; guided tours from $36 • ☎ 2773 4004, ⓦ ots.ac.cr/

The **Wilson Botanical Garden**, operated by the Organization for Tropical Studies, is among the best in Central America. Comprising over 30 acres, the gardens are home to over 2000 native plant species, including orchids and heliconias as well as several hundred endemic trees such as palms, ferns and massive bamboo. Resident biologists lead guided tours along the large network of paths that wind through the meticulously laid out garden, which is also primate habitat for numerous **butterfly** species; the sight of dozens of vibrantly coloured **butterflies** fluttering about the space of a couple of feet can be mesmerizing. **Bats** are common too, but aside from the tropical flora, perhaps the biggest draw is the hundreds of resident and migrating **bird** species, making this one of the country's top birdwatching spots.

ACCOMMODATION	WILSON BOTANICAL GARDEN
Las Cruces Biological Field Station Cabinas On a loop road off the main entrance road. You can stay at the gardens in comfortable *cabinas* with private bathroom and	floor to ceiling windows. Lodging includes three meals a day; reservations must be made in advance. __$105__

The Río Sereno border crossing

18km east of San Vito • Daily 8am–5pm • ☎ 2784 0130 • Few nationalities require a visa (see box, p.77)

About 9km east of San Vito along Hwy-613, the tiny village of **Sabalito** is the nearest community of any size to the Río Sereno border crossing into Panama. From here you can catch one of ten buses daily that arrive from San Vito and continue on to the border (15min). Ask the driver to drop you off at the Costa Rican *migración* to avoid walking up a hill with your bags: after clearing customs, you can walk to Panama's *migración*. Once in Río Sereno on the Panamanian side, walk down the main street to the station at the street's end. From here you can catch a bus that will take you on to David and La Concepción in Panama.

Parque Internacional La Amistad

Main entrance 25km northeast of San Vito • Daily 8am–4pm • $10 • ☎ 2200 5355

Created in 1982 as a biosphere reserve, the **PARQUE INTERNACIONAL LA AMISTAD** is a joint venture by the governments of Panama and Costa Rica to protect the Cordillera de Talamanca on both sides of their shared border. Amistad also encompasses several **indigenous reserves**, the most geographically isolated in the country, where Bribrí and Cabécar peoples are able to live with minimal interference from the Valle Central. It is the largest park in the country, covering 2070 square kilometres of Costa Rican territory.

In 1983 Amistad was designated a World Heritage Site, thanks to its immense scientific resources. The Central American isthmus is often described as being a crossroads or filter for the meeting of the North and South American eco-communities; the Amistad area is itself a "biological bridge" within the isthmus, where an extraordinary number of habitats, life zones, topographical features, soils, terrains and types of animal and plant life can be found. Its **terrain**, while mainly mountainous, is extremely varied on account of shifting altitudes, and ranges from wet tropical forest to high peaks where the temperature can drop below freezing at night. According to the classification system devised by L.R. Holdridge (see p.423), Amistad has at least seven (some say eight or nine) **life zones**, along with six transition zones. Even more important is Amistad's function as the last bastion of some of the species most in danger of **extinction** in both Costa Rica and the isthmus. Within its boundaries roam the jaguar and the puma, the ocelot and the tapir. Along with Corcovado on the Península de Osa, Amistad may also be the last holdout of the **harpy eagle**, feared extinct in Costa Rica.

Trails in the park

Its rugged terrain limits access to much of the park, but there are two **trails** that depart from the Altamira ranger station (see below). If you're hiking solo, your only option is the **Gigantes del Bosque** trail, a 3km-long round-route that meanders through mostly primary rainforest. There are two towers along the way, the first of which is ideal for **birdwatching**, particularly just after daybreak which is the best time to see some of the 400 species that live in the park. The path is reasonably well marked, but not always maintained, and tall grass often grows over parts of the latter half of the trail: allow between 2–3hr to make the loop.

Much longer and far more exhausting is the **Valle del Silencio** trail, which is 20km long and provides an excellent introduction to the varied habitats found in La Amistad. The trail climbs steadily to a campsite on a flat ridge near the base of Cerro Kamuk, offering stunning vistas of the park and further afield en route. There's a good chance of spotting **wildlife** along the way, possibly including quetzals and Baird's tapirs, the latter of which are thought to have larger populations here than anywhere else in the country. The trail takes about eight to ten hours round-trip and you cannot hike it without a guide; the park ranger at the Altamira station can make arrangements.

ARRIVAL AND INFORMATION	PARQUE INTERNACIONAL LA AMISTAD
By car Due to rough and unpredictable road conditions, the only reliable way to reach the Altamira ranger station is by car. From San Vito, head 27km north on Hwy-237 to Guácimo. From there turn onto a dirt road for about 17km through the village of El Carmén. 3km past El Carmén turn onto a dirt road that leads to Altamira.	**Tourist information** The small hamlet of Altamira functions as the park headquarters, with a nearby ranger station maintained by a full-time ranger who can provide information. The ranger station, 2km outside the village, is signposted from the centre.

ACCOMMODATION	
Altamira Ranger Station 2km from Altamira. You can camp or stay in a spartan dorm room at the ranger station,	where there are shower and toilet facilities as well as a small picnic area. Campsite and dorm bed each $\overline{5}6$

Ciudad Neily

If you're making your way south to the Paso Canoas border crossing, soporific **CIUDAD NEILY** makes a good spot to stock up on any last-minute supplies before you cross into Panama (18km away). Though it is one of the largest towns in the southern third of the country and the point where the Interamericana and Hwy-237 converge, there's not much to detain you and chances are you'll pass through it quickly en route to Panama.

Hwy-237 runs right down the middle of Ciudad Neily, before ending at the Interamericana; all the town's services are within a couple of blocks either side of it.

ARRIVAL AND DEPARTURE	CIUDAD NEILY
By bus Buses arrive at the Terminal TRACOPA (☎ 2221 4214), a couple of blocks uphill and east of Hwy-237 in the centre of town.	Destinations Paso Canoas (daily every 30min 6.30am–11.30pm; 30min); Puerto Jiménez (2 daily; 3hr); San Isidro de El General (10 daily; 4hr); San José (6 daily; 7hr).

ACCOMMODATION

Hotel Andrea ☎ 2783 3784, ⓦ hotelandreacr.com. If you need to stay overnight, make a beeline for the pretty *Hotel Andrea*, just west of the bus terminal, which has comfortable rooms with fans or a/c and an open-air restaurant that serves hearty and inexpensive *comida típica* meals. $50

DIRECTORY

Money and exchange There's a Banco Popular on Hwy-237 at the northern end of town and a Banco Nacional branch a couple of blocks south.

Supermarket The biggest supermarket in Ciudad Neily (and surely all of southern Costa Rica) is the Supermercado Hermanos Loaiza, a block northeast of the Banco Nacional.

The Paso Canoas border crossing

17km southeast of Ciudad Neliy • Usually 6am–10pm • ☎ 2732 2150 • Few nationalities require a visa (see box, p.77)

South of Neily duty-free shops and stalls start to line the Interamericana announcing the approach to **PASO CANOAS**, about 17km beyond Neily. As you come into town you'll pass the Costa Rican customs checkpoint, where everybody gets a going-over. Foreigners don't attract much interest, however; customs officials are far more concerned with nabbing Ticos coming back over the border with unauthorized amounts of bargain consumer goods. Barring a build-up of buses, the Paso Canoas crossing is generally quicker than the Río Sereno crossing (see p.405), if much less scenic.

ARRIVAL AND INFORMATION

By bus The TRACOPA (☎ 2221 4214) bus terminal is a block from the crossing. Buses run from the Panamanian border bus terminal to David, the first city of any size in Panama. From David it's easy to pick up local services, including the Ticabus to Panama City, which you can't get at the border. Destinations David (every hour or so until 5pm; 1hr 30min); San Isidro de El General (5 daily; 4hr 30min); San José (3 daily; 7hr 30min).

THE PASO CANOAS BORDER CROSSING

Immigration The *migración* is on the Costa Rican side, next to the TRACOPA bus terminal. You'll have to wait in line, especially if a San José–David–Panama City Ticabus comes through, as all international bus passengers are processed together. Arrive early to get through fastest.
Money and exchange There's no problem changing money: there's a Banco de Costa Rica on the Costa Rican side of the border and, beyond that, plenty of moneychangers.

ACCOMMODATION

Utterly without charm, Paso Canoas is not a place you'd choose to stay overnight unless arrival time dictates it. If you absolutely have to bed down here, there are about a dozen rock-bottom budget **cabinas** and **hospedajes**. These are all extremely basic, with cell-like rooms, private bathroom and cold water. They can also be full at weekends.

Cabinas Interamericano On a side road to the right after the TRACOPA bus terminal, heading towards the border ☎ 2732 2041. One place a cut above the pack is *Cabinas Interamericano*; the rooms are dull but are clean and not a bad deal; there's a restaurant, too. $23

SAN JOSÉ'S TEATRO NACIONAL, 1922

Contexts

History

Costa Rica was first inhibited, sometime around 10,000 BC, about 25,000 years after the first Homo sapiens had crossed the Bering Strait into what is now the Americas (though the only thing to support this tentative date is a single flint arrowhead excavated in the 1890s in Guanacaste). Archeologists know almost nothing of the various peoples of what is now modern-day Costa Rica before about 1000 BC. Certainly no written records were left, and what little knowledge we do have stems mostly from limited excavations of the Monumento Nacional Guayabo in the southeastern Valle Central.

Costa Rica before the Spanish

Pre-Columbian Costa Rica was a **contact zone** – a corridor for merchants and trading expeditions – between the Mesoamerican empires to the north and the Inca Empire to the south. Excavations of pottery, jade and trade goods, and accounts of cultural traditions, have shown that the pre-Columbian peoples of Costa Rica adopted liberally from both areas.

When the Spaniards arrived in Costa Rica at the beginning of the sixteenth century, it was inhabited by as many as 27 different **indigenous groups** or clans. Most clans were assigned names by the invaders, which they took from the **cacique** (chief) with whom they dealt. The modern-day Zona Norte was home to the **Catapas**, the **Votos** and the **Suerres**; the extreme south of the Talamancas held the **Cabécars** and the **Guayamís**, whose influence spread south to the Osa Peninsula. In the nearby Valle de Diquis and Valle de El General were the **Térrabas** and their subgroup, the **Borucas**. The Valle Central contained the **Huetars**, while modern-day Guanacaste – the most heavily populated and farmed area in pre-Columbian Costa Rica – was home to the **Chorotegas** and the older Nicoyan peoples. The Chorotegas, in particular, showed signs of cultural inheritance from the Olmec peoples of southern Mexico, while those of the extreme south and the Osa Peninsula had affinities with peoples in Panama and Colombia.

Clan society

Most of these groups existed in a state of almost constant **warfare**. However, unlike in the Mesoamerican states and in the Inca Empire, where victorious campaigns had led to the establishment of complex, far-reaching empires, in Costa Rica no one group gained ascendancy, and the political position of the clans seemed to remain more or less constant throughout the ages – like the forest-dwelling tribes in Amazonia to the south, these pre-Columbian peoples waged war not to increase their territory but to capture slaves, victims for potential sacrifice, marriage partners or simply for revenge.

c.4 million BC	c.10,000 BC	c.1000 BC
The collision of tectonic plates results in the creation of the Central American Isthmus	The first known peoples arrive in what we now know as Costa Rica	The Guayabo establish the town of the same name near modern-day Turrialba

The clans were, however, highly complex when it came to **religion**. Shamans were respected members of society, officiating at funerals, which were the most important rites of passage, especially in the Talamancan groups. Some clans had animal taboos that prevented them from hunting and killing certain beasts, and which neatly complemented each other – one group might not be able to hunt the tapir, for example, while the neighbouring clan would be prohibited from hunting the main prey of another group. This delicate balance played itself out on various levels, promoting harmony between man and nature. Like everywhere from southern Mexico to Brazil, the jaguar was much revered among all the groups, and only hunted to provide shamans with pelts, teeth and other ritualistic articles.

Gender divisions were, to an extent, along familiar lines: men made war and performed religious duties, while women were confined to domestic roles. However, women of the Boruca group in the southwest fought alongside men, and the Votos of the Zona Norte regularly had female chiefs. In many clans, the inheritance of names and objects was matrilineal.

People lived **communally** in stockaded villages, called **palenques** by the Spaniards. Whole groups, not necessarily related by kin, would live kibbutz-like in a village big-house. They organized work "gangs" who would tackle labour projects, usually agricultural. In most cases, land was held communally and harvests shared to ensure the survival of all. **Social hierarchy** was complex, with an ascending scale of *caciques* and shamans occupying the elite positions.

The Chorotegas in Guanacaste in particular developed a high level of **cultural expression**, possessing a written, symbol-based language, and harvesting and trading such diverse products as honey, natural dyes and cotton.

Costa Rica "discovered"

On September 18, 1502, on his fourth and last voyage to the Americas, **Christopher Columbus** sighted Costa Rica. Battered by a storm, he ordered his ships to drop anchor just off Isla Uvita, 1km offshore from present-day Puerto Limón. The group stayed seventeen days, making minor forays into the heavily forested coast and its few villages. The indigenous peoples Columbus met – as he could not fail to notice – were liberally attired in gold headbands, mirrored breastplates, bracelets and the like, convincing him of potential riches. In fact, the **gold** worn by those first welcoming envoys would have been traded or come to the peoples of the Caribbean coast through inter-tribal warfare. There was very little gold on this side of the country; rather, it came from the Valle de Diquis, in the southwest, the other side of the near-impenetrable hump of the Cordillera de Talamanca. With dreams of wealth, Columbus sailed on, charting the entire coastal region from Honduras to Panama, and naming it **Veragua**.

In 1506, King Ferdinand of Spain despatched **Diego de Nicuesa** to govern what would become Costa Rica. From the start, his mission was beset by hardship, beginning when their ship ran aground on the coast of Panama, forcing the party to walk up the Caribbean shore. There they met native people who, unlike those who had welcomed Columbus tentatively but politely with their shows of gold, burned their crops rather than submit to the authority of the Spanish. This, together with the

c.800 AD	1400	1502	1506
The Chorotegas arrive in Greater Nicoya (present-day Guanacaste)	Guayabo is mysteriously abandoned	Columbus "discovers" Costa Rica	Spain send their first governor to Costa Rica

GOLD, LAND AND SOULS

The first Spanish accounts of Costa Rican **indigenous peoples** were made in the sixteenth century by "**chroniclers**", the official scribes who accompanied mapping and evangelical expeditions. In general, these were either soldiers or missionaries who showed almost no talent for ethnography. Rather, they approached the pre-Columbian world as inventory-takers or suspicious accountants, writing terse and unimaginative reports liberally spiced with accounts of **gold** (although they found almost none). It was they who started the trend of portraying the cultures of the indigenous peoples of Costa Rica as "low" and underdeveloped; what they in fact meant was that there was little that could be expropriated for the Crown. Of the narratives that stand out is one by **Columbus** himself, who described the small welcoming party he received in 1502 in vivid and rather romanticized prose in his *lettera rarissima*, meant for the eyes of his sovereign.

Another, more important, account is by **Gonzalo Fernández de Oviedo**, whose comprehensive, nineteen-volume *Historia General de las Indias, Islas y Tierra Firme del Mar Oceano* was first published in 1535. Oviedo spent only ten or twelve days with the **Chorotega** peoples, but he had a fine eye for detail, and recorded many aspects of their diet, dress and social customs. He also noticed that they spoke a form of Nahua, the language of the Aztecs and the lingua franca of Mesoamerica, an observation that has since convinced most historians of a direct cultural link between the empires to the north and the peoples of pre-Columbian Costa Rica and Nicaragua.

One of the first things the Spanish chroniclers noticed was that the indigenous peoples in the **Talamancas** in the southeast and the **Greater Chiriquí** in the southwest practised **ritual sacrifice**. Every full moon, prisoners captured in the most recent raid would be ritually beheaded. The Spanish, of course, were repelled, and so began the systematic baptism campaigns, and the destruction of indigenous "idolatry".

impenetrable jungles, the creatures that lived in them and tropical diseases, meant that the expedition had to be abandoned.

Next came **Gil González Davila**, in 1521, who concentrated on Costa Rica's Pacific coast, which offered safer anchorage. González and his men covered practically the entire length of Pacific Costa Rica on foot, baptizing as they went: the expedition priest later claimed that some 32,000 souls had been "saved" in the name of the King of Spain. The indigenous peoples, meanwhile, began a campaign of **resistance** that was to last nearly thirty years, employing guerrilla tactics, infanticide, attacks on colonist settlements and burning their own villages. There were massacres, defeats and submissions on both sides, but by 1540 Costa Rica was officially a **Royal Province of Spain**, and a decade later, the Conquest was more or less complete. Most of the key areas of the country had been charted or settled, with the exception of the Talamanca region, which remained largely unexplored for centuries.

Indigenous people in the colonial period

During the first years of the Spanish invasion, those indigenous Costa Ricans who grouped themselves in large settlements, like the Chorotegas, proved more easily subjected, and were carted off by the Spanish to work in the mines, build the first Costa Rican towns or co-opted to general slavery in the guise of farm work. The more scattered groups fared better, in the main exiling themselves to the rugged Talamancas.

1524	1540	1563
Francisco de Córdoba founds Spain's first settlement, Villa Bruselas, on the Gulf of Nicoya	Costa Rica declared a Royal Province of Spain	Juan Vásquez de Coronado founds Cartago, the country's first capital

By then, however, the real conquerors of the New World had arrived: smallpox, influenza and measles. In the seventeenth and eighteenth centuries, huge pandemics swept the country, among them the so-called **Great Pandemic** of 1611–60, in which whole towns and villages disappeared virtually overnight. Although colonial censuses are notoriously inaccurate, in 1563 it is reckoned that an estimated 80,000 indigenous peoples lived in Costa Rica; by 1714, the official count was 999. Today, in a country of 4.7 million, less than two percent, or around 64,000, are indigenous (see box, p.420).

In 1560, **Juan de Cavallon** and **Juan Vásquez de Coronado** – the first true conquistadors of Costa Rica – succeeded in penetrating the Valle Central, the area that would become most significant in the development of the nation. As Cortés had done in Mexico, the Spaniards of Costa Rica took advantage of existing rivalries among the native groups and played them off against each other; in this way, they managed to dominate the groups of the Pacific coast with the help of tribes from the Valle Central.

The encomienda

In the early years of the colony, the Spaniards quickly established the **encomienda**, a system widespread in the Spanish Crown's Central American possessions that gave the conquistadors and their descendants the right to demand tribute or labour from the indigenous population. The *encomienda* applied to all indigenous males in Costa Rica between the ages of 18 and 50, and to a lesser extent to women, with quotas set for the donation of foods such as cacao fruit, corn, chicken, honey and chilli peppers.

Costa Rica's indigenous peoples resisted servitude to the colonials quite fiercely, and nor was there total acceptance of the way the native population was treated during this period. High-ranking clergymen protested to their Spanish overlords – as early as 1542, the **New Laws**, influenced by the passionate appeals of Fray Bartolomé de las Casas, decreed that colonizers had a duty to "protect" the indigenous peoples, and in 1711 the Bishop of Nicaragua, Fray Benito Garret y Arlovi, informed on the governor of Costa Rica for his brutal policies. These decrees assuaged the conscience of the Spanish Crown, but what happened on the ground in the colonies was, of course, quite a different matter.

The early settlers

It seems more appropriate to discuss the country's lack of colonial experience, rather than a bona fide colonization. In 1562, **Juan Vásquez de Coronado**, renowned for his favourable treatment of the indigenous peoples, became the second governor of Costa Rica. It was under his administration that the first settlement of any size or importance was established, and **Cartago**, in the heart of the Valle Central, was made capital of the colony. During the next century, settlers confined themselves more or less to the centre of the country. The Caribbean coast remained the haunt of buccaneers – mainly English – who put ashore and wintered here after plundering the lucrative Spanish Main; while the Pacific saw its share of pirate activity, too, most famously when Sir Francis Drake came ashore briefly in Bahía Drake in 1579.

This first epoch of the colony is remembered as one of unremitting **poverty**. Within a decade of its invasion Costa Rica was notorious throughout the Spanish Empire for its lack of gold. The settlers and their descendants, unlike those to the north and the south, who became wealthy on the gold of the Aztecs and Inca, never achieved their dreams of

1569	**1579**	**1611**	**1723**
The ruling Spanish establish the *encomienda* system	Sir Francis Drake lands at Bahía Drake on the Osa Peninsula	The start of the Great Pandemic, which lasts for nearly fifty years	Volcán Irazú erupts, virtually destroying Cartago in the process

instant aristocracy. Instead, they were confronted with almost insuperable obstacles, including tropical fever, hunger and belligerent natives. The Valle Central was fertile, but there was uncertainty as to what crops to grow. Coffee had not yet been imported to Costa Rica, nor had tobacco, so it was to subsistence agriculture that most settlers turned, growing just enough to live on. Spanish fabrics, manufactured goods and money itself became so scarce that by 1709 Valle Central settlers were forced to adopt cacao beans as currency; goat's hair and bark were used as clothing fabrics. In 1719, the governor of Costa Rica famously complained that he had to till his own land. With the emphasis on agriculture, and with little industry or trade, Costa Rica was unsurprisingly slow in founding urban settlements: in 1706, Cubujuquí (present-day Heredia) was established; in 1737, Villa Nueva de la Boca del Monte (later shortened, thankfully, to San José) was founded; and in 1782, it was the turn of Villa Hermosa (present-day Alajuela).

Beginnings of a national identity

The tough yeoman **settler farmers** who survived in these conditions are the most distinct figures in Costa Rica's early colonial history, and their independent, though impoverished, state is widely believed to be the root of the country's modern-day egalitarianism. Recent historical works, however, concede that while everybody in the early days of the colony may have been equally poor, social distinctions still counted, and where they did not exist, were manufactured: indeed, there is evidence to show that, had economic conditions permitted, a system of indentureship would have been imposed on the local *mestizo* (mixed-race) population, as happened in the highlands of Nicaragua, El Salvador and Guatemala.

Two other crucial factors went into the making of the modern nation: one was **coffee**, eventually to become Costa Rica's main export, a crop that requires many smallholders rather than large hacienda systems; the other was **ethnic** as, quite simply, the vast majority of peasants in Costa Rica were descendants of the Spanish colonists, rather than **indigenos** or **mestizos**, and as such were treated as equals by the ruling elite, who saw them as **hermaniticos**, or "little brothers".

Independence and prosperity

The nineteenth century was the most significant era in the development of Costa Rica. Initially, after 1821, when Central America declared **independence** from Spain, freedom made little difference to Costa Ricans. Although granted on September 15, 1823, the news did not reach Costa Rica until a month later, when a mule messenger arrived from Nicaragua to tell the astonished citizens of Cartago the good news. Rather than rejoicing in being freed from the Spanish – Spain had not paid much attention to the poor and isolated province anyway – a **civil war** promptly broke out among the inhabitants of the Valle Central, dividing the citizens of Alajuela and San José from those of Heredia and Cartago. The Alajuela–San José faction triumphed, and **San José** became the capital city in 1823.

Coffee kicks in

Costa Rica made remarkable progress in the latter half of the century, building roads, bridges and railways, and filling San José with neo-Baroque, European-style edifices. Virtually all this activity was fuelled by the **coffee trade**, bringing wealth that the settlers

1737	1775	1779
San José, then known as Villa Nueva de la Boca del Monte, is founded	Costa Rica's first conservation laws, an attempt to limit the impact of brush-burning, are passed	Coffee is introduced to Costa Rica

BANANA REPUBLIC: THE UNITED FRUIT COMPANY AND RACE RELATIONS

The history of **banana growing** in Costa Rica is inextricably linked to the creation of the railroads. The San José–Puerto Limón railway – the "Jungle Train" – was designed by American capitalist **Minor Keith** to establish an easy route for Valle Central coffee to reach the Caribbean coast; previously, the beans were transported via the Río Sarapiquí to Puntarenas then around Cape Horn. The railway took twenty years to build – its labour provided by an uneasy coalition of highlanders, imported Chinese "coolie" labour, Italians and Jamaicans fleeing economic difficulties in their home countries – and finally puffed its way out of the capital in 1890.

Minor had ingeniously planted bananas along the tracks in order to help pay for the route's construction, and as the fruit flourished and new markets opened up in Europe and the US, it became an exportable commodity: Costa Rica was the first Central American republic to grow bananas in bulk. In 1899, Keith and a colleague founded the **United Fruit Company**. The company, or **Yunai**, as it was called locally, came to transform the social, political and cultural face of Central America – and of all the countries in which it operated, it had the biggest dealings in Costa Rica. Opinions of Yunai oscillate between capitalist scourge and saviour of the nation. Almost from the beginning, the Company – from 1970 known as the **United Brands Company** and since 1990 **Chiquita** – gained a reputation for **antiunion practices**, deserting entire areas once the workforce showed any signs of being organized. While the banana companies have always generally offered high salaries, workers would often spend their income – for many years given in redeemable scrip instead of cash – on drink and dissipation. To a degree, this was a deliberate plan by the company to have their labour force continuously in hock and therefore pliable.

As long as the Company provided a steady flow of jobs, there was no real temptation for the **Jamaican population** (some 11,000 arrived in Costa Rica between 1874 and 1891) to leave the Caribbean coast, where they had effectively transported their own culture intact. In isolated Limón, they could retain their traditional food and religion and play West Indian games like cricket, preserving their culture in the face of a much larger highlands majority. They could also use their ability to speak English to their advantage – often Afro-Caribbeans attained high-ranking positions in the *bananeros* because they could communicate with the American foremen in their own language.

When the plantations began to close down in Limón in 1925 (as a result of the dreaded banana maladies Black Sigatoka and Panama disease), their fortunes began to change. The Company started to look for locations elsewhere in the country, acquiring land and planting bananas in the area around modern-day Quepos in the central Pacific, and Golfito in the

just a century earlier could hardly have dreamed of. Coffee beans were introduced to Costa Rica in 1779, though it was only when beans from Jamaica were first planted in the Valle Central in 1808 that the coffee story really begins. The plants thrived in the highlands climate, and by 1820 citizens of Cartago were being encouraged – ordered, even – to plant coffee in their backyards. But most significant in its early history was the arrival in 1844 of English merchant **William Le Lacheur**. His ship, the *Monarch*, had emptied her hold of its cargo, and Le Lacheur arrived in the Pacific port of Puntarenas looking for ballast to take back to Liverpool. He travelled to the Valle Central, where he secured a cargo of coffee beans, which he bought on credit, promising to return and pay in two years' time.

Until that point, most of Costa Rica's coffee had made its way to Chile, where it was mixed with a lower-grade South American bean, packaged for export under the brand

1782	1821	1823	1824
Alajuela (then called Villa Hermosa) is founded	Costa Rica gains independence from Spain	San José becomes the capital	Guanacaste secedes from Nicaragua, though residents in the north of the province vote against it

Zona Sur, and unbeknown to its Afro-Caribbean workers signed a contract with the government stipulating that **employment preference** be given to native Costa Ricans. It was not the first time the country's leaders had displayed such institutional racism. It is generally held that for the first half of the nineteenth century a law existed prohibiting the migration of Afro-Caribbeans to the Valle Central, while in 1933 the government had petitioned Congress to prohibit the entry of blacks into the country "because they are of a race inferior to ours" – and when the contract became public in September 1930, racial tensions rose to boiling point in Limón.

Afro-Caribbeans were trapped, unable to afford the passage home to Jamaica on the one hand and prohibited from working elsewhere in the country on the other, and in 1934 the most virulent **strike** yet seen in the Costa Rican *bananeros* began. It was organized by **Carlos Luis Fallas**, labour activist and novelist, who had been exiled to Limón as a result of his militancy on behalf of labour organizations in the Valle Central. Fallas proved a brilliant organizer, though initially the proposals he put forward to the Company were quite mild, requesting things like malaria drugs, snakebite serum and payment in cash rather than scrip. Nonetheless, the Company refused to recognize these proposals, and in August 1934 the strike began in earnest, tenaciously holding on in the face of physical harassment by the Company and police forces. For the next four years, strikes and worker opposition raged on, and in 1938 the Company pulled out of Limón Province for good, deserting it for the Pacific coast.

Left behind in the economic devastation and still unable to migrate within the country in search of work, the Afro-Caribbean population either took up cacao cultivation, hacked out their own smallholdings or took to fishing or other subsistence activities. Overnight, the schools, bunkhouses, US dollars, scrip economy, liquor and cigarettes disappeared, as did the US foremen and the ample plantation-style homes they had occupied. From about the start of the strike up until 1970, the region was virtually destitute, without much of a cash economy or any large-scale employers. It is only now beginning to recover in terms of banana production – under the aegis of the national banana-franchise operators **Dole** – and only at considerable cost to the environment, as more tropical forests are felled and more rivers polluted with pesticides.

You can get a flavour of the overwhelming presence of the Company in the banana towns of Limón's Valle Estrella and on the road from Jacó to Quepos, where you pass through a long corridor of African palm-oil plantations, its only major remaining investment in Costa Rica. The Company also left its mark on the collective consciousness of the region – Carlos Luis Fallas's **novels** *Mamita Yunai* (see p.435) and *Gentes y gentecillas*, García Márquez's *One Hundred Years of Solitude* and Guatemalan Asturias's masterly *El Papa Verde* all document its power in the everyday life of the *pueblitos* of Central America.

---

of **Café de Valparaíso** and sent to England, taking the long way around Cape Horn. With Le Lacheur's shipment, however, British taste buds were won round to the mellow, high-quality bean, and so began a trading partnership that saw the Costa Rican upper classes using Sheffield steel cutlery and Manchester linens for most of the eighteenth century.

The **coffee bourgeoisie** played a vital role in the cultural and political development of the country, and in 1848 the newly influential **cafetaleros** elected to the presidency their chosen candidate, Juan Rafael Mora. Extremely conservative and pro-trade, Mora came to distinguish himself in the battle against the American-backed filibuster William Walker in 1856, only to fall from grace and be executed in 1860 (see box, p.269).

1856	**1869**	**1890**
William Walker invades Costa Rica but is routed at La Casona	General Tomás Guardia Gutiérrez establishes free (and compulsory) primary education for all	The San José–Puerto Limón railway, or Jungle Train, opens, connecting the Valle Central with the Caribbean

The early twentieth century

The first years of the **twentieth century** witnessed a difficult transition towards democracy in Costa Rica. Universal male suffrage had come into effect during the last years of the nineteenth century, but class and power conflicts still dogged the country, with several **caudillo** (authoritarian) leaders, familiar figures in other Latin American countries, hijacking power. In general, however, these characters ended up in exile, and neither the army nor the church gained much of a foothold in politics. A number of radical labour initiatives were created during the 1920s, inspired by the Russian Revolution, though for much of the twentieth century Costa Rica's successive administrations, whatever their political colour, have proved no friend of labour relations, beginning in 1924 when most **strikes** were outlawed. In 1931, the Communist Party was formed, followed quickly by the National Republican Party in 1932. The latter dominated the political scene for most of the 1940s, with the election in 1940 of the Republican (PRN) candidate **Rafael Calderón Guardia**, a doctor educated in part in Belgium and a devout Catholic.

It was Calderón who instigated the social reforms and state support for which Costa Rica is still almost unique in the region. In 1941, he established a new **Labour Code** that reinstated the right of workers to organize and strike, and a social security system providing free schooling for all. Calderón also paved the way for the establishment of the University of Costa Rica, health insurance, income security and assistance schemes, and thus won the support of the impoverished and the lower classes – and the suspicion of the governing elites. One of those less than convinced by his policies was the man who would come to be known as **"Don Pepe"**, the coffee farmer **José Figueres Ferrer**, who denounced Calderón and his expensive reforms in a radio broadcast in 1941 and was then abruptly forced into exile in Mexico, from where he plotted his return.

The "revolution" of 1948 and after

The **elections of 1948** heralded the most eventful year of the twentieth century for Costa Rica. Constitutionally, Costa Rican presidents could not serve consecutive terms, so the election battle that year was between **Teodorico Picado**, widely considered to be a Calderón puppet, and **Otilio Ulate Blanco**, an ally of Figueres, who during two years in exile had become a heroic figure in some circles, returning to Costa Rica to play a key part in the **Acción Democrática**, a loose group of anti-Calderonistas. Ulate won the presidency, but the PRN won the majority in Congress – a fact that effectively annulled the election results.

Figueres, back on the scene and intent upon overthrowing Picado, who had stepped in and declared himself president in the face of the annulment, soon formed an opposition party, ideologically opposed to the PRN. In March, **fighting** around Cartago began, culminating in an attack by the Figueres rebels on San José. To a degree, the battles were fought to safeguard the system of democratic election in the face of corruption, and in order to stem the clannishness and personality cults that had dogged all Costa Rican political parties and presidential campaigns up until then.

Don Pepe takes control

While Figueres's rebel forces were well equipped with arms, some supplied through CIA contacts, the militia defending President Picado was not: the national army consisted of only about three hundred men at the time, and had to be supplemented

1895	1897	1899
Forest rangers, the forerunners of *guardaparques*, are established	Edward Porter Alexander officially defines the border between Costa Rica and Nicaragua, though the exact demarcation remains a bone of contention today	Minor Keith founds the United Fruit Company (now known as Chiquita)

by machete-wielding banana workers. Two thousand were dead by mid-April, when hostilities ceased. In May, the **Junta of the Second Republic** was formed, with Figueres as acting president, despite an after-the-fact attack from Nicaraguan Picado supporters in December.

Figueres wanted above all to engineer a complete break with the country's past, and especially the policies and legacies of the Calderonistas. Seeing himself as fighting both communism and corruption, he not only outlawed the PVP, the Popular Vanguard Party – formerly known as the Communist Party – but also nationalized the banks and devised a tax to hit the rich particularly hard, thus alienating the establishment. The new **constitution** drawn up in 1949 gave full citizenship to Afro-Caribbeans, full suffrage to women and codified the abolition of Costa Rica's army the previous year. In a way, the **abolition of the army** fitted with political precedents in Costa Rica. Nearly thirty years before, in 1922, former president Ricardo Jiménez Oreamuno had given a famous speech in which he said: "The school shall kill militarism, or militarism shall kill the Republic… We are a country with more teachers than soldiers… and a country that turns military headquarters into schools". Although the warming sentiment behind Jiménez's words is oft-repeated in Costa Rica, the truth is somewhat darker. Figueres's motives were not utopian but rather a pragmatic bid to limit the political instability that had been the scourge of so many Latin American countries, and an attempt to save valuable resources. Today, while the country still has no army, the police forces are powerful, highly specialized and, in some cases, heavily armed. Paramilitary organizations do exist, chief among them the Free Costa Rica Movement (MCRL); formed in 1961 and active until the mid-1980s, the MCRL was allegedly involved in a number of deeds more reminiscent of the Guatemalan army's death squads than the spirit of a harmonious and army-free Costa Rica.

In 1951, Figueres formed the **National Liberation Party**, or **PLN**, in order to be legitimately elected. He was a genius in drawing together disparate strands of society: when the elections came around the following year, he got the agricultural smallholder vote, while winning the support of the urban working classes with his retention of the welfare state. At the same time, he appeased the right-of-centrists with his essentially free-marketeering and staunch anti-communist stance.

The 1960s and 1970s

The **1960s and 1970s** were a period of prosperity and stability in Costa Rica, when the welfare state was developed to reach nearly all sectors of society. In 1977, the **Indigenous Bill** established the right of aboriginal peoples to their own land reserves – a progressive measure at the time, although indigenous peoples today are not convinced the system has served them well (see box, p.420). At the end of the 1970s, regional conflicts deflected attention from the domestic agenda, with the Carazo (1978–82) administration announcing its support for the FSLN revolutionary movement in Nicaragua, who, in dispatching President Anastasio Samoza into exile, had finally managed to end the family's forty-year dictatorship.

Storm in the isthmus: the 1980s

Against all odds, Costa Rica in the 1980s not only saw its way through the serious political conflicts of its neighbours, but also successfully managed predatory US

1910	1938	1940
An earthquake near Cartago kills 1750 people	The United Fruit Company cease operations in Limón, plunging the province into economic decline	Rafael Calderón Guardia, the founder of Costa Rica's regionally enlightened social policies, is elected president

interventionism, economic crisis and staggering debt. Like many Latin American countries, Costa Rica had taken out bank and government **loans** in the 1960s and 1970s to finance vital development. But in the early 1980s, the slump in international coffee and banana prices put the country's finances into the red. In September 1981, Costa Rica defaulted on its interest payments, becoming the first developing country to do so and sparking off a chain of similar defaults in Latin America that threw the international banking community into crisis. Despite its defaults, Costa Rica's debt continued to accumulate and by 1989 had reached a staggering US$5 billion, one of the highest per-capita debt loads in the world at the time.

Involvement in Nicaragua

To compound the economic crisis came the simultaneous escalation of the **Nicaraguan Civil War**. During the entire decade, Costa Rica's foreign policy – and to an extent its domestic agenda – would be overshadowed by tensions with Nicaragua and the US. Initially, the Monge PLN administration (1982–86) more or less capitulated to US demands that Costa Rica be used as a supply line for the Contra rebels, and Costa Rica also accepted military training for its police force from the US. At the same time, the country's first agreement for a structural adjustment loan with the IMF was signed. It seemed increasingly clear that Costa Rica was on the path to both violating its declared neutrality in the conflicts of its neighbours and condemning its population to wage freezes, price increases and other side-effects associated with the IMF restructuring.

In May 1984, the situation escalated with the events at the **La Penca** press conference, held by the US-backed Contra leader Edén Pastora in a simple hut on the banks of the Río San Juan. A bomb was apparently carried into the hut by a "Danish" cameraman, concealed within an equipment case, and was intended to kill all. Miraculously, an aide of Pastora's accidentally kicked the case over, so that when it was detonated the force of the blast went up and down instead of sideways, thus saving the lives of most of those within, including Pastora himself. Although nobody is quite sure who was behind the bombing – both the CIA and freelance Argentinian terrorists have been implicated – it seems that the point of the carnage was to implicate Nicaragua, thus cutting off international support and destabilizing the Sandinista government further. The immediate effect was to shock the Costa Rican government and the international community into paying more attention to the deadly conflicts of Nicaragua and, by association, El Salvador and Guatemala.

The Arias peace plan

In 1986, PLN candidate **Oscar Arias Sánchez** was elected to the presidency, and Costa Rica's relations with the US and Nicaragua took a different tack. The former political scientist began to play the role of peace broker in the conflicts of Nicaragua, El Salvador and, to a lesser extent, Honduras and Guatemala, mediating between these countries and also between domestic factions within them. In October 1987, just eighteen months after taking office, Arias was awarded the Nobel Prize for Peace, attracting worldwide attention.

Arias's **peace plan** focused on regional objectives, tying individual and domestic conflicts into the larger picture: the stability of the isthmus. It officially called for a ceasefire, the discontinuation of military aid to the Contra insurrectionists, amnesties for

1940	1948	1963
Marmita Yunai, Carlos Luis Fallas' novel about the banana plantations of Limón Province, is published	Following a six-week civil war, CIA-backed José Figueres Ferrer assumes the presidency from Teodorico Picado, and famously disbands the country's army	Thanks largely to the efforts of Karen Mogensen and Olof Wessberg, Reserva Absoluta Cabo Blanco becomes Costa Rica's first officially protected area

political prisoners and for guerrillas who voluntarily relinquished the fight, and, lastly and perhaps most importantly, intergovernmental negotiations leading to free and fair elections. The peace plan began, rather than ended, with the awarding of the Nobel Prize, dragging on throughout 1987 and 1988 and running into obstacles as, almost immediately, all nations involved charged one another with noncompliance or other violations. The situation deteriorated when the US stationed troops in southern Honduras, ready to attack Nicaragua. Meanwhile, Washington continued to undermine Costa Rica's declared neutrality, requesting in April 1988 that Arias approve Costa Rican territory as a corridor for "humanitarian aid" to the Contras. The same month, Arias met with US President George Bush in Washington, his diplomatic credibility enabling him to secure millions of dollars' worth of American aid for Costa Rica without compromising the country politically. For its part, the last thing the US wanted was internal unrest in Costa Rica, its natural (if not entirely compliant) ally in the region.

However, while Arias had stalled on the US using Costa Rica's northern border as a base from which to attack Nicaragua, he seemed to have fewer quibbles about what was happening in the south, in **Panama**. In July 1989, CIA-supported anti-Noriega guerrilla forces (many of them ex-Contras) amassed along the Costa Rica–Panama border in preparation for the US invasion of Panama that would take place in December.

Though Arias had gained the admiration of statesmen around the world, he proved to be less than popular at home. Many Costa Ricans saw him as neglecting domestic affairs, while increasing prices caused by the IMF's economic demands meant that by the end of the decade conditions within the country had not improved much.

The 1990s

In 1990, the mantle of power fell to **Rafael Ángel Calderón Fournier** (son of Calderón Guardia), who, in the 1980s, had been instrumental in consolidating the opposition that became the free-marketeering Partido Unidad Social Cristiana, or PUSC. A year later, Costa Rica was rocked by its most powerful **earthquake** since the one that laid waste to most of Cartago in 1910. Centred in Limón Province, the quake killed 62 people and caused extensive structural damage. At the same time, nationals of El Salvador, Honduras, Guatemala and especially Nicaragua were looking to Costa Rica – the only stable country in the region – for asylum, and tension rose as the **refugees** poured in. In 1992, Costa Rica faced more trouble as it was brought to law in US courts for its failure to abide by international **labour laws**, a continuing black mark on the country's copybook for most of the twentieth century.

Until 1994, elections in Costa Rica had been relatively genteel affairs, involving lots of flag-waving and displays of national pride in democratic traditions. The elections of that year, however, were probably the dirtiest to date. The PLN candidate – the choice of the left, for his promises to maintain the role of the state in the economy – was none other than **José María Figueres**, the son of Don Pepe, who had died four years previously. During the campaign, Figueres was accused of shady investment rackets and influence peddling. His free-market PUSC opposition candidate, Dr Miguel Ángel Rodríguez, fared no better, having admitted to being involved in a tainted-beef scandal in the 1980s. Figueres won, narrowly, though his term in office was plagued by a series of scandals. On a more positive note, in January 1995 a Free Trade agreement was

1968	1975	1977	1981
Volcán Arenal erupts, killing 78 people	Olof Wessberg is murdered on the Osa Peninsula	A network of 24 indigenous reserves is created	Costa Rica kick-starts a banking crisis by defaulting on its interest payments

INDIGENOUS PEOPLES IN MODERN COSTA RICA

You won't see much evidence of **native traditions** in Costa Rica today. Less than two percent of the country's population is of aboriginal extraction, and the dispersion of the various groups ensures that they frequently do not share the same concerns and agendas. Contact between them, apart from through bodies such as CONAI – the national indigenous affairs organization – is minimal.

Although a system of **indigenous reserves** was set up by the Costa Rican administration in 1977, giving aboriginal peoples the right to remain in self-governing communities, titles to the reserve lands were withheld, so that while the communities may live on the land, they do not actually own it. This has led to government contracts being handed out to, for example, mining operations in the Talamanca area, leading to infringements on the communities themselves, which are further hampered by the presence of missionaries in settlements like Amubrí and San José Cabécar. The 24 "Indian reserves" scattered around the country are viewed by their inhabitants with some ambivalence. As in North America, establishing a reservation system has led in many cases to a banishing of indigenous peoples to poor-quality land where enclaves of poverty soon develop.

In the last few decades, there has been a growing recognition of the importance of **preserving indigenous culture** and of providing reserves with increased services and self-sufficiency. In 1994, the first **indigenous bank** was set up in Suretka, Talamanca, by the Bribrí and Cabécar groups, to counter the fact that major banks have often refused indigenous business and initiatives credit; in the same year, indigenous people earned the **right to vote** in the country's elections for the first time. Political participation has been slow in coming, however, and basic rights such as control over their own land and its natural resources, and access to healthcare and an education that reflects their view of the world, are still wilfully disregarded. In 2008, the government amended the Biodiversity Law without consulting the communities whose land it affected; while Laura Chinchilla's **National Development Plan 2011–2014** was seen as another missed opportunity, failing to recognize indigenous rights when at one point it was hoped the plan might even include a long-mooted law granting autonomy to indigenous communities.

signed with Mexico in order to try to redress the lack of preference given to Costa Rican goods in the US market by the signing of the North American Free Trade Agreement (NAFTA), while Costa Rica's economy received a further shot in the arm in 1996 when the communications giant INTEL chose the country for the site of their new factory in Latin America, creating thousands of jobs.

In February 1998, PUSC candidate **Dr Miguel Ángel Rodríguez** was elected president, thus continuing the trend in Costa Rican politics for the past half-century, wherein power has been traded more or less evenly between the PLN and the PUSC. The new government committed itself to solving Costa Rica's most pressing problems, making improvements to the country's dreadful road system the top priority, but financing this and other major public works by private (usually foreign) investment, a strategy that is still the order of the day.

The new millennium

Rodríguez was succeeded in April 2002 by Abel Pacheco de Espriella, a psychiatrist also from the PUSC; it was the first time the party had been re-elected. One of the key

1985	1987	1991	2003
Oliver North orders the building of a secret airstrip in northern Costa Rica, in order to aid the CIA-backed Contras in Nicaragua	Oscar Arias receives the Nobel Peace Prize	An earthquake devastates much of Limón Province	Taiwan funds the Friendship Bridge, which connects the Costa Rican mainland to the Nicoya Peninsula

issues Pacheco faced was **CAFTA**, the Central American Free Trade Agreement, a proposed agreement with the US that Costa Ricans feared would erode the country's advanced social system. Pacheco added Costa Rica's name to those of all the other Central American nations, but fierce debate within the country would continue to stall its ratification. Meanwhile, in 2004, Costa Rica's squeaky-clean regional image was shattered by a series of **corruption** charges aimed at three of the country's former presidents: Rafael Ángel Calderón Fournier, José María Figueres and Miguel Ángel Rodríguez, all of whom were accused of accepting illegal financial kickbacks from foreign sources.

Promising to clamp down on government corruption, **Oscar Arias Sánchez** was elected president for the second time in February 2006, only narrowly beating rival Ottón Solís of the Partido Acción Ciudadana or Citizens' Action Party (PAC), founded just six years previously. The main issue dividing the candidates was CAFTA (Arias was strongly for it); post-election, the trade agreement continued to split the country, sparking fiery nationwide protests and leading to a first national referendum in October 2007. The "*Sí*" vote eventually scraped through with just over 51 percent, though continued opposition to the agreement meant that Arias spent the majority of his second term in office trying to push the deal through. Costa Rica finally **officially entered CAFTA** in January 2009 – the same month that the most powerful **earthquake** in more than 150 years struck the Valle Central (see box, p.138) – though wrangling over the wording of individual bills meant that it wasn't until May 2010 that the final piece of legislation, a controversial copyright law, was approved.

Laura Chinchilla and the drugs cartels

Despite the divisive force of CAFTA, it was the PLN candidate, **Laura Chinchilla**, who triumphed in the February 2010 election, and in doing so became Costa Rica's **first female president**. A former vice president, Chinchilla had pledged to continue the free-market policies of her predecessor, claiming 47 percent of the vote ahead of regular rival Ottón Solís. More important, perhaps, were her promises to tackle **violent crime**, an escalating problem in a country better known for its peaceful disposition. This alarming rise has been linked with the growing presence of **drug trafficking**, as Columbian and Mexican cartels increasingly use the country as a convenient pick-up point – the situation had grown so bad, so quickly, that in 2010 the US added Costa Rica to its "Top Twenty" list of major drug-trafficking countries. The fight against the cartels is a regional issue, and Chinchilla was quick to show her commitment to the Central American Integration System (or **SICA**) by touring Guatemala, El Salvador, Honduras and Nicaragua shortly after her victory, while the major impetus behind her visit to Mexico the following year was to improve cooperation against organized crime. Chinchilla's commitment to tackling the drug-supply route in Costa Rica was a hallmark of her presidency, so it was with bitter irony that less than a month after lobbying President Obama for Washington's help during his trip to Costa Rica in May 2013, she found herself embroiled in a drugs-related scandal. The fallout from her use of a jet with alleged links to drugs trafficking resulted in the resignation, among others, of Mauricio Boraschi, the head of Costa Rica's intelligence and security department and, ironically, the country's first anti-drugs commissioner.

2009	2009	2010	2010
Costa Rica enters CAFTA	The Cinchona earthquake ravages the Poás region	Laura Chinchilla becomes the country's first female president	Mauricio Boraschi named as the country's first anti-drugs commissioner, in an effort to tackle its growing drug-trafficking problem

INVASION BY INTERNET

On October 18, 2010, a group of Nicaraguan soldiers set up base on **Isla Calero**, an island on the south side of the Río San Juan, as part of an ongoing operation to dredge the river. With the centre of the San Juan serving as the historical border between Costa Rica and Nicaragua, the soldiers were technically occupying Costa Rican territory, but their commander had a simple, one-word justification for their apparent incursion: Google.

On their global mapping project, **Google Maps**, the internet giant had bestowed the island (some 1.7km of land at the river's eastern end) to Nicaragua – wrongly, according to Costa Rica, who believe that the border should follow the demarcation laid out in the **1897 Alexander Award**, but rightly according to Nicaragua, who feel that the **1858 Cañas–Jereüz Treaty**, which states that Isla Calero is in their territory, still holds true.

The "occupation" of Isla Calero is just the latest footnote in a dispute over the Río San Juan that stretches back over two hundred years, the arguments growing ever more intense as the river's delta dries out and the border shifts further northwards. This latest round of mud-slinging, however, involved the **Organization of American States** (**OAS**) and the **International Court of Justice** (**ICJ**), and it wasn't until December 2013, when the ICJ ordered Nicaragua to withdraw entirely from the area, never to return, that the matter was finally settled – officially, at least.

The 2014 elections and beyond

So far, CAFTA has been a success, enabling the privatization of the state-run insurance and telecoms industries and greatly increasing trade with the US – by the end of 2013, Costa Rica counted for forty percent of CAFTA exports to the States. Chinchilla's term in office was somewhat less of a triumph, though, and following a series of scandals and failed infrastructure projects, her administration bowed out with the lowest approval rating in two decades.

Perhaps understandably, fighting corruption was a key theme during the run-up to the 2014 elections, and a strong stance on this – along with the promise to address the country's growing social inequality, the worst in Latin America – helped PAC's **Luis Guillermo Solís** to a surprise run-off victory over PLN candidate Johnny Araya. As Solís begins his four years in office, the problems he faces are familiar ones. The influence of the drugs cartels grows ever larger, and will continue to do so as long as the country's security forces and Coast Guard remain undersized and underfunded, while the recent protracted border dispute with their northern neighbours (see box above) will influence that relationship for years to come. Public debt tops an uncomfortable fifty percent of GDP, yet Costa Rica's economy was predicted to grow by 4.5 percent in 2014, bolstered by the continued recent growth in **tourism**. While the country has bounced back well from the global recession, receiving a record number of visitors in 2013, the downturn was a timely reminder that summer visitors are notoriously fickle, and today's fashionable gated resort hotel can easily become tomorrow's five-star white elephant.

2012	2013	2013	2014
Costa Rica becomes the first Latin American country to ban hunting	5000 new species are added to the country's biodiversity list	Costa Rica receives a record 2.4 million annual visitors	Johnny Araya becomes first candidate to drop out of presidential run-off race

Landscape and habitat

Although smaller than West Virginia, Costa Rica has nearly as many habitats as the whole of the US, including forests, riverside mangroves, seasonal wetlands and coral reefs. Within this relatively small area, there is a remarkably varied terrain, ranging from the plains of Guanacaste, where there is often no rain for half the year, to the Caribbean lowlands, thick-forested and deluged with a liberal 6000mm of precipitation annually. In terms of elevation, too, the country possesses great diversity: from the very hot and humid lowlands of Corcovado, the terrain rises within just 150km to the chilly heights of Cerro Chirripó, at 3819m the country's highest point.

Because Costa Rica's territory is almost bewilderingly varied, with similar geographical features found in many different places, it is often considered in terms of **life zones**, a detailed system of categorization developed in 1947 by biologist L.R. Holdridge to describe particular characteristics of terrain, climate and the life they support. Although he conceived the system in Haiti, with temperature and rainfall being the main determinants, this system has been used to create ecological maps of various countries, including Costa Rica.

Tropical dry forest
The most endangered of all the life zones in Costa Rica is the **tropical dry forest** (see box, p.254), which needs about six dry months a year. Most trees here are deciduous or semi-deciduous; some lose their leaves near the end of the dry season, primarily to conserve water. They are less stratified than rainforests, with two layers rather than three or four, and appear far less dense. Orchids flower in the silver and brown branches, and bees, wasps and moths proliferate. Animal inhabitants include iguanas, white-tailed deer and some of the larger mammals, including the jaguar. The best examples are in the northwest, especially **Guanacaste and Santa Rosa national parks**.

Tropical wet forest
The **tropical wet forest** is home, metre per metre, to the greatest number of species of flora and fauna, including the bushmaster snake and tapir, along with the jaguar and other wild cats. Here, the canopy trees can be very tall (up to 80m) and, true to its name, it receives an enormous amount of rain – typically around 6000mm per year. Found in lowland areas, tropical wet forest is now confined to large protected blocks, chiefly the **Sarapiquí–Tortuguero** area and the large chunk preserved as **Parque Nacional Corcovado** on the Osa Peninsula.

ANATOMY OF A RAINFOREST
Rainforests can feature **primary forest**, which has not been disturbed for several hundreds, or even thousands, of years, and what's known as **secondary growth**, which is the vegetation that springs up in the wake of some disturbance, such as cutting, cultivation or habitation. A tropical rainforest is characterized by the presence of several **layers**, each interconnected by a mesh of horizontal lianas and climbers. At its most complex, it will be made up of four layers: the **canopy**, about 40 to 80m high, at the very top of which are emergent trees, often flat-topped; the **subcanopy**, beneath the emergent trees; the **understorey** trees, typically 10 to 20m in height; and finally the **shrub**, or ground layer.

Premontane wet forest

Premontane wet forests are found upon many of Costa Rica's mountains. Some trees are evergreen and most are covered with a thick carpet of moss. These forests typically exist at a high altitude and receive a lot of rain: the cover in **Parque Nacional Tapantí-Macizo Cerro de la Muerte** in the southeast Valle Central is a good example, as is **Parque Nacional Braulio Carrillo**, which has all five of the montane life zones within its boundaries. Many of the same animals that exist in the tropical wet forest live here, along with brocket deer and peccaries.

Cloudforest

Perhaps the most famous of Costa Rica's life zones are the tropical lower montane wet forests, or **cloudforests**, which occur in very isolated patches, mainly south of Cartago and on the Pacific slopes of the Cordillera de Tilarán (most famously at **Monteverde**). They're produced when the northwesterly trade winds from the Caribbean drift across to the high ridge of the Continental Divide, where they cool to become dense clouds that create a perennial near-one-hundred-percent humidity. The primeval-looking cloudforest hosts many bromeliads, including orchids, and has an understorey thick with vines, ferns and drooping lianas; its animal life includes tapirs, pumas and quetzals.

Tropical montane rainforest

Tropical montane rainforest occurs at the highest altitudes; the tops of **Poás** and **Irazú** volcanoes are good examples. Although large mosses and ferns can be seen, much of the vegetation has a shrunken, or dwarfed aspect, due to the biting wind and lofty altitude. Animals that live here include the Poás squirrel (endemic to that volcano) and some of the larger birds, such as raptors and vultures.

Tropical subalpine rain paramo

In and around the country's highest elevation, near **Cerro Chirripó**, is the only place you'll find **tropical subalpine rain paramo**, an inhospitably cold environment, with almost no trees. Costa Rica is the northern frontier of this particular Andean type of paramo. Except for hardy hawks and vultures, birds tend to shun this cold milieu, although at lower elevations you may spot quetzals.

Mangroves

The **mangrove** is an increasingly fragile and endangered ecosystem that occurs along tropical coastlines and is particularly vulnerable to dredging: among others, the *Hotel de Playa Tambor* in the central Pacific (see box, p.330) has been accused of irresponsibly draining mangroves. With their extensive root system, mangrove trees are unique for their ability to adapt to the salinity of seaside or tidal waters, or to areas where freshwater rivers empty into the ocean. Because they absorb the thrust of waves and tides, they act as a buffer zone behind which species of aquatic and land-based life can flourish unmolested. Meanwhile, the beer-coloured mangrove swamp water is like a nutritious primordial soup where a range of species can grow, including crustaceans, shrimp and fish as well as the turtles, caimans and crocodiles that feed on them, and their banks are home to a variety of bird life.

Wetlands

Birds and reptiles are especially abundant in the country's remaining **wetlands**, which are typically seasonal, caused by the flooding of rivers with the rains, only to shrink back to pleated mudflats in the dry season. The lagoons of the **Caño Negro** and **Mixto Maquenque** wildlife reserves in the Zona Norte, and the Río Tempisque, within the boundary of **Parque Nacional Palo Verde** in Guanacaste, are the prime wetlands in Costa Rica.

Rivers

Despite increasing silting and pollution caused largely by banana plantations, Costa Rica's **rivers** support a variety of life, from fish (including snook and tarpon) to migratory birds, crocodiles, caimans and freshwater turtles. The waterways that yield the best wildlife-watching are the **Tortuguero canals** and the ríos San Juan, Frío and Sierpe, as well as the **Río Tárcoles** in Parque Nacional Carara on the central Pacific coast.

Coral reefs

Costa Rica's **coral reefs**, never as extensive as those in Belize, are under threat. Much of the **Caribbean coast** was seriously damaged by the 1991 earthquake, which heaved the reefs up above the water. The last remaining ones on this side of the country are at **Cahuita** and a smaller one further south at **Manzanillo** in the Refugio de Vida Silvestre Gandoca-Manzanillo. Though the Cahuita reef has been under siege for some time from silting caused by the clearing of land for banana plantations, and from the pesticides used in banana cultivation, you can still see some fine (extremely localized) specimens of moose horn and staghorn coral. On the **Pacific coast**, the most pristine reef is at **Bahía Ballena**, protected within Costa Rica's first marine national park, and also the reef that fringes Isla del Caño, about 20km offshore from the northwest coast of the Osa Peninsula. Lying 535km southwest of Costa Rica's Pacific coast, **Parque Nacional Isla del Coco** remains the country's marine treasure, a coveted destination for experienced divers whose surrounding waters are home to more than thirty species of coral.

Conservation and tourism

Costa Rica is widely seen as being at the cutting edge of worldwide conservation strategy, an impressive feat for a tiny Central American nation. At the centre of the country's internationally applauded efforts is a complex system of national parks, wildlife refuges and biological reserves, which protect more than 25 percent of its territory, one of the largest percentages of protected land among western-hemisphere nations. These statistics are used with great effect to attract tourists and, along with Belize, Costa Rica has become virtually synonymous with ecotourism in Central America.

On the other hand, the National Parks Service does not possess the funds to protect adequately more than half the boundaries of these areas, which are under constant pressure from logging and agricultural encroachment, and to a lesser extent from mining interests. In addition, the question uppermost in the minds of conservationists and biologists is what, if any, damage is being caused by so many feet walking through the rainforests.

Conservation in the New World tropics

The **traditional view** of conservation is a European one of preserving, museum-like, pretty animals and flowers; an idea that was conceived and upheld by relatively wealthy Old World countries in which the majority of the forests have long-since disappeared. In the contemporary world, this definition of conservation no longer works, and certainly not in the New World tropics, besieged as they are by a lack of resources, huge income inequities, legislation that lacks bite and the continual appetite of the world market for tropical hardwoods, not to mention the Old World zeal for coffee and picture-perfect supermarket fruits.

There's a leftist perspective on conservation that sees an imperialistic, bourgeois and anti-*campesino* agenda among the large conservation organizations of the North. By this reckoning, saving the environment is all very well but does little for the day-to-day realities, say, of the twenty percent or so of Costa Rica's population who live below the poverty line. These people have, in many cases, been made landless and impoverished by, for instance, absentee landowners speculating on land (in the Zona Norte and in Guanacaste) or by the pulling-out of major employers like Chiquita (first in Limón Province and then in the Zona Sur near Golfito and on the Osa Peninsula). Many are left with simply no choice but to engage in the kind of activity – be it gold-panning, slash-and-burn agriculture or monobiotic fruit production – that is universally condemned by conservationists in the North.

Conservation in Costa Rica

Costa Rica has a long history of conservation-consciousness, although it has taken different forms and guises. As early as 1775, laws were passed to limit the destructive impact of *quemas*, or brush-burning, though the bulk of **preservation laws** were passed after 1845, concurrent with Costa Rica's period of greatest economic and cultural growth. That said, most of this legislation was directed at protecting resource extraction rather than the areas themselves – to guard fishing and hunting grounds and to conserve what were already seen as valuable timber supplies. In 1895, laws were passed protecting water supplies and establishing

THE CASE OF TORTUGUERO

National parks are now such an entrenched part of Costa Rica's landscape that they might be taken to have always been there. In fact, most have been established in the last forty years, and the process of creating them has not always been a smooth one…

Turtle Bogue (the old Miskito name for Tortuguero) has always been isolated. Even today, access is by boat or air only, and before the dredging of the main canal in the 1960s it was even more cut off from the rest of the country. Most of the local people were of Miskito or Afro-Caribbean extraction, hunting and fishing, and living almost completely without consumer goods. There was virtually no cash economy in the village, with local trade and barter being sufficient for most people's needs.

In the 1940s, **lumbering** began in earnest in the area. A sawmill was built in the village, and during the next two decades the area experienced a boom. The local lumber exhausted itself by the 1960s, but in the twenty-year interim it brought outsiders and a dependence on cash-obtainable consumer goods. Simultaneously, the number of **green turtles** began to decline rapidly, due to overfishing and egg harvesting, and by the 1950s the once-numerous turtle was officially endangered. The alarm raised by biologists over their precipitous decline paved the way for the establishment, in 1970, of **Parque Nacional Tortuguero**, protecting 30 of the area's 35km of turtle-nesting beach and extending to more than two hundred square kilometres of surrounding forests, canals and waterways. The establishment of this protective area put former sources of income off-limits to local populations, and villagers who had benefited from the wood-and-turtle economy either reverted to the subsistence and agricultural life they had known before or left the area in search of a better one. Nowadays, however, many locals make a good living off the increasing amount of tourism the park brings, especially those with their own independent businesses.

The establishment of Parque Nacional Tortuguero effectively broke the **boom-and-bust cycle** so prevalent in the tropics, whereby local resources are used to extinction, leaving no viable alternatives after the storm has passed. In Tortuguero, the hardwoods have made a bit of a comeback, and the green turtle's numbers are up dramatically from its low point of the 1950s and 1960s. Considering the popularity of the national park, there's no doubt that conservation and protection of Tortuguero's wetlands can have lasting benefits for local folk, as well as local flora and fauna.

guardabosques (forest rangers) to fight the *quemas* caused by the regular burning of deforested land and pasture by cattle-ranchers, while the forerunners of several institutions later to be important to the development of conservation in Costa Rica were founded by the end of the nineteenth century, including the Museo Nacional and the Instituto Físico Geográfico.

Much of the credit for helping establish Costa Rica's system of national parks in the second half of the twentieth century has to go to **Olof Wessberg** and **Karen Mogensen**, long-time foreign residents who in 1963, largely through their own efforts, founded the Reserva Natural Absoluta Cabo Blanco near their home on the southwest tip of the Nicoya Peninsula. The couple helped raise national consciousness through an extensive campaign in the mid-1960s, so that by the end of the decade there was broad support for the founding of a national parks service. In 1969, the Parque y Monumento Nacional Santa Rosa was declared, and in 1970 the **Servicio de Parques Nacionales** (**SPN**) was officially inaugurated. Spearheaded by a recently graduated forester, Mario Boza, the system developed slowly at first, as the law that established Santa Rosa really existed only on paper: neighbouring farmers and ranchers continued to encroach on the land for pasture and brush-burning as before.

Although it remains a mystery, the **murder of Olof Wessberg** in 1975 on the Osa Peninsula is an illustration of the powerful interests that are thwarted by conservation. Wessberg was conducting a preliminary survey in Osa to assess the possibility of a national park there (the site of modern-day Parque Nacional Corcovado). Although his assailant – the man who had offered to guide him – was caught, a motive was never discovered and the crime has not been satisfactorily solved.

MINAE, SINAC and Red

Nonetheless, despite the pressures of vested interests, the Costa Rican conservation programme moved forward in the early 1980s with the founding of **MINAE** (Ministerio del Ambiente y Energía), the government body entrusted with the overall control of the country's ecological resources. In 1988, the Arias government drafted a national conservation strategy, and, soon after his election victory in 1994, president José María Figueres started the drive to bring together all the various conservation efforts taking place throughout the country under direct government control. In 1995, the national parks, wildlife and forestry services were merged into **SINAC** (Sistema Nacional de Areas de Conservacion), a single agency within MINAE that had direct responsibility for the country's 29 national parks, 11 conservation areas and 167 other government-protected lands. For decades, much of the most important conservation work had been undertaken by privately (often foreign) funded initiatives, and so, in 1996, the **Red Costarricense de Reservas Naturales** was also founded, bringing the country's disparate patchwork of privately owned reserves and refuges (of which there are more than one hundred) under the control of a single administrative body subject to the same rules and regulations as state-owned parks. Privately funded conservation programmes are still vital, though, as they help to remove some of the financial burden from the beleaguered state coffers, which struggle to raise the revenue necessary to maintain the increasingly overstretched national parks. Indeed, private investment accounts for a large share of the funds the government is currently raising in order to triple the size of its protected marine areas by 2015, and in doing so boost its total protected areas to 26 percent of the country.

Eco-paradise lost: pesticides, pollution and poaching

There are, however, flaws in this Garden of Eden, chief among them the importance of the **agro-export** economy. It can take half a century for land used to grow pineapples to recover sufficiently enough to support anything else, while the damage wreaked by the **pesticides** used in banana plantations – the country's major agro-export – is becoming an increasing threat. Foreign consumers attach an amazing level of importance to the appearance of supermarket bananas and pineapples, and about twenty percent of potentially dangerous pesticides used in the cultivation of bananas serve only to improve the look of the fruit and not, as it is often thought, to control pestilence. Travellers who pass through banana plantations in Costa Rica or who take river trips, especially along the Río Sarapiquí in the Zona Norte, can't fail to notice the ubiquitous blue plastic bags – the pristine appearance of Costa Rican bananas is due largely to the fact that they grow inside these pesticide-lined bags, which make their way into waterways where they are fatally consumed by fish, mammals (such as the manatee) or iguanas. In the Río Tempisque basin, on the Pacific coast, armadillos and crocodiles are thought to have been virtually exterminated by agricultural pesticides.

Not that agriculture is purely to blame for the country's **pollution** problems. In recent years, several high-profile hotels have been fined for damaging their local environment, and in 2008 the *Hotel de Occidental Allegro Papagayo* in Manzanillo was shut down after it had been caught dumping sewage into a nearby estuary. Perhaps more alarmingly, the following year Parque Nacional Manuel Antonio – where conservation is always a balancing act thanks to the sheer number of visitors this tiny park receives – was found to be harming the very flora and fauna it was created to protect, and was almost closed after its leaking facilities were found to be polluting local rivers and coastline.

While Costa Rica became the first country in Central America to ban trophy hunting at the end of 2012, **poaching** in and around underprotected national parks and reserves is still a major issue. Turtle eggs are particularly vulnerable, being easily obtained and gathered in their hundreds, and while the beaches at Tortuguero are patrolled, those further south along the Caribbean coast at Moín are not. In the 2013 season, all but eight of the leatherback nests on Moín were ransacked by poachers. That year,

GOING, GOING, GONE

In a stunning indictment of the country's conservation policies, at the end of 2013 scientists announced the discovery of an incredible 5000 new species in Costa Rica, including 277 new types of wasp alone. But the national parks and protected biological corridors have come too late for some. The favoured upper-canopy habitat of the **harpy eagle**, arguably the world's most powerful raptor, has been ravaged to such an extent that the bird is thought to have disappeared forever from Costa Rica's jungles. The number of sightings of the **giant anteater** in the last quarter of a century can be counted on the fingers of one hand. And the iconic **golden toad**, once abundant in Monteverde, has gone the way of the dodo, declared extinct in 2004, fifteen years after one was last spotted.

conservation efforts in Moín had ceased in the face of armed threats from poachers, and in May 2013 the situation attracted global concern following the murder of 26-year-old conservationist Jairo Mora. At the time of writing, and despite discussions within MINAE that the area may be worth considering for national park status, Moín Beach remained under the poachers' control.

Conservation initiatives

In recent years, Mario Boza, a prominent conservationist who was heavily involved in the founding of the national parks system, has been advocating a strategy of **macro-conservation**. By uniting concerns and "joining up" chunks of protected land, he argued, macro-areas provide a larger protected range for animals that need room to hunt, like jaguars and pumas, or require sizeable migratory areas, such as the endangered great green macaw (see box, p.238). Most of all, they allow countries to make more effective joint conservation policies and decisions: macro-conservation projects currently include the Corredor Biológico Mesoamericano (the idea being to create an unbroken stretch of jungle throughout all of Mesoamerica) and the Parque Internacional La Amistad (Costa Rica and Panama).

Another initiative, even more promising in terms of how it affects the lives of many rural-based Costa Ricans, is the creation of "**buffer zones**" around some national parks. In these zones, *campesinos* and other smallholders can do part-time farming, are allowed restricted hunting rights and receive education about the ecological and economic value of the forest. Locals may be trained as nature guides, and *campesinos* may be given incentives to enter into nontraditional forms of agriculture and ways of making a living that are less environmentally destructive.

CONSERVATION ORGANIZATIONS IN COSTA RICA

The following list represents just a sample of the large number of **conservation organizations** working in Costa Rica, and there are many more local operations working towards the same common goal; several of these organizations offer a range of voluntary conservation opportunities (see p.76).

Fundación Amigos de la Isla del Coco Aptdo 276-1005, Barrio Corazón de Jesús, San José (☎ 2257 9257, ☯ cocosisland.org). Set up in 1994 to raise funds to preserve the unique flora and fauna of the remote Parque Nacional Isla del Coco (see box, p.326), a UNESCO World Heritage Site.

Fundación Neotrópica Aptdo 236-1002, Paseo de los Estudiantes, San José (☎ 2253 2130, ☯ neotropica.org). Well-established organization that works with several small-scale and (typically) local conservation initiatives in Costa Rica. Field offices in Turrialba, Puntarenas and on the Osa Peninsula; their main office in San José (opposite the Colegio Federado de Ingenieros y Arquitectos in Curridabat) sells posters, books and T-shirts in aid of funds.

Nature Conservancy. 4245 North Fairfax Drive, Suite 100, Arlington VA, 22203-1606, USA (☎ 202 628 6860) (☯ nature.org). US-based organization with a global remit – their work in Costa Rica focuses on the Cordillera Talamanca/Parque Internacional La Amistad and the Osa Peninsula. You can contact the local branch in Los Yoses in San José (☎ 2528 8800).

In the past, Costa Rica's **waste-disposal problems** have given the country a garbage nightmare, culminating in a scandal in 1995 with the overflowing of the Río Azul site, San José's main dump. The government fully recognizes the irony of this – rubbish lining the streets of a country with such a high conservation profile – and in an admirable, typically Tico grassroots initiative, legions of schoolchildren are now sent on rubbish-collecting after-school projects and weekend brigades. Even more ingenious is the national movement that sends Costa Rican schoolchildren to national parks and other preserves as **volunteers** to work on conservation projects during school holidays, thus planting the seeds for a future generation of dedicated – or at least aware – conservationists.

Tourism

Over two million tourists a year come to Costa Rica – mostly from the US, Canada and Europe – an incredible number, considering that its population is just 4.7 million. Along with the charms of the country itself, Costa Rica's popularity is linked with the growing trend toward **ecotourism** – for the most part, tourists with a genuine concern and interest in the country's flora, fauna and cultural life can choose from a variety of places to spend their money constructively, including top-notch rainforest lodges that have worked hard to integrate themselves with their surroundings (and those who want to rough it can still do so heroically in places like Corcovado and Chirripó). If managed properly, low-impact ecotourism is one of the best ways in which forests, beaches, rivers, mangroves, volcanoes and other natural formations can pay their way – in *dólares* – while remaining pristine and intact.

Several pioneering **projects** in Costa Rica have set out to combine tourism with sustainable methods of farming, rainforest preservation or scientific research. The **Rainforest Aerial Tram**, which adjoins Parque Nacional Braulio Carrillo (and is now known as the Rainforest Adventures Costa Rica Atlantic), one of the most advanced of its kind in the Americas, if not the world, provides a fascinating glimpse of the tropical canopy – normally completely inaccessible to human eyes – but it also offers a rare safe and stable method for biologists to investigate this little-known habitat. Income from visitors is funnelled into maintaining and augmenting the surrounding reserve. The **Reserva Biológica Bosque Nuboso Monteverde**, meanwhile, preserves a large piece of complex tropical forest, giving scientists a valuable stomping ground for taxonomic study. Tourism is just one of the activities in the reserve, which has been a research ground for tropical biologists from all over the world, and provides revenue for maintenance and, more importantly, continued expansion.

WHAT IS ECOTOURISM?

Ecotourism is a difficult term to define, and an authentic ecotourism experience even harder to pin down. One of the best attempts at a **definition** in recent years has been put forward by ATEC, the Asociación Talamanqueña de Ecoturismo y Conservación, which seeks to promote, as it says, "socially responsible tourism", by integrating local Bribrí and Afro-Caribbean culture into tourists' experience of the area, as well as giving residents pride in their unique cultural heritage and natural environment.

"Ecotourism means more than bird books and binoculars. Ecotourism means more than native art hanging on hotel walls or ethnic dishes on the restaurant menu. Ecotourism is not mass tourism behind a green mask. Ecotourism means a constant struggle to defend the earth and to protect and sustain traditional communities. Ecotourism is a cooperative relationship between the non-wealthy local community and those sincere, open-minded tourists who want to enjoy themselves in a Third World setting and, at the same time, enrich their consciousness by means of significant educational and cultural experience." ATEC

More people, more problems

The success of the country's ecotourism initiatives have brought their own problems, however. The huge **growth of tourism** worries many Costa Ricans, even those who make their living from it, and many, as yet unanswered, questions remain. Is it just a fad that will fade away, only to be replaced by another unprepared country-of-the-moment? What, if any, are the advantages of having an economy led by tourism instead of the traditional exports of bananas and coffee? Furthermore, how do you reconcile the need to attract enough visitors to make tourism economically viable while ensuring that this tourism remains low-impact?

MINAE vs the ICT

It is a problem made all the more difficult by ongoing arguments between two of the main organizations charged with managing the country's ecotourism industry: **MINAE**, the government body that, through SINAC, directly controls the country's network of national parks, and the **Costa Rican Tourist Board** (Instituto Costarricense de Turismo or **ICT**). Whereas MINAE is, despite severe underfunding, widely seen as having done a reasonably good job in ensuring that tourism doesn't overwhelm the parks' fragile ecosystems, the ICT is often regarded as putting commercial interests above environmental ones. In contrast to the somewhat impoverished state of MINAE, the ICT makes a lot of money out of tourism, much of it derived from the three percent tax collected on every occupied hotel room. This has led some to accuse the ICT of being more concerned with generating new accommodation (and thus money) than with the possible impact the increase in visitors could have on the environment and local communities.

The ICT has, however, taken a step in the right direction with their development of the **Certificate for Sustainable Tourism** (ⓦturismo-sostenible.co.cr). In an area that has traditionally been hard to quantify, the scheme helps shed light on the murky issue of just how eco an ecolodge or tour operator really is, by measuring how much they comply with the ICT's model of sustainable best practice and awarding them a rating of up to five "leaves"; as a company's rating increases, so do its benefits, which include publicity and promotion from the ICT, training and the like.

Foreign ownership, high prices and sex tourists

The question of who pays for Costa Rica's environmental well-being, though, is one that continues to provoke fierce debate. While the government actively welcomes contributions from **foreign sources**, many Costa Ricans are alarmed by what they see as the virtual purchase of their country by foreigners. Though many hotels and businesses are still Costa Rican-owned and- managed, North American and European ownership is on the rise, relegating many locals to low-paid jobs in the service sector. Gated **"gringo" communities** are springing up along the Pacific coast, and across the country **rising property prices** are having a drastic effect on Costa Ricans, with many being priced out of their own communities.

At times, the government seems bent on turning the country into a **high-income tourist enclave**. North Americans and Europeans will still consider many things quite cheap, but Costa Rica is already the most expensive country to visit in the region, and the government has admitted that they have no qualms about discouraging "backpackers" (meaning budget tourists) from coming to Costa Rica. Better-heeled tourists, the thinking goes, not only make a more significant investment in the country dollar for dollar, but are more easily controlled, choosing in the main to travel in tour groups or to stay in big holiday resorts – ironically, the type of places that are often dogged by environmental scandal (see box, p.330 & p.428).

Another flipside to Costa Rica's tourism success story is its ascendancy to one of the world's top **sex tourism** destinations. Prostitution with women over the age of 18 is legal, and it is estimated that approximately ten percent of foreign visitors are sex tourists. Disturbingly, paedophiles also come to Costa Rica, and they find no shortage of desperate underage prostitutes stricken by poverty and drug addiction. In 1999, Costa Rica's parliament passed a law against the sexual exploitation of minors, and while penalties are harsh and initiatives in place to educate taxi drivers, police officers, tour guides and hotel receptionists about the illegality of profiteering from promoting child prostitution, the problem is still prevalent.

Books

The most comprehensive volumes written on Costa Rica tend to be about natural history – many make better introductions to what you'll see in the country than the glossy literature pumped out by the government tourist board. Frustratingly, many of the most informative works on both natural and cultural history are out of date or out of print (designated "o/p" in the list below). You'll find a number of the titles listed below in San José bookshops, but don't expect to see them elsewhere in the country.

Those interested in **Costa Rican fiction** (which is alive and well, although not extensively translated or known abroad) will have much richer and varied reading with some knowledge of Spanish. Costa Rica has no single, internationally recognized, towering figure in its national literature, and in sharp contrast to other countries in the region the most sophisticated and best-known writers in the country are women. Carmen Naranjo is the most widely translated, with a number of novels, poems and short-story collections (plus some of the country's most prestigious literary awards) to her name, but there are a number of lesser-read writers, including the brilliant Yolanda Oreamuno, and an upsurge of younger women, tackling contemporary social issues like domestic violence and alcoholism in their fiction and poetry. The publication in 1940 of Carlos Luis Fallas's seminal novel *Mamita Yunai*, about labour conditions in the United Fruit Company banana plantations of Limón Province, sparked a wave of "proletarian" novels, which became the dominant form in Costa Rican fiction until well into the 1970s. Until recently, Costa Rican fiction also leant heavily on picturesque stories of rural life, with some writers – usually men – drawing on the country's wealth of fauna. There are also a number of *cuentos* (stories), fable-like in their simplicity and not a little ponderous in their symbolism, featuring turtles, fish and rabbits as characters.

TRAVEL NARRATIVE

Paul Theroux *The Old Patagonian Express: By Train Through the Americas*. Somewhat out of date (Theroux went through some 35 years ago), but a great read nonetheless. Laced with the author's usual tetchy black humour and general misanthropy, the descriptions of his two Costa Rican train journeys (neither of which still runs) to Limón and Puntarenas remain apt – as is the account of passing through San José, where he meets American men on sex-and-booze vacations.

CULTURE AND FOLK TRADITIONS

Roberto Cabrera *Santa Cruz Guanacaste: Una Aproximación a la Historia y la Cultura Populares*. The best cultural history of Guanacaste, written by a respected Guanacastecan sociologist. Verbal snapshots of nineteenth- and twentieth-century hacienda life, accounts of bull riding and details of micro-regional dances, such as the *punto guanacasteco* (adopted as the national dance).

★**Paula Palmer** *"What Happen": A Folk-History of Costa Rica's Talamanca Coast*. The definitive folk history of the Afro-Caribbean community on Limón Province's Talamancan coast. Palmer first went to Cahuita in the early 1970s as a Peace Corps volunteer, later to return as a sociologist. The oral histories she collected from older members of the local communities – atmospheric testimonies of pirate treasure, ghosts and the like – are complemented by photos and accounts of local agriculture, foods and traditional remedies.

Paula Palmer, Juanita Sánchez and Gloria Mayorga *Taking Care of Sibö's Gifts: An Environmental Treatise from Costa Rica's KéköLdi Indigenous Reserve*. Manifesto for the future of Bribrí culture and ecological survival of the *talamanqueña* ecosystems, and a concise explication of differing views of the land and people's relationship to it held by the *ladinos* and Bribrí on the KéköLdi Indigenous Reserve.

CONSERVATION

★**Catherine Caulfield** *In the Rainforest: Report from a Strange, Beautiful, Imperiled World*. Over twenty years old, but still one of the best introductions to the rainforest, dealing in an accessible fashion with many of the issues covered in the more specialized titles. Her chapter on Costa Rica is a wary elucidation of the destruction that cattle-ranching in particular wreaks, as well as an interesting profile of the farming methods used by the Monteverde community.

Gordon W. Frankie, Alfonso Mata and S. Bradleigh Vinson (eds) *Biodiversity Conservation in Costa Rica: Learning the Lessons in a Seasonal Dry Forest*. The first in-depth study of Guanacaste's endangered dry forest paints a detailed picture – biologically, environmentally, socially and politically – of this fragile ecosystem and its vital link to the country's other ecosystems.

Susanna Hecht and Alexander Cockburn *The Fate of the Forest: Developers, Destroyers and Defenders of the Amazon*. The best single book readily available on rainforest destruction, this exhaustive volume (updated in 2011) is written with a sound knowledge of Amazonian history. The beautiful prose dissects some of the more pervasive myths about rainforest destruction, and it's comprehensive enough to be applicable to any forested areas under threat in the New World tropics.

Luis Fournier Origgi *Desarrollo y Perspectivas del Movimiento Conservacionista Costarricense*. Seminal, if dry, survey of conservation policy from the dawn of the nation until the early 1990s, by one of Costa Rica's most eminent scientists and conservationists. In Spanish only.

HISTORY AND CURRENT AFFAIRS

Suzane Abel *Between Continents/Between Seas: Precolumbian Art of Costa Rica* (o/p). Produced as a catalogue to accompany the exhibition that toured the US in 1982, this is the best single volume on pre-Conquest history and craftsmanship, with illuminating accounts of the lives, beliefs and customs of Costa Rica's pre-Columbian peoples as interpreted through artefacts and excavations. The photographs, whether of jade pendants, Chorotega pottery or the more diabolical of the Diquis's gold pieces, are uniformly wonderful.

Elías Zamora Acosta *Etnografía Histórica de Costa Rica (1561–1615)*. Hugely impressive archival research that reconstructs the economic, political and social life in the province in the years immediately following the Spanish invasion. A masterwork, distressingly difficult to get hold of. In Spanish only.

Richard Biesanz, Mavis Hiltunen Biesanz and Karen Zubris Biesanz *The Ticos: Culture and Social Change in Costa Rica*. An intriguing blend of quantitative and qualitative research, supported by personal interviews with many Costa Ricans, this book seeks to get under the skin of Costa Rican society, examining (among other things) government, class and ethnic relations, the family, health and sport, and managing to be rigorous and

anecdotal at the same time.

Martha Honey *Hostile Acts: U.S. Policy in Costa Rica in the 1980s*. Those sceptical of elaborate conspiracy theories may have their minds changed by this exhaustively researched, weighty tome detailing the US's "dual diplomacy" against Costa Rica in the 1980s. In this heroic volume, and in contrast to her earlier findings in *La Penca: On Trial in Costa Rica*, Honey concludes that the 1984 La Penca bomber was a leftist Argentinian terrorist with connections to Nicaragua's Sandinista government.

★**Steven Palmer and Iván Molina** (eds) *The Costa Rica Reader: History, Culture, Politics*. One of the best introductions to the country, this book features more than fifty texts by Costa Ricans, from essays and memoirs to histories and poems, interspersed with photographs, maps, cartoons and fliers.

Mitchell A. Seligson *Peasants of Costa Rica and the Development of Agrarian Capitalism* (o/p). The best single history available in English, although only a university or specialist library will have it. Much wider in scope than the title suggests, this is an excellent intermeshing of ethnic and racial issues, economics and sociology along with hard-core analysis of the rise and fall of the Costa Rican peasant.

WILDLIFE, NATURAL HISTORY AND FIELD GUIDES

Mario A. Boza *Costa Rica National Parks (Parques Nacionales)*. Essentially a coffee-table book, this informed volume (it's written by one of the founders of the national-park system) is a great taster for what you'll find in the national parks. The text is in Spanish and English, with stunning photographs throughout.

A.S. and P.P. Calvert *A Year of Costa Rican Natural History*. Although now very old – the year in question is 1910 – this is a brilliant, insightful and charmingly enthusiastic travelogue/natural history/autobiography by an American

biologist and zoologist husband-and-wife team. It features much, much more than natural history, with sections such as "Blood Sucking Flies", "Fiestas in Santa Cruz" and "Earthquakes". The best single title ever written on Costa Rica, the only problem is finding it – try good libraries and specialist bookstores.

Joseph Franke *Costa Rica's National Parks and Preserves*. A park-by-park discussion of the system of national parks and wildlife refuges, with detailed information on hiking and trails, as well as a topographical and environmental profile of each park. Useful if you're intending to spend any time hiking in more than one or two parks.

★**Richard Garrigues and Robert Dean** *The Birds of Costa Rica*. This excellent, all-encompassing field guide to the country's myriad birdlife is fast threatening Stiles and Skutch's tour de force (see below) as the birdwatchers' bible – succinct and portable, it makes the ideal handbook for everyday use in the field.

★**Adrian Hepworth** *Costa Rica: A Journey Through Nature*. Cherry-picking from the author's extensive portfolio, the second edition of this best-selling coffee-table tome features more of the lavish wildlife photography that made the original one of the most popular visual souvenirs of Costa Rica.

Daniel H. Janzen (ed) *Costa Rican Natural History*. The definitive reference source, with accessible, continuously fascinating species-by-species accounts, written by a highly influential figure – Janzen was involved on a policy level in the governing of the national parks system. The introduction is especially worth reading, dealing in a cursory but lively fashion with tectonics, meteorology, history and archeology. Illustrated throughout with gripping photographs. Available in paperback but still doorstep-thick.

Sam Mitchell *Pura Vida: The Waterfalls and Hot Springs of Costa Rica*. Jolly, personably written but concise guide to the country's many little-known waterholes, cascades and waterfalls, complete with detailed directions and accounts of surrounding trails. Available in English in San José.

Donald Perry *Life Above the Jungle Floor: A Biologist Explores a Strange and Hidden Treetop World*. Nicely poised, lyrical account of Perry's trials and tribulations in conceiving and mounting his Rainforest Aerial Tram (see p.145). Most of the book deals with his time at Rara Avis, where he conceived and tested his tram prototype, the Automated Web for Canopy Exploration.

Fiona A. Reid, Twan Leenders, Jim Zook and Robert Dean *The Wildlife of Costa Rica*. This handy introduction to the main species you're likely to encounter, from mammals and birds to reptiles and amphibians, works well as a non-specialist field guide. The illustrations, particularly of the birds and mammals, are good and the species accounts detailed and informative – there's even a small section on insects, including butterflies, bullet ants and the extremely strange-looking tailless whip scorpion.

F. Gary Stiles and Alexander F. Skutch *A Guide to the Birds of Costa Rica*. Throughout Costa Rica, you'll see guides clutching well-thumbed copies of this seminal tome, illustrated with colour plates to aid identification. Hefty, even in paperback and too pricey for the amateur, but you may be able to pick up good secondhand copies in Costa Rica.

Mark Wainwright *The Mammals of Costa Rica*. The most comprehensive guide to the country's mammal species, including the oft-overlooked bats, is an amalgamation of hundreds of field researchers' work and features detailed but accessible information on natural history, conservation and, interestingly, mythology. The animal tracks are useful, though there are better illustrations in other books of this ilk.

Allen M. Young *Sarapiquí Chronicle: A Naturalist in Costa Rica* (o/p). Lavishly produced book based on entomologist Allen M. Young's twenty years' work in the Sarapiquí area and featuring a well-written combination of autobiography, travelogue and natural science, centring on the insect life he encounters.

FICTION

Miguel Benavides *The Children of Mariplata: Stories from Costa Rica*. A short collection of short stories, most of which are good examples of fable-like or allegorical Costa Rican tales. Many are written in the anthropomorphized voice of an animal; others, like *The Twilight Which Lost its Colour*, describe searing slices of poverty-stricken life.

Carlos Cortés *Cruz de Olvido*. Told in the macho, exhausted and regretful tone of a disillusioned revolutionary, this novel charts the return of a Costa Rican Sandinista supporter from Nicaragua to his home country, where "nothing has happened since the big bang". The narrative marries the storyteller's humorous disaffection with boring old Costa Rica and his investigation into the bizarre, excessively symbolic death of his son.

Fabián Dobles *Ese Que Llaman Pueblo* (Spanish only); *Years Like Brief Days*. Born in 1918, Dobles is Costa Rica's elder statesman of letters. Set in the countryside among *campesinos*, *Ese Que Llaman Pueblo* is a typical "proletarian" novel. *Years Like Brief Days* is the first novel by Dobles to be translated into English, an epistolary story told in the form of a letter written by an old man to his mother, describing the village he grew up in and his eventful life.

★**Carlos Luis Fallas** *Mamita Yunai: El Infierno de las Bananeras*. Exuberant and full of local colour, culture and diction, this entertaining leftist novel depicting life in the hell of the banana plantations is a great read. It's set in La Estrella valley in Limón Province, where Fallas, a pioneering labour organizer in the 1930s and 40s, was instrumental in forcing the United Fruit Company to take workers' welfare into account. In Spanish only.

Joaquín Gutiérrez *Puerto Limón*. One of the best books of the "proletarian" genre, by one of the nation's foremost literary figures, who was also a prominent journalist. While very much focused on the gritty realism of labour conditions in mid-twentieth-century Costa Rica, the writing is lyrical and beautifully simple.

★**Enrique Jaramillo Levi** (ed) *When New Flowers Bloomed: Short Stories by Women Writers from Costa Rica and Panama*. Collection of the best-known Costa Rican women writers, including Rima de Vallbona, Carmen Naranjo,

Carmen Lyra and Yolanda Oreamuno. Most of the stories are from the late 1980s, with shared themes of domestic violence – a persistent problem in Costa Rica – sexual and economic inequality and the tyrannies of female anatomy and desire. Look out especially for Emilia Macaya, a younger writer.

Tatiana Lobo *Assault on Paradise*. Costa Rica's first great historical novel tells the story of the arrival of the Spaniards and, as the title indicates, their destruction of the land and life of the indigenous peoples they encountered.

Carmen Naranjo *Los Perros no Ladraron*; *Responso por el Niño Juan Manuel*; *Diario de una Multitud*; *Ondina*; and *Sobrepunto*. In keeping with a tradition in Latin American letters but unusually for a woman, Naranjo occupied several public posts, including Secretary of Culture, director of the publishing house EDUCA and ambassador to Israel. She was widely considered to be an experimentalist, and her novels can be found throughout Costa Rica in Spanish only; her collection of stories *There Never Was Once Upon a Time*, however, is available in English.

★ **Yolanda Oreamuno** *La Ruta de su Evasión*. Oreamuno had a short life, dying at the age of 40 in 1956, but by the time she was 24 she had distinguished herself as the most promising writer of her generation with her novel *Por Tierra Firme*. *La Ruta* – concerning a child sent to look for his father, who has disappeared, possibly on a drinking binge – displays her continually surprising, lyrical style. The search is both actual and spiritual, the novel a complex weave of themes. In Spanish only.

Barbara Ras *Costa Rica: A Traveler's Literary Companion*. This anthology is probably the most accessible starting point for readers interested in Costa Rican literature, with flowing and well-translated stories arranged by geographical zone. The best stories are also the most heartrending – read *The Girl Who Came from the Moon* and *The Carbonero* for a glimpse of life beyond the tourist-brochure images.

Yasmín Ross *La Flota Negra*. Originally a journalist from Mexico, Ross's *La Flota Negra* is one of the best-received novels set in Costa Rica in recent years. It takes as its starting point the story of the Black Star Line, the shipping company that brought so many of the Caribbean immigrants whose descendants now make up the popula-tion of Limón, along with the Pan-Africanist Marcus Garvey's visit to the province. In Spanish only.

Anacristina Rossi *La Loca de Gandoca* (*The Madwoman of Gandoca*). Rossi's popular novel is really "faction", documenting in businesslike prose and with tongue firmly in cheek the bizarre and byzantine wranglings over the Refugio de Vida Silvestre Gandoca-Manzanillo, including the surveying of the indigenous Bribrí on the KéköLdi reserve. In Spanish only.

Rima de Vallbona *Flowering Inferno: Tales of Sinking Hearts*. Slim volume of affecting short stories by one of Costa Rica's most respected (and widely translated) writers on social life, customs and – most poignantly, in the case of *Flowering Inferno* – the position of women.

Spanish

Although it is commonly said that everyone speaks English in Costa Rica, it is not really the case. Certainly, many who work in the tourist trade speak some English, and there are a number of expats who speak anything from English to German to Dutch, but the people you'll meet day to day are likely to speak only Spanish. The one area where you will hear English widely spoken is on the Caribbean coast, where many of the Afro-Caribbean inhabitants are of Jamaican descent, and speak a distinctive regional creole.

If you want to get to know Costa Ricans, then it makes sense to acquire some **Spanish** before you arrive. Ticos are polite, patient and forgiving interlocutors, and will not only tolerate but appreciate any attempts you make to speak their language.

Pronunciation

The rules of **pronunciation** are pretty straightforward. Unless there's an accent, all words ending in "l", "r" and "z" are stressed on the last syllable, all others on the second to last. Unlike in the rest of Latin America, in Costa Rica the final "d" in many words sometimes gets dropped; thus, you'll hear "*usté*" for "*usted*" or "*¿verdá?*" for "*¿verdad?*" Other Costa Rican peculiarities are the "ll" and "r" sounds. All vowels are pure and short.

A somewhere between the A sound in "back" and that in "father"

E as in "get"

I as in "police"

O as in "hot"

U as in "rule"

C is soft before E and I, hard otherwise: *cerca* is pronounced "serka"

G works the same way: a guttural H sound (like the ch in "loch") before E or I, a hard G elsewhere: *gigante* becomes "higante"

H is always silent

J is the same sound as a guttural G: *jamón* is pronounced "hamon"

LL may be pronounced as a soft J (as in parts of Chile and Argentina) instead of Y: *ballena* (whale) becomes "bajzhena" instead of "bayena"

N is as in English, unless it has a tilde (accent) over it, when it becomes NY: *mañana* sounds like "manyana"

QU is pronounced like the English K

R is not rolled Scottish burr-like as much as in other Spanish-speaking countries: *carro* is said "cahro", with a soft rather than a rolled R

V sounds more like B: *vino* becomes "beano"

Z is the same as a soft C: *cerveza* is thus "servesa"

WORDS AND PHRASES

BASICS

Yes, No	Sí, No	With, Without	Con, Sin
Please	Por favor	Good, Bad	Buen(o)/a, Mal(o)/a
Thank you	Gracias	Big, Small	Gran(de), Pequeño/a
You're welcome	De nada	More, Less	Más, Menos
Where?	¿Dónde?		
When?	¿Cuando?	**GREETINGS AND RESPONSES**	
What?	¿Qué?	Hello, Goodbye	Hola, Adiós
Why?	¿Por qué?	Good morning	Buenos días
Here, There	Aquí, Allí	Good afternoon/ night	Buenas tardes/noches
This, That	Este, Eso	See you later	Hasta luego
Now, Later	Ahora, Más tarde	Sorry	Lo siento/Discúlpame
Open, Closed	Abierto/a, Cerrado/a	Excuse me	Con permiso/Perdón

How are you?	¿Cómo está (usted)?
I (don't) understand	(No) Entiendo
What did you say?	¿Cómo?
Do you speak English?	¿Habla (usted) inglés?
I don't speak Spanish	(No) Hablo español
My name is…	Me llamo…
What's your name?	¿Como se llama usted?
I am American/	Soy estadoudinense/
English/Australian/	inglés(a)/australiano(a)/
New Zealander/	nuevo(a) zelanda/
South African	africano del sur

DIRECTIONS

Do you know…?	¿Sabe…?
I don't know	No sé
How do I get to…?	¿Como llega a…?
Left, Right,	Izquierda, Derecha,
Straight on	Derecho
Where is…?	¿Dónde está…?
…the nearest bank	…el banco más cercano
…the post office	…el correo
…the toilet	…el baño/servicio
Is there a (hotel) near	¿Hay un (hotel) cerca de
here?	aquí?

ACCOMMODATION

Do you have a room…?	¿Tieneun cuarto/una
	habitacíon…?
…with two beds/	…con dos camas/
a double bed	una cama matrimonial
a single bed	una cama sencilla
It's for one person	Es para una persona
(two people)	(dos personas)
…for one night	…para una noche
(one week)	(una semana)
It's fine, how much is it?	¿Está bien, cuánto es?
Don't you have	¿No tiene algo más
anything cheaper?	barato?
Can one…?	¿Se puede…?
…camp (near)	¿…acampar (cerca de)
here?	aquí?
Hot water	Agua caliente
Cold water	Agua fría
Air-conditioned	Aire-acondicionado
Shared bath	Baño colectivo/
	compartido
Ceiling fan	Abanico
Check-out time	Hora de salida
Taxes	Impuestos

TRANSPORT

| Boat | Barco |
| Bus | Autobus |

Train	Tren
Plane	Avion
Where is the bus station?	¿Dónde está el estación
	autobuses?
Where does the bus	¿De dónde sale el
to…leave from?	autobus para…?
I'd like a (return)	Quisiera un tiquete (de
ticket to…	ida y vuelta) para…
What time does it	¿A qué hora sale
leave (arrive in…)?	(llega en…)?
First	Primero/a
Last	ltimo/a
Next	Próximo/a

SHOPPING

I want to buy…	Quiero comprar…
I would like…	Quisiera…
Give me…	Deme…
(one like that)	(uno así)
What's that?	¿Qué es eso?
How much does it cost?	¿Cuanto cuesta?
It's too expensive	Es demasiado caro
What's this called in	¿Como se llama éste
Spanish?	en español?
ATM	Cajero de automatico
Credit card	Tarjeta de credito
Money	Dinero
Market	Mercado
Shop/store	Tienda

NUMBERS

1	un/uno/una
2	dos
3	tres
4	cuatro
5	cinco
6	seis
7	siete
8	ocho
9	nueve
10	diez
11	once
12	doce
13	trece
14	catorce
15	quince
16	diez y seis
20	veinte
21	veintiuno
30	treinta

31	treinta y uno	It's half past (ten)	Es (las diez) y media
40	cuarenta	Yesterday	Ayer
50	cincuenta	Today	Hoy
60	sesenta	Tomorrow	Mañana
70	setenta	Monday	lunes
80	ochenta	Tuesday	martes
90	noventa	Wednesday	miércoles
100	cien(to)	Thursday	jueves
101	ciento uno	Friday	viernes
200	doscientos	Saturday	sábado
201	doscientos uno	Sunday	domingo
500	quinientos		
1000	mil	January	enero
2000	dos mil	February	febrero
1990	mil novocientos noventa	March	marzo
1991	…y uno	April	abril
		May	mayo
First	Primero/a	June	junio
Second	Segundo/a	July	julio
Third	Tercero/a	August	agosto
		September	septiembre
		October	octubre

TIME, DAYS AND MONTHS

What time is it?	¿Qué hora es?	November	noviembre
It's (9) o'clock	son las (nueve)	December	diciembre

A COSTA RICAN MENU READER

BASICS

Aceite	Oil
Aceitunas	Olives
Ajo ("al ajillo")	Garlic (in garlic sauce)
Cebolla	Onion
Cilantro	Coriander
Frijoles	Beans
Huevos	Eggs
Leche	Milk
Queso	Cheese
Salsa	Sauce

MEAT (CARNE), FISH (PESCADO) AND SEAFOOD/SHELLFISH (MARISCOS)

Atún	Tuna
Bistec	Steak
Cerdo	Pork
Corvina	Sea bass
Jamón	Ham
Langosta	Lobster
Lomito	Cut of beef (filet mignon)
Pargo	Red snapper
Trucha	Trout

FRUITS (FRUTAS)

Aguacate	Avocado
Anona	Custard fruit; sweet, thick ripe taste: one of the best fruits in the country
Banano	Banana
Carambola	Starfruit
Cas	Pale-flesh fruit with sweet-sour taste
Chinos	Usually used for *refrescos*
Fresas	Strawberries
Guanábana	Soursop; very large green mottled fruit, with sweet white flesh tasting like a cross between a mango and a pear; mostly found on the Caribbean coast
Guayaba	Guava; very sweet fruit, usually used for making spreads and jams
Limón	Lemon
Mamones chinos	Spiny-covered red or yellow fruits that look diabolical but reveal gently flavoured lychee-type fruit inside; somewhat like peeled green grapes, but sweeter and more fragrant. Usually sold in

	small bags of a dozen on street corners or buses
Maracuyá	Passion fruit; small yellow fruits, sharp and sweet
Moras	Blackberries
Naranja	Orange
Papaya	Papaya/pawpaw; large, round or oblong fruit with bland orange flesh. Best eaten with fresh lime juice, and very good for stomach bugs
Pejibaye	A Costa Rican speciality, you'll find this small green-orange fruit (known as the peach palm fruit) almost nowhere else. Like its relative, the coconut, it grows in bunches on palm trees: the texture is unusual, as is the nutty flavour
Piña	Pineapple
Sandía	Watermelon
Tamarindo	A large pod of seeds, covered in a sticky, light-brown flesh; the unique taste – at once tart and sweet – is best first sampled in a *refresco*
Zapote	Large sweet orange fruit, with a dark-brown outer casing

VEGETABLES (*VERDURAS*)

Chayote	Resembling a light-green avocado, this vegetable is tender and delicate when cooked, and excellent in stews and with meat and rice dishes
Fruta de pan	Breadfruit; eaten more as a starch substitute than a fruit
Hongos	Mushrooms
Palmito	Heart-of-palm; the inner core of palm trees, usually eaten in salads, with a somewhat bitter taste and fibrous texture
Plátanos	Plantains; eaten sweet
Zanahorias	Carrots

TYPICAL DISHES (*PLATOS*)

Arreglados	Meat and mayonnaise sandwiches on greasy bread buns
Arroz…	Rice…
…**con pollo**	…with chicken
…**con carne**	…with meat
…**con pescado**	…with fish
…**con mariscos**	…with seafood
…**con camarones**	…with shrimps/prawns
Bocas	Small snacks, usually eaten as an accompaniment to a beer
Casado	Plate of meat or fish, rice and salad, sometimes served with fried plantains
Ceviche	Raw fish, usually sea bass, "marinated" in lime juice, onions, chillies and coriander
Chicarrones	Fried pork rinds
Chilasquilas	Tortillas and beef with spices and battered eggs
Empanadas	Meat or vegetable patties
Frijoles molidos	Mashed black beans with onions, chilli peppers, coriander and thyme
Gallo pinto	"Painted rooster"; breakfast dish of rice and beans
Gallos	Small sandwiches
Pan de maíz	Corn bread; white rather than yellow
Picadillo	Potatoes cooked with beef and beans
Sopa negra	Black-bean soup with egg and vegetables
Tacos	Tortilla filled with beef or chicken, cabbage, tomatoes and mild chillies
Tamal	One of the best local specialities, usually consisting of maize flour, chicken or pork, olives, chillies and raisins, all wrapped in a plantain leaf
Tortilla	Thin, small and bland bread, served as an accompaniment to meals and, especially in Guanacaste, breakfast

DESSERTS (*POSTRES*)

Cajeta	Dessert made of milk, sugar, vanilla and sometimes coconut
Helado	Ice cream
Milanes	Delicate chocolate fingers
Queque	Cake
Queque seco	Pound cake
Tamal asado	Cake made of corn flour, cream, eggs, sugar and butter
Tres leches	Boiled milk and syrup-drenched cake

REGIONAL DISHES
CARIBBEAN

Pan bon	Sweet glazed bread with fruit and cheese
Patacones	Plantain chips, often served with frijoles molidos (see opposite)
Rice and beans	Rice and beans cooked in coconut milk
Rundown	Meat and vegetables stewed in coconut milk

GUANACASTE

Chorreados	Corn pancakes
Horchata	Hot drink made with corn or rice and flavoured with cinnamon
Natilla	Sour cream
Olla de carne	Rich, hearty meat stew
Pinolillo	Milky corn drink
Rosquillas	Corn doughnuts
Tanelas	Scone-like corn snack

Idioms and slang

Costa Rican Spanish is a living language full of flux and argot. Local slang and usage are often referred to as **tiquismos** (from *Costarriqueñismos*, or Costa Ricanisms) or, as Costa Ricans will say when enlightening the foreigner as to their meaning, "*palabras muy ticas*". Some of the expressions and terms discussed below may be heard in other countries in the region, especially in Nicaragua and El Salvador, but still they are highly regional. Others are purely endemic, including *barbarismos* (bastardizations) and *provincialismos* (words particular to specific regions of Costa Rica).

The noun "Tico" used as a short form for Costa Rican comes less from a desire to shorten "Costarriquense" than from the traditional trend towards **diminution**, which is supposed to signal classlessness, eagerness to band together and desire not to cause offence. In Costa Rica, the common Spanish diminution of "ito" – applied as a suffix at the end of the word, as in "herman*ito*" ("little brother") – often becomes "itico" ("herman*itico*"). That said, you hear the -ito or -itico endings less and less nowadays.

Costa Rican Spanish often displays an astounding **formality** that borders on servility. Instead of "*de nada*" ("you're welcome"), many Costa Ricans will say, "*Para servirle*", which means, literally, "I'm here to serve you". When they meet you, Costa Ricans will say "*Con mucho gusto*" ("It's a pleasure"), and you should do the same. Even when you leave people you do not know well, you will be told "*Que le vaya bien*" ("May all go well with you").

A COSTA RICAN DICTIONARY

An entertaining, illustrated dictionary of slang and *dichos* (sayings) for Spanish-speakers interested in understanding heavily argot-spiced spoken Costa Rican Spanish, **Nuevo diccionario de Costarriqueñismos**, by Miguel Ángel Quesada Pacheco, is a fascinating compendium, giving the regional location of word usage and sayings, what age group uses them and some etymology. It also reveals a wealth of localisms developed to describe local phenomena – witness, for example, the number of different words for "wasp".

Nicknames and a delight in the informal mix with a quite proper formal tone used in spoken Costa Rican Spanish. Nicknames centre on your most obvious physical characteristic: popular ones include *flaca* (thin); *gorda* (fat); and *macha* (light-skinned). Terms of endearment are also very current in popular speech; along with the ubiquitous *mi amor*, you may also get called *joven* (young one).

Intimate address

It's difficult to get your head round forms of **second-person address** in Costa Rica. Children are often spoken to in the "*usted*" form, which is technically formal and reserved for showing respect (in other Spanish-speaking countries, children are generally addressed as "*tu*"). Even friends who have known each other for years in Costa Rica will address each other as "*usted*". But the single most confounding irregularity of Costa Rican speech for those who already speak Spanish is the use of "**vos**" as personal intimate address – generally between friends of the same age. Many people on a short trip to the country never quite get to grips with it.

Now archaic, "*vos*" is only used widely in the New World in Argentina and Costa Rica. It has an interesting rhythm and sound, with verbs ending on a kind of diphthong-ized stress: *vos sabés, vos quires* (you know, you want), as opposed to *tu sabes/ usted sabe* or *tu quieres/usted quiere*. If you are addressed in the "*vos*" form, it is a sign of friendship, and you should try to use it back if you can. It is an affront to use "*vos*" improperly, with someone you don't know well, when it can be seen as being patronizing. Again, Costa Ricans are good-hearted in this respect, however, and put errors down to the fact that you are a foreigner.

Everyday expressions

Here are some everyday **peculiarities** that most visitors to Costa Rica will become familiar with pretty quickly:

!Achará! Expression of regret: "What a pity!", like "¡Qué lástima!"

Adiós "Hi", used primarily in the campo (country) when greeting someone on the road or street. Confusingly, as in the rest of Latin America, adiós is also "goodbye", but only if you are going away for a long time.

¿Diay? Slightly melancholic interjection in the vein of "Ah, but what can you expect?"

Fatal Reserved for the absolutely worst possible eventuality: "Esta carretera para Golfito es fatal" means "The road to Golfito is the very worst".

Feo Literally "ugly", but can also mean rotten or lousy, as in "Todos los caminos en Costa Rica están muy feos"("All the roads in Costa Rica are in really bad shape").

Maje Literally "dummy", used between young men as an affirmation of their friendship/maleness: it's used like "buddy, pal" (US) or "mate" (UK). There is no equivalent for women, unfortunately.

!Pura vida! Perhaps the best-known *tiquismo*, meaning "Great!", "OK!" or "Cool!".

Qué mala/buena nota Expression of disapproval/approval – "How uncool/great".

Luck and God

Both **luck** and **God** come into conversation often in Costa Rica. Thus, you get the pattern:

| ¿Cómo amaneció? | "How did you sleep?" (Literally, "How did you wake up?") | Muy bien, por dicha, ¿y usted? | "Very well, fortunately, and you?" |
| | | Muy bien, gracias a Dios. | "Very well, thank God." |

Also, you will hear *dicha* and *Dios* used in situations that don't seem to have much to do with luck or divine intervention: "¡Qué dicha que usted llegó!" ("What luck that you arrived!"), along with such phrases as "*Vamos a la playa esta fin de semana, si Dios quiere*" ("We'll go to the beach this weekend, God willing"). Even a shrug of the shoulders elicits a "*¡Dios sabe!*" ("God only knows"). And the usual forms "*hasta luego*" or "*hasta la vista*" become in Costa Rica the much more God-fearing "*Que Dios le acompañe*" ("May God go with you").

"Where is your boyfriend?"

"*¿Dónde está su novio?/padres?*" ("Where is your boyfriend/family?") is a query women, especially those travelling alone, will hear often. **Family** is very important in explaining to many Costa Ricans who you are and where you come from, and people will place you by asking how many brothers and sisters you have, where your family lives, whether your grandmother is still alive… It's a good idea to get to grips with the following:

madre/padre	mother/father	**hermano/hermana**	brother/sister
abuelo/abuela	grandfather/grandmother	**tío/tía**	uncle/aunt
hijo/hija	son/daughter	**primo/prima**	cousin

Glossary

abastecedor a general store, usually in a rural area or *barrio* (neighbourhood) that keeps a stock of groceries and basic toiletries

agringarse (verb) to adopt the ways of the gringos

agua potable drinking water

aguacero downpour

ahorita "right now" (any time within the coming hour)

area de acampar camping area

area restringido restricted area

bárbaro fantastic, cool (literally "barbaric")

barrio neighbourhood (usually urban)

bomba petrol station

botica pharmacy

burro can refer to the animal (donkey), but is usually an adjective denoting "really big", as in *"Vea este bicho sí burro"* ("Come see this really big insect")

campesino peasant farmer, smallholder

campo literally countryside, but more often in Costa Rica "space", as in "seat" when travelling; thus, *"¿Hay un campo en este autobus?"* means "Is there a (free) seat on this bus?"

cantina bar, usually patronized by the working class or rural labouring class

capa rain gear, poncho

carro car (not *coche*, as in Spain)

cazadora literally, huntress; a beaten-up old schoolbus that serves as public transport in rural areas

chance widely used Anglicism to denote chance, or opportunity; like *oportunidad*

chiquillos kids; also *chiquititos*, *chiquiticos*

chivo cute

chorreador sack-and-metal coffee-filter contraption, still widely used

choteo quick-witted sarcasm, something Costa Ricans admire, provided it's not too sharp-tongued

colectivo an open-back truck used as a form of public transport in remote rural areas

conchos yokels, hicks from the sticks

cordillera mountain range

correo post office

dando cuerda colloquial expression meaning, roughly, to "make eyes at", in an approximation of sexual interest (men to women, hardly ever the other way around)

entrada entrance

evangélico usually refers to anyone who is of a religion other than Catholic, but particularly Protestant even if they are not evangelical; such religions are also called *cultos*, belying a general wariness and disapproval for anything other than Catholicism

finca farm or plantation

finquero coffee grower

foco flashlight/torch

galletas biscuits

gambas buttresses, the giant above-ground roots that some rainforest trees put out

gaseosa fizzy drink

gasolina petrol

gringo not-at-all pejorative term for a North American (a European is usually *europeo*)

guaca pre-Columbian burial ground or tomb

güila child

güisqui whisky (usually bad unless imported, and astronomically expensive)

hacienda big farm, usually a ranch

hospedaje very basic *pensión*

humilde humble, simple; an appearance and quality that is widely respected

ICE Instituto Costarricense de Electricidad, the country's principal telecommunications provider

ICT Instituto Costarricense de Turismo, the national tourist board

indígena an indigenous person; preferred term among indigenous groups in Costa Rica, rather than the less polite *índio* (Indian)

invierno winter (May–Nov)

jornaleros day labourers, usually landless peasants who are paid by the day, for instance to pick coffee in season

josefino resident of San José

malecón seaside promenade

mal educado literally, badly educated; a gentle if effective insult, especially useful for women harassed by hissing, leering men

marimba type of large xylophone played mainly in Guanacaste; also refers to the style of music

mestizo person of mixed race indigenous/Spanish; not usually pejorative

metate pre-Columbian stone table used for grinding corn, especially by the Chorotega people of Guanacaste

MINAE Ministry of Environment and Energy

mirador lookout or viewing platform

morenos offensive term for Afro-Caribbeans (the best term to use is *negros* or *Limonenses*)

muelle dock

Neotrópicos Neotropics: tropics of the New World

Nica Nicaraguan, from *Nicaragüense*

PAC Citizens' Action Party, the ruling political party

palenque a thatched-roofed longhouse inhabited by indigenous people; more or less equivalent to the Native American longhouse

pasear to be on vacation/holiday; literally, to be passing through

peón farm labourer, usually landless

personaje someone of importance, a VIP, although usually used pejoratively to indicate someone who is putting on airs

PLN National Liberation Party, the main opposition party

precarista squatter

puesto post (ranger post or ranger station)

pulpería general store or corner store

purrujas spectacularly annoying, tiny biting insects encountered in lowland areas

PUSC Social Christian Unity Party, historically one of Costa Rica's leading political parties

quebrada stream

rancho palm-thatched roof, also smallholding

redondel de toros bullring, not used for bullfighting but for local rodeos

refresco drink, usually made with fresh fruit or water; sometimes a fizzy drink, although this is most often called *gaseosa*

regalar (verb) usually to give, as in to give a present, but in Costa Rica the usual command or request of *"Deme uno de estos"* ("Give me one of those"), becomes *"Regáleme"*; thus *"¿Regáleme un cafecito, por favor?"* ("Could you give me a coffee?")

rejas security grille, popularly known in English as The Cage: the iron grille you see around all but the most humble dwellings in an effort to discourage burglary

río river

sabanero Costa Rican cowboy

salida exit

sendero trail

SINAC National System of Conservation Areas

soda cafeteria or diner; in the rest of Central America, it's usually called a *comedor*

temporada season: *la temporada de lluvia* is the rainy season

temporales early-morning rains in the wet season

terreno land, small farm

Tico/a Costa Rican

UCR Universidad de Costa Rica (in San Pedro, San José)

UNA Universidad Nacional (in Heredia)

verano summer (Dec–April)

volcán volcano

Small print and index

A ROUGH GUIDE TO ROUGH GUIDES

Published in 1982, the first Rough Guide – to Greece – was a student scheme that became a publishing phenomenon. Mark Ellingham, a recent graduate in English from Bristol University, had been travelling in Greece the previous summer and couldn't find the right guidebook. With a small group of friends he wrote his own guide, combining a highly contemporary, journalistic style with a thoroughly practical approach to travellers' needs.

The immediate success of the book spawned a series that rapidly covered dozens of destinations. And, in addition to impecunious backpackers, Rough Guides soon acquired a much broader readership that relished the guides' wit and inquisitiveness as much as their enthusiastic, critical approach and value-for-money ethos.

These days, Rough Guides include recommendations from budget to luxury and cover more than 120 destinations around the globe, as well as producing an ever-growing range of eBooks.

Visit **roughguides.com** to find all our latest books, read articles, get inspired and share travel tips with the Rough Guides community.

Rough Guide credits

Editor: Rachel Mills
Layout: Nikhil Agarwal, Ankur Guha
Cartography: Katie Bennett
Picture editor: Tim Draper
Proofreader: Diane Margolis
Managing editor: Mani Ramaswamy
Assistant editor: Dipika Dasgupta

Production: Charlotte Cade
Cover design: Nicole Newman, Tim Draper, Nikhil Agarwal
Editorial assistant: Rebecca Hallett
Senior pre-press designer: Dan May
Programme manager: Helen Blount
Publisher: Joanna Kirby
Publishing director: Georgina Dee

Publishing information

This seventh edition published October 2014 by
Rough Guides Ltd,
80 Strand, London WC2R 0RL
11, Community Centre, Panchsheel Park,
New Delhi 110017, India
Distributed by Penguin Random House
Penguin Books Ltd,
80 Strand, London WC2R 0RL
Penguin Group (USA)
345 Hudson Street, NY 10014, USA
Penguin Group (Australia)
250 Camberwell Road, Camberwell,
Victoria 3124, Australia
Penguin Group (NZ)
67 Apollo Drive, Mairangi Bay, Auckland 1310,
New Zealand
Penguin Group (South Africa)
Block D, Rosebank Office Park, 181 Jan Smuts Avenue,
Parktown North, Gauteng, South Africa 2193
Rough Guides is represented in Canada by Tourmaline
Editions Inc. 662 King Street West, Suite 304, Toronto,
Ontario M5V 1M7
Printed in Singapore by Toppan Security Printing Pte. Ltd.

Help us update

We've gone to a lot of effort to ensure that the seventh
edition of **The Rough Guide to Costa Rica** is accurate
and up-to-date. However, things change – places get
"discovered", opening hours are notoriously fickle,
restaurants and rooms raise prices or lower standards. If
you feel we've got it wrong or left something out, we'd like
to know, and if you can remember the address, the price,
the hours, the phone number, so much the better.

Please send your comments with the subject line
"**Rough Guide Costa Rica Update**" to ✉ mail@uk
.roughguides.com. We'll credit all contributions and send a
copy of the next edition (or any other Rough Guide if you
prefer) for the very best emails.
Find more travel information, connect with fellow
travellers and plan your trip on ⊕ roughguides.com.

ABOUT THE AUTHORS

Keith Drew Worryingly addicted to *gallo pinto*, Keith Drew is also co-author of the *Rough Guide to Morocco* and, closer to home, the *Rough Guide to Bath, Bristol and Somerset*, which has a similarly friendly populace but distinctly fewer volcanoes. A managing editor at Rough Guides, he lives in Winchester with his wife, Kate, and their three children, Maisie, Joe and Lilah.

Steven Horak A contributor to several other Rough Guides, including Canada, the USA and the Czech Republic. He has also written children's books and travels regularly for his photography (⊛stevenhorak.smugmug.com) from his home in Santa Fe, New Mexico.

Shafik Meghji A travel writer, journalist, editor and photographer, Shafik Meghji is based in South London but has travelled extensively throughout Costa Rica. He has co-authored more than twenty Rough Guides, including those to Argentina, Bolivia, Chile, Ecuador, India and Nepal, as well as the Buenos Aires Essential Guide app. Shafik's travel writing has been published in three anthologies, and he contributes regularly to newspapers, magazines and websites around the world. He blogs at ⊛unmappedroutes.com and you can follow his tweets @ShafikMeghji.

Acknowledgements

Steven Horak Thanks to Rachel Mills for her skillful editing, enthusiasm and steady hand. Thanks as well to Mani Ramaswamy for her guidance, and to Shafik and Keith for their helpful tips. In Costa Rica many thanks to all those who provided invaluable information and assistance, including Marco Montoya, Natalie Ewing, Offi, Ballardo Diaz, Mariana, Rocio López, Mayra Güell, Rick Vogel, Terry Lillian Newton, George Schwarzenbach, Tiziana Sambucci, Chris and Charlie Foerster, Yolanda and Sepp, Nichole DuPont, Terri and Mark Lovis, and the guides of Jinetes de Osa. Lastly, thank you to the Rough Guides crew in the Delhi and London offices whose skill and hard work made this edition possible.

Shafik Meghji Many thanks to all the Ticos and travellers who helped me out with my research. A special *muchas gracias* must go to: Mani Ramaswamy and Rachel Mills at Rough Guides; Steven Horak; Glenn and Teri Jampol; Natalie Ewing; Keith Flanaghan; Jayne Lloyd-Jones; Dana Cohen; Jean, Nizar and Nina Meghji; and Sioned Jones.

Readers' updates

Thanks to all the readers who have taken the time to write in with comments and suggestions (and apologies if we've inadvertently omitted or misspelt anyone's name):

Elissa Dennis, Bjorn O. Hem, Mr Karel P.L. Henkemans and Rachel Manser

Index

Maps are marked in grey

Map symbols

The symbols below are used on maps throughout the book

✈	International airport	⊠	Gate/entrance	— —	Ferry
✈	Domestic airport/airstrip	🔽	Viewpoint	- - - -	Footpath
♦	Place of interest	▲	Mountain peak	-·-·-·-	Unpaved road
●	Museum	/▲	Volcano	▒▒▒▒	Pedestrian road
✉	Post office	◈	Springs	◁▷	Railway
ⓘ	Tourist information	◠	Cave	━━━	Wall
@	Internet access	🏛	Waterfall	▒	Building
ⓒ	Telephone office	⋮⋮	Ruins/archeological site	▢	Market
⊞	Hospital	🏠	Ranger station	◯	Stadium
ⓢ	Bank	⛺	Campsite	🪦	Cemetery
★	Transport stop	🐘	Zoo	♦ National Reserve/park
⛽	Fuel station	⛴	Boat tour		Beach
Ⓟ	Parking	🏰	Tower		Swamp
⊤	Gardens				Coral

Listings key

■	Accommodation
●	Restaurant/café
■	Bar/club
●	Shopping

ROUGH GUIDES
A CHRONOLOGY

1982 The First *Rough Guide to Greece* – written and researched by Mark Ellingham, John Fisher and Nat Jansz – is published, shortly followed by Spain and Portugal **1983** *Amsterdam* – written by Martin Dunford – is published **1986** The first Rough Guides' offices set up in Kennington, South London **1987** Rough Guides set up as independent company **1989** BBC2 commission a Rough Guides TV series presented by Magenta Devine and Sankha Guha

1990 Rough Guides first published in the US under the name The Real Guides **1994** The first Reference titles – *World Music*, *Classical Music* and *The Internet* – are published • World Music Network starts selling Rough Guides compilation CDs **1995** roughguides.com is launched **1997** New York office set up

2001 First eBooks launched **2002** Rough Guides moves to Penguin headquarters at 80 Strand, London • Delhi office established • Rip-proof city maps series launched **2003** New colour sections added to the guides • First commissioned photographic shoots take place **2004** The *Rough Guide to a Better World* published in association with DFID **2006** First full-colour Rough Guide – *World Party* – is published • **2007** 25s series launched in honour of the 25th anniversary • *Make the Most of Your Time on Earth* becomes best-selling RG and is nominated in Richard and Judy Book Club awards **2008** A new RG TV series is broadcast on Channel 5 **2009** The first hardback picture book – *Earthbound* – featuring our commissioned photography goes on sale

2010 All guides are printed on FCO approved paper **2011** The new full-colour Pocket Guides series is launched • The first city guide iPhone/iPad apps are released **2012** Rough Guides' travel books are relaunched in time for our 30th anniversary, using full colour throughout • The first Rough Guide eBooks made specifically for the iPad go on sale **2013** roughguides.com is relaunched